PUBLIC BUDGETING SYSTEMS

NINTH EDITION

ROBERT D. LEE, JR.
THE PENNSYLVANIA STATE UNIVERSITY

RONALD W. JOHNSON
RTI INTERNATIONAL, RETIRED

PHILIP G. JOYCE
UNIVERSITY OF MARYLAND

JONES & BARTLETT
LEARNING

World Headquarters
Jones & Bartlett Learning
5 Wall Street
Burlington, MA 01803
978-443-5000
info@jblearning.com
www.jblearning.com

Jones & Bartlett Learning books and products are available through most bookstores and online booksellers. To contact Jones & Bartlett Learning directly, call 800-832-0034, fax 978-443-8000, or visit our website, www.jblearning.com.

Substantial discounts on bulk quantities of Jones & Bartlett Learning publications are available to corporations, professional associations, and other qualified organizations. For details and specific discount information, contact the special sales department at Jones & Bartlett Learning via the above contact information or send an email to specialsales@jblearning.com.

Production Credits
Publisher: Michael Brown
Managing Editor: Maro Gartside
Editorial Assistant: Kayla Dos Santos
Editorial Assistant: Chloe Falivene
Production Manager: Tracey McCrea
Production Assistant: Alyssa Lawrence
Senior Marketing Manager: Sophie Fleck Teague
Manufacturing and Inventory Control Supervisor: Amy Bacus
Composition: DiacriTech
Cover Design: Michael O'Donnell
Cover Image: © Photos.com
Printing and Binding: Edwards Brothers Malloy
Cover Printing: Edwards Brothers Malloy

Library of Congress Cataloging-in-Publication Data
Lee, Robert D.
 Public budgeting systems / Robert Lee, Ronald Johnson, and Philip Joyce.—9th ed.
    p. cm.
 Includes bibliographical references and index.
 ISBN 978-1-4496-2790-4 (casebound) — ISBN 1-4496-2790-0 (casebound)
 1. Budget—United States. 2. Budget process—United States. 3. Program budgeting—United States. I. Johnson, Ronald Wayne, 1942- II. Joyce, Philip G., 1956- III. Title.
 HJ2051.L4 2013
 352.4'80973—dc23
                        2012004762
6048

Printed in the United States of America
16 15 14 13 12   10 9 8 7 6 5 4 3 2 1

Dedicated to
Ann, Rob, Tatiana, Craig, Dan, Cameron, and Bob
and to
Sally, Ron, Jennifer, Zac, Landen, Lucas, Abi, Scott, and Amber
and to
Rita, Christopher, Mariah, and Samuel

Table of Contents

Preface

This is a general book on public budgeting. Its purpose is to survey the current state of the art of budgeting among all levels of government in the United States. Where their inclusion would be illustrative, examples from other countries and from some nongovernmental organizations are used. In addition, we emphasize methods by which financial decisions are reached within a system and ways in which different types of information are used in budgetary decision making. We stress the use of program information because budget reforms for decades have sought to introduce greater program considerations into financial decisions.

Budgeting is considered within the context of a system containing numerous components and relationships. One problem of such an approach is that because all things within a system are related, it is difficult to find an appropriate place to begin. Although we have divided the text into chapters, the reader should recognize that no single chapter can stand alone. Every chapter mentions some topics and issues that are treated elsewhere in the book.

A discussion of budgeting may be organized in various ways. Historical or chronological sequence is one possible method of organization, although this approach would require discussing every relevant topic for each time period. Another strategy is to arrange topics by level of government, with separate sections for local, state, and federal budgeting. Such an approach again would involve extensive rehashing of arguments and information. Yet another approach is to focus on phases of the budget cycle from preparation of the budget through auditing of past activities and expenditures. Rigid adherence to this approach would be inappropriate because the budget cycle is not precisely defined and many issues cut across several phases of the cycle. Another approach would be to organize the discussion around the contrast between the technical and political problems of budgetary decision making.

The organization of this book is a combination of these approaches. Although we have not formally divided the book, readers will see that the chapters are separated into five sections. The first four chapters lay out an overall framework for budgeting, budget decisions, and budgeting systems. The discussion is of U.S. budgeting, but the framework is applicable for the most part to any budgeting system whether national, state, or local, or whether it is in Europe or any other continent. Chapter 1, *Introduction*, begins with the concepts of budgets and budgeting systems. It provides a general discussion of the nature of budgetary decision making, including distinctions between private and public budgeting, the concepts of responsibility and accountability in budgeting, the possibility of rationality in decision making, and the nature of budgeting and budget systems. Chapter 2, *The Public Sector in Perspective*, addresses the issues of the size of the public sector and the arguments about what is appropriate for the public sector vis-a-vis the private sector. It reviews the scope of the public sector, the magnitude of government, the sources of revenues, and the purposes of government expenditures.

Chapter 3, *Government, the Economy, and Economic Development*, has been relocated in this *Ninth Edition* from its place at the end of previous editions. This chapter goes into detail, primarily for the United States, in discussing government's responsibilities for and impacts upon the overall health of the economy. Specific attention is given to the most recent recession that began in 2007, the worst recession since the Great Depression. Budget cycles are the topic of Chapter 4, which summarizes the basic steps in budgeting: preparation and submission, approval, execution, and auditing. Chapter 4 forecasts the more detailed discussions in the following two groups of chapters. Together the first four chapters provide a basic framework for the remainder of the book.

The next six chapters are organized around budget decision-making processes and the principal actors involved from the initial steps of budget preparation through budget approval by legislative bodies. These chapters set up the subject of budget decisions for the annual, recurrent budget, also called the operating budget. The topics are revenues and expenditures; reform efforts that have focused on improving annual budget decisions; and detailed budget preparation and approval. A separate chapter is devoted to the U.S. congressional approval process and its outcomes. In these six chapters we treat budget decisions on both the preparation and approval sides, and on revenues and expenditures. We note that reform efforts have focused almost exclusively on the expenditure side.

The purpose of these six chapters is to provide the reader with an understanding of the types of deliberations involved in developing a proposed budget. Chapter 5, *Budgeting for Revenues: Income Taxes, Payroll Taxes, and Property Taxes*, considers the different sources from which governments obtain their funds, the criteria for evaluating revenue sources, and specific sources such as income, payroll, and property taxes. Chapter 6, *Budgeting for Revenues: Transaction-Based Revenue Sources*, continues the discussion of revenues by considering sales taxes, user fees, and the like. Chapter 7, *Budget Preparation: The Expenditure Side*, discusses early budget reform efforts and contemporary approaches to developing proposals for funding government programs. Chapter 8, *Budget Preparation: The Decision Process*, examines the process of putting together a budget proposal that includes recommended revenue and expenditure levels, and then reviews the types of budget documents that are used in government.

Chapters 9 and 10 deal with the budget approval process. Chapter 9, *Budget Approval: The Role of the Legislature*, provides a general account of the processes used by legislative bodies. Chapter 10, *Budget Approval: The U.S. Congress*, separately treats the special factors and problems associated with congressional budgeting.

The third grouping contains two chapters that concentrate on the execution, audit, and evaluation phases of budgeting. Chapter 11, *Budget Execution*, considers the roles played by the chief executive, the budget office, and the line agencies. The chapter discusses the topics of tax administration, cash management, procurement, and risk management. Chapter 12, *Financial Management: Accounting, Reporting, and Auditing*, presents the basic features of accounting systems and processes, reviews the various types of reports that flow from accounting systems, and explains the types of audits that are conducted. These chapters provide considerable detail on how budgets actually are implemented once the formal decision cycle through approval is complete, and how honesty and integrity are attained, or at least sought, through the accounting, reporting, and auditing systems and processes.

The fourth group of chapters focuses entirely on systems for making long-term investment decisions and financing long-term capital assets, in contrast to the previous six chapters that focus mainly on the annual operating budget. Of course much of the political processes involved in decisions on the annual operating budget apply to capital budget decisions as well. However, Chapters 13 and 14 deal only with decisions to purchase assets or make investments that will not be consumed or exhausted in a single year and, in many cases at the state and local level, will be financed over a long time period, sometimes as much as 20 to 30 years.

Chapter 13, *Capital Assets: Planning and Budgeting, Analysis, and Management*, examines capital budgeting as a decision process. Decision processes that focus on long-term capital budgeting and methods for financing capital investments differ significantly from decision processes for the annual revenues and expenditures discussed in Chapters 5 through 10. Decisions about capital budgeting actually occur throughout the budget process, although capital programming occurs during budget execution. Chapter 14, *Capital Finance and Debt Management*, considers the financing of long-term capital investments through debt and equity instruments.

The final chapter is separate unto itself in that it is more about the interactions among levels of government—in the United States, federal, state, and local—and not on specific decision processes. Chapter 15, *Intergovernmental Relations*, examines the financial interactions among governments, the types of fiscal assistance in use, and possible means of restructuring intergovernmental relationships.

The book closes with some brief concluding remarks on themes that can be expected to receive considerable attention from budgeting practitioners and scholars in the next several years. The bibliographic note provides guidance on keeping informed about changes in the field of budgeting.

Overall, this edition retains much of the structure of the eighth edition with the major exception of grouping *Government, the Economy, and Economic Development* together with the other three chapters that establish the overall framework for public budgeting systems. As with the eighth edition, this *Ninth Edition* includes increased attention to some topics, such as the recession that started in 2007 for which massive fiscal and monetary programs were put in place to first arrest and then to combat the recession's effects. Various revenue sources, capital budgeting, and state and local debt management also receive additional attention. This text also reflects the continuing impact of the need to combat potential and actual acts of terrorism and of the large increase in the costs of natural disasters and their human and economic impacts. Text, tables, and exhibits have been completely updated.

Drs. Lee and Johnson began the first edition as faculty members in the Institute of Public Administration at The Pennsylvania State University. Eight editions later, Dr. Lee is Professor Emeritus of Public Administration and Professor Emeritus of Hotel, Restaurant, and Recreation Management at The Pennsylvania State University. Dr. Johnson has retired as Executive Vice President for International Development and Senior Policy Advisor at RTI International. This *Ninth Edition* is now the third edition in which Dr. Philip G. Joyce plays a key role as an integral member of our writing team. He is Professor of Management, Finance, and Leadership at the University of Maryland's School of Public Policy.

Our hope is that this new edition will be useful to readers from many backgrounds and with widely diverse purposes.

Acknowledgments

Having gone through eight previous editions, this *Ninth Edition* is the product of numerous individuals, not just its three authors. We are indebted to current and former colleagues at The Pennsylvania State University, RTI International, and the University of Maryland. Professor Joyce was ably assisted in the preparation of this edition by two research assistants from the Maryland School of Public Policy—Michael Gallaher and Evan Cook; Gallaher also assisted Dr. Johnson in searching out updated data for Chapters 2 and 3. Colleagues and students at other institutions, including a variety of colleges and universities, have provided valuable advice. Practitioners in the United States and many developing countries have helped refine our understanding with real-world situations. In preparing the book, we received considerable advice from expert practitioners in the executive and legislative branches of federal, state, and local governments and from their counterparts in nonprofit organizations. The responsibility for the final product, of course, belongs to us alone.

Introduction

In what many characterize as the *information age*,[1] it is to be expected that any book dealing with large organizations operating in the world economy would focus extensively on information. This text is about complex governmental institutions that operate in a world economy and society, and its extensive focus on information is no surprise. We consider budgets, budgeting systems, and budgeting processes; the nature of the decisions that are made; and the processes by which those decisions are made. Budgeting has always been about information, and budget systems are about gathering the best information available, whether that information be primarily of a technical nature or of a political nature, and bringing that information to bear on decisions about allocating resources to purposes.

Public budgeting involves the selection of ends and the means to reach those ends. It involves the division of society's economic and financial resources between the public sector and the private sector, as well as the allocation of such resources among competing public sector needs. Public budgeting systems are systems for making choices of ends and means. These choices are guided by theory, by hunch, by partisan politics, by narrow self-interest, by altruism, and by many other sources of value judgment, including avarice and perceptions of the public interest.

Public budgeting systems work by channeling various types of information about societal conditions and about the private and public values that guide resource allocation decision making. Complex channels for information exchange exist. Through these channels, people process information on what is desired, make assessments of what is or is not being achieved, and analyze what might or might not be achieved. Integral to budgeting systems are intricate processes that link both political and economic values. In making decisions that ultimately determine how resources are allocated, the political process uses sometimes bewildering and often conflicting information about values, actual conditions, and possible condition changes. This text analyzes procedures and methods—past, present, and prospective—used in the resource allocation process.

This chapter examines some basic features of decision-making and budgeting systems. First, some major characteristics of public budgeting are explained through comparison and contrast with private forms of budgeting. Second, the development of budgeting as a means of holding government accountable for its use of society's resources is reviewed.

Next, budgets and budgeting systems are defined. Finally, the role of information in budgetary decision making is considered.

DISTINCTIONS REGARDING PUBLIC BUDGETING

Budgeting is a common phenomenon. To some extent, everybody does it. People budget time, dollars, food—almost everything. The family hardware store budgets, Wal-Mart budgets, and governments budget. Moreover, important similarities exist in the budgeting done by large public and private bureaucracies.[2]

Budgeting is intended as a mechanism for setting goals and objectives, for allocating the resources necessary to achieve those objectives, for measuring progress toward objectives, for identifying weaknesses or inadequacies in organizations, and for controlling and integrating the diverse activities carried out by numerous subunits within large bureaucracies, both public and private. Budgeting is the manifestation of an organization's strategies, whether those strategies are the result of thoughtful strategic planning processes, the inertia of long years of doing approximately the same thing, or the competing political forces within the organization bargaining for shares of resources. Once resources are allocated through the budgetary process, the organization's strategies become apparent even if they have not been articulated as strategies. Budgeting means examining how the organization's resources have been used in the past, analyzing what has been accomplished and at what cost, and charting a course for the future by allocating resources for the coming budget period. Whether this process is done haphazardly or after exhaustive analyses, whether it is carried out by order of the chief executive officer or requires the extensive input of citizens, it is still budgeting.

Public budgeting is also about assigning responsibility for accomplishing the results intended by the executive and legislative actors that ultimately set the budget. Budgets are generally executed by individuals in large bureaucracies. Budget allocations identify not only the amounts to be spent and the intended purposes of those expenditures, but also the unit within the bureaucracy—and by implication, the individuals managing that unit—responsible for achieving the intended results. In the contemporary age in which much of the value in any process, whether producing a commercial good or producing a public service, is in the information or knowledge applied, responsibility for budget decisions and budget implementation is vastly more complicated. First, the information available to the decision makers, whether they choose to use it or not, is much more extensive. Second, decision-making processes are highly visible to citizens and other stakeholders. Thus, for practical reasons, and because strong central government controls are politically less feasible than in the past in most countries, budgetary decisions are more decentralized than ever.

Public and Private Sector Differences in Objectives

Resource Availability

Important differences exist between the private and public spheres. In the first place, the amount of resources available for allocation in the budget process varies greatly. Both family and corporate budgeting are constrained by a relatively fixed set of available resources, even if vastly different in size. Income is comparatively fixed, at least in the short run, and therefore outgo must be equal to or less than income. Of course, income can be expanded by increasing the level of production and work, such as a member of the family taking a second job, or temporarily by borrowing, but the opportunities for increasing income are limited.

Governments, in contrast, are bound by much higher limits. In the United States, at least, government does not use nearly all of the possible resources available. Only in times of major crises, such as World War II and the recession that began in 2007, has the government of the United States begun to approach the upper limits of its resources. In those two crises, the federal government borrowed an amount that eventually came close to equaling or even exceeding the total production of the economy in a year. During World War II, the government borrowed an amount about equal to the total economy's production, called *gross domestic product* (GDP), and the government spent most of it directly and indirectly on the war effort. Rationing, price controls, and other measures were imposed so as to severely limit private sector consumption and in its place allocate most of society's resources to the government. In the most recent recession, government again borrowed enough, on top of decades of annual budget deficits, that total government debt equaled and exceeded total GDP. That borrowing had a different purpose, of course—to stimulate the economy and to put money in the hands of producers and consumers.

During times not characterized by crisis, much of the total economy is left to the private sector, with government using only a fraction of society's workforce, goods, and services. In 2010, combined federal, state, and local government expenditures amounted to 36% of total GDP, with about three-fifths of that from the federal government. That percentage was several points higher, a result of government stimulus programs to combat the recession, than the 25% to 30% that has been typical since 1960, but it was still on the lower end compared to most industrialized countries (see the chapters on the public sector and economic development).[3] Government has the power to determine how much of society's total resources will be used for public purposes. Private parties operate within the limits of their ability to acquire resources through their market activities: selling their labor, selling goods, and so forth.

Profit Motive

Another major distinction between private and public budgeting is the motivation behind budget decisions. The private sector is characterized by the profit motive, whereas government undertakes many things that are financially unprofitable. In the private sector, profit serves as a ready standard for evaluating previous decisions. Successful decisions are those that produce profits (as measured in dollars). Some companies, of course, focus on short-term profits, and others may take a longer-term view, but in the end, failure to achieve a profit or at least break even means the company goes out of business.

The concept of profit, however, can lead to gross oversimplifications about corporate decision making. Not every budget decision in a private firm is determined by the criterion of making an immediate profit. Corporations sometimes forgo profits in the short run. In the case of price wars, they attempt to increase their share of a given market even if it means selling temporarily at a loss. At other times, they incur large debts and take other, apparently unprofitable, actions to combat a hostile takeover, an attempt by an outsider to purchase enough stock to exercise control over a corporation's assets. Their major objectives are sometimes to produce a good product and to build public confidence. They have enough confidence in their pursuit of customer service that the result will be sustained, long-run profits. At other times, they undertake actions for mainly social motives, wishing to make a contribution to the society that sustains their corporate existence, a concept known as corporate social responsibility (CSR).[4] Still, in private sector firms, revenues must exceed costs over the long run.

Large firms also budget significant resources for research and development (R&D) activities, only a few of which will eventually lead to a product that generates large sales and profits. An R&D division can be evaluated over the long term by how many of its developments contribute to profits, but this kind of evaluation is difficult. Often, the results of R&D are subtle improvements in existing products, and measuring the amount of investment relative to the incremental profit gain is impossible. In this regard, private budgeting for R&D is no less difficult than the federal government's support of R&D. Overall, the evidence is that investing in R&D yields positive returns on that investment.[5]

Regardless of the role profit plays in the private sector, government decision making in general lacks even this standard for measuring activities. Exceptions to this generalization are government activities that yield revenues. State control and sale of alcoholic beverages, whether undertaken for profit or for regulation of public morals, can be evaluated, like any other business, in terms of profit and loss. Similarly, the operation of a water system, a public transit authority, or a public swimming pool can be evaluated in business profit-and-loss terms. This does not mean that each of these should turn a profit. After all, operating a public swimming pool may be the result of a decision to provide subsidized recreation to a low-income neighborhood whose residents cannot afford other private recreational alternatives. The budgeting process, however, can be used to assess the operation as a business to clarify the subsidy level and to aid decision makers in comparing costs with those for other public services provided free of direct charge (see the chapter on capital assets).

Nevertheless, the majority of private sector budget decisions pertain to at least long-term profits, and most public sector budget decisions do not. Governments undertake some functions deliberately instead of leaving them to the private sector. Public budgetary decisions, for example, frequently involve allocation of resources among competing programs that are not readily susceptible to measurement in dollar costs and dollar returns. For example, there are no easy means of measuring the costs and benefits of a life saved through cancer research, although the value of future earnings is sometimes used as a surrogate measure of the value of life. The U.S. government undertakes large programs to control or eradicate malaria and other tropical diseases in Africa, based not on economic or financial returns, but on a broad concept of the public interest in eradicating diseases that affect low-income populations in developing countries. Nor is there a ready means of clearly separating private incentives from public incentives. For example, although the National Cancer Institute spends millions of public dollars annually on cancer research, the amount is minuscule compared with the amount spent by private companies on research for cancer prevention and treatment.

Just because most public sector activities are not intended to be profitable does not mean that business-like measurement of results in relation to costs is useless. Although not susceptible to bottom-line or profit-and-loss measurement, many government programs are able to measure their results in terms of output (efficiency) and outcome (effectiveness). The tropical disease eradication programs undertaken by the U.S. government for reasons of the public interest, for example, can and are measured by the efficiency and effectiveness with which the programs are implemented. Legislation passed in 1993 mandated the use of performance measures to improve the federal government's accountability for the results of its expenditures. That act was reaffirmed and updated in 2010 with the GPRA Modernization Act (GPRAMA).[6]

Public and Private Sector Differences in Services Provided

Public Goods

Some government services yield public or collective benefits that are of value to society as a whole, whereas corporate products are almost always consumed by individuals and specific organizations. When Ford Motor Company produces automobiles, people buying the automobiles use them to meet their own personal needs. When the Departments of Defense and Homeland Security produce a network for preventing nuclear devices from entering the nation's ports, that network benefits the public in general. Economists call these kinds of products and services *public goods.* They have two properties. The first is *nonexcludability.* Once the network is in place, no one can be excluded from its benefits, even if they are unwilling or unable to pay for them.[7] The second is *nonrivalness.* One person's use of the good or service does not diminish another person's use. For example, a second person can "consume" national defense without lessening the benefits that the first person gets from that public good. Of course, few public products and services qualify as pure public goods, and many goods and services produced by governments are also produced by the private sector. Police protection is a public service, but communities, companies, and individuals also purchase various forms of protection against crime from private security companies.

Externalities

Another class of government services consists of those from which individuals can be excluded but for which the benefits, or costs, extend beyond those who are the immediate targets of the service. When Ford Motor Company sells a car, its stockholders enjoy the benefits of the profits, but those profits do not spill over to society at large. However, when a child is educated through a school system, not only does the child benefit, but society's productive capacity is also enhanced. Many private schools educate children for a profit, and the owners of the schools enjoy the benefits of the profits along with the children and society. However, it seems unlikely that these same for-profit schools would willingly provide equivalent education to all children who cannot make tuition payments. Economists label the benefits that spill over to the rest of society *externalities.* Governments provide at least some services that produce significant externalities because the private sector would provide these only to the extent that profit could be made. Education, if left entirely to the private sector, would presumably be available only to those who could pay, or would be provided in insufficient quantity and quality for the needs of society.

Pricing Public Services

Defining just what is clearly public in nature and determining what the private sector presumably cannot or will not provide is controversial. During the 1980s and 1990s, the federal government cut back on transfers to state and local governments, which also faced more stringent tax and spending limitations inspired by their voters (see the chapter on transaction-based revenue sources). As a consequence, many services once thought to be exclusively public were converted to private services or to public services provided by private firms on a contract basis.[8] That trend continued when state and local budgets shrank dramatically in the two recessions of the first decade of the 2000s, though there is some evidence that smaller jurisdictions or smaller private contracting for public services has waned somewhat, while large contracts seem to be increasing.[9]

This trend advanced throughout many developing countries with public sectors even larger than in the United States. The Margaret Thatcher government, in privatizing many formerly public services such as the water utilities throughout the United Kingdom, served as a model for the early 1980s movement in the United States and around the world (see the discussion of various forms of privatization and private participation in public services).

This type of conversion is not a new idea, but public sector budget pressures have changed the landscape to require those who benefit directly from a government service to pay for its cost. For example, in the 1990s the U.S. Coast Guard stopped providing towing services to disabled boats unless a genuine emergency exists; it instead notifies private operators, who charge the cost to the disabled boat captain. That practice has cut back significantly on calls for towing in general, with prices providing a rationing mechanism. What is private and what is public varies over time, and public budgeting is affected by those variations.[10]

Other Public and Private Sector Differences

Whatever objectives, other than profit, that private corporations may have, to stay in business they must seek economic efficiency and obtain the greatest possible dollar return on investments. In contrast, governments may be intentionally inefficient in resource allocations, undertaking services that the private sector would be reluctant to provide at all. For example, government-financed medical care for the elderly may be inefficient in the sense that other government programs provide greater economic returns to society, but it has been agreed that at least some support should be provided to the elderly. Governments are also charged with other unique responsibilities such as intervention in the economy (see the chapter on government and the economy).

Another difference between private and public organizations lies in the clientele and the owners of the means of production. In theory, at least, both corporations and governments are answerable to their stockholders and clients. In the private sector, these individuals can disassociate themselves from firms. Their counterparts in the public sector are denied this choice except through the extreme act of emigration. Private stockholders expect dollar returns on their investments, and if they are not satisfied, they sell their shares. Because government costs and returns are not so easily evaluated, the electorate has no simple measure for assessing the returns on the taxes they pay, and they have no means to sell their shares, other than to move to another country. Even so, many state and local governments provide annual reports to citizens that are similar in purpose to stockholder reports. These reports emphasize the investments government is making and the benefits citizens are receiving in lieu of profits. Of course from time to time the stockholders of corporations and of governments force management to change, the latter through regular elections.

Corporate budgetary decision making is usually more centralized than government decision making. Corporations can stop production of economically unprofitable goods such as Hummer vehicles. Given the nature of the public decision-making process, however, governments encounter more difficulty in making decisions both to inaugurate programs and to eliminate them. For example, though there was an apparent large majority consensus for more than two decades that the Medicare program that assists the elderly in financing health care should include some form of prescription drug coverage, it was not until 2006 that a program was finally implemented.

RESPONSIBLE GOVERNMENT AND BUDGETING

The emergence and reform of formal government budgeting can be traced to a concern for holding public officials accountable for their actions.[11] The government performance monitoring movement represents the most recent manifestation of a rather ancient concern that public officials be held accountable for their actions.[12] No matter the particular reform terminology in vogue, in a democracy, budgeting is a device for limiting the powers of government. Two issues recur in the evolution of modern public budgeting as an instrument of accountability: responsibility to whom and for what purposes.

Responsible to Whom?

Responsibility to Constituency

Basically, responsibility in a democratic society entails constituents holding their officials answerable, usually through elections. Elected executives and legislative representatives at all levels of government are, at least in theory, held accountable through the electoral process for their decisions on programs and budgets. In actuality, budget documents are not the main source of information for decisions by the electorate. Obviously, most voters do not diligently study the U.S. budget before casting their votes in presidential and congressional elections. However, when the government's share of the total economy grows, it is increasingly clear that voters do hold elected representatives responsible for the overall budget, the budget deficit, and the general performance of the economy. That the electorate holds presidents responsible for the economy was evidenced in 1992 by President George H. W. Bush's defeat in his bid for reelection. Eight years later, the 2000 election showed that even in the midst of a booming economy, many voters were more concerned about apparent ethical and moral lapses in the White House than their happiness with the economy.

The 2010 midterm elections changed the majority party control of the U.S. House of Representatives from Democratic to Republican hands and reduced the Democratic majority in the Senate. The 2010 election issues spoke to the voters' concerns about the economy and the national debt.

State and local governments have specific creditors: the purchasers of bonds issued to finance long-term capital improvements. The interest rates that state and local governments have to pay on their bonds are affected by their ability to provide creditors with convincing evidence of their creditworthiness (see the chapter on capital finance and debt management). Hence, financial institutions that purchase bonds and ratings institutions that rate state and local bonds are important constituents to whom these governments are accountable.

Because the public in a large society cannot be fully informed about the operations of government, the United States has used the concepts of *separation of powers* and *checks and balances* as means of providing for responsible government. Power is divided among the executive, legislative, and judicial branches, and each provides some checks on the others. Although the president is held responsible to Congress for preparation and submission of an executive budget, only Congress can pass the budget. Specifically, the U.S. Constitution, in Article 1, Section 9, states that "no money shall be drawn from the Treasury, but in consequence of appropriations made by law...." In most states and many localities, the chief executive has a similar responsibility to recommend a plan for taxes and expenditures. The legislative body passes judgment on these recommendations and subsequently holds the executive branch responsible for carrying out the decisions. Local government practice varies more since some local governments do not have an elected chief executive.

Development of the Executive Budget System

The development of an executive budget system for holding government accountable was a long process that can be traced as far back as the Magna Carta in 1215. The main issue that resulted in this landmark document was the Crown's taxing powers. The Magna Carta did not produce a complete budget but concentrated only on holding the Crown accountable to the nobility for its revenue actions.[13] At the time, the magnitude of public expenditures and the use of these funds for public services were of less concern than the power to levy and collect taxes. It was not until the English Consolidated Fund Act of 1787 that the rudiments of a complete system were established. A complete account of revenues and expenditures was presented to Parliament for the first time in 1822.[14]

The same concern in eighteenth-century England for executive accountability was exhibited in other countries. It was carried over to the American experience even prior to the ratification of the Constitution in 1789. Fear of a strong executive branch was evidenced by the failure to provide for such a branch in the Articles of Confederation in 1781. Fear of "taxation without representation" probably explains why the Constitution is more explicit about taxing powers than the procedures to be followed in government spending.

The first decade under the Constitution saw important developments that could have resulted in an executive budget system, but the trend was reversed in subsequent years. The Treasury Act of 1789, establishing the Treasury Department, granted to the secretary the power "to digest and prepare plans for the improvement of the revenue ... [and] to prepare and report estimates of the public revenue and expenditures."[15] Alexander Hamilton, secretary of the treasury, in interpreting his mandate broadly, asserted strong leadership in financial affairs. Although the act did not grant the secretary power to prepare a budget by recommending which programs should and should not be funded, such a development might have subsequently occurred.

Instead, Hamilton's apparent lack of deference to Congress strengthened that body's resolve for greater legislative control over financial matters. To curtail the discretion of the executive branch, Congress resorted to the use of increasing numbers of line items, specifying in narrow detail for what purposes money could be spent.[16] The pattern emerged that each executive department would deal directly with Congress, thereby curtailing the responsibilities of the secretary of the treasury. The budgetary function of the Treasury Department became primarily ministerial. The Book of Estimates, prepared by the secretary and delivered to Congress, could have become the instrument for a coordinated set of budgetary recommendations. Instead, it was simply a compilation of departmental requests for funds. A. E. Buck wrote, "Thus budget making became an exclusively legislative function in the national government, and as such it continued for more than a century."[17]

Modern Executive Budgeting

By the beginning of the twentieth century, changing economic conditions stimulated the demand for more centralized and controlled forms of budgeting. E. E. Naylor wrote that before this time there was little "enthusiasm for action … since federal taxes were usually indirect and not severely felt by any particular individual or group."[18] By 1900, however, existing revenue sources no longer consistently produced sufficient sums to cover the costs of government. At the federal level, the tariff could not be expected to produce a surplus of funds, as had been the case. Causes of this growing deficit were the expanded scope of government programs and, to a lesser extent, waste and corruption in government finance. The latter is often credited as a major political factor stimulating reform.

Local government led the way in the establishment of formal budget procedures. Municipal budget reform was closely associated with general reform of local government, especially the creation of the city manager form of government. In 1899, a model municipal corporation act, released by the National Municipal League, featured a model charter that provided for a budget system whose preparation phase was under the control of the mayor. In 1907, the New York Bureau of Municipal Research issued a study, "Making a Municipal Budget," that became the basis for establishing a budgetary system for New York City.[19] By the mid-1920s, most major U.S. cities had some form of budget system.

Substantial reform of state budgeting occurred between 1910 and 1920. This reform was closely associated with the overall drive to hold executives accountable by first giving them authority over the executive branch. The movement for the short ballot, aimed at eliminating many independently elected administrative officers, resulted in governors being granted greater control over their bureaucracies. Ohio, in 1910, was the first state to enact a law empowering the governor to prepare and submit a budget. A. E. Buck, in assessing the effort at the state level, suggested that 1913 marked "the beginning of practical action in the states."[20] By 1920, some budget reform had occurred in 44 states, and all states had a central budget office by 1929.[21]

Simultaneous action occurred at the federal level, and much of what took place there contributed to the reforms at the local and state levels. Frederick A. Cleveland, who was director of the New York Bureau of Municipal Research and who played a key role in national reform, asserted that "it was the uncontrolled and uncontrollable increase in the cost of government that finally jostled the public into an attitude of hostility."[22] In response to this public concern, President William H. Taft requested and received from Congress in 1909 an appropriation of $100,000 for a special Commission on Economy and Efficiency. Known as the Taft Commission, the group was headed by Cleveland and submitted its final report in 1912, recommending the establishment of a budgetary process under the direction of the president. This report was to spur activity at the state and local levels.

The Budget and Accounting Act, which established the new federal system, was not passed until 1921.[23] In the interim, deficits were recorded every year between 1912 and 1919, except for 1916. The largest deficit occurred in 1919, when (largely because of the need to finance World War I) expenditures were three times greater than revenues ($18.5 billion in expenditures as compared with $5.1 billion in revenues). During this period, vigorous debate centered on the issue of whether budget reform would in effect establish a superordinate executive over the legislative branch. In 1920, President Wilson vetoed legislation that would have created a Bureau of the Budget and a General Accounting Office on the grounds that the latter, as an arm of Congress, would violate the president's authority over the executive branch. The following year, President Warren G. Harding signed virtually identical legislation into law.

Thus, an executive budget system was established, despite a historical fear of a powerful chief executive. In 1939, as a result of recommendations made by President Franklin D. Roosevelt's Committee on Administrative Management (the Brownlow Committee), the Bureau of the Budget was removed from the Treasury Department and placed in the newly formed Executive Office of the President. This shift reflected the growing importance of the bureau in assisting the president in managing the government. Ten years later, the budgetary task force of the First Hoover Commission on the Organization of the Executive Branch recommended that the Bureau of the Budget be reinstated in the Treasury Department, but the commission as a whole opposed the recommendation.[24] The Budget and Accounting Procedures Act of 1950 reinforced the trend of presidential control by explicitly granting the president control over the "form and detail" of the budget document.[25] The Second Hoover Commission in 1955 endorsed strengthening the president's power in budgeting as a means of restoring the "full control of the national purse to the Congress."[26] A president, who had full control of the bureaucracy, could be held accountable by Congress for action taken by the bureaucracy.

One of the stated goals of the reform movement was to bring the sound financial practices of business to the presumably disorganized public sector—a goal often expressed by current reformers. Available evidence, however, indicates that business practices were not particularly exemplary at the turn of the century, suggesting that the reforms were largely invented in the public sector rather than being transferred into government from the outside.[27] It remains popular to advocate bringing good business practices to government, but the corporate accounting scandals that revealed false revenue claims in such giants as Enron and the subprime mortgage investment practices of the major financial market institutions suggest that private practices are not always exemplary.

Responsible for What?

Revenue Responsibility

The earliest concern for financial responsibility centered on taxes. As indicated above, the Magna Carta imposed limitations not on the nature of the Crown's expenditures but on the procedures for raising revenue. The same concern for the revenue side of budgeting was characteristic of the early history of budgeting in this country. The Constitution is more explicit about the tax power of the government than about the nature or purposes of government expenditures.

Expenditure Control, Management, and Planning

The larger the budget has become, the more the concern has shifted to expenditures. Increasing emphasis has been placed on the accountability of government for what it spends and for how well it manages its overall finances. Expenditure accountability may take several different forms. Budgeting scholar Allen Schick described the focus on accountability in U.S. budgeting as having gone through three stages by the 1960s.[28]

The first stage he characterized as concern for tight control over government expenditures. The most prevalent means of exerting this type of expenditure control is to appropriate by line item and object of expenditure. Financial audits are then used to ensure that money is, in fact, spent for the items authorized for purchase. This information focuses budgetary decision making on the things government pays for, such as personnel, travel, and supplies—the objects of expenditure—rather than on the accomplishments of government activities. In other words, responsibility is achieved by controlling the resources or input side.

Schick's description of the second stage was that of a management orientation, with emphasis on the efficiency of ongoing activities. Historically, this orientation is associated with the New Deal through the First Hoover Commission (1949). The emphasis was on holding administrators accountable for the efficiency of their activities through methods such as work performance measurement. Budgeting by activity achieves accountability by measuring the activities carried out for the money expended.

The third stage of budget reform Schick identified was based on the post–Hoover Commission concern regarding the planning function served by budgets. The traditional goal of controlling resource inputs may be accommodated in the short time frame of the coming budget year. Managerial control over efficiency, although aided by a longer time perspective, also may be accommodated in a traditional budget-year presentation. The planning emphasis focuses on a longer time frame. Many objectives of government programs cannot be accomplished in one budget year. A multiyear presentation of the budget is thus necessary to indicate the long-range implications, both financial and program results, of current budget decisions.

The advent of program budgeting in the 1960s with its focus on multiyear planning and the ultimate results of government programs was the culmination of the planning focus on outcomes that must be measured outside the government itself. Control-oriented information such as objects of expenditure and managerial-oriented information such as the outputs produced by government activities (and the costs to achieve those outputs) do not really require measurement outside the orbit of governmental agencies. A focus on outcomes requires much more extensive information that is not generated by the accounting system. Understanding outcomes requires information about what happens as a result of government expenditures. Typically, these outcomes are achieved only by commitment of resources over many budget years.

Some services provided by government lend themselves well to measures of accomplishment, and some do not. Federal responsibilities for defense and foreign policy certainly have visible consequences, but narrowing down to particular budget decisions on expenditures and particular defense or foreign policy outcomes is both conceptually and practically difficult at best. Local government services such as water, streets, solid waste collection and disposal, and so forth are much more susceptible to results measurement. The planning approach epitomized by program budgeting reforms stressed outcome measurement over a multiyear horizon. Are society's ends being achieved as a result of program expenditures?

Financial Management, Financial Condition, and Program Performance

Since those three stages were first characterized in the 1960s, additional improvements in using information to ensure responsible government budgeting have become standard practice. Some have suggested that these efforts since the 1960s constitute additional or new stages of budget reform. One author has offered up prioritization, characterized by budget cutbacks in both federal and state government budgeting in the 1980s, as a fourth stage, and accountability, emphasizing performance measurement, as a fifth stage.[29] Another has suggested a similar fourth stage, labeling it limitation, emphasizing the attempts in the 1980s to shrink the federal budget and state taxing and expenditure limitations (see the chapter on budgeting for revenues and taxes).[30]

While it is clear that budgeting at the federal, state, and local levels continues to change in terms of emphasis and focus, the labeling of additional stages is somewhat in the eye of the beholder. It is difficult to discern a major difference between *limitation* and *control*, for example. It is also clear that some additional budgetary analysis and planning tools have become important in public budgeting systems since the three-stages description was first put forward. One of these is performance measurement and performance management, which enhances the ability to budget for the achievement of results. Another is financial management, which entails greater attention to the financial soundness of public sector institutions and new and enhanced tools to measure and report on financial soundness. Measuring financial health and increased use of business-like financial management tools enhances the ability of elected leaders to exert control over resources.

Performance Management

Performance measures associated with work activities and with long-term results are not new, as already noted. However, performance measurement has evolved and expanded since the 1980s. Program budgeting was much more an approach for the executive to gain greater understanding and control over spending by focusing on plans and results. Today, performance measurement and management have a strong emphasis on public reporting on progress and redefining programs based on citizen response to the measured progress. This emphasis on public reporting is a logical extension of the broader concept of *accountability for results* that characterizes budgeting systems and reforms in budgeting. Newer information tools are focused on external communications. Local government budgeting increasingly focuses on performance budgeting as the major tool for communicating with the public and garnering public support for the budget.[31]

With or without a complete budgetary system overhaul such as program budgeting entails, all levels of government in the United States, and especially state and local government, typically have extensive performance management systems.[32] The "reinventing government" movement and the National Performance Review of the Clinton administration were two examples of the trend toward more measurement and management of results, but with a much greater emphasis on public reporting.[33] The George W. Bush administration built on that progress even while ending the National Performance Review, but moved toward the use of performance ratings with its Program Assessment Rating Tool and the President's Management Agenda. The GPRA Modernization Act in 2010 included provisions intended to enhance both congressional and executive emphases on performance measurement and management.

Performance management emphasizes setting objectives and then motivating managers to be entrepreneurial in their pursuit of those objectives. Of course, since managing growth in government and achieving efficiencies is such a strong focus in performance management, the tools may also be used to shrink programs for other than managerial reasons. Other countries also have given the same emphases to results-oriented or value-driven budgeting as a primary tool in increasing the efficiency and reducing the size of the public sector.[34]

Financial Management

Another feature that has seen heightened focus is the financial health of the governmental entity or the entire government. There are two facets to this: (1) improved public reporting on the financial condition of government, and (2) a significant focus on the value and condition of long-lived assets such as infrastructure systems. Publicly traded corporations have always had to answer to their stockholders for the financial condition of the corporation, and privately held companies at a minimum have to demonstrate sound financial condition to secure debt financing from lenders. But the application of financial management concepts to focus on the financial condition of government agencies was new in the late 1980s. The emphasis has been on creating tools for measuring the financial condition of government, adapted from private financial and managerial accounting practices, and new mechanisms for ensuring that the government remains in a sound financial position.

One of the motivations behind the concern to hold government accountable for its long-run financial position was the New York City budget crisis of the mid-1970s. Following on the heels of that near-bankruptcy, both financial institutions that purchased municipal bonds and citizens who wondered about their own cities sought to improve the reporting of the long-term financial position of governments.[35] At the time, the general operating budget and related accounting reports often did not reveal the overall financial position of the government entity. Now, virtually every large local and state government in the United States, as well as the federal government, routinely produces reports, often with much public fanfare on their financial condition.[36]

Fixed Asset Management

Concern at the federal level has led to a much greater emphasis on fixed asset management and increased attention in the annual budget to investments in long-lasting assets. The Governmental Accounting Standards Board Statement No. 34 (GASB 34) requires state and local governments and other public entities to report on their fixed assets (see the chapters on financial management and capital assets). Some government expenditures are really investments in future economic productivity. Others primarily consume resources with little hope of any future payoff. Investment means creating additional productive capacity, such as improving transportation networks that reduce the cost of private sector economic activity through more efficient means of transportation and upgrading education systems that enhance the long-term intellectual ability of students to develop new products and new processes.

All governments budget for these activities, but not all government budgeting systems make explicit the consumption-versus-investment tradeoffs in budget decisions. The argument can be made that some funds should be diverted away from social welfare programs that fail to produce new capability and toward investment opportunities that stimulate regional and national economic development. While most state and local governments employ formal capital budgeting techniques, federal agencies typically do not, although in specific types of investments, such as information technology, formalized capital investment planning and analysis now are required (see the chapter on capital assets).[37]

The notion of stages in budgeting can be overemphasized. Whether one decides ultimately to label trends as new stages, it is clear that there is a stronger emphasis on program and performance measurement and on financial management and reporting with significant efforts and new information tools at all levels of government. Most of the emphasis in this text is on the budget as an instrument for financial and program decision making at all levels of government—federal, state, and local. The one responsibility that most sharply differentiates federal budget decisions from state and local decisions is the federal government's responsibility for the overall state of the economy. Not only does the federal budget allocate resources among competing programs, but it is also an instrument for achieving economic stability and growth (see the chapter on government and the economy). The responsibility to use it as an instrument of economic policy has been a part of the federal budgetary process since the Employment Act of 1946.[38]

Budgeting is an important process by which accountability or responsibility can be provided in a political system. As has been discussed, responsibility varies both in terms of the people to whom the system is accountable and in terms of its purposes. Given the various forms of accountability and the types of choices that decision makers have available to them, different meanings can be attached to the terms *budget* and *budgeting system*. Depending on the purposes of a budget, decision makers will need different kinds and amounts of information to aid them in making choices. The following sections focus on the kinds of information required for different budgetary choices and the kinds of procedures for generating the necessary information.

BUDGETS AND BUDGETING SYSTEMS

What Is a Budget?

Budget Documents

In its simplest form, a budget is a document or a collection of documents that refers to the financial condition and future plans of an organization (family, corporation, government), including information on revenues, expenditures, activities, and purposes or goals.

In contrast to an accounting operating statement, which is retrospective in nature, referring to past conditions, a budget is prospective, referring to anticipated revenues, expenditures, and accomplishments. Of course, budgets always contain some information about past revenues and expenditures that is consistent with accounting records. Historically, the word *budget* referred to a leather pouch, wallet, bag, or purse. More particularly, "In Britain the term was used to describe the leather bag in which the Chancellor of the Exchequer carried to Parliament the statement of the Government's needs and resources."[39]

The status of budget documents is not consistent across political jurisdictions. In the federal government, the budget has limited legal status. It is the official recommendation of the president to Congress, but it is not the official document under which the government operates. As will be seen later, the official operating budget of the United States consists of several documents—namely, appropriation acts. In contrast, local budgets proposed by mayors may become official working budgets adopted in their entirety by the city councils.[40]

In still other instances, there may be a series of budget documents instead of one budget for any given government. These may include (1) an operating budget, which handles the bulk of ongoing operations; (2) a capital budget, which covers major new construction projects; and (3) a series of special fund budgets that cover programs funded by specific revenue sources (see the chapter on financial management). Special fund budgets commonly include those for highway programs financed through gasoline and tire sales taxes. In such cases, revenue from these sources is earmarked for highway construction, improvement, and maintenance. As another example, fishing and hunting license fees may constitute the revenue for a special fund devoted to the stocking of streams and the provision of ample hunting opportunities.

The format of budget documents also varies. On the whole, budget documents tend to provide greater information on expenditures than on revenues, which are usually treated in a brief section. On the expenditure side, budgets are multipurpose, in that no single document and no single definition can exhaust the functions budgets serve or the ways they are used. At the most general level, budgets can be conceived of as (1) descriptions, (2) explanations or causal assertions, and (3) statements of preferences or values.

Budgets as Descriptions

Budgets are first descriptions of the status of an organization, whether it is an agency, a ministry, or an entire government. The budget document may describe what the organization purchases, what it does, and what it accomplishes. Descriptions of organizational activity are also common in budget documents. Expenditures may be classified according to the activities they support. For example, a revenue department may be concerned with initial tax collection, taxpayer assistance, and audit/enforcement. Another type of description, organizational accomplishments, states the consequences of resource consumption and work activities for those outside the organization. For example, successful job placements for individuals finishing a vocational rehabilitation program constitute one type of outcome or consequence of a public expenditure. These statements require external verification of the effects of the organization on its environment.

As descriptions, budgets provide a discrete picture of an organization at a point or points in time, in terms of resources consumed, work performed, and external effects. The dollar (or euro or pound sterling) revenues and expenditures, according to these types of descriptions, may be the only quantitative information supplied. Alternatively, information may be supplied about the number and types of personnel; the quantity and kinds of equipment purchased; measures of performance, such as the number of buildings inspected or the number of acres treated; and measures of impact, such as the number of accidents prevented, the amount of crop yield increases, and so forth. Generally, the more descriptive material supplied, the more the organization can be held accountable for the funds spent, the activities supported by those expenditures, and the external accomplishments produced by those activities. Much of the history of budget reform reflects attempts to increase the quantity and quality of descriptive material available both to decision makers and to the public.

Budgets as Explanations

When they describe organizations in terms of purchases, activities, and accomplishments, budgets also at least implicitly serve a second major function—explanation of causal relationships. The expenditure of a specific amount for the purchase of labor and materials that will be combined in particular work activities implies the presumed existence of a causal sequence that will produce certain results. Regardless of how explicit or how vague the budget document or the statements of organization officials may be, budgetary decisions always imply a causal process in which work activities consume resources to achieve goals. Some organizations may have little accurate information about accomplishments, especially public organizations whose accomplishments are not measured in terms of profit and loss. Governments may choose not to be explicit about particular results because they are difficult to measure, politically sensitive, or both. Regardless of the availability of information or the willingness of an organization to collect and use it, the budget is an expression of a set of causal relationships.

Budgets as Preferences

Budgets are statements of preferences. Whether intended or not, the allocation of resources among different agencies, among different activities, or among different accomplishments reveals the preferences of those making the allocations. These may be the actual preferences of a few decision makers, but more often they are best thought of as the collective preferences of many decision makers arrived at through complex bargaining. A preference schedule reflects, if not any one individual's values, an aggregate of choices that become the collective value judgment for the local government, state, or nation.

What Is a Budgeting System?

Systems

Budgeting can best be understood as a kind of system, a "set of units with relationships among them."[41] Budgetary decision making consists of the actions of executive officials (both in a central organization such as the governor's office or the mayor's staff and in executive line agencies), legislative officials, organized interest groups, and perhaps unorganized interests that may be manifested in a generally felt public concern about public needs and taxes. All these actions are related, and understanding budgeting means understanding the interrelationships. Such understanding is best achieved by thinking in terms of complex systems.

A complex social system is composed of organizations, individuals, the values held by these individuals, the norms they act upon, and the relationships among these elements. A system may be thought of as a network typically consisting of many different parts with messages flowing among the parts. The elements of systems interact with each other to produce system results, or consequences, and the network of interactions may produce the same set of results through several different paths, or the same path may from time to time produce different outcomes.[42] Budgeting systems involve political actors, economic and social theories, numerous institutional structures, and competing norms and values, all of which produce outputs in patterns not immediately evident from studying only budget documents.

Budget System Outputs

In a budgetary system, the outputs flowing from the network of interactions are budget decisions, and these vary greatly in their overall significance. Not every unit of the system will have equal decisional authority or power. A manager of a field office for a state health department is likely to have less power to make major budgetary decisions than the administrative head of the department, the governor, or the members of the legislative appropriations committees. Yet each participant does contribute some input to the system. The field manager may alert others in the system to the emergence of a new health problem and, in doing so, may contribute greatly to the eventual establishment of a new health program to combat that problem. Modern information technology and the greater emphasis on responsibility at all levels of the organization for achieving results means the lower-level staff in an agency are much more influential than they have been in the past. Even actors not in the formal budgeting system may influence the decisions. For example, doctors and hospitals, who are part of surveillance for early detection of the latest flu, in effect are providing inputs to the budgeting system.

Like the outputs of any other system or network, budget decisions are seldom final and more commonly are sequential. Decisions are tentative, in that each decision made is forwarded for action to another participant in the process. This does not mean that all decisions are reversible. Major breakthroughs, such as passage of the Elementary and Secondary Education Act of 1965, which provided substantial federal aid to education, are abandoned only in response to powerful political pressure.[43] The No Child Left Behind Act, which reauthorized major elements of federal assistance to elementary and secondary education, continued most of the key elements of the original 1965 legislation, although giving great emphasis to testing student achievement as a means of ensuring accountability at the classroom level (see the discussion in the chapter on intergovernmental relations).[44] Likewise, the introduction of prescription drug care into Medicare in 2006 was only after years of debate and proposals. Despite dissatisfaction, eliminating such hard-won programs once in place is nearly impossible. Subsequent budget decisions, therefore, are in large part bounded by previous decisions. The subsequent decisions tend to center on the question of changing the level of commitment—allocating more resources, fewer resources, or different kinds of resources—to achieve desired levels of impact or different types of impact.

System Interconnectedness

Another feature of a system is that a change in any part of it will alter other parts. Because all units are related, any change in the role or functioning of one unit necessarily affects other units. In some instances, changes may be of such a modest nature that their ramifications for other parts of the system are difficult to discern. However, when major budgetary reforms are instituted, they assuredly affect most participants. For example, if one unit in the system is granted greater authority, individuals and organizations having access to that unit have their decisional involvement enhanced, whereas those groups associated with other units have diminished roles.[45] Thus, each individual and institution evaluates budget reforms in terms of how political strengths will be realigned under the reforms.

INFORMATION AND DECISION MAKING

Types of Information

To serve the multiple functions described in the preceding section, budgeting systems must produce and process a variety of information. Most of the major reforms, whether attempted or proposed, in public budget systems have been intended to reorganize existing information and to provide participants with new and greater quantities of information. Basically, two types of information exist: program information and resource information. The latter is more traditional. People are accustomed to thinking of budgets in terms of resources, such as monetary units and personnel. A budget would not be a budget if it did not contain dollar, ruble, or other monetary figures. Similarly, budgets commonly contain data on employees or personnel.

Conventional accounting systems provide much of the information that public organizations use for budgetary decisions. This type of information is limited to the internal aspects of organizations—for example, the location of organizational responsibility for expenditures and the resources purchased by those expenditures. When the decision-making system incorporates information about the results or implications of programs, one must leave the boundaries of the organization to examine consequences for those outside it. This step requires more extensive and more explicit clarification of governmental goals and objectives (see the chapter on the expenditure side of budget preparation) and increases the importance of analysis. This feature of budget reforms, such as program budgeting, zero-base budgeting, managing for results, and performance budgeting, with their emphasis on program information and priority setting, has generated the most heat among critics of budget reform.[46]

Decision Making

Much of the criticism of reform has involved the argument that reform of decision-making systems must take into account the limitations on human capabilities to use all the information that might be collected and analyzed.[47] Although sometimes subtle differences distinguish theories of decision making, the various theories are often classified into three basic approaches: pure rationality, muddling through or incrementalism, and limited rationality.[48] An early application of these notions to public sector decision making was Graham Allison's study of the 1962 Cuban Missile Crisis, *The Essence of Decision*, in which he characterized three models as rational, organizational, and governmental/political.[49] These are descriptive theories as well as prescriptions for how decisions ought to be made.

Rational Decision Making

Decision making according to the pure rationality approach consists of a series of ordered, logical steps. First, all of an organization's or a society's goals are ranked according to priority. Second, all possible alternatives are identified. The costs of each alternative are compared with anticipated benefits. Judgments are made as to which alternative comes closest to satisfying the relevant needs or desires. The alternative with the highest payoff and/or least cost is chosen. Pure rationality theories assume that complete and perfect information about all alternatives is both available and manageable. Decision making, therefore, is choosing among alternatives to maximize some objective function. The rational choice model is built on microeconomics and the notion of the individual actor making an optimal choice to maximize the decision maker's utility.

The applicability of the rationality model is limited, and few argue that it is a description of how ordinary human beings make most decisions. It is most consistent with notions of technical or economic rationality, where objectives can be stated with some precision and the range of feasible alternatives is finite.[50] Also, the model can be of use where accurate predictions of behavior are possible, such as in the private market, where assumptions regarding rational behavior can be used to predict future economic trends.[51]

As a description of how government budgeting works, the pure rationality model is obviously misleading. Meeting the complete requirements of even a few of the steps is impossible. It has been argued that the costs of information are so high as to make it rational to be ignorant—that is, to make decisions on the basis of a limited search and limited information. Some attempts at budget reform have been criticized as attempts to impose an unworkable model, pure rationality, on government financial decision making. The use of program information has been a particular target for criticism.[52] However, this criticism is somewhat misdirected in that it is not so much the information search cost that is limiting, but rather the individual decision maker's perspective. Public budgeting decisions are made in a larger political context with numerous actors involved, a more complicated situation than the clear-sighted approach toward an agreed-upon objective that is the essence of the rational choice model.

Incrementalism

The second approach to decision making, muddling through or incrementalism, is more akin to the organizational and political processes of actual decision making identified by Allison. It has been advocated as more realistic by critics of pure rationality, such as Charles E. Lindblom, Aaron Wildavsky, and others.[53] According to this view, decision making involves a conflict of organizational and individual interests and a corresponding clash of information that results in the accommodation of diverse partisan interests through bargaining.

"Real" decision making is presumed to begin as issues are raised by significant interest groups that request or demand changes from the existing state. Decision making is not some conscious form of pure rationality, but is a process of incrementally adjusting existing practices to establish or reestablish consensus among participants. Alternatives to the status quo are normally not considered unless partisan interests bring them to the attention of the participants in the decision-making process. There is only a marginal amount of planned search for alternatives to achieve desired ends. The decision process is structured so that partisan interests have the opportunity to press their desires at some point in the deliberations. Decisions represent a consensus on policy reached through a political, power-oriented bargaining process.

The most important characteristic of the muddling through, or incrementalist, approach is its emphasis on the proposition that budgetary decisions are necessarily political. Its descriptive appeal is that it more accurately depicts a process in which numerous actors, each with a different point of view, negotiate and bargain for a consensus. The larger the issue, the more difficult it is to achieve consensus for radical change, which results most often in incremental adjustments to the status quo. Whereas a purely rational approach might suggest that budgetary decisions are attempts to allocate resources according to economic or other "objective" criteria, the incrementalist view stresses the extent to which political considerations outweigh calculations of optimality. The strongest critics of many budget reforms have tended to equate those reforms with seeking to establish the pure rationality model or a solely economic model, a description rarely accepted by those proposing budget reforms. As will be seen throughout this text, any "real" budget reform is forced to accommodate the political nature of decision making. In reality, elements of rationalism and incrementalism pervade the budgetary process.[54]

Limited Rationality

The third approach to decision making, a compromise between the other two approaches, is called limited rationality. This model recognizes the inadequacies in the assumptions behind the pure rationality description of decision making as applied to complex problems. While acknowledging the inherent constraints of human cognitive processes, limited rationality does not suggest that a deliberate search for alternative approaches to goal achievement is of no avail. Searching for alternatives is used to find solutions that are satisfactory but not necessarily optimal.

Substantial evidence, cited by some of the giants in budgeting (Wildavsky) and decision making (Lindblom), indicates that many decisions are indeed incremental, and clearly each budget decision does not require a thorough review of all options and careful calculations of the possible outcomes of each option. Yet major decisions that depart dramatically from the past are made from time to time in the budgetary process. Non-incremental change, especially at the macro level, addressing major deficits and surpluses, does occur.[55] And, of course, major events such as terrorist threats and creating a new agency such as the Department of Homeland Security cause non-incremental change, although the core of federal budgeting did not change significantly after September 11, 2001.[56] Furthermore, decision makers often do attempt to achieve public values and are motivated more by the social and economic problems their agencies must address than by bureaucratic budget maximizing and interest-group pressures.[57]

Limited rationality suggests that large forces are marshalled at times for major change, and incremental adjustments are made at other times for issues that do not generate demand for substantial departure from the status quo. Decision theories do differ in how they view the values that decision making serves and the capacities of decision makers to serve those values. One model assumes virtually no limits on human capacities for processing information, another suggests that decision making should be sensitive only to partisan political interests, and still another attempts to strike a balance between the other models. The history of budgeting and budget reform, we argue, reflects the tensions among these approaches to decision making.

SUMMARY

Public budgeting involves choices among ends and means. Public budgeting shares many characteristics with budgeting in the private sector, but it often requires the application of criteria different from those used by private organizations. Chief among these differences is that few public sector decisions can be assessed in terms of profit and loss. Private sector decisions, in contrast, ultimately must consider the long-run profit or loss condition of the firm.

Budgeting systems involve the organization of information for making choices and the structure of decision-making processes. Public budgeting systems have evolved as one means of holding government accountable for its actions. Budgetary procedures are developed to hold the government in general accountable to the public, the executive branch accountable to the legislature, and subordinates accountable to their managers. Budgetary procedures also are developed to specify what the executive is accountable for. Concern for the financial solvency of some city governments and the size of the federal budget deficit and total debt have led to reform proposals to use budgeting as a device for holding governments accountable for their long-term financial position. Renewed interest is evident in citizens demanding that governments report regularly on their performance.

Budgetary systems work through information flows. However, each participant in the budgetary process pays selective attention to information. The various theories of decision making differ in terms of how much information decision makers are willing and able to consider. The decision-making approach that seems best to characterize budgetary systems is the limited rationality approach. This approach underlies the discussions throughout this text.

NOTES

1. Warsh, D. (2006). *Knowledge and the wealth of nations: a story of economic discovery*. New York, NY: W. W. Norton; Ferguson, N. (2011). *Civilization: the west and the rest*. London, UK: Penguin.
2. Downs, A. (1967). *Inside bureaucracy*. Boston, MA: Little, Brown; Wilson, J. (2000). Preface. In *Bureaucracy: what government agencies do and why they do it*. New York, NY: Basic Books.

3. U.S. Council of Economic Advisers (2011). *Economic report of the president: 2011.* (pp. 283, 287). Washington, DC: U.S. Government Printing Office. Note: state and local current expenditures available for 2010 only in national income and product accounts.

4. Porter, M., & Kramer, M. (2006). Strategy and society: the link between competitive advantage and corporate social responsibility. *Harvard Business Review, 84,* 78–92.

5. Hall, B., et al. (2009). *Measuring the returns to R&D.* NBER Working Paper No. 15622. Retrieved December 4, 2011, from http://www.nber.org/papers/w15622.pdf; Deloitte and Thomson-Reuters (2011). *R&D value measurement: is R&D earning its investment?* London, UK: Deloitte. Retrieved December 4, 2011, from http://www.deloitte.com/assets/Dcom-UnitedKingdom/Local%20Assets/Documents/Industries/Life%20Sciences/UK_LS_RD_ROI.pdf.

6. Government Performance and Results Act of 1993 (P.L. 103-62); GPRA Modernization Act of 2010 (P.L. 111-352).

7. Rosen, H. (2005). *Public finance* (7th ed.). New York, NY: McGraw-Hill; Hyman, D. N. (2010). *Public finance: a contemporary application of theory to policy* (10th ed.). Mason, OH: Cengage.

8. Brooks, R. (2004). Privatization of government services: an overview and review of the literature. *Public Budgeting, Accounting and Financial Management, 16,* 467–491; Leavitt, W., & Morris, J. (2007). Public works services arrangements in the twenty-first century: the multiple sector partnership as an alternative to privatization. *Public Works Management Policy, 12,* 325–330.

9. Rubin, I. (2006). Budgeting for contracting in local government. *Public Budgeting & Finance, 26,* Spring, 1–13; Little, R. (2011). The emerging role of public-private-partnerships in mega-project delivery. *Public Works Management Policy, 16,* 240–249.

10. Brown, T., et al. (2006). Managing public service contracts: aligning values, institutions and markets. *Public Administration Review, 66,* 323–331; Vining, A., & Boardman, A. (2008). Public-private partnerships: eight rules for governments. *Public Works Management Policy, 13,* 149–161.

11. White, M. (1978). Budget policy: where does it begin and end? *Governmental Finance, 7,* 2–9. Credits W. F. Willoughby's *The problem of a national budget* (1919) with an early statement of budgeting as a process for holding government accountable.

12. Osborne, D., & Plastrik, P. (1997). *Banishing bureaucracy: the five strategies for reinventing government.* Reading, MA: Addison-Wesley. For the critics' view, see Williams, D. (2000). Reinventing the proverbs of government. *Public Administration Review, 60,* 522–534.

13. Webber, C., & Wildavsky, A. (1986). *A history of taxation and expenditure in the western world.* New York, NY: Simon & Schuster.

14. Burkhead, J. (1956). *Government budgeting* (pp. 2–4). New York, NY: Wiley.

15. Treasury Act of 1789. Ch. 12, 1 Stat. 65.

16. Smithies, A. (1955). *The budgetary process in the United States* (p. 50). New York, NY: McGraw-Hill.

17. Buck, A. (1919). *Public budgeting* (p. 17). New York, NY: Harper and Brothers.

18. Naylor, E. (1941). *The federal budget system in operation* (pp. 22–23). Washington, DC: Author.

19. Burkhead, J. (1956). *Government budgeting,* 12–13.

20. Buck, A. (1919). *Public budgeting,* 14.

21. Burkhead, J. (1956). *Government budgeting,* 23; Willbern, Y. (1967). Personnel and money. In J. Fesler (Ed.), *The 50 states and their local governments* (p. 391). New York, NY: Knopf.

22. Cleveland, F. (1915). Evolution of the budget idea in the United States. *Annals, 62,* November, 22.

23. Budget and Accounting Act of 1921. Ch. 18, 42 Stat. 20.

24. U.S. Commission on Organization of the Executive Branch of the Government (1949). *General management of the executive branch.* Washington, DC: U.S. Government Printing Office.

25. Budget and Accounting Procedures Act of 1950. Ch. 946, Title I, part I, 64 Stat. 832.

26. U.S. Commission on Organization of the Executive Branch of the Government (1955). *Budget and accounting* (p. ix). Washington, DC: U.S. Government Printing Office.

27. Rubin, I. (1993). Who invented budgeting in the United States? *Public Administration Review, 53,* 438–444.

28. Schick, A. (1966). The road to PPB: the stages of budget reform. *Public Administration Review, 26,* 243–258; Caiden, N. (2010). Challenges confronting contemporary public budgeting: retrospectives/prospectives from Allen Schick. *Public Administration Review, 70,* 203–210.

29. Tyer, C., & Willand, J. (1997). Public budgeting in America: a twentieth century retrospective. *Journal of Public Budgeting, Accounting and Financial Management, 9,* 189–219.

30. Bartle, J. (2001). Budgeting, policy, and administration: patterns and dynamics in the United States. *International Journal of Public Administration, 24,* 21–30.

31. Yang, K., & Holzer, M. (2006). The performance-trust link: implications for performance measurement. *Public Administration Review, 66,* 114–126; Berman, B. J. (2006). *Listening to the public: adding the voices of the people to government performance measurement and reporting.* New York, NY: Fund for the City of New York; Epstein, P. D., et al. (2006). *Results that matter: improving communities by engaging citizens, measuring performance, and getting things done.* Hoboken, NJ: Jossey-Bass.

32. Holzer, M., et al. (2009). *Literature review and analysis related to measuring local government efficiency.* Newark, NJ: Rutgers University School of Public Affairs and Administration.

33. National Performance Review (1993). *Mission driven, results-oriented budgeting.* Washington, DC: U.S. Government Printing Office; Thompson, J. (2000). Reinvention as reform: assessing the national performance review. *Public Administration Review, 60,* 508–521.

34. McCormack, L. (2007). Performance budgeting in Canada. *OECD Journal on Budgeting, 7*(4), 1–18. See also, in the same journal issue, articles on performance budgeting in Denmark, Korea, and the Netherlands. The journal regularly publishes articles detailing performance budgeting in a large number of countries. Journal contents can be viewed online at http://www.oecd.org/document/14/0,3746,en_2649_33735_2074062_1_1_1_1,00.html.

35. Johnson, R., & Lewin, A. (1984). Management and accountability models of public sector performance. In T. Miller (Ed.), *Public sector performance: a conceptual turning point* (pp. 224–250). Baltimore, MD: Johns Hopkins University Press.

36. A good example is Comptroller, State of New York (published annually since 2003; see most recent year). *State of New York financial condition report.* Albany, NY: Comptroller's Office of Public Information. Retrieved December 5, 2011, from http://www.osc.state.ny.us/finance/index.htm.

37. Office of Management and Budget (2011). *Circular A-11: Part 7, The planning, budgeting acquisition and management of capital assets.* Retrieved December 5, 2011, from http://www.whitehouse.gov/sites/default/files/omb/circulars/a11/current_year/s300.pdf.

38. Employment Act of 1946. Ch. 33, 60 Stat. 23.

39. Burkhead, J. (1956). *Government budgeting,* 2.

40. Bland, R. (2007). *A budgeting guide for local governments* (2nd ed.). Washington, DC: International City Management Association.

41. Miller, G. (1965). Living systems: basic concepts. *Behavioral Science, 10,* 200.

42. Kendall, K., & Kendall, K. (2010). *Systems analysis and design* (8th ed.). New York, NY: Prentice-Hall.

43. Elementary and Secondary Education Act of 1965 (P.L. 89-10).

44. No Child Left Behind Act of 2001 (P.L. 107-110).

45. Jones, L., & McCaffery, J. (1994). Budgeting according to Aaron Wildavsky: a bibliographic essay. *Public Budgeting & Finance, 14,* Spring, 16–43.

46. Wildavsky, A., & Caiden, N. (2000). *The new politics of the budgetary process* (4th ed.). New York, NY: Longman Press; Kelly, J. (2003). The long view: lasting (and fleeting) reforms in public budgeting in the twentieth century. *Public Budgeting, Accounting and Financial Management, 15,* 309–326; Kasdin, S. (2010). Reinventing reforms: how to improve program management using performance measures. Really. *Public Budgeting & Finance, 30,* Fall, 51–78.

47. Knoll, M. (2010). The role of behavioral economics and behavioral decision making in Americans' retirement savings decisions. *Social Security Bulletin, 70*(4). Retrieved December 5, 2011, from http://www.ssa.gov/policy/docs/ssb/v70n4/v70n4p1.html.

48. Brewer, G., & de Leon, P. (1983). *The foundations of policy analysis.* Chicago, IL: Dorsey.

49. Allison, G., & Zelikow, P. (1999). *Essence of decision: explaining the Cuban missile crisis* (2nd ed.). New York, NY: Longman.

50. The terms *technical* and *economic rationality* are the names of two of five basic types of rationality identified by Diesing, P. (1962). *Reason and society.* Urbana, IL: University of Illinois Press.

51. Friedman, M. (1953). *Essays in positive economics.* Chicago, IL: University of Chicago Press.

52. Wildavsky, A. (1979). *Speaking truth to power: the art and craft of policy analysis.* Boston, MA: Little, Brown.
53. Lindblom, C. (1959). The science of "muddling through." *Public Administration Review, 19,* 79–88; Jones, L. (1997). Changing how we budget: Aaron Wildavsky's perspective. *Journal of Public Budgeting, Accounting and Financial Management, 9,* 46–71.
54. Reddick, C. (2002). Testing rival decision-making theories on budget outputs: theories and comparative evidence. *Public Budgeting & Finance, 22,* Fall, 1–25.
55. Reddick, C. (2003). Budgetary decision making in the twentieth century: theories and evidence. *Journal of Public Budgeting, Accounting and Financial Management, 15,* 251–274; Reddick, C. (2007). State resource allocation and budget formats: towards a hybrid model. *Journal of Public Budgeting, Accounting and Financial Management, 19,* 222–245.
56. Joyce, P. (2005). Federal budgeting after September 11th: a whole new ballgame, or is it déjà vu all over again? *Public Budgeting & Finance, 25,* Spring, 15–31.
57. Reddick, C. (2004). Rational expectations theory and macro budgetary decision-making: comparative analysis of Canada, UK, and USA. *Journal of Public Budgeting, Accounting and Financial Management, 16,* 316–356.

The Public Sector in Perspective

Depending on how we are affected personally by government and our general philosophical views about the roles of the public and private sectors, we have different and sometimes contradictory views about the public sector. Sometimes it is too big; sometimes it is too small. Often we do not think of the government at all, except when government intrudes in obvious ways. Federal income tax filing time in the United States is one of those intrusions, and it often leads one to say: "Government is too big; I pay too much in taxes." The 2010 oil spill resulting from the explosion of the BP deep well rig in the Gulf of Mexico is another dramatic occasion. It led many people to demand faster and more massive response from both federal and state governments.

One danger of generalizing about the size of the public sector of society is that any single generalization necessarily ignores important information. Although the statement "government is vast" may be valid, it fails to recognize the difficulties in determining what is and is not government or the fact that government is also small in some respects. This chapter describes the size and extent of the public sector, discusses the relative and absolute growth rates of government, and considers the general level of taxes and other revenue sources and the societal functions that these revenues support.

The chapter explores three main topics. The first is the relative sizes of the private and public sectors of society and the reasons for the growth of government. The second is the magnitude of government and the historical growth of local, state, and federal finances. The third section contrasts the purposes of government expenditures with the sources of revenue used by the three main levels of government in the United States.

RELATIVE SIZES OF THE PRIVATE AND PUBLIC SECTORS

Basic to all matters of public budgeting is the issue of the appropriate size of the public sector. This issue is inherently political, not only in the partisan sense but also in the sense that it involves fundamental policy questions about what government should and should not do, and what it can and cannot do. At stake are congeries of competing public and private wants and needs and competing philosophies of the role of the public sector in society. Many of the framers of the Constitution wanted to keep the central government small to protect individual liberty. However, other early leaders, such as Alexander Hamilton, sought a more active role for the new government.[1]

Reasons for Growth

Value Questions

The issue of size relates to the values of freedom and social welfare. Keeping government small has been advocated as a means of protecting individuals from tyranny and stimulating individual independence and initiative. In contrast, critics charge that sometimes reliance on the private sector causes the underfinancing of public programs and the failure to confront major social problems.[2] Some people argue that the wave of corporate scandals that occurred in 2002 (Enron and WorldCom, for example) and the stock market volatility due in part to the behavior of large mortgage lending institutions later in the decade were in part caused by placing too much faith in an unfettered—or more precisely, deregulated—private sector. Debates over the rise of the welfare and warfare states have been especially acrimonious.

The U.S. political system, of course, is not structured in such a way that any single and overriding decision is made as to the size of this sector. The multiplicity of governments makes it virtually impossible to reach any single decision about overall governmental size. Decisions relevant to size are made in a political context within and between the executive and legislative branches and among the three major levels of government—local, state, and federal. Each set of decisions contributes to an ultimate resolution of the question, but a decision on the appropriate size really results from tallying many individual choices. And any time we decide to measure the size of the public sector, we are only capturing a snapshot at that point in time. Significant changes in public sector size occur over time, sometimes quite rapidly.

Government Responses

Why government expands has been the subject of extended debate.[3] One of the two main reasons is that government is "responsive" to the demands of society. Wagner's law, originally proposed in the 1880s, holds that economic development creates opportunities for new activities that government alone can perform.[4] The second reason is that government has a supposed propensity to grow. In this case, government grows as a result of empire building by government bureaucrats, supported by political leaders.[5] Among the numerous factors suggested as stimulating responses from government are the following:[6]

- *The need for collective goods.* Because defense, homeland security, disaster response, and some other programs benefit all citizens and cannot be handled readily by the private sector, the government becomes involved. When wars occur, governments grow in size. After the conflict, they tend to remain larger than during the prewar period. Education is another important collective good. Educated people tend to be more productive and increase the total wealth of the society, and the private sector cannot be relied on to provide an appropriate level of public education.

- *Demographic changes.* Increases in total population and in the numbers of newborns and the elderly stimulate the creation and expansion of government programs.
- *Changes in living patterns.* As people move from rural to urban areas, and then from cities to suburbia, demands for government services follow them. Governments must then provide more schools, roads, public utilities, and public safety.
- *Externalities.* Industrial firms, which are concerned mainly with making a profit, may pollute the air and water. Government is expected to control the social costs arising from these private actions.
- *Economic hardships.* Depressions and other negative economic situations stimulate the growth of government.
- *High-risk situations.* When risks are high, the private sector is unlikely to invest large quantities of resources, so government is called upon to support programs. Examples include the development of nuclear energy as a source of electrical power and the creation of the space program. Once the risks of certain aspects of space activity became manageable as a result of government intervention, commercial interests engaged in space research and moved into the launching of private vehicles and satellites.
- *Technological change.* With the advent of new technology, government has provided support, as in the case of roads and airports, to accommodate improved transportation modes and information highways, such as the Internet, and to regulate new industries, as in the case of railroads, radio, and television.

These reasons are helpful in explaining why government is necessary and why it has expanded over time. Proposals to expand or contract the scope of the public sector also reflect many political considerations. Principally, any proposal for the expansion of services that results in an increase in taxes is likely to have unfavorable political repercussions. Therefore, the size issue always relates to both government expenditures and revenues (taxes). Decision makers, no matter how crude or approximate their methods of calculating, attempt to weigh the merits of coping with the current situation with the available resources against the merits of recommending new programs that may alleviate problems but at the same time raise the ire of taxpayers. The success of the Tea Party movement in capturing enough seats in the U.S. House of Representatives in the 2010 congressional elections to unseat the Democratic Party control, in addition to the changeover in many state legislatures, may have in part reflected taxpayer uneasiness with the size of government.

Private and Public Sector Boundaries

Major problems are encountered when attempts are made to gauge the sizes of the public and private sectors and to distinguish between one government and another. Government has become so deeply involved in society that one may frequently have difficulty discerning what is not at least quasi-public. Moreover, governments have extensive relationships with each other, to the point where a discussion of any single government becomes meaningless without a discussion of its relationships with other governments.

Statistical data on government revenues and expenditures fail to reflect adequately the size of government. For instance, the entire political campaign process is clearly governmental in that substantial sums of money are spent to elect people to political offices. These funds are not recorded as government expenditures, but nonetheless are "governmental" in nature.[7] Federal Election Commission statistics show that spending in the 2008 presidential election exceeded $1.7 billion, more than four times the amount spent in the 2000 election.[8] Also, the size of government tends to be understated in cases where government activities require relatively little money and personnel but have a substantial impact on the private sector or other governments. This is especially true with respect to regulatory activities, such as the federal government's control of interstate commerce, occupational safety, and environmental health.

Nonexhaustive Expenditures

It can be misleading to rely exclusively on revenue and expenditure data for measuring size for another reason. Sometimes the assumption is made that all government expenditures represent a drain on the private economy. In fact, government expenditures can be nonexhaustive as well as exhaustive. Exhaustive expenditures occur when government consumes resources, such as facilities and manpower, that might otherwise have been used by the private sector. Nonexhaustive expenditures occur when government redistributes or transfers resources to components of the society instead of consuming them. Interest payments on the national debt, unemployment compensation, aid to the indigent, and old-age and retirement benefits are major examples of nonexhaustive government expenditures.

Another form of nonexhaustive expenditures is investment for the future, whether for capital facilities (see the chapters on capital assets and capital finance) or for services, as in education for children. Government aid to small businesses, support of research and development, and similar activities are forms of investment in future economic development. As a result of these kinds of expenditures, the cost of government is actually less than the total dollar figures reported in budgets. Money that is spent by governments will generate future revenue for both society and its governments.

Effects on the Private Sector

Government expenditures have specific effects on industries, occupations, geographic regions, and subpopulations. These effects are especially evident in the field of defense. During the Cold War, clusters of firms and their employees became highly dependent upon defense outlays, resulting in what President Eisenhower in 1961 decried as the military-industrial complex. The case could be made that a dangerous symbiotic relationship developed between the military, with its penchant for new weaponry, and corporations eager to supply such weaponry. Periodic scandals in defense contracting offer seeming confirmation of the fears expressed by President Eisenhower.

The effects of defense are particularly pronounced in regard to employment, despite the downsizing that has occurred since the end of the Cold War. In 2010, civilian employment in the Department of Defense accounted for just over 0.5% of the private sector labor force and more than one-fourth of the federal government's civilian labor force. In addition, in 2010 the federal government employed more than 1.4 million active duty armed services personnel, including more than 1.1 million within the borders of the United States or its territories. Total military and civilian defense employment constituted 1.5% of total U.S. employment in 2010.[9] Those figures were almost unchanged from 2005, despite the continued buildup of the military during the heights of the Iraq and Afghanistan wars.

The effects of defense expenditures on the private economy also have been substantial. Defense expenditures account for a significant percentage of jobs in various industries. The creation of defense-related jobs entices people into educational programs that train them to develop the requisite skills. As a result, people are attracted to technical career fields that are dependent upon continued defense spending. These people suffer or flourish based on which policies prevail.

Geographic and Industry Effects

Military research, development, and procurement are of such great magnitude that many specific industries and corporations become quasi-public institutions. In 2009, the Department of Defense spent $327.4 billion in total contracts. Of this amount, $303.4 billion went to business firms in the United States. The remainder was provided to nonprofit or education institutions in the United States, intergovernmental contracts, or work done outside the United States.[10] Defense expenditures greatly influence the private sector—in firms that engage in shipbuilding, aircraft construction, and communications, to name just three examples—and the importance of defense expenditures on the private sector increases in periods of defense buildup. Besides providers of military equipment, such as Boeing, General Dynamics, General Electric, and General Motors, numerous consulting and research and development firms are dependent on military expenditures. Nondefense contracting firms are similarly dependent, with 60% to 80% of their revenues coming from government contracts. The role of contractors in Iraq and Afghanistan in performing what had historically been military functions, and in the massive reconstruction programs, received special attention from government watchdog agencies, such as the Government Accountability Office, as charges of poor oversight, waste, fraud, and simply an excessive reliance on contractors mounted.[11]

Employees of these varied private sector firms, judging from their length of service on government projects, are doing work that otherwise would be done (and, in many cases, used to be done) by career civil servants. One difference between these contractors and the civil servants they supplant is that the pay of managerial staff in these firms is often higher than that of similarly trained government employees. Professional salaries, such as for engineers and scientists, tend to be relatively equal, because government must meet private sector salaries to recruit and retain professionals. Another difference is that private sector employees do not constitute a permanent expense to the government. These workers are not protected by civil service laws and are ineligible for government pension benefits. Furthermore, when these workers' services are not needed, government has no obligation to them as it would to its own employees.

The geographic effects of defense expenditures are equally important because they are not uniformly distributed throughout the nation. In 2009, the Department of Defense spent $504 billion. Five states—Virginia, California, Texas, Florida, and Maryland—accounted for $192 billion, or about 38% of that total.[12] In addition to direct expenditures, the Department of Defense also spent $332 billion for procurement contracts and grants in the same year. When payments to these various firms are totaled, the states of Virginia, California, Texas, Maryland, and Connecticut respectively rank as the top five locations of these recipients, accounting for 41% of all contracts and grants.[13]

Defense, while the most striking example of private dependence upon public outlays, is not the sole example. Highway construction also involves large sums of public money. The employees of construction firms specializing in bridge and highway construction are, in effect, government employees. The same is true for suppliers of road-building equipment. Much of the emphasis on job stimulation in the various federal programs adopted starting in 2008 was on highway construction projects that could start immediately and put people back to work (see the chapter on government and the economy). In addition, the 1990s and early 2000s saw a continued emphasis on contracting out as a means of producing public services. In 2005, 10.5 million individuals were employed under federal grants and contracts, up from 7 million in 1999.[14]

In some cases, the impact of government on an industry is greater as a result of what government does *not* do than what it *does* do. The federal government's choice not to tax interest paid on home mortgages (see the chapter on budgeting for revenues and taxes), for example, has a far greater effect on the housing industry than all federal expenditures for public housing and redevelopment.

The lack of clear-cut distinctions between the public and private sectors and between one government and another is evident in education. Elementary and secondary education is a function of local school districts, but about half the funds used by these districts come from state governments, with additional funds coming from the federal government and local sources of revenue, primarily property taxes. The states have a primary role in funding public higher education, with important federal support, especially in the form of student aid and research financing. Governments also selectively subsidize private colleges and universities. Private corporations also make important contributions to both public and private schools. In 2002, the U.S. Supreme Court ruled that it is constitutional for governments to use public funds to provide vouchers to parents whose children attend private or parochial schools.[15] Since that ruling, some states have adopted statutes permitting school vouchers, but most have not. In addition, the level of funding may understate the degree of federal involvement in elementary and secondary education. The federal government can, as a condition of the receipt of federal assistance, insist that state and local governments adopt policies they might otherwise have chosen not to adopt. The best recent example of this is the federal No Child Left Behind Act, which forced state and local governments to adopt specific accountability standards in the form of testing requirements in order to continue to receive federal funds.[16] Under the constitutionally provided federal system, the national government cannot directly compel states and localities to establish such standards, but the threat of the loss of federal funds is sufficient to encourage most to go along with the federal requirements. The Obama administration, while continuing to enforce the act, introduced measures in the reauthorizing legislation to allow states more flexibility, but reauthorization stalled in Congress. Stimulus programs to provide both additional funding and flexibility to states, such as the Race to the Top program in the American Recovery and Reinvestment Act of 2009, did give states more choice in designing their education programs, with the Obama administration using waivers to allow states to set their own standards.[17]

Subpopulation Effects

Taxes and expenditures affect different subpopulations in different ways. In the example given earlier of the federal government allowing income tax deductions for interest paid on home mortgages, the middle and upper classes benefit far more than lower-income groups, who are typically renters rather than homeowners. This tax expenditure—namely, the government's not taxing something that could be taxed—has a redistributional effect in favor of the middle and upper classes (see the chapter on budgeting for revenues and taxes).

Government actions also have important effects on generations, including those yet to be born. Taxing and spending policies can help or harm children (born and unborn) through health and education programs, the working-age population through transportation programs, and the elderly through government-sponsored nursing care and the like. Future generations benefit from government programs that encourage investment in economic development, but excessive debts that governments may accumulate may harm these same people in the future.

THE MAGNITUDE AND GROWTH OF GOVERNMENT

There are many ways to measure the magnitude of government, but measurements of dollars and people are generally the easiest. By focusing on revenues, expenditures, and numbers of employees, we can use comparable standards in contrasting governments with each other and with private organizations. These measures, then, are the main ones used in this section. While care has been taken in making these comparisons to obtain the most recent and accurate data possible, some of the data here must be considered approximate.[18]

Revenues

One approach to assessing the size of government is to compare many governments with each other, as well as with large private sector organizations. **Table 2–1** makes such comparisons, using revenues or receipts, which allows comparisons among private and public organizations.[19] Table 2–1 ranks the 25 largest governments and industrial corporations in the world, as measured by revenues. Thirteen of the 25 are governments, with the U.S. federal government ranked first. One U.S. state government, California, makes the list as the nineteenth largest organization in the world. Significantly, 12 of the world's 25 largest organizations are not governments but private sector corporations (all multinational), with Wal-Mart coming in as the ninth largest. The listing is replete with intriguing contrasts. For example, Austria's government budget is smaller than the budget of California, and both have budgets much smaller than Wal-Mart's.

Figure 2–1 shows central government revenue as a percentage of GDP for 2009 for Organization for Economic Cooperation and Development (OECD) countries, excluding five with no data for 2009. On that list, the United States ranks third from the bottom, probably surprising to most U.S. citizens. Note, however, that the figures are for central government revenues only. Many OECD countries are unitary states, so that all government revenues are central, whereas government in the United States, as noted in this chapter, includes substantial financial roles for state and local governments. Thus, comparing the

Table 2–1 Twenty-Five Largest Governments and Industrial Corporations in the World by Revenues, 2009

Rank	Governments	Revenues (Billions of Dollars)	Private Corporations
1	United States (Federal)	$2,105.05	
2	Germany (1)	$1,231.88	
3	France	$1,111.03	
4	Italy	$919.60	
5	Japan	$795.75	
6	United Kingdom	$747.50	
7	Spain	$448.55	
8	Canada	$421.42	
9		$408.21	Wal-Mart Stores
10		$285.13	Royal Dutch Shell
11		$284.65	Exxon Mobil
12		$246.14	BP
13	Korea	$213.24	
14		$204.11	Toyota Motor
15	Belgium	$203.64	
16		$202.20	Japan Post Holdings
17	Sweden	$188.33	
18		$187.52	Sinopec
19	California	$186.31	
20		$184.50	State Grid
21		$175.26	AXA
22		$165.50	China National Petroleum
23		$163.53	Chevron
24		$163.20	ING Group
25	Austria	$162.98	

Sources: Data from U.S. Council of Economic Advisers (2011). *Economic report of the president (p. 285)*. Washington, DC: U.S. Government Printing Office; Bureau of the Census, U.S. Department of Commerce (2009). *State government finances 2009: summary table*. Retrieved March 28, 2011, from http://www.census.gov/govs/state/; CNN Money (2009). *Global 500*. Retrieved May 21, 2011, from http://money.cnn.com/magazines/fortune/global500/2010/full_list/; Organization for Economic Cooperation and Development (2010). *Revenue statistics: comparative tables*. Retrieved May 23, 2011, from http://www.oecd-ilibrary.org/taxation/data/revenue-statistics/comparative-tables_data-00262-en?isPartOf=/content/datacollection/ctpa-rev-data-en.

U.S. federal government only with countries that have no state and local governments is somewhat misleading. Adding state and local revenues to federal revenues and dividing by GDP moves the United States two more places up the list, but it is still near the bottom. One other observation is important, and that is that the revenue figures do not consider borrowing. U.S. expenditures as a percent of GDP are considerably higher—36%—than U.S. revenues (see the chapter on government and the economy for a discussion of deficits and debt). This difference is due to expenditures financed by borrowing.

A comparison of organizations only in the United States also demonstrates the significant size of the governmental sector. A list of the top 50 organizations (including corporations, the federal government, and state governments) in the United States includes seven state governments (see **Table 2–2**). These states, in order of appearance, are California, New

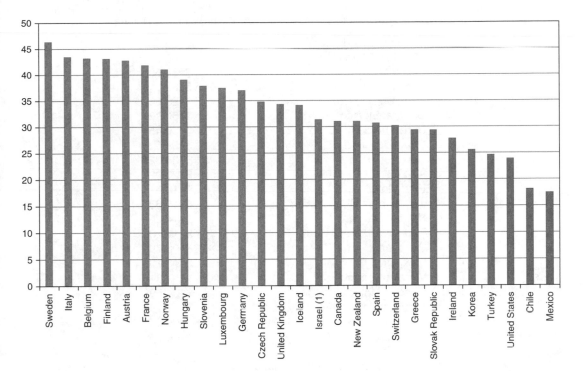

Figure 2–1 Central Government Revenue as a Percentage of GDP: Selected OECD Countries 2009.
Source: Data from Organization for Economic Cooperation and Development (2010). *Revenue statistics: comparative tables.*
Retrieved October 12, 2011, from http://www.oecd-ilibrary.org/taxation/data/revenue-statistics/comparative-tables_
data-00262-en?isPartOf=/content/datacollection/ctpa-rev-data-en

York, Texas, Florida, Pennsylvania, Illinois, and Ohio. If cities were included in the ranking, New York City would be 42nd on the list, just below Pennsylvania and above Illinois and Ohio.[20]

These statistics dramatically underscore the need for caution in generalizing about governments or private corporations. It is necessary to recognize the important differences in the functions of government and industry and the methods by which these organizations make decisions. Differences also abound within these two types of organizations. The services provided and methods of decision making are not identical in the governments of Japan, Germany, and the United Kingdom, nor are they the same in such private corporations as General Motors, IBM, and Wells Fargo. In contrast, using the standard of revenue size may provide more insights into the operations of organizations than simply classifying organizations as public or private, national or local, and so forth. Revenue is a key measure of the economic impact of an organization—revenue collected from the private sector by governments or sales by private companies (see the chapter on government and the economy). Though not all industrial firms are like General Motors, nor are all state governments like California's, all organizations of any given size, regardless of their private or public character, may exhibit some common traits, and all of a similar size represent similar proportions of the total economy. And many large private organizations in the United

Table 2–2 Fifty Largest U.S. Organizations by Revenues, 2009 (in Billions of Dollars)

1	United States (Federal)	$2105.05
2	Wal-Mart Stores	$408.21
3	Exxon Mobil	$284.65
4	California	$186.31
5	Chevron	$163.53
6	General Electric	$156.78
7	Bank of America Corp.	$150.45
8	ConocoPhillips	$139.52
9	New York (State)	$135.22
10	AT&T	$123.02
11	Ford Motor	$118.31
12	J.P. Morgan Chase & Co.	$115.63
13	Hewlett-Packard	$114.55
14	Berkshire Hathaway	$112.49
15	Citigroup	$108.79
16	McKesson	$108.70
17	Verizon Communications	$107.81
18	General Motors	$104.59
19	American International Group	$103.19
20	Cardinal Health	$99.61
21	CVS Caremark	$98.73
22	Wells Fargo	$98.64
23	International Business Machines	$95.76
24	Texas	$95.25
25	UnitedHealth Group	$87.14
26	Procter & Gamble	$79.70
27	Kroger	$76.73
28	AmerisourceBergen	$71.79
29	Costco Wholesale	$71.42
30	Valero Energy	$70.04
31	Archer Daniels Midland	$69.21
32	Boeing	$68.28
33	U.S. Postal Service	$68.09
34	Home Depot	$66.18
35	Target	$65.36
36	WellPoint	$65.03
37	Florida	$64.24
38	Walgreen	$63.34
39	Johnson & Johnson	$61.90
40	State Farm Insurance Cos.	$61.48
41	Pennsylvania	$60.73
42	Medco Health Solutions	$59.80
43	Microsoft	$58.44
44	Illinois	$55.58
45	Ohio	$54.44
46	United Technologies	$52.92
47	Dell	$52.90
48	Goldman Sachs Group	$51.67
49	Pfizer	$50.01
50	Best Buy	$49.69

Sources: CNN Money (2009). *Global 500-U.S. only.* Retrieved May 23, 2011, from http://money.cnn.com/magazines/fortune/global500/2010/countries/US.html; U.S. Council of Economic Advisers (2011). *Economic report of the president* (p. 285). Washington, DC: U.S. Government Printing Office; Bureau of the Census, U.S. Department of Commerce (2009). *State government finances 2009: summary table.* Retrieved March 28, 2011, from http://www.census.gov/govs/state/.

States received massive bailout funds during the most recent recession, such as General Motors, further blurring private versus public distinctions.

Although total revenues or expenditures are useful as approximate guides in measuring the size of government, these data need to be assessed in light of the varied capabilities of societies to support government. Unfortunately, reliable international data are often unavailable. Therefore, drawing useful comparisons among international organizations is difficult.

Even given these limitations, it is obvious that the U.S. economy is one of the most prosperous in the world. The high per capita GDP in the United States, $42,723 in 2010, has allowed for both big government and a large private sector.[21] While the size of federal, state, and local government as a proportion of GDP has grown—from about 31% in 2005 to 36% in 2010—the growth is not as dramatic as it might seem given the depth of the recession that started in 2007.[22] This figure, however, is misleading in regard to the size of the public sector in that just under half of the per capita expenditures go toward the purchase of goods and services—the other half is used for transfer payments and interest payments on debt.

Expenditures

Because early records on state and local finance are spotty, federal expenditure data must be used to obtain some overall perspective on the growth of government since the eighteenth century. **Table 2–3** shows federal spending from 1789 through 2010. During this period, expenditures rose from only $4.3 million in the first few years to almost $3.5 trillion annually in fiscal year 2010 (bear in mind that an important contributor to this difference is inflation).[23]

The twentieth century has seen important differences in the expenditure patterns of the federal government and those of state and local governments. Federal expenditures have fluctuated most, primarily because of war-related activities. The first year in which federal expenditures exceeded $1 billion was 1865, the peak year of the Civil War. Later, in response to World War I, federal expenditures jumped from $0.7 billion in 1916 to $18.5 billion in 1919, then dropped to $6.4 billion the following year. They also increased from $13.3 billion in 1941, the year the United States entered into World War II, to $92.7 billion in 1945, then declined just after the war. During the Korean War, expenditures rose from $42.6 billion in 1950 to $74.3 billion in 1953, and then dropped to $68.4 billion in 1955, after the war.[24]

In general, the past century has seen a pattern where federal expenditures have risen during wartime and then declined, but not to prewar levels, resulting in a cumulative increase over time. The Vietnam War era, however, departed from this pattern: federal expenditures rose both during and after the war. One of the reasons for the continued high spending from the 1960s onward was the creation and growth of large entitlement programs, such as Social Security, Medicare, and Medicaid. More recently, the Afghanistan and Iraq wars resulted in increases in federal spending as a proportion of GDP, as Table 2–3 shows, and a substantial increase in federal debt (see the chapter on government and the economy). The addition to the federal debt from the approximately $1.3 trillion in war-related expenditures over ten years accounted for about 25% of the increase in federal

Table 2–3 Federal Government Expenditures, Selected Years, 1789–2010 (Millions of Dollars)

1789–91	4	1885	260	1975	332,332
1800	11	1890	318	1980	590,947
1805	11	1895	356	1985	946,423
1810	8	1900	529	1990	1,253,198
1815	33	1905	567	1995	1,515,837
1820	18	1910	694	2000	1,789,216
1825	16	1915	746	2001	1,863,190
1830	15	1920	6,358	2002	2,011,153
1835	18	1925	2,924	2003	2,160,117
1840	24	1930	3,320	2004	2,293,006
1845	23	1935	6,412	2005	2,472,205
1850	40	1940	9,468	2006	2,655,100
1855	60	1945	92,712	2007	2,728,700
1860	63	1950	42,562	2008	2,982,500
1865	1,298	1955	68,444	2009	3,517,700
1870	310	1960	92,191	2010	3,455,800
1875	275	1965	118,228		
1880	268	1970	195,649		

Sources: Data from Bureau of the Census, U.S. Department of Commerce (1975). *Historical statistics of the United States: colonial times to 1970* (part 2, p. 1114). Washington, DC: U.S. Government Printing Office; U.S. Office of Management and Budget (2007). *Historical tables, budget of the United States government: fiscal year 2007* (pp. 53–54). Washington, DC: U.S. Government Printing Office; U.S. Congressional Budget Office (2011). *The budget and economic outlook: fiscal years 2011–2021* (pp. 54, 87). Washington, DC: U.S. Government Printing Office.

debt (see the chapter on government and the economy). The remainder is attributable to domestic, civilian programs, mainly the anti-recession measures.

State and local expenditures, in contrast, have fluctuated less. In 1902, state and local expenditures were $1.1 billion, and they have continued to grow steadily over the past 100 years, to $2.4 trillion in 2008, with no significant reductions during any period.[25]

Important shifts have occurred in the extent to which the nation relies on different levels of government. At the turn of the century, local governments were by far the biggest spenders, followed by the federal government and then the states. During the Great Depression, federal spending spurted above local expenditures, and the gap has continued to widen. As of 2008, federal expenditures stood at $3 trillion,[26] compared with $1.7 trillion for states and $1.6 trillion for local governments.[27] Caution should be exercised in interpreting these numbers, in that each includes intergovernmental transfers—namely, grants from one government to another. Total spending for all governments was $5.8 trillion in 2010, of which $3.7 trillion represented federal expenditures and $2.1 trillion represented state and local expenditures. (Note that data are not as readily available for local government finances, so when separating local from state, the data are not as current.) These last numbers take out the effect of intergovernmental transfers— $0.5 trillion. Therefore, taxes collected at the federal level (for example) but spent at the state or local level are counted as federal spending.[28]

One means of looking at the growth of government over time, while controlling for price changes, is to consider government expenditures as a percentage of GDP. **Figure 2–2** shows that, from 1926 to 2010, the cost of government rose from 12% to 36% of GDP. Increases first occurred in the 1930s due to the Great Depression, and World War II brought expenditures to an all-time high at about half of GDP. A sharp cutback followed in the postwar years, and expenditures dropped to a low of just under 20% by 1948. The Cold War and the Korean War occasioned another sharp increase in the early 1950s, and— after reductions in military spending in the late 1950s—the Great Society programs and the Vietnam War resulted in increased spending again during the 1960s; the spending has persisted since that time. Although there has been some year-to-year fluctuation, the percentage of GDP devoted to government remained relatively stable between 28% and 34% since 1970, rising to 36% in 2010 as a result of economic stimulus programs and defense spending.

Public Employment

Another way to measure the size and growth of government is to examine trends in the number of government employees. In 1816, there were fewer than 5,000 full- and part-time civilian employees in the federal service. Much more growth in public employment followed the Civil War. In 1871, there were more than 50,000 federal employees, and this number doubled to 100,000 by 1881. The period of fastest growth was from the Great Depression through World War II. In 1931, there were still only 610,000 employees, but by 1945—the peak of the wartime economy—the federal civilian workforce had climbed to

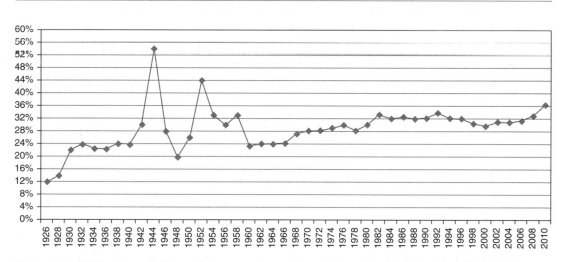

Figure 2–2 All Government Expenditures as a Percentage of Gross Domestic Product, 1926–2010.
Sources: Data from Bureau of Census, U.S. Department of Commerce (1969). *Historical statistics on governmental finances and employment* (pp.1, 36–37). Washington, DC: U.S. Government Printing Office; U.S. Council of Economic Advisers (2011). *Economic report of the president* (pp. 283, 287). Washington, DC: U.S. Government Printing Office.

nearly 4 million. Within a year, however, it was reduced to fewer than 3 million employees, and since then, only once (in 1950) has the federal workforce dropped below 2 million. Federal civilian personnel averaged approximately 3 million between 1970 and 2000, but decreased to about 2.7 million by 2005 and increased about 3% to 2.8 million by 2010.[29]

Although the size of the federal bureaucracy is extraordinarily large, the government's personnel are geographically dispersed. In 2009, California had 169,000 federal civilian employees, a figure equal to almost one-third of Wyoming's population. Federal employees (excludes military personnel) are also numerous in other states, including Virginia, with 147,000; Texas, with 140,000; and Maryland, with 124,000.[30] In the 1990s, such states became painfully aware of their dependence on federal employment as the government began to downsize the military, because about one of every three federal civilian jobs is in defense. Similar effects on states with high defense-related employment likely will occur as the post–Iraq and Afghanistan defense period budgets decline, relative to the total federal budget, assuming no major defense crisis occurs.

At the state and local levels, the number of employees has also increased. State employment grew from 3.8 million in 1980 to 4.4 million in 2009. In the same period, local employment increased from 9.6 million to 12.4 million.[31] However, both state and local employment had declined by 2010 with cutbacks in most categories of state and local employees. Significantly, the growth at the local level has been accompanied by a decline in the number of local governments. In 2007, there were more than 89,000 local governments, 29,000 fewer than five decades earlier. This decline is largely attributable to school district consolidation. Since 1972, the number of local governments has been increasing gradually, due mainly to increases in the number of special districts—that is, governments that typically provide a single service such as water provision or recreation services. There were more than 37,000 of these special district governments in 2007.[32]

SOURCES OF REVENUE AND PURPOSES OF GOVERNMENT EXPENDITURES

In general, government does not simply get money and spend it. Rather, governments obtain revenue from specific sources and spend it on specific public goods and services. The following discussion considers the relationships between income and outgo—that is, the ways in which revenue is generated and the purposes of government expenditures.

Federal Revenues and Expenditures

The federal government obtains revenues from several different sources. The major source of revenue for the federal government is the individual income tax. In fiscal year 2010, 42% of all federal revenues came from this source. Social insurance taxes (payroll taxes for Social Security and Medicare) accounted for another 40% of the total, a sharp increase from 35% in 2006. Adding in the almost 15% contributed by corporate income taxes, these three sources accounted for 91% of all federal revenues. This distribution represents a substantial shift from the early 1900s, when customs duties and excise taxes were the major revenue sources. These sources now account for 4% of total federal revenues. **Table 2–4** shows a summary of federal revenues and expenditures.

There are two main types of federal spending: discretionary spending, which is provided for through the annual appropriations process, and mandatory spending, which is provided for through "permanent" law. Discretionary appropriations provide for most of the core functions of government, including the operations of major federal departments. This category accounted for about 39% of all federal spending in 2010, and just over half of this amount went for defense. This represents a substantial decline in the relative importance of discretionary spending from the 1970s. In 1973, 50% of expenditures were discretionary, and the figure was 65% in 1967.[33] Increased defense spending associated with military activities in Iraq and Afghanistan has increased the percentage of the budget accounted for by discretionary spending in recent years, reversing a trend of several decades. As recently as 2001, discretionary spending represented less than 35% of total federal spending.[34]

Mandatory spending (chiefly entitlements) accounted for about 55% of federal spending in 2010. This was a substantial increase in the proportion of the budget that went to mandatory spending since 1970, when the figure was 35%. The major single entitlement—36% of total mandatory spending—is Social Security. The health entitlements (Medicare and Medicaid) together make up another 41% of all mandatory spending. The expansion of mandatory spending since the mid-1960s (fueled by the federal role in health care costs and smaller "Great Society" programs of the Johnson administration) has increased the proportion of the federal budget devoted to mandatory spending.

Table 2–4 Federal Revenues and Expenditures, 2010 (Billions of Dollars)

Revenues			Expenditures		
Source	Dollars (Billions)	Percent	Source	Dollars (Billions)	Percent
Individual Income	899	41.6	Social Security	701	20.3
Corporate Income	191	8.8	Medicare	520	15.0
Social Insurance	865	40.0	Medicaid	273	7.9
Excise	67	3.1	Other Spending	600	17.4
Estate and Gift	19	0.9	Offsetting Receipts (3)	−184	−5.3
Total Taxes	**2,041**	**94.4**	**Total Mandatory**	**1,910**	**55.3**
Customs Duties	25	1.2	Defense	689	19.9
Federal Reserve	76	3.5	Nondefense	660	19.1
Miscellaneous	20	0.9	**Total Discretionary**	**1,349**	**39.0**
Total Receipts	**2,162**	**100.0**	**Net Interest**	**197**	**5.7**
			Total Outlays	**3,456**	**100.0**

Source: Modified from U.S. Congressional Budget Office (2011). *The budget and economic outlook: fiscal years 2011–2021* (pp. 54, 87). Washington, DC: U.S. Government Printing Office.

The other category of federal spending is net interest. The federal government's spending on interest has increased and decreased, depending on the federal government's reliance on deficit financing and on interest rates. In 2010, it was 6% of the budget. In 1995, that figure was 15%. The reason for the much lower interest percentage in 2010, with a much larger debt, is historically low, near zero, interest rates. The Congressional Budget Office projected net interest to grow again to 12% by 2021 as a result of deficits driven by stimulus programs and defense expenditures and expected interest rate increases.[35] Extreme partisan differences in the U.S. Congress have made compromise on sufficient expenditure decreases and/or revenue increases extraordinarily difficult.

State and Local Revenues and Expenditures

State and local revenues and expenditures are summarized in **Table 2–5**. The first thing to note about state revenues shown in the table is that nearly 28% comes from other governments, mostly from the federal government. Typically, insurance trust revenues, the majority of which are for employee retirement, have constituted a significant portion of revenues—more than 20% in 2007. However, unrealized gains and losses from security holdings such as for public employee retirement systems are accounted for as revenues, and 2008 included significant unrealized losses. As a result, insurance trust revenues in 2008 were only at 5%. Sales and gross receipts taxes account for 22% of state government revenue. States obtain another 17% from individual income taxes, and 18% comes from user charges, such as tuition at state universities. Not every state taps into each of the varied revenue sources that the states use. Some states have both a sales tax and an individual income tax. Others have only one or the other, and two states (Alaska and New Hampshire) have neither.

Local governments obtain one-third of their money from other governments and the rest mainly through property tax and other sources. Of all local revenue, 26% comes from property tax. A little over 21% is obtained from charges, miscellaneous general revenue, and utility fees. While some local governments have income and sales taxes, these sources contribute only about 7% of all local revenues in aggregate.

State and local expenditures also follow different patterns. Some expenditures that are important for the federal government are nonexistent in states and localities. For example, neither the states nor their local governments are responsible for defense, postal service, or space exploration. When looking at direct expenditures (that is, expenditures that are actually made directly by the government, as opposed to assistance provided to some other level), public welfare is the largest expense for states, with education spending (primarily for higher education) ranked second. Other significant areas of state expenditure include highways and corrections.

Education spending is by far the largest category of local expenditures. The 38% spent on education is more than three times the percentage that is devoted to the second-ranked category, utility expenditure. Other significant areas of expenditure include public safety (police and fire), hospitals, and highways.

Table 2–5 State and Local Revenues and Expenditures, 2007–2008 (in Millions of Dollars)

Source	State and Local	State	State Percent	Local	Local Percent
Total Revenue	2,660,475	1,619,128	100.0%	1,530,814	100.0%
General Revenue	2,425,778	1,513,904	93.5%	1,401,341	91.5%
General Revenue from Own Sources	1,944,398	1,067,795	65.9%	876,604	57.3%
Taxes	1,330,412	781,647	48.3%	548,765	35.8%
Property	409,686	12,691	0.8%	396,995	25.9%
Sales and Gross Receipts	448,689	358,522	22.1%	90,166	5.9%
Individual Income	304,627	278,373	17.2%	26,255	1.7%
Corporate Income	57,810	50,759	3.1%	7,051	0.5%
Motor Vehicle Licenses	21,344	19,719	1.2%	1,626	0.1%
Other Taxes	88,256	61,584	3.8%	26,673	1.7%
Charges and Miscellaneous	613,987	286,148	17.7%	327,839	21.4%
Utility Revenue	139,142	16,523	1.0%	122,620	8.0%
Liquor Store Revenue	7,243	6,128	0.4%	1114	0.1%
Insurance Trust Revenue	88,312	82,574	5.1%	5,738	0.4%
Intergovernmental Revenue	481,380	446,109	27.6%	524,738	34.3%
From Federal Government	481,380	423,150	26.1%	58,230	3.8%
From State Government				466,508	30.5%
Total Expenditures	2,338,836	1,733,862	100.0%	1,593,088	100.0%
Intergovernmental	4,761	477,085	27.5%	15,790	1.0%
Direct by Function	2,834,075	1,256,777	72.5%	1,577,298	99.0%
Direct General Expenditure	2,400,204	1,024,666	59.1%	1,375,539	86.3%
Capital Outlay	307,448	107,058	6.2%	200,390	12.6%
Other Direct General Expenditures	2,092,757	917,608	52.9%	1,175,149	73.8%
Education and Libraries	837,674	232,658	13.4%	605,017	38.0%

(continued)

Table 2–5 State and Local Revenues and Expenditures, 2007–2008 (in Millions of Dollars)

Source	State and Local	State	State Percent	Local	Local Percent
Public Welfare	404,624	354,048	20.4%	50,576	3.2%
Hospitals	128,853	51,938	3.0%	76,916	4.8%
Health	79,704	40,033	2.3%	39,671	2.5%
Social Insurance and Veterans' Services	5,172	5,155	0.3%		
Highways	153,515	90,645	5.2%	62,871	3.9%
Other Transportation	27,806	3,258	0.2%	24,550	1.5%
Police Protection	89,676	12,034	0.7%	77,642	4.9%
Fire Protection	39,683			39,683	2.5%
Corrections	72,904	47,239	2.7%	25,665	1.6%
Protective Inspection and Regulation	14,937	9,298	0.5%	3,766	0.2%
Natural Resources	29,917	19,942	1.2%	9,974	0.6%
Parks and Recreation	40,646	5,510	0.3%	35,136	2.2%
Housing and Community Development	50,974	10,857	0.6%	40,118	2.5%
Sewerage	46,679	1,273	0.1%	45,406	2.9%
Solid Waste Management	23,757	2,439	0.1%	21,318	1.3%
Governmental Administration	126,997	52,102	3.0%	74,895	4.7%
Interest on Debt	100,055	44,719	2.6%	55,336	3.5%
Other General	126,630	41,520	2.4%	85,110	5.3%
Utility Expenditures	193,353	26,073	1.5%	167,280	10.5%
Liquor Store	5,934	4,945	0.3%	989	0.1%
Insurance Trust	234,584	201,094	11.6%	33,490	2.1%

Source: Data from of the Census, U.S. Department of Commerce (2011). State and local government finances summary: 2007–2008 (pp. 6–11). Retrieved October 16, 2011, from http://www2.census.gov/govs/estimate/08statesummaryreport.pdf.

SUMMARY

Government is indeed large. The growth pattern of the public sector has been upward, and drawing a definitive line today between the public and private sectors is virtually impossible. If present trends continue, government can be expected to become even larger, albeit at a slower rate, providing more services directly or ensuring the provision of services by regulating the private sector.

Governments in the United States differ in the types of revenue sources used and main areas of expenditure. The federal government relies primarily on personal and corporate income taxes and social insurance taxes. Federal expenditures are concentrated in defense, medical entitlements, and social insurance. States obtain almost one-fourth of their revenue from the federal government and the remainder largely from sales and individual income taxes. Their expenditures are concentrated in education, social services, and welfare. Local governments, in contrast, receive one-third of their funds from other governments and one-fourth from property taxes, while their most expensive function is education.

NOTES

1. Zuckert, M., & Webb, D. (Eds.). (2009). *The anti-federalists writing of the Melancton Smith circle.* Indianapolis, IN: Liberty Fund; Beer, S. H. (1993). To make a nation: the rediscovery of American federalism. Cambridge, MA: Belknap Press; White, L. D. (1948). The federalists: a study in administrative history, 1789–1801. New York, NY: Free Press.
2. Galbraith, J. K. (1973). *Economics and the public purpose.* Boston, MA: Houghton Mifflin.
3. Musgrave, R. A., & Musgrave, P. B. (1989). *Public finance in theory and practice* (5th ed.). New York, NY: McGraw-Hill; Hyman, D. N. (2010). *Public finance: a contemporary application of theory to policy* (10th ed. online). Florence, KY: Cengage Books; Rosen, H. S. (2005). *Public finance* (7th ed.). New York, NY: McGraw-Hill Irwin.
4. Lamartini, S., & Zaghini, A. (2008). *Increasing public expenditures: Wagner's law in OECD countries.* Frankfurt: Center for Financial Studies. Retrieved September 15, 2011, from http://www.ifk-cfs.de/fileadmin/downloads/publications/wp/08_13.pdf.
5. Berry, W. D., & Lowery, D. (1987). Explaining the size of the public sector. *Journal of Politics, 49,* 401–440; Larkey, P. D., et al. (1981). Theorizing about the growth of government. *Journal of Public Policy, 1,* 157–220.
6. Beck, M. (1981). *Government spending: trends and issues.* New York, NY: Praeger; Lewis-Beck, M. S., & Rice, T. W. (1985). Government growth in the United States. *Journal of Politics, 47,* 2–30.
7. Polsby, N. W. (2004). *Presidential elections* (11th ed.). New York, NY: Chatham House.
8. Salant, J. D. (2008). Spending doubled as Obama led first billion dollar race in 2008. *Bloomberg News.* Retrieved September 25, 2011, from http://www.bloomberg.com/apps/news?pid=newsarchive&sid=aerix76GvmRM.
9. Bureau of the Census, U.S. Department of Commerce (2012). *Statistical abstract of the United States* (Online ed.). Washington, DC: U.S. Government Printing Office. Calculated September 29, 2011, from http://www.census.gov/compendia/statab/cats/labor_force_employment_earnings.html. All figures cited in this paragraph are from the same source.
10. Bureau of the Census, U.S. Department of Commerce (2012). *Statistical abstract of the United States.* Calculated September 29, 2011, from http://www.census.gov/compendia/statab/2012/tables/12s0506.pdf.

11. U.S. Government Accountability Office (2009). *Hard lessons: the Iraq reconstruction experience.* Washington, DC: Government Printing Office.

12. Bureau of the Census, U.S. Department of Commerce (2012). Statistical abstract of the United States. Calculated September 29, 2011, from http://www.census.gov/compendia/statab/2012/tables/12s0506.pdf.

13. Bureau of the Census, U.S. Department of Commerce (2012). *Statistical abstract of the United States.* Calculated September 29, 2011, from http://www.census.gov/compendia/statab/2012/tables/12s0506.pdf.

14. Light, P. C. (2003). *Fact sheet on the new true size of government.* The Brookings Institution, September 5. Retrieved September 15, 2006, from http://www.brookings.edu/gs/cps/light20030905.htm; Light, P. C. (2006). *The new true size of government,* August 2006. Retrieved September 17, 2011, from http://wagner.nyu.edu/performance/files/True_Size.pdf.

15. *Zelman v. Simmons–Harris* (2002). 536 U.S. 639.

16. Smith, E. (2005). Raising standards in American schools: the case of No Child Left Behind. *Journal of Education Policy, 20*(4), 507–524.

17. American Recovery and Reinvestment Act of 2009 (P.L. 111-5).

18. All illustrations in the book were prepared using the most current data available. Federal cutbacks in the 1980s resulted in fewer data collections, such as detailed information on state and local government finances. When comparing across levels of government, complete data for federal, state, and local vary in availability, so some tables and figures necessarily use the most common denominator—meaning if the most recent local government data available are from 2009, then all comparisons with state and federal also use 2009 data, even though more recent federal figures may be available. Another important note is that unlike governments that are generally stable, corporations can change dramatically in size, and consequently their rankings reflected in Tables 2–1 and 2–2 may go up or down sharply within the span of a few years. This could occur, for example, as the result of a major IPO (initial public offering). Changes in corporate rankings reflect their relative successes and failures in sales and also reflect various forms of corporate mergers.

19. The original idea of comparing private and public organizations was suggested by Robert J. Mowitz, then Director, Institute of Public Administration, The Pennsylvania State University, for the first edition of *Public Budgeting Systems.*

20. Independent Budget Office (2009). *Analysis of the Mayor's Preliminary Budget for 2010.* New York, NY: Independent Budget Office, 1. Retrieved September 24, 2011, from http://www.ibo.nyc.ny.us/iboreports/March2009final.pdf.

21. U.S. Council of Economic Advisers (2011). *Economic report of the president* (p. 227). Washington, DC: U.S. Government Printing Office.

22. U.S. Council of Economic Advisers (2011). *Economic report of the president,* 202, 287.

23. U.S. Office of Management and Budget (2011). *Budget of the United States government: fiscal year 2011, historical table* (p. 342). Washington, DC: U.S. Government Printing Office.

24. Bureau of the Census, U.S. Department of Commerce (1975). *Historical statistics of the United States: colonial times to 1970,* (part 2, p.1114). Washington, DC: U.S. Government Printing Office.

25. U.S. Council of Economic Advisers (2011). *Economic report of the president,* 291.

26. U.S. Office of Management and Budget (2011). *Budget of the United States Government: fiscal year 2011, historical tables,* 342.

27. Bureau of the Census, U.S. Department of Commerce (2011). *State and local government finances summary: 2007–2008.* Retrieved October 10, 2011, from http://www2.census.gov/govs/estimate/08statesummaryreport.pdf.

28. U.S. Council of Economic Advisers (2011). *Economic report of the president,* 288–290.

29. Bureau of the Census, U.S. Department of Commerce (2012). *Statistical abstract of the United States.* Retrieved September 30, 2011, from http://www.census.gov/compendia/statab/2012/tables/12s0497.pdf.

30. Bureau of the Census, U.S. Department of Commerce (2012). *Statistical abstract of the United States.* Retrieved October 5, 2011, from http://www.census.gov/compendia/statab/2012/tables/12s0498.pdf.

31. Bureau of the Census, U.S. Department of Commerce (2012). *Statistical abstract of the United States.* Retrieved October 10, 2011, from http://www.census.gov/compendia/statab/2012/tables/12s0466.pdf.

32. Bureau of the Census, U.S. Department of Commerce (2012). *Statistical abstract of the United States.* Retrieved October 10, 2011, from http://www.census.gov/compendia/statab/2012/tables/12s0428.pdf.

33. U.S. Congressional Budget Office (2006). *The budget and economic outlook: fiscal years 2007–2016* (p. 44). Washington, DC: U.S. Government Printing Office.

34. U.S. Congressional Budget Office (2006). *The budget and economic outlook: fiscal years 2007–2016,* 144.

35. U.S. Congressional Budget Office (2011). *The budget and economic outlook: fiscal years 2011–2021* (p. 54). Washington, DC: U.S. Government Printing Office.

Government, the Economy, and Economic Development

The sheer size of the government sector in the U.S. economy guarantees that government action will have a major impact on overall economic performance. Total government expenditures as a percentage of gross domestic product (GDP)—a measure of the size of the economy—are more than 36%, and the federal share alone exceeds 25%.[1]

This chapter focuses on the impact of government budgets—primarily the federal government's budget—on the overall economy. The first section introduces basic concepts in measuring the economy. These concepts are used throughout the chapter. The second section considers the U.S. economy and its interdependence with the economies of other nations. Other governments and private individuals in other countries react to actions taken by the U.S. federal government, and actions taken by these external parties cause economic changes within the United States. To understand government and the economy, one first has to understand the conditioning factors of the world economy.

The third section summarizes the major objectives sought by U.S. government economic policy. Included is a discussion of deficit control and management of the federal debt. In contrast to state and local borrowing, which is basically used as a means to finance capital investment, federal deficit spending and subsequent borrowing function more as macro-economic policy tools.

The fourth section briefly discusses how governments and businesses attempt to forecast the economic future, and the fifth examines the principal tools used to influence the economy. For the federal government, these tools conventionally include fiscal and monetary policy. The chapter gives special attention to the major recession that started in 2007. In a separate section, we consider the combination of fiscal and monetary tools used in attempts to combat that recession. For state and local governments, tools to influence their economies include infrastructure investments and taxing or spending decisions that are intended to affect the local and state business climate. The final section focuses on the role of government in securing equity through influencing the distribution of income and other social goods in society.

MEASURING THE SIZE OF THE ECONOMY

Economists measure the economy in many ways. Two basic concepts, production and income, characterize the economy in terms of the total value of goods and services produced and the income derived from the production of those goods and services. These two concepts are at the base of all the size measures discussed in this section. In principle, these two concepts are the same. The costs of goods and services sold (the value of the output) are equal to the receipts received by the producers (the value of the income). In practice, there are imperfections in the measurement, whether one is measuring production costs including costs of goods purchased, cost of labor, and so forth or whether one is measuring firms' and households' incomes.

Gross Domestic Product

Gross domestic product (GDP) is the basic measure of economic output. It is the value of the total goods and services produced by the nation. Gross domestic product is the aggregate of personal consumption expenditures, gross private domestic investment, net exports of goods and services, and government purchases of goods and services.

Gross National Product

An indicator similar to GDP, gross national product (GNP), for many years was the common indicator of total production. In 1992, the federal government and most analysts switched to GDP for comparison purposes, since most other countries report production in terms of GDP. The main difference between the two is that GDP excludes the earnings of U.S. businesses and residents abroad, and excludes earnings of foreign workers in the United States that are remitted abroad. Thus, GDP reflects production within the U.S. economy as opposed to production by U.S. economic entities.

For the United States, GDP and GNP typically do not differ much because income earned abroad and income remitted abroad tend to balance. For some economies, especially developing economies, remittances from citizens working abroad are a significant source of national income. In 2010, remittances from the United States and many other economies to Central and South America totaled more than $58.5 billion, down nearly 10% from previous years as the impact of the recession, especially in industrialized countries, was felt. For example, net remittances for El Salvador amounted to more than 15% of national income in 2010. For Egypt it was 3.5%, and Morocco 7.4%.[2]

Net National Product and National Income

Two related indicators, both derivatives of GDP, are net national product (NNP) and national income (NI). Gross domestic product includes all capital investment, some of which does not create new productive capacity but instead replaces capacity that has been used up, such as obsolete equipment no longer capable of producing. Net national product measures only capital investment net of depreciation. Capital replacement expenditures do not count in NNP. In 2009, the U.S. GDP was $14.1 trillion, while the U.S. NNP was $12.4 trillion, meaning that approximately $1.7 trillion of GDP represented no new production capacity.[3] Tracking NNP provides clues about future production because if the economy is using up capital stock and not replacing it, the production of goods and services that depends on that decreasing capital stock will decline or grow at a slower rate.

National income is derived from NNP by eliminating indirect business taxes included in the price of goods sold and business transfer payments. The table contained in **Exhibit 3–1** summarizes the relationships among GDP, GNP, NNP, and NI of the U.S. economy from 1960 through 2009. Note that beginning in 2004, the statistical tables prepared by the president's Council of Economic Advisers lumped indirect business taxes, business transfer payments, and net surpluses of government enterprises into *statistical discrepancy*, masking somewhat the underlying differences among the measures. The text in the illustration assesses some of the underlying changes in the U.S. economy revealed by evaluating GDP, GNP, NNP, and NI over a 49-year time period, 1960–2009.

Exhibit 3–1 Relationships among GDP, GNP, NNP, and NI

There are several measurements of the size of the economy. They are all based on the value of production in the economy, or the income derived from that production. Production and income are the opposite sides of the coin. Accurate measurement is complicated and beyond the scope of this text. But understanding how the different measures relate to each other is important because, as discussed in the text, each basic measure of the size of the economy captures somewhat different concepts. The following table shows how each measure is derived from gross domestic product.

Year	GDP	+ Income receipts from rest of the world	– Income payments to rest of the world	= GNP	– Consumption of fixed capital			= NNP	– Statistical discrepancies	= NI
					Total	Private	Government			
1960	526.4	4.9	1.8	529.5	55.6	40.5	15.0	473.9	–0.9	474.9
1965	719.1	7.9	2.6	724.4	70.7	51.9	18.9	653.7	1.5	652.2
1970	1038.3	12.8	6.4	1044.7	108.3	81.7	26.6	936.4	6.9	929.5
1975	1637.7	28.0	15.0	1650.7	190.4	150.4	39.9	1460.3	16.3	1444.0
1980	2788.1	79.1	44.9	2822.3	344.1	282.3	61.8	2478.2	45.3	2433.0
1985	4217.5	112.4	85.9	4244.0	505.4	412.8	92.7	3738.6	42.3	3696.3
1990	5800.5	188.5	154.1	5838.0	691.2	560.4	130.8	5143.7	84.2	5059.5
1995	7414.7	229.3	199.6	7444.3	869.5	704.6	164.8	6574.9	52.5	6422.3
2000	9951.5	380.5	342.8	9989.2	1184.3	996.8	197.5	8804.9	–134.0	8938.9
2005	12638.4	573.0	475.9	12735.5	1541.4	1290.8	250.6	11194.2	–79.7	11273.8
2009	14119.0	629.8	483.6	14265.3	1861.1	1535.8	325.3	12404.2	179.1	12225.0

Source: Extracted from U.S. Council of Economic Advisers (2011). *Economic report of the president: 2011* (p. 220). Washington, DC: U.S. Government Printing Office.

(continued)

The adjustments to gross domestic product to derive several other measures of the size of the economy reveal changing characteristics of the U.S. economy. For the earlier years represented in the table, GDP is about 10 percent larger than NI, whereas gross national product and GDP are within 1 percent of each other for all the years. Income earned abroad by U.S. concerns and income earned in the United States and remitted abroad by non-U.S. entities generally balance each other out. Beginning in the 1980s, GDP relative to NI is increasing, exceeding NI closer to 14% to 15%. This is caused by increases in the consumption of fixed capital by both the private sector and government. Phrased differently, neither the private sector nor government is investing in fixed assets, meaning the kind of assets that will yield future production, at the same rates relative to the existing capital stock as in earlier years. Discussion of gross and net savings rates later in the chapter reveals that the United States in recent decades saves less from within the economy and relies more on investments in capital from abroad to finance private sector capital investment and the government budget deficit.

THE UNITED STATES AND THE WORLD ECONOMY

Cross-Border Economic Shocks

Most U.S. citizens after World War II thought of the United States as not only the most significant contributor to, but also the economic controller of, the world economy. The U.S. economy's dependence on imported oil was of little note until the Organization of Petroleum Exporting Countries (OPEC) curtailed oil production in 1973 and 1974, and U.S. citizens for the first time in the postwar era realized the significant effects of other actors in the world economy on U.S. prices. High gasoline prices since 2005, brought on by higher consumption worldwide—particularly in major newly emerging economies such as Brazil, Russia, India, and China (sometimes referred to as the BRIC countries)—and various turbulent events in many oil-producing regions reemphasize the interconnectedness among economies.

Similarly, economic growth in several nations with economies once considerably smaller than that of the United States, including the Japanese and German economies, and the more recent emergence of Brazil, Russia, India, and China as major participants in the world economy, mean that the United States, although still a major component of the world economy, is merely one among several important national economies.[4]

Since that first oil shock and the strengthening of other economies relative to our own, citizens are more attuned to how much U.S. economic well-being depends on the economic behavior of billions of individuals around the world and on the economic policy decisions of dozens of other governments. It is the economies of both underdeveloped and developing nations, not just those of industrialized nations, that can have huge impacts on the United States and other industrialized economies, and vice versa.

The Asian financial crisis that started in 1997 caused economies first throughout Asia, then other emerging markets, to tumble. The ripple effects of that crisis included investors rapidly selling off their emerging-market portfolio holdings, and many reinvested in the U.S. and other Western industrial markets. Industrialized financial markets soared temporarily, exacerbating the situation in emerging markets as many investors exited those economies. The financial collapse of Western industrial markets in 2007 made some newly strong economies, such as Brazil, Russia, India, and China, even more attractive as investors looked to alternatives to industrialized country investments. Both situations show that when investors quickly sell off their holdings if there is any hint that economic conditions are declining, markets in the affected countries can swing wildly. These portfolio investments, as opposed to longer-term investments in fixed assets such as factories and other capital-intensive industries, can allow for wide, rapid swings in emerging economy stock markets.

Contributing to further entwining among economies is investment in productive assets, such as factories and retail establishments, across borders. *Foreign direct investment* (FDI) is the largest single source of capital inflow to developing economies. Foreign direct investment accounts for nearly 30% of the GDP of developing economies, up from less than 10% in 1980. The importance of FDI flows is no longer mainly a developing country phenomenon. FDI as a percentage of GDP in developed economies rose from less than 10% in 1990 to just over 30% in 2010. In that time period, for the United States the increase was from just over 9% to nearly 24%; for the United Kingdom, the increase was from 20% to 48%.[5] Unlike portfolio investments in stocks and bonds, FDI flows directly create productive assets and are not easily divested during downturns in the target economy. Changes in FDI flows thus tend to reflect investors' predictions about long-term trends in the target economies.

Another economic variable linking economies across the world is the simple purchase of goods and services across borders. If you buy a vehicle manufactured in another country, or if your business sells pumps to oil companies in other countries, the result is a cash flow inward or outward, to or from one's own economy. The value of international trade—exports plus imports—grew from 16% of U.S. GDP in 1975 to more than 26% in 2005, and then fell back to 16% in 2009, reflecting the worsening economy.[6]

Other cross-border shocks can cause significant economic disruption, particularly when economic conditions are already fragile. The 2011 earthquake and subsequent tsunami in Japan disrupted markets in many countries other than Japan. For the United States, the automobile industry, which was getting back on its feet after almost disappearing, felt the effects for most of the remainder of 2011 as parts and other supplies from Japanese manufacturers disrupted by the catastrophe-slowed U.S. production.[7]

The notion that there is now a global economy, and that the United States is a part of that global economy but not the controlling agent, is accepted by most people, albeit for some quite uncomfortably. Of course, the United States is also vehemently criticized for its size and the influence of its economy in some other countries.

The United States as a Debtor Nation

A second major factor influencing today's world economy involves the debt of U.S. individuals, corporations, and governments. Citizens notice price increases in gasoline and other products dependent on imports and dramatic political conditions such as terrorism. Not as obvious are the credit flows among nations and how the United States is both actor and reactor to worldwide economic forces. In 1985, the United States became a net debtor nation for the first time. Formally, that meant that the value of foreign investments in the United States exceeded the value of U.S. investments abroad. In 2009, the value (measured at current market price) of foreign investments in the United States was approximately $21.1 trillion, and U.S. investments abroad were valued at $18.4 trillion; both more than doubled since the mid-1990s. Of that $21 trillion, just under 25% was held by official foreign investors (governments and government institutions).[8] Most of that official foreign investment was in U.S. Treasury securities and other U.S. government debt, reflecting official U.S. borrowing from abroad (discussed in more detail later in this chapter).

The net difference, about $2.7 trillion, reflects a long-term pattern. Investments in the United States continue to be more attractive to foreign investors than investments abroad are to U.S. investors, although economic and stock market fluctuations affect the short term from time to time. For example, when the U.S. stock market tumbled in 2001, foreign investors sold off relatively more of their U.S. assets than did U.S. investors, and the proportionate value of foreign holdings in the United States dropped. This did not recur to any significant degree in the market collapse of 2007 and subsequent years, largely because financial markets in other industrialized countries looked generally even less attractive to investors than the United States.[9]

Since 1985, the United States has remained a net debtor, with the cumulative value of foreign-owned assets in the United States exceeding the value of assets in other countries owned by U.S. investors.

In 2009, 16% of the foreign asset holdings in the United States were in financial derivative products in the U.S. financial markets. Other investments in U.S. stocks and bonds were about 25% of the total. Foreign asset holdings in the United States in descending order are in: (1) debt and equity securities of U.S. companies through portfolio investment; (2) U.S. Treasury securities held by official governments and private investors as noted above; and (3) fixed assets, including resorts, factories, and even public utilities such as water companies through direct foreign investment.[10] Prior to the surge in U.S. government debt beginning in the early 2000s, more foreign investments were going into the U.S. stock market plus fixed assets and less into U.S. government securities such as Treasury bills (see the chapter on budget execution). The U.S. federal budget surplus of the late 1990s had substantially reduced federal borrowing needs. Rising federal budget deficits of course require federal borrowing, much of it from foreign investors, so the trend since 2001 has been for relative growth in foreign purchases of U.S. government debt.

The inflow of foreign capital has helped keep U.S. interest rates low because it fills part of the demand for borrowing created by federal budget deficits, and it finances high levels of consumption, including imported products, by U.S. households. In addition, foreign investment produces jobs in the United States. On the other hand, when the net inflow of foreign capital replaces domestic capital for investment, it makes the economy even more linked to the rest of the world's economies. The U.S. savings rate is too low to finance all the demand for investments, leaving the economy increasingly dependent on the confidence of foreign investors in the U.S. economy. U.S. households' high consumption patterns, which include huge purchases of imported goods, and government budget deficits require importing foreign capital to finance consumption and debt.

As long as foreign investors are confident in the U.S. economy, these patterns may not be a problem. Major threats to foreign confidence, such as the stock market drop in 2000–2002, the disasters of September 11, 2001, and ongoing problems with the wars in Afghanistan and Iraq, have caused some concerns among foreign investors, but by comparison with other investment opportunities, the U.S. economy remains attractive. The 2007 financial market collapse had a temporary effect, but debt crises in several European Union countries discouraged flight from the United States to other Western economies.[11] As countries like Brazil, Russia, India, and China increasingly relax currency restrictions and open their rapidly growing economies more fully, the relative attractiveness of the United States, and other older industrialized economies, could start to decline. If confidence in the U.S. economy were to wane significantly, then interest rates in the United States most likely would have to rise to attract investors. Such rates would be guided by monetary policy actions (discussed later in this chapter) taken by the Federal Reserve Board.

Value of the U.S. Dollar in the World Economy

The third phenomenon relates to changes in the value of the dollar in the world economy. When relatively few citizens traveled abroad, and trade accounted for less than 10% of the U.S. economy, most Americans never thought about the value of the dollar against foreign currencies.

Americans now travel extensively abroad and have for the past 30 years or more, and most Americans purchase imported goods. Likewise, citizens from countries around the world travel extensively in the United States. Changes in the value of the dollar relative to other currencies now are quite visible to most consumers and travelers. Early in the 1970s, the dollar purchased a lot of goods and services in or from other countries, as the dollar value was high relative to most major currencies.

By 1987, the value of the dollar relative to other currencies had reversed. U.S. residents watched the incoming flood of tourists as European and Asian visitors came to the United States, while prices for comparable trips for U.S. residents abroad climbed to new highs. Imported cars, stereos, and televisions that had been bargains a year before became unaffordable for many. This reversal occurred for two reasons. Per capita incomes grew faster in several other countries that increased their purchasing power and drove up prices for goods produced in those economies. Second, the value of the U.S. dollar, with the exception of a brief period during the budget surplus period of 2000 to 2002, fell relative to most other major world currencies. **Figure 3–1** illustrates the latter for the time period 1990 through 2010. The figure compares the value of the U.S. dollar against an index of other major world currencies. The base year for the index value of 100 is 1973, when the value of the dollar against the index was 1.00. Changes up or down in the figure reflect increases or decreases in the purchasing power of the dollar against other major currencies such as the British pound, the EU euro, and the Japanese yen.

One of the major factors affecting the value of the dollar has been the introduction of a common currency in most of Europe—the euro. Initially, the dollar and the euro were valued within about 10% of each other. The U.S. economy was booming and there were federal budget surpluses. From 2007 through late 2011, the euro-to-dollar ratio varied

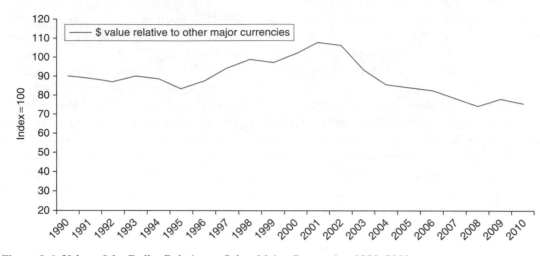

Figure 3–1 Value of the Dollar Relative to Other Major Currencies: 1990–2010.
Source: Data from U.S. Council of Economic Advisers (2011). *Economic report of the president: 2011* (p. 316). Washington, DC: U.S. Government Printing Office.

from as low as 1.20 euro/dollar to 1.59 euro/dollar.[12] The euro appreciated against the dollar in part because of cyclical economic changes, but also because the prices of goods and services in the various former European country currencies settled into stable relationships in euro terms after adopting the common currency.

Economic crises in 2011, however, raised concerns that the euro might not survive and that European countries would revert to their individual currencies. A new treaty that was hammered out under great international pressure, and pressure from within, particularly by Germany and France, probably saved the euro, though not all countries currently in the euro zone may remain.[13]

Economists now understand that the value of the dollar fluctuates with changes both within the influence range of the U.S. private economy and government action and with changes in other economies. Since the mid-1980s, the dollar no longer dominates world currencies, but is merely one of several dominant currencies.

Competitiveness of the U.S. Economy

A fourth key economic phenomenon is the competitiveness of the U.S. economy relative to that of other emerging industrial powers. Ordinary Americans first took note of this competitiveness issue on a large scale in the 1980s. Although "cheap foreign labor" had been considered a threat by many traditional U.S. industries, such as textiles, for more than two decades, the 1980s saw problems in industries in which innovation and technology had constituted the U.S. competitive edge. For the first time, the United States encountered competitors in computer design, electronics, and other high-technology areas, who began to produce not only cheaper but, in the minds of many consumers, better products.[14]

A surge in the 1990s in U.S. productivity, led by significant private sector restructuring and manifested in part by downsizing of the workforce in many industries, helped move the issue of government stimulation of U.S. competitiveness further off the national agenda. Aided by private sector restructuring and a balanced budget, by the late 1990s the U.S. economy experienced both overall growth and strong competitiveness with other economies. A significant factor at that time was the massive investment in computer software and hardware to avoid some problems associated with old software that would not recognize dates beyond the year 1999 (the "Y2K" problem) and overall growth in the information and communications technology sector. Investment in new computer technology after the Y2K scare of 1999–2000 slowed. Nonetheless, since then, U.S. labor competitiveness has increased relative to the economies of the European Union, with the gap widening since 2001.[15] The major contributor to the U.S. economy's competitiveness relative to other major industrial countries is the competitiveness of the U.S. services industry.[16]

Of growing concern in the United States since the recession that started in 2007 leading to unemployment rates exceeding 9% (see discussion of unemployment later in this chapter) is the increasing competitiveness of emerging economies such as the BRIC countries. Economic production in those economies has grown at rates near 10% or more, even during the recession. These economies have enjoyed the contribution to production growth of expanding labor forces. In addition, with investments in industrial modernization, any labor-based economy will experience significant growth in production. The United States and other industrial economies, however, achieve productivity gains only through increasing the productivity of a labor force that grows in size slowly, if at all.[17] Labor productivity in the United States and western Europe has not improved significantly, relative to that of the larger emerging market countries, in the past decade. Russia is an exception in the emerging market powers in that its population is not growing. The role of productivity in achieving economic growth is discussed in detail in the next section.

The U.S. economy is so interdependent with those of other nations that no significant actions that the United States takes lack repercussions around the world. Likewise, no significant economic events in other major industrial nations or groups of developing nations fail to have repercussions in the United States. As populous countries like China and India continue to industrialize, demand for resources, especially oil, becomes a major variable in every economy in the world. Understanding the role of the government in the U.S. economy thus means casting a wider net and considering the actions and reactions of the country's major trading partners and major creditors.

OBJECTIVES OF ECONOMIC POLICY

The role of the federal government in the economy consists of several interrelated functions. First, the government provides the legal framework in which economic transactions take place. Second, it directly produces services and some goods, and it regulates private production. Also, it purchases significant quantities of goods and services and redistributes income among individuals and groups. Some argue that governments should also promote their countries' economic competitiveness in the global marketplace. There is a major divide between those who argue that government should invest directly in economic promotion and those who argue that the more appropriate government role is creating the right economic climate for growth.[18]

One goal of the government's regulation of economic transactions through setting the legal framework is sometimes described as maintenance of a "level playing field"—making sure that all economic actors play by the same rules and succeed or fail solely on the basis of their own strengths and weaknesses. The stock market scandals in which companies such as Enron and WorldCom apparently inflated earnings by using unacceptable accounting practices resulted in major civil and criminal prosecutions and significant federal legislation, notably Sarbanes-Oxley (see the chapter on financial management). Similarly, the financial crisis that started in 2007, set off by the weakly regulated use of esoteric derivatives in the U.S. mortgage market, created demands for increasing regulations in the securities market. Setting the legal framework is the subject of texts on regulation, business, and constitutional law. This section and the following one focus on the government's effects on the economy's overall performance.

In 1932, Franklin D. Roosevelt promised to involve the federal government in the solution to economic problems brought on by the Great Depression, but it was not until after World War II that the overall role of the government in stimulating the economy was formalized through legislation. The Employment Act of 1946, later amended by the Full Employment and Balanced Growth Act of 1978, set several macroeconomic policy objectives for the federal government.[19] Primary among these were full employment, price stability, and steady economic growth. Though not formalized in legislation, two additional objectives are accepted in policy now—equilibrium in the balance of transactions between the U.S. economy and other economies, and debt management.[20]

Most industrial nations share these objectives, whether they rely primarily on the private market, central planning, or a mix of central control and market activity to achieve them. Less industrial, developing, and emerging market countries also share these objectives, but the most prominent economic policy objective for these nations is the promotion of economic development. The mood in most industrial economies has consistently favored a less activist role for government, but the success of Japan's economy through the 1980s and the apparent causal role played by the Japanese government's activist production and trade promotion policies intensified the debate on the proper role of the government in promoting development. The U.S. economy's outstanding performance for decades without significant government stimulation quieted (at least in the United States) the call for government intervention to stimulate competitiveness with key exceptions discussed below.

The first three objectives of the federal government are primarily domestic in nature. In many respects, they can be summarized in a single prescription: achieve a level of economic growth that produces full employment without unacceptable inflation. Economic growth is the engine that drives demand for employees. However, running that engine too fast or with too rich a fuel mixture may cause prices to rise unacceptably. Reformulating these objectives into a single statement brings out the causal connection between economic growth and employment. It also brings into the discussion two key value-laden terms: full employment and unacceptable inflation.

Full Employment

Definition of Full Employment

As a measure of economic performance, employment is the number of civilians over age 16 outside of institutions who are working in formal income-producing jobs. About 60,000 households, consisting of about 110,000 individual eligible adults and statistically representative of the country, are surveyed each month. The survey asks the respondent about his or her activities during the preceding week. If a person responds that he or she worked at a job for pay, or in a family enterprise without being paid, or was on vacation or some other similar situations, the individual is employed. If a person did not work in any of these situations or is not temporarily ill, on vacation, and so forth, and is looking for a job, he or she is unemployed. All others are considered not in the labor force. To be considered unemployed, a person currently does not have a job, has actively looked for work in the prior four weeks, and is currently available for work. If a person is temporarily laid off and waiting to return to work, that person is considered unemployed.[21]

The most commonly used measure of employment is the unemployment rate. The unemployment rate is the proportion of the workforce not employed at a given time. To be considered unemployed, one must be seeking employment as measured in the survey by such activities as sending out resumes, visiting unemployment offices, calling about employment, placing ads, conducting online job searches, and so forth. The definition of seeking employment was refined in 1994 to exclude individuals who reported that they were discouraged by failure to find work, but who had not looked for work in the past 12 months. Merely looking at want ads or online employment opportunities does not count. Individuals who have taken no active steps such as the above during the four weeks prior to the interview are not counted in the labor force.

There is no legislated definition of full employment, although an unemployment rate of 3% to 4% was often cited as the criterion of full employment after the 1946 Employment Act. Until the 1980s, the thinking was that about 3% to 4% of the workforce at any given time will be between jobs or otherwise temporarily unemployed, and thus we can never achieve unemployment below that threshold. Some members of the workforce are considered at least temporarily unemployable because of changes in the nature of jobs and skill requirements. Some economists do not count these "structurally" unemployed as part of the base for calculating full employment. Homemakers returning to the workforce, young people voluntarily switching jobs, and fluctuations in demand in the global economy also make it difficult to achieve a 3% to 4% target.

The unemployment rate has been around 4% or below only 12 times in the 64 years from 1948 through 2011, and it was not better than 4.9% from 1970 until 1998, when for four consecutive years the unemployment rate ranged from about 4% to 4.7%, and again in 2006 and 2007, when it was 4.6%.[22] Most in the United States have come to accept an unemployment rate higher than 4% as consistent with the term "full employment."

The acceptance of a higher unemployment rate as the criterion of full employment is connected to the fact that the U.S. economy is much more susceptible to external events than it once was. As external economic shocks occur and consumer tastes change more rapidly, U.S. businesses simply cannot react as quickly as they once could, leading at times to downturns and unemployment. When unemployment dropped below 5% in 1997, coupled with low inflation rates and an unexpectedly high rate of growth in GDP, the U.S. economy had reached its strongest point in decades and it was sustained for almost five years. During that period, debate centered on whether the United States had entered a new era of lower unemployment accompanied by low inflation, fueled by the greater value-added contribution of knowledge to production and a decline in the physical capital contribution to total production.

However, some of that prosperity was the paper wealth associated with the stock market boom, especially in Internet, telecommunications, and related industry stocks. It also was apparent that at least some of the late 1990s spending on information technology was a concentrated spurt that would not be sustained annually. Post September 11, 2001, with wars in Afghanistan and Iraq and renewed, large federal budget deficits, unemployment rates returned to the 5% to 6% range except for 2006–2007. Even aside from the extremely high unemployment rates above 9% starting in 2009, the patterns since the late 1990s reinforce the old notion of 3% to 4% as unsustainable.

Political Acceptability of Unemployment

The political system has a varying capacity to accept unemployment. A nationwide unemployment rate of 9% or 10%, a rate reached in the early 1980s and again after 2007, is clearly unacceptable by current standards but is substantially lower than the peak of 24% unemployment during the Great Depression of the 1930s. As the rate declines toward 5%, acceptance increases. The extent to which society tolerates unemployment is partially dependent on who is unemployed. Although there may be a tendency to accept high unemployment among low-skilled, minority group, or younger workers, tolerance for unemployment quickly dissipates when it reaches middle-income, white-collar workers. The Occupy Movement of 2011, claiming to represent the 99% of the population hurt by the recession, was led in part by well-educated young people who claimed they were unable to find employment.

Politically, the unemployment rate is not the only important issue. Since the late 1980s, when the rate hovers around 5% or less, citizens have been more concerned with the types of new jobs that are being created. The concern is that many new jobs have been either service jobs that pay only the minimum wage or part-time jobs that pay few or no benefits, especially health care and retirement benefits. That certainly was a criticism in the 1990s boom and again in the middle of the first decade of 2000, but the 9%-plus unemployment rate by the end of that decade overshadowed any concern about what kind of jobs are created. Of greater concern to some than job quality has been the concentration of wealth in the United States in the top 5%, top 2%, and top 1% of individuals. We discuss this issue in a section on equity later in the chapter.

Another issue is the controversy over part-time work. Many people choose part-time work, but companies also have increased the number of workers they hire either as part-time workers or as temporary workers in order to reduce total wage costs by not paying fringe benefits to temporary or part-time workers. When companies downsize their workforces during downturns, an increasing percentage of the national labor force works part-time and in temporary activity. Although their total employment often amounts to full

40-hour or more weeks, these workers lack the job security of regular employment and the benefits of health insurance and retirement plans.

Controlling Inflation

Relationship Between Unemployment and Inflation

The more the unemployment rate declines, the more difficult it becomes to find workers. As a result, wage rates may be bid up, creating inflationary pressures. Certainly through the mid-1960s, the traditional assumption that rising employment leads to price increases and declining employment to price decreases seemed to hold up. However, the mid-1970s recession saw both rising unemployment and rising prices. At the peak, 1974 prices rose 11% over those of the year before, and 1975 prices rose another 9%. During that time, unemployment peaked at more than 8%. In 2010, the year-over-year change in consumer prices was a drop of 1.5%, with unemployment increasing to a high of 9.6%.

Figure 3–2 illustrates this heretofore unconventional relationship. During the 1980s, the more conventional pattern held, with inflation and unemployment moving in opposite directions until the sustained growth period of the 1990s. By 2000, the economy was achieving both the lowest inflation rates in 40 years and low unemployment rates, as Figure 3–2 illustrates. Subsequent increases in inflation and unemployment from 2000 to 2005, unconventionally, tracked together. The last part of the decade dramatically shows the conventional inverse relationship with high unemployment and low inflation rates.

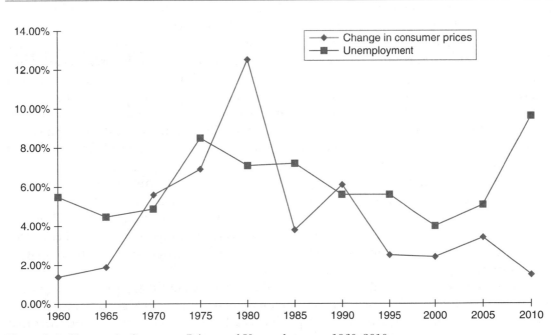

Figure 3–2 Changes in Consumer Prices and Unemployment, 1960–2010.
Source: Data from U.S. Council of Economic Advisers (2006). *Economic report of the president: 2006* (pp. 332, 356). Washington, DC: U.S. Government Printing Office; *Economic report of the president: 2011*, 264.

The 1990s experience had economists, primarily those that emphasize monetary policy over fiscal policy (see discussion later in this chapter) reestimating the natural rate of unemployment and the *nonaccelerating inflation rate of unemployment* (NAIRU). The latter was proposed as the rate of unemployment below which excess demand for labor is thought to set off wage and price inflation. That rate was previously considered to be in the 5% to 6% range. Unemployment below this range presumably would set off wage-led inflation. Milton Friedman in 1968 proposed to the American Economic Association that there is a natural rate of inflation on which the economy stabilizes for any given unemployment rate. At this natural rate, a rise in employment will set off no inflation, or a fall in employment will bring no price reductions.[23] The NAIRU concept particularly gained currency in the 1990s.

Figure 3–2 illustrates that a lower rate of unemployment (at or below 5%) did not result in wage-induced inflation between 1960 and 2010, with the possible exception of 1990, when unemployment had fallen not below 5% but had risen to near 6% from 8%, and prices also rose. If the natural rate or nonaccelerating inflation rate (they are different but related concepts) can be calculated accurately, then monetary policy actions to control inflation need be taken only when the actual unemployment rate falls below the NAIRU. There is no exact measure of NAIRU, and various methods yield ranges of plus or minus 1% to 2%.

The natural and noninflationary rates can change over time. For instance, severe drought conditions or a hard winter freeze in major citrus-growing regions can cause food prices to increase, contributing to overall higher consumer prices, unrelated to wage pressures. Increased worker productivity can increase output without setting off price deflationary pressures, and more workers can be hired as long as the productivity rate remains constant or increases without putting pressure on wages. This balance is one of the explanations for the pre-recession ability of the U.S. economy to have low inflation and low unemployment. In addition, greater pressure on jobs from foreign competition holds wage rates down regardless of what is happening in the domestic economy. If wage demands grow too high too rapidly, companies may intensify their search for foreign production sources.

Since the recession that began in 2007, concern has increased about structural unemployment. By early 2012, more than 40% of the six million unemployed Americans had been unemployed longer than six months. Although the financial markets had recovered most of their losses by mid-2011 and corporate profits were growing significantly, unemployment in excess of 9% gave rise to concerns about long-term unemployment.[24] Congressional Budget Office projections were for the unemployment rate to stay above 5.5% until 2015.[25] Proposed stimulus programs in 2011, including the proposed American Jobs Act (see discussion of fiscal and monetary policy tools later in this chapter), and concerns voiced by the Chairman of the Federal Reserve Ben Bernanke suggested that there may be more structural problems.[26]

Increased structural unemployment in the United States or any other country in the future may be the result of world economic conditions and greater fluidity across borders as companies choose where to produce their goods and services. In those circumstances, countries that are able to increase the productivity of their workforce through technology and infrastructure investments are more likely to both increase production and decrease unemployment.[27]

Economic Growth

Economic Productivity

Unemployment is not the only—and perhaps not the best—measure of the economy's health. Even if the rate of unemployment and the rate of inflation are both at acceptable levels, the overall productivity of the economy could be seriously declining. The change in GDP is sometimes used as an indication of economic productivity. The preferred measure is GDP per capita, which normalizes GDP for population differences. For the United States, the average annual growth rate in productivity or GDP per capita from 1970 through 2009 was 1.6%. For Japan, the comparable figure was 1.8%.

Figure 3–3 compares the United States, France, Canada, Germany, Japan, and the United Kingdom for several periods between 1979 and 2010. The figure adjusts for inflation and population differences by displaying *real GDP per capita.* By 1990, Japan's economy had reached mature status, yielding growth rates similar to those of the United States and other advanced economies. Japan had much higher growth rates from the 1960s through the 1980s, when its economic base was much smaller.

Since 1979, the United States, Canada, and the United Kingdom generally have outperformed most of the countries of the European Union. Higher labor productivity and

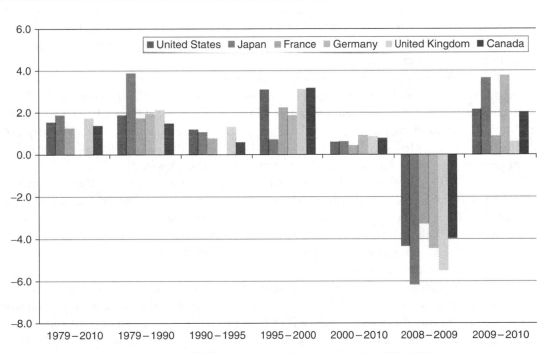

Figure 3–3 Percent Change in Real GDP Per Capita: Selected Countries, 1979–2010.
Source: Data from Office of Productivity and Technology, Bureau of Labor Statistics, U.S. Department of Labor (2011). *International comparisons of GDP per capita and per hour: 1960–2010.* Retrieved November 13, 2011, from http://www.bls.gov/fls/intl_gdp_capita_gdp_hour.pdf.

technological innovation are generally cited as explaining the U.S. and U.K. advantage. Being more open to international trade is another factor explaining higher U.S. and U.K. productivity.[28] More generally, labor shifting from low-productivity work to higher productivity work is the most compelling factor explaining overall economic growth, also explaining the patterns for the newly emerging major economic powers, such as Brazil, Russia, India, and China.[29]

Inflation varied in the countries illustrated during the period covered by Figure 3–3, but it does not affect the GDP results since the figure is based on *real GDP per capita.* Japan's measured GDP per capita growth was largely unaffected by inflation during that time, whereas the United States and Canada experienced more inflation. Using *nominal* (unadjusted for inflation) GDP, the United States and Canada would have been much higher in some periods, masking similarities and differences across countries. This demonstrates the importance of looking at real GDP in order for the measure not to appear larger than warranted.

Impact of Government on Productivity

Most economists think that the primary impact of the government on economic productivity and long-term growth is due to influences on knowledge development and investment in productive capacity. Presidents William Clinton, George W. Bush, and Barack Obama all emphasized the importance of government support for knowledge development. President Obama appointed a council of corporate CEOs to advise on how to boost U.S. economic productivity and proposed a program of investment in research and development (R&D), technology, and education.[30] The proposal was consistent with competitiveness measures advocated by his predecessors in office.

In 1981, Congress passed a temporary measure to encourage more private R&D and renewed it regularly until 2005. Congress considered a proposal in 2001 to make the R&D tax credit permanent, but the measure failed. However, in 2004, 2006, and 2010, Congress temporarily extended the tax credit, making the provisions retroactive to the expiration of the last temporary extension. Temporary extensions seem the only politically acceptable way in Congress to keep that particular competitiveness stimulus in place.

The impact of the direct and indirect actions of government on improving the productivity of the economy can be measured only in the long run. For example, even if businesses substantially increase their expenditures for R&D as a result of government incentives, the payoff in productivity terms will show up only years into the future. A majority of U.S. states offer a variety of general tax credit programs for businesses. A few additional states have more targeted tax credit programs for R&D investments in specific geographic areas of the state, or for specific industries or technologies, such as encouraging the growth of the biotechnology industry.[31]

Worldwide, the focus is somewhat more on the factors that make an economy attractive for foreign direct investment and that facilitate domestic investment than on direct stimulative activities. **Exhibit 3–2** describes research on measuring the ease of doing business in economies around the world as a way of evaluating the effects of government regulations and interventions, or lack thereof for some issues, in order to target changes that would improve the business climate.

Exhibit 3–2 The Ease of Doing Business Around the World

Greater emphasis in the last decade has been placed on reducing the barriers to private economic investment and activity than on direct promotional activities of government. The World Bank produces an annual report on *Doing Business* that ranks 181 countries on the ease of doing business. Ten subjects are the basis for the measurement:

1. Starting up a business (how long it takes, how much red tape, how many actors must be involved)
2. Dealing with licenses (permitting, renewals, inspections)
3. Employment (hiring rules, firing rules and costs, working hour mandates)
4. Commercial property registration (time it takes, cost, clarity on property rights)
5. Access to credit (legal/regulatory practices, access to information about credit)
6. Investor protection (shareholder suits, disclosures on company transactions)
7. Taxes (complexity/time taken to file, total taxes as percent of income)
8. Export/import regulations (transactions and permits required, duties, ease of movement of goods and capital across borders)
9. Enforceability of contracts (effectiveness of legal system, cost of enforcing, sanctity of contract)
10. Closing a business (costs, bankruptcy rules)[1]

The five top-ranked economies, in order, are Singapore, Hong Kong (China), New Zealand, the United States, and Denmark. The five lowest-ranked economies are Chad, Central African Republic, Republic of Congo, Eritrea, and Guinea.[2] The World Bank program aims at transforming economies by in part transforming the rules and conditions in which economic activity takes place. Looking at the entire set of rankings, it is not just that overall level of economic development measured by size matters, but government actions and failure to take action to create a favorable climate has a great influence on the productivity of the economy.

1. World Bank (2011). *Ease of doing business: 2012*. Retrieved November 14, 2011, from http://www. doingbusiness.org/reports/global-reports/doing-business-2012.
2. World Bank (2011). *Doing business: economy rankings*. Retrieved November 14, 2011, from http:// www.doingbusiness.org/rankings.

A Government Technology Policy

The question of whether the government should be more active in protecting and promoting critical high-technology industries first emerged in the late 1980s when the U.S. economy began to lose ground in all areas, not just markets dominated by inexpensive labor. The concept has persisted as a key policy issue. The George H. W. Bush administration was widely criticized for not protecting critical industries such as microelectronics, and President Clinton made stimulation of high-technology development an economic policy priority. The George W. Bush administration designated corporate tax reduction, repeal of taxes on dividends, and the R&D tax credits as the most important tools with which to support economic development. President Obama made technology promotion, particularly in developing green energy and other advanced environmental improvement technologies, a focal point in his first budget proposals and as part of separate stimulus packages.[32] Congress has been reluctant to support most of these initiatives, though as noted above, R&D tax credit programs have been "temporarily" extended periodically.

The problem with providing more support to one segment of the economy than to another is that government rather than the marketplace "picks winners and losers," and there is little evidence that governments are good in that role. The federal support for the Solyndra Corporation, a solar panel technology developer and manufacturer, is a case in point. As part of a larger federal push to commercialize green energy technologies, the Solyndra Corporation was a recipient of a major federal loan program. When Solyndra's particular solar panel technology proved commercially not viable, at least in the context of energy prices prevailing at the end of the first decade of 2000, the company declared bankruptcy (this case is discussed in additional detail in the discussion of recession stimulus efforts).[33]

The decades of Japan's double-digit growth seemed to many observers sufficient evidence that government-led development was the proper path, but recent decades have altered that view considerably. Singapore is sometimes held up as an example of successful and significant government intervention, but as Exhibit 3–2 notes, Singapore ranks first in the world in ease of doing business, brought about more by the climate created by government than by government choosing and directing industry targets for growth. The federal government has difficulty determining what particular elements in a volatile industry such as electronics or alternative energy technologies will be the most important determinants of U.S. global competitiveness in high-technology markets five or ten years from now.[34] The more widely accepted view is that government actions, rather than overtly promoting particular industries, should be directed toward improving the human and capital base, should encourage savings and investment, and should promote the international exchange of ideas, goods, and services.

There has been an ebb and flow over time to arguments that government should develop a technology policy.[35] The first major federal programs for higher education, focusing on science and math, were launched in 1958, the year immediately after the Soviet Union launched the first satellite, Sputnik. Anxiety over Japan's remarkable growth in the 1970s spurred concern about the government not doing enough to ensure U.S. competitiveness in the world economy. More recently, the rapid growth of Brazil, India, and China stimulates debate. The American Jobs Act proposed by the Obama administration in 2011 had a dual focus on job creation and making U.S. businesses more competitive in world markets.[36] The president called for investment in education, scientific research, and infrastructure to move ideas as well as goods.[37]

Equilibrium in International Financial Flows

Important elements of government policy in this era of the global marketplace are actions designed to affect the balance of trade and other financial transactions among nations. Related to this balance is U.S. reliance on world capital markets to finance its budget deficit. The U.S. financial position vis-à-vis the rest of the world is discussed in this section. A review of the overall deficit situation and debt management follows.

As noted earlier, since 1985, more capital has flowed into the United States in the form of investments in United States private assets and U.S. government Treasury debt than the U.S. has invested in other economies. This means that there are more foreign demands on U.S. assets than there are U.S. claims on assets in other countries. Those demands on U.S. assets constitute claims against private parties in the United States and on the U.S. government. In 2009, the U.S. economy received financial flows of various kinds from the rest of the world in the amount of $2.2 trillion while paying individuals, companies, and governments in other countries $2.6 trillion. Thus, the United States paid out approximately $.4 trillion more than it received. Of that amount, about 25% was U.S. government debt repayments to other governments and individuals outside the United States.[38]

Most of the imbalance is due to companies and individuals in the United States purchasing more abroad than is sold to other countries (creating a trade imbalance). That is one contributing factor for the United States. The other major factor, as noted earlier, is the net balance of investments abroad and foreign investments in the United States. It is of concern to government economic policy in part because the larger the government budget deficit, the more the government borrows from the capital markets, potentially driving up interest rates. It is also of concern to government economic policy because it means an imbalance in payments to investors abroad versus payments from investors abroad.

Balance of Payments

Balance of payments refers to the value of goods and services and the financial assets and liabilities flowing between the United States and other countries. Historically, the balance of payments policy objective was to avoid a situation in which imported goods and services plus financial transactions created the potential for drawing down on the U.S. gold reserve. Today, with the rate of exchange between the U.S. dollar and other currencies freely set by the market and unrelated to gold reserves, the balance of payments objective is primarily a matter of maintaining equitable trade relationships between the United States and other countries. Trade negotiations between the United States and South Korea or between the United States and China, for example, are contentious because of the much larger value of goods that U.S. businesses and citizens purchase from those two countries than customers in those countries purchase from the United States.

The balance of payments consists of several components or measures. The net balance of goods purchased abroad versus goods sold abroad is the simple trade balance. It is called the *current account surplus* or *current account deficit*. In 2010, for example, the current account deficit was at an all-time high of $798 billion.[39] A current account deficit has been the pattern for the United States for all but one year since 1982. To remedy an excess in net imports via trade in goods and services, the U.S. economy would have to (1) produce and sell more goods and services abroad, which would mean an increase in GDP; (2) consume less of the goods currently produced in the United States so they could be sold abroad, assuming there is demand for them; (3) reduce consumption of goods from abroad; or (4) achieve some combination of the first three.

Besides the trade balance, financial transactions help determine the current account surplus or deficit. The net flow of capital investments (debt and equity investments, purchases of assets) is called the *capital account surplus* or *deficit*. By definition, if there is a current account (trade flows) deficit, then there must be a capital account (financial flows) surplus to pay for the value of goods and services imported in excess of goods and services exported.

Between 1995 and 2010, the total value of exports from the United States to the rest of the world almost doubled, whereas the value of imports from the rest of the world to the United States increased by more than 120%.[40] There is no universal agreement, however, on the extent to which a long-term current account deficit and its counterpart capital account surplus is a problem. On the downside, it can mean that consumer purchases of goods from abroad exceed the ability of the economy to produce goods and services demanded abroad. In other words, an economy may be unable to produce the goods and services that its residents desire, at a price its residents are willing to pay. The funds that flow abroad for those purchases are not available, therefore, for investment in the U.S. economy for increased production. To some extent, that is the case. United States consumers do purchase large quantities of consumer goods from other countries, and of increasing importance, the United States purchases an ever larger proportion of total fuel consumed in the United States from other countries.

The imbalance in trade of goods and services, however, has not been the main issue for the United States. As noted earlier, the U.S. capital markets are attractive to foreign investors, and they have been especially attractive during world financial crises such as the Asian and emerging-market collapses of the late 1990s and the market collapse of 2007. Thus, the inflow of investments from abroad is a more important explanation for the current account deficit than is the purchase of goods from abroad. There is a demand in other countries to invest in assets in the United States, independent of its trade position with the rest of the world.

The danger in the volume of capital account surplus lies in its role in financing investment in future growth that otherwise would have to come from savings in the United States. To the extent that our future economic growth can be financed only from abroad, because of low savings in the United States (discussed below), then a major shock to the U.S. economy that causes investors from abroad to pull out large amounts of funds would both decrease the funds available for investment and decrease current consumption. The post–September 11 period initially did lead to some pullback from the U.S. capital market, but that was short lived, in part due to actions by the Federal Reserve Board (discussed later in this chapter) to hold down interest rates. As some foreign investments pulled out of the stock market and the decline in the value of the dollar against major foreign currencies decreased consumer purchases from abroad, the current account deficit shrunk marginally. Even with as bad a situation as the U.S. financial markets experienced following the 2007 market collapse, by 2011 the United States was again a more attractive target of financial investors than most other countries. Still, in 2011, foreign investors owned only about 11% of U.S. financial assets, signifying that foreign ownership of U.S. private sector assets is not a major worry.[41]

Financing the U.S. Economy

The flows of capital across international boundaries and the financing of investment will continue to be major focal points of both economists and governments. Globalization, while widely discussed, is still not entirely understood. Historically, investments made in other countries were substantially in productive capacity. When a company or an investment banking group invested in a factory abroad, the productive capacity in that country increased, and it was no easy matter for the investors to take their investment out quickly. Since the late 1980s, international transactions in financial instruments, such as stocks and bonds as opposed to physical capital, have substantially increased. One of the main reasons for the rapidity of the Asian and emerging-market collapses in the 1990s was the amount of foreign investment in tradable financial instruments that allowed investors to pull their funds out quickly.[42] That did not recur to any significant degree in the United States following the 2007 market collapse. However, other countries, such as Portugal, Italy, Greece, and Spain, experienced more severe pressures on their financial markets as investors withdrew portfolio investments in those countries.

The importance of these movements in the trade balance lies in their implications for how the economy is financed. From the mid-nineteenth century until the mid-1980s, the U.S. economy was financed domestically. National saving was sufficient to provide funds for national investment, with the surplus national saving being invested abroad. To the extent that households spend heavily on consumer goods and save little, and the government budget is in deficit, investment has to be financed from sources outside the economy. An important part of the U.S. economy has been financed not by domestic savings but rather by foreign investments in the United States. These foreign investments represent a future claim on U.S. assets that are not matched by equal U.S. claims on foreign assets.

Were the same foreign investments made in U.S. industry's stocks and bonds, and not in government debt, financing would be available for economic expansion. To the extent that the investment in U.S. government debt does not produce expansion of domestic U.S. production capacity, the government's need for this financing competes with industry's need for investment finance. In macroeconomic terms, this external financing of the budget deficit creates a situation in which a greater quantity of U.S. goods and services has to be sold abroad in the long term to meet payments to foreign holders of U.S. public sector debt. That quantity then is not available for U.S. consumption or investment. Thus the trade balance, as well as the overall balance of payments disequilibrium, is intertwined with the federal government budget deficit.

The late 1990s boom in the U.S. economy illustrates this point. The federal budget achieved balance in fiscal year 1998. Not only did the U.S. government not need to issue long-term securities to finance a deficit, but for three years the Treasury actually bought back higher-denominated debt with part of the budget surplus. By the end of the twentieth century, foreign borrowing to finance the deficit was becoming less of an issue, but a return to large federal deficits starting in 2002 again spotlighted the role foreign investors play in financing federal budget deficits. The situation further highlighted the comparatively low savings rate of U.S. households.

The upside of foreign investments in the U.S. economy is that they represent foreign confidence in the economy. In the market turmoil of 2011, the confidence in the U.S. economy relative to other countries might not have been as much the strength of the U.S. economy overall, but the relatively weaker investment choices offered in other countries.[43] Foreign investors have found U.S. Treasury notes an attractive investment because of the interest rates offered and because of their safety. Although the U.S. Congress stalled until the last possible moment in 2011 in raising the ceiling on the amount of debt the U.S. government could legally incur, creating concerns in world financial markets about the ability of the United States to pay all its bills in a timely fashion, a compromise was reached tying the increase in the debt ceiling to a plan to reduce the federal deficit (see discussion later in this chapter).[44]

The Decline in National Savings

Except for the four budget surplus years from 1998 to 2001 (see the chapter on budget approval and the U.S. Congress), the U.S. economy has generated falling amounts of savings to finance investment in the economy, relative to the size of the economy. National savings represent the source of funds for new investment in equipment, plants, and other physical facilities that allow total production to grow. Economists generally measure savings as gross and net national savings as a percentage of GDP. *Gross national savings* is the sum of household saving, corporate saving, and government saving. Household saving may be literally in the form of savings accounts or more likely in investment in securities through individual investments and individual and corporate contributions to pension plans. Government saving may be in the form of investment in fixed assets such as roads and bridges or, though rare, a budget surplus. Corporate saving is investment in fixed assets such as factories, equipment, land improvement, and so forth, plus net changes in inventory. These government and corporate investments, financed by purchases of equity and debt in companies or taxes in the case of government, create the economy's capacity to produce goods and services.

Not all investments by governments and corporations actually produce an increase in productive assets, of course, because they must replace older facilities and equipment that are no longer useful. Machinery purchased to replace obsolete equipment would not result in an increase in productive capacity. The term *net national savings* captures the difference between investment in productive capacity, whether government or corporate, that adds to new production by subtracting the value of fixed assets replaced.

The U.S. gross national savings rate has ranged from a high of 22% in 1965 to a low of just under 11% in 2009. However, taking into account the consumption of fixed capital (see Exhibit 3–1), the net national savings rate hit its low in 2009, a negative 2.3%. The previous high net savings rate since the early 1960s was in 1965 (12%).

Figure 3–4 shows U.S. gross and net savings rates (savings as percentage of GDP) from 1962 through 2010. It is clear that both savings rates have declined steadily, with occasional and sometimes significant bumps upward. Typically it has not been an increase in personal savings that has caused the rates to go up temporarily, but temporary decreases in the government budget deficit, such as the increased savings rate in the late 1990s. The data indicate that the United States is increasingly a consumption-based economy, with declining private sector and public sector investments that would support future growth (see the chapter on capital assets for a discussion on low levels of public investment in infrastructure).

How does the U.S. savings rate fare compared with that of other industrialized countries? **Figure 3–5** compares the United States with the United Kingdom, Japan, South Korea, and Germany. It is clear that with the exception of 2000, when the United States experienced a federal budget surplus, the United States lags behind each of the other countries. South

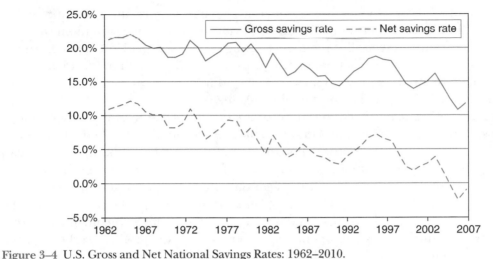

Figure 3–4 U.S. Gross and Net National Savings Rates: 1962–2010.
Note: Savings rates are gross and net savings, respectively, as a percentage of GDP.
Source: Data from U.S. Council of Economic Advisers (2011). *Economic report of the president: 2011* (pp. 220, 228). Washington, DC: U.S. Government Printing Office.

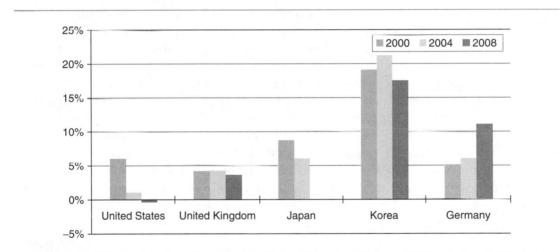

Figure 3–5 Net National Savings Rates for the United States and Selected Other Industrial Countries: 2000, 2004, and 2008.
Sources: Data from Organization for Economic Co-operation and Development (2006). *OECD statistics, V. 2.6*, Paris: OECD, Retrieved July 15, 2006, from http://stats.oecd.org/wbos/degault.aspx?datasetcode=ANA TABLE 2. Japan data is 2000 and 2003. Note: the OECD table from which 2000 and 2004 were extracted is no longer accessible at that URL. 2008 source: *Net saving rate: percentage of GDP*, Paris: OECD, Retrieved November 14, 2011, from http://www.oecd-ilibrary.org/economics/national-accounts-at-a-glance-2009/net-saving-rate_9789264075108-table7_1-en.

Korea's net savings rate is comparable to that of other newly advanced industrial economies, benefiting from substantial increases in labor productivity due to investments in manufacturing technology and a shift in the labor force from less to more productive occupations, such as from small-scale agriculture to manufacturing. Overall, as noted earlier, most of the capital formation that occurred in the U.S. economy was absorbed by replacing obsolete or unusable assets.

The substantial decline in U.S. net national savings has been relatively unique, as the small sample in Figure 3–5 illustrates. Even countries like the United Kingdom that run a capital account surplus typically have higher savings rates than the United States. In the economic boom of the 1990s, net national savings was relatively high, in part because of substantial investment in the U.S. capital markets and in part because of low government budget deficit, including some years of budget surplus.

The compensating factor that offsets some of the problems that might otherwise be created by a sustained low savings rate is in the technology advantage that the U.S. economy enjoys relative to most other countries, though Brazil, Russia, India, and China are increasingly competitive in new technology investments.[45] The measures of savings discussed in this section capture those elements in the economy that are investments in fixed assets (i.e., physical or tangible objects). Classically, land, labor, and capital were the three elements that combine to produce goods and services. But increasingly, the main factor that still enables the United States to have the highest gross domestic product, and one of the highest levels of GDP per capita, is technology.

Typically, when a company replaces an obsolete piece of equipment, the new equipment is highly likely to be much more productive than what it replaced. Net national savings would not capture this increased productive capacity due to the more sophisticated knowledge built into the new equipment. If one were able to measure the production of the old equipment when it was operating at full capacity, and the production of the new piece of equipment operating at full capacity, then one would not fully subtract the cost of the new equipment from gross national savings. But in the total economy, the measurement problems in trying to capture the value of technology are currently insurmountable. So to the extent that new technology built into new fixed assets is not measured in terms of contribution to productivity, net national savings understates the ability of the economy to continue to produce goods and services. The value of knowledge generated within the economy and the attractiveness of the U.S. economy are what have enabled the U.S. economy, despite lower savings rates and despite frequent government budget deficits, to continue to enjoy higher standards of living than almost any other country in the world.[46]

Deficits and Debt Management

State and local debt are primarily tools for financing long-term investment in physical infrastructure and other capital assets. It is therefore prudent for state and local governments to use short-term borrowing only for meeting the demands of short-term contingencies and to ensure that long-term borrowing is linked to the expected life of the investments financed. Federal debt policy, in contrast, relates more to macroeconomic policy considerations than to capital investment requirements. Deficits in the federal budget accumulate as spending exceeds revenues, regardless of whether the spending finances investments in long-term growth, meets operating expenses, pays interest on previous debt, provides transfer payments, or pays the costs of war. While it is possible to make a numeric comparison between the investment levels in the federal budget and the size of the deficit, federal budget deficits have not been the result of conscious investment planning.

Developing-Country Debt Management

Developing countries' debt-management issues are generally not comparable to those of the United States or other longtime industrialized economies that incur substantial public debt as fiscal policy measures. For developing countries, prudent debt management is more comparable to that of U.S. state and local governments. Developing countries as a rule have excess or idle labor capacity. For these countries, the long-run economic strategy is to invest in education to improve the productivity of labor and in physical infrastructure to facilitate the production and flow of goods and services produced by the private sector. Typically, a shortage of physical infrastructure, such as transportation and communications facilities, retards the economic investment that would employ the excess labor capacity. Governments in developing countries borrow from donor agencies, such as the World Bank, and from banks in industrial countries to increase their physical infrastructure and other capital investments. If they are economically sound, the investments will produce long-run economic growth sufficient to repay the indebtedness.

More often than not, however, developing countries encounter debt troubles when borrowing finances current consumption rather than investment and when physical infrastructure assets that have been built are not maintained. The economy then does not maintain a sufficient level of growth, revenues do not increase as expected, and debt exceeds capacity to repay.

U.S. Government's Use of Debt

In the post-Depression era, the federal budget deficit was used as an overt tool to influence total demand in the economy and thus overall economic performance. According to the prevailing economic theory of that era, deficits should be managed to stimulate the economy without creating inflationary pressure. However, by the 1980s, the size of the deficit had reached proportions that were out of step with economic policy objectives. In actuality, the federal budget achieved a surplus in 1998, in part due to deliberate management, but largely due to tax receipts increasing with rapid economic growth. As already noted, 2002 marked a return to a federal deficit with an economic downturn and the effects of September 11. These (in retrospect) relatively modest deficits were followed by the major recession starting in 2007, which ushered in three consecutive years (2009, 2010, and 2011) with deficits in excess of $1.2 trillion, which overshadow the deficits caused by Afghanistan and Iraq. Furthermore, independent of these presumably short-term problems, the federal budget has a built-in deficit for the foreseeable future unless major changes are made in expenditures and/or revenue sources.[47]

Distinguishing between presumably temporary use of debt as a deliberate stimulus and debt that accumulates as a result of policy decisions about revenues and expenditures is critical to informed public policy. The confusion between the two is demonstrated, on the one hand, by the debates over a variety of stimulus packages starting as early as 2007. On the other hand, the deficits that reflect an apparent inability for the executive and legislative branches, and the two major parties, to agree on combinations of expenditure cuts and revenue measures when the economy is more normal is not a fiscal policy decision.

The debates also demonstrate each side seeking political advantage by mixing the two main causes of a growing federal debt.[48]

The 2011 Economic Report of the President emphasized two themes underlying the major programs to encourage an economy that showed signs of turning around from the previous two years of recession:

1. the need to continue to make major investments in education, energy independence, and new technologies to create entirely new industries to fuel future U.S. economic growth, such as green environmental businesses;
2. the need to ensure that necessary budget cuts did not affect primarily lower-income and middle-class families, and did not come without higher-income Americans paying more of a share.[49]

The Congressional Budget Office, in its *Budget and Economic Outlook*, issued at about the same time as the *Economic Report of the President*, emphasized long-term projections (to 2021) of the budget surplus/deficit comparing CBO's baseline projections with projections that assume continuation of specific policies. These policies included indexing of the Alternative Minimum Tax (AMT), no reduction in physician reimbursement rates for Medicare payments, and the Job Creation Act of 2010 (P.L. 111–312). With these assumptions, CBO's policy continuation scenario forecast a federal budget deficit as a percentage of GDP at about the highest level since the early 1970s, with the exception of the peak (or more aptly valley) in 2008–2010.[50] **Figure 3–6** shows deficits as a percentage of GDP since the 1950s.

The clash between incurring deficits as a temporary stimulus and deficits that are a result of a long-term political inability to achieve a balance between expenditures and revenues

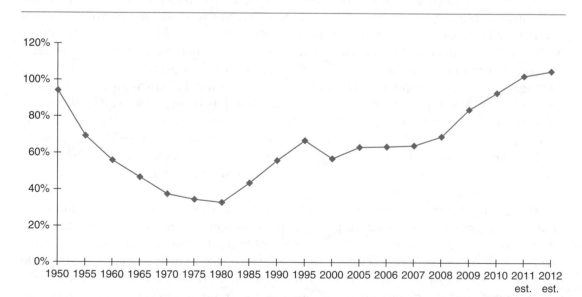

Figure 3–6 Federal Debt as a Percentage of Gross Domestic Product, 1950–2012 (2011 and 2012 estimated)
Source: Data from U.S. Council of Economic Advisers (2011). *Economic report of the president: 2011* (p. 284). Washington, DC: U.S. Government Printing Office.

culminated in the debate over and resolution of the federal debt ceiling in 2011. The maximum size of the federal debt is set by law, and from time to time as the debt has grown, new legislation raising the debt ceiling is necessary. Typically, though not without a considerable amount of political rhetoric, Congress has more or less automatically raised the debt ceiling. When the parties have become more contentious, the increase is modest and forces new legislation within a year or two. At other times, the increase has been sufficient for several years. Not so in 2011. Months of political argument between the two major parties and even within those parties brought the United States to the brink of being unable to meet, at least on a timely basis, all of its payment obligations. The Republican Party's position generally held to the view that government spending is simply too high and that taxes should remain low on upper-income households and corporations since they are the primary producers of new jobs. The Democratic Party's position generally held to the view that there should be shared sacrifice in the extreme economic conditions and that some tax increases on wealthier Americans were warranted in order not to cut into programs benefiting primarily the lowest-income Americans.

On August 2, 2011, legislation was signed for a new debt ceiling sufficient to last at least through the 2012 presidential elections. Approval in Congress for the ceiling increase was won with an agreement to cut the federal budget by $2.1 to $2.4 trillion by 2021. No one really thought the deal actually addressed the underlying twin problems of low rates of economic growth and a budget deficit fueled by major tax cuts in the 2000s and growth in so-called mandatory spending.[51] Mandatory spending consists of programs whose spending levels are stipulated by legislation, such as Social Security and Medicare, and cannot be cut without legislative change.

To achieve the $2 trillion-plus in expenditure cuts, the debt ceiling legislation established a 12-member Joint Select Committee on Deficit Reduction (supercommittee), divided equally between the House and Senate and between the two political parties. Approximately $900 billion in budget cuts were identified in the legislation. The supercommittee's job was to agree upon an additional $1.5 billion in reductions. A forcing function if the supercommittee did not agree to at least $1.2 trillion were automatic cuts divided equally between defense and Medicare. The hope was that those automatic cuts would be so politically unpalatable to both parties that the committee would reach a more rational compromise.

On November 21, 2011, the supercommittee announced that it had been unable to achieve its objective. The draconian automatic cuts are to take place beginning in 2013. The president's response was to promise to veto any legislation passed to rescind or modify the automatic budget cuts. The 2012 Republican Party primaries to choose a nominee to run against Barack Obama and the election itself made it seem unlikely that the deficit would be addressed in any major way until 2013 or beyond.

Size of the U.S. Federal Debt

To shed more light on the debate about government debt in recent years, it is important to understand the relative size of the federal debt and to consider its origins and implications. Figure 3–6 shows that the total federal indebtedness in 1950 equaled 94% of GDP, reflecting the financing of World War II. That figure steadily declined until it reached postwar lows around 35% between 1970 and 1982. Steady increases after that brought federal debt up to 67% of GDP in 1995, the highest level since 1955. Federal debt dropped briefly as a result of the budget surpluses at the end of the Clinton administration and started to climb again with the George W. Bush administration tax cuts and the 2001–2002 recession. Debt then increased dramatically as a result of the recession that started in 2007. Estimates for 2011 and 2012 show federal debt exceeding 100% of GDP, for the first time since World War II and its immediate aftermath.[52]

Effects of Economic Performance on the Size of the Federal Debt

Two circumstances explain the rapid rise in the federal government's debt at the end of the last century and into the twenty-first century. First, the federal budget, in terms of both revenues and expenditures, is affected by the overall performance of the economy. Oil price shocks and high inflation led to unbalanced federal budgets throughout the 1980s. Overall growth in the economy in real terms was virtually zero for that decade. This lack of growth created pressure on the budget because of automatic increases in expenditures for some social welfare programs that expand as unemployment goes up. It also caused a decline in federal revenues. A brief reversal occurred in the mid-1990s, as low unemployment and increased production combined to produce decreased demand for federal social welfare assistance and increased tax revenues. Two simultaneous wars, high prices for imported oil, rising costs for some federal programs such as Medicare, and the disastrous recession starting in 2007 renewed the longer-term trend toward higher deficits. The stimulus programs to address some of the recession's effects added significantly to the debt, as reflected in the return to World War II debt levels.

Effects of Tax Cuts on the Size of the Federal Debt

The second set of circumstances affecting the long-term growth in the deficit are tax policy decisions beginning with the administration of President Ronald Reagan. On taking office, President Reagan, with approval by Congress, initiated a sweeping set of economic reforms, including a major series of tax cuts beginning in 1981 and significant budget reductions in non-defense spending. However, as the program evolved, it proved politically impossible to reduce non-defense spending sufficiently to match increases in defense expenditures, and overall spending remained at prior levels or even went higher than before the tax cuts.

The theory behind the tax cuts at that time was that the funds not collected by the government would be better invested by the private sector, yielding a future revenue dividend in the form of increased tax yields from the heightened economic activity. In reality, the so-called *fiscal dividend* never materialized. Federal revenue levels grew more slowly than at any time since the 1960s, while defense spending, entitlement program outlays, and interest on the debt soared to new heights.

Since those initial tax cuts, annual increases in federal revenue have fluctuated between 5% and 10%, with only a couple of years below 5% or above 10%. The tax cuts adopted in 1997, unlike those of 1981, were accompanied by offsetting expenditure reductions, so there was not as much of a reduction in federal revenue. Again, as in the 1980s, there was no appreciable dividend in higher productivity, and therefore federal revenues did not increase. The exceptions were three economic boom years already attributed in this chapter to an unusual stock market expansion in high-technology stocks. The Economic Growth and Tax Relief Reconciliation Act of 2001 and the Jobs and Growth Tax Relief Reconciliation Act of 2003 made it still more difficult to achieve a budget surplus.[53] In fact, total federal revenues were lower for three consecutive fiscal years after the 2001 tax cut was passed. This decline in revenues largely explains the movement of the budget from surplus into deficit over that period.[54] Since that time, the costs of the wars in Afghanistan and Iraq and the recession that started in 2007 have made it impossible without major policy changes even to approach a more balanced budget.

ANTICIPATING ECONOMIC CONDITIONS

Both the private and public sectors need tools to measure economic change and anticipate economic trends. If businesses are to make sound investment decisions (including the decision to hire new workers or build new plant capacity), they have to anticipate future economic developments. If interest rates are expected to fall, it is not the time to borrow to buy new production equipment. If a tax incentive that reduces overall tax liability when funds are invested in new productive capacity is about to expire, it is a good time to make new investments before the expiration. Some of these events can be predicted with relative certainty. An investment tax credit may have a specific expiration date, as did the R&D tax credit, but experience has shown that Congress is reluctant to give up such credits, continually renewing them. In contrast, it may not be as easy to predict how much change will occur in interest rates. Forecasting tools are a vital ingredient in business economic planning.

If the federal government is to achieve its economic policy objectives, it also needs sensitive and valid measures with which to predict the direction of the economy. Likewise, it needs models of change that predict what will happen if specific policy changes, such as a change in the maximum corporate income tax rate or changes in major entitlement programs such as Social Security, are enacted. Although forecasting techniques are beyond the scope of this text, some familiarity with the measures that are watched closely by business and government and with the analytical models used by forecasters is important for understanding government economic policy.

Business and government forecasters watch closely a number of individual economic indicators. Some indicators are related to the labor force, including unemployment, average weekly hours worked, and average hourly earnings. Other indicators reflect financial conditions, such as interest rates and new starts in home building. Businesses, forecasters, and public policy makers examine such indicators to understand current economic conditions and to predict turning points when the economy will begin to move up or down from its current state.

Of particular importance for anticipating economic turning points are cyclical indicators, also known as *leading, coincident,* and *lagging indicators.*[55] Leading indicators presumably predict what the economy will do, revealing the turning points, whereas lagging indicators report what already has occurred. Formerly, the Bureau of Economic Analysis of the U.S. Department of Commerce released the cyclical indicators monthly. In October 1995, the Department of Commerce awarded a contract to the Conference Board, a private, not-for-profit economics research and business membership organization to maintain the Business Cycles Indicators database. Since 1996, the Conference Board has served as the official source of the indices.

Coincident Indicators

Coincident indicators, which report what the economy is doing now, are the indicators that most commonly reach the public's attention. They include measures of industrial production, personal income, and manufacturing and trade sales.

Prices

Earlier, we described the basic measures of national product and income that indicate what is happening to the levels of production and income. Prices are another measure of what is happening. Wholesale prices may provide an earlier warning of potential problems than measures of national product because they indicate probable changes in prices about to be paid by consumers. The wholesale or producer price index covers about 2,800 commodities.

The *consumer price index* (CPI) is based on the cost of goods and services bought by urban wage and clerical workers. It is estimated from three data sources—a periodic sample survey of about 50,000 housing units and 23,000 retail establishments in 87 urban areas around the country to determine buying habits, and monthly calls and visits to retail establishments and other vendors to collect price information on most commodities. The household sample includes two population groups—all urban consumers and urban wage earners and clerical workers.[31] Change in the CPI is widely cited as an indicator of inflation. One of its most important uses is to adjust various government benefit programs, most prominently Social Security, for the effects of inflation. Social Security payments are automatically increased based on increases in the CPI.

How the CPI is constructed is controversial, largely because of the effect it has on the government budget and the deficit. The actual household survey of buying habits can occur as long as four or five months prior to the publication of the index. A National Academy of Sciences panel in 2002 made a series of recommendations for improvement in CPI methods, some of which were adopted.[56] Changes in the CPI are not the major variables that affect budget forecasts. The Congressional Budget Office focuses on changes in real GDP growth, interest and inflation rates, and wage and salary share of GDP in its long-term (ten-year) budget projection.[57]

Unemployment

Two other measures provide good indications of the current state of the economy—unemployment and industrial production. Unemployment, a percentage measure of the people within the labor force who are not employed, is a common public policy target indicator. This measure is politically charged. A change in the unemployment rate of half a percent up or down is enough to send the president before the news media to announce significant economic progress or to have opposition leaders charge that the economy is failing. However, unemployment is subject to wide seasonal fluctuations, and the measurement of unemployment is subject to manipulation. Some job seekers may become discouraged and fall out of the count altogether. Women and members of ethnic minority groups may not be well represented in the count of job seekers because they may be convinced that there are no jobs to seek or no jobs worth seeking. Therefore, unemployment data always have to be interpreted with some care.

Unemployment figures can vary widely among regions of the country, states, and substate regions. For instance, rural areas may be hard hit economically while urban areas are less harmed. State economies dependent upon tourists traveling by automobile may be more sensitive to the effects of higher gasoline prices, and the result may be higher unemployment in those states.

Industrial Production

The industrial production index, prepared by the Federal Reserve System, is a measure of the manufacture of durable and nondurable goods. The durable portion of manufacturing is watched closely, particularly key industries such as steel. Sales of steel and other hard inputs into manufacturing reflect future intentions of manufacturing concerns. Rising sales may indicate the possibility of future investments in capital facilities. Falling sales may indicate lack of confidence in the economy and attempts by firms to keep inventories low. The value of this index has declined somewhat as the size of the manufacturing segment of the economy relative to the services segment has declined.

Leading Indicators

Although the coincident indicators are useful measures of the current or recent state of the economy, they often do not provide the lead time necessary to devise intervention strategies. The forecaster as a result turns to the leading indicators. Leading indicators include such items as average duration of unemployment, commercial and industrial loans, change in the consumer price index for services, and inventories-to-sales ratios in manufacturing and trade.

Employment-Related Indicators

A key leading indicator is the *average weekly hours in manufacturing*. Its usefulness is based on the practice of most manufacturers of cutting back on the length of the workweek rather than laying off workers if the demand for production starts to decline. A somewhat later indicator is the *average weekly initial claims for unemployment insurance*. This indicator provides evidence of the extent to which layoffs are increasing or decreasing. Both measures indicate employers' estimates of the direction of change in the economy.

Housing Starts

Private, non-farm housing starts, measured by the number of building permits issued for new private housing units, provide a measure of the faith of builders and financial investors in the health of the economy. A decline in the number of starts can signal future economic decline. Housing is thought to be sensitive in that it reflects willingness to tie up investment dollars for several months to a year in an expensive commodity for which there may be no buyer at the time construction begins. For example, on a substate basis, Flint, Michigan, was heavily hit by cutbacks in automobile manufacturing employment, resulting in a major downturn in housing construction in the mid-2000s. The situation was so dire that not only were housing construction workers out of jobs, but so were government housing inspectors, since they lacked anything to inspect. Bursting of the mortgage market bubble in 2007 affected all states, but some states, such as Florida and Nevada, were hit harder than others.

Housing starts are also extremely sensitive to mortgage rates. During periods of extremely high rates, such as the early 1980s, many potential buyers were forced out of the market. In both the 1990s and again in the first decade of the 2000s, mortgage rates fell to their lowest points in nearly 50 years, and housing starts increased, even after September 11, 2001. A significant portion of 2001–2002 financing activity was in refinancing existing mortgages as opposed to financing newly constructed homes.

In recent years, housing starts have become a somewhat less reliable leading indicator. Growth in the use of adjustable-rate mortgages allows home buyers to hedge against cyclical swings in interest rates, which in turn keeps demand for housing higher in the initial stages of rising interest rates. However, increasingly complex financial instruments and weak scrutiny of borrowers resulted in a boom in housing construction later in the decade, only to collapse into record-setting foreclosures when the bubble burst. Since the housing industry in the United States is typically a leader in recovery from recession, the 2007 housing bubble burst had particularly severe repercussions for housing construction playing any role in turning the economy around.[58]

Stock Markets

Stock markets are watched closely by the business community and government analysts, but their volatility makes them difficult to use as leading indicators. The New York Stock Exchange (NYSE) historically was the market most carefully watched. The NASDAQ (National Association of Security Dealers Automated Quotation), where the large majority of technology stocks are traded, has become as important—and to some, more important—due to the substantial increase in the information and communications technology sector's share of the economy. The Tokyo and London markets are watched as well. A substantial increase in investments in emerging markets and the swings in these markets have given prominence to several other markets, especially after the volatility of the late 1990s. The Hang Seng (Hong Kong) stock market index is reported daily, for example.

Several composite indexes of stock exchange transactions are used, the most notable being the Dow Jones Industrial and Standard & Poor's indexes. Changes are infrequent in the stocks listed in these indexes, although they became more frequent in the late 1990s as stock values for some of the companies included in these indices fell to near zero and some went out of business. For example, the 30-stock Dow Jones Industrial Average (DJIA), which includes such giant firms as Walt Disney Company and ExxonMobil Corporation, remained largely intact from 1980 until 1997, when it made a major change and dropped four stocks and added four others. Since 1997, Dow Jones has dropped Enron after the scandal of its inflated and fraudulent earnings came to light, and added Bank of America, Chevron, and Kraft Foods. Kraft replaced American International Group, which was devastated by the market collapse in 2007. As the U.S. economy continues to rely on service industries and technology industries, more frequent additions and deletions are necessary. For example, Wal-Mart was added to the index to capture more of the services component of the economy, and companies like Microsoft and Hewlett-Packard, which represent information technology, have been added. A major initial public offering of a privately held company, such as Facebook, also causes adjustments to the list of 30 stocks in the DJIA.

Stock transactions are useful as leading indicators in that they reflect the faith of investors in the stocks traded on the open market and thus in the companies whose stocks are traded. Stock transactions may be helpful as a barometer of investor confidence. In principle, the value of a stock reflects the health of the firm. In reality, stocks may surge or decline wildly as a result of corporate takeover attempts and fights to prevent takeover or as a function of irrational investor behavior showing faith in unlimited growth potential in stock prices.

Criticism of stock analysts' recommendations abounded after the market crash of 2007. The Dow Jones Industrial Averages (DJIA) hit a low of 7,500 in February 2009, half of a previous high of just over 15,000 in September and October 2007. By November 2011, the market had moved back to around 12,000, representing recapture of about 60% of losses.[59] To the extent that stock prices reflect factors other than the economic health of the corporations, prices will be misleading as an economic indicator.

Composite Indexes

A variety of combined indexes are used to gauge economic changes and trends. As noted earlier, the private Conference Board took over the database and calculations of leading, lagging, and coincident indicators. The Conference Board's indicators and composites reflect the overall economy. Composite indices are published by the board monthly, combining several individual indices.

One type of composite is a *diffusion index*. It measures the proportion of individual components of the index that are moving in the same direction. The numerical value of a diffusion index is equal to the percentage of components of the index that are moving in the same direction. For example, the diffusion index of the leading composite index assigns values of 1, 0.5, or 0 to each component based on change of 5% or more, less than 5%, or no change or drop, respectively.[60] Stock analysts and trade publications also compute and publish indices of the major markets.

Forecasting

Despite the availability of a wide range of indicators and extensive historical series, forecasting remains a risky business. It is common to find two or more major federal organizations in substantial disagreement over expected economic trends. Rarely do the Office of Management and Budget (OMB) and the Congressional Budget Office (CBO) agree, for example, on the forecast of the federal deficit. However, the CBO calculated that the mean percentage error in forecasts of more than a dozen economic indicators was rarely more than 1% for the CBO, administration forecasts, and private economic forecasters. CBO did observe that its estimates were (barely) more accurate than administration forecasts. In addition, the CBO notes that its forecasts compare favorably to a consensus survey of private forecasters, called the *Blue Chip Consensus*.[61] Of course, the longer the forecast period, the greater the variances that might be expected among forecasters and the greater inaccuracy of the forecasts.

To the extent that discrepancies arise, forecasts by the president's advisers, reflected in the annual budget, have tended to overestimate economic performance so that government receipts fall short of original estimates, and expenditures tend to be higher due to programs such as unemployment benefits that kick in automatically. The CBO has also been optimistic but often is more accurate than OMB.

Economic forecasts are based on informed judgment or a combination of judgment and sophisticated econometric models. Several private organizations employ econometric models that include numerous variables—from around 100 to as many as 1,200. Among the more famous private models is DRI-WEFA (a merger of Data Resources, Inc., and the former Wharton Econometric Forecasting Associates).[62] Several organizations, including the Institute for Survey Research at the University of Michigan, conduct surveys of ordinary consumers and expert analysts to obtain estimates of economic trends. Judgment is regularly used to adjust the sophisticated mathematical models.

Not surprisingly, during major economic changes both business and government are sometimes criticized for not having anticipated the degree of change or sometimes even the direction of change. The recession year of 1982 had been predicted in 1981 to be a year of modest economic growth. The recovery in 1983 was predicted to be a period of slow growth, whereas actual growth in GDP turned out to be more than twice the growth that had been forecast. The recession that plagued the last two years of the George H. W. Bush administration was reputed to be momentarily ending, but the Clinton campaign was able to make the case that recovery had not yet begun. Some economists, especially in Europe, forecasted annually from 1995 through 2000 that the American economic bubble would burst. Finally, in 2001, they were right. Models seem to fail when major structural changes are occurring, such as OPEC's gain of control over oil production in the early 1970s or the rapid rise in fuel prices in 2006. In addition, models fail when asset prices are significantly overvalued, such as in the 2007 market collapse when the complex derivatives that had fueled the housing finance growth came unraveled. Given the conflicting interpretations possible even with sound information, economic forecasters as well as political leaders interpret the data from their own perspectives. The technical problems involved are great, but inevitably, forecasting succumbs not to technical problems but to political resolutions. The president and his staff may focus on one set of indicators that show signs of progress, while members of Congress from the opposing party may focus on another set of indicators. State and local political leaders are just as susceptible to coloring judgment with hope by trying to appear confident in the economic future while sometimes failing to address serious underlying economic and fiscal weaknesses. We return to the issues involved in conflicting theories of economic behavior and the implications for government economic policy in the next section.

TOOLS AVAILABLE TO AFFECT THE ECONOMY

In this section, we first discuss the actions government may take to affect the economy. Some are not deliberate actions, but rather occur automatically. Most of the focus in this section, however, is on deliberate actions taken by government. These fall into two categories: fiscal policy and monetary policy. The next section is an illustration of the application of these tools to the economic crisis that unfolded beginning in 2007.

Automatic Stabilizers

Government actions intended to achieve economic policy objectives can be either discretionary or automatic. In the case of discretionary actions, policy makers discuss alternatives and reach a decision as to how to intervene in specific circumstances. Automatic or built-in stabilizers, in contrast, do not require policy makers to take any special steps. Some government revenues and expenditures rise or fall automatically with changes in the economy. Revenues are especially sensitive to economic performance, with tax revenues falling due to falling incomes. State and local government revenues rise and fall without intervention as economic conditions change. In some cases, the requirement that states balance their budget forces them to cut expenditures as revenues from sales and income taxes fall. The federal government, in contrast, historically does not immediately reduce expenditures to match a revenue decline.

Figure 3–7 shows the relationship between the change in GDP and the change in federal revenues from 1963 through 2010. With few exceptions, GDP declines are matched

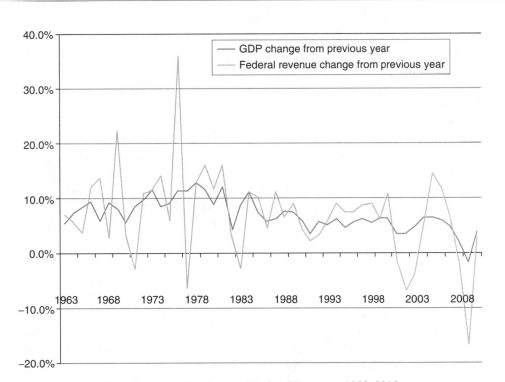

Figure 3–7 Changes in Gross Domestic Product and Federal Revenue, 1963–2010.
Source: Data from U.S. Council of Economic Advisers (2011). *Economic report of the president: 2011* (pp. 188, 283). Washington, DC: U.S. Government Printing Office.

by declines in revenues, and vice versa, though not always at the same rate. For example, the slight increase in GDP from 1987 to 1988 was exceeded by a much larger increase in federal revenue. Similarly, the drop in GDP from 2008 to 2009 was accompanied by a much larger drop in federal revenue. In most of the years illustrated in the series, the directional changes occur in the same year. There is little lag between a declining GDP and a decline in federal revenue since much of federal revenue derives from taxes on components of GDP (corporate and personal income). Government expenditures, at least at the federal level, do not automatically fall with declining economic performance. In fact, they tend to increase. The combined tax revenue declines and expenditure increases have an automatic stimulative effect tending to encourage economic growth.

The progressivity of the tax structure is another example of a built-in or automatic stabilizer. As the economy declines, corporate profits decline and workers' salaries decrease. Both corporate and personal taxes go down with the result that proportionately more funds are left available to the private sector for investment, stimulating demand. Similarly, tax revenues rise as the economy expands, providing some brake on growth so it does not lead to inflationary pressures. Unemployment insurance is another example of an automatic stabilizer, as it kicks in immediately as the unemployed file claims.

Nongovernmental stabilizers are also an inherent part of the economy and individual economic behavior. Recessions are resisted by individuals and corporations that use savings to maintain established levels of activities. Conversely, expansionary trends are resisted. As income rises, greater proportions of income are placed in savings rather than being used for consumption.

Discretionary Policies

Discretionary interventions vary widely. They are based on economic theories of behavior, both micro- and macroeconomic, that anticipate the economy's responses to government actions involving taxing and spending and alterations in the money supply and the flow of funds through the monetary system. The former actions are called fiscal policy. The latter are dubbed monetary policy. Fiscal policy and monetary policy are first reviewed separately, and then their integration into an overall strategy is discussed. A separate section then follows to illustrate how these tools were used to combat the effects of the recession, starting with a fiscal policy stimulus package in late 2008 endorsed by the outgoing President George W. Bush and the incoming President Barack Obama.

Fiscal Policy Instruments

The essential tools of fiscal policy are revenues, expenditures, and the implied surplus or deficit. Their use evolved during the twentieth century and has continued into the twenty-first, changing as different views of the role of government in the economy have held sway. The prevailing view had been that little government intervention was necessary. If the economy seemed to be faltering, the government's role should be limited to an incremental increase in expenditures over revenues to "prime the pump." During the Great Depression of the 1930s, demand fell so rapidly and to such a depth, however, that small actions by the government had virtually no effect. It was only the extraordinary production demands of World War II, financed largely by federal budget deficits, that stimulated sufficient growth to pull the economy out of its freefall. The immediate postwar period rode on the demand for consumer goods that had been in short supply during the war, and there seemed to be little for the government to do for the economy one way or the other.

Keynesian Economics

Ideas about what the government should do in the event of a downturn have not stood still. John Maynard Keynes had argued in 1936 that the main cause of downturns was lack of demand.[63] According to this view, the government's aim should be to stimulate demand by spending, thereby ensuring that idle productive capacity is used. By 1946, the federal government had assumed a formal, legislatively mandated role in the economy, and that role was guided by the prescriptions of Keynesian economics.

Keynes focused on the problem of cuts in production in response to declining demand. Such cuts result in less purchasing power for consumers, which further reduces demand for goods and services. This still further decline in demand results in further reductions in production levels. The emphasis, according to Keynesians, should be on maintaining demand levels. The way to maintain demand levels, in their view, is for government to spend at a level higher than revenues—in other words, to incur a deficit whenever economic fluctuations threaten to reduce demand to levels that will generate unemployment and general economic decline. President Richard Nixon famously declared during the major recession during his administration: "I am a Keynesian in economics."[64] President Obama in his first Economic Report to Congress stressed the need to stimulate demand, as noted earlier in this chapter, falling short, however, of declaring himself a Keynesian.

Supply-Side Economics

Keynesian economics was widely accepted until the 1970s, when a contrasting view of the basic problem in a fluctuating demand cycle was given wide circulation. Some economists argued that the basic problem lay not on the demand side, but on the supply side.[65] So-called *supply-side economics* became the dominant viewpoint of the Reagan and George W. Bush administrations. The supply-side view has held that high tax burdens are the major contributor to reduced economic performance. The more taxes are collected, the less money is available for private investment and the less incentive there is to produce. If taxes are cut, production will presumably be stimulated and additional workers will be hired. Although the tax rates are lower, the actual revenue yield will be higher because of increased corporate profits and increased take-home pay for workers. Furthermore, the increased supply of goods and services available should have a dampening effect on inflation. Instead of stimulating demand with federal expenditures, the supply-side approach emphasizes stimulating the economy by increasing the income available to consumers to spend by reducing taxes.

The more extreme version of the supply-side view provided the basis for the 1981 tax cuts (Economic Recovery Tax Act of 1981). However, the expected revenue windfall did not materialize. Consumer spending and to some degree corporate spending did increase, but the gain in federal revenue from the growth stimulated by the reduced taxes did not offset the tax losses, and the deficit increased. As noted earlier, the tax cuts of the George W. Bush administration similarly did not produce the desired effects. The prevailing explanation of why tax cuts have not produced consumer and business spending sufficient to make up for the loss in revenue is not necessarily inconsistent with the theory that tax cuts generally stimulate growth. The accepted view is merely that tax revenues from that growth are usually less than necessary to offset the government revenue loss.

This explanation is complicated by the circumstances surrounding tax cuts in the 1980s and again in the 2000s. Often the periods during which large tax-cut packages have been introduced have coincided with economic downturns so that federal revenues fell not only as a result of the tax cuts, but also because of the general decline in economic activity, as Figure 3–7 illustrates. Furthermore, the economic period of the George W. Bush administration was dominated much more by the September 11 attacks and the subsequent wars in Afghanistan and Iraq than by tax cuts and other economic programs. It is impossible to guess whether the federal budget deficit would have just been smaller without the wars, or if it would have headed toward at least short-term balance. That guess would have to be based largely on a guess about the receptiveness of Congress to the aggressive tax cuts proposed by the president and the willingness or political ability to reduce expenditures and to address major long-term issues in financing Social Security and Medicare.

The 2010–2011 period shows that a closely divided Congress does not portend well for addressing the combination of expenditure and revenue decisions. Public opinion polls seemed to indicate that a majority of Americans would accept an increase in taxes. For example, the *Washington Post/ABC News* opinion survey conducted in July 2011 found that 34% of Americans said they preferred to see the budget deficit solved by spending cuts alone, 2% by revenue increases alone, and 62% by a combination of both.[66] Nevertheless, Congress was unable to agree on any budget package that included tax increases, influenced most heavily by promises made by many Republicans to never vote for a tax increase.

Differences between the demand-oriented economists and the supply-oriented economists have moderated, though the differences between politicians on either side of that debate have not. The middle-of-the-road view is that specific and directed tax decreases or reductions in tax liabilities can be helpful, such as investment tax credits to encourage businesses to invest in capital facilities and an R&D tax credit to encourage private expenditures on research. A major multiplier effect, in which tax reductions yield tax revenue increases, is unlikely, however. Capital gains tax changes seem to produce the greatest level of response. Prevailing views tended to emphasize somewhat more the supply-side view than efforts to stimulate demand, until the recession started in 2007 in which initially bipartisan efforts produced the first of several programs to stimulate demand.

Multiplier Effects

Extracting taxes from the economy or adding expenditures will have not only immediate effects but also multiplier effects, as any transaction will generate several other transactions. For each government expenditure resulting in payments to industry or an individual, part is taxed, while the remainder is divided between consumption and investment. The private citizen or firm spends and, in doing so, places dollars in the hands of others. Some of those dollars will in turn be taxed and the rest spent or invested. Therefore, an increase of $100 in government expenditures will be multiplied in its effect on the economy.

Expenditures have a stimulative effect when they exceed revenues. An initial government expenditure financed by the deficit puts money in the hands of producers and consumers, who in turn pay a portion in taxes, save a portion, and spend a portion. An excess of revenues over expenditures has a dampening effect. An extremely large federal deficit, however, confounds the fiscal policy effects, such as has been experienced since 2007.

Response Lags in Fiscal Policy

One problem with implementing a modest fiscal policy is the gap between the time a revenue or expenditure response is seen as necessary and the time it can actually occur. The lack of complete information about the economy produces a *perception lag*, the period of time that elapses between an event—such as the beginning of an inflationary or a recessionary period—and its recognition. The perception lag contributes to a *reaction lag*, the time between recognition and the decision to act. Pluralistic or decentralized political systems, and systems characterized by deep partisan divides, are often unable to avoid substantial reaction lags. In addition, once agreement is reached, there is typically an *implementation lag*, the time required before the action taken actually affects the economy. Tax measures are clearly felt within a short period of time. The Economic Stimulus Act of 2008 contained tax rebates to taxpayers, some of whom received their rebates within three to four months of the act's passage.[67] The introduction of a new tax does require time to establish the specific regulations and mechanisms for collection. Once the tax is established, however, comparatively little time is required to make the necessary adjustments to the tax rate.

In contrast, extended implementation lags are likely when expenditures are adjusted for fiscal policy purposes. An example is the American Recovery and Reinvestment Act of 2009, which contained an infrastructure spending component intended to go to *shovel-ready* projects—projects that state or local governments were already executing, but which could be expanded or speeded up without major engineering design and procurement steps.[68] While funds were allocated rapidly in many instances, by 2011 unexpended funds remained in the program.

In the short term, the apportionment process that allocates funds to agencies may have some marginal influence on spending patterns during the various quarters of the fiscal year (see the chapter on budget execution). Potentially more powerful tools include budget impoundments, which, within certain limits, allow the president to defer or rescind expenditures (see the chapter on budget approval and the U.S. Congress). Many expenditures, however, are basically uncontrollable in the immediate future because of previous commitments (for example, entitlement programs that provide assistance to the elderly and the poor). Furthermore, a large component of the federal budget is now devoted to meeting interest payments on the debt or to refinancing previous debt, expenditure commitments that must be met.

Effects of Global Capital Flows

As noted at the outset of the chapter, in the United States, changes in world markets were of little consequence for most of the twentieth century. Changes in the U.S. economy, such as occurred during the Great Depression and other serious recessions, rippled through other economies, but economic declines in other countries had less effect on the U.S. economy. We have already discussed the current interdependencies among the United States and other economies. The Asian and emerging-market financial crisis of the late 1990s had ripple effects through financial markets around the world as portfolio investors rapidly pulled their funds from investments in the region. Banks in industrialized countries, especially Japan, had large loans denominated in local currencies—the Thai *baht* and the Indonesian *rupiah*. The government of Thailand was unable to maintain the pegged value of the baht against the dollar, and ultimately devalued the currency. That meant that lenders who had lent yen or dollars and had not denominated the repayments in yen or dollars found their loans almost worthless. An important part of the problem for the world economy, and especially for Japan, was that there was no market information about the extent of exposure of foreign banks to losses due to lending in Thailand, Indonesia, and other emerging market countries in local currencies.[69]

Severe economic distress in Greece and Italy in 2010–2012 created similar ripple effects in other economies. Unlike the Asian financial collapse in the 1990s, the problems in some countries in the European Union came when the U.S. economy was starting to emerge from the recession that started in 2007. The threat of massive loan defaults in Greece, though affecting European banks more than U.S. financial institutions, caused concern that the U.S. economic recovery would be stalled.[70] A similar set of concerns over Italy's debt followed closely on the heels of Greece's problems.[71] U.S. government borrowing from the central banks of several nations, including Japan and China, has caused some concern. Reliance on borrowed dollars from central banks of other countries that hold large dollar reserves is unprecedented in modern U.S. economic history. Many analysts continue to argue that the underlying strength of the United States is still attractive. Those countries whose central banks hold large dollar reserves are willing to continue to lend because their economies depend substantially on purchases by the U.S. economy. Some other analysts express real concern about this unprecedented borrowing from central banks. There is no historical base from which to understand what could make those central banks lose confidence and reduce their levels of lending to the U.S. government.[72] If other emergent economies such as the BRIC countries continue to get stronger, some central banks of other countries may see alternative investments sufficient to reduce their appetite for U.S. government debt. Were that to happen, federal borrowing from the U.S. markets would have to increase, causing interest rates to rise, or dramatic tax increases and/or expenditure decreases would have to occur to reduce the deficit.

Monetary Policy

Control of the Money Supply

Both demand-side and supply-side economists focus on the role of taxing and spending in the economy. Although supply-side economists did not launch a major critique of demand-side theories until the late 1970s, other economists since the 1950s have argued that the government's main effect on the economy should not come through fiscal policy at all. Originally led by Milton Friedman, these economists argue that the main effects of government policy on the private sector should come through control over the money supply. In a simple economy, a government controls the money supply through its monopoly power over the printing of money. As the economy expands, the demand for money increases, and government ultimately meets this demand by printing more money. In a sense, the government can literally print currency and use that currency to meet its spending requirements.

The increase in the money supply (over and above printing replacements for worn currency) is called *seignorage*. Clearly, if the government resorts to printing money without regard to demand, the value of the currency printed declines. U.S. news media in the early 1980s showed film footage of individuals in Bolivia actually pushing carts full of currency to pay for a few dollars' worth of goods as the annual inflation rate reached several thousand percent. Inflation affected currencies so much in Russia and Poland shortly after the demise of the Soviet Union that the governments issued new currency, eliminating three zeros to ease the use of currency in ordinary transactions. Indonesia followed suit after the financial collapse in the 1990s. In the early 1990s, Ukraine suffered a period of hyperinflation as the economy opened up, and Zimbabwe in 2006 experienced hyperinflation.

The main money supply is characterized by the Federal Reserve as M1 and M2. To the average citizen, money is cash—paper money and coinage—and the amount of that is strictly controlled by the government. In the United States, only the federal Treasury Department may print currency or mint coins. But in any complex economy, paper money and coinage in circulation are not the major component of the money supply. In the United States, less than 50% of the readily circulating money supply takes the form of paper money and coinage. Slightly more than 50% of the readily circulating money consists mainly of checkable deposits in banking institutions. Together, currency, coinage, demand deposits such as checking accounts, and small time deposits constitute the component of money supply called M1. In late 2011, M1 was at about $2.1 trillion and represented about 22% of the total money supply in circulation. To M1 would be added savings deposits and small-denomination time deposits, including retail money market accounts. M1 plus these additional components is called M2. M2 is considered the measure of total money supply in circulation, which in 2011 was approximately $9.6 trillion. Familiar paper money and coins thus are about 10% of total money in circulation. Excluded from M2 are large time deposits and institutional money market accounts, IRA and Keogh accounts, deposits that are attributable to foreign institutions, and U.S. federal deposits. Added to M2, these additional accounts measure total money supply in the economy, which stood at $12.0 trillion in 2011.[73]

The banking deposit component of the money supply expands through credit or borrowing. When an individual borrows to purchase a new car, the bank increases the individual's bank balance though the individual has not deposited funds in the bank for this increase. The individual then can write a check to the car dealer. When corporations borrow from financial institutions or issue debt in the stock market, they secure funds for investment. In this case, the money supply grows by the amount of the loan. If interest rates are low, both consumer and business borrowing are encouraged, and the economy expands. Similarly, banks can borrow from the Federal Reserve System, which also adds to the money supply. Deregulation of the banking industry and the growth of various stock and bond funds have further increased the number and types of negotiable instruments that constitute the money supply. Influencing the money supply thus grows ever more complicated.

Role of the Federal Reserve System

In the United States, control over the money supply and interest rates, and hence monetary policy, is exercised by the Federal Reserve System, a quasi-public institution.[74] The system is headed by a board of governors consisting of seven members appointed by the president with the advice and consent of the Senate. The chairperson and vice chair are designated by the president, also with the advice and consent of the Senate. The Federal Reserve Bank and its 12 branches are augmented by all national banks and by state banks and trust companies that wish to join the system.

The Federal Reserve serves as a bank to the banking community. Financial transactions among banks and other financial institutions are cleared through the Federal Reserve. The system lends money to the member banks, which the banks can then relend to their customers. In setting its lending rates to banks, the Federal Reserve influences the direction and magnitude of interest rates in the entire economy, in turn dampening or stimulating the credit system. The system also buys and sells government bonds ranging from short-term Treasury notes to long-term bonds (open market operations). In addition, the Federal Reserve controls the reserve requirements for member banks—the amount of money a bank must have available as a proportion of the total demand deposits of customers.

Using these three tools—lending, open market operations, and control of reserve requirements—the Federal Reserve controls the money supply. In this way, it attempts to moderate demand that might lead to inflationary pressures by reducing the growth in the money supply, or to stimulate demand when the economy is faltering by allowing the money supply to grow. The board, in describing the purposes of the Federal Reserve System, refers explicitly to the 1978 Full Employment and Balanced Growth Act (discussed earlier in this chapter) describing the three main monetary policy objectives of "maximum employment, stable prices and moderate long-term interest rates" contributing to the legislatively mandated government roles in the economy.[75]

Discount Rate

The Federal Reserve's means to directly influence the level of borrowing is through its lending rate to member institutions (the banks). Called the discount rate, this tool has increased in prominence as a monetary tool. Banks borrow from the Federal Reserve to meet customers' demands for money. As the Federal Reserve increases the interest rate, the rate charged to final borrowers increases, which in turn decreases the demand for funds. Since the 1980s, these operations have become the main focus of Federal Reserve actions to control inflation in rapid-growth periods such as the late 1990s and again in 2004–2006. In the boom of the 1990s, until the stock market decline of 2000–2001, the Federal Reserve was quite successful in using small adjustments in the discount rate to control inflation while not depressing the economy. Beginning in 2000, the Federal Reserve—or the Fed, as it is often called—steadily reduced the federal funds rate from more than 6% in 2000 to less than 2% by the end of 2001, declining further to around 1% in 2004.

In 2004, the Fed began raising interest rates to slow the rate of growth in the economy out of concern that inflation would get out of control, mainly because of increased consumer spending and borrowing by the government to finance the deficit. The first increase in June 2004 was followed by regular quarterly increases until August 2006, the longest period of consecutive increases in recent history. The rate at that point in August 2006 was 5.25%, meaning that banks borrowing from the Fed to meet their obligations and maintain required reserves repaid the Fed at an annual rate of 5.25%.[76] These actions by the Fed to adjust the interest rate are watched closely by the stock markets. How the Fed chairman announces a rate change or announces that there will be no rate change at this time can create rapid reaction in the markets.

Open Market Operations

Open market operations do not get as much citizen attention but are highly visible to the financial community because they occur daily. In open market operations, the Federal Reserve buys or sells government bonds (or, less frequently, gold or foreign currency) on the open market. Open market operations can be particularly important when the federal funds rate drops to near zero or actual zero, as it did in 2011. At that point, lowering interest rates has reached the limit in terms of expanding the money supply. However, the Fed's purchase or sale of long-term securities, or open market operations, also can expand or contract the money supply. As the Federal Reserve purchases bonds from the banking system, it increases the reserve holdings of the member institutions selling the bonds and hence increases their ability to lend money. This increase in turn stimulates economic activity, because more investment funds are made available. As member banks buy bonds from the Federal Reserve, their cash reserves decrease, reducing their ability to loan and thereby reducing the total supply of funds available to the economy. The purchase of long-term securities is sometimes described as *quantitative easing.*[77]

Reserve Requirement

Another tool available to the Federal Reserve is changing the reserve requirements of member institutions. This is not frequently used. For every dollar in deposits, member banks are required to retain a specific percentage. By increasing this percentage, the Federal Reserve can immediately curtail the amount banks can lend and thus the amount of money available. Historically changed only every few years, the reserve requirement in the 1980s became a more prominent feature of monetary policy, with adjustments often occurring on an annual basis.

Putting all of these monetary tools together, the government's monetary policy is described as *loose* or *tight* (or as *expansionary* or *contractionary*). Loose monetary policy usually involves lowering the prime rate, purchasing securities from member banks, and perhaps lowering reserve requirements. These actions permit banks to lend more to customers. As a result, private investment goes up and unemployment falls. The side effects are lower interest rates and higher prices.

A tight monetary policy entails the reverse: the prime rate increases, the Federal Reserve sells securities, and reserve requirements may increase. These actions reduce the ability of banks to lend. Tight monetary policy is pursued generally to dampen inflationary pressures and to slow down a speeding economy. In contrast, loose monetary policy is pursued to stimulate growth and reduce unemployment.

Role of the Chairperson of the Federal Reserve Board

For much of the history of the Federal Reserve, it seems unlikely that many Americans ever knew the name of an incumbent or former chair. However, Chairman Alan Greenspan was almost a household name in the 1990s, especially to the millions of Americans who became first-time investors in the stock market or started paying attention for the first time to the value of their company pension fund investments in the market. As chair of the Federal Reserve, Greenspan appeared regularly on the news networks and was widely quoted in the press. When he described in 1996 investors' attitudes toward growth in the value of stocks as "irrational exuberance," stock prices plummeted the same and following days.[78] When he stepped down in 2005, replaced by Ben Bernanke, it was almost as if an icon had retired, leaving difficult shoes for Bernanke to fill.[79] Bernanke has proved to be a less flamboyant personality than Greenspan, but the ability of a statement by the chair in a public speech or in testimony before a congressional committee to influence the stock market has not diminished.

While the chair is clearly the spokesperson for the Federal Reserve, it is more likely that the news media and the investing public are now highly sensitive to actions by the Federal Reserve, and hence the chair is watched carefully for indications of where the Federal Reserve is going. Internally, the chair presides over a seven-member group and wields his or her influence through personality, force of argument, and relative prestige. The chair and the Federal Reserve are not synonymous.

Political Criticism of the Federal Reserve Board

Although the Federal Reserve Board is protected from direct coercion from the president and the Congress because its members' terms are fixed without threat of removal, the board is periodically criticized for appearing to respond to political pressure. While there is little evidence of overt behavior in support of incumbent presidents, some evidence indicates that the Federal Reserve Board has done less than it could in some periods (for example, in the 1960s and 1970s) to offset cyclic movements in the money supply and that this lack of action coincided with the interests of incumbent administrations.[80]

Until the stock market boom of the 1990s, the Federal Reserve was seen in a loose sense as somewhat more Republican Party–oriented, mainly because of its role in managing monetary policy, with the association between monetarists such as Milton Friedman and more conservative public policies focusing on lower levels of federal spending, tax cuts, and balanced budgets. The achievement of a balanced budget during the Clinton administration, though obviously a cooperative result from both political parties and more the result of a sustained economic boom, put the Democratic Party in the mainstream of monetary and fiscal policy, apparently diminishing some of the previous partisan differences over economic policy. Republicans now are as frequently critical of the Fed as any other group.

Combining Fiscal and Monetary Policy

Although economists differ on the emphasis given to fiscal versus monetary policy, the two sets of tools operate at the same time, whether deliberately or not. Sometimes they are complementary. At other times the effects of fiscal policy actions are offset by monetary policy actions. Many analysts are wary of advocating frequent changes in fiscal or monetary policy in response to changing economic conditions. The inability to predict economic change sufficiently far in advance and the slow response of governments suggests to many economists that fiscal policy should be oriented toward long-term economic objectives and that monetary policy should be used for effecting short-term adjustments. Although fiscal and monetary policy advocates disagree vigorously, most economists agree that the budget deficits of the 1980s, early 1990s, and after 2002 have been harmful.

Who Is in Charge?

When it comes to fiscal and monetary policy, different organizational entities are involved, sometimes raising the question, "Who is in charge of overall economic policy?"

Monetary policy is somewhat clear-cut in that the Federal Reserve System is in charge. The tools that were discussed are under the control of the board with the leadership of the chair.

Fiscal policy is more complicated. The president is responsible for recommending policy and Congress for setting it. The Council of Economic Advisers as well as other key advisers provide input into the president's decision making as to what to recommend to Congress. Historically, about the only time Congress has looked at the total picture of the budget and economic policy is during the annual budget resolution (see the chapter on budget approval and the U.S. Congress). Target revenue and spending levels are set, along with a projected deficit (or, occasionally, surplus). Tax rates are set by law periodically, with continuing debate over whether they should be adjusted upward or downward. The Treasury Department, then, has responsibility for administering the taxes. Spending is set by a series of appropriation bills handled by separate appropriation subcommittees, with each executive agency being responsible for carrying out the mandates specified in these bills. The Office of Management and Budget (OMB) has some influence on spending patterns through the apportionment process (see the chapter on budget execution).

Recognizing the importance of the federal government's role in economic affairs, President Clinton created the National Economic Council (NEC) in 1993. The NEC is responsible for coordinating economic policy, and its parallel organization, the National Security Council (NSC), for national security concerns. The NEC serves as a coordinator among the numerous cabinet and Executive Office of the President agencies advising the president, including the Council of Economic Advisers (CEA), the OMB, and the Department of the Treasury.[81] The NEC functions to ensure that actions of the executive branch affecting the economy are consistent with the president's economic policy.

In recent times, the inability to pass a complete set of appropriations bills, the apparently unmanageable, in a political sense, federal deficit, and the deep division between expenditure cuts and revenue enhancements have all focused most of the attention onto the overall budget and economic picture. The apparent power to reach compromises, or at least to negotiate in pursuit of compromise, has narrowed the focus to the president, speaker of the House, Senate majority leader, and a few other key members of Congress, along with the Federal Reserve Board chair.

Public Investment Role of Government

Government Investment in Infrastructure

Fiscal policy and monetary policy are basically tools of central governments. State and local governments typically have balanced budget requirements, making it inadvisable to incur debt strictly for fiscal policy reasons, and neither type of government has a major influence on the overall money supply. However, state and local governments have significant impacts on regional economies, and state and local governments are increasingly adopting explicit economic development strategies. In this regard, state and local governments pursue strategies to create an effective climate to foster economic growth.

Also, these governments inevitably change taxes and spending in response to general economic conditions, which, whether deliberate or not, has at least regional economic effects. Since state and local budgets typically need to be balanced, these governments must respond to economic trends. During the 1990s, 44 states cut taxes.[82] When an economic downturn leads to reduced revenues, expenditures need to be reduced and taxes possibly need to be increased. As a consequence, citizens may find that services they need are no longer available or are in scarcer supply. In the case of local governments, one of the biggest problems during recessions is that many people fall in arrears with their local property taxes. For state governments, economic downturns often lead to decisions to raise tax rates at a time when people can least afford tax increases, though in 2001–2002, fewer than ten states raised tax rates. More took other temporary revenue measures, such as using rainy-day funds, securitizing tobacco settlement revenue (see the chapter on capital finance and debt management), and postponing expenditures.[51]

In fiscal year 2010, states enacted revenue increase measures affecting 2010 in the amount of $24 billion, proposed revenue increases of about $7 billion for 2011, and planned about $14 million in revenue increases in 2012.[83] The primary reason for these revenue increases was the requirement that most state and local budgets (current budgets, excluding capital expenditures) must be balanced.

One of the major strategic elements available is public sector investment in the physical infrastructure necessary for business expansion. Serious concern emerged in the United States during the early 1980s and remains to this day regarding the loss in economic productivity due to deterioration in the infrastructure base of roads, bridges, streets, water and sewer systems, and other public facilities. According to some, fewer technological innovations, decreases in labor productivity, and inadequate capital investment in infrastructure were the major contributors to an overall worsening of the U.S. economy then[84] and now.[85]

State and Local Incentives for Private Sector Investment

Governments are a major source of total capital formation in many developing countries. Public sector investment in infrastructure, including state-owned enterprises, historically accounted for most of the capital formation in developing countries. With privatization of state enterprises and growth of the private sector, however, the public sector role in capital formation has diminished. Although state and local governments in the United States do not invest as high a proportion of their finances in infrastructure, their role in creating a favorable economic climate is important. Some state employee pension funds, for example, have been used as sources of venture capital and to capitalize industrial development funds to attract new business. Federal policies, such as giving municipal bonds tax-exempt and other tax-preference status, also influence state and local investment spending (see the chapter on capital finance and debt management).

Similarly, even in the face of reduced federal financial assistance and difficult fiscal circumstances, state and local governments have over the past several decades increased both their relative share of infrastructure financing and the absolute amounts spent on public infrastructure. This stimulative effect, of course, required state and local tax increases.

State and local governments also actively compete over the location of major industrial facilities.[86] However, to the extent that state and local governments offer special incentives, such as tax breaks and below-market-cost facilities for industrial expansion, little national economic growth is stimulated. Certainly it may be possible to induce a business to relocate or to locate a planned expansion by offering special incentives, but such a move represents for the national economy only a relocation of economic activity rather than net new economic growth. Of course, from a national point of view, attracting firms from other countries results in net growth within the national economy, albeit at the potential expense of some other country. More generally, however, attracting an investment to a particular location may readily benefit that region, but if it is not net new investment, but rather is due to the closing of a facility in another U.S. location, then the net economic benefit to the national economy is limited. The net economic benefit is only the possible result of increased productivity from closing an older facility and putting in its place, in another location, a technologically more sophisticated and more competitive facility.

Link Between Public Infrastructure and Economic Growth

The causal link between public infrastructure investment and real economic growth depends on two conditions. The lack of facilities or infrastructure has to be a barrier to investment, and the costs of the investment have to be in principle recoverable through economic gains. For example, if poor road conditions slow the movement of goods and services, then the costs of those goods and services increase. In addition, firms may hold back on new investments because of the expected difficulty in transportation. Investment in road improvements under these conditions reduces transportation costs, which in turn either provides additional funds for investment or is passed on in savings to consumers, who can subsequently increase either savings or investment. If the economic returns on the road improvements exceed their costs, the result is a net economic gain to the economy. Conversely, if there are insufficient centers of production and consumption linked by those roads, then the volume of transportation will not be sufficient to yield enough economic gain, and the investment will not have been warranted.

Unfortunately, determining when an investment will yield a sufficient economic return is often difficult. Many local governments in the United States have invested in downtown revitalization, business incubator facilities, industrial parks, and other facilities without appropriate analysis of the local economy and have been disappointed with the returns. Some investments that seem to have substantial benefits initially turn out later to be white elephants when the businesses some years later decide to relocate elsewhere. Charlotte, North Carolina, lost its first National Basketball Association team to New Orleans because it would not build a new stadium, though other factors—such as less-than-full arenas—were cited by the owners. Seattle similarly lost its basketball team, which moved to Oklahoma

City. An expansion team was later awarded to Charlotte, but Charlotte first had to promise to build a new facility. One study of U.S. highway investments suggested that instead of significant new capital investment in highways, greater economic impact could occur from decreasing congestion and other planning improvements—for little more spending than current levels. Other studies have reached similar conclusions about a wide range of infrastructure investments.[87] In developing countries, inadequate consideration of whether there are genuine economic opportunities to be stimulated by an infrastructure investment at times has led to indiscriminate construction of roads where there were no real market and production centers to link.

PUTTING IT ALL TOGETHER: FISCAL AND MONETARY POLICY ACTIONS TO COMBAT THE 2007–2009 RECESSION

In this section, we discuss the major fiscal and monetary policy actions taken in the George W. Bush and Barack Obama administrations to combat the most significant recession since the Great Depression. This section starts with a description of the characteristics of the recession, showing the information that led the press, policy makers, and the public to describe the situation informally as a recession and then to make official pronouncements of a recession. The discussion then turns to the combination of legislative and nonlegislative actions to combat the recession. We describe these interventions in the same terms as the previous section's discussion of fiscal and monetary policy actions. Finally, the section concludes with a discussion of the results achieved by those interventions, although in most cases the full effects are not yet measured, and many likely will not be known for several years after the recession has started to recede from memory.

What Went Wrong, and What Made It Officially a Recession?

Following a slump in 2001–2002, when GDP grew at less than 2% compared with a year-over-year growth rate just over 4% in 2000, the U.S. economy began a recovery period that lasted about four years. From 2003 through early 2007, GDP growth rates were between 2.5% and 3.5%.[88] That growth was fueled substantially by a residential housing construction boom. Housing starts in 2000 were at about 1.5 million. By the end of 2005, they had surpassed 2.1 million. Contributors to this rapid increase in new home starts were Federal Reserve actions to lower interest rates during the 2000–2001 economic slump and the development of the subprime mortgage market with a number of complex financial products. These derivative mortgage products encouraged lenders to look to borrowers who previously might not have qualified for mortgages. The Fed's low interest rate policy was maintained even after the economy started picking up again in 2003, a move that contributed to what we all know in hindsight was an unsustainable bubble in the housing market.[89]

Financiers took advantage of the Fed's easing access to credit and encouraged first-time home buyers with attractively low interest rates on variable-rate mortgages. Under the assumption that housing prices would continue to rise, loans that otherwise might be questionable in terms of conventional analysis of a borrower's ability to repay, so-called *subprime* loans, became an increasing proportion of financial institutions' portfolios, including the two federally sponsored government enterprises—Fannie Mae (Federal National Mortgage Association) and Freddie Mac (Federal Home Mortgage Corporation).

Most of the subprime mortgages were not actually held intact by the lenders. Motivated in part by a desire to spread the risks from these subprime loans to a larger pool of investors, and partly by a desire to obtain the revenue stream from repayments more quickly than the term of the loans, financial institutions securitized the repayment streams. These new securities then were sold to a much larger pool of investors, including commercial banks who themselves were not mortgage lenders. These securities were made more complex as the revenue streams from mortgage repayments were stripped out, and for the most part lost the association with the underlying mortgages. Different time streams from the repayments and repayments from loans of widely varying loan quality were bundled together into new securities. Investors in these new securities, as it turned out, rarely could trace the repayment flow they were supposed to receive back to any identifiable individual mortgages.

Many new home purchasers had made little upfront equity investment (down payment) in their homes, and some expected to sell the property in a few years as housing prices went up, and before their adjustable mortgage rates increased. However, when prices stabilized and then fell, and substantial adjustments upward occurred in their mortgage rates, many buyers were unable to meet their mortgage payments. The risks to the lenders and investors in these complex derivative instruments became apparent as home prices fell below the purchase price.[90]

Housing prices fell more than 30% overall. About one-fourth of homeowners owed more than the value of their homes, a phenomenon known as being *under water*, and nearly 10 million homeowners fell delinquent in their mortgage payments.[91] Construction of new housing units also fell dramatically. That in turn threw people out of work.

Though no recession has a single cause, the consensus view is that the primary contributor to the recession was the collapse in the financial markets caused by a collapse in mortgage markets.[92] An investigations subcommittee of the U.S. Senate Committee on Homeland Security and Governmental Affairs concluded that the financial markets collapse was caused by lack of regulatory oversight. That lack of regulatory oversight, particularly the lack of oversight of Fannie Mae and Freddie Mac, enabled the development of "a mortgage market saturated with risky loans, and financial institutions that were supposed to hold predominantly safe investments instead held portfolios rife with high risk [and] poor quality mortgages. . . . Regulatory failures were a proximate cause of the financial crisis."[93]

Figure 3–8 illustrates with several key economic indicators the dramatic changes that followed the rapid drop in new housing construction. By the end of the second quarter of 2007, residential investment had fallen by greater than 20%, as shown in Figure 3–8.

Year over year from 2005 through 2009, GDP growth rates fell from 3.1% to 2.7%, to 1.9%, to 0.0 in 2008 and to –2.6% from 2008 to 2009. The quarterly data in Figure 3–8 show that GDP growth fell every quarter—with the exception of the second quarter of 2008—from the third quarter of 2007 to the first quarter of 2009. For most of that period, not only was each quarter's growth rate lower than the previous, but there was also an absolute drop in GDP.

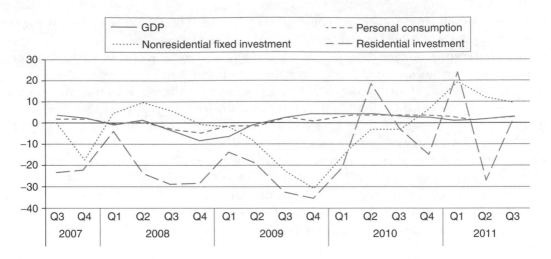

Figure 3–8 Quarterly Changes in Key Indicators Related to Recession: 2007–2011.
Notes: All data points are percent change from previous quarter; figures are revised for 2007 through first quarter 2011.
Source: Data from Bureau of Economic Analysis, U.S. Department of Commerce (2011). *Overview of the economy: tables.*
Retrieved November 16, 2011, from http://www.bea.gov/newsreleases/glance.htm.

There is no legal definition of a recession. A simple rule of thumb is often cited in the media—when the economy, measured by GDP, drops two consecutive quarters, then it is a recession. By that definition, the United States entered into a recession in 2007, as illustrated in Figure 3–8. More variables than just GDP are involved in a recession, of course. The National Bureau of Economic Research(NBER), a highly respected nonprofit independent economic research organization, is often cited as the recognized source by both business and government for interpreting the meaning of changes in the business cycle.[94] NBER's Business Cycle Dating Committee looks at a more inclusive range of economic indicators as well as GDP growth, including indicators of change in income, employment, production, and sales. That committee dates the beginning of the recession also as the last quarter of 2007. Though GDP growth started increasing again in the fourth quarter of 2008, the dating committee's analysis of the more comprehensive set of indicators determined that the recession ended in June 2009.[95] That definitive statement does not mean that the economic indicators described a strong economy by mid-2009. It means only that the indicators had turned in a positive direction for a sufficient period of time to say formally that the recession was over. Indeed, a large portion of the general population had felt no relief by then and were convinced the recession continued unabated.

In addition to aiding in identifying the time period for the recession, Figure 3–8 also illustrates some of the consequences during and since the recession. Nonresidential investment, mainly investment by businesses, dropped steadily from the second quarter of 2008 through the fourth quarter of 2009. From the first quarter of 2010 through the first three quarters of 2011, nonresidential investment showed steady growth for all but one quarter. Housing investment was much more erratic, dropping precipitously in 2008, recovering briefly for the first half of 2009, and then dropping sharply for the rest of that year. At the beginning of 2010, housing investments went up and down. Many of the investments were in the purchase of existing homes on the market, including repossessions and short sales, and not new construction.

Notably, personal consumption has shown very little variance. There was very little growth, and little decline, in personal consumption throughout the latter part of 2007 through three quarters of 2011. Some of that may be attributable to some of the provisions of various stimulus packages that included temporary tax reductions and extensions of unemployment benefits, and to households maintaining consumption levels by reaching into savings. As discussed earlier (Figure 3–2), unemployment rates grew rapidly to nearly 10% during the recession and remained through 2011 at around 9%.

Behind the statistics, of course, are fundamental issues. Paramount is the increase in long-term unemployment: individuals remain unemployed for extended periods or do not return to the workforce. One consequence of long-term unemployment is a significant reduction in lifetime earnings. For example, it is estimated that a worker laid off when unemployment is 9% or greater faces a loss of 20% on average in lifetime earnings.[96] However, in contrast to unemployment figures, by mid-2011 the stock markets had regained much of the loss experienced when the housing bubble burst. The high rate of unemployment, combined with a substantial rebound in stocks, became a major social and political issue and is discussed in the chapter's concluding section on equity.

Fiscal and Monetary Policy Responses to the Recession

The first response to the financial markets collapse included attempts to deal with the drop in the value of assets held by major investment banks and other financial industry giants. Washington Mutual Bank became the largest bank failure in the United States. Lehman Brothers became the largest bankruptcy filing in U.S. history. Merrill Lynch was acquired by Bank of America. Bear Stearns collapsed and was acquired by JPMorgan Chase. The two government-sponsored enterprises (GSE) that have been the mainstay of the U.S. housing mortgage market, Fannie Mae and Freddie Mac, were bailed out of their losses by commitments from the Federal Reserve Bank. Both GSEs, though sponsored by the federal government, were private firms that had been operating independently, and their shares were traded publicly on the New York Stock Exchange. The bailout involved the United States acquiring 80% of their stock, and the two entities were taken under conservatorship by the Federal Housing Finance Agency. These early steps were intended to deal with the asset values of institutions in the housing industry.

Starting in 2008, actions were taken to address the losses faced by a much broader swath of the economy: consumer spending dropped, credit dried up for both individuals and businesses, exports dropped, unemployment rose rapidly, and the economy went into full recession. Major programs to support the automobile industry, including both credit and government purchase of equity in General Motors and loans to Chrysler and Tesla, were among those actions. Among the major U.S. automakers, only Ford Motor Company survived without an infusion of government support, although Ford did borrow through one of the programs that combined economic stimulus and environmental objectives, as documented in **Exhibit 3–3**.

When unemployment benefits started running out, legislation extended unemployment benefits in some cases up to 99 weeks and beyond, depending on individual state laws. To stimulate employment, programs were put in place to support infrastructure construction through grants to state and local governments. Federal agency spending that could be speeded up, such as research and development funds, was put on a faster track. Exhibit 3–3 documents the major fiscal and monetary policy actions to address these two profound facets of the crisis: financial sector collapses and broader economic losses across most of society.

The Federal Reserve periodically reduced the federal funds rate, the rate that member banks pay to borrow from the Fed, and purchased securities in open market operations to enable banks and other financial institutions to issue more credit. *Quantitative easing*, discussed earlier in the section on the Federal Reserve, was practiced when real interest rates converged on zero. The Federal Reserve also purchased asset-backed securities in a variety of financial institutions other than Fannie Mae and Freddie Mac, without the federal government taking management control.

Exhibit 3–3 shows the legislative authority under which each action was taken where appropriate. Actions taken by the Federal Reserve under its statutory authority did not require specific individual statutes as did almost all of the stimulus packages. The exhibit also illustrates implementation of programs established through legislation pre-dating the financial crisis and recession that were in some cases speeded up in order to achieve a stimulus effect. For example, provisions of the Clean Energy Policy Act of 2005 and the Energy Independence and Security Act of 2007 authorized actions that were expanded or speeded up or both during the recession in order to achieve a stimulus effect.[97] The Supplemental Appropriations Act of 2009 included additional appropriations for those earlier acts in order to extend or expand these acts to achieve stimulus objectives.[98]

Exhibit 3–3 Fiscal and Monetary Policy Actions Taken 2007–2011

Beginning with the collapse of the mortgage market in 2007, the federal government undertook a number of fiscal, monetary, and regulatory actions to stimulate the economy back into growth, and to address the market failures that caused the slump. The following table lists the fiscal and monetary policy actions with a brief description of each program.[1]

Stimulus	Description
Fiscal Policy Actions to Stimulate Demand Through Public Spending and Tax Incentives	
Economic Stimulus Act of 2008 (P.L. 110-185)	Provided tax rebates to low- and middle-income taxpayers, gave tax credits to employers to hire workers, and raised limit on size of mortgages that could be purchased by Fannie Mae and Freddie Mac

Stimulus	Description
Fiscal Policy Actions to Stimulate Demand Through Public Spending and Tax Incentives	
Emergency Economic Stabilization Act of 2008 (P.L. 110-343) • Division A: Troubled Assets Relief Program (TARP)	TARP provided up to $700 billion to purchase troubled assets, primarily intended for mortgages and mortgage instruments. Authorized the Fed to purchase commercial paper (short-term notes) from non-financial institutions.
• Division B: Energy Improvement and Extension Act	Provided tax credits for electric hybrid vehicles, renewable energy projects, and other energy efficiency initiatives.
• Division C: Tax Extenders and Alternative Minimum Tax Relief Act	Increased threshold for Alternative Minimum Tax applicability, extended unemployment insurance, and extended or expanded a variety of tax credit programs such as the Child Tax Credit.
Toxic Asset Purchase Program 2009 (uses authorization in Economic Stabilization Act of 2008)	Allocated approximately $100 billion in unobligated TARP funds and authorized low-interest loans to entice private sector financial institutions to purchase troubled or toxic assets.
American Recovery and Reinvestment Act of 2009 (P.L. 111-5)	Estimated up to $787 billion for infrastructure projects (intended to be shovel ready) mostly through grants to state and local governments, extended unemployment insurance, state and local assistance for health and education, temporary tax credits including to first-time homebuyers, and tax relief for low-and middle-income individuals and for businesses.
Consumer Assistance to Recycle and Save Act Provisions incorporated in the Supplemental Appropriations Act of 2009 (P.L. 111-32)	So-called *Cash for Clunkers* program provided rebates to consumers purchasing new cars or light trucks that were more fuel efficient; initial authorization of $1 billion expanded to $3 billion due to high demand.
Worker, Homeownership and Business Assistance Act of 2009 (P.L. 111-92)	Extended tax credits for first-time homebuyers, extended unemployment insurance particularly in states with highest long-term unemployment, extended small-business tax credits in current year against prior years losses and expanded to include medium and large businesses.

(continued)

Stimulus	Description
Fiscal Policy Actions to Stimulate Demand Through Public Spending and Tax Incentives	
Tax Relief, Unemployment Insurance Reauthorization, and Job Creation Act of 2010 (P.L. 111-312)	Extended for two years cuts in personal and corporate income tax rates enacted in 2001 and 2003, extension of unemployment benefits, and one-year reduction in Social Security tax.
Monetary Policy Actions to Affect Supply of Credit, Money Supply, and Support Participants in Credit Markets	
Actions to improve liquidity of member banks (depository banking institutions) and other financial institutions • Changes in federal funds rate to member banks • Primary credit lending • Secondary credit lending • Seasonal credit lending • Term Auction Facility (TAF)	Federal funds rate reduced effectively to zero (from 5.25% at outset in 2007). Extended term of primary, secondary, and seasonal credit lending to depository banks. Opened access to borrowing to financial institutions other than banks, for first time in Fed history. Temporary program (TAF) to extend credit to depository institutions to 84 days.
Operations to increase money supply, quantitative easing	Purchase of Treasury bonds, Fannie Mae and Freddie Mac securities, and other purchases of securities expands the monetary base; actions taken both to increase credit after federal funds rate approached zero and also to shore up by taking approximately 80% of equity in Fannie Mae and Freddie Mac.
Actions to restore liquidity of financial institutions • Commercial Paper Funding Facility • Asset-Backed Commercial Paper Money Market Mutual Fund Liquidity Facility • Money Market Investor Funding Facility • Term Asset-Backed Loan Facility • Primary Dealer Credit Facility • Term Securities Lending Facility • Term Securities Lending Facility Options Program	Variety of temporary programs, each mostly aimed at different participants in the financial markets, or at different specific credit needs. Lending to primary dealers in the credit market, increase access to credit for money market funds, and purchase of asset-backed commercial paper (short-term borrowing practiced by most firms for cash flow and very short-term credit needs) are examples of institutions or credit needs met by these programs. Each one was characterized by it being a temporary facility, each designed for very specific borrowing needs or participants, and each intended to enable easier access to credit.

Stimulus	Description
Fiscal Policy Actions to Stimulate Demand Through Public Spending and Tax Incentives	
Actions to support specific institutions • Bear Stearns • AIG • Citigroup • Bank of America	Federal Reserve Bank of New York created and extended credit to an LLC, Maiden Lane LLC, to acquire the assets of Bear Stearns to enable an orderly acquisition of assets by J.P. Morgan Chase. $85 billion line of credit to American International Group to enable it to meet its credit requirements; restructured to reduce LOC to $25 billion, and Maiden Lane II created and extended credit to purchase mortgage-backed securities from AIG. Restructured third time to enable AIG divestiture of major assets as part of a company restructuring. Guaranteed against losses in a mortgage-backed assets pool in exchange for preferred shares of stock; acquired additional preferred shares subsequently with $20 billion from TARP. Ultimately terminated by Citigroup for an exit fee when support became unnecessary. Pledge of support to Bank of America that proved ultimately unnecessary and Bank of America paid an exit fee to withdraw from the program.
Actions for mutual support of liquidity in dollar reserves and foreign currency reserves in Federal Reserve and other central banks	Program to extend, and receive, liquidity credit to and from other central banks to stabilize fluctuations in demand for the dollar and other currencies. Ended in early 2010 and restarted in mid-2010 in response to increasing pressure on dollar.
Term Asset-Backed Securities Loan Facility (TALF)	One-year program to stimulate highly rated (AAA) asset-backed securities such as credit card and student loan securities by lending to holders of such securities. Up to $200 billion planned, $70 billion loaned.

A variety of other actions were taken by the two administrations under the authority provided by legislation passed prior to the financial crisis and prior to the overt development of various stimulus programs. The Energy Policy Act of 2005 (P.L. 109-58) created a loan guarantee program to support clean, renewable energy and to support the development of innovative clean energy technologies. The American Recovery and Reinvestment Act of 2009 amended the Energy Policy Act to expand the scope of energy technologies eligible

(continued)

for support under the loan guarantee program and to speed up the program in order to stimulate the economy. The Energy Independence and Security Act of 2007 (P.L. 110-140) was signed into law in the George W. Bush administration as part of several initiatives to increase energy independence through renewable fuels, energy-efficient manufacturing processes, energy efficient vehicles, and alternative fuels. The FY 2009 Supplemental Appropriations Act (P.L. 111-32) included appropriations for loans for development of electric vehicles under the Advanced Technology Vehicles Manufacturing loan program to support ATVM in the United States. Nissan Motors, Ford Motor Company, and Tesla received the first loans under the ATVM program, about $10 billion.[2] Publicity about the loans focused not only on the advanced technology support but also on the job creation stimulus consequences, particularly in hard-hit states in the upper Midwest.[3]

1. Congressional Budget Office (2011). *Budget and economic outlook: fiscal years 2011–2010* (pp. 33–36). Washington, DC: Government Printing Office; White House (2009). *Fact sheet: the worker, homeownership, and business assistance act of 2009.* Retrieved November 17, 2011, from http://www.whitehouse.gov/the-press-office/fact-sheet-worker-homeownership-and-business-assistance-act-2009; Federal Reserve (2011). *The Federal Reserve's response to the crisis* (follow links on overview page to each program carried out by the Fed during the crisis). Retrieved November 16, 2011, from http://federalreserve.gov/monetarypolicy/bst_crisisresponse.htm; Laeven, L., and Valencia, S. (2010). Resolution of banking crises: the good, the bad and the ugly. Washington, DC: International Monetary Fund. Retrieved November 17, 2011, from http://www.imf.org/external/pubs/ft/wp/2010/wp10146.pdf; Binder, A. (2010). *How the great recession was brought to an end.* Retrieved November 18, 2011, from http://www.economy.com/mark-zandi/documents/End-of-Great-Recession.pdf. Sources also consulted included online archives of news stories from *Washington Post, New York Times,* and *Wall Street Journal,* in addition to press releases from the White House. Some of these sources are cited in endnotes in the chapter. Where descriptive information is repetitive of main sources cited here, individual URLs are not listed here.
2. Loan Programs Office, U.S. Department of Energy (2011). *ATVM.* Retrieved November 17, 2011, from https://lpo.energy.gov/?page_id=43.
3. Nissan, Ford and Tesla get U.S. loans to build green vehicles. *LA Times* online edition, June 2, 2009. Retrieved November 15, 2011, from http://articles.latimes.com/2009/jun/24/business/fi-autos24.

Not included in the table are proposals made in 2011 for additional stimulus programs that were not considered by Congress or, when considered, did not generate sufficient support for passage. In September 2011, the Obama administration proposed a major new stimulus program. The proposed American Jobs Act would have:

- extended unemployment insurance for the long-term unemployed
- cut payroll taxes for employers on the first $5 million in wages
- expanded Small Business Administration Loans
- provided assistance to states and local governments to avoid or prevent layoffs of teachers, firefighters, and police, and
- introduced a new infrastructure construction program.

The bill did not come to a full vote.

The deeply partisan nature of the arguments about stimulus programs during the recession is illustrated by the Solyndra case. The Solyndra Corporation, a manufacturer of solar panels, was the first recipient (2009) of a $500 million loan guarantee. Solyndra's selection as the first borrower was made by the Department of Energy during the George W. Bush administration. The loan was restructured in 2011 after the company raised $75 million in private equity investment; the restructuring put the private equity investors ahead of the government. When Solyndra declared bankruptcy in September 2011, a storm of political criticism developed because the private equity investors were given primacy over the government loan and over the possible role of pressure from the White House on the Department of Energy to approve the restructuring because of the administration's commitment to show success in the complex solar technology industry.[99]

Nonbudgetary and Budgetary Effects of Fiscal and Monetary Policy Actions

The extent to which the various stimulus actions addressed the problems of the recession will not be felt for years after the stimulus programs were put in place. However, some results were clearly visible by 2011, particularly in addressing crisis in the financial system and the capital markets. Virtually all of the temporary credit facilities shown in Exhibit 3–3 that were put in place by the Federal Reserve either were ended early or were allowed to lapse at the end of the planned temporary period. Many did not use the majority of authorized credit or did not reach the limit—many banks and other financial institutions, after the initial industry restructuring that took place, no longer needed the special programs.

Detailed information on each program and the changes in the Federal Reserve's balance sheets caused by purchase and sales of assets is available on the institution's website.[100] The website and publication of hundreds of briefings and reports were the result of congressional requirements that the actions of the Federal Reserve be reported to Congress in detail.[101] The website documents the repayment of most of the loans extended and the repurchase of stock acquired by the government, such as General Motors stock. The major exception to the government's recapturing loans and investments in financial institutions are the two GSEs, Fannie Mae and Freddie Mac, which remained under federal supervision.

The banking industry underwent considerable consolidation. About 2% of U.S. banks failed in 2009, compared with twice that number in the 1989 S&L crisis. The banks that failed in the more recent crisis held about 6% of total deposits, considerably less than the deposits held by failed financial institutions in the 1989 S&L crisis. The rapidity and breadth of the responses appear to account for both the reduced severity and the accelerated recovery of the banking sector.[102]

As noted above, after the initial emphasis on assisting financial institutions and the financial markets to recover, the emphasis was placed on restoring economic growth and stimulating employment. **Figure 3–9** summarizes key indicators of change in production (measured as a percentage of GDP) and employment (measured as jobs created). Figure 3–9 uses both Congressional Budget Office and Council of Economic Advisers estimates of the impact of the stimulus packages, mainly the American Recovery and Reinvestment Act of

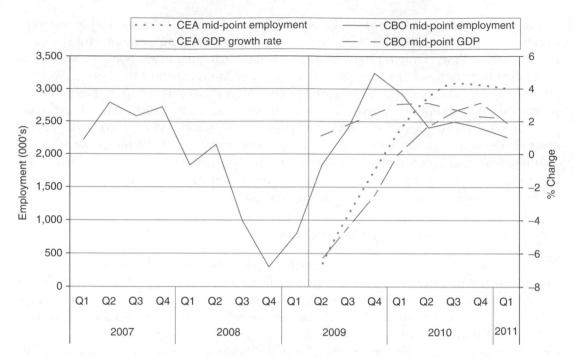

Figure 3–9 CBO and CEA Estimates of Effects of Stimulus on GDP Growth and Employment (GDP growth = % change; Employment in 000s).

Sources: Data from U.S. Congressional Budget Office (2011). *Estimated impact of the American Recovery and Reinvestment Act on employment and economic output* (p. 3). Washington, DC: U.S. Government Printing Office; Council of Economic Advisers (2011). *The economic impact of the American Recovery and Reinvestment Act: seventh quarterly report.*

2009. For the figure, we selected the midpoints between high and low estimates calculated by each of those institutions.

The figure shows change in GDP (solid line) starting prior to the start of the financial crisis. As discussed earlier, the drop in two consecutive quarters in GDP growth, marking the beginning of the recession, shows in the figure. CBO and CEA estimates are very close in the estimated timing of the impacts and in the magnitude, with the exception that CEA estimates a much higher rate of economic growth attributable to the stimulus efforts in the fourth quarter of 2009. The CEA's estimate falls more closely in line with CBO's estimates within two quarters. Both CEA and CBO show almost identical trends in increased employment, and very close estimates of the millions of jobs created, from 339,000 (CEA) and 400,000 (CBO) jobs created in the second quarter of 2009, rising to around 3 million (CEA) in the second quarter 2010 through first quarter 2011, versus CBO estimates in those same quarters about 500,000 less.[103] One economist's analysis describes these effects of the fiscal stimulus as "very substantial."[104]

Still, at the end of 2011, the effects of the recession showed a seriously down economy. Factors included conservative growth in private sector investment, much slower return to consumer spending levels than after previous recessions, continuing stagnation in housing prices and housing construction, and unemployment rates in excess of 9%. The Federal Reserve, as a result of its purchases of securities and holding securities as collateral on loans extended, had a significantly larger share of private sector securities in its balance sheet.[105] As Figures 3–8 and 3–9 both show, though GDP growth turned significantly positive in 2010, it did not continue regular growth. It ranged from a high of 3.4% in the first quarter of 2010 to a low of .4% in the first quarter of 2011, back to 2.5% in the third quarter of 2011 (Figure 3–8 includes percent change in GDP through three quarters of 2011, whereas Figure 3–9 illustrates estimates of impact of stimulus programs on GDP growth and extends only through the first quarter of 2011). The primary explanation for the volatility in stock markets and GDP is a continuing economic slump in most industrialized countries, and particularly major concerns over Greek and Italian public sector debt.[106]

The budgetary consequences will remain with policy makers and the public for years to come. As noted earlier, total federal debt climbed to nearly 100% of GDP. The stimulus packages and the decisions to enter into larger deficit spending were the result of actions of both major political parties and both the executive and legislative branches. The failure of the supercommittee to achieve its goal of identifying budget cuts in excess of $2 trillion did not portend well for the political process resolving the budgetary consequences of actions taken to address the recession.

EQUITY AND GOVERNMENT ECONOMIC POLICY

The formal, legislatively mandated objectives of government economic policy for the United States include only full employment, price stability, and steady economic growth, as discussed in this chapter. Except in the indirect results of employment policy, the distribution of economic gain is not a formal economic policy objective for the United States. In many other countries, however, economic growth *and* equity are formal objectives of government policy.[107] Specific and intentional steps to improve the distribution of wealth are matters of formal policy. Government economic policy actions have redistributive effects, however, whether these are policy objectives or not. The World Bank's 2006 world development report, *Equity and Development*, defines equity as "equal opportunity . . . and . . . avoidance of deprivation in outcomes."[108] People should have equal chances at achieving similar life goals, and outcomes produced by society and government should not result in deprivation of some in favor of others.

Unintentional Redistributive Effects

To this point, we have been concerned with the overall performance of the economy. Government involvement in the economy also has consequences for specific subsectors or individuals. Fiscal and monetary policy actions taken to manage overall economic growth and price stability are not necessarily neutral in their effects on individuals and industries. If the government lowers corporate tax rates to stimulate business investment but increases other taxes to neutralize the effects on the budget balance, then those for whom taxes are raised are paying for the economic benefits whether they share in those benefits or not. Many developing country governments have attempted to address problems of the urban poor by imposing price controls on agricultural products. While the short-run effect may be to lower food prices in urban areas, the longer-run effect is to decrease agricultural production. In the short run, economic costs are imposed on one group, rural producers, for the benefit of another group, urban consumers. In the long run, overall economic performance declines.

Economic policies aimed at stabilization also can have unintentional redistributive effects. Under inflationary conditions, persons on fixed or relatively fixed incomes lose purchasing power. This is especially true for retired persons living on pensions, but it is also true for workers who cannot command increases in wages. If the government takes no action to slow the rate of inflation, its inaction "redistributes" income from those on fixed incomes to those whose wages or other income rises with inflation. Higher interest rates favor income earnings from investments, usually held by upper-income families. Large federal deficits, which ultimately impose repayment costs on future generations, may also create intergenerational inequity (see the chapter on financial management).

Addressing Inequality

Equity as a concept of "equal chances" as defined above is easy to describe but difficult to measure directly. Inequality in absolute terms is somewhat easier to measure and therefore is often used in discussions of equity and inequity, such as inequality in the distribution of income. Since the 1960s, the degree of inequality of income distribution in the United States has increased significantly. Analysis from the Organization for Economic Cooperation and Development (OECD) shows that between the mid-1980s and the late 2000s, the United States increased on one measure of inequality by an average annual rate of half a percent per year. This rate of increase in inequality, however, was about the same as or lower than most other Western industrial countries.[109] The sharp increase in inequality during the 1980s is attributed by many to the significant cuts in federal corporate and personal income taxes, benefiting mainly the already wealthy, and cuts in programs of assistance to the poor.[110] The stock market booms of recent decades substantially widened the gap between the top and the bottom, though the gaps did decrease during subsequent crashes. However, the crash in the market led by the housing bubble that burst in 2007 affected middle-income taxpayers in two major ways. First, housing values plummeted, and for many middle-income households, their house is their primary capital asset. Second, the same middle-income taxpayers depend on their pension savings, which are invested in the financial markets, for a majority of their post-retirement income. Upper-income households, of course, are affected by both decline in the value of homes and stock market declines, but they tend to have more diversified sources of wealth.

Some economists argue that the government should mitigate the negative distributional effects of economic growth that leave only the middle- and upper-income classes better off.[111] According to these economists, policies such as aggressive employment subsidies to reduce the number of unemployed should be implemented as direct measures to lower unemployment.[112]

In the United States, the recession starting in 2007 and its aftermath brought inequality and equity issues to a head in the political arena. The two major parties were deeply divided on the question of the role of taxes in resolving the budget deficit problem. Republicans generally argued that the rich are the primary sources of investment to fuel economic growth and job creation.[113] Democrats generally argued that previous tax cuts had dispro-portionately favored the wealthy. The candidates for the Republican Party nomination and President Obama demonstrated the divide in the rhetoric about reducing government spending without tax increases versus the view that everyone has to pay a fair share.[114]

Measuring inequality, as in the OECD analysis discussed above, involves some kind of comparison between a norm that is argued to represent equality and deviations from that norm. **Exhibit 3–4** illustrates the concept of equity and its measurement, and compares income inequality for several nations. The idea is to measure the extent to which an ineq-uity exists, and then devise deliberate government policies to reduce the inequity.

Exhibit 3–4 Measuring Income Inequality and Selected Country Results

For governments that endorse an overt policy to reduce inequality, or advocate for decreasing inequality, at the macro level, how does one best characterize the degree of inequality? One approach is to use the *Gini index.*

The Gini index concept is illustrated graphically in what is called a *Lorenz curve* as the area between a line that depicts perfect equality and a line (curve) that depicts the actual measured distribution in a specific society or economy. The line depicting per-fect equality is a measurement concept, not some kind of universal norm. It is a social and political question in any given society as to what extent deviation from the line is reasonable and acceptable.

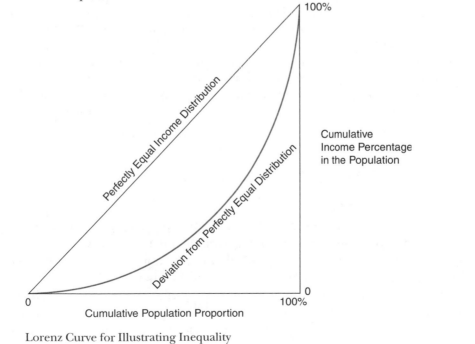

Lorenz Curve for Illustrating Inequality

(continued)

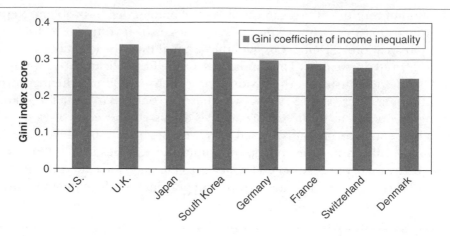

A Lorenz curve plots the cumulative percentage of income (or other valued good) held by income groups against the cumulative percentage of income groups. For example, in a perfectly equal distribution of income, the lowest population decile in income would have 10% of the income, the first and second lowest deciles would have 20% of the income, and so forth. That perfectly equal distribution would plot as a straight 45-degree line on an *x, y* graph. The difference between the actual plotted Lorenz curve and the perfectly equal distribution is measured as the area between the two curves— the *Gini coefficient of inequality*.

The graphic above looks at the income distribution of a selected group of countries. The Gini indices reported essentially measure the distance between the theoretical construct of exactly equal distribution and the actual distribution of income. The higher the index number, the greater the deviation from a perfectly equal distribution.

The graph is helpful in visualizing the differences among countries. The United States has the highest index of income inequality, with the United Kingdom close behind. Japan and South Korea form a cluster closer to .3. France, Switzerland, and Denmark show similar indices below .3; Denmark, at .25, is the lowest among the 34 countries the OECD measured. The OECD average across the 34 countries was .31. Thought for discussion: what tools might policy makers use to address inequalities as reflected in such measures?

Source: Data from *Society at a glance 2011: OECD social indicators.* Paris: OECD. http://www.oecd.org/document/24/0, 3746,en_2649_34637_2671576_1_1_1_1,00.html#data.

Income Stabilization Policies

Income stabilization policy is one way to address the problem of economic inequality, with the most deliberate approach being a negative income tax. This would involve determining an appropriate income guarantee, a benefit reduction rate, and a break-even income. The income guarantee is the amount of the transfer when the family income is zero, the benefit reduction rate is the rate at which the amount transferred is reduced as family income increases, and the break-even income is the point where family income reaches a level beyond which the family no longer qualifies for a transfer. The United States has no negative income tax, but its principles are incorporated to varying degrees in several income-related transfer programs.

Transfer Programs

Several transfer programs (food stamps; Supplemental Feeding Program for Women, Infants, and Children; Medicaid) provide a minimum or floor level of benefits comparable to the income guarantee. Major reforms in the welfare system, however, have severely curtailed benefits by imposing lifetime limits on the amount individuals may receive and imposing strict work requirements (see the chapter on intergovernmental relations).

Tax Policies

Expenditure programs are not the only form of income redistribution. Different taxes have different impacts on various groups. In addition, the overall structure of the entire tax system may operate to redistribute income among different groups. In the Tax Reform Act of 1986, lower-income groups benefited from sharply reduced taxes, middle-income groups benefited from modest reductions, and upper-income individuals and corporations experienced tax increases. In 1993, there were sharp increases in the top tax bracket. In 1997, tax decreases focused on both ends of the income spectrum. The 2001 and 2003 tax changes substantially benefited upper-income groups.

Tax expenditures, discussed in the chapter on budgeting for revenues and taxes, are often redistributive in effect. Not taxing interest on municipal bonds redistributes income toward the purchasers of municipal bonds, who tend to be retirees, either directly or through pension fund investments. Allowing interest on mortgages, including second homes, to be deducted from taxable income has a redistributive effect toward middle- and upper-income individuals. The problem with the redistributive effects of tax expenditures is that they are much less transparent as a policy instrument. A tax expenditure does not appear plainly as an expenditure, nor does it appear directly as a tax reduction.

While economic policy affects the distribution of income, it cannot be expected to address structural features of the labor market. For example, workers with minimal or obsolete skills have difficulty finding employment even during periods of rapid growth. Economic policy is also of limited assistance in coping with readjustments in the economy, such as might occur with changes in homeland security and defense operations in the United States and overseas. Other policies, of course, are designed to deal with more basic structural problems. Expenditures on education, both academic and vocational, are expected to increase the overall human resource base for the economy. Regulatory policies are expected to reduce private incentives to pollute the environment, a problem that imposes an eventual economic cost when the environmental damage is repaired.

No redistributive policy is neutral in its economic impact. Indeed, no economic act, no matter what its intended effects, is automatically neutral with regard to distribution of income. There is no consensus among experts as to whether addressing major budget deficits by redistributing income through tax increases is neutral or positive in its impact on economic growth, or in fact stunts economic growth.[115]

Designing redistributive policies should take into account the potential reduction in economic efficiency and try to mitigate any losses. During a recessionary period, both the labor force and total plant capacity are underemployed, so that government action to stimulate the economy may do just that without causing significant unintended redistributive effects. At some point, political unrest results when public policy is seen as inequitable. The Occupy Movement began in 2011 as Occupy Wall Street and spread to cities throughout the United States and around the world. Protestors set up camps and demonstrated, claiming that the economic system aided the top 1% of the population and worked against the other 99%, and public policy did little to correct that distortion.

SUMMARY

Representing more than 36% of total economic activity in the United States, federal, state, and local government budgets have a tremendous combined effect on the economy. The federal government deliberately intervenes in the economy to achieve aggregate economic objectives. The major economic policy objectives of most central governments include economic growth, full employment, stable prices, and balance in the flow of funds into and out of the economy. Increasingly, as national economies become more interdependent, governments, including the U.S. federal government, are including specific competitiveness objectives as part of national economic policy. Because federal budget deficits sometimes soar to unacceptable (politically and economically) heights, management of the deficits and the overall government debt also has been added as a major economic policy objective in the United States. For some countries, achieving some degree of equity in income and social status is a formal policy objective. Although equity is not a legislatively mandated policy objective in the United States, income inequality has become a major political issue and a focal point of fairness arguments about alternative means to addressing the federal budget deficit.

Fiscal policy and monetary policy are the main tools used to influence macroeconomic performance. Fiscal policy encompasses the use of the government's taxing and spending powers to stimulate or dampen economic activity. An excess of expenditures over revenues (a deficit) stimulates demand and thus employment. A possible consequence, however, may be inflation. An excess of revenues over expenditures (a surplus) has a dampening effect on the economy. Monetary policy affects economic activity through control over the money supply. By changing interest rates and reserve requirements and by buying or selling bonds, the Federal Reserve can speed up or slow down the pace of economic activity. The federal response in two administrations to address the financial markets crisis and the 2007–2009 recession was the most extensive combination of fiscal and monetary policy actions since the Great Depression. The impact of those actions on the federal budget deficit became a major focal point in the political competition leading up to the 2012 presidential election.

Although state and local governments do not exercise fiscal and monetary control, their role in providing the basic infrastructure required for private sector business activity is important to regional economic performance. In this respect, state and local governments and developing country governments pursue similar ends. For developing country governments, their effective use of borrowed funds from donor agencies and commercial banks depends on putting the funds to use in increasing economic productive capacity.

Government policy interventions also have consequences for income redistribution. Changes in tax policy and increases or decreases in expenditures are almost never neutral as regards income distribution. In addition, there is general agreement that some level of redistribution of income is appropriate to address the problems of individuals with very low incomes. How extensive these programs should be, however, remains perennially controversial.

NOTES

1. U.S. Council of Economic Advisers (2011). *Economic report of the president: 2011* (pp. 283, 287). Washington, DC: U.S. Government Printing Office. Note: state and local expenditures available for 2010 only in national income and product accounts.
2. International Association of Money Transfer Networks (2010). LAC: money transfers bring order in chaos. *Money Transfers, 31,* 5. Retrieved November 11, 2011, from http://www.iamtn.org/files/Money_Transfers_Monthly_April_2010.pdf; World Bank (2011). *WDI Data Catalogue.* Retrieved November 11, 2011, from http://data.worldbank.org/data-catalog#Tables. Note: WDI Data Catalogue searchable online by country or downloading selected databases.
3. U.S. Council of Economic Advisers (2011). *Economic report of the president: 2011,* 220.
4. Friedman, T. (2006). *The world is flat: a brief history of the twenty-first century* (Expanded ed.). New York, NY: Farrar, Straus & Giroux; Friedman, T., & Mandelbaum, M. (2011). *That used to be us: how America fell behind in the world it invented and how we can come back.* New York, NY: Farrar, Straus & Giroux.
5. United Nations Conference on Trade and Development (2011). Annex table 7. In *World Investment Report.* Retrieved November 13, 2011, from http://www.unctad.org/sections/dite_dir/docs/WIR11_web%20tab%207.pdf.
6. U.S. Council of Economic Advisers (2006). *Economic report of the president: 2006,* (pp. 310, 312). Washington, DC: U.S. Government Printing Office; U.S. Council of Economic Advisers (2011). *Economic report of the president: 2011,* 218.
7. Chen, V. (2011). Fed economists: 2012 recession odds top 50%. *Bloomberg News,* November 14. Retrieved November 15, 2011, from http://www.bloomberg.com/news/2011-11-14/fed-economists-say-odds-of-2012-u-s-recession-exceed-50-on-europe-crisis.html.
8. U.S. Council of Economic Advisers (2011). *Economic report of the president: 2011,* 313.
9. I wouldn't start from here. (2011). *The Economist, 401,* October 15, 80–81.
10. U.S. Council of Economic Advisers (2011). *Economic report of the president: 2011,* 313.
11. I wouldn't start from here. (2011). *The Economist,* 80–81.
12. OANDA (2011). *Historical exchange rates.* Retrieved December 11, 2011, from http://www.oanda.com/currency/historical-rates/.
13. Beware the Merkozy recipe. (2011). *The Economist, 401,* December 10, 56.
14. Executive Office of the President (1993). *Technology for America's economic growth: a new direction to build economic strength.* Washington, DC: U.S. Government Printing Office.
15. Mischke, J., et al. (2010). Why Europe lags behind the United States in productivity. *McKinsey Quarterly,* October, 5. Retrieved November 1, 2011, from https://www.mckinseyquarterly.com/PDFDownload.aspx?ar=2684.
16. Mischke, J., et al. (2010). Why Europe lags behind the United States in productivity, 5.
17. Malhotra, V., & Manyika, J. (2011). Five misconceptions about productivity. *McKinsey Quarterly,* March, 1. Retrieved November 3, 2011, from https://www.mckinseyquarterly.com/Five_misconceptions_about_productivity_2760.
18. The World Bank (2004). *World development report 2005: a better investment climate for everyone.* Klapper, L., & Love, I. (2010). New firm creation: what has been the effect of the financial crisis? *Viewpoint,* no. 324, September 30. Retrieved November 13, 2011, from http://rru.worldbank.org/PublicPolicyJournal/.
19. Employment Act of 1946 (P.L. 79-304); Full Employment and Balanced Growth Act of 1978 (P.L. 95-253).
20. Musgrave, R. A., & Musgrave, P. B. (1989). *Public finance in theory and practice* (5th ed.). New York, NY: McGraw-Hill; Hyman, D. N. (2010). *Public finance: a contemporary application of theory to policy* (10th ed. online). Florence, KY: Cengage Books; Rosen, H. S. (2005). *Public finance* (7th ed.). New York, NY: McGraw-Hill Irwin.
21. U.S. Department of Labor, Bureau of Labor Statistics (2011). *How the government measures unemployment.* Retrieved November 10, 2011, from http://www.bls.gov/cps/cps_htgm.htm#where.
22. U.S. Council of Economic Advisers (2011). *Economic report of the president: 2011,* 240.

23. Federal Reserve Bank of San Francisco (1998). Economic Letter 98–28: *The natural rate, NAIRU, and monetary policy.* San Francisco, CA: Federal Reserve Bank of San Francisco. Retrieved August 2003 from http://www.frbsf.org/econrsrch/wklyltr/wklyltr98/el98–28.html. Discussion and examples of NAIRU in this paragraph rely on this source. See also Mitchell, M., & Nyusken, J. (2008). *Full employment abandoned; shifting sands and policy failures.* Cheltenham, UK: Edward Elgar.
24. The ravages of time. (2011). *The Economist, 401,* October 1, 33.
25. U.S. Congressional Budget Office (2011). *The budget and economic outlook: fiscal years 2011–2021* (p. 128). Washington, DC: U.S. Government Printing Office.
26. The ravages of time. (2011). *The Economist,* 33.
27. Malhotra, V., & Manyika, J. (2011). Five misconceptions about productivity.
28. McGukin, R., & van Ark, B. (2006). *Performance 2005: productivity, employment and income in the world's economies.* New York, NY: Conference Board.
29. MacMillan, M., & Rodrik, D. (2011). *Globalization, structural change and productivity growth.* NBER working paper 17143, June. Retrieved November 14, 2011, from http://www.nber.org/papers/w17143.
30. Superville, D. (2011). Obama calls for investments in education, R&D: West Coast swing highlights vision of making U.S. more competitive globally. *MSNBC.com.* Retrieved November 13, 2011, from http://www.msnbc.msn.com/id/41669273/ns/business-personal_finance/t/obama-calls-investments-education-rd/.
31. Federal Reserve Bank of San Francisco (2005). *The rise and spread of state R&D tax credits.* Retrieved August 24, 2006, from http://www.frbsf.org/publications/economics/letter/2005/el2005-26.html.
32. White House (2011). *Blueprint for a secure energy future.* Washington, DC: U.S. Government Printing Office.
33. Solyndra and the White House: letting sunlight in. (2011). *The Economist, 401,* September 24, 36.
34. Grossman, G., & Helpman, E. (2001). *Innovation and growth: technological competition in the global economy.* Cambridge, MA: MIT Press.
35. Samuelson, R. (2006). Cooling off about keeping up. *Washington Post.* Retrieved August 12, 2006, from http://www.realclearpolitics.com/articles/2006/08/experiencing_another_competiti.html.
36. The White House (2011). *We can't wait: Obama administration announces two steps to help businesses create jobs, strengthen competitiveness* [press release]. Retrieved November 13, 2011, from http://www.whitehouse.gov/the-press-office/2011/10/28/we-cant-wait-obama-administration-announces-two-steps-help-businesses-cr.
37. National Economic Council (2011). *A strategy for American innovation: securing our economic growth and prosperity.* Retrieved November 6, 2011, from http://www.whitehouse.gov/innovation/strategy.
38. Council of Economic Advisers (2011). *Economic report of the president: 2011,* 218.
39. Council of Economic Advisers (2011). *Economic report of the president: 2011,* 218.
40. Council of Economic Advisers (2011). *Economic report of the president: 2011,* 219.
41. Council of Economic Advisers (2011). *Economic report of the president: 2011,* 93.
42. Krugman, P. (1999). *The return to depression economics.* New York, NY: W. W. Norton.
43. Nowhere to hide. (2011). *The Economist, 401,* October 15, 15.
44. The debt ceiling deal: no thanks to anyone. (2011). *The Economist, 401,* August 6, 24.
45. A game of catch-up: the shift in economic power from west to east is accelerating. (2011). *The Economist, 401,* September 24, 35.
46. Walsh, D. (2006). *Knowledge and the wealth of nations: a source of economic discovery.* New York, NY: Norton.
47. U.S. Government Accountability Office (2006). *Fiscal year 2005 U.S. government financial statements: sustained improvements in federal financial management is crucial to addressing our nation's financial condition and long-term fiscal imbalance.* Washington, DC: U.S. Government Accountability Office; U.S. Congressional Budget Office (2011). *The budget and economic outlook: fiscal years 2011–2021.*
48. The debt ceiling deal: no thanks to anyone. (2011). *The Economist,* 24; America's missing middle. (2011). *The Economist, 401,* November 5, 15.
49. U.S. Council of Economic Advisers (2011). *Economic report of the president: 2011,* 1–7.

50. U.S. Congressional Budget Office (2011). *The budget and economic outlook: fiscal years 2011–2021*, 16.
51. The debt ceiling deal: no thanks to anyone. (2011). *The Economist*, 24.
52. U.S. Council of Economic Advisers (2011). *Economic report of the president: 2011*, 284.
53. P.L. 107-16 and P.L. 108-27, respectively.
54. U.S. Congressional Budget Office (2006). *The budget and economic outlook: fiscal years 2007–2016*.
55. The Conference Board (2001). *Business cycles indicator handbook*. New York, NY: Conference Board.
56. Schultze, C. (2003). The consumer price index: conceptual issues and practical suggestions. *Journal of Economic Perspectives, 17*, Winter, 3–22.
57. U.S. Congressional Budget Office (2011). *Budget and economic outlook: fiscal years 2011–2021*.
58. Housing and the economy: rising from the ruins. (2011). *The Economist, 401*, November 5, 37.
59. *Dow Jones Industrial and Transportation averages*. (2011). Retrieved November 17, 2011, from http://www.thumbcharts.com/1343/dow-jones-industrial-and-transportation-averages.
60. The Conference Board (2011). *How to compute diffusion indexes*. Retrieved November 13, 2011, from http://www.conference-board.org/data/bci/index.cfm?id=2180.
61. U.S. Congressional Budget Office (2009). *CBO's economic forecasting record: 2009 update* (p. 17). Washington, DC: U.S. Government Printing Office.
62. DRI-WEFA (2011). *DRI-WEFA's Macroeconomic models*. Retrieved November 13, 2011, from http://www.iccfglobal.org/pdf/DRI_WEFA_USMacroModel.pdf.
63. Keynes, J. M. (1936). *The general theory of employment, interest and money*. New York, NY: Harcourt Brace.
64. Variously quoted in newspapers and other media on several occasions. Most commonly cited is a speech at Harvard University, January 4, 1971.
65. Laffer, A., & Seymour, J. (Eds.). (1979). *The economics of the tax revolt: a reader*. New York, NY: Harcourt Brace Jovanovich.
66. *Washington Post–ABC News poll*. (2011). Retrieved November 15, 2011, from http://www.washingtonpost.com/wp-srv/politics/polls/postabcpoll_071711.html.
67. Economic Stimulus Act of 2008 (P.L. 110-185).
68. American Recovery and Reinvestment Act of 2009 (P.L. 111-5).
69. Fuhrer, J., & Schuh, S. (1998). Beyond shocks: what causes business cycles? an overview. *New England Economic Review*, November/December, 3–24.
70. Papandreou's people. (2011). *The Economist, 401*, November 5, 61.
71. That's all folks. (2011). *The Economist, 401*, November 12, 19.
72. Nowhere to hide. (2011). *The Economist*, October 15, 15.
73. Federal Reserve Board (2011). *Federal Reserve statistical release: money stock measures*, December 8. Retrieved December 15, 2011, from http://www.federalreserve.gov/releases/h6/current/.
74. The Federal Reserve Board (2011). *The federal reserve system: purposes and functions*. Washington, DC: U.S. Government Printing Office.
75. The Federal Reserve Board (2011). *The federal reserve system: purposes and functions*, 15.
76. The discount rate or federal funds rate at different time periods is readily accessible from various historical statistical series and current weekly and quarterly reports from the system's website, www.federalreserve.gov. Daily reports are also accessible.
77. Bernanke, B. (2010). *Central bank independence, transparency, and accountability*. Speech by the Chairman of the Federal Reserve Board before the Institute for monetary and economic studies international conference, Bank of Japan, Tokyo, Japan, May 25. Retrieved November 14, 2011, from http://www.federalreserve.gov/newsevents/speech/bernanke20100525a.htm.
78. Greenspan lets things simmer. (1999). *The Economist, 346*, July 1. Retrieved August 23, 2006, from http://economist.com/displayStory.cfm?Story_ID=218974.
79. Big Ben strikes gold. (2005). *The Economist, 352*, October 29. Retrieved September 4, 2006, from http://economist.com/opinion/displaystory.cfm?story_id=E1_VDRQGVV.
80. Beck, N. (1991). The Fed and the political business cycle. *Contemporary Policy Issues 9*, 25–38.
81. Exec. Order No. 12835, 3 C.F.R. 6189; National Economic Council (2011). *Overview*. Retrieved November 14, 2011, from http://www.whitehouse.gov/administration/eop/nec.

82. Johnson, N., & Filipowich, B. (2006). Tax cuts and continued consequences: states that cut taxes the most during the 1990s still lag behind. *New Republic*, December 19. Retrieved January 14, 2007, from http://www.cbpp.org/12-19-06sfp.htm.

83. National Association of State Budget Officers (2011). *Fiscal survey of the states: 2011* (p. 40). Lexington, KY: National Association of State Budget Officers.

84. Kinnander, O. (2001). As infrastructure crumbles, engineers scream for investment. *The Bond Buyer, 335*, March 9, 40.

85. Van Ark, B. (2009). *Innovation and U.S. competitiveness: reevaluating the contributors to growth.* New York, NY: Conference Board.

86. Ulbrich, H. (2002). Economic aspects of business tax incentives. *Public Policy and Practice, 2*, October. Retrieved January 16, 2007, from http://ipspr.sc.edu/ejournal/businesstax.asp.

87. Small, K., et al. (1989). *Road work.* Washington, DC: Brookings Institution; Krohl, R. (2001). The role of public capital in the economic development process. *International Journal of Public Administration, 24*, 1041–1060; U.S. Congressional Budget Office (2010). *Public spending on water and transportation infrastructure* (p. 14). Washington, DC: U.S. Government Printing Office.

88. U.S. Council of Economic Advisers (2011). *Economic report of the president: 2011*, 193. All yearly figures cited in this section are from this source.

89. Taylor, J. (2009). *The financial crisis and the policy responses: an empirical analysis of what went wrong* (p. 3). NBER working paper w14631. New York, NY: National Bureau of Economic Research.

90. Morgenson, G., & Rosner, J. (2011). *Reckless endangerment: how outsized ambition, greed, and corruption led to economic Armageddon.* New York, NY: Times Books; Acharya, V., et al. (2011). *Guaranteed to fail: Fannie Mae, Freddie Mac, and the debacle of mortgage finance.* Princeton, NJ: Princeton University Press.

91. Rising from the ruins. (2011). *The Economist, 401*, November 5, 37.

92. Taylor, J. (2009). *The financial crisis and the policy responses*, 3.

93. Permanent Subcommittee on Investigations, U.S. Senate Committee on Homeland Security and Governmental Affairs (2011). *Wall Street and the financial crisis: an anatomy of a financial collapse* (p. 5). Washington, DC: U.S. Government Printing Office.

94. NBER is noted for having had among its research associates a large number of Nobel laureates in economics, former chairs of the Council of Economic Advisers, and other well-known economists.

95. National Bureau of Economic Research (2010). *Business cycle dating committee report*, September 20. Retrieved November 12, 2011, from http://www.nber.org/cycles/sept2010.html.

96. The ravages of time. (2011). *The Economist, 401*, October 1, 33.

97. Energy Policy Act of 2005 (P.L. 109-58); Energy Independence and Security Act of 2007 (P.L. 110-140).

98. Supplemental Appropriations Act of 2009 (P.L. 111-32).

99. Solyndra and the White House: letting sunlight in. (2011). *The Economist, 401*, September 24, 36.

100. The Federal Reserve's response to the crisis. (2011). *FederalReserve.gov*. Retrieved November 16, 2011, from http://federalreserve.gov/monetarypolicy/bst_crisisresponse.htm. Follow links on overview page to each program carried out by the Fed during the crisis.

101. A provision in the American Recovery and Reinvestment Act of 2009 (P.L. 111–5).

102. Laeven, L., & Valencia, F. (2010). *Resolution of banking crises: the good, the bad and the ugly.* International Monetary Fund (IMF) Working Paper no. 10/146, 19.

103. U.S. Congressional Budget Office (2011). *Estimated impact of the American Recovery and Reinvestment Act on employment and economic output* (p. 3). Washington, DC: U.S. Government Printing Office; Council of Economic Advisers (2011). *The economic impact of the American Recovery and Reinvestment Act: seventh quarterly report.* Retrieved February 18, 2012, from http://www.whitehouse.gov/sites/default/files/cea_7th_arra_report.pdf.

104. Binder, A., & Zandi, M. (2010). How the great recession was brought to an end. *Economy.com*. Retrieved November 18, 2011, from http://www.economy.com/mark-zandi/documents/End-of-Great-Recession.pdf.

105. Federal Reserve Board (2011). *Credit and liquidity programs and the balance sheet.* Retrieved November 17, 2011, from http://federalreserve.gov/monetarypolicy/bst_fedsbalancesheet.htm; Bernanke, B. (2009). *The crisis and policy response* [speech]. Retrieved November 18, 2011, from http://federal reserve.gov/monetarypolicy/bst_crisisresponse.htm.
106. Europe's debt crisis; rushing for the exits. (2011). *The Economist 401*, November 12, 32.
107. The World Bank (2005). *World development report 2006: equity and development.* New York, NY: Oxford.
108. World Bank (2005). *World development report 2006* (p.vii). New York, NY: Oxford.
109. *Society at a glance 2011: OECD social indicators.* (2011). Paris: OECD. Retrieved November 20, 2011, from http://www.oecd.org/document/24/0,3746,en_2649_34637_2671576_1_1_1_1, 00.html#data.
110. Niggle, C. (1989). Monetary policy and changes in income distribution. *Journal of Economic Issues, 23*, 809–822.
111. Classlessness in America: the uses and abuses of an enduring myth. (2011). *The Economist, 401*, September 24, 44.
112. Up the NAIRU without a paddle. (1997). *The Economist, 344*, March 8, 92.
113. Diving into the rich pool. (2011). *The Economist, 401*, September 24, 83.
114. Hunting the rich. (2011). *The Economist, 401*, September 24, 13.
115. Hunting the rich. (2011). *The Economist,* 13.

Budget Cycles

Public budgeting systems consist of numerous participants and various processes that bring the participants into interaction. The purpose of budgeting is to allocate scarce resources among competing public demands so as to attain societal goals and objectives. Those societal ends are expressed not by philosopher kings but by mortals who must operate within the context of some prescribed allocation process—namely, the budgetary system.

This chapter provides an overview of the participants and processes involved in budgetary decision making. First, the phases of the budget cycle are reviewed. Any system has some structure or form, and budgetary systems are no exception. As will be seen, the decision-making process has several steps. This chapter outlines the process and discusses the intermingling of the budget's cycles, both within government and among governments.

THE BUDGET CYCLE

The discrete activities that constitute budgeting are geared to a cycle. The cycle provides the timetable for the system to absorb and respond to new information and, therefore, allows government to be held accountable for its actions. Although existing budget systems may be less than perfect in guaranteeing adherence to this principle of responsibility, periodicity contributes to achieving and maintaining limited government. The budget cycle consists of four phases: (1) preparation and submission, (2) approval, (3) execution, and (4) audit and evaluation.

Preparation and Submission

The preparation and submission phase is the most difficult to describe because it has been subjected to the most reform efforts. Experiments in reformulating the preparation process abound. Although institutional units may exist over time, both procedures and substantive content vary from year to year.

Chief Executive Responsibilities

The responsibility for budget preparation varies greatly among jurisdictions. Budget reform efforts in the United States have pressed for executive budgeting, in which the chief executive has exclusive responsibility for preparing a proposed budget and submitting it to the legislative body. At the federal level, the president has such exclusive responsibility, although many factors curtail the extent to which the president can make major changes in the budget. In parliamentary systems, the prime minister (chief executive) typically has responsibility for budget preparation and submits what is usually called the "government budget" to the parliament.

Preparation authority, however, is not always assigned to state governors and local chief executives. While a majority of governors have responsibility for preparation and submission, some share budget-making authority with other elected administrative officers, civil service appointees, legislative leaders, or some combination of these parties.

In parliamentary systems, if a coalition of several parties is necessary to form a government, and the coalition is held together by each of the main parties in the coalition controlling one or more ministries, the prime minister may have very little control over budget preparation. Such was the case with the first government under the Iraq constitution adopted in 2005. Belgium holds the modern record for parliamentary systems for failure to form a government and thus name a prime minister; as of the end of 2011,[1] Belgium had failed to form a coalition government for almost two years.

At the municipal level, the mayor may or may not have budget preparation powers. In cities where the mayor is strong—has administrative control over the executive branch—the mayor normally does have budget-making power. This is not necessarily the case in weak-mayor systems and in cities operating under the commission plan, where each councilor or commissioner administers a given department. Usually, city managers in council-manager systems have responsibility for budget preparation, although their ability to make budgetary recommendations may be tempered by their lack of independence. City managers are appointed by councils and commonly lack tenure. Even in a city in which the mayor or chief executive does not have budget preparation responsibility, this duty is still likely to be in the hands of an executive official such as a city finance director. Thus, a majority of cities follow the principle of executive budget preparation.

Location of Budget Office

Budget preparation at the federal level is primarily a function of a budget office that was established by the Budget and Accounting Act of 1921[2]—the Bureau of the Budget (BOB), which became a unit of the Treasury Department. Over time, the role of the BOB increased in importance. In 1939, it became part of the newly formed Executive Office of the President. Given that the BOB was thought to be the "right arm of the president"—a common phrase in early budget literature—the move out of the Treasury, a line department, into the Executive Office of the President placed the BOB under direct presidential supervision. In 1970, President Nixon reorganized the BOB, giving it a new title, the Office of Management and Budget (OMB). The intent of the reorganization was to bring "real business management into Government at the very highest level."[3]

The state budget office is contained within the governor's office in only 10 states in the United States. It is a freestanding agency in 10 other states. Most commonly (in 21 states), the budget office is within an office of management and/or administration. Notably, in 39 of the 50 states, the governor's office sets budget targets for executive branch agencies.[4]

Information about professional personnel in state budget offices is presented in **Tables 4–1** and **4–2**. Given the significant variation in state sizes, the number of personnel assigned to budget agencies, not surprisingly, varies widely. In 2008, there were 1,675 staff assigned to budget agencies in the 50 states.[5] Of those, the largest number were assigned to budget

---

Table 4–1 Functional Roles of Budget Agency Personnel in the Fifty States

	Budget Analysts	*Tech/Computer*	*Administrative*	*Other*
Average Number	23	4	64	120
Most	245 (NY)	43 (FLA)	112 (NY)	281 (CA)
Fewest	3 (WVA)	1 or 0 (28 states)	1 or 0 (12 states)	17 (17 states)
Total Budget Staff (1,675)	1,151	204	320	605

Source: Adapted from Head, J., and Sigritz, B. (2008). *Budget processes in the states* (p. 15). Washington, DC: National Association of State Budget Officers.

Table 4–2 Education of Personnel in State Budget Offices, 2005

	Percent
Level of Education	
High School	2
Two Years	1
Baccalaureate	38
Master's	54
Doctorate	4
Total (*n* = 41 states)	100
University Degree Major	
Public Administration	31
Business Administration	24
Accounting	13
Economics	8
Other Social Sciences	8
Other Professional Majors	6
Mathematics/Sciences	3
Liberal Arts	3
Humanities	2
Other	2
Total (*n* = 35 states)	100

Source: Data from Burns, R. C. (2006). Unpublished data from Survey of State Budget Offices, 2005. Morgantown, WV: Recreation, Parks, and Tourism Program, University of West Virginia.

analyst positions, as shown in Table 4–1. Another 200 were in technology- or computer-related positions. New York had the most personnel classified as budget analyst—245—and West Virginia the fewest, with only three.

Professional training of budget professionals also is diversified. As of 2005, most professional staff at least had a baccalaureate degree, and more than half had a master's degree or higher. Table 4–2 shows that the largest degree field was public administration (31%), followed by business administration and accounting. The professional staff size varied from five to 278 employees, with the mean being 30 and the median 20.[6]

Steps in the Preparation Stage

In the federal government, budget preparation starts in the spring, a full year and a half before the budget year starts, or even earlier for large agencies. Agencies begin by assessing their programs and considering which programs require revision and whether new programs should be recommended. At approximately the same time, the president's staff makes estimates of anticipated economic trends to determine available revenue under existing tax legislation. The next step is for the president to issue general budget and fiscal policy guidelines, which agencies use to develop their individual budgets. In late summer, these budgets are submitted to the OMB. Throughout the fall and into the later months of the year, OMB staff members review agency requests and hold hearings with agency spokespersons. Not until late in the process, usually in November, December, and into January, does the president become deeply involved in the process. It culminates in February with the submission of a proposed budget to Congress for the forthcoming fiscal year that starts in October of that same calendar year.

At the state and local levels, a similar process is used where executive budgeting systems prevail. The central budget office issues budget request instructions, reviews the submitted requests, and makes recommendations to the chief executive, who decides which items to recommend to the legislative body. In jurisdictions not using executive budgeting, the chief executive and the budget office play minor roles. In this type of system, the line agencies direct their budget requests to the legislative body.

Political Factors

The preparation phase, as well as the other three phases in the budget cycle, is replete with political considerations, both bureaucratic and partisan, in addition to policy considerations. Each organizational unit is concerned with its own survival and advancement. Line agencies and their subunits attempt to protect against budget cuts and may strive for increased resources. Budget offices often play negative roles, attempting to limit agency growth or imposing agency budget cuts. Budget offices are always conscious of the fact that the chief executive (the governor or mayor, for example) can overrule whatever they propose. All members of the executive branch are concerned with their relationships with the legislative branch and the general citizenry. The chief executive is especially concerned about partisan calculations: Which alternatives will be advantageous to his or her political party? Of course, there is concern for developing programs for the common good, but this concern plays out in a complicated game of political maneuvering.[7]

Fragmentation

One complaint about the preparation phase is that it tends to be highly fragmented. Organizational units within line agencies tend to be concerned primarily with their own programs and frequently fail to take a broad perspective. Even the budget office may be myopic, although it will be forced into considering the budget as a whole. Some agencies also will privately and some not so privately engage in separate discussions with the legislative branch to try to restore cuts made by the budget office, thereby weakening the notion of the *executive* budget. Only the chief executive is unquestionably committed to viewing the budget in its entirety in the preparation phase.

Approval

Revenue and Appropriation Bills

The budget is approved by a legislative body, such as Congress, a state legislature, a county board of supervisors, a city council, or a school board. The important role of the legislature in the United States traces back to the American rebellion against "taxation without representation." For this reason, the "power of the purse" is considered to be a crucial responsibility of the people's representatives. The legislature reviews the executive's budget recommendations and often has access to the original agency budget requests, which enables it to make comparisons. At the federal level, revenue measures are enacted separately and are controlled by House and Senate committees other than the appropriations committees. This is not the case in many states, however.

Congress is normally not privy to original budget requests, although ways are often found to obtain this information, such as questions being put to agency representatives in committee hearings. The fragmented approach to budgeting in the preparation phase is not characteristic of the approval phase at the local level. A city council may have a separate finance committee, but normally the council as a whole participates actively in the approval process. Local legislative bodies may take several preliminary votes on pieces of the budget but then adopt the budget as a whole by a single vote.

Most states, like the federal government, separate tax and other revenue measures from appropriations or spending bills. Some states place most or all of their spending provisions in a single appropriation bill, whereas others create hundreds of appropriation bills. Most state legislatures are free to augment or reduce the governor's budget, but some are restricted in their ability to increase the budget. Likewise, many parliamentary systems allow the parliament to modify—but not increase—the government's budget proposal.

At the federal level, the revenue and appropriation processes have been markedly fragmented and involve numerous committees and subcommittees. Not only have revenue raising and spending been treated as separate processes, but the expenditure side is handled in many different major appropriation bills instead of being treated as a whole. Reforms introduced in 1974 attempted to integrate these divergent processes and pieces of legislation, but the system had numerous flaws.[8] The chapter on budget approval and the U.S. Congress discusses in detail efforts at reforming the congressional budget process.

The legislature holds a series of hearings at which the central budget office and the individual agencies testify. These hearings can be lovefests in which the committees that oversee agencies are eager to recommend increased appropriations for the agencies' programs. Conversely, tensions are common in such hearings. An executive may emphasize the need to restrain expenses, while legislators may seek expansion of various programs and corresponding increases in expenditures. Tensions are sometimes particularly keen between Congress and the president's budget director, especially during periods of divided government in which the president is of one party and Congress is controlled by the other.

In both the preparation and the approval phases, one or two issues often dominate budget deliberations. If a state government is projecting a major decline in revenues due to a weakening of the economy, closing the gap between low revenues and higher expenditures will be a major concern. At the federal level, wrestling with a huge budget deficit was a primary focus in budgeting from the 1980s until the mid-1990s, and renewed again with the return of large budget deficits associated with the recession starting in 2007 and the large stimulus measures adopted to try to restart the economy, all financed entirely by borrowing.

Since September 11, 2001, both the president and Congress have been deeply concerned with fighting terrorism on a global scale and increasing domestic security. The result has been huge outlays of funds without comparable revenue increases, turning the budget surpluses of the 1990s into record-breaking deficits. With the budget so far out of balance, budget proposals considered of highest priority, particularly proposals to fight terrorism and continue the ongoing wars and to stimulate the economy in the latter part of the decade, have been placed in a favored position relative to other priorities in the budget. Some measures were introduced to cut spending in less favored programs, but these were relatively minor compared with the deficit increases.

Executive Signature or Veto Powers

The final step of the approval stage is signing the appropriation and tax bills into law. The president, governors, and, in some cases, mayors have the power to veto. A veto sends the measure back to the legislative body for further consideration. Most governors (44 of them) have item-veto power, which allows them to veto specific portions of an appropriation bill but still sign it. In no case can the executive augment parts of the budget beyond that provided by the legislature. However, 38 governors have the authority to reduce the enacted budget without legislative approval.[9] The president was given a form of item veto that took effect in 1997, but it was invalidated by the Supreme Court the following year (see the chapter on budget approval and the U.S. Congress).

Execution

Apportionment Process

Execution, the third phase, commences with the beginning of the fiscal year—October 1 for the federal government and July 1 for most state governments. Some form of centralized control during this phase is common at all levels of government and is usually maintained by the budget office. Following congressional passage of an appropriation bill and its signing by the president, agencies must submit to the OMB a proposed plan for apportionment (see the chapter on budget execution). This plan indicates the funds required for operations, typically on a quarterly basis. The apportionment process is used in part to ensure that agencies do not commit all their available funds in a period shorter than the 12-month fiscal year. The intent is to avoid the need for supplemental appropriations from Congress.

The apportionment process is substantively important in that program adjustments must be made to bring planned spending into balance with available revenue. Because an agency most likely did not obtain all the funds requested, either from the president in the preparation phase or from Congress in the approval phase, plans for the coming fiscal year must be revised. To varying degrees, state and local governments also use an apportionment process.

Impoundment

The chief executive may assert control in the apportionment process through a form of item veto known as "impoundment," which is basically a refusal to release some funds to agencies. Thomas Jefferson often is considered the first president to have impounded funds. President Nixon impounded so extensively that Congress took legislative action. The 1974 legislation, in a sense, was a treaty between Congress and the White House allowing limited impoundment powers for the president. These limited impoundment powers have resulted in very little reduction in spending.

Allotments

At the federal level, once funds are apportioned, agencies and departments make allotments. This process grants budgetary authority to subunits such as bureaus and divisions. Allotments are made on a monthly or quarterly basis, and like the apportionment process, the allotment process is used to control spending over the course of the fiscal year. Control is often extensive and detailed, requiring approval by the department budget office for any shift in available funds from one item to another, such as from travel to wages. Some transfers may require clearance by the central budget office. At other levels, it is a one-stage allotment process, typically without using the term *apportionment*.

Preaudits

Before an expenditure is made, a form of preaudit is conducted. Basically, the preaudit ensures that funds are committed only for approved purposes and that an agency has sufficient resources in its budget to meet the proposed expenditure. The responsibility for this function varies widely, with the budget and/or accounting office being responsible for it in some jurisdictions and independently elected comptrollers being responsible for it in others. Later, after approval is granted and a purchase is made, the treasurer or other responsible official writes a check or makes an electronic fund transfer for the expenditure.

Execution Subsystems

During budget execution, several subsystems are in operation. Taxes and other debts to government are collected. The Internal Revenue Service (IRS) in the Treasury Department is responsible for this set of tasks at the federal level. Cash is managed in the sense that monies temporarily not needed are invested. Supplies, materials, and equipment are procured, and strategies are developed to protect the government against loss or damage of property and against liability suits. Accounting and information systems are in operation. For state and local governments, bonds are sold and the proceeds are used to finance construction of facilities and the acquisition of major equipment.

Audit and Evaluation

The final phase of the budgetary process is audit and evaluation. The objectives of this phase are undergoing considerable change, but initially the main goal was to guarantee executive compliance with the provisions of appropriation bills, particularly to ensure honesty in dispensing public monies and to prevent needless waste. In accord with this goal, accounting procedures are prescribed and auditors check the books maintained by agency personnel. In recent years, the scope of auditing has been broadened to encompass studies of the effectiveness of government programs.

Location of the Audit Function

In the federal government, considerable controversy was generated concerning the appropriate organizational location of the audit function. In 1920, President Woodrow Wilson vetoed legislation that would have established the federal budget system on the grounds that he opposed the creation of an auditing office answerable to Congress rather than to the president. Nevertheless, the General Accounting Office (GAO) was established in 1921 by the Budget and Accounting Act and was made an arm of Congress, with the justification being that an audit unit outside of the executive branch should be created to provide objective assessments of expenditure practices.

The GAO over the years underwent a gradual and major set of changes that led to its name being changed in 2004 to the Government Accountability Office.[10] It obviously retained its initials of "GAO."

GAO Functions

The GAO is headed by the comptroller general, who is appointed by the president, upon the advice and consent of the Senate, for only one term of 15 years. The comptroller general can be removed by Congress only by impeachment or joint resolution. There has never been such an effort, and as of 2011, there had been only eight people in this position since its creation in 1921.

The GAO does not maintain accounts, but rather audits the accounts of operating agencies and evaluates their accounting systems. With major reforms in accounting and auditing undertaken by the executive branch at the direction of Congress, and especially with the creation of independent inspectors general within executive departments and agencies, the GAO conducts far fewer audits than it once did.

The GAO provides a variety of other services. It gives Congress opinions on legal issues, such as advising on whether a particular agency acted within the law in some specific instance under consideration. It also resolves bid protests over the awarding of government contracts.

Where the GAO has gained major responsibility is in the arena of assessing the results of government programs. Comptroller General David Walker has said that the GAO's "activities [are] designed to determine what programs and policies work and which ones don't. This also involves sharing various best practices and benchmarking information. It means looking horizontally across the silos of government and vertically between the levels of government."[11] This responsibility for evaluating government programs has sometimes led to criticism of the GAO. In particular, some members of Congress have claimed that the office has lost its neutrality and become a policy advocate.

The GAO's focus of course can change over time as the result of specific congressional direction, or more generally to resonate with the most critical issues of the time. The newest comptroller general, Eugene Dodaro, reflected in his opening statement at his confirmation hearing the criticality of the size of the budget and budget deficits: "It is critical for GAO to provide insights into the government's financial condition and outlook and to seek ways to contribute to a more efficient and fiscally sustainable government. This includes working to help agencies identify and reduce billions of dollars in improper payments; identifying areas of duplication, overlap and fragmentation, as well as other opportunities to save money and enhance revenue; and helping promote more effective financial, information technology, acquisition, and performance management practices that can lead to eliminating wasteful approaches, provide greater efficiency, and ensure better accountability of taxpayer dollars."[12]

In 2002, the General Accounting Office engaged in a historical conflict with the White House. President George W. Bush had created the National Energy Policy Development Group (NEPDG) to recommend a new energy policy for the government. Vice President Dick Cheney chaired the group. After the group completed its work, the GAO asked to see important records. Of particular concern was the list of companies and individuals from industry that had supplied advice. The energy giant Enron had collapsed, leaving many stockholders with huge losses and company employees without retirement benefits. Some suspected that Enron, which had close ties to President Bush before he left Texas for Washington, had exerted undue influence on the design of the energy policy.

The White House refused to release the requested documents, which prompted the GAO to file suit in U.S. district court against Vice President Cheney and the NEPDG.[13] This move marked the GAO's first suit in its history against a high-ranking government official. The GAO contended that taxpayers' dollars were used by the group, and consequently, the GAO had a right to know how those dollars were spent. The White House's position was that it had a right to obtain information and advice on a confidential basis and should not be required to release the documents. A U.S. district court ruled that the comptroller general had not been harmed by the withholding of information and therefore lacked standing—namely, the right to bring suit.[14] The GAO decided not to appeal the ruling.

State and Local Auditors

At the state and local levels, the issue of organizational responsibility for auditing has been resolved in different ways. The alternatives are to have the audit function performed by a unit answerable to the legislative body, to the chief executive, to the citizenry directly, or to some combination of these. The use of an elected auditor is defended on the grounds that objectivity can be achieved if the auditor is independent of the executive *and* legislative branches. The opposing arguments are that the electorate cannot suitably judge the qualifications of candidates for auditor and that the election process necessarily forces the auditor to become a biased rather than an objective analyst. States primarily use elected and legislative auditors.

Sample Cycle

Figure 4–1 is a sample budget cycle. It is the one used in Pennsylvania, which, like most states, has a fiscal year beginning July 1. As can be seen, preparation begins with budget instructions being issued in August. Pennsylvania also issues Program Policy Guidelines (PPGs), which provide substantive policy guidance to agencies for preparing their budget requests. Submission by the agencies occurs in October, followed by budget office analysis and the governor's review from October through January. In February, the governor submits the budget to the legislature, which deliberates through the spring. The budget is adopted by the legislature by July 1, the beginning of the new fiscal year. Agencies then submit to the budget office what Pennsylvania calls a "rebudget." This is a reworking of their budget requests to reflect what the legislature approved as distinguished from what the agencies requested. The diagram does not show the audit phase that begins at the end of the fiscal year.

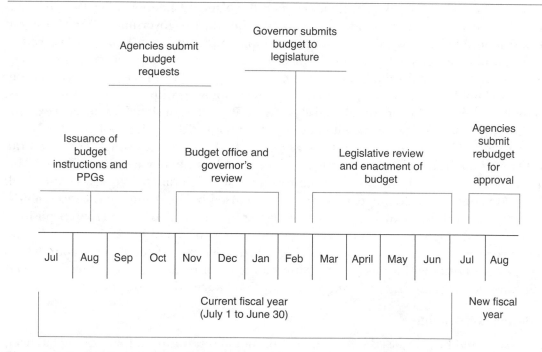

Figure 4–1 Budget Cycle in Pennsylvania.
Source: Adapted from Office of the Budget (2011). The budget process in Pennsylvania. Harrisburg, PA: Commonwealth of Pennsylvania, retrieved October 14, 2011, from http://www.budget.state.pa.us/portal/server.pt/community/office_of_the_budget_home/4408.

States that operate with biennial budgets—there are 23 of these states—operate with a 24-month cycle. North Carolina, for example, adopts a two-year budget in odd-numbered years. By April of the even-numbered years, the governor submits to the legislature recommendations for adjustments necessary for the second year of the budget. The state legislature meets to act on the governor's recommendations. This is called the *short session,* because constitutionally the legislature can deal with only a limited number of issues, primarily making adjustments to the two-year budget adopted in the previous year.[15]

SCRAMBLED BUDGET CYCLES

Although it is easy to speak of a budget cycle, no single cycle actually exists. Instead, a cycle exists for each budget period, and several cycles are in operation at any given time. The decision-making process does not simply proceed from preparation and submission to approval, execution, and finally audit. Decision making is complicated by the existence of several budget cycles for which information is imperfect and incomplete.

Overlapping Cycles

A pattern of overlapping cycles can be seen in **Figure 4–2**, which shows the sequencing of five budget cycles typical of a large state with an annual budget process. Only cycle 3 in the diagram displays the complete period covering 39 months. The preparation and submission phase requires at least nine months, approval six months, execution 12 months, and audit 12 months. The same general pattern is found at the federal level, except that the execution phase begins on October 1, giving Congress approximately eight months to consider the budget. As indicated by the diagram, three or four budget periods are likely to be in progress at any point in time.

Budget preparation is complicated by this scrambling or intermingling of cycles. In the first place, preparation begins perhaps 15 months before the budget is to go into effect. Moreover, much of the preparation phase is completed without knowledge of the legislature's actions in the preceding budget period.

Figure 4–2 Scrambled Budget Cycles.

Federal Experience

At the federal level, this problem has proved especially thorny. Congress historically has been slow to pass appropriation bills, and the approval phase was rarely completed by the start of the fiscal year when it began July 1. The usual procedure was to pass a continuation bill permitting agencies to spend at the rate of the previous year's budget while Congress continued to deliberate on the new year's budget. Although the budget calendar adopted in the 1970s gave Congress an additional three months, which was expected to permit completion of the approval phase, agencies' preparation problems for the following year's budget request persisted. In any given year, an agency begins to prepare its budget request during the spring and summer, even as Congress deliberates on the agency's upcoming budget. Despite the additional time granted to Congress to act on the budget, work on the budget was completed on time in only three out of 36 years from the time the new budget calendar went into effect through 2010.[16] This obviously compounds the problem of scrambled budget cycles.

Links Between Budget Phases

While a budget is being prepared, another one is being executed. The budget being executed may be for the immediately preceding budget year, but it can also be for the one before. As can be seen in Figure 4–2, in the early stages of preparation for cycle 4 the execution phase is in operation for cycle 2. Under such conditions, the executive branch may not know the effects of ongoing programs but is nevertheless required to begin a new budget, recommending changes upward or downward. Sometimes a new program may be created, and an agency must then recommend changes in the program for inclusion in the next budget without any opportunity for assessing its merits.

Length of Preparation Phase

The cycle, particularly the preparation phase, may be even longer than indicated above, especially when agencies must rely upon other agencies or subunits for information. For example, in preparing the education component of a state budget, a department of education will require budget information and requests from state universities and colleges early to meet deadlines imposed by the governor's budget office. The reliability and validity of data undoubtedly decrease as the lead time increases. Therefore, the earlier these schools submit their budget requests to the state capital, the less likely it is that such requests will be based on accurate assessments of future requirements.

Other Considerations

Besides the factors already mentioned, other issues further complicate budget cycles—most notably, intergovernmental considerations and the timing of budget years.

Intergovernmental Factors

Another problem arises from intermingled budget cycles because the three main levels of government are interdependent. For the federal government, the main problem is assessing needs and finding resources to meet these needs. A state government must assess its needs and those of local governments and must then search for funds by raising state taxes, providing for new forms of taxation by local governments, or obtaining federal revenues. In preparing budgets, governors take into account whatever information is available on the likelihood of certain actions by the president and Congress. For instance, the president may have recommended a major increase in educational programs that would significantly increase funds flowing to the states, but considerable doubt will exist as to whether Congress will accept the recommendation. In such a case, how should a governor shape the education portion of the state budget? The problem is even worse at the local level, which is dependent on both the state and federal governments for funds.

Budget Years

Budget cycles are further complicated by a lack of uniformity in the budget period. Although most state governments have budget years beginning July 1, four states do not: New York's begins April 1; Texas's begins September 1; and Alabama's and Michigan's begin the same day as the federal fiscal year—October 1.[17] Consistency does not even exist within each state. It is common for a state to begin its fiscal year on July 1 but to have to deal with local governments operating with different start dates, such as January 1, April 1, or September 1.

A case can be made for staggering the budget year for different levels of government. This practice might assist decision makers at one level by providing information about action taken at other levels. For example, the federal government might complete action on its budget by October 1. States could then begin a budget year on the following April 1 and local governments on July 1. Under such an arrangement, states could base their budgetary decisions on knowledge of available financial support from Washington. Local governments, in turn, would know the aid available from both Washington and their respective state capitals.

Rearranging the dates for fiscal years is no panacea, however. Information about financial support from other governments is only one of many items used in decision making. Also, any slippage by the legislature in completing its appropriations work by the time a fiscal year begins would void the advantages of staggered budget cycles. In addition, there is no direct translation from appropriations to aid to other governments. Money does not automatically flow to states and communities as soon as Congress passes an appropriation bill. Instead, state and local governments must apply for assistance, a process that typically requires many months.

Annual and Biennial Budgets

Not only is there inconsistency in the date on which budget years begin, but the length of the budget period also varies. Whereas the federal government and most local governments operate under annual budgets, as noted above, 23 states have biennial (two-year) budgets. Such a system violates the once-standard principle of annuality.[18] The argument is that annual budgets allow for careful and frequent supervision of the executive by the legislature and that this approach serves to promote greater responsibility in government. The problem with the annual budget, however, is that little breathing time is available. Both the executive and legislative branches are continuously in the throes of budgeting. The biennial approach, on the other hand, relieves participants of many routine budget matters and may allow greater time for more thorough analysis of government activities.

The 1993 National Performance Review recommended that the federal government adopt biennial budgeting as a means of eliminating "an enormous amount of busy work."[19] The idea continues to hold interest for some reformers (see the chapter on budget execution and the U.S. Congress). In October 2011, the Senate Budget Committee sent a letter endorsing the biennial budget idea to the joint Senate-House supercommittee established to try to reach agreement on budget cuts in excess of $1.5 trillion.[20]

One of the greatest dangers of a biennial system is that it may obstruct—if not prohibit—a prompt response to new conditions. The costs of not being able to adjust to changing conditions may far outweigh any benefits accruing from time saved. This consideration may explain why most of the more populous states are on annual budget systems and why many states with biennial budgets make provision for "reopening" the two-year budget at midpoint.

Still another consideration is whether under "normal" conditions sufficient amounts of new information become available to warrant annual systems. If program analysis were a well-established part of the budgetary process, then conceivably, new insights into the operation of programs would continually occur. In such instances, an annual process might be preferable. In other cases, in which decision makers operate one year with virtually the same information as was available the preceding year, there seems to be little need for annual budgets. Partially for this reason, proposals have been made for selectively abandoning the annual budget cycle. Under such a system, new programs or proposed changes in existing programs would be submitted in any given year for legislative review, whereas continuing programs would be reviewed only periodically.

SUMMARY

The four phases of the budget cycle are preparation and submission, approval, execution, and audit and evaluation. In general, the first and third phases are the responsibility of the executive branch, and the second is controlled by the legislative branch. The fourth phase in the federal system is directed by the GAO, which is answerable to Congress and not the president, and a set of independent auditors known as inspectors general. Auditing at the state and local levels is normally the responsibility of either independently elected officials or officials who report directly to the legislature.

A standard criticism of budgeting, especially at the federal level, is that the budget is seldom considered in its entirety during its preparation phase. Within the executive branch, only the president and his or her immediate staff view the budget as a whole. Agencies are primarily concerned only with their own portions of the total. The same disjointed approach has been characteristic of the approval phase at the federal level. More basically, the budget is rarely adopted in its entirety by the beginning of the fiscal year, requiring a series of continuing appropriations either for some agencies or for the entire federal government.

Budget cycles are intermingled. As many as four budget cycles may be in operation at any time in a single government. This phenomenon complicates decision making. For example, budget preparation is often forced to proceed without knowledge as to what action the legislature will take on the previous year's budget. Moreover, the interdependent nature of the three levels of government contributes to a scrambling of cycles. One possibility would be conversion to biennial budgets, a practice that is common at the state level. It is introduced frequently in proposed reform legislation at the federal level, but the idea has never gained traction.

NOTES

1. Belgium's lame duck government sets a world record. (2011). *DW-World*, March 3. Retrieved December 7, 2011, from http://www.dw-world.de/dw/article/0,,14952394,00.html.
2. Budget and Accounting Act of 1921. Ch. 18, 42 Stat. 20.
3. Nixon, R. M. (1970). *New York Times*, June 11; Dawes, C. G. (1923). *The first year of the budget of the United States*. New York, NY: Harper and Brothers.
4. Head, J., & Sigritz, B. (2008). *Budget processes in the states* (pp. 18, 30). Washington, DC: National Association of State Budget Officers.
5. Head, J., & Sigritz, B. (2008). *Budget processes in the states*, 15.
6. Burns, R. C. (2006). Unpublished data from Survey of State Budget Offices, 2005. Morgantown, WV: Recreation, Parks, and Tourism Program, University of West Virginia.
7. Wildavsky, A., & Caiden, N. (2004). *The new politics of the budgetary process* (5th ed.). New York, NY: Longman.
8. Congressional Budget and Impoundment Control Act of 1974. P.L. 93-344.
9. Head, J., & Sigritz, B. (2008). *Budget processes in the states*, 38.
10. GAO Human Capital Reform Act of 2004. P.L. 108-271.
11. Walker, D. M. (2002). The role of GAO and other government auditors in the 21st century. Address to the 14th Biennial Forum of Government Auditors, Providence, RI, 2002. Retrieved September 1, 2006, from http://www.gao.gov/cghome/14thbf.html; see Walker, D. M. (2004). *Evolving role of public service auditors*. Retrieved September 1, 2006, from http://www.gao.gov/cghome/erpsa/.
12. Dodaro, E. (2010). *Testimony of Eugene L. Dodaro to be comptroller general of the United States U.S. Government Accountability Office*. Retrieved August 15, 2011, from http://www.gao.gov/new.items/testimony_confirmation_hearing2010nov18.pdf.
13. U.S. General Accounting Office (2002). *Decision of the Comptroller General concerning NEPDG litigation*. Retrieved February 24, 2012, from http://www.gao.gov/cgdecnepdg.pdf.
14. *Walker v. Cheney* (2002). 230 F. Supp. 2d 51 (D.D.C.).
15. Governor's Office of North Carolina (2010). *The North Carolina state budget: recommended adjustments, 2010–2011*. Retrieved October 15, 2011, from http://www.osbm.state.nc.us/files/pdf_files/2010_budget.pdf.
16. Streeter, S. (2006). *Continuing appropriations acts: brief overview of recent practices* (p. 6). Washington, DC: Congressional Research Service. Updated by authors for 2006–2010.
17. Head, J., & Sigritz, B. (2008). *Budget processes in the states*, 4.
18. Sundelson, J. W. (1935). Budgetary principles. *Political Science Quarterly, 50*, 236–263.
19. National Performance Review (1993). *From red tape to results: creating a government that works better and costs less*. Washington, DC: U.S. Government Printing Office.
20. Senate Budget Committee (2011). *Conrad/Sessions bipartisan letter to Joint Select Committee on Deficit Reduction*. October 14. Retrieved December 7, 2011, from http://budget.senate.gov/democratic/index.cfm/documents—analyses?ContentRecord_id=a40bfffc-3314–48ce-aede-787cadf677cf&ContentType_id=94b7f973–e764–43ef-9365–d24d20a41170&Group_id=21c20bfa-d4fd-4bac-b73c-4808d6c5efe9.

Budgeting for Revenues: Income Taxes, Payroll Taxes, and Property Taxes

CHAPTER

5

This chapter and the next one describe the principles of taxation and the institutional characteristics of the major revenue sources used by governments. This chapter covers income taxes, payroll taxes, and property taxes while the next one covers sales taxes, user fees, and gambling revenues. The availability of revenues sets the tone for deciding on the level of expenditures and the decision process for allocating expenditures among competing priorities.

Historically, taxation has been a fundamental concern of the citizenry. Citizens may be less concerned about how government spends its money than about how that money is raised to support programs. The property tax bill, federal income tax return, and the water bill are more visible than most of the services citizens receive. The tax bill also almost always seems larger than the value of any individual service, so it is a stark reminder of the cost of government. In developing a budget package, political leaders are always mindful that program initiatives leading to higher expenditures and, therefore, to higher taxes may have negative effects on the possibility of winning reelection to their offices.

This chapter includes two sections. The first section discusses principles of taxation, covering such issues as the adequacy of various revenue sources, equity considerations, economic efficiency concerns, and the ability to collect revenues at a relatively low cost. The second, and longer, section details various revenue sources that rely on income or property as a base, including the individual income tax, the corporate income tax, payroll taxes, and property taxes. The discussion of each of these taxes focuses on such characteristics as their adequacy as a revenue source, their fairness, ease of collection, and so forth, and on the mechanics of how the tax base and tax rates are determined.

PRINCIPLES OF TAXATION

A chief concern that public officials have for any tax is the extent to which that tax will generate adequate revenue to fund the services provided by the government. The major revenue sources used by governments—income taxes, property taxes, and sales taxes—are used in large part because the number and value of taxable events or the value of the base are so large and therefore have the potential to generate so much income. There are other reasons, aside from the adequacy of revenue, however, to choose one particular revenue

133

source over another. These can include the equity (or fairness) of the revenue source, the extent to which the revenue source distorts economic choices, the cost of administering the tax, and the political feasibility of particular revenue sources. Few, if any, governments rely on a single source of revenue, and therefore, issues arise over how much any one source should contribute to the total budget of a government.

Adequacy of Revenue

Not all revenue sources have the same potential for growth. In general, as an individual's wealth or income goes up, he or she tends to demand more from government. For this reason, governments normally seek to avoid sources of revenue that do not have the potential to grow as fast as income or wealth. In addition, as noted above, some sources of revenue can produce large amounts of income for the government at relatively low rates, because of the sheer size of the tax base. To illustrate these points, consider the federal income tax and taxes on cigarettes. The federal income tax runs off a large tax base, and because of its progressive rate structure, higher levels of income are taxed at higher rates. A tax on cigarettes, on the other hand, runs off a relatively smaller base (sales of cigarettes), and demand for cigarettes does not tend to grow with income. For this reason, the progressive income tax is a much more productive revenue source than the cigarette tax. Taxes on cigarette sales, however, do not generate nearly as much controversy among a majority of voters and therefore may be more attractive to lawmakers.

In addition to the sheer size of the base, it is important for tax policymakers to take into account the potential of the tax base to respond to changes in tax rates. For many taxes, as tax rates increase, they discourage engaging in the taxed activity. Thus, a higher sales tax increases the price of goods (thus decreasing the amount of goods sold), and high marginal income tax rates may encourage some individuals to choose "leisure" over work, at least at the margin. One study of a range of taxes in North Carolina confirmed the existence of this relationship between tax rates and the tax base.[1] Conversely, where demand for a given good is "inelastic" (that is, where demand does not respond to price), an increase in the tax rate is much less likely to discourage consumption. This tends to be true, for example, of the cigarette tax, since many people are addicted to the good in question. However, there is evidence that higher prices do discourage consumption among some smokers, including young adults age 18 to 24.[2] The important implication for the adequacy of revenue is that behavioral responses to taxes must be factored in when doing revenue estimates, lest these estimates overstate the amount of revenue that will be generated for a given tax rate.

Equity

As important a question of how much money is going to be raised from a tax is the question of who will pay that tax. In fact, the question of "who pays" is often the central question of taxation. Consider the debate about whether or not to extend the Bush tax cuts enacted in 2001 and 2003, and for whom. Republicans have generally argued that all of the tax cuts should be extended. Democrats, on the other hand, have taken the position that only those households whose incomes are less than $250,000 per year should continue to enjoy these tax cuts. The result of the Democratic-supported policy would be a significant tax increase for upper-income taxpayers and an income tax system where a higher proportion of taxes are paid by these wealthier taxpayers. President Obama and the Congress agreed to extend the tax cuts for everyone for 2011 and 2012, or beyond the point of the 2012 presidential election.[3]

There are two general principles of tax equity. The first is the ability to pay principle, which says that the taxpaying capacity of different taxpayers should be taken into account in designing the tax system. The second is the benefit principle, which says there should be some relationship between the benefits received by the taxpayer and taxes paid.

Ability to Pay

Different taxpayers have different levels of income and wealth and, therefore, may have different capacities to bear the cost of financing government.[4] One sense of equity relates to the "ability to pay" principle. A tax should be related to the taxpayer's income or wealth or, more generally, to the taxpayer's ability to pay the tax. A taxpayer who can afford to pay more should pay more. Some consider that equitable. This principle implies that a tax imposes the same loss of utility for each taxpayer or, as economists refer to it, the *equal absolute sacrifice*.[5] Equity has both horizontal and vertical dimensions.

Horizontal Equity

Horizontal equity refers to charging the same amount to different taxpayers whose ability to pay (usually measured by income levels) is the same. If two taxpayers living in the same jurisdiction are the same on relevant dimensions, and they pay different levels of tax, that tax would violate the principle of horizontal equity. That can occur, for example, because the way a tax is administered may erroneously identify two taxpayers as being the same, when in fact they are different. This can be a particular problem for the property tax, because the level of tax paid is usually a direct function of assessed values of property. If two parcels are erroneously valued the same, when in fact one could sell for more on the market, then these two taxpayers are being treated as if they are the same, when they in fact may be quite different. It is important to note that whether two taxpayers are "the same" is frequently in the eye of the beholder. If two taxpayers have the same level of income, for example, but one is supporting a family of five on that income while the other is a single taxpayer with no dependents, simply differentiating tax paid on the basis of income fails to account for real differences in ability to pay. In this case, a tax that appears to be horizontally equitable may not be at all.

Vertical Equity

While there is nearly universal agreement that horizontal equity should be adhered to, vertical equity is a somewhat harder principle on which to obtain consensus. Put simply, vertical equity has to do with "treating different taxpayers differently." Normally, this implies knowledge of how a given tax affects different people, or income groups, in the society. Vertical equity is normally measured by computing the *effective tax rate*, which is computed by dividing the tax paid by a given individual by some measure of wealth or income. The computation of the effective tax rate can yield conclusions that a given tax, or tax system, is:

- *Progressive*, if effective tax rates are higher for higher-income taxpayers than for lower-income taxpayers;
- *Proportional*, if effective tax rates are essentially the same across different income categories; or
- *Regressive*, if lower-income taxpayers experience higher effective tax rates than higher-income taxpayers.

Knowing whether a tax is progressive, proportional, or regressive involves knowing more than just the tax rate. For example, a sales tax on purchases seems to treat all taxpayers equally but is often actually regressive in that poorer families may spend a greater proportion of their incomes on taxed items than wealthier families do.

Most people would argue for tax systems that are either proportional or progressive. But even if there is general agreement that a tax system should be progressive (as is generally true for the federal income tax), this does not mean that there is agreement concerning *how* progressive the tax should be. Since debates about progressivity are actually debates about the portion of the tax burden to be borne by different taxpaying groups, they are important and can create substantial controversy. In addition to the direct tax burden borne by different taxpayers, some Republicans in Congress have wanted to make the income tax less progressive, arguing that many upper-income taxpayers are "job creators" and that lower tax rates therefore have a positive effect on employment.[6]

Overall, the entire U.S. system of revenue, at the national level, is progressive, but that masks some variation by revenue source. While the federal income tax is quite progressive, the payroll tax (for Social Security and Medicare) is actually regressive, because there is an income ceiling above which Social Security taxes are not paid. In 2011, taypayers and employers were assessed the payroll tax only on the first $106,800 of payroll income.[7] The revenue system cannot be judged independently of certain government expenditure programs. Transfer payments, such as various forms of aid to poor families, are somewhat like "negative" taxes in their effect and increase the progressivity of the tax and transfer system considered together.

A Congressional Budget Office (CBO) study of the incidence of federal taxes—individual income, social insurance, corporate income, and excise taxes—found that, in 2007, the highest quintile (the one-fifth of households earning the most incomes) experienced an overall effective tax rate of 25.1% for all federal taxes. This compared to 17.4% in the next highest quintile, and only 4.0% for the lowest quintile. While the individual and corporate income taxes are even more progressive than the overall system, both excise taxes and social insurance taxes tend to be more regressive. Another measure of the level of progressivity of the federal individual income tax is illustrated by the fact that households in the top quintile (one fifth of all taxpaying households) paid 86% of all income taxes in 2007. This was the main reason that these same taxpayers paid two-thirds (69%) of all federal taxes in the same year. The top 1% of households, by income, targeted by the "Occupy" protests in 2011, pay 28% of all federal taxes and 40% of all individual income taxes.[8]

Benefit Received

Another concept to keep in mind is that of benefit received. Some revenue is derived from payments by recipients for services rendered or benefits received. User charges or fees are notable examples—for example, municipal parking garage fees, bus fares, and water and sewer charges. People who park in the garage pay for that service. The principle of payment for services results in an efficient allocation of public sector resources, because people will use only the amount of a particular service for which they are willing to pay. This process is similar to the way in which the private market works. That is, the private market produces no more of those goods than people are willing to purchase.

However, if all government services were paid for by fees, some people would be unable to pay and necessarily would be excluded. Elementary and secondary education, for example, is the most expensive local government service. If government provided this service entirely by charging parents and students the cost of providing education, many parents would be unable to send their children to school. This situation would lead to segments of the society being uneducated and unable to secure employment that required the ability to read, write, and the like. Because of the *spillover effects* (the fact that lack of education would adversely affect others in the society), many government services cannot be appropriately supported solely through user fees.

In addition, the public supports education for equity reasons. Everyone should have access to at least some level of education regardless of their ability to pay for it. Similarly, public goods have positive *externalities*—that is, they benefit all citizens regardless of whether one actually uses the service. Education, for example, benefits the entire community by making it more attractive to businesses making location decisions, and it benefits the entire economy by increasing the productivity of the workforce. The benefit received principle simply cannot be applied uniformly to all government services.

Moreover, particular taxes may be structured to permit the overall tax system to better adhere to the benefit principle. For example, the State of Florida has a sales tax but no income tax. This permits substantial taxation of visitors to the state to obtain revenue from individuals who are causing state services to be provided, but might otherwise not pay the cost of any of these services. Tourists would not pay income taxes were the state to have one, yet tourists impose burdens on government services. Therefore, sales taxes help to make tourists pay for the costs they impose. Of course, tourists not only generate costs, but also generate jobs and income for Florida. If the state were to impose what was perceived as an onerous sales tax rate, that might drive tourists away to other states.

The problem of nonresident service provisions is also the justification for nonresident income taxes (so-called commuter taxes) in many metropolitan areas, which tax income earned in a jurisdiction, even by nonresidents, as a means of exacting payment from them for services provided. Some major metropolitan areas with a significant population of suburban commuters impose commuter taxes. An important exception is Washington, D.C., which has been prohibited by Congress from levying such a tax and is prohibited by the federal courts from imposing such a tax without the approval of Congress.[9]

Economic Efficiency

According to the related concept of efficiency, an efficient tax is one that does not appreciably affect the allocation of resources in the private sector, such as between consumption and saving or among competing items for consumption. Taxes on alcohol, for example, seem to have no appreciable effect on consumption of alcoholic beverages. However, taxes can be used for regulatory purposes, as opposed to purely efficient revenue-raising purposes. Increased taxes on tobacco obviously increase the price of cigarettes, and studies have found that higher prices do discourage consumption among some smokers, including young adults age 18 to 24.[10] Other tax provisions that exclude some items from taxation, such as selected tax deferrals on personal income saved for retirement, are designed to influence behavior and may not be neutral or simply efficient.

Tax systems that are progressive can be inefficient and have unintentional consequences. If tax rates are particularly high for wealthy persons, for instance, then the system may encourage them to spend more time on leisure and less on working and earning more income. In many European countries, that effect—encouraging people to spend more time on leisure and less on purely income-earning activities—might be perceived as a positive outcome of the tax.

Tax system design generally tries to consider both equity and efficiency objectives. Use of taxes to regulate behavior, as in increased tobacco taxes, is generally not considered in the overall design of a tax system, but rather is typically legislated separately. Extensive research has focused on how to consider both principles simultaneously while developing optimal tax structures that are designed to achieve an optimal balance between efficiency and equity objectives.[11]

Cost of Administration

Generally, taxes that are expensive to administer should be avoided. Money spent to collect taxes represents a net loss to society, and therefore, the less spent on tax administration, the better. There are a number of specific costs associated with tax collection. Some costs are to the government, some to the taxpayer, and some to an intermediary, such as the shopkeeper who collects the sales tax. The individual income tax, for example, may be relatively cheap for the government to administer (given the level of revenue produced), but it can be quite costly for individuals to comply with all of the specific requirements of reporting income and calculating taxes owed. These high compliance costs occur primarily because of the complexity of the tax system. But this complexity, in part, represents the cost of attempting to promote equity. Most of the allowable deductions and credits for the federal income tax, for example, stem from attempts to adjust the tax to allow for individual taxpayer conditions.

On the other hand, there are taxes where the cost of compliance is relatively low, but the cost of initial collection by the government is high. Consider the case of the local property tax. Because the government is obliged to place a value on properties, it needs to expend substantial resources to identify the amount of taxes required to be paid and to collect those taxes in the first instance.

In addition to the cost of initial collection, there is the separate cost to the government of enforcement. Enforcement tends to be more difficult and costly in cases where the laws and rules surrounding the revenue source are complex, and where the responsibility for initial collection (for determining the amount of tax to be paid) lies with the taxpayer. Thus, the income tax is relatively costly to enforce, while the property tax is much less costly. In the latter case, there is much less room for interpretation by the taxpayer—the amount is not normally in dispute. (See the chapter on budget execution, which includes a section on tax administration that goes into greater detail on particular techniques and issues.)

Political Feasibility

Even taxes that score well on adequacy, equity, efficiency, and ease of administration still may fall short if they cannot be raised in the current political environment. States without an income tax will probably find it almost impossible to enact one, despite whatever other appeals such a tax may have. Tobacco-growing states probably will find it difficult to raise cigarette taxes, while such taxes may be relatively appealing in states that do not grow tobacco. In fact, it is not surprising that there is wide variation in the per-pack tax rates in different states. For example, Virginia and Kentucky, which are major tobacco-growing states, taxed cigarettes at 30 cents per pack in 2010. In contrast, Rhode Island taxed them at $2.46 per pack.[12]

INCOME, PAYROLL, AND PROPERTY TAXES

Many of the major revenue sources used by governments are based on income or wealth—property values being the primary wealth that is taxed in the United States to generate revenue. These bases are partially desirable because they are large; a relatively large amount of revenue can be raised at relatively low rates. They are also used because it is easy to adjust the tax to individual taxpayer conditions; that is, those taxpayers with relatively higher incomes have a relatively greater ability to pay taxes. Similarly, taxpayers with a great deal of property wealth may be viewed as having an extraordinary ability to pay, though that is not necessarily true for the elderly, who may have a valuable residence but after retirement have much less income with which to pay the tax. The major revenue sources in this category are the personal income tax, the corporate income tax, the payroll tax (primarily used for Social Security and Medicare), and the property tax.

The Personal Income Tax

The income tax is a relatively recent, but important, addition to the revenue sources used by governments. Until the passage of the 16th Amendment to the Constitution, ratified in 1913, the taxation of income was not permitted in the United States.[13] Since that time, the income tax has become the most important revenue source for the federal government, in addition to being an important source for many state and local governments. By tradition and for convenience, state and local income taxes tend to operate in a way that is similar to the federal income tax, albeit with very different rate structures. This section describes the structure of the federal income tax system, and then discusses briefly the particular characteristics of state and local personal income tax systems. Income taxes, in general, have the following structure:

1. The computation of income (in the case of the federal income tax, *adjusted gross income*, or AGI), which is the initial calculation of the tax base.
2. Reductions to adjusted gross income because of individual taxpayer characteristics. These take the form of *deductions* (standard or itemized) or *exemptions* (for the taxpayer and dependents).
3. The application of *tax rates* (graduated in the case of the federal income tax) to taxable income, which is the result of AGI minus deductions and exemptions.
4. Reductions in the tax paid as a result of *tax credits*, which are dollar-for-dollar reductions in taxes paid.

Computing Adjusted Gross Income

Not all income is taxed. In the case of the federal government, decisions have been made about precisely which types of income should be subject to taxation and which should not. Economists have historically embraced a very broad definition of income, called the *Haig-Simons definition*, which defines income as any increase in an individual's potential ability to consume.[14] This includes some of the income used in the federal definition, including salaries, wages, commissions and tips, dividends, interest, rents, alimony, and unemployment compensation. Excluded from the federal definition, however, are most employee benefits (such as employer-provided health insurance and contributions to pension funds), disability retirement, workers' compensation, food stamps, and interest earned on some state and local bonds.

This arguably advantages people who have more of the excluded income. For example, two individuals whose adjusted gross income is the same may in fact be not equally well off, if one of them is being provided a subsidy by his employer for health insurance and retirement benefits (not counted in adjusted gross income, and therefore not taxed), while the other is not. For this reason, the more sources of income included in the tax base, the more equitable the income tax. When the base excludes sizable segments of income, vigorous debates immediately arise over whether some interests are receiving undue favoritism as a result of legislative lobbying.[15]

Tax codes also provide for adjustments to gross income that typically have the effect of removing portions of income from the base. For example, the federal tax code excludes expenses for moving to accept a new job, some job-related educational expenses, and some employer-paid business reimbursements. The result of the components of income that are included (above), less these adjustments, becomes the base from which exemptions and deductions are subtracted, or adjusted gross income.

Exemptions and Deductions

Individual exemptions and deductions may further reduce the individual income tax base. Exemptions are reductions to the tax base that literally result from one's existence. If you file income taxes, you can claim yourself as an exemption. Moreover, the more dependents that a taxpayer claims on his or her return, the more exemptions, and therefore the greater the dollar amount from exemptions. In 2011, the federal exemption was $3,700 for most taxpayers. This means that a married couple filing jointly could claim $7,400 in exemptions. If they had three children, that rose to $18,500. There is one caveat to this. As a result of changes to income tax laws in 1993, the personal exemption was, until 2009, reduced for higher-income taxpayers (those who are married filing jointly with incomes greater than $250,200 in 2009, for example) and were eventually phased out entirely. This phase-out is not in effect for 2010, 2011, and 2012, but it is scheduled to resurface, under current law, in 2013.[16]

More important than exemptions for many people are deductions. Each taxpayer is permitted to claim a *standard deduction* without providing any documentation. This standard deduction varies according to the filing status of the taxpayer. In 2011, the standard deduction was $5,800 for a single person, and $11,600 for married people filing jointly (regardless of the number of dependents).

Itemized deductions are much more complicated. These deductions literally attempt to adjust taxable income to reflect differences in individual taxpayer conditions. As such, they can vary widely from one taxpayer to another, but they also require that the taxpayer maintain supporting evidence for the deduction. Taxpayers itemize their deductions when their totals are greater than the standard deductions. The main itemized deductions include:

- *Home mortgage interest*—the interest paid on borrowed funds for a taxpayer's first two properties can be deducted from income. This represents an important subsidy for homeowners and establishes a significant incentive for home ownership. It decreases the progressivity of the federal income tax system, however, since more tax benefits are provided to higher-income individuals, a higher proportion of whom are homeowners.[17]

- *Unreimbursed health expenses*—health care expenses, to the extent that they are not reimbursed, may be deducted from income. An important caveat, however, is that only those unreimbursed expenses that exceed 7.5% of adjusted gross income can be deducted. This means that a taxpayer with an AGI of $100,000, and unreimbursed medical expenses of $8,000, could deduct only $500 from his or her taxes.

- *State and local taxes*—many taxes paid to state and local governments are exempt from federal taxation. This includes all state and local income and property taxes, and many vehicle licensing and registration fees. Since 2004, it has also included sales taxes paid (an earlier sales tax deduction had been repealed in 1986), but taxpayers are not permitted to deduct both income taxes and sales taxes. Historically, the real property tax and state income taxes have been the taxes most frequently claimed as deductions from federal taxes.[18]

- *Charitable contributions*—payments made by cash or check to recognized nonprofit organizations are deductible. In addition, items donated to such institutions may also be deducted (provided there is evidence of both the donation and its value), as well as miles driven on behalf of a charity.[19]

- *Business expenses*—particularly for self-employed individuals, a wide variety of business expenses can be deducted. These include the cost of providing for retirement and health benefits, and even a portion of home mortgage costs provided the taxpayer uses the deducted portion of his home solely for business. Even non-self-employed individuals can deduct a variety of expenses, especially related to unreimbursed job costs and certain entertainment expenses. The Internal Revenue Service, however, has been relatively vigilant concerning unwarranted business expense deductions.

These exclusions, inclusions, adjustments, and deductions to the income base are intended to yield income figures for individuals and families that further horizontal and vertical tax equity. These factors together are meant to recognize variations in total income and the circumstances involved in earning that income and meeting living expenses. Individuals earning the same income but having different numbers of family members and expenses will be treated differently, while others with unequal gross incomes ultimately may have the same ability to pay when adjustments and deductions are taken into account.

Rate Structure

The vertical equity of the tax system at the federal level is also affected by the use of a progressive rate structure. Tax law changes since 2001 have altered tax brackets, reducing the amount of taxes that almost all taxpayers are liable to pay. In 2011, the federal income tax had six tax brackets, which varied from 10% (for the first $17,000 in taxable income for a married couple) to 35% (for taxable income in excess of $379,150 for married taxpayers). It is important to note that the nature of the income tax is such that different portions of income are taxed at different rates. Therefore, even someone with taxable income of $1,000,000 will see the first $17,000 of that income taxed at only 10%. This taxpayer would experience each of the tax brackets for various portions of income. **Exhibit 5–1** shows a tax calculation for a hypothetical taxpayer, demonstrating the sequence of taxation, from the calculation of AGI, to taxable income, to tax paid.

Exhibit 5–1 Example of Computation of the Federal Income Tax in 2011

John and Bernadette Public are a married couple who file their taxes jointly. They have two dependent children. Their adjusted gross income, consisting of $150,000 in salaries and $20,000 in interest, was $170,000 in 2011. They claim a $1,600 tax credit for the care of their dependent children. They itemize deductions, and have three such deductions in 2011: $15,000 in home mortgage interest, $2,000 in state and local taxes, and $1,000 in charitable contributions. The calculation below shows how they compute their federal income tax liability for 2011. The personal exemption (claimed for each of them plus their dependents) is $3,700.

In calculating the Publics' taxes, we first compute their taxable income. Next, we reduce the taxable income by the sum of their itemized deductions (they have chosen to itemize because their itemized deductions exceed the standard deduction) and personal exemptions, to arrive at taxable income. Tax liability is then computed by applying the tax rates from the tax table below to their taxable income (recall that in doing this, different portions of their income are taxed at different rates). Finally, the tax liability is reduced by the tax credit in order to arrive at the total tax paid.

Step 1: Adjusted Gross Income
Salaries—$150,000
Interest—$20,000
Total AGI—$170,000

Step 2: Taxable Income
Adjusted gross income—$170,000
Less: Itemized deductions—$18,000
Less: Personal exemptions—$14,800
Total Taxable Income—$137,200

Step 3: Tax Liability
Total taxable income—$137,200
Calculating tax paid for different components of income:
$17,000*.10=$1,700
$52,000*.15=$7,800
$68,200*.25=$17,050
Total Tax Liability—$26,550

Step 4: Total Tax Paid
Tax liability—$26,550
Less: Tax credit—$1,600
Total Tax Paid—$24,950

2011 Tax Table: Married Filing Jointly

If taxable income is over	But not over	Marginal tax rate is
$0	$17,000	10%
$17,000	$69,000	15%
$69,000	$139,350	25%
$139,350	$212,300	28%
$212,300	$379,150	33%
$379,150	No limit	35%

Some have proposed a flat rate income tax, or alternatively a national sales tax, to replace the existing federal income tax system. Either of these taxes would likely impose relatively high rates in order to replace the revenue from the existing income tax. In addition, both would be less progressive than the current federal system, although recent research suggests that taxpayers who support such a change do not believe the current system is as progressive as it is, and do not believe that a "reformed" system would be as regressive as it would be.[20] The original "9–9–9" proposal from Republican Presidential hopeful Herman Cain in 2011 would have imposed a flat individual income tax rate of 9%, coupled with a national sales tax of 9%, and a corporate income tax rate of 9%.[21]

In 2010, chairs of the President's Commission on Fiscal Responsibility, otherwise known as the Bowles-Simpson Commission, recommended as part of their deficit reduction proposals the elimination of a number of exemptions and deductions. At the same time, they proposed reducing individual income tax rates. Since the package was designed to reduce the federal budget deficit, and to slow the growth in federal debt, the loss of revenue from reductions in rates was more than offset by the added revenue that would come from the elimination of these tax breaks. Among the tax preferences targeted by the Bowles-Simpson Commission were some of the largest and most popular, including the provision of retirement and other benefits by employers and the home mortgage interest deduction.[22]

Tax Credits

Unlike tax deductions, tax credits are dollar-for-dollar reductions in taxes that are applied after all the preceding steps have been completed. Perhaps the largest tax credit is the *earned income tax credit* (EITC), established in 1975. This is a tax credit for the "working poor" and can behave like a *negative income tax*, in that individuals can receive a credit in excess of the tax that they are required to pay. In this case, they receive a check from the government for the amount by which the credit exceeds their liability.[23] Research shows that the EITC is heavily used by low-income individuals because it has been around so long, and because it is effectively targeted to low-income individuals.[24] Other tax credits are provided for children (provided that the taxpayer's income is less than $110,000 for married taxpayers filing jointly) and for child and dependent care expenses (for example, having a caregiver come into your home to care for a child or an aging relative).

The Alternative Minimum Tax

The *alternative minimum tax* (AMT) is a feature of the federal income tax system. First introduced in 1969, its intent is to collect taxes from wealthy individuals who might be able to shelter that income from the regular income tax system.[25] The AMT is literally a shadow income tax system. Taxpayers are required to calculate their taxes in two ways—under the regular tax system and the AMT—and are required, in effect, to pay the higher amount.

The AMT has become more controversial in recent years because it applies to more and more taxpayers. CBO estimates that 4 million people paid the AMT in 2009. The AMT has expanded its reach for two reasons. First, unlike many of the features of the regular tax system, the parameters of the AMT are not indexed for inflation. Second, because many people are experiencing reduction in taxes under the regular tax system due to the recent tax cuts, they are pushed onto the AMT.[26] Because more people have been affected by the AMT over time, there has been substantial pressure to reform or eliminate the AMT. This is particularly true because more and more taxpayers who do not consider themselves wealthy are nonetheless paying the AMT. For example, until 2000 there was never any year in which the AMT affected more than 1% of taxpayers.[27] The vast majority of those taxpayers had very high levels of income. CBO estimated that, without changes to the law by 2010, 84% of taxpayers with incomes between $100,000 and $200,000 would have paid the AMT. Eliminating the AMT, however, would be costly. CBO estimated that abolishing the AMT would result in $620 billion in lost revenue from fiscal year 2010 to fiscal year 2019, representing a loss of roughly 4% in individual income tax receipts over that period. Over the past several years, the government has passed legislation to "patch" the AMT by adjusting rate brackets, exemptions, deductions, and credits, thus limiting its effect on additional taxpayers.[28]

State and Local Income Taxes

Most personal income taxes levied by the states and local governments are modeled on the federal tax. The states sometimes use the federal base or a modification of it. Some state income taxes, such as Colorado, Illinois, Indiana, and Pennsylvania, are simply a proportion of the federal tax owed. Most states have some kind of graduated rate structure, although the marginal tax rates are uniformly lower than federal marginal rates. Hawaii and Oregon had the highest marginal tax rates (11%) in 2010.[29] When the federal government modifies its tax laws, changes inadvertently occur in state taxes. Local income taxes tend to be simple to calculate and involve flat, rather than progressive, tax rates.

Indexing

The federal government and some states use indexing in various forms to adjust income taxes in accordance with changes in price levels. If tax brackets are not altered and prices subsequently rise, then inflation will produce higher tax revenues because rising incomes will place citizens in higher tax brackets without any real increase in buying power. Besides adjusting tax brackets, other indexing techniques include modifying the standard deduction or personal exemption. A controversial issue is the measure of inflation used to adjust tax brackets (and many other revenue and expenditure elements). The consumer price index historically has been used, but many now feel that it overstates inflation, causing taxes to be lower than they should be and, more importantly, causing federal benefit programs to extend benefits greater than should be, as discussed in the chapter on government and the economy.

Enforcement

A key income tax issue is enforcement. As noted above, the individual income tax relies heavily on honest self-reporting by taxpayers. Although employers withhold an important proportion of total individual income taxes paid, thereby enforcing tax collection for the Internal Revenue Service (IRS), enforcement remains a problem—and an especially difficult problem when taxpayers think the tax is unfair. Much income is never identified and thus never becomes part of the tax base. A large underground economy operates in which transactions occur in trade, payments in kind, and unrecorded payments in cash never become part of the income tax base. Measuring the size of that invisible economy is naturally difficult, but the World Bank estimated in 2010 that the "informal sector" for Organization of Economic Cooperation and Development (OECD) countries was 16.6% of gross domestic product (GDP).[30] According to this same study, for the United States, income equal to an estimated 8.4% of GDP is unrecorded and therefore untaxed. In addition to this unrecorded income, the U.S. income tax relies heavily on self-reporting, which may also contribute to an exaggeration of deductions, which also has the effect of reducing the tax collected.

Tax Expenditures

Revenues that could be, but are not, collected constitute tax expenditures and can aid or hinder attempts to achieve an optimal balance. According to federal law, tax expenditures are "revenue losses … which allow a special exclusion, exemption, or deduction from gross income or which provide a special credit, a preferential rate of tax, or a deferral of tax liability."[31]

Tax expenditures are not new. Home mortgage interest payments (on up to two homes) have been deductible from income since 1910, for example. While tax expenditures may exist for any tax, the individual income tax, at the national and state levels, includes by far the largest number of tax expenditures, primarily because of the significant number of permitted deductions from gross income. Numerous exemptions from taxation or deductions from income for corporations have crept into law over the years as well.[32]

The largest income tax expenditures in the federal budget (with estimates of fiscal year 2012 revenue losses) are the exclusion of employer contributions for medical insurance ($184 billion), the mortgage interest deduction on owner-occupied homes ($99 billion), contributions to 401(k) plans ($67 billion), the step-up basis of capital gains at death ($61 billion), and the exclusion of imputed rental income ($51 billion). Together, these five income tax expenditures were estimated to cost the federal government more than $450 billion in 2012.[33]

Tax expenditures are not automatically bad. The public policy goal for the home mortgage interest deduction is to encourage and enable individual family home ownership. Exclusion of employer pension and medical insurance contributions is meant to increase savings for pensions and reduce the cost of health care. The housing exemption may help make housing affordable to moderate-income families, but it also benefits more affluent taxpayers and may be of no benefit to low-income families. Is the housing exemption, then, a factor that furthers or detracts from equity? Given the recent wave of foreclosures, there is also some reason to believe that the mortgage interest deduction, along with other policies that reduced the cost of housing, encouraged people who could not afford homes to buy them.

Since the 1970s, tax expenditures have become an important issue in debates over tax reform. These measures reduce the revenue flowing into government treasuries and can represent "loopholes" for the wealthy. Increasingly, policymakers and analysts also recognize that these tax expenditures represent an alternative form in which to confer benefits to citizens. That is, if the goal of a program is to encourage affordable housing, there is no difference between sending a potential developer a check for $50,000 or giving the same developer a $50,000 tax break. Benefits conferred on the spending side, however, tend to be much more transparent than those provided through the tax code.

Like the federal government, some state governments routinely report estimates of tax expenditures as a part of their budgets.

Corporate Income Taxes

Taxes on corporate earnings have been defended as appropriate given the size of corporate economic power and the fact that some individuals might be able to escape taxation by "hiding" their income in corporations. On the other hand, corporate income taxes seem to result in double taxation. First a corporation is taxed, and then individuals are taxed on dividends paid on their corporate stock holdings. There have been proposals to replace the corporate income tax with a tax on net business receipts to avoid this double taxation, but these proposals have not attracted much interest. Proposals to exclude dividends from individual income taxation also have been unsuccessful.

Tax Base

Corporate taxes use net corporate earnings as a base. Whereas the individual income tax base basically considers income before expenses, except for some deductions and exclusions, corporate income taxes apply only to net profit after operating expenses. In addition, some deductions are allowed for capital losses, operating losses, depreciation of capital investments, charitable contributions, and expenditures for research and development. How these deductions are applied is often controversial, such as how rapidly a corporation can depreciate capital investments. The federal corporate tax rates gradually increase from 15% to 35% as net earnings increase.

As a percentage of GDP, receipts from the federal corporate income tax are actually lower than those of every other OECD country with the exception of Turkey.[34] Many states have corporate income taxes as well, although the importance of the corporate income tax has declined at the state level in recent years. In 2010, corporate income taxes accounted for approximately 5% of overall state revenues, about one-half of the level of two decades earlier.[35]

In addition to the overall amount of money collected from the corporate income tax, these taxes can also be compared, across countries, in terms of their overall rate structures. In 2010, including both national and state/local government corporate taxes, the United States corporate tax rates, at 39.2%, were higher than those of any other OECD countries with the exception of Japan, which had a rate of 39.5%. Looking at national government taxation of corporate income, only France (at 34.4%) and Belgium (at 34%) exceeded the top rate in the United States (32.7%).[36]

Tax Incidence

The primary issue as regards corporate taxation is who actually carries the burden of corporate taxes. Corporations may be able to increase prices and, in effect, make consumers pay the tax, or they may limit wage increases to workers and, in effect, have them pay the tax. Another option is to take taxes out of profits, thereby reducing dividends for investors. Corporations probably use some combination of these shifts.

An issue involving state corporate taxes is whether they affect decisions to locate and expand operations in one state over another. Legislators and executives in a state government fear that any increase in their corporate income taxes will discourage corporations from locating in the state and encourage others to move out of the state. The expectation is that what a state loses in tax revenue, it will gain from companies already there expanding their operations in the state and from companies relocating to the state (see discussion of what is sometimes called smokestack chasing in the intergovernmental chapter).

Payroll Taxes

Insurance trust funds, which are separate accounts set up to hold certain earmarked revenues (see the chapter on financial management), are financed by means of charges on salaries and wages (the charges are paid by employees, employers, or both). These are typically referred to as payroll taxes, and they are differentiated from income taxes because they are taxes on wages and salaries only, as opposed to more comprehensive taxes on income. These charges are not taxes inasmuch as they do not generate revenue to be used to pay for services; instead, the programs provide benefits to the people who are covered by them. Employers and employees pay into these systems, and people earn benefit credits through contributions made during their working careers. As of 2011, the full rate paid for Social Security taxes was 12.4%, and for Medicare taxes it was 2.9%. Each of these was equally divided between employees and employers. Two other caveats apply for Social Security taxes. First, as of 2011, they were paid on the first $106,800 of payroll income. Second, they were temporarily reduced to 8.4% for 2011 and 2012 as part of an economic stimulus effort. Social insurance receipts rose as a percentage of GDP from 4.5% in 1972 (as low as 3% in the early 1960s) to 0% in 2010.[37]

Social Security and Supplemental Security Income

Social Security is a trust program of vast proportions. Its complexities far exceed the scope of this text. Here we sketch its overall structure.

Three major programs are administered directly by the Social Security Administration. The first, Old Age and Survivors Insurance, is a benefits program for retired workers and their survivors. The second program, Disability Insurance (DI), provides benefits for covered workers who are disabled and cannot work. In 2010, the Social Security Administration paid out benefits to 52.5 million individuals, including 36.4 million retired workers, 9.7 million disabled workers, and 6.4 million spouses, children, or survivors of retired or disabled workers. In fiscal year 2010, benefits paid out for Old Age and Survivors Insurance benefits totaled $557.2 billion. Total benefits for DI in the same year totaled $118.3 billion.[38]

The third major program under Social Security provides monthly benefits to people who are aged, blind, and disabled. This program is known as Supplemental Security Income (SSI).[39] SSI funds come from general tax revenues, rather than from employer-employee contributions. Unlike DI, SSI does not require work credits for eligibility but does require that recipients be needy. It is possible to qualify for both programs, although qualifying for DI has the effect of reducing SSI benefits. In 2009, 7.7 million people received $46.6 billion in benefits under the SSI program.[40]

Legislation passed in 1983 greatly modified the financing of Old Age and Survivors Insurance to improve the solvency for the long term. Estimates then were that the trust fund would be insolvent before 1990 unless corrective actions were taken. While the increases in both the employer and the employee contribution rates and an increase in the amount of annual income subject to the tax will satisfy the fund's needs for some decades, the consensus is that the program will need revising again, and that the longer reform is postponed, the more dramatic will be the changes required.

For some time, various analysts have projecting that the point would come when Social Security benefit outlays would exceed payroll taxes in the trust fund. Taken together, the Social Security trust funds are projected to be in deficit, excluding interest paid to them, in each year beyond 2010, for at least 75 years (without any changes). As a whole, the Social Security trust funds were still in surplus for fiscal year 2010, largely because of interest paid to the trust funds from the balance of the federal government.[41] CBO estimates that Social Security will have enough revenues to cover all scheduled benefits until fiscal year 2038, because of the repayment of funds that the trust funds have loaned to the non–Social Security portion of the federal budget. After 2038, however, unless there is an additional infusion of funds into the trust funds, Social Security will be able to pay only 79% of the full amount of current projected benefits.[42] Such a change would inevitably create a political crisis of overwhelming magnitude.

Several issues have fueled the debate over Social Security reform, and the motivations for reform among many groups are not necessarily consistent. First is the issue we might label "violation of trust." This issue is based on a misunderstanding in some circles concerning the nature of the Social Security trust funds. Many citizens assume that the funds they and their employers contribute to the system are being held in trust, invested much like pension funds to yield the benefits that will be paid out to them in the future. Politicians make a similar claim in their criticisms of Social Security. In reality, each year's payments into the Social Security Trust Fund are used to pay claims to beneficiaries in that year. Historically, at least for the past 25 years, the payments into the fund have exceeded payments to beneficiaries out of the fund. Those excess payments created a surplus in the fund, and that surplus in turn has been lent to the U.S. Treasury at the equivalent of the 30-year Treasury bond to finance part of other federal spending. The alternative to the Treasury borrowing from the Social Security fund is to force the Treasury to borrow from the U.S. and overseas capital markets. Under such a scheme, the surplus Social Security funds would need to be invested rather than sit idle—perhaps in the stock market (discussed below).

Thus, one motivation for reform is the political point of view that the fund should behave as a revolving fund, with proceeds paid into the fund being invested, as in most pension funds. That view somewhat naively assumes that private pension funds pay out benefits commensurate with the results of investment of funds paid in. That statement is true of defined contribution plans (retirement plans where individuals pay a set amount into a retirement plan, but are not guaranteed a specific return), but defined benefit plans pay out specific levels of benefits regardless of whether the fund investments are sufficient to meet those benefit payouts. Just as an employer with a defined benefits pension fund is obligated to meet the benefit payouts defined in the plan, from business net profits if necessary, so the federal government is obligated to meet whatever Congress determines will be the benefit structure, first from the trust fund itself and then from other federal revenues as necessary. Unless Congress fails to appropriate funds to meet legislated benefits (if and when the surplus in the fund turns into a deficit) or passes legislation so as to lower benefits, then the trust fund issue really is not an issue. Instead, it is a convenient political football for both parties to kick around.

A second motivation for reform is closely linked to the debates on the federal budget surplus or deficit. Because the fund shows a surplus, and all revenue to the fund counts as part of the federal government's revenue total, the size of the federal deficit is lower than if Social Security figures were excluded. The more fiscally conservative believe that the practice of using the trust fund surplus to finance part of other spending is inappropriate. Such a practice, according to this argument, represents a nontransparent imposition of taxes, as tax payments that were advertised as supporting Social Security are, at least in the short run, used to finance other government spending.

A third issue discussed by advocates for reform is that the funds being paid into Social Security should be earning more than the implicit 30-year Treasury bond rate. The bull market of the 1990s particularly fueled this aspect of the debate, as stocks earned dramatic returns—two and three times the rate of the 30-year Treasury bond. Proposals have been advanced to invest the funds flowing into the trust fund in the stock market, so as to earn higher benefits for future pensioners. This notion has gotten a lot less traction recently, as the effect of the recession that started in 2007 on the U.S. stock market now gives some pause when it comes to the investment of Social Security assets in riskier equities than U.S. Treasury securities.

Medicare

Medicare, the largest federal health insurance program, is administered by the Centers for Medicare and Medicaid Services (CMS) in the Department of Health and Human Services. Medicare provides basic health insurance to the elderly, with a separately funded catastrophic coverage component, and is funded by payroll tax contributions, premiums paid by persons covered under the program, and general revenues. Medicare also covers people on DI once they have been receiving DI benefits for 24 months. These beneficiaries are under age 65.

Medicare has become one of the major contributors to rapidly rising federal expenditures for health care. Medicare outlays totaled more than almost $520 billion in fiscal year 2010.[43] In 2002, Congress and the Bush administration passed the Medicare Modernization Act, which established, for the first time, a prescription drug benefit for Medicare that took effect in 2006. Estimates of the 10-year cost of this entitlement expansion ranged from $400 billion to $500 billion, although subsequent estimates suggest that this original cost assumption was overstated.[44]

The combination of the same demographic factors that are driving the Social Security imbalance and the pace of medical care inflation contribute to an even bleaker long-term outlook for Medicare than for Social Security. In fiscal year 2010, the two Medicare trust funds combined had a deficit of $21 billion, consisting of a surplus of $9 billion in the Supplementary Medical Insurance (Part B) fund, which was more than offset by a deficit of $30 billion in the Hospital Insurance (Part A) fund.[45] The Patient Protection and Affordable Care Act (PPACA) of 2010, to the extent that it aims to reduce health care costs in the overall system, is designed to reduce Medicare costs as well, at least in the long run.[46] According to estimates by the Congressional Budget Office, while overall health care costs (and Medicare costs) will be reduced somewhat, the reform does not involve a major downward shift in health care costs.[47]

Reform proposals have been especially aimed at reducing the incentives for physicians and hospitals to order expensive treatments for Medicare patients and to reduce the possibilities for fraudulent charges. Holding down reimbursement rates slowed the slide toward a Medicare deficit, and on the agenda for longer-term reform is moving more people into managed care organizations and away from individual physicians. Perhaps the most controversial reform proposal in recent years was the reform suggested by Congressman Paul Ryan (R-WI), as part of the House budget resolution in 2011. The Ryan plan would have created a cap on the amount that the federal government could spend on each beneficiary. Spending over the amount of the cap would be the responsibility of the consumer. This proposed change would have fundamentally changed Medicare and shifted much of the financial risk to beneficiaries. In addition, the House budget resolution advocated increasing the Medicare eligibility age from 65 to 67, beginning in 2022.[48]

Medicaid

The second-largest federal health program, but one that is not funded by the payroll tax, is Medicaid. It is funded by federal and state tax revenues as opposed to payroll taxes. In aggregate, the federal government pays about 57% of the costs of Medicaid, with state and local governments paying the remainder. This federal percentage will increase, as the federal government has committed, as a part of the new health reform law, to pick up 100% of the cost of newly eligible beneficiaries through 2016, and 90% of the cost after that through 2020.[49] From 1970 through 2010, total federal Medicaid spending increased from $2.7 billion to almost $273 billion, which represented a sixfold increase in the size of the program as a percentage of GDP (from 0.3% to 1.9%).[50] Medicaid provides medical care to the poor and the medically indigent (persons who are not classified as poor but who cannot afford medical care). Medicaid and SSI are not trust programs as defined earlier, because their funds come from general tax revenues and not revenues earmarked for special trust funds. (For a discussion of Medicaid, see the chapter on intergovernmental relations.)

Unemployment Insurance

The second largest insurance trust for state governments is unemployment insurance (UI). This program is administered by the states within a framework imposed by the federal government. A floor on benefits is set nationally, with states having the option of exceeding the floor. The program is supported by payroll taxes paid mainly by employers, although in a few states employees are required to make supplementary payments. It is expected to generate sufficient revenues during prosperous periods to cover payments to unemployed workers during recessionary periods. State programs can sometimes run into a deficit situation, such as during a sustained recession or occasionally because of temporary timing differences between payments into the funds and payments out. In such cases, the federal government lends money to the states but expects repayment with interest. Obviously, a state with a declining tax base can face severe problems in financing its unemployment insurance program. In addition, a sustained period of unemployment will deplete state resources and will typically require the federal government to step in and extend unemployment benefits beyond the regular UI benefits. In fact, during the recession that started in 2007, state governments had to borrow $42 billion from the federal Treasury just to finance their UI costs.[51]

Workers' Compensation

Another important insurance trust at the state level is workers' compensation, which provides cash benefits to persons who, because of job-related injuries and illnesses, are unable to work. Accidents at work may disable people temporarily or permanently. Poor working conditions can cause physical and mental health problems. In addition to cash benefits, the program pays for medical care and rehabilitation services.

Property Taxes

Taxes on wealth are based on accumulated value in some asset rather than on current earnings from the asset. Real and personal property, financial assets, and equipment are important types of wealth that sometimes are subject to taxation. The wealth tax that is most important in the eyes of taxpayers, however, is the real property or real estate tax. The property tax is the one most reviled by taxpayers, largely because it is regarded by many as the most unfair. In fact, in a 2005 Gallup poll more than twice the Americans responding to a survey question (42%) rated the property tax as the "worst" (least fair) tax after the next most hated tax, the federal income tax (20%).[52]

This tax is the almost exclusive domain of local governments. Despite forecasts of its demise, the property tax remains the largest single own-source generator of revenue for local governments (it is exceeded only by intergovernmental revenue), although it has declined in recent years relative to other state and local taxes.

The property tax funds almost 75% of locally raised school district revenues. In recent years, courts in at least 17 states, however, have overturned their states' financing systems that relied heavily on local property taxes.[53] The argument is that despite state aid to local school districts, almost sole reliance on the property tax to finance education at the local level means unequal education opportunities across the state (see the chapter on intergovernmental relations). The property tax is also the most important source of local own-source revenue for funding urban services in developing countries, although user charges (discussed in the chapter on budgeting for transaction-based revenues) may be a faster growing source of local revenue in the more prosperous emerging market economies.[54]

The justification for using the property tax as the major revenue source for local government is that the services provided by local government supposedly increase the economic value of one's property. It is widely thought that people select their place of residence based on the quality of local schools and other public services. In high-quality service jurisdictions, housing costs are typically higher, reflecting higher costs for delivering services and higher expectations of home buyers for quality services. Property taxes reimburse local government for higher-quality services. The argument goes as follows: If more general taxes, such as the sales tax, were used to finance services that benefit property owners, then property owners would be less aware of the costs of those services and therefore insist on more and higher-quality services. Evidence has been found to support this argument in developing countries, where demand for urban services is much higher in cities that do not use property and other local taxes and charges to finance those services.[55]

The property tax is also less susceptible to tax avoidance than other broad-based taxes because it is clearly visible and is immobile. People can buy goods in other jurisdictions or order goods over the Internet and easily avoid paying sales tax. Property taxes, by comparison, are difficult to avoid. To the extent that they operate as a quasi-price for the public services provided in a given jurisdiction, property taxes are justified on the basis of the benefit principle, as described above. One argument is that homeowners understand that the value of local public services substantially affects the value of their homes, and that they are vigilant in their control of local government largely for that reason.[56]

One way to tie the benefits of services affecting property values to taxes on property is through *tax increment financing* (see the chapter on capital finance and debt management for discussion of bond issues backed by expected tax incremental increases). Tax increment financing has been used in redevelopment of inner cities to capitalize on the economic and financial gains that stem from a major rehabilitation project for a contiguous area usually characterized by urban blight and abandoned properties. Prior to city government action, many property owners in such areas derive no benefits from their properties, and the city is able to collect little or no property tax. A redevelopment project changes conditions so that the property in the redeveloped area attains new value, and the property tax gains from that new value are set aside to pay for financing the redevelopment. Some use also has been made of tax increment financing in rural areas, but it is not as valuable a tool there. Property tax rates are typically much lower in rural areas, land values are more volatile, and investors in bonds to support rural infrastructure tax increment funded projects perceive higher risks.[57]

The main policy issue with the property tax is its regressive nature. Higher-income taxpayers tend to have a larger proportion of their wealth in assets that are not subject to the property tax. As a consequence, these taxpayers generally pay a disproportionately lower property tax (as a percentage of their income) as compared with middle- and lower-income taxpayers, whose only major asset may be their homes. For middle- and lower-income taxpayers, most of their wealth is being taxed each year. For renters, the regressive effects of the property tax depend on the extent to which the landlord can pass on the property tax through the rent. For all these reasons, the regressive nature of the property tax fuels controversy. In addition, the property tax is relatively complicated to implement and to maintain. Because the local jurisdiction must establish the tax base (the value of each property within the jurisdiction) rather than basing it on some external objective source, updating the tax base for the property tax is always controversial when carried out.

Tax Base

The base of the real property tax is the assessed value of the land and any improvements on it, such as homes, factories, and other structures. The value is what the property would sell for if placed on the market. Value for commercial and industrial property is sometimes reflected in the income earned by a corporation from the property or facility.

Often the assessed value of property may increase beyond the ability of taxpayers to afford the tax bills. One leading example of this would be in cases where there are rapidly rising property values, and longtime residents (who might not be able to afford to buy their houses in the current market) experience ever-increasing tax bills. These residents may be "property rich" but "income poor." Many states and localities have instituted *homestead exemptions* to address this sort of problem. Under these exemptions, a set initial amount is excluded from assessed valuation. This would tend to benefit those individuals with homes that have lower assessed values, since a higher percentage of the assessed value would be exempt from the property tax for those properties.

Another such issue arises in the case of farmland in metropolitan areas. As metropolitan areas expand and encroach upon farming areas, the value of the land increases even though the use remains unchanged. Situations emerge in which taxes rise beyond what farmers can afford and create a market incentive for the land to be sold and subdivided for homes and other development. All states provide some form of protection for farmland as a means of preserving rural land and discouraging urban sprawl, with reduced tax assessments for farming and other undeveloped land being the most common method. Often these tax breaks are really postponements. If the land is later sold for subdivision and housing at a value much higher than the land's worth as farmland, the seller must then pay back property taxes reflecting the residential use tax rate. As with other tax preferences, property tax reductions to preserve farmland can have unintended consequences. One study of Pennsylvania's program concluded that it preserved land in rural areas where population pressure is light, so the need for preservation is small.[58] Many states also buy the development rights from property owners as a way of preserving land for open space or other purposes.

Many properties are completely tax exempt in the United States. Federal and state land is normally exempt from local property taxes, for example, although these jurisdictions may make payments in lieu of taxation. Places of worship, such as churches, synagogues, and mosques, are tax exempt, as are most parsonages and other related properties. Nonprofit hospitals, YMCAs and YWCAs, nonprofit cemeteries, and the like are usually tax exempt as well.

When tax-exempt properties account for a large proportion of a jurisdiction's potential tax base, the effects of tax exemption can be severe. Some governments have aggressively challenged the tax-exempt status of some nonprofit organizations. The basis for the challenge is that some nonprofit organizations produce for-profit goods and services. Philadelphia, for example, has employed a five-part test. To remain exempt from property and other taxes, a nonprofit has to prove that it "advances a charitable purpose; gives away a substantial portion of its services; benefits people who are legitimate subjects of charity; relieves government of some of its burden; and operates entirely free of profit motives."[59] However, Philadelphia lacks the authority to force those nonprofits that do not meet the tests to pay property taxes. Instead, it asks, with some success, for voluntary payments in lieu of taxes.

A different situation may exist in cases where state governments grant blanket local property tax exemptions. In this case, the state government makes decisions that cost local governments money, and these exemptions may not be directly targeted toward those individuals that most need tax relief. In many such instances, the lost local property tax revenue is replaced by the state government. A study of a homestead exemption program in New York State suggests that there is some evidence that local governments are less efficient in the provision of local public services because those services are funded to a lesser extent by local taxes than by state assistance. The argument here is that, to the extent that state taxes are financing these services, this reduces pressure on local officials to cut back on costs to provide a given level of output.[60] The recession that began in 2007 differed from other recent recessions in that there were substantial dislocations in the housing market, which resulted in depressed property tax bases across the entire country.[61]

Assessment

After registering all properties in the taxing jurisdiction, the first major step to generating revenue from the tax is to assess the value of the properties. Local governments do not, in fact, have a direct way of measuring the actual market value of all properties in their jurisdiction. At any given time, the local government can know directly what recent properties have sold for, but this is only a small fraction of all the properties in the registered base. This creates a substantial challenge, in that they need to establish an assessed value for each property absent real information on the sales price of most properties.

Many governments use the *market data approach* to assessment. In this method, properties that have not sold are assessed by comparison to similar properties where a market price can be observed. The greatest challenge here is ensuring that properties that are assumed to be comparable are comparable in fact. The probability of doing this can be improved by inspecting individual properties and cataloguing their characteristics, but this is a time-consuming process, particularly if done on an annual basis. Adjustments to property values may be done annually or only once every several years.

While the goal in many jurisdictions is to assess each property at its full market value, in practice many jurisdictions assess parcels at a percentage or fraction of the full market value. The ratio of the assessed value to the market value is known as the *assessment ratio*. A home whose market value is $120,000 would be assessed at only $24,000 if the assessment ratio were 20%. In practice, it should make no difference whether the full value or a fraction of it is used. Fractional assessment simply requires a higher tax rate than market value assessment to produce the same revenue.

Taxpayers may find some psychological solace in fractional assessment, but problems arise in cases where properties within the same jurisdiction are assessed at different fractions of their market values. This occurs, for example, if reassessments are done on different properties at different times. If some properties are assessed at one percentage of market value and other properties at a different percentage, then the tax burden is no longer proportionate to the value of the property. This is less likely to be an issue where properties are assessed at 100% of market value, particularly because taxpayers are much more likely to know whether their property has been overassessed in this case. Even where the goal is assessing at full market value, fractional assessment may be used to differentiate types of properties. For example, rural property may be assessed at a lower fraction than highly developed property.

Inaccurate and inconsistent assessment practices can cause problems of both horizontal and vertical equity. Horizontal equity problems exist because properties that have the same market value in fact are assessed at different rates, resulting in taxpayers who should be paying the same level of tax paying different levels. Numerous studies have found evidence of horizontal inequity because of lack of data, assessor error, or bias.[62] Vertical equity concerns exist when properties of different market values are assessed at different percentages of those market values. A study found that, in particular, lower-valued houses were assessed at closer to their full market value than higher-valued houses. This means that less-affluent taxpayers pay a higher percentage of local property taxes than would be the case were all properties valued at the same percentage of full market value.[63]

For a local government instituting the property tax for the first time, the valuation process is almost overwhelming. Traditional valuation procedures involve comprehensive tax mapping to locate every property. An assessor must visit each property, measuring the foundation to determine square footage, noting construction details, and recording information about the condition of the structure.

For most jurisdictions in the United States, properties have been constructed under building permits that require supplying information about construction details to the local jurisdiction. Periodic inspections of the properties when under construction, conducted by local code enforcement officers or building inspectors, provide additional information. A database, then, can be devised using existing building records and information about sales of properties when deeds are transferred. As new structures are built, they can be added to the database.

Exhibit 5–2 shows a property tax valuation system in Orange County, North Carolina, that is considered a model for the country. Techniques such as those used in Orange County help to foster a perception of fairness among taxpayers. Property owners conclude that they are paying their fair share and are not being overcharged while other taxpayers are being undercharged. If these equity considerations are met, then the likelihood of a taxpayer revolt is minimized. However, it does not make the property tax popular, as it is likely that it is the most hated tax in the country.

Exhibit 5–2 Property Tax Valuation in Orange County, NC

Orange County, North Carolina, has what is considered a model property tax valuation system.

It is fully computerized and includes diverse information about each property in the county. Besides information about the location of each lot, the size of the structure, and the number of baths, a drawing of the lot and the location of the structure on it are included in the computerized file and can be displayed onscreen. Of course, printed maps of properties are available as well.

Characteristics of Properties
- Property address
- Plot map and reference to deed register
- Area of lot (square footage)
- Occupancy (single-family dwelling, two-family, multifamily)
- Size of dwelling (square footage of living space)
- Number of structures
- Number of stories of each structure
- Basement, slab, or crawl space
- Foundation construction method

- Exterior construction method
- Roof type and roofing materials
- Number of rooms
- Number of bathrooms
- Number of bedrooms
- Year built
- Number of fireplaces
- Interior finish
- Floor type
- Built-in appliances
- HVAC system
- Special features (spas, etc.)
- Landscaping
- Land topography
- Utility connections
- Paved or unpaved driveway
- Last sale price and date

Source: Data extracted from Office of the Tax Assessor (2002). Orange County database. Hillsborough, NC: Orange County.

Tax Rates

Property tax rates are a percentage of assessed value. The rate is expressed in mills, with one mill being one-tenth of 1%. As applied to property taxes, a one-mill rate yields $1 of revenue for every $1,000 of assessed value. A property tax rate of 68.5 mills as applied to a $120,000 property assessed at 20% of market value would yield $1,644 ($120 \times 0.2 \times 68.5 = 1,644$).

Local jurisdictions often determine the annual property tax rate by calculating backward from projected expenditures minus other revenues. The property tax increase is then expected to make up the budget gap. The community's decision makers simply determine how many additional mills will be needed to close the gap. Of course, attempts are made to avoid such tax increases by keeping expenditures as low as considered possible. The process of adjusting the tax rate to match expenditure requirements probably accounts for the great popularity of the property tax among local officials. This tax is one over which officials have considerable control, unlike other taxes that depend on the economy (income and sales taxes) or intergovernmental aid.

Many local governments in areas of rapidly increasing property values have found that they are able to accommodate budgetary increases above the base level at declining property tax rates. In most of these cases, the rate of assessment increase exceeds the percentage of rate reduction, thus resulting in a rising tax bill. The key decision for any local government involves how often to reassess properties. With the housing boom of the 1990s and 2000s, substantial incentives existed to reassess properties frequently in order to take advantage of increasing property values and therefore be able to produce increasing levels of revenue at declining property tax rates. This may result from increased demands on the part of citizens for additional services, or from desires by government officials to expand government.[64] As noted above, these trends toward "easy money" from the property tax at declining rates reversed themselves dramatically after 2008. Taxpayers expected governments to downgrade the assessed value of their property, since they knew that in many cases there had been precipitous declines in market values. Even though property values had dropped, however, this did not decrease the need that local governments had for property tax revenue. This left most local governments in the difficult position of having to raise property tax rates or reduce service levels, or both.

Circuit Breakers

As taxes rise, some property owners may encounter considerable difficulty in paying their tax bills and may even be forced to sell their homes and move into rental housing. To alleviate this problem, several states use *circuit breaker* systems that set a limit on taxes, particularly for low-income elderly persons. A qualified homeowner pays an amount up to the limit, and the state pays any additional amount owed. Often a state bases the limit on some income criterion: when property taxes exceed a specified percentage of the taxpayer's income, the state pays the difference.[65]

Personal Property

Besides taxing real property, some jurisdictions tax personal property. For individuals, such property includes furniture, vehicles, clothing, jewelry, and the like. Intangible personal property includes stocks, bonds, and other financial instruments such as mortgages. For corporations, personal property includes equipment, raw materials, and items in inventory. Taxes on personal property are unpopular and subject to considerable evasion.

Taxing and Spending Limitations

Although citizens seemingly have had little opportunity to affect taxes and spending other than through the process of selecting elected representatives, 1978 changed all that. In that year, California voters approved Proposition 13, an initiative that limited the property tax rate to 1% of market value. That provision by itself would have required a rollback in taxes, but an additional provision further cut taxes. Property assessments were to be returned to their values in 1975, when property was considerably less expensive.

Although tax limitation measures were not new, Proposition 13 began a new era in which government officials were forced to consider taxpayer reaction and to limit taxes and spending.[66] Many state and local governments followed California's lead during the late 1970s and early 1980s by passing statutory limits or, in some cases, adding restrictions to state constitutions. California voters approved Proposition 4 in 1979, which limited both state and local government expenditures. In the following years, restrictive measures were adopted in about half of the states. Massachusetts, which had come to be known as "Taxachusetts," gained notoriety in 1980 as a result of its passage of Proposition 2 1/2. This measure required that local governments reduce taxes by 15% each year until they equaled 2.5% of market value.[67]

"By 1990, 21 states had enacted potentially binding limitations and 13 had enacted nonbinding limitations on the finances of their local governments."[68] The elections of 1994 and 1996 brought more conservative control to many state legislatures and ushered in a new round of tax limitation proposals.[69] Oregon, Colorado, and Missouri also passed tax or spending limitations in the mid- to late 1990s.

The original stimulus behind what came to be known as the taxpayers' revolt was the sharp rise in property values and, consequently, tax bills, but a more generally negative attitude emerged—the attitude that government officials have an insatiable appetite for spending. This attitude has been on display once again in recent years, with the rise of the Tea Party movement. This movement has, as one of its core values, the notion that virtually all taxes, at all levels of government, are too high. Besides taxing too much, governments allegedly use the revenues to interfere needlessly in the lives of citizens and the operations of corporations. Property taxes remain one of the most criticized forms of taxation. This is probably because of dissatisfaction with the results school systems are producing, which are funded almost entirely by property taxes.[70] The result has been several types of tax and expenditure limitations. One review classified them into five categories:

1. Overall property tax limitation (for example, limit maximum annual percentage increase)
2. Specific property tax limitation (for example, limit use of property tax to finance education)
3. Property tax levy limit (for example, implement ceiling on amount of tax)
4. General revenue or general expenditure increase limit (for example, limit annual expenditure increase to a specific limit)
5. Property tax assessment increase limit (limit the assessed value increase)[71]

Most of these limitations focus on the property tax specifically, but the fourth (overall revenue or expenditure limits) is more broadly restrictive and can apply at the state as well as the local level. Taxpayers' concerns have caused many state and local governments to increase communication with the public on what is accomplished with tax dollars and how taxes are kept to a minimum. Minnesota, for example, enacted a law requiring the construction of an overall index calculating the cost of everything residents pay to the government as a percentage of personal income. Not only are taxes included, but so are all fees, charges, and any other payment to government. The index is kept for different state departments and individual local governments so that citizens throughout the state can compare their own government with others and with limitation guidelines.[72]

The effects of these limitations has varied, but in most cases local governments made up for the revenue loss through other sources, usually non-general-revenue sources. In some cases, state governments almost immediately made up for the shortfall.[73] Overall, spending may have declined in some jurisdictions, but not enough to show up in aggregate figures for individual states. There is some evidence, however, that these limitations are more constraining on local property taxes in the long run than in the short run.[74] The main effects seem to have been sixfold.

First, state legislatures and local governments are much more reluctant to initiate new programs and especially to propose tax increases or new taxes. In the case of new programs, this is presumably because there is more uncertainty surrounding the affordability of these programs in the future. The reluctance to impose tax increases probably relates to knowledge of the underlying disposition of taxpayers toward these increases in states with tax and expenditure limitations (TELs).

Second, combined with major cutbacks in federal aid to states and localities, as well as state aid to local governments, the limitation movement set these governments on an imaginative hunt for alternative finance measures. The significantly greater use of impact fees, discussed earlier, and other direct charges to those benefiting from services was an outgrowth of the tax revolt.

Third, states provided increased financial assistance to hard-pressed local governments. For example, when Michigan ran into problems with property tax funding for education, the state increased the sales tax and, in turn, used state funds for formerly local education funds. A more explicit example is Oregon's experience with Ballot Measure 5, which required the state to replace lost property tax revenue with state aid, thus shifting many of the fiscal effects of the initiatives to the state government.[75] Sometimes that state aid has come at a price—namely, various strings attached by states for their aid. One simple example is that Oregon prohibited local governments from giving their employees salary increases greater than those given to state employees.

Fourth, overall expenditures have been cut somewhat and some services have been reduced, either in quality or quantity, as a means of curbing spending.[76] Essential services such as law enforcement and fire protection have been maintained, albeit at decreased levels. Budget problems forced cutbacks in maintenance of buildings and purchase of new vehicles and equipment.[77] Overall, however, tax and expenditure limitations did not materially change the relative amounts that state and local governments spend on government functions.[78] Some evidence indicates that spending cuts have produced long-term quality decline, at least in some services. For example, public school student performance has declined in several states that have imposed expenditure limitations, even after controlling for a number of other possible influences.[79] Moreover, a 2006 study argues that TELs tend to have had a positive increase on economic growth at the state level, while local-level effects on economic growth have been negative, but only in the short run.[80]

Fifth, tax and expenditure limitations have had differential effects on the capacity of local governments to rely on local property taxes to deliver services. A nationwide study found that these limitations do not offer a uniform constraint across jurisdictions, but rather represent a greater constraint for some than others. In the case of both general-purpose governments (cities or counties) and school districts, there is significant variation across these jurisdictions within single metropolitan areas. In particular, the effects seem to be "greatest within counties comprising the urban core and those with relatively more disadvantaged populations."[81]

Sixth, tax and expenditure limitation enacted through citizen referenda have been found to be more constraining than those enacted through legislation. A 2010 study concluded that the legislatively enacted TELs are more likely to have loopholes that enable governments to wiggle out of them when they become too constraining.[82]

One clear conclusion that can be reached about TELs is that their effects are complex and go far beyond simply constraining taxing and spending. This conclusion has been sustained over 30 years of research and experience with TELs. A 2009 Lincoln Institute of Land Policy study surveyed officials in municipalities that had enacted TELs, and the results were decidedly mixed. While 36% said that their TELs had impacted budgets, for example, 40% said they had had no clear effect. Furthermore, while 20% said that the TELs in their cities had reduced service provision, 13% said that they had sought out new revenue sources.[83] It is difficult to reach the conclusion that tax and expenditure limitations clearly limit either taxes or spending; their effects are much more complicated. Still, the rise of the Tea Party movement likely signals a renewed interest in such budget-limiting rules.

SUMMARY

Governments use numerous revenue sources to support their operations, with taxes obviously being one of the most important types. In devising a tax system, governments need to consider the adequacy of the tax revenue being produced, the equity of the tax system (on both ability-to-pay grounds and on the basis of who benefits from local public services), economic efficiency, collectability, and political feasibility. Taxes on personal and corporate income are important sources of income for the federal government and state governments. They are highly complex taxes, and the personal income tax in particular is usually adjusted to individual taxpayer conditions. Payroll taxes are typically used to finance particular services, and are earmarked for those purposes. By far the largest payroll taxes are for Social Security and Medicare. The property tax, which is the largest tax for local governments, is heavily influenced by assessment practices, which can substantially affect the equity and the production of the tax. The use of property taxes is constrained by the imposition of constitutional or statutory limitations.

NOTES

1. Walden, M. (2003). Dynamic revenue curves for North Carolina taxes. *Public Budgeting & Finance, 23*, Winter, 49–64.
2. Farrelly, M. (2008). The impact of tobacco control programs on adult smoking. *American Journal of Public Health, 98*, 304–309.
3. Herszenhorn, D., & Stolberg, S. (2010). Obama defends tax deal, but his party stays hostile. *New York Times,* December 7.
4. Lambert, P., & Naughton, H. (2009). The equal absolute sacrifice principle revisited. *Journal of Economic Surveys, 23*(2), 328–349.
5. The House Republican plan for America's job creators. (2011). *GOP.gov.* Retrieved February 21, 2012, from http://www.gop.gov/indepth/jobs/taxes.
6. Internal Revenue Service (2010). *Circular E: Employers tax guide,* December 29, 1.
7. U.S. Congressional Budget Office (2010). *Average federal tax rates in 2007* (p. 6). Washington, DC: U.S. Government Printing Office. Retrieved February 24, 2012, from http://www.cbo.gov/sites/default/files/cbofiles/attachments/AverageFedTaxRates2007.pdf.
8. U.S. Congressional Budget Office (2010). *Average federal tax rates in 2007,* 6.
9. Weiss, E. (2005). D.C.'s bid to impose commuter tax denied. *Washington Post,* November 5.
10. Farrelly, M. (2008). The impact of tobacco control programs on adult smoking. *American Journal of Public Health, 98*, 304–309.

11. McClure, C. E., Jr., & Zodrow, G. R. (1994). The study and practice of income tax policy. In J. M. Quigley & E. Smolensky (Eds.), *Modern public finance* (p. 185). Cambridge, MA: Harvard University Press.

12. Tax Foundation. (2010). *State Sales, Gasoline, Cigarette, and Alcohol Taxes.* Washington, DC: Tax Foundation. Retrieved February 24, 2012, from http://www.taxfoundation.org/news/show/245.html.

13. Buenker, J. (1981). The ratification of the federal income tax amendment. *Cato Journal, 1*(1), 183–223.

14. Nelson, S. C., & Cronin, J. (2006). Adjusted gross income. In J. Cordes, R. Ebel, & J. Gravelle (Eds.), *Encyclopedia of taxation and tax policy* (p. 3). Washington, DC: The Urban Institute Press.

15. Pollack, S. (1996). *The failure of U.S. tax policy: revenue and politics.* University Park, PA: Pennsylvania State University Press.

16. Perez, W. (2011). Tax planning guide. *About.com.* Retrieved December 20, 2011, from http://taxes.about.com/od/preparingyourtaxes/a/personal_exempt.htm.

17. Green, R. (2005). Mortgage interest deduction. In J. Cordes, R. Ebel, & J. Gravelle (Eds.), *Encyclopedia of taxation and tax policy*, 260–261.

18. Maguire, S. (2005). State and local tax deductibility. In J. Cordes, R. Ebel, & J. Gravelle (Eds.), *Encyclopedia of taxation and tax policy*, 367–370.

19. Randolph, W. (2005). Charitable deductions. In J. Cordes, R. Ebel, & J. Gravelle (Eds.), *Encyclopedia of taxation and tax policy*, 51–53.

20. Slemrod, J. (2006). The role of misconceptions in support for regressive tax reform. *National Tax Journal, 59,* 57–75.

21. Ohlemacher, S. (2011). 999 plan: Herman Cain's proposal would raise taxes on 84 percent, study shows. *Huffington Post,* October 18. Retrieved February 21, 2012, from http://www.huffingtonpost.com/2011/10/18/999-plan-herman-cain_n_1018462.html.

22. Marron, D. (2011). Cutting tax preferences is key to tax reform and deficit reduction. *Testimony Before Senate Committee on the Budget* (p. 4). February 2. Retrieved February 21, 2012, from http://www.taxpolicycenter.org/publications/url.cfm?ID=1001492.

23. Dowd, T. (2005). Distinguishing between short-term and long-term recipients of the earned income tax credit. *National Tax Journal, 58,* 807–828.

24. Dickert-Conlin, S., Fitzpatrick, K., & Hanson, A. (2005). Utilization of tax credits by low-income individuals. *National Tax Journal, 58,* 743–785.

25. Weiner, D. (2006). Alternative minimum tax. In J. Cordes, R. Ebel, & J. Gravelle (Eds.), *Encyclopedia of taxation and tax policy*, 11.

26. U.S. Congressional Budget Office (2010). *The Individual Alternative Minimum Tax* (p. 1). Washington, DC: U.S. Government Printing Office.

27. U.S. Congressional Budget Office. (2010). *The Individual Alternative Minimum Tax,* 1.

28. U.S. Congressional Budget Office. (2010). *The Individual Alternative Minimum Tax,* 1.

29. Rosenberg, C., & Reuben, K. (2010). State individual income tax rates. *Tax Notes,* May 10, 697.

30. Schneider, F., Buehn, A., & Montenegro, C. (2010). Shadow economies all over the world. *World Bank,* July, 24.

31. Congressional Budget and Impoundment Control Act of 1974 (P.L. 93–344, 88 Stat.), 297, 299.

32. Gravelle, J. G. (2006). Tax expenditures. In J. Cordes, R. Ebel, & J. Gravelle (Eds.), *Encyclopedia of taxation and tax policy*, 406–408.

33. U.S. Office of Management and Budget (2011). *Budget of the United States government, fiscal year 2012, analytical perspectives* (p. 252). Washington, DC: U.S. Government Printing Office.

34. U.S. Congressional Budget Office (2005). *Corporate income tax rates: international comparisons* (p. 22). Washington, DC: U.S. Government Printing Office.

35. Cornia, G., Edmiston, K., Sjoquist, D., & Wallace, S., et al. (2005). The disappearing state corporate income tax. *National Tax Journal, 48,* 115–138; United States Bureau of the Census (2010). *State government tax collections: summary report.* Washington, DC: Bureau of the Census.

36. Organization for Economic Cooperation and Development (2010). *Corporate income tax rates* [spreadsheet]. Paris, France: OECD.

37. U.S. Congressional Budget Office (2011). Historical budget tables. From *The budget and economic outlook: fiscal years 2012 to 2021.* Washington, DC: U.S. Government Printing Office.

38. U.S. Social Security Administration (2010). *Annual statistical supplement to the Social Security Bulletin*, 1. Retrieved February 21, 2012, from http://www.ssa.gov/policy/docs/statcomps/supplement/.

39. Daly, M. C., & Burkhauser, R. V. (2000). *The Supplemental Security Income program.* San Francisco, CA: Federal Reserve Bank of San Francisco.

40. U.S. Social Security Administration (2010). *Annual statistical supplement to the Social Security Bulletin*, 1.

41. U.S. Congressional Budget Office (2011). *The budget and economic outlook: fiscal years 2012 to 2021* (pp. 122–123). Washington: U.S. Government Printing Office.

42. U.S. Congressional Budget Office (2011). *CBO's long-term projections for Social Security: additional information* (August, p. 8). Washington, DC: U.S. Government Printing Office. Retrieved February 24, 2012, from http://www.cbo.gov/publication/41644.

43. U.S. Congressional Budget Office (2011). Historical budget data. Appendix E of *The budget and economic outlook: fiscal years 2012 to 2021*, 141.

44. See Chapter 4 of Joyce, P. (2011). *The Congressional Budget Office: honest numbers, power and policymaking.* Washington, DC: Georgetown University Press.

45. U.S. Congressional Budget Office. (2011). Trust funds and measures of federal debt. In *The budget and economic outlook: fiscal years 2012–2021*, 122.

46. The Patient Protection and Affordable Care Act (P.L. 111-148).

47. See Chapter 7, "The Obama Health Reform," in Joyce, P. (2011). *The Congressional Budget Office: honest numbers, power and policymaking.*

48. U.S. House of Representatives, Committee on the Budget (2011). *The path to prosperity*, April 5. Retrieved February 21, 2012, from http://budget.house.gov/UploadedFiles/PathToProsperity FY2012.pdf.

49. MacGillis, A. (2010). Study of health care law rebuts state protests on Medicaid costs. *Washington Post*, May 26.

50. Historical budget data. In U.S. Congressional Budget Office (2011). *The budget and economic outlook: fiscal years 2011 to 2021.*

51. Burtless, G. (2011). The administration's new plan to revamp the unemployment insurance tax: a good policy that can be greatly improved [blog post]. *Brookings Up Front Blog*, March 20.

52. Fisher, G. W. (1996). *The worst tax? a history of the property tax in America.* Lawrence, KS: University Press of Kansas; Taxes [Gallup poll]. (2011). *Gallup.com.* Retrieved December 20, 2011, from www.gallup .com/poll/1714/taxes.aspx?

53. Fischel, W. A. (2002). School finance litigation and property tax revolts: how undermining local control turns voters away from public education. In *Developments in school finance: fiscal proceedings from the annual state data conference, July 1999 and July 2000* (p. 79–127). Washington, DC: National Center for Education Statistics. For a discussion of the trends toward school litigation focused on problems with the property tax, see Kenyon, D. (2007). *The property tax-school funding dilemma.* Cambridge, MA: Lincoln Institute of Land Policy.

54. Johnson, R. W., & McCullough, J. S. (1996). *Case study on urban local government finance.* Paper presented at the Asian Development Bank seminar on Urban Infrastructure Finance in Asia, Research Triangle Park, North Carolina, Research Triangle Institute, April 17.

55. Bahl, R. W., & Linn, J. F. (1992). *Urban public finance in developing countries.* New York, NY: Oxford University Press; Bird, R. M. (1992). *Tax policy and economic development.* Baltimore, MD: Johns Hopkins University Press.

56. Fischel, W. (2001). Homeowners, municipal corporate governance, and the benefit view of the property tax. *National Tax Journal, 54*, 157–173.

57. Petersen, J. E. (2000). TIFs in the hinterlands. *Governing, 13*, August, 68.

58. Kelsey, T. W., & Kreahling, K. S. (1996). Preferential tax assessments for farmland preservation: influence of population pressures on fiscal impacts. *State and Local Government Review, 28*, 49–57.

59. Lemov, P. (1995). Tin-cup taxation: local governments are pressuring nonprofits to chip in to cover the costs of the services they use. *Governing, 8*, October, 25–26.

60. Eom, T., & Rubenstein, R. (2006). Do state-funded property tax exemptions increase local government efficiency? An analysis of New York State's STAR program. *Public Budgeting & Finance, 26*, Spring, 66–87.

61. Urban Institute (2008). The housing crisis and what it means for state and local governments. *Urban Institute Policy Nutshells*, February 26.
62. Allen, M., & Dare, W. (2002). Identifying determinants of horizontal property tax inequity: evidence from Florida. *Journal of Real Estate Research, 24*, 153–164.
63. Allen, M. (2003). Measuring vertical property tax inequity in multifamily property markets. *Journal of Real Estate Research, 25*, 171–184. For a good overview of the extant research on both vertical and horizontal property tax inequity, see Sirmans, G., Gatzlaff, D., & Macpherson, D. (2008). Horizontal and vertical inequity in real property taxation. *Journal of Real Estate Literature,16*(2), 167–180.
64. Stine, W. (2005). Do budget maximizing public officials increase the probability of property reassessment? *Applied Economics, 37*, 2395–2405.
65. Monk, D. H. (1990). *Educational finance: an economic approach* (pp. 158–160). New York, NY: McGraw-Hill.
66. Rueben, K. (2000). The impact of initiatives on state and local government finance. *Municipal Finance Journal, 20*, 20–25; Hoene, C. (2004). Fiscal structure and the post-proposition 13 fiscal regime in California's cities. *Public Budgeting & Finance, 24*, Winter, 51–72.
67. Ladd, H. F., & Wilson, J. B. (1983). Who supports tax limitations: evidence from Massachusetts' proposition 2 1/2. *Journal of Policy Analysis and Management, 2*, 256–279; Moscovitch, E. (1985). Proposition 2 1/2. *Government Finance Review, 1*, October, 21–25; Wallin, B. (2004). The tax revolt in Massachusetts: revolution and reason. *Public Budgeting & Finance, 24*, Winter, 34–50.
68. Mullins, D. R., & Joyce, P. G. (1996). Tax and expenditure limitations and state and local fiscal structure: an empirical assessment. *Public Budgeting & Finance, 16*, Spring, 75–101.
69. Gold, S. D. (1996). State tax cuts of 1995: is something new afoot? *Public Budgeting & Finance, 16*, Spring, 3–22; National Association of State Budget Officers (1997). *1996 state tax initiatives.* Retrieved January 22, 2007, from http://www.nasbo.org/Policy_Resources/Taxes_Fees/taxib.html.
70. Bradbury, K. L., et al. (1998). School quality and Massachusetts enrollment shifts in the context of tax limitations. *New England Economic Review*, July/August, 3–20.
71. Mullins, D., & Joyce, P. (1996). Tax and expenditure limitations and state and local fiscal structure, an empirical assessment. *Public Budgeting & Finance, 16*, Spring, 77.
72. Minnesota Budget Project (2006). *Minnesota tax burdens: who pays and how much?* Retrieved January 20, 2007, from http://www.mncn.org/bp/incid01.htm (source no longer accessible).
73. McGuire, T. J. (1999). Proposition 13 and its offspring: for good or for evil? *National Tax Journal, 52*, 129–138.
74. Dye, R., et al. (2005). Are property tax limitations more binding over time? *National Tax Journal, 58*, 215–225.
75. Thompson, F., & Green, M. (2004). Vox populi? Oregon tax and expenditure limitation initiatives. *Public Budgeting & Finance, 24*, Winter, 73–87.
76. Brown, T. (2000). Constitutional tax and expenditure limitation in Colorado: the impact on municipal governments. *Public Budgeting & Finance, 20*, Fall, 29–50.
77. King-Meadows, T., & Lowery, D. (1996). The impact of the tax revolt era state fiscal caps: a research update. *Public Budgeting & Finance, 16*, Spring, 102–112.
78. Joyce, P. G., & Mullins, D. R. (1991). The changing fiscal structure of the state and local public sector: the impact of tax and expenditure limitations. *Public Administration Review, 51*, 244–245.
79. Downes, T. A., & Figlio, D. N. (1999). Do tax and expenditure limits provide a free lunch? evidence on the link between limits and public sector service quality. *National Tax Journal, 52*, 113–128.
80. Deller, S., & Stallman, J. (2006). Tax and expenditure limitations and economic growth. *Marquette Law Review, 90*, 497–554.
81. Mullins, D. (2004). Tax and expenditure limitations and the fiscal response of local government: asymmetric intra-local fiscal effects. *Public Budgeting & Finance, 24*, Winter, 111–147.
82. New, M. (2010). U.S. state tax and expenditure limitations: a comparative political analysis. *State Politics and Policy Quarterly, 10*, 25–50.
83. Brooks, L., & Phillips, J. (2009). Municipally imposed tax and spending limits. *Land Lines.* Lincoln Institute of Land Policy, April.

Budgeting for Revenues: Transaction-Based Revenue Sources

In addition to income, payroll, and wealth-based taxes covered in the previous chapter on budgeting for revenues, governments raise revenue from a number of sources that are based on largely voluntary transactions. The largest and most important of these is the general retail sales tax. There are also a number of sales taxes levied on specific goods, including taxes on luxury goods such as expensive automobiles, so-called sin taxes on liquor and cigarettes, and benefit-based excises on items like motor fuel. Governments have expanded their use of fees and charges, many of which are used to finance related services. Over the past 35 years, the use of lotteries and games of chance as a revenue source for state governments has mushroomed. Although having grown over the years, neither charges nor gambling revenues represent a primary source of revenue for general-purpose governments. Many special districts such as water and sewer authorities get the majority of their revenue from charges, however.

This chapter reviews each of these revenue sources, discussing their applications and the political and economic issues surrounding them. In doing so, we discuss how these revenue sources stack up relative to other criteria.

RETAIL SALES AND OTHER CONSUMPTION TAXES

Sales taxes are one of the most important sources of revenue for state governments. Forty-five of the 50 states (all but Alaska, Delaware, Montana, New Hampshire, and Oregon) levy a general sales tax, and it is the largest state-generated source of revenue for many of them.[1] All states have at least some selective sales taxes. Overall, the general and selective sales taxes account for more than 23% of total state general revenues from all sources. Income taxes are the second largest single general revenue source, at 19%, followed by user charges, which account for about 11% of general revenues. However, all taxes account for just more than 50% of state general revenues. If one looks at the sales tax as a proportion of tax revenues only, sales taxes account for almost half of state tax revenue.[2]

There are two types of sales taxes. The general sales tax is a tax on all (or most) consumed goods and sometimes services. Specific sales taxes are taxes on a particular type of good or service. There are also two varieties of sales tax. *Ad valorem* taxes are levied as a percentage of the purchase price of an item. If an item subject to a sales tax costs twice as much as another item subject to a sales tax, the tax paid is twice the amount as well. General sales taxes are *ad valorem* taxes.

Unit taxes, on the other, hand, are levied per unit of the item sold, without regard to price. This means that more expensive brands are taxed at the same level as less expensive brands. Gasoline, or cigarette, or liquor taxes, are usually unit taxes, since taxation is based on the gallons (in the case of gasoline or liquor) or packs (in the case of cigarettes) sold. The production from *ad valorem* taxes, for obvious reasons, tends to rise as prices increase, while unit taxes yield relatively flat revenues.

General Sales Taxes

The general sales tax is the largest revenue source for state governments and is used by many local governments as well. Many state governments raise as much as one-fourth to one-third of state tax revenue from this source. Some states raise as much as one-half. Sales tax revenues result from the size of the tax base—in this case, the value of the taxed goods that are sold—and the rates applied to that base.

Tax Base

While all three levels of government rely on some form of consumption tax, state governments are the most dependent, particularly on retail sales taxes. The base of any consumption tax is a product or class of goods (sometimes services) whose value is measured in terms of retail gross sales or receipts. The base is a function of which products and services are included and excluded. All states except Illinois exempt prescription medicines (Illinois taxes these at a lower rate of 1%), and 31 of the 45 states with sales taxes exclude food, except for that sold in restaurants, delis, or some specialty foods sold in grocery stores.[3] Some states have opted for reducing the sales tax rate on food compared to other taxed items, rather than eliminating it altogether.

Other commonly excluded items are clothing, household fuels, soaps, and some toiletries. Some items may be exempt from the general sales tax only because they are subject to another sales tax. Cigarettes, gasoline, and alcoholic beverages are examples of specific goods exempted from the general sales tax for this reason. States generally are not precluded from levying two taxes on one sale. Such double taxation may occur, for example, when a general sales tax and a specific sales tax are placed on cigarettes and alcoholic beverages.

The justification for these commodities' exemptions is typically that they make the sales tax less regressive, to the extent that the nontaxed items are necessities. The clearest case is food, where lower-income persons spend a larger percentage of their income on this commodity than higher-income persons. This same justification applies to the exemption for prescription and other medicines.[4] Tax exemptions for clothing are less clear on vertical equity grounds, although some states exempt only a portion of the cost of a given article of clothing (the first $100, for example) in an effort to offset this problem.

The most notable items not included in most sales tax bases are services, such as the professional services of doctors and lawyers, dry cleaners, or accountants. A Council of State Governments study found that consumption expenditures for tangible goods are less than those for services.[5] States that exclude services from the sales tax base may forgo considerable revenue, depending on the distribution between the "goods" and "services" economy in that state.

However, applying the sales tax to services is so unpopular that few states have implemented that option. Only three states (Hawaii, New Mexico, and South Dakota) tax most services.[6] In fact, when the State of Florida passed a law that applied the sales tax to services in 1986, it was forced to repeal that tax the next year when citizens and affected interests "discovered" the tax.[7]

The most debated current issue regarding the application of the sales tax concerns the ability of states to tax mail-order or Internet sales. As more and more commerce has switched from traditional retail outlets to mail-order or Internet outlets, state and local governments have lost substantial revenue because of the difficulty in enforcing the use tax (a tax paid by the purchaser on items where sales tax was not paid at purchase). **Exhibit 6–1** discusses the issues surrounding the taxation of mail-order and Internet sales.

Exhibit 6–1 Taxation of Mail-Order and Internet Sales

States currently have only limited authority to tax mail-order sales and have been lobbying Congress to pass legislation allowing full taxation. The reason is a simple one. Mail-order sales vastly increased starting in the 1980s and constitute a potentially lucrative source of revenue.

U.S. Supreme Court interpretations of the due process and interstate commerce clauses have been fairly restrictive on states' ability to tax interstate sales. A 1967 case (*National Bellas Hess, Inc. v. Department of Revenue, State of Illinois*) concluded that a mail-order firm had to have a substantial nexus of business in a state in the form of a physical presence. A 1992 case (*Quill Corporation v. North Dakota*) relaxed the so-called nexus doctrine, holding that the due process clause of the Constitution does not bar enforcement of North Dakota's use tax on the Quill Corporation, but on other grounds it still refused to overrule *Bellas Hess*.[1]

An additional complication is the growth of sales through cable and satellite television and other electronic commerce. Use of the Internet as a mechanism to place orders shipped interstate has become a significant mode of commerce, and it will continue to grow as more users gain access to electronic sources. One estimate put national losses from the failure to tax Internet sales nationwide at $11 billion in 2012, and at least $52 billion over the six-year period between 2007 and 2012. States with relatively large revenue losses, according to this estimate, included California ($8.7 billion), Texas ($4.0 billion), New York ($4.0 billion), and Florida ($3.7 billion).[2] Although the principle has not been tested in any court case so far, Internet commerce is being treated the same as interstate mail-order and phone sales. Recent research demonstrates a small, but statistically significant, relationship between the state sales tax rate and the propensity of consumers to purchase online, with higher sales tax rates leading to more online spending.[3]

There are a number of significant policy problems raised by the mail-order and Internet sales issue. First, as noted above, is the sheer magnitude of the revenue loss. This puts those states that rely more heavily on the sales tax (for example, those with only a

(Continued)

sales tax) at a significant disadvantage compared to states with both an income and a sales tax, or only an income tax. Second, there is the problem that it creates for traditional "bricks and mortar" businesses, whose costs—rent, for example—are higher than for online businesses, and who must include the tax in the cost of the price of their goods. Third, to the extent that some taxpayers can avoid paying the sales tax through Internet or mail-order purchasing, the tax burden is shifted to those who do not engage in these kinds of transactions. To the extent that traditional sales fall more heavily on lower-income individuals without access to the Internet, this would tend to make the sales tax more regressive.

In 1998, Congress passed the Internet Tax Freedom Act, which has been subsequently extended, the last time in 2007.[4] That act placed a moratorium on taxing Internet sales, or other taxes on Internet services or transactions. This moratorium is currently in effect through 2014. The initial 1998 Act included the appointment of an Advisory Commission on Electronic Commerce to deal with the issue.[5] The commission deadlocked without effectively solving the problem. In its wake, some states have taken matters into their own hands. Some states attempt to tax Internet purchases by asking taxpayers filing individual income tax returns to report on goods purchased from out of state through online sources, but have not created any effective enforcement mechanisms.

More generally, state governments have joined together to create the Streamlined Sales Tax Project. This project intends to simplify and make consistent across the states the application and administration of the sales tax. Success with this approach might overcome judicial objections to requiring retailers to collect sales taxes for all 45 states, each of which has a different system, as an undue burden.[6] Some research suggests that, under some circumstances, firms might have incentives to comply voluntarily with the collection of sales tax on Internet sales. The authors of this study, however, were not sanguine about the ability of states to simplify tax administration sufficiently to create widespread voluntary compliance.[7]

1. Coleman, H. A. (1992). Taxation of interstate mail-order sales. *Intergovernmental Perspective* 18, Winter, 9–14; *National Bellas Hess, Inc. v. Department of Revenue, State of Illinois* (1967). 386 U.S. 753; *Quill Corporation v. North Dakota* (1992). 504 U.S. 298.

2. Sparks, C., McCoskey, M., & Alvis, J. (2004). Can internet sales be taxed? *Public Finance and Mangement, 4*, 126; Bruce, D., Fox, W., & Luna, L. (2009). *State and local government sales tax revenue losses from electronic commerce.* Unpublished paper, April 13.

3. Alm, J., & Melnik, M. (2005). Sales taxes and the decision to purchase online. *Public Finance Review, 33*, 184–212.

4. Internet Tax Freedom Act (1998). P.L. 107-75; Internet Tax Non-Discrimination Act (2004). P.L. 108-435; for an updated source, see Griffin, K., McMurtrey, M., & Smith, L. (2008). To tax or not to tax? foreign and domestic taxation of the Internet. *Proceedings of the Academy of Legal, Ethical, and Regulatory Issues, 12*, 1–5.

5. Goolsbee, A., & Zittrain, J. (1999). Evaluating the costs and benefits of taxing Internet commerce. *National Tax Journal, 52*, 413–428.

6. Swope, C. (2000). E-tax outrage turns into action. *Governing, 13*, September, 86. See the website at http://www.streamlinedsalestax.org.

7. Cornia, G., Sjoquist, D., & Walters, L. (2004). Sales and use tax simplification and voluntary compliance. *Public Budgeting and Finance, 24*, Spring, 1–31.

Tax Rates

State sales tax rates vary from as low as 2.9% (Colorado) to as high as 8.25% (California).[8] To avoid levies of a fraction of a cent, bracket systems are used in which a set amount is collected regardless of the specific sale. For example, a 5% tax might yield 5 cents on any purchase starting at 81 cents or 90 cents. With computers and electronic scanners at check-out counters in stores, determinations can be quickly made as to whether an item is taxable and how much tax, if any, should be charged.

Many states permit a separate local sales tax on top of the state sales tax. Local sales tax rates vary widely, from a low of only 0.03% in Idaho to a high of 4.69% in Louisiana.[9] Local sales taxes are typically collected by the state and remitted to the local treasury.

Sales taxes are regressive in that higher-income consumers typically have more discretionary income and may spend it on items not subject to sales taxes. As noted above, the more the base of the sales tax excludes necessities (such as food and prescription drugs) and includes luxury or nonessential goods and services, the less regressive the tax is likely to be.

This regressive nature of the sales tax may represent a somewhat counterintuitive result, since sales taxes almost always employ a single rate (as opposed to the federal income tax, for example, which has graduated rates). Because of that single rate, some people may think of them as not regressive at all, but rather proportional. Even though sales taxes are levied on a flat-rate basis, however, does not mean that everyone pays the same portion of their income in tax. On the contrary, the vertical equity implications of the tax are substantially dependent on the portion of an individual's income that is spent on taxed items.

Consider a case where one taxpayer earns $50,000 in income and spends $40,000 of that on items subject to the sales tax, while a second taxpayer earns $80,000 and spends $60,000 of that on tax items. The first taxpayer will pay $2,000 in tax ($40,000 times 5%), which represents an effective tax rate of 4% ($2,000/$50,000). The second taxpayer pays more in tax ($3,000, or $60,000 times 5%), for an effective tax rate of 3.75% ($3,000/$80,000). Even if the sales tax rate is 5% for each taxpayer, the lower income taxpayer will have a higher effective tax rate than the higher-income taxpayer. Thus a tax that appears proportional may actually be regressive. As noted above, the exemption of necessities such as food and drugs tend to have the effect of making the tax less regressive and even progressive in some cases.

The general sales tax continues to be a relatively popular and widespread form of taxation, but state and local governments increasingly see threats to the sales tax as a revenue source, for several reasons. First, as noted in Exhibit 6–1, the threat to the productivity of the tax resulting from sales to remote vendors is a real one. Second, the trend is toward more services (that tend not to be taxed) and fewer goods (that are subject to the tax), which impacts the productivity of the tax. Third, legislatures have had a tendency in recent years to provide tax exemptions (in particular, in the form of tax "holidays" to encourage shopping in the state during specific time periods such as the weekend before school starts) that have questionable results but impose substantial revenue losses. For these reasons, one noted sales tax expert is concerned about the viability of the sales tax as a revenue source, and sees those states that rely heavily on the sales tax as having a more difficult time keeping pace with demands for services.[10]

The Value-Added Tax

Increased concerns about the robustness of the U.S. tax system, especially the intergovernmental system of taxation and revenue transfers (see the chapter on intergovernmental relations), have led some to advocate adoption of a value-added tax (VAT).[11] The United States is one of the few industrialized countries without a VAT. As its name implies, a VAT is a consumption tax on the value added by producers and distributors at every stage in the production, distribution, and sales process. Interest in the VAT in the United States seemed to peak in the early 1990s. Proposed during the 1992 election by then-candidate Bill Clinton, the VAT did not get serious attention in Congress. During recent presidential campaigns, it has not been mentioned at all, but has instead been superseded by various candidates' proposals for fundamental income tax reform, including various flat-tax alternatives. Tax professionals argue that it is superior to many other forms of consumption taxation, but it just has not generated much enthusiasm in the United States.[12]

Efforts to reduce the federal budget deficit have revived calls for some kind of national sales tax in the United States. The highest profile of these was proposed by the Bipartisan Policy Center's (BPC) debt reduction proposal. This BPC initiative was headed by former Senator Pete Domenici (R-NM) and CBO founding director Alice Rivlin. The Domenici-Rivlin proposal was for a 6.5% "debt reduction sales tax," phased in over two years.[13]

Selective Sales Taxes

Selective sales taxes are normally referred to as *excise taxes*. There are three general categories of excise taxes: luxury excises, sumptuary excises, and benefit-based excises. They differ according both to the specific types of sales that are taxed and to the fiscal or social goals of the tax.

Luxury Excises

These excise taxes are levied on items that are "uniquely or predominantly consumed by the rich," meaning that the act of purchasing the good itself is considered to be evidence of an extraordinary ability to pay taxes.[14] At one time, federal excise taxes were levied on a wide range of luxury goods, such as jewelry, yachts, and expensive automobiles. The logic of these taxes rests on the assumption that the purchase of such goods is prima facie evidence that the consumer can afford the tax. The overall effect of these taxes, then, is to make the tax system more progressive. There are some problems created by luxury excises. One problem is that the definition of what is a "luxury" is in no way fixed. That is, a watch is not a luxury, but an "expensive watch" may be. A car is not a luxury, but an "expensive car" may be. The problem, of course, is that there is no standard definition for "expensive," so any definition used is by necessity somewhat arbitrary. Some families may have a need to purchase a more expensive car in order to accommodate their family. For a single person, the purchase of such a vehicle may be a luxury. Thus, the definition of a luxury item is clearly open to debate and interpretation.

Another issue with luxury excises is that they can create distortions between taxed and untaxed goods. The luxury tax itself changes the relative price of the luxury item compared to items that are not subject to the tax. This means that tax policy is discriminatory against these luxury items relative to other goods that may be purchased. This has the effect of discouraging, at the margin, purchases of these items, which has the related effect of disadvantaging retailers and producers of luxury goods, perhaps to the point of driving them out of business. In 1990, a new federal luxury tax on yachts was criticized as bankrupting yacht producers and sellers, although it was difficult to evaluate the specific cause of the problems experienced by producers and sellers since the imposition of the tax occurred virtually simultaneously with the economic recession of the early 1990s.

Luxury excise taxes tend not to exist at the state level, and the federal luxury tax has ebbed and flowed according primarily to political factors. The most recent experience with expanding federal luxury taxation was under the Omnibus Budget Reconciliation Act of 1990, when luxury taxes on boats (over $100,000), automobiles (over $30,000), airplanes (over $250,000), and furs and jewelry (over $10,000) were imposed. These taxes proved unpopular, however, and all have since been repealed.[15]

Sumptuary Excises

These sales taxes are regulatory in nature. Taxes on alcohol and tobacco have been justified as deterring people from consuming these commodities. In reality, the evidence suggests that the demand for these products is relatively *inelastic*, casting doubt on whether taxes discourage usage. These items tend to be relatively demand inelastic in large part because they are addictive in nature. Therefore, a smoker is unlikely to stop smoking, or even cut back, because of higher taxes on a pack of cigarettes.

In the 1990s, a substantial tax increase on tobacco was proposed as an important source of financing for federal health care reform. The rationale was that smokers are one of the major sources of health care insurance utilization and that those who create those costs should be the ones to pay taxes to fund them—a sort of reverse benefit principle. The proposal, however, did not get serious review in Congress. Nevertheless, some states have substantially increased tobacco taxes both as a revenue measure and as a health regulatory measure. Large increases in tobacco taxes have reportedly discouraged youth from smoking.

Sumptuary excises, regardless of their regulatory nature, tend to be somewhat regressive, for two reasons. First, there is a tendency toward greater alcohol and cigarette consumption among lower-income groups than higher-income groups. Second, and perhaps even more important, since these taxes are unit taxes instead of ad valorem taxes, effective tax rates are higher for lower-priced brands. While this is likely less of an issue for cigarettes (because the price difference between brands is not great) it is a much larger issue for alcoholic beverages, where there is a huge price range for bottles of wine or spirits (or even six-packs of beer). As an example, if the tax on wine amounted to 50 cents per bottle, this would represent a 10% tax on a $5 bottle, but only a 2% tax on a $25 bottle.

There is a federal alcohol beverage tax, and many states levy liquor taxes as well. Both federal and state alcohol taxes are levied on a unit basis. In fiscal year 2010, the federal tax was $13.50 per "proof gallon" (about $2.14 for an 80-proof bottle) of distilled spirits, $18 per 31-gallon barrel of beer (or $0.58 per gallon, and roughly 5 cents per can), and $1.07 per gallon (about 21 cents per bottle) of table wine (provided that the alcohol content was 14% or less).[16]

Table 6–1 shows the state tax rates for both the cigarette tax (per pack of cigarettes) and the tax on distilled spirits (per gallon) in 2010. Several things are notable from this table. First, while every state taxes cigarettes, the cigarette tax varied widely from state to state. South Carolina had the lowest tax in the nation, at only 7 cents per pack, while Rhode Island's cigarette tax was 35 times that level, at $3.46 per pack. Overall, there were 29 states (including the District of Columbia) with a tax of more than $1.00 per pack, and eight states with taxes of less than 50 cents per pack. Distilled spirits showed substantial variation but not as much as cigarettes, with a range of $1.50 (Maryland) to $12.80 (Alaska), not including those 18 states where the state sells liquor directly, thus earning the majority of revenue from direct profit rather than from taxation.

Table 6–1 State Gasoline, Cigarette, and Alcohol Taxes

	Gas Tax Per Gallon[a,b]	Cigarette Tax Per 20–Pack	Spirits Tax (Per Gallon)
Alabama	$0.21	$0.43	$18.78[d]
Alaska	0.08	2.00	12.80
Arizona	0.19	2.00	3.00
Arkansas	0.22	1.15	2.58
California	0.47	0.87	3.30
Colorado	0.22	0.84	2.28
Connecticut	0.42	3.00	4.50
Delaware	0.23	1.60	5.46
Florida	0.35	1.34	6.50
Georgia	0.12	0.37	3.79
Hawaii	0.44	2.80[c]	5.98
Idaho	0.25	0.57	10.96[d]
Illinois	0.39	0.98	8.55
Indiana	0.34	1.00	2.68
Iowa	0.22	1.36	12.47[d]
Kansas	0.25	0.79	2.50
Kentucky	0.23	0.60	6.46[e]
Louisiana	0.20	0.36	2.50
Maine	0.31	2.00	5.21[d]
Maryland	0.24	2.00	1.50
Massachusetts	0.24	2.51	4.05
Michigan	0.35	2.00	10.91[d]
Minnesota	0.27	1.50	5.03
Mississippi	0.19	0.68	6.75[d]
Missouri	0.17	0.17	2.00
Montana	0.28	1.70	8.62[d]
Nebraska	0.28	0.64	3.75
Nevada	0.33	0.80	3.60
New Hampshire	0.20	1.78	0.00[f]
New Jersey	0.15	2.70	5.50
New Mexico	0.19	0.91	6.06
New York	0.45	2.75	6.44
N. Carolina	0.30	0.45	13.39[d]

	Gas Tax Per Gallon[a,b]	Cigarette Tax Per 20–Pack	Spirits Tax (Per Gallon)
N. Dakota	0.23	0.44	2.50
Ohio	0.28	1.25	9.04[d]
Oklahoma	0.17	1.03	5.56
Oregon	0.25	1.18	24.63[d]
Penn.	0.32	1.60	6.54[d]
Rhode Island	0.33	3.46	3.75
S. Carolina	0.17	0.07	5.42[g]
S. Dakota	0.24	1.53	3.93[h]
Tennessee	0.21	0.62	4.40
Texas	0.20	1.41	2.40
Utah	0.25	0.70	11.41[d]
Vermont	0.25	2.24	0.68[d]
Virginia	0.20	0.30	20.13[d]
Washington	0.38	2.03	26.45[d]
West Virginia	0.32	0.55	1.85[d]
Wisconsin	0.33	2.52	3.25
Wyoming	0.14	0.60	0.00[f]
D.C.	0.24	2.50	1.50

[a] In addition to the 18.4 cpg federal gasoline tax.
[b] The American Petroleum Institute has developed a methodology for determining the average tax rate on a gallon of fuel. Rates may include any of the following: excise taxes, environmental fees, storage tank fees, other fees or taxes, general sales tax, and local taxes. In states where gasoline is subject to the general sales tax, or where the fuel tax is based on the average sale price, the average rate determined by API is sensitive to changes in the price of gasoline. States that fully or partially apply general sales taxes to gasoline: CA, CO, GA, IL, IN, MI, NY. Rates shown are as of April 3, 2009.
[c] Hawaii's cigarette excise tax increased to $3.00 on July 1, 2011.
[d] States where the state government controls all sales. The implied excise tax rate is calculated using methodology designed by the Distilled Spirits Council of the United States (DISCUS).
[e] There is an additional 11% wholesale sales tax on all alcoholic beverages.
[f] Control state where the implied excise tax rate as calculated by DISCUS is less then zero.
[g] Includes a wholesale tax of $5.36 per case.
[h] There is an additional 2% wholesale tax on wine and spirits.

Sources: Tax Foundation, State Sales, Gasoline, Cigarette, and Alcohol Tax Rates by State, 2000-2010, http://www.taxfoundation.org/taxdata/show/245.html, accessed April 11, 2012.

One of the arguments in favor of liquor taxes is that they reduce alcohol consumption. Studies have shown that heavy and moderate drinkers tend to reduce their consumption in response to higher taxes, since these taxes affect the price of a fifth of liquor, a bottle of wine, or a six-pack of beer. Young and underage drinkers are thought to be particularly responsive to price.[17] The tax, then, is thought to assist in helping these individuals to recognize the external costs that their drinking has on society.[18]

Benefit-Based Excises

These taxes are justified on the basis of the "benefit received" concept discussed in the prior chapter on budgeting for revenues. The assumption here is that the tax should be levied on individuals who cause particular services to be provided and that the proceeds from the tax should go to finance that particular service.

Motor vehicle fuel taxes are the classic case. In most states and for the federal government, revenues from taxes on gasoline and diesel fuels are used for transportation purposes. This includes road and bridge construction and maintenance, as well as mass transportation in many cases. The argument here is a simple one. Those individuals who purchase more motor fuel tend to use the highways more than those who purchase a lesser amount of motor fuels. To the extent, then, that the motor fuel tax is used to finance these transportation services, the result is that a greater portion of the cost of financing these services is borne by users. Furthermore, the greater the service consumption, the more the tax paid. Even in cases where gasoline taxes are used to finance mass transportation, the argument holds, since encouraging use of mass transportation creates benefits for drivers who are driving on roads that are less congested.

Taxes are typically levied on different types of motor fuels, such as gasoline, diesel, and gasohol. Table 6–1 includes a column showing the tax rates for gasoline only. As with the excise taxes discussed earlier, gasoline tax rates per gallon differ from state to state, although the range here is much narrower, from a low of 8 cents (Alaska) to 47 cents (California). The tax rates in the vast majority of the states (48 out of 51, including the District of Columbia) fall somewhere between 15 and 40 cents per gallon.

Other such excises include taxes on airline tickets. The revenues from these taxes are used to maintain airports and airport security. There are numerous such taxes at the national level in the United States, including the U.S. Domestic Transportation Tax (7.5%), the U.S. International Departure Tax ($13.40 as of 2011), the Arrival Tax (also $13.40), and a $3.70 Federal Flight Segment Tax.[19]

USER CHARGES

All governments have user charges, and almost all public sector functions are partially supported by user charges. As noted earlier, user charges and fees for services are the fastest-growing state and local revenue source. For example, admission fees are charged to national and some state parks and to local tennis courts, other recreational facilities, and exercise and athletic programs. Some elementary and secondary schools charge for textbooks, and higher-education institutions charge tuition. Hospitals, transit systems, water and sewer operations, and refuse collection revenues come mainly from fees and charges. Some jurisdictions own electric and telephone facilities, which they finance through user fees. Police departments charge fees for fingerprinting and special assignments, such as patrolling at sports events.

Rationale for Charges and Fees

The employment of user charges to raise revenues is based on the principle that citizens ought to pay for the cost of public services as a control on the amount of services produced. The more technical argument for their employment holds that the amount of a service provided is closer to the *optimal level of service*, as determined by consumer preferences, when the cost of service is borne directly by the consumer.[20] If the cost of a service is part of general taxes, then citizens tend to demand more of that service than they are actually willing to pay. Furthermore, user charges adhere very closely to the benefit principle, in that it is the beneficiaries of the service in question that pay for that service.

At the federal level, the growth in user charges and fees began with the Reagan administration's opposition to tax increases. With massive annual federal deficits and a president opposed to raising taxes, federal agencies in need of additional revenues selectively considered fees as an alternative. The philosophy of federal user charges, that "each service, sale, or use of Government's goods or resources provided by an agency to specific recipients be self-sustaining," is expressed in Office of Management and Budget Circular A-25.[21] Presidents and members of Congress have found it financially useful and politically acceptable to increase user fees while holding taxes steady or even cutting taxes. President Obama's fiscal year 2012 budget proposed new or expanded user fees that would have resulted in almost $50 billion in additional revenue between fiscal year 2012 and fiscal year 2016.[22]

Types of Charges

Fees vary in the extent to which they are voluntary. Charges for entrance into a museum or a municipal swimming pool are clearly voluntary. Other leisure options are available if citizens prefer not to pay for these public services. On the other hand, charges for sewers and trash collection are usually mandatory. If a municipal sewer system exists, citizens normally have no choice but to use it and pay the requisite fee. The largest federal user fees are levied by the U.S. Postal Service. These charges may be considered partially voluntary in that alternatives for at least some postal services exist. Other services lie between these extremes. Paying a bus or subway fare may be voluntary, but for many people without other transit options, the fees are required. Differentiating between a mandatory fee and a tax is difficult.

The federal government classifies user charges as offsetting collections and offsetting receipts. Generally speaking, the former represent collections from the public that the Congress authorizes agencies to spend when collected, while the latter are authorized to be spent by a law enacted subsequent to their collection. Between these two types of charges, the U.S. government is expected to collect $488 billion in user charges in fiscal year 2012. **Table 6–2** lists the most common of these fees, as collected in fiscal year 2010. The largest two sources of fees were the Postal Service, which collected fees worth $68 billion, and the Department of Health and Human Services, whose Medicare Part B insurance premiums accounted for $61 billion. Other significant charges were for Tennessee Valley Authority sales of energy ($29 billion), federal employee insurance premiums ($12 billion), and

Table 6–2 Major Federal User Charges, Fiscal Year 2010

Department/Agency	Description	$Billions
Postal Service	Stamps and other fees	67.9
Health and Human Services	Medicare Part B premiums	60.8
Tennessee Valley Authority	Sale of energy	29.2
Various	Employee contributions for health	11.6
Defense	Commissary charges	5.9
Other		142.6
Total User Charges		318.0

Source: Data from U.S. Office of Management and Budget (2011). *Budget of the United States government, fiscal year 2012, analytical perspectives* (p. 224). Washington, DC: U.S. Government Printing Office.

Department of Defense commissary payments ($6 billion). Taken together, these five sources represent more than $175 billion of the total $318 billion in user charges, or 55% of the total.[23]

State and local governments also generate substantial user charges. In fiscal year 2008, state governments in aggregate collected $151 billion in these levies. Of this amount, more than $84 billion (55%) was for higher education, primarily for tuition and room and board. The other large user charge area was hospitals, at $36 billion (24%). States also collect charges for highway travel (through tolls), use of natural resources, recreation, and numerous other activities, but none of these other individual categories account for more than 5% of total state charges. Local governments collected $223 billion in charges in the same year, with hospitals as the largest single source ($61 billion, or 27%). Other significant local charges were for sewerage ($38 billion, or 17%), education ($25 billion, or 11%), and air transportation ($16 billion, or 7%). The aforementioned four categories accounted for more than 60% of all local charges.[24]

Some fees are continuous, whereas others are applied only for special occasions. Transit fares and sewer and water charges are examples of continuous fees. Special-occasion charges include a building permit fee that a contractor has to pay prior to erecting a house, an office building, or some other structure. Although many jurisdictions use general tax revenues to repave and improve streets, other communities levy special assessments on the property owners whose streets will be improved. Similarly, when a community installs a sewer system for the first time, property owners are assessed connection or hookup fees. These charges are calculated on a front footage basis—namely, the number of linear feet that a lot faces or fronts a street. User charges are increasingly being seen as effective revenue sources for social and human services as well.

Special assessments are used in more general ways to support municipal services. Firms that construct new office buildings in a city may have an option to provide on-site parking or pay a fee that is used to construct municipal parking facilities. The State of Virginia, for example, permits high growth areas to impose "Road Impact Fees." These fees are used to "offset the cost of transportation improvements that are necessary due to new development."[25] By charging impact fees to developers, Orange County, Florida, "require[s] growth and development to share in the burdens of growth by paying its pro rata share for the reasonably anticipated costs of major road network systems improvements."[26]

Other services financed through impact fees include water and sewer treatment and education facilities. The City of Bozeman, Montana, requires new development to pay an impact fee for water and sewer treatment facilities based on the size of new water meters.[27] Also, King County, Washington, has imposed a school impact fee for every new dwelling unit built in a school district.[28] Some jurisdictions even impose moratoriums on new development if adequate infrastructure, such as schools, is not available. For instance, in Montgomery County, Maryland, the Adequate Public Facilities Ordinance (APFO) for 2009 through 2011 stated, "If projected enrollment exceeds 120% of projected capacity, then the entire school cluster is in moratorium for residential development approvals."[29] However, user charges have had a limited role to play in financing local education services, despite the fact that education is the largest area of expenditure at the local level. Fees for school lunches represent the single case where substantial use has been made of charges to recover costs for local public services. Other fees that could be charged, but often are not, are for services such as transportation, textbooks, or activities. Some have argued that education fees could be expanded substantially, particularly for auxiliary services (services over and above the basic educational market basket), including such services as transportation, after-school care, and other services beyond the scope of a typical K–12 curriculum. The argument for charging for these services is usually made on the basis of efficiency. That is, the argument is that parents are more likely to demand careful accounting for the costs of these services if they are required to pay these costs. This would have the effect of reducing overall costs for those services.[30]

Charges and Tax Subsidies

Although user charges can be substantial, they often fail to cover the costs of the services they support. Entrance fees for a municipal swimming pool usually do not provide adequate funds to operate the pool. Therefore, tax revenues are used. An important example of such a subsidy is in the operation of municipal transit systems. If transit fares were set high enough to generate the required operating revenues, the rates would be so high that poor commuters could not afford to use the system and higher-income commuters would shift to alternative modes of travel—private vehicles and taxicabs. Pricing policies for some services can be quite complicated, making it difficult to determine whether the actual costs are fully recovered by the tariff structure.[31] Furthermore, recovery of the capital cost of constructing facilities such as swimming pools and transit systems would increase the cost still more than just fees to recover operating costs. However, the failure to include capital cost recovery in user charges also likely leads to underinvestment in capital facilities, or significant subsidy from the general fund, at the expense of all taxpayers.

Subsidies aid all who use a service. If transit fares remain artificially low because of a tax subsidy, then both the wealthy and the poor who use the system benefit, though the wealthier could certainly afford to pay for the service. Alternative mechanisms include providing free service to the poor, such as free bus tokens, or setting fees on a sliding scale. For example, a government-operated mental health clinic might charge poor and moderate-income families little or nothing for services while charging higher-income families at a rate that covers costs.

Some local governments that own profitable utilities, such as public electricity companies and sometimes water enterprises with substantial industrial customers, use utility fee revenue to decrease the taxes otherwise needed to finance other, unrelated services. For those local governments owning such profitable enterprises, the overall cost of other government services to citizens is often lower per capita than for other comparable local governments.[32] Caution is in order, however, before one automatically assumes that local governments should seek to become utility owners. The sometimes hidden costs of diverting public management talent to the operation of an essentially private business could adversely affect the municipality's overall management efficiency, although that may be difficult to quantify.

Besides the various revenue sources discussed so far, there are still others that can be mentioned only briefly here. Governments operate revolving loan programs that produce revenue as borrowers make principal and interest payments. Licenses are issued that usually require fees. The purpose of these fees may be to cover costs (for example, building permit fees are used to pay the salaries of building inspectors) or to raise revenues beyond costs. Charitable contributions, such as gifts to municipal hospitals, county nursing homes, state universities, and the like, constitute another revenue source.

LOTTERIES, CASINOS, AND OTHER FORMS OF GAMBLING

For the past 40 years in the United States, state governments have increasingly operated lotteries and other games of chance in an effort to raise revenues. In addition, more and more states have permitted casino gambling and slot machines over recent years, and have taxed and regulated these activities. Governments had taxed gambling activities, such as horse and dog racing, for many years earlier, but with the advent of lotteries in the 1960s the states became more directly involved in the operation of games of chance.

Lotteries and Gambling

Since 1963, when New Hampshire began the first modern state lottery, all but eight states have launched lottery programs. In 2009, states generated $17.7 billion in net revenue from all lottery games.[33] This represented just under 3% of overall state revenues from their own sources (that is, excluding grants and other intergovernmental revenues).

There is wide variation from state to state in the importance of the lottery as a revenue source. The State of New York raised $2.5 billion from the lottery in 2009, or 2.9% of its own-source general revenue of $86 billion. Income from lotteries in other large states varied substantially, with California collecting about 0.8% and Florida almost 3% of their own-source general revenue from lotteries. Some small states raise substantial sums from their lotteries. West Virginia raised 9% of its own-source general revenue from the lottery in 2009, while the figure was 8% in Rhode Island and 6% in Delaware.[34]

Revenues generated from the programs can vary considerably from year to year, depending on lottery activity in adjacent states, the size of jackpots, and the extent to which a lottery has "matured" and lost the public's interest. State lottery revenues rose rapidly in the late 1980s and early 1990s, then leveled off by the mid-1990s. Recent years have seen a resurgence in interest by both the public, attracted in part by very large, multistate payouts, and the states, in attempts to recover from the economic downturn of the early 2000s and the recession that started in 2007. Still, the biggest increase in lottery sales came between 1985 and 1995, when sales more than tripled. Since 1995, lottery sales have leveled off, more closely tracking the rate of inflation over that period.[35] During the recession that started in 2007, lottery proceeds were relatively stable, and were certainly less volatile than income and sales tax revenues. Between 2007 and 2008, lottery proceeds to states increased by approximately 2%, and then dropped by that same 2% between 2008 and 2009. By contrast, state income tax revenues declined by more than 11%, and general sales tax revenues by 6%, between 2008 and 2009.[36]

Even with all of this activity, the lottery is not a significant revenue source for most states. Recent research not only demonstrates that lotteries do not raise much revenue, but also provides evidence that the revenue that is raised from the lottery often comes at the expense of revenues from other sources, especially sales and excise taxes. Put simply, either taxpayers may substitute spending on the lottery for other spending subject to the sales tax, or politicians may feel less pressure to raise taxes from other sources because of the revenue generated by the lottery.[37]

Lotteries can be regressive in that lower-income individuals are more likely to participate than middle- and upper-income individuals.[38] A review of the research on lotteries consistently found the lottery to be among the most regressive "taxes" at the state level. This same article went a step further and argued that, in states with lotteries, the regressive nature of the tax contributed to the concentration of wealth toward higher-income taxpayers.[39] A partial exception to this trend was found in the high-stakes "Powerball" game, where, for higher jackpots, the lottery tends to become significantly less regressive, suggesting that higher-income people are willing to play the lottery if the potential returns are high enough.[40] The regressive nature of the lottery is considered particularly problematic given the substantial effort—in the form of advertising—that is made by states to convince citizens to play the lottery. It should be noted, however, that the odds against winning substantial sums from playing the lottery are astronomically high.

In addition to their regressive nature, one factor that distinguishes lotteries from other forms of taxation is their relatively high administrative costs. According to data from the U.S. Census Bureau, in 2009, out of the total money spent on lottery tickets, 61% of those funds went back to lottery players in the form of prizes, 34% went to the state in net revenue, and the remaining 5% went for administrative costs.[41] This means that, given conventional ways of calculating administrative costs of taxes (administrative costs as a percentage of revenue), the lottery, at 14%, is a very expensive tax to administer. This tax costs so much to administer primarily because of the high cost of advertising. Again, as noted above, there is no other tax where the government expends so much time and money trying to convince people to pay it.

In the early 2000s, there were calls to privatize lotteries in some states, with private firms "buying" the right to operate the lottery and reap annual profits in exchange for a one-time payment to the state that could then be used either for immediate spending (on capital improvements, for example) or to produce an annual revenue stream. The states of Indiana and Illinois actively pursued such lottery privatizations.

Illinois Governor Rod Blagojevich first proposed selling his state's lottery in the spring of 2006, and continued to propose it during his 2006 gubernatorial reelection campaign.[42] In January 2007, Blagojevich took the first steps toward privatizing the lottery. Under the proposal, the new owners would give the state several billion dollars up front (the governor's earlier estimate was that the state might receive as much as $6 billion) in exchange for receiving the right to all revenue and profit for 75 years.[43] Mitch Daniels, the governor of neighboring Indiana, proposed his own privatization of that state's Hoosier Lottery. Under the Daniels proposal, a private firm would have paid more than $1 billion in order to gain a 30-year right to sell lottery tickets.[44] Other states, including California, Colorado, Florida, Michigan, New Jersey, New York, and Texas, also considered leasing lotteries, on a long-term basis, to private firms, exchanging the rights to annual lottery proceeds for one-time or annual payments.[45]

Proposals to privatize lotteries hit a snag in October 2008, when the U.S. Department of Justice issued an opinion that states could not enter into long-term leases with non-state actors to operate lotteries. The Justice Department argued that federal law required the state to "exercise actual control over all significant business decisions made by a lottery enterprise and retain all but a minimal share of the equity interest in the profits and losses of the business." It is permissible, according to this opinion, for the state to contract out provision of goods and services necessary to operate the lottery, but ultimate control over the lottery must remain with the state.[46] In September 2010, Illinois became the first state to hand over management of its lottery to a private firm, although the state (as required by the Justice Department) will "retain ownership and regulatory oversight."[47]

Casino Gambling

In addition to lotteries, a number of states have legalized casino gambling and similar forms of amusement, such as slot machines. While in 1988, legalized casino gambling existed only in Nevada and New Jersey, in 2011, 29 states had Native American casinos, 15 states had non–Native American casinos as standalone properties, and 7 other states that did not have standalone casinos had casinos at racetracks.[48] Native American casinos operate substantially differently than non–Native American casinos. In the case of the former, states negotiate with tribes for the state "take" of casino revenues. In the latter case, taxes are levied on gross receipts or adjusted gross receipts (gross receipts less winnings). Some states use a flat scale, while others use an adjusted scale. States also raise money from licensing fees and fees for gaming devices, such as slot machines. The chapter on intergovernmental relations discusses the relationships between states and Native American tribes concerning casino gambling.

Most states raise little or no money from amusement taxes. In 2009, there were only 10 states that raised more than $100 million in revenues from these taxes.[49] Although in some states, such as Louisiana, casino gambling has cut into state lottery revenues, other states are generating significant revenues from such ventures. Some states receive substantial support from amusement taxes, including the obvious leader, Nevada (home of Las Vegas and Reno), which generated $832 million in amusement taxes in 2009, or 12% of total own-source revenues in that year. Other significant contributions from amusement taxes came in Indiana (4.3%), Louisiana (4.1%), and Mississippi (3.4%). Nationwide research suggests that, while there is significant "cannibalization" of lottery revenues from casinos, states as a whole seem to benefit, from a revenue perspective, from having both lotteries and casino gambling.[50]

Overall, however, the enthusiasm for tax and economic benefits from lotteries, casinos, and other legalized gambling has waned somewhat, except in those states where neighboring states seem to be attracting residents of nonlottery states to cross state borders to purchase lottery tickets. For example, one argument used in 2002 in North Carolina to support a lottery proposal was the amount of money that North Carolina residents were spending in the neighboring Virginia and South Carolina lotteries. The Commonwealth of Pennsylvania introduced slot machines in November 2006, an action that arguably could have been influenced by the existence of casinos in neighboring New Jersey. The economic benefits in terms of employment and increased tax revenues have been less than expected, though definitely positive. Hard evidence of social consequences has been difficult to find, although opponents of legalized gambling anecdotally argue that the social costs exceed the economic benefits.[51]

One of the selling points often used to market the lottery and other forms of gambling revenues is that their proceeds will be used to support spending for some specific (usually popular) policy area. For example, many states earmark lottery revenues, or other gaming revenues, for education or senior citizen programs. It is frequently difficult, however, to make the case that this earmarking actually leads to a net increase in funding for these areas. In cases where funds are dedicated to education, for example, lottery earmarking may simply have the effect of freeing up other revenues that would have been spent on education to be used for other purposes.[52] This is because of the *fungibility* of revenues, given that some sources can be substituted for others without increasing spending for particular programs (see the chapter on intergovernmental relations). In some states where lottery earnings are earmarked to support education, state legislatures have cut other state education spending by commensurate amounts.[53]

An exception was found to this general rule in Georgia, where lottery revenues have stimulated additional spending in the areas advertised by lottery proponents. According to the authors of this study, this occurred because of the specific structure of the earmark, the transparency of the budget process, and the commitment of the governor to increase funds rather than substitute them.[54]

Pari-Mutuel Wagering Taxes

In addition to lottery and amusement taxes, some states allow betting on sporting competitions, primarily horse racing (although some states also have legalized dog racing and jai-alai). These are more similar to amusement taxes than lotteries in the sense that the activity is not operated by the state, but is regulated and taxed by the state. Nationwide, pari-mutuel taxes generated only $232 million in 2007. This represented only 0.02% of total own-source revenue for states in that year. Only California ($37.5 million), New York ($28.1 million), Florida ($28.1 million), and Pennsylvania ($24.7 million) raised more than $20 million in that year, but in each of these cases, the revenue from this source made an inconsequential contribution to state revenues.

SUMMARY

Some revenue sources, instead of being taxes on income or wealth, are taxes on individual transactions. Among these are general and specific sales taxes, user charges, and revenue raised from games of chance, such as lotteries. These revenue sources have in common that they are levied on a more or less voluntary basis. That is, individuals have relatively more "choice" in whether they engage in the transaction or pay the tax.

The general sales tax is the largest single revenue source for state governments, and is also used by many local governments. The tax is levied on sales made at the retail level. Many states exclude particular transactions from the tax base. Among the most frequent exclusions are food and prescription drugs. By and large, these exclusions make the tax less regressive, since they are necessities and thus tend to represent a larger percentage of total spending for lower-income taxpayers than for higher-income taxpayers. In recent years, the viability of the sales tax has been threatened by the increased spending by consumers from remote vendors, including both mail-order and Internet sales. States and local governments lack a reliable way to collect taxes on these transactions.

Sales taxes are also levied on particular types of transactions. There are three general categories of these selective sales, or excise, taxes. First, luxury excises are levied on items (such as boats or luxury automobiles) the purchase of which is viewed as evidence of an extraordinary taxpaying ability. Second, sumptuary excises (so-called sin taxes) are levied on items such as cigarettes and liquor, ostensibly to discourage consumption of these goods that are thought to cause harm to both the individual who consumes them and society as a whole. Third, benefit-based excises operate as a quasi-price by taxing individuals and then using the proceeds of those taxes to finance benefits used by the specific taxpayers on whom the tax is levied. A classic example of this is gasoline taxes used to finance transportation projects, especially highways.

Increasingly, governments charge citizens directly for their purchase of individual services, or have dedicated revenue from charges for particular spending programs or functions. In this way, government services can be made to resemble market transactions. User charges have been growing at all levels of government and include such varied items as federal postal service fees, state university tuition, and local water and sewer fees.

Many state governments rely on revenue from gambling to finance a portion of state government services. While most states do not raise much money from gambling, games of chance have been a growth industry for states. There are substantial differences between lotteries and other forms of gaming revenue. In the case of lotteries, the games are operated directly by the government, with games marketed, tickets sold, and proceeds paid directly to state coffers. In the case of other games of chance, such as casino gambling, the games are not operated by the state but are taxed by the government. Casino gambling has been on the increase in recent years, including both Native American and non–Native American components.

NOTES

1. Tax Foundation (2010). *State sales, gasoline, cigarette, and alcohol taxes.* Retrieved December 7, 2011, from http://www.taxfoundation.org/files/state_various_sales_rates_2000-2010.pdf.
2. U.S. Bureau of the Census (2011). State government finances summary: 2009. *Governments Division Briefs*, January. Retrieved February 24, 2012, from http://www2.census.gov/govs/state/09statesummaryreport.pdf.
3. Federation of Tax Administrators (2011). *State sales tax rates and food and drug exemptions.* Retrieved December 7, 2011, from http://www.taxadmin.org/fta/rate/sales.pdf.
4. Due, J., & Mikesell, J. (2005). Retail sales tax, state and local. In J. Cordes, R. Ebel, & J. Gravelle (Eds.), *Encyclopedia of taxation and tax policy* (p. 337). Washington, DC: Urban Institute Press.
5. CanagaRetna, S. (2010). *State fiscal issues.* Presentation at the Southern Legislative Conference of the Council of State Governments, at the 2010 Division of Insurance and Research Economist and Analyst Meeting Federal Deposit Insurance Corporation (FDIC), Dallas, Texas, October 7. Retrieved December 7, 2011, from http://knowledgecenter.csg.org/drupal/content/state-fiscal-issues.

6. Due, J., & Mikesell, J. (2005). Retail sales tax, state and local. In J. Cordes, R. Ebel, & J. Gravelle (Eds.), *Encyclopedia of taxation and tax policy*, 337.

7. The Government Performance Project: Florida (2003). *Governing.* Retrieved November 7, 2006, from http://www.governing.com/gpp/2003/gp3fl.htm.

8. Tax Foundation (2010). *State sales, gasoline, cigarette, and alcohol taxes.*

9. Tax Foundation (2010). *Fiscal fact # 240.* August 19. Retrieved December 7, 2011, from http://www.taxfoundation.org/files/ff240.pdf.

10. Mikesell, J. (2004). The prospects for general sales taxation in American state and local government finance: challenges for a fiscal workhorse unready for the new millennium. *Journal of Public Budgeting, Accounting and Financial Management, 16,* 63–79.

11. Rivlin, A. M. (1992). *Reviving the American dream: the economy, the states and the federal government.* Washington, DC: Brookings Institution.

12. Zodrow, G. R. (1999).The sales tax, the VAT, and taxes in between—or, is the only good NRST a "VAT in drag"? *National Tax Journal, 52,* 429–442.

13. Debt Reduction Task Force (2010). *Restoring America's future* (pp. 20–43). Washington, DC: Bipartisan Policy Center.

14. Davie, B., updated by D. Zimmerman (2005). Luxury taxes. In J. Cordes, R. Ebel, & J. Gravelle (Eds.), *Encyclopedia of taxation and tax policy*, 245–247.

15. Davie, B., updated by D. Zimmerman (2005). Luxury taxes.

16. Pogue, T. (2005). Alcohol beverage taxes, federal. In J. Cordes, R. Ebel, & J. Gravelle (Eds.), *Encyclopedia of taxation and tax policy*; 2010 taxes confirmed by Department of the Treasury, Alcohol and Tobacco Tax and Trade Bureau, at http://www.ttb.gov/tax_audit/atftaxes.shtml.

17. Chaloupka, F., Grossman, M., & Saffer, H. (2002). *The effects of price on alcohol consumption and alcohol-related problems.* National Institute on Alcohol Abuse and Alcoholism of the National Institutes of Health. Retrieved December 7, 2011, from http://pubs.niaaa.nih.gov/publications/arh26-1/22-34.htm.

18. Pogue, T. (2005). Alcohol beverage taxes, federal. In J. Cordes, R. Ebel, & J. Gravelle (Eds.), *Encyclopedia of taxation and tax policy*, 5.

19. U.S. Department of State (2011). *Airport taxes and fees update.* Retrieved December 7, 2011, from http://www.state.gov/ofm/resource/imp/tax/20129.htm.

20. Johnson, R. W., & McCullough, J. S. (1996). *Case study on urban local government finance.* Paper presented at the Asian Development Bank Seminar on Urban Infrastructure Finance in Asia. Research Triangle Park, NC: Research Triangle Institute.

21. U.S. Office of Management and Budget (1993). *Circular A-25.* Retrieved January 21, 2007, from http://www.whitehouse.gov/omb/circulars/a025/a025.html.

22. U.S. Office of Management and Budget (2011). *Budget of the United States government, fiscal year 2012, analytical perspectives* (pp. 228–229). Washington, DC: U.S. Government Printing Office.

23. U.S. Office of Management and Budget (2011). *Budget of the United States government: fiscal year 2012, analytical perspectives*, 224.

24. U.S. Bureau of the Census, U.S. Department of Commerce (2011). State and local government finances summary: 2008. *Governments division briefs,* April 11, 6. Retrieved February 24, 2012, from http://www.census.gov/prod/2011pubs/g08-alfin.pdf.

25. *House Bill 3202: Road impact fees.* (2007). Retrieved February 24, 2012, from http://www.hb3202.virginia.gov/roadimpactfees.shtml.

26. Orange County, Florida, Orange County Road Impact Fee Ordinance, Art. IV, Section 23-87, Intent and Purpose. Retrieved February 17, 2012, from http://www.orangecountyfl.net/Portals/0/Resources/Internet/DEPARTMENTS/Public_Works/ARTICLEIVRoadImpactFee.pdf.

27. City of Bozeman (2011). *Impact fee schedule.* Retrieved December 7, 2011, from https://www.bozeman.net/Departments-(1)/Planning/Impact-Fees-(1).

28. King County (1994). *Chapter 21A.43 impact fees.* Retrieved December 7, 2011, from http://www.mrsc.org/subjects/planning/kcc21a.43.pdf.

29. Montgomery County (2010). *2009–2011 adequate public facilities guidelines*. Retrieved December 7, 2011, from http://www.montgomeryplanning.org/research/growth_policy/growth_policy09/2009_2011_adequate_public_facilities_guidelines.shtm.

30. Wassmer, R., & Fisher. R. (2002). Interstate variation in the use of fees to fund K–12 public education. *Economics of Education Review, 21*, 87–100.

31. Foster, B. D., & Fujita, G. (2000). Rate setting for municipal utilities: Detroit's combined sewer overflow facilities. *Government Finance Review, 16*, June, 33–40.

32. Khan, A., & Stumm, T. J. (1994). The tax and expenditure effects of subsidization by municipal utility enterprises. *Municipal Finance Journal, 15*, 68–81; Stumm, T. J., & Khan, A. (1996). Effects of utility enterprise fund subsidization on municipal taxes and expenditures. *State and Local Government Review, 28*, 103–113.

33. U.S. Bureau of the Census, U.S. Department of Commerce (2005). *Income and apportionment of state-administered lottery funds: 2004*. Retrieved February 24, 2012, from http://www2census.gov/govs/state/04lottery.pdf.

34. Calculations by author from U.S. Bureau of the Census, U.S. Department of Commerce (2010). *Income and apportionment of state-administered lottery funds: 2009*. Retrieved February 24, 2012, from http://www2.census.gov/govs/state/09lottery.pdf; and U.S. Bureau of the Census (2011). *State government finances summary: 2009*.

35. Calculations by author from U.S. Bureau of the Census, U.S. Department of Commerce (2011). *Income and apportionment of state-administered lottery funds: 2009;* and U.S. Bureau of the Census (2011). *State government finances summary: 2009*.

36. Calculations by author from U.S. Bureau of the Census, U.S. Department of Commerce (2010). *Income and apportionment of state-administered lottery funds: 2009;* and U.S. Bureau of the Census (2011). *State government finances summary: 2009*.

37. Fink, S., Marco, A., & Rork, J. (2004). Lotto nothing? The budgetary impact of state lotteries. *Applied Economics, 36*, 2357–2367.

38. Clotfelter, C. T., & Cook, P. J. (1990). On the economics of state lotteries. *Journal of Economic Perspective, 4*, Fall, 105–119.

39. Freund, E., & Morris, I. (2005). The lottery and income inequality in the states. *Social Science Quarterly, 86*, 996–1012.

40. Oster, E. (2004). Are all lotteries regressive? Evidence from the Powerball. *National Tax Journal, 57*, 179–187.

41. U.S. Bureau of the Census, U.S. Department of Commerce (2005). *Income and apportionment of state-administered lottery funds: 2004*. Retrieved February 24, 2012, from http://www2census.gov/govs/state/04lottery.pdf.

42. Bellandi, D. (2006). Blagojevich says state could get more money by privatizing lottery. *Associated Press*. Retrieved January 23, 2007, from http://web.lexis-nexis.com.proxygw.wrlc.org/universe/document?_m=7f31fe756f82363a6f.4845691a4b40eb&_docnum=1&wchp=dGLbVtb-zSkVA&md5=e07f7e9c38137cd4eccb5d17f8e873d1.

43. Duhigg, C., & Anderson, J. (2007). Illinois is putting lottery on block for quick payoff. *New York Times*, January 23. Retrieved January 23, 2007, from http://www.nytimes.com/2007/01/23/business/23lottohtml.

44. Hinnefeld, S. (2006). Governor Daniels proposes privatizing lottery, using profits on higher education. *Bloomington (Ind.) Herald-Times*. Retrieved January 23, 2007, from http://web.lexis-nexis.com.proxygw.wrlc.org/universe/document?_m=7f31fe756f82363a6f4845691a4b40eb&_docnum=2&wchp=dGLbVtb-zSkVA&md5=073b938da312b1adfb7c3ce8d0d99a46.

45. Duhigg, C., & Anderson, J. (2007). Illinois is putting lottery on block for quick payoff. *New York Times*, January 23. Retrieved January 23, 2007, from http://www.nytimes.com/2007/01/23/business/23lotto.html?scp=1&sq=Illinois+is+putting+lottery+on+block+for+quick+payoff&st=nyt.

46. Smith, M. (2008). Daniels drops plan to privatize lottery after feds say no. *Associated Press*, October 25. Retrieved February 24, 2012, from http://www.news-sentinel.com/apps/pbcs.dll/article?AID=/SE/20081025/NEWS/810250332.

47. Illinois lottery goes private. (2010). *NBCChicago.com*, September 15. Retrieved February 24, 2012, from http://www.nbcchicago.com/news/business/illinois-lottery-privatization-103016309.html.

48. American Gaming Association (AGA) (2011). *AGA 2011: Fact sheet—types of gaming by state*. Available at http://www.americangaming.org/industry-resources/research/fact-sheets/states-gaming.

49. American Gaming Association (2011). *AGA 2011: FAQs*. Available at http://www.americangaming.org/industry-resources/faq.

50. Elliott, D. E., & Navin, J. (2002). Has riverboat gambling reduced state lottery revenue? *Public Finance Review, 30*, 235–247.

51. U.S. General Accounting Office (2000). *Impact of gambling: economic effects more measurable than social effects*. Washington, DC: U.S. Government Printing Office.

52. Gribbin, D., & Bean, J. (2006). Adoption of state lotteries in the United States, with a closer look at Illinois. *The Independent Review, 10*, 360.

53. Spindler, C. J. (1995). The lottery and education: robbing Peter to pay Paul? *Public Budgeting & Finance, 15*, Fall, 54–62.

54. Lauth, T., & Robbins, M. (2002). The Georgia lottery and state appropriations for education: substitution or additional funding? *Public Budgeting & Finance, 22*, Fall, 89–100.

Budget Preparation: The Expenditure Side

By the end of the first decade of the 2000s, the federal government's Office of Management and Budget (OMB) was emphasizing rigorous performance evaluations throughout the government to help determine the strengths and weaknesses of programs and to assist in allocating resources in the budgetary process, publishing assessments online for the public to view at a newly created website, *www.performance.gov.*[1] State and local governments similarly were widely using program information in their budget processes. These were the outgrowth of changes that began in the early 1900s. Budgeting had come a long way.

In the budget preparation phase, important decisions about expenditures are made simultaneously with decisions concerning revenues. The two general types of information relevant for budgeting are program and resource information. Program information consists of data on what government does and what those activities accomplish. Resource information consists of the inputs necessary to perform those activities. The inputs include dollars, facilities, equipment, supplies, and personnel, and have been a long-established feature of budgetary systems. The use of program information, on the other hand, has slowly emerged as an integral part of budgeting.

The critical argument relating to these two types of information is that they must be considered in combination if budgeting is to be a sensible process of allocating resources. The budget is expected to relate the accomplishments of government to the resources available. The history of budgetary reform can be viewed as a struggle to create such budget systems.

This chapter examines the various approaches used in assembling the expenditure side of budgets. The first section of this chapter discusses early reform efforts. The second section describes the types of program information used to varying degrees in budget systems. The last section explores the numerous budget systems that have been used, including performance, program, zero-base, and hybrid budgeting systems.

EARLY DEVELOPMENTS

As noted earlier, budgeting can focus on expenditure control, management of resources, and planning for future allocation decisions.[2] By "planning," we are specifically referring to efforts to associate means with ends in order to attain goals and objectives in the future. While the development of these three emphases has been sequential over time to some extent, they are not rigidly fixed to specific time periods, and both the management and planning phases have involved greater utilization of program information. Not only is there a blurring of distinctions between these stages in terms of the dates of their popularity, but use of planning coupled with program information also was advocated at least as far back as the early part of the twentieth century.

Program Information

1910–1939

Before the establishment of the federal budgetary system, budgeting was often advocated as a means of allocating resources to obtain program results.[3] Two of the most notable proponents were President Taft[4] and the 1912 Taft Commission on Economy and Efficiency. At one point in its report, the Commission stated, "In order that he [the administrator] may think intelligently about the subject of his responsibility he must have before him regularly statements which will reflect *results in terms of quality and quantity*; he must be able to measure quality and quantity of results by units of cost and units of efficiency" (emphasis added).[5] Although there was an obvious interest in economizing—in saving dollars—there was also an interest in obtaining the best return in program terms for resources spent.[6]

Other important spokespersons for program results in budgeting in the 1910s included Frederick A. Cleveland[7] and William F. Willoughby.[8] The 1920s and 1930s brought more proponents for program results being included in budgets, including Lent D. Upson,[9] A. E. Buck,[10] Wylie Kilpatrick,[11] and the 1937 President's Committee on Administrative Management.[12] A. E. Buck's classic *Public Budgeting* (1929) admittedly lacked a strong program information orientation, but Buck did express interest in reforms that would concentrate on measuring the products of government activities.

1940–1960

Although the use of program information and planning was advocated throughout the first four decades of the twentieth century, this issue received far greater attention beginning in the 1940s. V. O. Key, Jr., challenged previous budgetary literature as largely mechanical and criticized it for failing to focus on the "basic budgeting problem" of comparing the merits of alternative programs: "On what basis shall it be decided to allocate X dollars to activity A instead of activity B?"[13] The 1949 Commission on Organization of the Executive Branch of the Government, commonly known as the First Hoover Commission, recommended that the federal budget be "based upon functions, activities, and projects: this we designate as a performance budget." Budgeting should be in terms of "the work or the service to be accomplished."[14]

More proponents of the same viewpoint emerged in the 1950s. Noted scholars included Verne B. Lewis,[15] Frederick C. Mosher,[16] Catheryn Seckler-Hudson,[17] and Arthur Smithies.[18] The Second Hoover Commission supported the recommendations of its predecessor.[19] Smithies suggested the use of program information in budgeting as a primary means of improving both executive and legislative decision making. Jesse Burkhead's *Government Budgeting* (1956), while basically descriptive rather than normative, devoted considerable discussion to performance and program budgeting.[20]

By the 1950s, the use of program information in budgeting had become a mainstream reform issue. At the same time, another school of thought led by Charles E. Lindblom, Aaron Wildavsky, and others challenged the budget reform movement on the grounds that political decision systems were not readily adaptable to program planning. Lindblom advanced the "muddling through" model of decision making that ran counter to budgetary reform efforts. Wildavsky was to become the most outspoken skeptic of the feasibility of using program information in budgeting. In 1969 he concluded, "No one knows how to do program budgeting."[21]

Nonbudgetary Developments

An alternative school of thought led by David Novick, Charles J. Hitch, Roland McKean, and others was rooted in a set of theoretical and technological fields that developed after World War II. These fields and technologies were highly compatible with the budget reform movement and served as the theoretical foundation for planning-programming-budgeting (PPB) systems attempted in the 1960s.[22] Of central importance were the following six conceptual fields and technologies:

1. Operations research, a technique that involves specifying objectives, designing a model representing the situation under investigation, and collecting and applying relevant data.[23]
2. Economic analysis, a process of determining whether benefits exceed costs of a current or contemplated program.[24]
3. General systems theory, an approach that focuses on how components of a system relate to one another.[25]
4. Cybernetics, the science of control and communication.[26]
5. Information technology, the methods by which data are manipulated to produce information suitable for analysis and supportive of the decision-making process.[27]
6. Systems analysis, an eclectic form of analysis that draws upon the previous five items.[28]

These fields and technologies were developed outside the budget reform movement but were highly compatible with it. The six constituted the theoretical and technological foundation for what became the PPB system in the Department of Defense in the 1960s.

The reform efforts from the early 1900s to 1960 that emphasized the use of program information, coupled with this series of other nonbudgetary developments, constitute the foundation for more recent budget system innovations and for contemporary budget systems.

STRUCTURING THE REQUEST PROCESS

Except in the smallest organizations, a central budget office alone cannot prepare a budget. As noted in the chapter on budget cycles, budget preparation begins with the almost simultaneous amassing of supporting information in the operating agencies and the issuance of budget instructions from a central budget office.

The information developed at this stage depends partially on how each agency chooses to make its case and partially on the way decisions are expected to be made within an organization. If only dollar requests are prepared, obviously no information will be available with which to make judgments on program effectiveness. On the other hand, a central budget office may not necessarily use program information in its deliberations, even if it requires its submission. Still another factor determining what information will be prepared is the known information demands from other budget participants, most notably, the legislative body. Much data may be amassed, not because the agency or the chief executive has any intention of using them for decision purposes, but simply because each year the legislative body demands that information. Program efficiency or effectiveness information may be used in executive branch decisions about appropriations requests sent to the legislature, but that information may be largely ignored by the legislative body in the actual appropriations process.

Preparation Instructions

Budget preparation practices vary considerably within agencies. Different degrees of participation by field office staff and other line personnel occur, but while such variation exists, the overall process is guided by a set of instructions issued by a central budget office of a government.

At the federal level, such instructions are contained in OMB Circular A-11, *Preparation, Submission, and Execution of the Budget*. This document, issued annually, contains considerable detail about most aspects of federal budgeting and, counting text and supporting illustrations, runs more than 700 pages in length. The sections specifically pertaining to budget preparation and submission cover about 140 pages. The circular is available on the Internet, and agencies can submit much of their budget request information through a computer template system.[29] **Table 7–1** indicates the vast array of materials that agencies must submit. Much of this information is mandated by various statutes, such as performance information being required by the Government Performance and Results Modernization Act of 2010 and its predecessor, the Government Performance and Results Act of 1993.[30] Revisions in OMB Circular A-11 have decreased the extensiveness of requirements for including program results information in agency budget submissions to OMB. Program activity descriptions remain heavily featured, as does the traditional budget accounting information.

Table 7–1 Selected Materials that Federal Agencies Must Submit as Part of Their Budget Requests

Section Title of OMB Circular A-11	Description
I. General Policies and Requirements	
25 – Summary of Requirements	Overview of materials they must submit
31 – Compliance with Administrative Policies and Other General Requirements	Confirm that budgets comply with president's spending levels, president's management agenda, management improvement agenda, and other requirements
32 – Personnel, Compensation, Benefits, and Related Costs	Estimate expenditures for employee pay and benefits
32 – Estimates Related to Specific Types of Programs and Expenditures	Estimate expenditures for construction, leases of capital assets, hospitals, advisory committees, taxes, and tax expenditures

Section Title of OMB Circular A-11	Description
II. The Budget Submission	
51 – Basic Justification Materials	Summarize justification of programs, analysis of resources, agency restructuring, performance goals, measures and indicators, loan and loan guarantee programs, and acquisition of capital assets
52 – Information on Financial Management	General reporting requirements, policies addressed by reports, description of required Report on Resources for Financial Management Activities
53 – Information Technology and E-Government	Report information technology spending and efforts to expand public access to information through technology (e-government)
54 – Rental Payments for Space and Land	Show expenditures for rental of buildings, other structures, and land; justification of budget for space requirements
III. MAX Data and Other Materials Required after Passback	
79 – Budget Data System	Overview of MAX budget system, which provides computer support for the budget process, account identification codes
80 – Development of Baseline Estimates	Overview of preparing baseline estimates on discretionary and mandatory spending, supplemental requests, governmental receipts
81 – Policy and Baseline Estimates of Budget Authority, Outlays, and Receipts	Project budget authority, outlays, and receipts for future years based on existing laws (current services projections)
82 – Combined Schedule X	Budget obligations by program activity, budgetary resources available for obligation, other detailed resource accounting
83 – Object Classification	Submit information about personnel, contractual services, acquisition of assets, and grants and fixed charges
84 – Character Classification (Schedule C)	Report expenditures as to whether they are investments or non-investments and whether they provide funding to state and local governments
85 – Estimating Employment Levels and the Personnel Summary	Estimate the full-time equivalent (FTE) of personnel by program activity
86 – Special Schedules	Provide balance sheets that summarize financial transactions
95 – Budget Appendix and Print Material	Instructions on detailed appropriations language, narratives, more detailed budget request supporting information

Source: Adapted from U.S. Office of Management and Budget (2011). *Preparation, submission, and execution of the budget*, Circular No. A-11. Retrieved October 13, 2011, from http://www.whitehouse.gov/sites/default/files/omb/assets/a11_current_year/a_11_2011.pdf.

Table 7–2 provides a comparable summary of budget preparation instructions for New York State. One striking characteristic is the attention devoted to capital expenditures, such as monies for the purchase of land, buildings, and large pieces of equipment—nine of 17 required budget request schedules pertain to capital assets. This is not a surprising contrast to federal budget instructions, as New York State, like almost all state governments and unlike the federal government, has a separate capital budget (see the chapter on capital assets).

Instructions such as those contained in Circular A-11 and New York State's budget instructions include forms to be completed, reducing uncertainty among agencies as to what the budget office expects of them. Typically, a calendar will be provided explaining when requests are due for submission to the budget office and indicating a period when agencies may be called for hearings with the budget office (see the chapter on budget

Table 7–2 Selected Materials that New York State Agencies Must Submit as Part of Their Budget Requests

Subject	Description
Commissioner's Statement	Indicate agency's mission, funding requirements, and changes requested
Agency Summary Recapitulation	Show appropriations by fund type, aid to localities, capital projects, and debt service
Program Recapitulation	Summarize current appropriations by program/fund and show requested changes
Miscellaneous Receipts	Report miscellaneous receipts
State Operations and Aid to Localities	Provide expenditures by objective classification and report aid to localities
State Operations Request for Replacement/Additional State Vehicles	Indicate request for vehicles including type of vehicle and type of fuel
State Operations Nonpersonal Services	Submit information on all equipment and real property that requires installment payments out of state bond proceeds
Special Revenue Funds—Federal	Report existing and new federal grants
Reappropriations of Current Appropriations in Force	Request reappropriation when an existing appropriation will not be expended by its expiration date
Commissioner's Capital Plan Overview	Report major changes in five-year capital plan
Capital Projects Summaries	Provide detailed data on capital projects
Non-Highway and Highway Appropriation Request	Request approval of new capital projects
Capital Commitments	Report expected dollar value of contracts expected to be awarded
Capital Projects Codes	Supply departmental and budget codes for each capital project

Subject	Description
Capital Maintenance Plan Report	Provide overview of plans for maintenance of capital
Description of Maintenance Projects	Show detailed information about planned maintenance projects
Requested Maintenance Appropriations, Reappropriations, and Disbursements	Request approval of maintenance appropriations
Summary of Capital Assets	Indicate age, useful life, and value of agency assets
Summary of Maintenance Plan Evaluations	Supply narrative discussing the evaluation of plans to maintain agency assets

Source: Adapted from New York State Division of the Budget (2006). Budget request manual. Retrieved October 18, 2011, from http://www.budget.state.ny.us/brm/item2.pdf. Individual schedules available separately.

cycles). The instructions, then, determine the type and amount of information that will be required of the agencies, although the budget office may request additional information from particular agencies.

In the case of the federal government, Circular A-11 describes a two-step process. The circular is released in the summer, and agencies have varying deadlines to submit their requests. Then the agencies receive feedback, or "passback," on their proposals and must submit revised and more detailed requests using the computer support system. This second stage occurs in November, leading up to the president's submission of the budget to Congress after the first of the year.

No matter what the jurisdiction, standard items can be found in virtually all budget instruction manuals. Where appropriate, agencies are asked to submit revenue data (e.g., an agency operating a loan program with a revolving fund). Most of the instructions, however, concentrate on expenditures. The expenditures are keyed with the accounting system, using objects of expenditures such as personnel and supplies (see the chapter on financial management). There may also be detailed breakouts on the number of persons in a given unit, their job titles, and their current salaries. The instructions usually allow for the agencies to provide narrative statements to justify their requests.

Separate sets of instructions may be provided for the operating and capital fund budgets as well as other funds, as Table 7–2 illustrates for New York State. Instructions for the latter, which are used extensively at the state and local levels, are required to distinguish requests for appropriations that must be accounted for in different funds, other than the state general fund. Examples include funds meant primarily for major fixed assets such as buildings and equipment, special funds that segregate certain federal revenues, revenues from state enterprises, and others. Federal agencies are required to separate out their investments in fixed assets, although no distinctions are made between investments in assets, or capital, and operating or current expenses when Congress appropriates funding for the agencies (see the chapters on capital assets and capital financing).

Program Information

Budget systems are making increased use of program information, starting with the emphasis on planning reforms that began in the latter half of the previous century, as discussed earlier in this chapter. Preparation instructions specify which types of program data are to be supplied. The measures typically will have been negotiated between the budget office and the agencies before budget preparation time. In other words, when the agencies receive the request instructions, they already know what program information they need to submit. Determining what information to collect and present in budget requests is a concern at all levels of government in the United States and abroad. The umbrella term most often used to describe the overall field of program information is *performance measurement*.[31] Such measurement is seen as a means for holding agencies accountable for results from the expenditure of tax dollars and other public resources.

Social Indicators

Of the variety of program information, social indicators are the broadest or most general type. These measures of the physical, social, and economic environments are intended to reflect what sometimes is called *quality of life*.[32] The percentage of the workforce unemployed broken out by age, sex, race, and income constitutes a set of important social indicators. Other commonly used social indicators gauge family stability/broken homes, income for individuals and families, and health-related topics such as infant mortality. Measures of this type are useful in assessing past and current trends and provide decision makers with some insights into the need for programs.

Social indicators are rarely used as measures of program performance because they are so broad as to defy demonstrating causal linkage between a specific program expenditure and a change in one of these indicators. But they are important in identifying the problems on which government may need to focus and in identifying long-term trends, whether the trends are positive or negative. Part of the *Analytical Perspectives* document in the president's annual federal budget includes a section on social indicators. The section acknowledges that social indicators do not link directly to specific federal program performance: "They do not measure the outcomes of Government policies, because they do not show the direct results of Government activities, but they do provide a quantitative measure of the progress or lack of progress toward some of the ultimate ends that Government policy is intended to promote."[33]

Broad social indicators are used at state and local levels as well. One volunteer network in the Seattle area developed, in 1993, a set of 40 such indicators to determine whether the region is maintaining "sustainability"—namely, preserving its "cultural, economic, environmental and social" conditions. In the 1990s, the group found that the region was declining in sustainability in such areas as wetlands, energy use, and children living in poverty. In the 2000s, the City of Seattle strove for sustainability while at the same time fostering development.[34]

One limitation of the original Seattle measures, as well as other social indicators, is their lack of direct linkage with any given government service, meaning that the indicators are of little use for making yearly budget decisions. Children live in poverty as a result of many factors, and no government program alone could be expected to solve the problem.[35] At the same time, social indicators about communities in a state may give rise to decisions about how to help each of the communities in need.[36] Seattle addressed to some degree this connectivity issue with a several-year review of its sustainability indicators program. With the fourth iteration of the sustainability program, the community reorganized the program into a new organization: *www.B-Sustainable.org*. The major revision developed indicators at a lower level of aggregation, including down to the neighborhood level, in part to more closely link indicators with actions to improve conditions.[37]

Outcomes

Measures of more direct relevance to budgeting are outcomes, also called impacts. Measures of this type concentrate on *effectiveness*—whether desired effects or consequences are being achieved. When a government action has affected "individuals, institutions [or] the environment," an impact has occurred.[38] In the case of employment, an outcome measure might be the average earnings of nonwhite men who completed a job training program or, even more narrowly focused, the average increase in hourly earnings after completion of the program compared with prior earnings. Such a measure needs to be assessed carefully because earnings may have increased in a given time period mainly as a result of inflation or an upturn in the economy. Outcomes can be seen as a method of gauging the value of government services or determining whether expenditures are accomplishing what decision makers wished to achieve.

One approach may be to think of some outcomes as "raw" and others as "adjusted." Raw outcomes might be various measures of performance by school children on a standardized achievement test. Adjusted measures might take into account the children's characteristics, their families' socioeconomic backgrounds, and the neighborhoods in which they live.[39]

Myths or doctrines sometimes lead to problems in the selection of impact measures. For example, in providing funds to police departments, the assumption is often made that crime will be controlled. This assumption leads to the selection of crime rates as impact measures despite the fact that police have only limited control over crime.

Outputs

In contrast with outcome measures, output measures reflect the immediate products or services being provided. Returning to the employment example, the number of graduates of the training program would be the output. The percentage of persons enrolled who graduate, or the completion rate, can be calculated from year to year. Such measures are far easier to calculate than many impact measures because the data sources are within the organization. One needs simply to keep accurate records of who enrolled and who graduated. Impacts, on the other hand, are external. From this example, if we look at earnings of graduates, a monitoring or follow-up system for the graduates is necessary to obtain the appropriate outcome data.

Similarly, a program to spray for malaria is easy to measure in terms of the number of households sprayed, because the agency responsible for spraying keeps track of the output. But it may be a different part of the same agency, or sometimes a different agency altogether, or even a private party, that measures health status, the presumed intended outcome. Furthermore, there may be many additional factors involved in reducing the incidence of malaria, and it can be difficult to measure the extent to which the outcome is attributable to the spraying program or some other program or change in environmental conditions, such as a drought reducing the opportunity for the next season of mosquitoes to breed.

When it is known that a relationship exists between outputs and outcomes, then allocating resources may be straightforward. For example, measles inoculations are known to prevent the disease; therefore, allocating funds for the inoculations is warranted, presuming a disease threat exists. In the case of smallpox, vaccination programs ceased when the disease was basically eradicated, though recent recurrences in isolated regions of the world have stimulated new smallpox vaccination programs.

One drawback of using output measures alone is that an erroneous assumption can be made about causal relationships. Focusing on the graduation rate of a job training program makes sense only if it is known that training improves employability. Unless data are collected to verify anticipated results (i.e., a higher rate of employment at the end of the job training), the program is being maintained without outside corroboration of its goal.

Outputs, then, may encourage *suboptimization*, or the improvement of operations for attaining subobjectives, while risking the possibility of moving away from larger values. If the job training program was ineffective but the emphasis was placed on outputs, then decision makers would focus attention on increasing the quantity of outputs at reduced unit costs without realizing that the expenditures were altogether ineffective—not producing the desired employment results.

During the George W. Bush administration, in order to avoid this suboptimization problem, the U.S. Office of Management and Budget expected agencies to use outcome measures and required special justifications when agencies recommend using only output measures in the Program Assessment Rating Tool (PART) program.[40] However, Government Accountability Office (GAO) reports on the performance of the PART program suggested that agencies seemed to emphasize primarily efficiency—the ratio of inputs to outputs.[41] The chapter on the budget decision process goes into more detail on output and outcome measures.

Activities and Workload

Activities are the work that is done to produce outputs. The total hours of instruction could be a measure for a job training program, or the measure might be more tightly focused, such as hours of instruction in lathe operations. Activities are sometimes measured as workload. The number of applications processed and the number of enrollees in a program are both workload measures. If the number of applicants increases even though enrollments are kept constant because of space limitations, the workload will still increase, because more applications must be screened. Both activities and outputs are far easier to measure than impacts, a factor that contributes to the extensive use of the former in budgeting and more limited use of the latter.

Productivity

A term having many different meanings is *productivity*.[42] This term is sometimes used to cover virtually all forms of program measurement. A different approach is to limit the concept of productivity to comparisons of resource inputs and work. Ratios are typically used for productivity measurement, such as the total cost of a job training program divided by the number of graduates, yielding an average cost per graduate. If average cost remains constant from one year to another despite increases in salary rates and various supplies, then the assumption is that the unit is more productive. OMB Circular A-11 provides that agencies should report gains in *efficiency*, which is sometimes a synonym for productivity.

Productivity measures often require extensive recordkeeping. If a group of employees together performs several different activities, then a reporting system is needed to account for the hours committed to each activity by each employee. This accounting is sometimes accomplished by means of daily report forms. State and local police often must submit daily reports on hours spent patrolling, investigating, testifying in court, and report writing itself. Less complicated systems may use weekly, monthly, or quarterly report forms. On the cost side, accounting systems need to capture nonpersonnel expenditures related to activities.

Need

A final type of measure gauges the need for a program. The need measure indicates the gap between the level of service and the need for it. In the case of the job training program, one need measure would be the number of persons who are without adequate job skills and, therefore, require training.

In discussing need, we have come full circle back to social indicators, prompting a few words of caution. We have relied here on several examples to show differences among types of measures, but it should be understood that the differences might not always be so obvious. For example, the dollar value of fire damage in a city might be considered a social indicator, an impact of the fire department, and an indicator of fire service need.

Using Program Measures

A major challenge facing any budget system is deciding how to use these diverse types of information. Which types of information will be used, in what combination, and to what extent? An initial temptation is to use every imaginable measure of government operations. Such an approach is doomed to failure. If carefully and thoroughly executed, it would produce massive amounts of data that could not be comprehended by decision makers. Indeed, such data produce what is called "noise" rather than information.

Reformers for decades have been concerned that budgeting keep its focus on the missions of government and on the goals and objectives to be achieved. Osborne and Gaebler's popular work *Reinventing Government* stresses the need to keep mission primarily in mind when making decisions in government.[43] *Mission* refers to the fundamental reasons why a government program exists.

Although scholars and practitioners in the field of budgeting have yet to reach any consensus on what constitutes a goal as distinguished from an objective, one approach is to think of goals as broadly stated ideal conditions, such as the absence of crime. *Goals*, under this definition, are unlikely to be achieved but function as desired states that governments can continuously work toward attaining. *Objectives*, on the other hand, are more focused and immediate, and impact data are used to gauge whether a program is moving toward achieving its objectives. A jurisdiction might focus on reducing burglaries and could specify a quantitative target for the future, such as a 10% reduction in burglaries. In setting goals and objectives, decision makers must understand that some desired results can be achieved in a comparatively short period, such as a year, whereas other results will require many years of effort to achieve.[44]

The program measures that agencies develop may be a reflection of their overall types of missions. One research team defined four mission types: distributive, redistributive, regulatory, and market emulators.[45] *Distributive* encompasses the provision of services such as defense and transportation. *Redistributive* refers to making transfer payments, as with rent subsidies, and programs targeted at special groups, such as health benefits for the needy. *Regulatory*, as the term suggests, concentrates on control, such as controlling would-be air polluters or controlling food producers as a means of protecting the nation's food supply. *Market emulators* are those government operations that are run like a business, such as public utilities. Operations such as public electric utilities, municipal golf courses, parking garages, and institutions of higher education may operate somewhat like businesses.

The OMB's PART effort defined seven types of program measures that federal agencies were to develop depending upon the principal means by which a program's activities were to accomplish their objectives.[46] **Table 7–3** shows that the types are direct federal, competitive

Table 7–3 Typology of Federal Programs and Agencies

Program Type	Description	Example
Direct Federal	Services provided primarily by federal employees	State Department's Visa and Consular Services program
Competitive Grant	Competition used to award grants to state and local governments, organizations, and individuals	Health Centers at the Department of Health and Human Services
Block/Formula Grant	Formula used in awarding grants to state and local governments and other entities	Department of Energy's Weatherization Assistance program
Regulatory Based	Rulemaking and enforcement used to accomplish mission	Environmental Protection Agency's Mobile Source Air Pollution Standards and Certification program
Capital Assets and Service Acquisition	Goals accomplished by acquisition of "land, structures, equipment, and intellectual property" or purchase of services	Navy Shipbuilding
Credit	Goals served by providing loans, loan guarantees, and direct credit	Export-Import Bank's Long-Term Guarantees program
Research and Development	Knowledge creation and its application	Solar System Exploration program of National Aeronautics and Space Administration

Source: Data from U.S. Office of Management and Budget (2006). *Program assessment rating tool guidance no. 2006-02*, 6.

grant, block/formula grant, regulatory based, capital assets and service acquisition, credit, and research and development. The table provides illustrative federal programs for each type.

Selecting measures for any given program depends on perceptions about the program's mission. Individuals may differ widely on what they consider to be a specific program's mission. In a broad sense, the vision one has of a program is related to one's perception of what the public interest is. In a narrow sense, individuals may have specific expectations of what government programs should accomplish. Renters may want a city housing program to focus on affordable rental housing, while homeowners may be largely concerned with city policies that will protect property values and keep taxes low. Owners of rental properties, in contrast, may be chiefly interested in achieving substantial returns on their financial investments. Ultimately, the success of many, if not most, government programs will be evaluated in terms of several measures rather than only one or two. The need to use multiple measures makes analysis of a program's achievements more challenging than if a single measure is used.

Interpreting measures, especially social indicators and impacts, poses an additional problem. Because conditions in society result from a wide assortment of variables, isolating government's contribution to any given situation is difficult. One of the most difficult tasks in developing program measures is to select those that reflect what a particular government accomplishes. The federal government faces considerable challenges in this arena, because national programs are carried out through a variety of means. Means and actors vary, such as direct action of multiple federal agencies or indirect actions of other parties who are assisted through grants—for example, state and local governments, and nonprofit organizations—and providing or guaranteeing credit, as Table 7–3 illustrates. If a given program is successful, to what extent is the success due to partial funding by a particular federal agency?

Choosing Among Program Results

Inevitably some tradeoffs occur when trying to decide among programs. Consequently, *equity* becomes a concern: Are different segments of the citizenry benefiting according to some standard of fairness? The perceived severity of a problem to be addressed by government enters into such deliberations, such as the perception that a community has a major illegal drug problem or that the nation must address the problem of conquering acquired immune deficiency syndrome (AIDS). In both of these examples, a tempering factor is whether government programs are able to use infusions of resources effectively. Large budget allocations for combating drug abuse will not necessarily resolve such problems.

Governments are at a disadvantage in making these difficult choices in comparison with private corporations, which have the profit motive as their primary concern. Put simply, a private corporation will invest in those product lines that are expected to yield the highest rate of return on investments. Governments utilize some combination of the types of program information discussed here but cannot readily convert them into a single measure of profit. Instead, they must choose among disparate commodities such as fire protection, air pollution reduction, and public transit. Making comparisons may help in this situation. Where government actions such as physical capital investments can be measured more easily on the cost and result side with a common metric—monetary—then a single measure of return on investment comparable to private sector metrics can be and is used (see the chapter on capital assets).

SYSTEMS OF BUDGETING

If the central budget office simply instructed agencies to request budgets for the coming year, the result most likely would be several different types of responses based on different assumptions about the coming budget year. One agency might respond by requesting what it felt was needed. Another might respond in light of what resources it thought were available, resulting in a much lower request. Others might use combinations of these and other approaches. The consequences would be budget requests based on varied assumptions, and these requests would require different reactions from the budget office. To avoid such disparities in the assumptions made by requesting agencies, budget instructions often provide guidance to agencies.

Preparation Assumptions

Current Services Budgeting

One type of guidance is to assume essentially no change in programs. A department's current budget is considered its base, and any increases are to be requested only to cover additional operating costs, such as increased costs for personnel, supplies, and so on. An assumption is made that the government is committed or obligated to continue existing programs. Often, this base approach has been used only implicitly, but since the 1960s and 1970s, many governments have had their budgets explicitly indicate levels of commitment for agencies and programs.

The federal budget has included current services estimates since the 1970s. For the federal government, current services estimates are frequently referred to as "baseline" budget estimates. A baseline budget, like a current services budget, estimates the effects of continuing current tax and spending policies into the future. North Carolina segregates *continuation budgets* from *expansion budgets* requiring agencies to submit on separate forms and worksheets their budgets for *continuation* of current programs at current levels and their proposed budgets for new or *expanded* programs.[47] The chapter on the budget decision process presents a variety of samples from budget documents, including baseline estimates for the federal government.

Nonprofit organizations sometimes consider the base, or current services, budget to be last year's budget less specific projects that were intended to have a starting and stopping point. Other special projects may be included in the new budget request, but the baseline total budget does not include the costs of projects that have been completed in the previous year. For example, a youth nonprofit organization might have received a three-year grant for after-school programming for teens. The grant money, since it is temporary, would not be considered part of the base and would be budgeted accordingly.

Explicitly determining the current commitments is difficult because programs often are created without any forthright statement of commitment. In the easiest cases, there is an obligation to serve all claimants on the system. School districts, for example, are obligated to serve all eligible children. Therefore, budget requests from units within the school district would be based on the expected number of enrolled children. In other cases, the commitment may be in terms of the level of service, specifically outputs and workload. Using job training as an example again, the unit could have a commitment to maintain the same number of graduates or, alternatively, the same number of students. Budgeting, then, can be seen as adding increments to or subtracting them from the base.

Fixed-Ceiling Budgeting

One alternative to the current commitment approach is fixed-ceiling budgeting. Under this system, a dollar limit is set government-wide, then factored into limits for departments, bureaus, and other subunits. The advantage is that budget requests are created that do not, when totaled, exceed the desired ceiling. The disadvantage is that some organizational units may receive inadequate funding and others may be overfunded in terms of program priorities. This imbalance can result from the unavailability of adequate information about program requirements when limits are set. Fixed-ceiling budgeting is most useful during periods of stability, although fixed-ceiling approaches are used quite frequently by governments to encourage line agencies to make fewer expenditure demands during periods of fiscal stress. A weakness of both the base and fixed-ceiling approaches is that by themselves they offer no suggestions for program changes. If the budget office and chief executive have only these types of budget requests, they lack information about alternative resource allocations. In response to this lack of information, several "what-if" approaches to budget requests have been devised. These approaches ask agencies to develop alternatives by asking, for example, "What if more dollars were available?" or "What if program improvements were to be made in specific areas?"

Open-Ended Budgeting

One of the most common what-if approaches is open-ended budgeting. The question is asked, "What if resources were available to meet all anticipated needs?" This approach is sometimes called "blue sky" budgeting, in which the sky is the limit in requesting new funds. Agencies are expected to ask for what they think they need to deal with problems assigned to them. Open-ended budgeting should not be confused with the absence of guidance, in which some agencies might request "needed" funds and others might ask for lesser amounts. The advantage of the open-ended approach is that it brings perceived needs for services to the surface. The open-ended budget, in contrast with the current services budget, can serve as the basis for discussions of preferred funding levels. The disadvantage is that open-ended requests may exceed the economic and political capabilities of the jurisdiction, making the requests seem like fanciful wish lists. The harsh realities at federal, state, and local levels starting in 2007 rendered notions of open-ended budgets for all practical matters useless.

Performance Budgeting

A flurry of budget reform activity aimed at bringing greater program data into the budget decision-making process occurred in response to the First Hoover Commission (1949), which proposed the use of performance budgeting. In response to the Commission's recommendation, Congress specifically provided in the National Security Act Amendments of 1949 that performance budgeting be used in the military.[48] The following year saw passage of the Budget and Accounting Procedures Act, which in essence required performance budgeting for the entire federal government.[49] State and local governments followed suit.

Among federal, state, and local agencies, performance budgeting was geared mainly toward developing workload and unit cost measures of activities. For the postal service, the number of letters that could be processed by one employee was identified. Armed with this knowledge and an estimate of the number of letters to be processed, postal officials could calculate the personnel required for the coming budget year.[50] In the name of performance budgeting, the Department of Defense in 1950 adopted a single set of budget categories that were applied to all services. These categories, most of which were still in use in the 2000s, included personnel, maintenance and operation, and research and development.

Although reconstructing the past is difficult, little evidence suggests that performance budgeting ever became the basis upon which decisions were made in federal, state, or local budget processes. Nevertheless, some lasting effect is evident. Performance budgeting did introduce on a wide scale the use of program information in budget documents as well as the use of performance information for various purposes. Both program and performance information gained increasing attention in later years.[51]

Planning-Programming-Budgeting and Program Budgeting

The origin of the term *planning-programming-budgeting* is uncertain. Mosher used it in his 1954 book on Army program budgeting.[52] During the early 1960s in the Department of Defense, PPB stood for program package budgeting, because a package was presented in terms of the resource inputs (personnel, equipment, and so forth) and outputs.[53] By 1965, when President Lyndon Johnson extended the system to civilian agencies, PPB had come to mean planning-programming-budgeting. It should be recognized that planning and programming are not distinct from each other but differ only in degree. They have been defined as follows:

- *Planning* is the production of the range of meaningful potentials for selection of courses of action through a systematic consideration of alternatives.
- *Programming* is the more specific determination of the manpower, material, and facilities necessary for accomplishing a program.[54]

Today, PPB is generally used to refer to a series of budgetary reform efforts in the 1960s. The terms *program budgeting* and *performance budgeting* are more generic and apply to systems intended to link program costs with results.

Defense

There are several reasons why PPB started in the Department of Defense. Probably the most important one was that, despite having the authority to manage the military, the secretary of defense did not have the necessary management support. Secretary Robert S. McNamara in 1961 had the determination to initiate change. In coming to the Pentagon, he brought with him several people from the RAND Corporation who earlier had done extensive work related to program budgeting. David Novick of RAND published reports in the 1950s recommending such a system for the Department of Defense.[55] The key person for program budgeting under McNamara was Charles J. Hitch, who became assistant secretary of defense (comptroller). McNamara, Hitch, and others made use of the development of operations research, computers, and systems analysis, all of which were complementary to the mainstream of budgetary reform.

The central component of the Department of Defense (DOD) system is the Future Years Defense Program (FYDP), which projects costs and personnel according to missions or programs over a five-year period. The programs form the *program structure*, a classification system that begins with broad missions and factors them into subunits and activities. The structure groups like activities together regardless of which branches of the service conduct them, thereby allowing for analyses across organizational lines. The major programs are published in DOD Handbook 7045.7-H. The main program elements are generally consistent over time. **Exhibit 7–1** explains the relationship between program elements and budget appropriations accounts, and lists the most recent DOD program elements.

Changes in the FYDP are accomplished by the Office of the Secretary of Defense issuing guidance, to which the services respond by preparing *program objective memoranda*, which contain budget proposals for modifying the FYDP.[56] The program objective memoranda suggest programmatic and resource incremental changes to the base established in the FYDP.

Exhibit 7–1 Department of Defense Future Years Defense Program

The FYDP relates the appropriated funds and other resources to the Defense Department's 11 major programs. Resource requirements are specified in three broad categories: dollars, manpower, and forces (either equipment or combat units). The FYDP considers the following 11 program elements the *outputs* purchased by the resource requirements (inputs):

- Strategic forces
- General-purpose forces
- Command, control, communications, and intelligence
- Mobility forces
- Guard and reserve forces
- Research and development
- Central supply and maintenance
- Training, medical, and other general personnel activities
- Administration and associated activities
- Support of other nations
- Special operations forces

Source: Summarized from *Department of Defense future years defense program (FYDP) structure.* Retrieved October 21, 2011, from http://www.dtic.mil/whs/directives/corres/pdf/704507h.pdf, Section two, FYDP structure concepts and rules: major force programs, 6–11.

In addition to this elaborate process, the Department of Defense undergoes a Quadrennial Defense Review every four years, the most recent being the 2010 QDR.[57] The QDR provides the opportunity for a high-level strategic review of the nation's security threats and defense posture. There is no direct linkage to budget decisions except that QDR results feed into DOD strategic planning, which in turn feeds into the budget process.

A similar process for the State Department and the U.S. Agency for International Development, the Quadrennial Diplomacy and Development Review, took place in 2010 and 2011.[58] It too had only limited links to the budgetary process. Despite extensive documentation of program costs and outputs, Congress has continued to appropriate funds for defense, based on object classifications, with the main ones including military personnel; operation and maintenance; procurement; research, development, test, and evaluation; and military construction.

In 1995, the Commission on Roles and Missions of the Armed Forces, created by the National Defense Authorization Act for Fiscal Year 1994, issued a wide-sweeping set of recommendations, including a call for a major overhaul of the defense budget process. Earlier, the National Performance Review (NPR) had suggested changes in the process, but the 1995 Commission made recommendations that would fundamentally revise the system.[59] The report stated, "The current PPB system reexamines the entire multiyear defense program annually, uses too many people, takes too long, goes into too much detail, and leaves little time for reflection and creativity."[60] Despite these recommendations and much discussion, the Clinton, George W. Bush, and Obama administrations made few defense budget system changes, though reforms initiated under Defense Secretary Donald Rumsfeld during George W. Bush's second term merged the once separate program and budget review processes, allowing for some streamlining of the system.[61]

Federal Civilian Reforms

Turning to the civilian side of government, use of PPB by federal agencies was announced in 1965 by President Johnson, who had been impressed with the Department of Defense budget system. This action sparked massive reform efforts throughout all levels of government in the United States.

The federal civilian system was intended to be similar to the Department of Defense model. Multiyear plans, known as program and financial plans, were to be devised for each department. Changes were to be made through the submission of program memoranda. However, by 1969, when Richard M. Nixon became president, PPB had not been fully implemented by the civilian agencies. In 1971, OMB relieved agencies of the duty to prepare program and financial plans and program memoranda. As a major budget system, PPB was allowed to die quietly.[62]

A study conducted by the Bureau of the Budget (now OMB) found six factors that characterized the more successful efforts to introduce PPB:[63]

1. The number of analysts was sufficient.
2. Analysts were well qualified.
3. Analysts had formal access to agency heads and managers.
4. Analysts had informal access.
5. Agency heads and managers gave strong support for use of analysis.
6. Analysis was viewed as a valuable tool by agency heads and managers.

This study and others found that lack of understanding of and commitment to program budgeting on the part of leadership tended to deter success, as did an agency's general "underdevelopment" in the use of analytic techniques. Agencies administering "soft" social programs had difficulty devising useful program measures. Bureaucratic infighting also reduced the chances of successful implementation. These findings are instructive for any government that undertakes to restructure the operations of its budget system.[64]

State and Local Reforms

The use of PPB did not revolutionize state and local decision making in the 1960s any more than it revolutionized federal decision making. Most of the states that experimented with PPB emphasized the development of program structure, multiyear plans, and program memoranda, while only a few concentrated on analysis as their main thrust. By the mid-1970s, the emphasis had swung away from the structural features of PPB to the use of measures of effectiveness and efficiency and program analysis. In the 1960s, many states and municipalities took only cautious first steps and established no timetable for completion of the installation process. Others began the effort on a pilot basis, attempting PPB in one department before expanding its use.

By the close of the 1960s, it was difficult to identify many ongoing PPB systems at the state and local levels. The reasons for failure or lack of major success were similar to those already mentioned for federal agencies. State and local governments usually did not have sufficiently sophisticated management practices to be able to undertake the expected transformation. Additionally, people simply expected too much to result from conversion to PPB and did not realize the financial and administrative costs associated with the conversion. Legislative bodies often showed little support for the new budget system, and this fact was interpreted by some as legislative hostility toward change.[65]

Change, however, did occur as a result of efforts to introduce PPB systems. Perhaps the biggest single achievement was that governments began to make greater use of program information in budgetary decision making, albeit information largely of the output variety.[66]

Zero-Base Budgeting

Zero-base budgeting (ZBB) is another form of "what-if" budgeting. "Traditional" ZBB—that is, not the type used by the federal government during the Carter administration—asks, "What if a program were to be eliminated?" Rather than assuming that a base exists, the approach asks what would happen if a program were to be discontinued. Each program is challenged to justify its very existence in every budget cycle.

Early Use

The U.S. Department of Agriculture engaged in an experiment with ZBB in the early 1960s, and the results were disappointing.[67] ZBB, it was found, wasted valuable administrative time by requiring the rehashing of old issues that had already been resolved. The system was unrealistic, since many programs were mandatory in the political arena and could not be dismantled no matter how compelling the available data and analysis. Decision makers within the agency could not adequately review the excessive paperwork that was generated.

The disadvantage of ZBB is analogous to that of open-ended budgeting. Both approaches make basically unrealistic assumptions. Whereas open-ended budgeting assumes unlimited resources, the zero-base approach assumes that decision makers have the capacity to eliminate enough programs to justify the time spent in evaluating them. In reality, the political forces in any jurisdiction are such that few programs in any given year can be abandoned. For this reason, ZBB may be better applied to selective programs in any one year rather than government-wide. A cycle of reviews can be established such that some programs are thoroughly reviewed each year using ZBB, and all programs are reviewed in any five-year period.

The 1970s

Zero-base budgeting gained new popularity in the 1970s.[68] Much attention focused on Georgia and its governor, Jimmy Carter, who subsequently brought a new version of ZBB to the federal government upon becoming president in 1977.[69] The Carter administration's version had three major characteristics:[70]

1. *Decision units* were identified for which budget requests, called decision packages, were to be prepared. Approximately 10,000 of these were prepared each year.
2. Alternative funding levels were used for each package:

   - The *minimum level*, which entailed providing services below present levels;
   - The *current level*, which maintained existing services and reflected increased costs for personnel, supplies, and the like; and
   - An *enhancement level*, which provided for upgraded services.

3. Alternative funding levels of decision packages were to be ranked by importance.

The ZBB experiment at the federal level was criticized on several counts. The most frequently heard complaint related to the amount of time required to prepare requests and the corresponding deluge of paperwork. The ZBB system, contrary to what President Carter had promised, did not require agencies to justify every tax dollar they received. Administrators puzzled over how a minimum level below current operations could exist when the statute under which an agency operated specified benefits, as in the case of Social Security.

Rarely did ZBB eliminate unnecessary programs, curtail their growth, or result in reassigning priorities among programs.[71] In some isolated instances, savings were achieved by funding programs at the minimum level, but that produced agency resentment. Administrators of these programs saw themselves as being punished because they had identified how their programs could operate with less than the current budget. More often, however, the system was seen as involving excessive paperwork that ultimately had little or no impact on policy making. Shortly after President Reagan took office in January 1981, the new administration announced that ZBB would no longer be practiced.

The experience at the state and local levels was comparable to that of the federal government. Although ZBB initially seemed to hold great promise, ultimately it was abandoned, even if some governments continued to describe their budget systems as founded on the concept.

One observation was that ZBB efforts in the 1970s were doomed because of the immense amount of data that needed to be processed with technology that would seem ancient compared with today's standards. An extension of such reasoning is that today's technology may make possible ZBB and other reforms that failed in earlier times.[72] That observation seems reasonable with respect to the steady increase in the use of program information in budgetary decision making, but does not gainsay the pessimism based on many attempts for total systemic reform in budgetary processes.[73] However, the main reason ZBB is unlikely to be considered seriously again is that literally starting with base zero on an essential function, such as police services, is nonsensical.

Strategic Planning and Guidance

Planning

Many governments, in part following the lead of private sector organizations, have engaged in strategic planning efforts, which focus attention on missions, goals, and objectives.[74] In strategic planning, options are identified and chosen in light of fundamental values and purposes. Annual budgeting is then used to allocate resources according to the established priorities. Some have called budget systems that use strategic planning and performance measurement *performance-based budgeting* (PBB),[75] but that is an overly broad way to conceive of performance-based budgeting. A strategic plan and performance measures do not necessarily have anything to do with the budget process. Performance-based budgeting is not to be confused with performance budgeting (mentioned earlier). Performance-based budgeting differs, as did program budgeting, in that it focuses on results rather than on workload or activity.

Strategic planning can be an extremely time-consuming process in which various plans, often presented in great detail, are drafted, reviewed, and then modified. This process usually involves developing an overall plan and then revising the plan annually to reflect new information and revised priorities. Comparisons can be drawn here with the Department of Defense's FYDP, mentioned earlier. The process of devising and revising plans is sometimes considered as valuable as the actual written plans themselves, in that the process fosters extensive thinking within a government about its core values in serving the citizenry.

Policy and Program Guidance

A less ambitious but nevertheless useful approach is to provide broad policy guidance or more narrowly focused program guidance to departments and agencies before they begin to prepare their budget requests. At the federal level, the OMB often instructs specific agencies regarding which program funding proposals are likely to receive favorable review and instructs them to prepare issue papers on specific programs for which concern exists about the efficacy of resource utilization. Some state and local budget offices provide program guidelines that indicate to agencies the concerns of their governors or mayors—namely, the issues that have high priority for the coming budget year.

In response to such guidance, agencies prepare detailed program requests. A discussion of the range of available alternatives is likely to take place, possibly with detailed costing and the expected results of each. Where guidance is not directed at any one agency, two or more may submit competing requests, each attempting to show how its proposed alternative would deal with a problem. For example, both the city police and the recreation departments might submit budget proposals for dealing with juvenile gangs.

The advantage of such guidance is that agencies prepare requests that are likely to be favorably received by the chief executive and are spared many hours of needless work in preparing requests that are fated for rejection. Policy or program guidance, however, does not ensure executive approval of agency requests. The requests may be rejected simply because of inadequate funds or because the arguments for the proposed changes fail to persuade decision makers.

Other Budgeting and Management Systems

Numerous other budgeting and management systems exist. These include management by objectives, total quality management, and managing for results.

Management by Objectives

Workload is often the focus of management by objectives (MBO) and other participative management techniques that were developed in the 1950s and 1960s.[76] Although many diverse activities have been carried out in government under the rubric of MBO, a common theme tends to be prescribing objectives for organizational units, managers, and workers in terms of the work they are expected to accomplish. Participative management systems such as MBO emphasize involvement of all strata of the bureaucracy in the development of objectives.

Total Quality Management or Continuous Quality Improvement

Total quality management (TQM)—also called continuous quality improvement—is not a budget system but, as envisioned by its creator, W. Edwards Deming, is a management system that focuses on the end products or results of organizations.[77] Available space does not allow a thorough discussion of TQM, but it should be noted that the system relies heavily on program measurement and that one of Deming's 14 TQM recommendations is to avoid management by objectives. The latter management system is seen as setting quotas for workers rather than empowering them to think creatively and allowing them to achieve results that might well be beyond any expected quotas.

Managing for Results

A term that gained popularity in the United States after 2000 is *managing for results* (MFR). The term may have its roots in the United Kingdom, Australia, and New Zealand. The term is often associated with performance management efforts.[78] A key factor in MFR efforts is that managers must be held accountable for their operations *and* must have the authority to get done whatever tasks are required.[79]

Hybrid Techniques

Many of the techniques discussed here can be used in combination to form hybrid systems. ZBB, for example, can be used selectively for some agencies undergoing intensive review even as others use a fixed-ceiling approach. A government may use fixed-ceiling budgeting to allocate monies among major departments but then allow each department to use *entrepreneurial* budgeting—namely, allocating funds within the department with only a minimum of control from the central budget office.[80] *Target-base budgeting* is also sometimes used, such as in California, for example. In this type of budgeting, agencies prepare budget requests based on fixed ceilings but then may propose budget increases above the ceilings.[81] Governments can use a current services budget in conjunction with priority listing of decision packages in an approach akin to the Carter administration's version of ZBB. The base approach can be combined with open-ended budgeting, in which agencies request funds for what they perceive to be their needs. Program guidance can be linked with priority listings.

Multiyear Requests

All budget requests are multiyear in that they cover at least the current year plus the coming budget year and probably the past year as well. States with biennial budgets obviously have multiyear requests. One issue is whether budget requests should extend beyond the budget year and, if so, how a multiyear perspective is to be included in the budget. The argument for multiyear requests is simple: Without looking beyond the budget year, commitments of resources may be made that were never intended. This argument applies particularly to proposed expansions and new programs (see the chapter on capital assets). A key distinction is between multiyear budget forecasting, or estimating, and multiyear appropriations requests. The DOD's QDR, for example, is a five-year planning perspective estimating future year budget requirements, but the DOD appropriations request, like all other federal agencies, is for a single year.

Time Horizons

In theory, the time horizon of a budget request should be geared to the life cycle of each program. This life cycle is clearest in specific projects or programs that have an obvious beginning and conclusion. A weapons system is one of the best examples. The cycle begins with research and concludes when the system is judged to be obsolete.

On the other hand, many government programs have no foreseeable conclusion. The need for education, roads, law enforcement, recreation, and the like will always exist. Each may have unique properties that suggest possible time horizons. Given the length of time required to design and construct schools, projections of several years are needed. Multiyear requests can reveal when roads will require major repairs, redesigns, and expansions. Indeed, the necessity for multiyear planning is often part of the justification for the separate capital budgeting processes pursued by many governments.

Because an appropriate life cycle for multiyear requests is often not obvious, an arbitrary set of years may be imposed. The most common is the budget year plus the four succeeding years, known as a five-year projection. Making projections beyond five years is difficult because of the many unknowns. Using the road example, it may be largely unknown what the typical commuting pattern will be 10 or more years from now. Furthermore, political leaders have limited incentives to focus on costs or benefits that occur many years in the future, because these future costs and benefits will likely arise outside of their electoral window.

Cost and Program Projections

Assuming they can be made, projections can be limited to finances or can include program data projections. The state of the art tends to limit projections to finances, showing anticipated future financial requirements. When program impacts and outputs are projected, the requests show what resources will be needed in future years as well as the benefits that will be accrued.

Multiyear projections using cost and program data can prove helpful in coping with severe economic conditions. Where program reductions are necessary, agency requests can illustrate the consequences over a longer time period. Cuts in an agency's budget made this year may seem essential but produce undesirable future consequences. To live within available revenues, a city may reduce its road maintenance program, with no noticeable reduction in road quality in the first year. However, by the second or third year following these cuts, the city may have a road network of substantially lower quality than before, and that in turn can lead to more costly capital investments to rehabilitate the road network.

Use of Budget Techniques: Federal

Numerous congressional and presidential initiatives over the past two decades have continued the pattern of planning reforms by emphasizing the use of program measures, either or both output and outcome measures, to improve program performance. Generally, new budget concepts have not been developed. Each recent administration has put its own particular emphasis on budget reform, generally rejecting the primary label attached to the previous administration's reform initiative and introducing at least a new description of how the new administration intends to improve governmental performance. During that same time period, Congress has weighed in with two major government performance improvement statutes. Each presidential and congressional initiative is discussed in brief in the following subsections.

National Performance Review

Upon taking office in 1993, President Clinton established the National Performance Review (NPR) under the direction of Vice President Gore. The NPR's initial report, issued in 1993, contained a host of recommendations intended to streamline all aspects of the government.[82] Later in the Clinton administration, NPR became known as the National Partnership for Reinventing Government and had as its focus *reengineering* or *reinventing* government. The intent was to redesign processes carried out by agencies so as to improve their efficiency and effectiveness. *Benchmarking* was an important component in which best practices elsewhere, whether in government or the private sector, were identified and used as a guide for revising how government operates.[83] Customer satisfaction surveys were an important part of the reinventing government movement. As **Exhibit 7–2** illustrates, customer satisfaction surveys, both those conducted by government and those conducted by independent, external organizations, have had some continuity.

Government Performance and Results Act

Occurring coincident with the NPR was congressional passage of the Government Performance and Results Act (GPRA, pronounced "gip-ra") of 1993.[84] This law resulted from a congressional and presidential concern about "waste and inefficiency" in government and "insufficient articulation of program goals and inadequate information on program performance." It was based on the premise that agencies (1) need to define their missions and desired outcomes, (2) measure performance, and (3) use the performance information to revise programs.[85]

Exhibit 7–2 Customer Satisfaction Surveys and Government Performance

The American Society for Quality, the University of Michigan's Ross School of Business, and the CFI Group have developed the American Customer Satisfaction Index, which has been used in gauging satisfaction with services in both the private and public sectors. Some of the 2010 results for government are reported below. As can be seen, government as a whole received a score of 66.9 on a scale of 100. This score was in the same range as previous years dating back to 1998. Local satisfaction was 68.3, and federal satisfaction was 65.4. The table shows just a small sampling of agencies and their customers. For instance, while individual taxpayers filing electronically gave the Internal Revenue Service (IRS) a score of 77, large and international corporate taxpayers gave the IRS a score of only 53.

American Customer Satisfaction Scores for Public Sector, Local Government, Federal Government, and Selected Customer Segments, 2010

	Customer Segment	2010 Score
Public Administration/Government		66.9
Local Government		68.3
	Solid Waste/suburban (metro)	79
	Solid Waste/central city (metro)	77
	Police Service/central city (metro)	66
	Police Service/suburban (metro)	65
Federal Government		65.4
National Weather Service, Commerce	Users of weather services	85
General Services Administration	Users of Federal Supply Service	83
Small Business Administration	Applicants for Homeowner Loan	74
Internal Revenue Service, Treasury	Individual electronic filers	77
Internal Revenue Service, Treasury	Large and international business corporate tax filers	53

Source: Data from American Society for Quality, University of Michigan Ross School of Business, and CFI Group (2011). ACSI Scores. Retrieved October 15, 2011, from http://www.theacsi.org/index.php?option=com_content&view=article&id=132&Itemid=196 and http://www.theacsi.org/index.php?option=com_content&view=article&id=238:acsi-scores-for-us-federal-government-2010&catid=14&Itemid=298.

In late 2010, GPRA was amended by the GPRA Modernization Act (GPRMA).[86] This modernization was the accumulation of several years of congressional effort, stimulated by a major GAO analysis of GPRA's accomplishments and shortcomings. The GAO reported that GPRA:

- "established a solid foundation of results-oriented performance planning, measurement, and reporting in the federal government"; and
- had "begun to facilitate the linking of resources to results"; but
- it had issues such as "federal managers continue to have difficulty setting outcome-oriented goals, collecting useful data on results, and linking institutional, program, unit, and individual performance measurement and reward system."[87]

In the Clinton administration, the White House established a formal structure for implementing GPRA. The president designated deputy secretaries in the various departments to serve as chief operating officers, and assigned to them responsibility to direct implementation of GPRA. The George W. Bush administration continued that practice, and by executive order, the Bush administration created the role of performance improvement officer (PIO).[88] These formal structures were not formalized in the legislation, however. This was corrected by GPRMA, which conveys a statutory requirement for the PIOs, and for the Performance Improvement Council, also previously established under presidential authority prior to GPRMA. OMB Circular A-11, which instructs agencies on how to prepare their budgets, provides guidance on the implementation of GPRMA.

GPRA required federal agencies to have strategic planning processes and plans in place, starting by the end of fiscal 1997. GPRMA requires that agency strategic plans be published annually on their agency websites, reflecting an increasing emphasis in both the executive and legislative branches to give more public visibility to planning and budgeting, with a particular focus on results accomplished, or not, by federal programs. According to OMB Circular A-11, plans must cover at least six years—the budget year plus the next five years. Plans must show agency mission, strategic goals, and means and strategies planned for achieving goals. Updates and revised plans must be submitted to the president (i.e., OMB) and Congress at least every three years.

Given the diversity of agencies within the federal government and the immensity of the task of implementing GPRA, unevenness in the quality of the annual plans was inevitable. GAO reviewed weaknesses in the implementation of GPRA that were intended to be resolved by GPRMA's enhancements of the original act. GAO identified five major areas for improvement:

- greater coordination across overlapping and crosscutting programs;
- improved management capabilities in the areas of financial, human capital, information technology, procurement, and acquisition;
- improved quality and usefulness of performance information;
- sustained leadership commitment to accountability for results; and
- partnering with Congress to shape agency goals, identify appropriate performance measures, and increase consultation.[89]

George W. Bush's Management Agenda

In his first year in office, President Bush announced a five-prong president's management agenda (PMA). The items were human capital, competitive sourcing, financial performance, e-government, and budget/performance integration (BPI). The budget/

performance integration component was called the linchpin of the Bush management agenda, since without an effective budgeting and performance management system the other four parts of PMA were most likely to fail.[90]

The Bush management agenda included rating each department in the five management emphasis areas by the President's Management Council. "Green" indicated success. "Yellow" was for mixed results. "Red" indicated unsatisfactory. In 2006, for example, the Treasury Department received "greens" on human capital and competitive sourcing, "yellows" on e-government and budget/performance integration, and "red" on financial performance. OMB received no "greens," "yellows" on human capital and e-government, and "reds" on competitive sourcing, financial performance, and budget/performance integration. In contrast, the Labor Department received "greens" on all five items. The National Science Foundation (NSF) and the Social Security Administration (SSA) each received four "greens." NSF's and SSA's weak area was competitive sourcing ("red" and "yellow," respectively). Results were reported on the website *www.results.gov*, which was replaced by *www.performance.gov* when the Obama administration established its own reform agenda.

The rating tool introduced by President Bush was known as the Program Assessment Rating Tool (PART). Its purpose was to systematically evaluate the operations of government and to move budget reform forward. The reform was in keeping with the mainstream of budget reform, bringing to bear greater program information to the allocation of scarce resources. *Performance budgeting* is the term used, but this should be distinguished from the performance budgeting of the 1950s.

The PART process was used "to assess the performance of federal programs and to drive improvements in program performance."[91] The starting point for the PART was the identification of 1,000 programs in the federal budget. In 2003, the Bush administration pledged to evaluate 200 of these programs each year for five years. The key goals of the PART were to identify which programs worked and how well they worked. In the final PART annual report of the Bush administration, OMB reported that 1,017 federal programs representing 98% of the federal budget had been reviewed. The report identified several key achievements with respect to meeting performance goals and increasing the use of program information:

- 63% of program performance goals were met in 2008, compared to 74% in 2007;
- 57% of 2008 program measures improved performance results over the prior year, compared to 45% in 2007;
- 88% of programs have at least one outcome-oriented performance measure, up slightly from 86% in 2007; and
- 94% of programs have at least one efficiency measure, up from 90% in 2007.[92]

It is important to note that these comparisons between years do not mean that the same programs were rated each of those two years, and the differences reflect improvements or lack of improvement in the same programs. The numbers reference whatever programs were rated in those two different years.

The PART consisted of a series of mainly yes-or-no questions that agencies had to answer about their programs. There were four groups of questions:

1. *Program Purpose and Design:* to assess whether the program's purpose and design are clear and sound (20%),
2. *Strategic Planning:* to assess whether the program has valid long-term and annual measures and targets (10%),
3. *Program Management:* to rate the program's management, including financial oversight and program improvement efforts (20%), and
4. *Program Results/Accountability:* to rate program performance on measures and targets reviewed in the strategic planning section and through other evaluations (50%).[93]

Exhibit 7–3 is a sample of the detailed guidance that the Office of Management and Budget provided for agencies in using PART. The emphasis was on outcome measures and not outputs. The guidance required at least one efficiency measure as well. Of particular significance is that an agency and its corresponding resource management office (RMO) within OMB had to agree on measures, or the answer to the question is an automatic "no." OMB guidance suggested this was a "collaborative" process, but some agencies undoubtedly felt the heavy hand of OMB in rejecting measures they preferred and advocating measures less favorable to the agencies' budget reviews.

After scoring and weighting the four groups of questions, overall PART scores were tabulated. Programs were judged to be effective (85 to 100), moderately effective (70 to 84), adequate (50 to 69), or ineffective (0 to 49). When a program failed to have approved long-term and annual performance measures, the program automatically received a rating of "results not demonstrated." This last category included programs that possibly were ineffective and programs that may be effective but for which suitable measures had not been developed.

The PART program ultimately got mixed reviews. It was generally perceived as more useful in the executive budgeting process, but of more limited utility in congressional appropriations decision making, in part because committee staff did not feel the process of developing performance measures included congressional consultation.[94] The PART did force agencies to be mindful about justifying their programs through specific measures. At the same time, OMB did not use PART results to slash underachieving programs. The President's Management Council explicitly denied budget cutting as a major PART agenda, saying:

> The Administration wants programs to work. The primary purpose of the PART is to make sure that federal programs live up to their congressionally-mandated intent and are effectively managed to provide the best value for taxpayers. The PART is rarely the only basis for program termination proposals. If a program is ineffective, it may well need more money.
>
> There are numerous examples of programs rated effective that received budget cuts and programs rated ineffective that received more funding. For example, although the Office of the Coordinator of U.S. Assistance to Europe and Eurasia (Support for East European Democracy/Freedom Support Act) was found to be effective at promoting democratic, economic, and other types of reform, its budget was proposed for reduction because Romania, Bulgaria, and Croatia graduated from U.S. assistance.[95]

Exhibit 7–3 Question on Annual Performance Measures in Program Assessment Rating Tool

---

Does the program have a limited number of specific annual performance measures that can demonstrate progress toward achieving the program's long-term goals?

Purpose: To determine whether a limited number of annual performance measures have been identified that directly support the long-term goals evaluated in Questions 2.1 and 2.2. The measures should be logically linked to the long-term goals in a manner that enables them to demonstrate progress toward achieving those long-term goals.

Elements of *Yes*: A *Yes* answer needs to clearly explain and provide evidence of each of the following:

Question 2.3: Quick Tips	
Answer Options	*Yes, No*
Question Linkages	If *No* on 2.1, must provide explanation of how annual performance goals contribute to long-term outcomes and purpose to get *Yes* on 2.3.
Additional Guidance	Block Grant R&D Capital Assets and Service Acquisition

✓ A limited number of discrete, quantifiable, and measurable annual performance measures have been established for the program.

✓ Annual performance measures adequately measure the program's progress toward reaching the long-term goals evaluated in Questions 2.1 and 2.2. The explanation must clearly state how the outcomes help achieve the long-term goals of the program.

✓ Annual performance measures focus on outcomes. Measures may focus on outputs if the program can adequately justify why it is unable to define satisfactory quantifiable outcome measures. The justification for not adopting outcome measures and the explanation of how output measures show progress toward desired outcomes must be clearly presented in the explanation and/or evidence sections.

The annual performance measures may be those developed by the agency to comply with GPRA [Government Performance and Results Act], if the performance measures meet the criteria listed above.

Elements of *No*: A *No* must be given if the agency and OMB have not reached agreement on measures that meet PART requirements.

Programs must have at least one efficiency measure as part of their annual measures. Credit for efficiency measures is given in Question 3.4.

Source: Reprinted from U.S. Office of Management and Budget (2006). *Guide to the program assessment rating tool (PART)*, 25. Retrieved August 1, 2006, from http://www.whitehouse.gov/omb/part/fy2006/2006_guidance_final.pdf.

An assessment after the first three years of implementation concluded that PART had an impact on agency resource allocation decisions, but had not caused significant changes in program and agency management.[96] The term *performance budgeting* seems to suggest that budget decisions are based on performance, but in actuality, performance information is more of an aid to decision makers. Use of such information is tempered by a variety of factors that includes assessments of the quality of information and the reality of the political environment. Still, the PART may well have influenced budget decisions. One study found that PART scores were related to OMB budget recommendations, particularly for small and medium-sized programs.[97] Another study found that the PART enhanced OMB's control over the budget, which is important in that the agency is responsible for overseeing the budget on behalf of the president.[98] Congress, on the other hand, did not seem to respond to nor make much use of PART information.[99] A harsher comment noted that the Congress "generally ignored the OMB-initiated PART performance evaluations."[100]

The Obama Administration Management and Budget Initiatives

Similar to the predecessor administration, the Obama administration introduced both an overall government management improvement agenda and specific budget reforms. Much of the emphasis at the outset was on recovery from the financial crisis and the resulting recession. Six management initiatives were described in the first budget of the new administration:

- Replacing the PART with a new Performance Improvement and Analysis Framework;
- Ensuring responsible spending of Recovery Act funds;
- Transforming the federal workforce;
- Managing across sectors;
- Reforming federal contracting and acquisition; and
- Increasing transparency, implementing new technology, and encouraging participatory democracy.[101]

The PART was described as having improved the use of performance measures in federal agencies, but not being very successful in using measurement as a device to actually improve performance. Under the Obama administration, emphasis has been placed on assessing what works and does not work, and on the role of formal evaluations that are published on a new website, *www.performance.gov*. Published on the new website are agency multiyear strategic and annual plans, reports on evaluations of agency programs, and summative annual agency reports. An early assessment of the new site critiqued it as "underperforming."[102] Although a new framework for performance improvement and analysis was forecast, what actually developed were specific initiatives to conduct more rigorous program evaluations and publish the results.

The fiscal year 2011 budget stressed an Obama administration pledge to deliver *high-performance government* by asking each agency head to identify a few, less than 10, high-priority performance goals.[103] These priority areas are to become the focal point for most performance measurement efforts aimed at measuring not only process but impact, using the most appropriate evaluation research methods to document real impact of federal programs. An important feature of the reform agenda was to hold agency officials at the highest level accountable for achieving goals that they themselves selected, and to communicate those achievements widely across government, to Congress, and to the public.

As a response to the deepening recession that started in 2007 and growth in the federal deficit, formal budget processes began to move away from broader system or process reforms and focus instead on individual initiatives to address specific issues, mainly related to the recession and the deficit. For example, to ensure responsible spending of Recovery Act funds, (see the chapter on government and the economy) agencies were required to distinguish Recovery Act funds from all other funding requests in their budget proposals. The contracting and acquisition initiative focused across all agencies on reducing the number of *no-bid* or *sole-source* contracts, decreasing the use of large indefinite quantity or task order contracts, and decreasing wherever possible the size of individual federal procurement actions.

The major formal budget reforms in the first years of the Obama administration were not those of the administration itself, but were contained in GPRMA (2010), discussed above. This, of course, was a congressional and not an administration initiative, though it does formalize many features of GPRA that were vague or not spelled out in the legislation, and had been implemented by executive order. Specific provisions were included in the act to make the results of evaluations of federal programs much more accessible to the public, to focus intensively on spending programs to address the effects of the recession, and to increase funding for more rigorous and extensive program evaluations. These provisions continued the trend toward greater production and use of performance information, even if they did not solve all the problems of actually using the information in budget and appropriations decisions.[104]

Use of Budget Techniques: State, Local, and Other Countries

State Techniques

States have also moved in major ways toward requiring performance measurement as part of their budget processes, with many states demonstrating commitments to revising their budget systems to use program information in decision making. A National Association of State Budget Officers study found that 49 of 50 states described their budget systems as either program or performance budget systems, and 40 states collect performance measures. However, only 14 state legislatures in those 40 states participate formally in the performance measurement system. In 26 states, performance measures are formally reviewed or audited regularly.[105] A Pew Center on the States study found that states' use of strategic planning and performance measurement also improved budgetary decision making. The study detailed five objectives for systems to improve budget decision making:

- Ensure a lead role for strategic planning;
- Implement high-value performance measures and rigorous measurement;
- Provide analysis of performance information to see if and how results are being achieved;
- Use the results in decision making; and
- Make performance information available to the public.[106]

One study of states' use of performance-based budgeting (PBB) during different economic conditions found that executive branch participants tend to use performance measures and related features much more than legislators, similar to findings reported above about the federal government. In addition, the study found that performance measures and other features of PBB were used more often during good economic conditions, whereas during economic downturns with pressures on state budgets, performance approaches tended to move off center stage.[107] This finding is consistent with results reported above on the Obama administration's emphasis on efforts to deal with the recession and the budget deficit, and the generally lower interest of the U.S. Congress in performance measurement and related planning reforms.

Intriguingly, an earlier survey of state executive and legislative budgeters found disagreement in eight states regarding whether PBB had been implemented. These states were Alabama, Georgia, Idaho, Minnesota, New Hampshire, Ohio, Vermont, and Washington. Nine states reported not implementing PBB, and 29 states reported implementing PBB.[108] On the plus side, the vast majority of the respondents said that PBB had improved their understanding of state government operations (82%). On the minus side, a substantial majority said the system had increased their workload (75%).

The Government Performance Project (GPP), an activity sponsored by the Pew Charitable Trusts and conducted by a consortium of researchers and journalists, has been studying management capacity in both state and local governments. Using a letter-grade system, the project found a wide range of performance in managing for results in 1999, 2001, 2005, and 2008. In their summary of the 2008 project, the authors state: "Information is king."[109] The GPP grades states in their management of money, people, infrastructure, and information. Though the study reported that all four categories are important to improving state performance, it also said that in 2008 "the elements that make up the information category—planning, goal-setting, measuring performance, disseminating data and evaluating progress—overlap with the other three fields to a greater degree than ever before. Information elements, in short, are key to how a state takes care of its infrastructure, plans for its financial future and deals with the dramatic changes affecting the state workforce."[110]

The information category focuses a great deal of attention on the availability and use of performance information in state governments. The 2008 results identified Illinois, Michigan, Utah, Virginia, and Washington as the top performers in their use of information for management. Each of these states received a grade of "A." The lowest-rated states were New Hampshire and South Dakota, with "D" grades. The study found, just as in the 2005 survey, that states are making more use of performance information for budgeting and for managing their day-to-day activities than in the past. Whereas during the 1990s it was still relatively rare to have extensive use and publication of information, it is commonplace now. The use of performance information for budgeting, however, often does not extend to legislative use of performance data in appropriating funds.[111]

There is reason to question whether report cards oversimplify matters and whether they provide useful information to consumers, whether the users are the general public or government decision makers, such as legislators.[112] On the other hand, governments may well embrace management reforms partially in pursuit of improved ratings. The GPP has received extensive publicity, and low grades for a state not only are embarrassments but also may have political repercussions. As a consequence, states may strive to improve their management so as to improve their ratings.

Local Techniques

Use of program information at the local level is more limited than at the state level, but there has been progress since the 1990s.[113] A mid-1990s study of members of the Government Finance Officers Association found that 51% of local governments still used line-item budgeting.[114] Performance budgeting and zero-base/target-base budgeting were used by 2% to 3%, while program budgeting was used by 10% of the local governments. Thirty-five percent reported using a hybrid system. In contrast, a survey of city and county administrators and budgeters done in the early 2000s found performance measurement to be "pervasive."[115] A case study analysis of Indianapolis documented the importance of the role of performance measures in departmental budgeting.[116]

In addition to grading the states, the Government Performance Project graded the nation's largest cities and counties in 2000 on several factors, including managing for results.[117] Though the 2000 study has not been repeated, at that time it found cities lagging behind state governments, not surprisingly, but increasing in the use of performance measures, especially in reporting to the public. Milwaukee, which earned a high grade in the GPP 2000 study, has attracted attention as a city that successfully achieved comprehensive management and budget reform.[118] A National League of Cities database of city practices shows about 24% of almost 150 entries include performance reports to citizens or other performance measurement dissemination practices.[119] Atlanta has gained recognition for its "Atlanta Dashboard" system. Its CitiStats program is designed to create a "performance management culture in the City of Atlanta"[120] through its performance management system designed to identify the effectiveness of city programs.[121] Baltimore also has a well-regarded CitiStat program.

While performance measurement has clearly gained ground at the local level, the use of program information in decision making may be more limited. A study of counties found that of those reporting usage of performance measurement in budgeting, 78% said measures were used in preparing departmental budget requests, 68% said measures helped county commissioners review the executive budget, and 80% said measures were used for monitoring the efficiency and effectiveness of services.[122] A study of cities and counties found that administrators had doubts about the extent that program measurement was being used in decision making.[123]

Techniques in Other Nations

Efforts to include performance measurement in budgeting are common in other countries.[124] In the mid-1990s, New Zealand was said to be furthest along in developing a resource allocation system that relied heavily on quantified performance.[125] The financial and fiscal crisis in the United States and most industrialized countries brought on by the recession starting in 2007, as noted earlier in this chapter, has focused more attention on the efficiency side of governmental performance. Local governments in the United Kingdom underwent a performance management initiative in the 1990s that produced a data set known as the Best Value Performance Indicators. These were replaced in 2008 by a single set—the National Indicators Set. This was revised again in 2011 to produce the Single Data List for Local Government.[126] A survey of local governments in the Australian state of Victoria found that 50% of the respondents thought budget reforms changed attitudes in favor of planning, and 47% thought the reforms influenced resource allocations.[127] Singapore has made extensive use of performance information and is increasing its emphasis on outcome measures. However, Singapore, while using program information in budgetary decision making, does not attempt to directly link performance and budget data.[128] A study of five governments in Canada, England, and the United States found that performance reporting was being used in strategic planning and agency decision making.[129] A scan of the table of contents of the *OECD Journal on Budgeting* shows articles on the introduction or implementation of performance measurement, performance budgeting, or similar topics in Poland (2011), Turkey (2010), Lithuania (2010), Moldova (2010), People's Republic of China (2010), and the Philippines (2010) in just a two-year period.[130]

Management reforms, including those in the budgeting arena, in Australia, New Zealand, the United Kingdom, and to a lesser extent, Canada, have been called the *New Public Management* (NPM).[131] This concept is generally associated with the concern that public sector management theories gave almost exclusive attention to technological reforms, neglecting the role of values and the political process through which values affect decisions. Over time, the movement spread throughout Europe, especially into Austria, Germany, and Switzerland. NPM has reached the United States from the standpoint of scholars trying to understand what constitutes NPM, whether it has accomplished anything in other countries, and whether it is on the upswing or downswing. For example, some scholars have declared NPM dead, though that is disputed.[132] It should be noted, at a minimum, that NPM is more than a budgeting reform. It typically covers myriad other changes, including privatization and increased flexibility for managers.

Reasons for Adopting Reforms

Why do some governments adopt budget reforms while others do not—or adopt them at a slower pace?[133] Researchers have identified several factors:

- Fiscal stress caused by the inability of governments to finance all programs at what seems to be a minimal standard stimulates searches for alternative budget techniques. Improved budgeting is seen as a means for improving the "health" of the government and the economic health of the economy.[134] On the other hand, when fiscal stress becomes severe, governments may simply attempt to cope during a crisis rather than improve their ability to manage themselves.[135]

- Governments search for techniques that facilitate dealing with the knottiest of problems and provide them with the sense of being in control of current and future operations. Emphasis is on increasing the efficiency and effectiveness of operations. The concern is to link programmatic goals with results.[136] When an agency is under pressure from higher-level decision makers about its effectiveness and even existence, the agency may initiate budget changes using performance measures on its own as a means of strengthening its position in the political-administrative arena.[137]

- Government structure is sometimes important. Local governments with professional managers are more likely to adopt program and performance budgeting than are those with strong mayor systems.[138] This seems to be true internationally with national governments.[139]

- Having an elected and appointed political leadership that is committed to budget reform is another important ingredient, because reforms that are generated exclusively from lower levels in the bureaucracy are unlikely to be effective. Leadership not only must be committed but must also have the leadership skills necessary to forge ahead.[140]
- Governments need trained professional staffs and computer capabilities to undertake many budget reforms.[141] Involvement by employees and incentives for their involvement may increase the chances for success.[142] Agencies led by "prospectors" as distinguished from "defenders" and "reactors" may be more likely to introduce performance management and be successful in the endeavor.[143] Any such changes that are undertaken should be expected to take time. Expectations of quick results are likely to lead to disappointments.
- A desire on the part of legislators for enhanced information as an aid in exercising oversight of the executive branch is another important factor.[144] On the other hand, when the budget structure and appropriations are not aligned with performance information, the legislature may send a signal to the executive branch that performance is not all that important.[145]
- Legal requirements, such as the 1993 and 2010 federal legislation instructing agencies to prepare strategic and annual performance plans, and other mandates and incentives are important (GPRA and GPRMA).
- Another potential influence of major proportions relates to professions. The professional accounting field has shown interest in mandating that accounting systems be linked to program measurement. The Governmental Accounting Standards Board (GASB) strongly encourages voluntary reporting of *service efforts and accomplishments* and in 1994 moved toward adopting a requirement that governments link *service efforts and accomplishments* to their accounting systems.[146] The Government Finance Officers Association, in opposing the GASB proposal, favored a voluntary system, maintaining that the GASB, as an accounting organization, would overstep its bounds and area of expertise were it to require service efforts and accomplishments reporting.[147] In 2008 GASB Concept 5 reemphasized the voluntary nature of its recommendations on service efforts and accomplishments reporting (see discussion in the chapter on financial management).[148]
- Involvement of customers/citizens in the process has been identified as facilitating the adoption and use of performance measurement in budgeting.[149]

This listing is in no way exhaustive but simply illustrates some of the factors that can be important in whether a government successfully implements some form of budget reform that is results oriented.

Impediments to Reform

Perhaps one of the most difficult barriers to reform is overcoming the past. So-called new management practices arise with great frequency. Governments may feel pressure to jump on the most current bandwagon, but then later they jump from that bandwagon to another. Any person involved in policy making and administration can easily become cynical about the prospects for any new management practice actually being implemented. Experienced administrators inevitably question whether the latest technique will have any real effect on how decisions are made and what outcomes they produce. Administrators may also feel that the only reason for adopting the latest technique is the desire for a new administration to put its own identity stamp on the budget process.

Other factors that complicate or deter reform include the following:

- Major difficulties can be expected in setting goals and measures and gaining acceptance of those goals.[150] For example, environmental and conservation interests hold differing views on which goals the U.S. Forest Service should pursue.[151] This lack of clarity would be much less of a problem for an agency such as the U.S. Weather Service, which operates with the luxury of an agreed-upon mandate—to forecast the weather in an accurate and timely manner.

  Even when there is agreement on the goal, operationalizing it so that it is clear when it has been achieved can be a thorny problem. For instance, there is no easy method for determining how much defense is enough. The problem is that defense is mainly a matter of deterrence and preparedness. The military is expected to have sufficient strength to deter an attack by a potential aggressor and to be sufficiently prepared for war or other emergencies if they do occur. The deterrent strategy is working when no attack has been launched.

  Preparedness, on the other hand, can be tested only in real combat and other military situations. Even then, agreeing upon the goals and the measures of accomplishment is sometimes impossible. Was the objective in the Iraq war the limited one of removing Saddam Hussein from power and leaving it to the Iraqis to form a new government? In that case, the objective was accomplished in December 2003. Or was it a complex combination of military and political objectives, including reconstructing Iraq and promoting a democratic government as a source of stability in the Middle East?[152] In the latter case, years after U.S. military personnel left the country, it may not be clear whether or not the objective was achieved.

  When multiple federal agencies are required to accomplish a set of objectives, it can be too complicated to arrive at a clear set of common objectives. When state, local, and private agencies are part of the equation, identifying a clear set of performance objectives and the appropriate measures of success defy imagination. Hurricanes Katrina, Rita, and Wilma of 2005, Hurricane Irene of 2011, and the Deepwater Horizon gulf oil catastrophe of 2010 are notable examples of how federal, state, and local government agencies and private organizations, most noticeably the American Red Cross, can be called upon for disaster relief. The suffering inflicted by the earlier storms on the residents of New Orleans and throughout the Gulf Coast brought attention to the inadequacies of disaster responses, no matter how thorough program measures may have existed for the U.S. Federal Emergency Management Agency (FEMA) and comparable state and local bodies.[153]

- Another concern is whether strategies lead to accomplishment of goals. Do the numerous efforts of the Department of Homeland Security really reduce the influx of illegal aliens entering the United States?[154]

- More generally, producing believable data presents a major problem. Simple errors can occur in collecting and tabulating data. Organizations and individuals may be tempted to falsify or misrepresent their accomplishments, or may feel under such great pressure to perform that they cheat on performance measures. For example, teachers and administrators in numerous districts, from New York City to Atlanta, from New Jersey to Washington, have exaggerated student performance on standardized achievement scores or even reported exaggerated results obtained by assisting students with the test.[155] Data need to be valid (measures are appropriate) and verified (for completeness, accuracy, consistency, and the like).[156]

- Agencies have overlapping missions, and consequently any outcomes or impacts may actually result from several agencies' work. Managing for results suggests prospects for collaboration across agencies but can work in the other direction, leading to battles over administrative "turf."[157]

- Measuring the accomplishments of regulatory agencies is particularly challenging, and much of what the federal government does is of a regulatory nature.[158] The regulatory units are located both in departments, such as the Food and Drug Administration in the Department of Health and Human Services, and in stand-alone bodies, such as the Environmental Protection Agency, the Securities and Exchange Commission, and the Federal Communications Commission. The banking crisis that began in 2008 raised the question of whether it could have been avoided had the regulators not, in effect, been asleep on the job.

- Obtaining accurate data in a uniform format and on a timely basis can be a nightmare for federal agencies that depend on information from state and local governments and private enterprises. The same problem arises for state agencies in obtaining data from local governments.

- Some governments have used adjusted performance measures that attempt to take into account the extent to which external factors (i.e., those outside an organization's control) influence outcomes. These techniques are themselves subject to criticism, but with attention to methodology they can yield more accurate results.[159]

- Linking program data with cost data is complicated by the limited abilities of accounting systems and inconsistencies across accounting systems (see the chapter on financial management). Accounting systems may track financial transactions in formats that do not match up well with the needs of a program manager. Comparisons between units may be thwarted because the units use different accounting system rules.

- The lack of incentives can doom efforts to use performance measurement in budgeting. If high-level executives and legislators show little or no interest in using performance data for decision making, lower-level administrators will consider data collection and program planning to be merely a paper exercise.[160] Equally as troublesome is holding executives and managers accountable for results but not giving them the means to accomplish the desired outcomes. Due to revenue declines, budgets may be cut, but departments may be expected to accomplish what was originally planned.

- Managers often find it unpleasant, if not downright repulsive, to have their operations compared with operations in other departments or in other governments. Yet benchmarking is frequently regarded as a desirable technique. As discussed earlier, benchmarking involves comparing one's operations with those of others. Serious problems of comparison arise in that governments operate in different environments, may measure their activities differently, and may account differently for their use of resources. Managers have become more comfortable with comparative performance measurement as methodologies have improved and as it has become commonplace. The Council of State Governments launched a project in 2009 to assess the state of the art and develop comparative performance measures across states.[161] State comparisons are published at *www.StatesPerform.org*. Benchmarking holds the prospect of being able to compare schools to determine which are performing better in educating children, but in doing so it threatens those who run the schools. The federal government's No Child Left Behind Act, for example, requires testing of individual students to hold teachers and administrators accountable for educational outcomes. As noted above, the pressure to meet the act's requirements has generated considerable controversy and numerous instances of false reporting and cheating by threatened school administrators, teachers, and entire districts. Citizen satisfaction can be measured across governmental boundaries, such as determining whether one community is more satisfied with its recreation services than other communities.[162]

If all of these problems were not enough, additional factors could become influential. The public sector routinely borrows management ideas from the private sector, and one that is emerging is the "balanced scorecard," developed and popularized by Robert S. Kaplan and David P. Norton.[163] Its underlying premise is that the private sector has been too focused on the "bottom line" of profit and loss and needs to be concerned with other matters, such as customer satisfaction and employee satisfaction. While public sector performance measurement often includes customer satisfaction, employee satisfaction may be of limited concern. The balanced scorecard suggests that government should step back and rethink how it measures its activities and results.

Finally, the question must be asked whether budget reforms aimed at fostering performance management have any bearing on global rethinking about the purposes of government and how those purposes or goals are pursued.[164] Yes, budget systems may be tied to strategic planning, but do these systems address, in any real sense, fundamental questions about government and draw attention to key issues, such as immigration, terrorism, international trade imbalance, and the like?

SUMMARY

One of the main themes running through budgetary literature has been the need to use the budgetary process as a vehicle for planning. In particular, this need has facilitated an attempt to incorporate program data into the system along with resource data, such as dollar and personnel costs.

During and after World War II, a set of theoretical fields and technologies emerged that had a great influence on budgetary reform. These include operations research, economic analysis, general systems theory, cybernetics, computer technology, and systems analysis.

Budget requests are prepared by agencies in accordance with instructions provided by the central budget office. In addition to data on finances and personnel, request instructions increasingly require program data, including social indicators, impacts, outputs, workloads, and activities, as well as data on the need or demand for services. Productivity measures are used to relate resource consumption, as measured in dollars and personnel, to the work accomplished and the product of that work.

Budget request manuals take varied approaches to providing guidance on how agencies should request resources. These approaches include current commitment, fixed-ceiling, and open-ended budgeting. Reform efforts since the 1960s have focused on PPB systems, or more generally program budgeting. Strategic planning and policy and program guidance have also proved popular. Current emphasis is on performance measurement. Governments tend to use hybrids of these systems.

NOTES

1. Orszag, P. (2009). *Memorandum for heads of executive departments and agencies: increased emphasis on program evaluations* [memorandum]. Retrieved November 1, 2011, from http://www.whitehouse.gov/sites/default/files/omb/assets/memoranda_2010/m10-01.pdf.
2. Schick, A. (1966). The road to PPB: the stages of budget reform. *Public Administration Review, 26,* 243–258; Caiden, N. (2010). Challenges confronting contemporary public budgeting: retrospectives/prospectives from Allen Schick. *Public Administration Review, 70,* 203–210.
3. Williams, D. W. (2004). Evolution of performance measurement until 1930. *Administration & Society, 36,* 131–165; Meyers, R., & Rubin, I. (2011). The executive budget in the federal government: the first century and beyond. *Public Administration Review, 71,* 334–344.
4. Taft, W. H. (1912). *Economy and efficiency in the government service.* House Doc. No. 458, 16.
5. Commission on Economy and Efficiency (1912). *The need for a national budget.* House Doc. No. 854, 4–5.
6. Williams, D. W. (2003). Measuring government in the early twentieth century. *Public Administration Review, 63,* 643–659.
7. Cleveland, F. A. (1915). Evolution of the budget idea in the United States. *Annals, 62,* 15–35.
8. Willoughby, W. F. (1918). *The problems of a national budget.* New York, NY: Appleton.
9. Upson, L. D. (1924). Half-time budget methods. *Annals, 113,* 69–74.
10. Buck, A. E. (1929). *Public budgeting.* New York, NY: Harper and Brothers.
11. Kilpatrick, W. (1936). Classification and measurement of public expenditures. *Annals, 183,* 19–26.
12. President's Committee on Administrative Management (1937). *Report.* Washington, DC: U.S. Government Printing Office.
13. Key, V. O., Jr. (1940). The lack of a budgetary theory. *American Political Science Review, 34,* 1138–1144. See Light, P. C. (2006). The tides of reform revisited: patterns in making government work, 1945–2002. *Public Administration Review, 66,* 6–19; and Posner, P. (2009). Introduction to the mini-symposium on the federal budget process: the persistence of reform. *Public Administration Review, 69,* 207–210.
14. Commission on Organization of the Executive Branch of the Government (1949). *Budgeting and accounting* (p. 8). Washington, DC: U.S. Government Printing Office; U.S. Office of Management and Budget (2010). *Budget of the U.S. government: analytical perspectives, 10. Social indicators* (pp. 95–102). Washington, DC: U.S. Government Printing Office.
15. Lewis, V. B. (1952). Toward a theory of budgeting. *Public Administration Review, 12,* 42–54.
16. Mosher, F. C. (1954). *Program budgeting: theory and practice with particular reference to the U.S. Department of Army.* Chicago, IL: Public Administrative Service.
17. Seckler-Hudson, C. (1952). Performance budgeting in the government of the United States. *Public Finance, 7,* 327–345.
18. Smithies, A. (1955). *The budgetary process in the United States.* New York, NY: McGraw-Hill.
19. Commission on Organization of the Executive Branch of the Government (1955). *Final report to Congress.* Washington, DC: U.S. Government Printing Office; Commission on Organization of

the Executive Branch of the Government (1955). *Budgeting and accounting*. Washington, DC: U.S. Government Printing Office.

20. Burkhead, J. (1956). *Government budgeting* (pp. 133–182) New York, NY: Wiley.

21. Wildavsky, A. (1969). Rescuing policy analysis from PPBS. *Public Administration Review, 29,* 193.

22. The early thinking on this topic was suggested by Robert J. Mowitz, Director of the Institute of Public Administration, Pennsylvania State University.

23. Churchman, C. W., et al. (1957). *Introduction to operations research*. New York, NY: Wiley; van Gigch, J. P. (1995). The paradigm of the science of management: in celebration of C. West Churchman's 80th birthday. *Interfaces, 25,* 81–88.

24. For an early survey of the economic analysis field, see Prest, A. R., & Turvey, R. (1965). Cost-benefit analysis: a survey. *Economic Journal, 75,* 683–735.

25. Von Bertalanffy, L. (1951). General system theory: a new approach to unity of science. *Human Biology, 23,* 303–361.

26. Wiener, N. (1956). *The human use of human beings*. Garden City, NY: Doubleday.

27. Ouchi, W. G. (1970). A short history of the development of computer hardware. In T. L. Whisler (Ed.), *Information technology and organizational change* (pp. 129–134) Belmont, CA: Wadsworth.

28. Fisher, G. H. (1966). *The analytical bases of systems analysis*. Santa Monica, CA: RAND Corporation.

29. U.S. Office of Management and Budget (2011). *Preparation, submission, and execution of the budget,* Circular A-11. Retrieved October 17, 2011, from http://www.whitehouse .gov/sites/default/files/omb/assets/a11_current_year/a_11_2011.pdf.

30. Government Performance and Results Act of 1993 (P.L. 103-62); Government Performance and Results Modernization Act of 2010 (P.L. 111-352).

31. Joyce, P. (2011). The Obama administration and PBB: building on the legacy of federal performance-informed budgeting? *Public Administration Review, 71,* 356–367. For historical reviews, see Hatry, H. P. (1999). *Performance measurement: getting results*. Washington, DC: Urban Institute; Walters, J. (1998). *Measuring up: governing's guide to performance measures for geniuses (and other public managers)*. Washington, DC: Congressional Quarterly; Klitgaard, R., & Light, P.C. (Eds.) (2005). *High-performance government: structure, leadership, incentives*. Santa Monica, CA: RAND Corporation; U.S. Government Accountability Office (2005). *Performance measurement and evaluation: definitions and relationships*. Washington, DC: GAO.

32. See the *Social Indicators Research* journal, which has been publishing research and information on social indicators since 1974.

33. U.S. Office of Management and Budget (2011). *Budget of the U.S. government 2012, analytical perspectives: 10. Social indicators,* 95.

34. Sustainability Seattle (1998). *Indicators of sustainability community*. Seattle: Sustainability Seattle; Department of Planning and Development, City of Seattle (2006). *Sustainable communities*. Retrieved July 25, 2006, from http://www.seattle.gov/dpd/GreenBuilding/SustainableCommunities/Overview.

35. Aristigueta, M. P., et al. (2001). The role of social indicators in developing a managing for results system. *Public Performance & Management Review, 24,* 254–269.

36. Murphey, D. A. (1999). Presenting community-level data in an "outcomes and indicators" framework: lessons from Vermont's experience. *Public Administration Review, 59,* 76–82.

37. Sustainable Seattle (2011). *Fourth set of indicators*. Retrieved October 18, 2011, from http://sustainableseattle.org/component/content/article/124; for a list of all indicators, see http://www.b-sustainable.org/indicator_index.

38. Mowitz, R. J. (1970). *The design and implementation of Pennsylvania's planning, programming, budgeting system*. Harrisburg, PA: Commonwealth of Pennsylvania.

39. Rubenstein, R., et al. (2003). Better than raw: a guide to measuring organizational performance with adjusted performance measures. *Public Administration Review, 63,* 607–615.

40. U.S. Office of Management and Budget (2006). *Program assessment rating tool guidance no. 2006-04.* Washington, DC: OMB.

41. U.S. Government Accountability Office (2010). *Streamlining government: opportunities exist to strengthen OMB's approach to improving efficiency.* Washington, DC: GAO.
42. See current issues of *Public Performance and Management Review,* a quarterly journal.
43. Osborne, D., & Gaebler, T. (1992). *Reinventing government: how the entrepreneurial spirit is transforming the public sector.* Reading, MA: Addison-Wesley; Osborne, D., & Plastrik, P. (1997). *Banishing bureaucracy: the five strategies for reinventing government.* Reading, MA: Addison-Wesley; Rondinelli, D. A., & Cheema, G. S. (Eds.) (2003). *Reinventing government for the twenty-first century: state capacity in a globalizing society.* Bloomfield, CT: Kumarian.
44. Spicer, M. (2004). Public administration, the history of ideas, and the reinventing government movement. *Public Administration Review, 64,* 353–362; Kim, P. S., et al. (2005). Toward participatory and transparent governance: report on the sixth global forum on reinventing government. *Public Administration Review, 65,* 646–654.
45. Whicker, M. L., & Mo, C. (1998). *Impact of agency mission on agency budget strategy.* Paper presented at the national conference of the Association for Budgeting and Financial Management, Washington, DC.
46. U.S. Office of Management and Budget (2006). *Program assessment rating tool guidance no. 2006-02,* 4–6.
47. North Carolina Office of Management and Budget (2010). *2009–11 budget instructions: what's due?* Retrieved October 15, 2011, from http://www.osbm.state.nc.us.
48. National Security Act Amendments of 1949. Ch. 412, 63 Stat. 578.
49. Budget and Accounting Procedures Act of 1950. Ch. 946, 64 Stat. 832;
50. Schick, A. (1966). The road to PPB, 252–253.
51. Organization for Economic Cooperation and Development (2009). *Evolutions in budgetary practice: Allen Schick and the OECD senior budget officials.* Paris, France; OECD.
52. Mosher, F. C. (1954). *Program budgeting,* 34–47.
53. Massey, R. J. (1963). Program packages and the program budget in the Department of Defense. *Public Administration Review, 23,* 30–34.
54. Novick, D. (1965). The Department of Defense. In D. Novick (Ed.), *Program budgeting: program analysis and the federal budget* (p. 91). Cambridge, MA: Harvard University Press.
55. Novick, D. (1956). *Efficiency and economy in government through new budgeting and accounting procedures.* Santa Monica, CA: RAND Corporation.
56. Jones, L. R. (1991). Policy development, planning, and resource allocation in the Department of Defense. *Public Budgeting & Finance, 11,* Fall, 15–27; U.S. General Accounting Office (2004). *Future Years Defense Program: actions needed to improve transparency of DOD's projected resource needs.* Washington, DC: GAO.
57. U.S. Department of Defense (2010). *QDR panel calls for more force structure changes.* Retrieved October 28, 2011, from http://www.defense.gov/news/newsarticle.aspx?id=60303.
58. The Quadrennial Diplomacy and Development Review can be retrieved from http://www.state.gov/s/dmr/qddr/.
59. National Performance Review (1993). *Creating a government that works better and costs less: Department of Defense.* Washington, DC: U.S. Government Printing Office.
60. Commission on Roles and Missions of the Armed Forces (1995). *Directions for defense.* Washington, DC: U.S. Government Printing Office.
61. Jones, L. R., & McCaffery, J. L. (2005). Reform of the planning, programming, budgeting system, and management control in the U.S. Department of Defense: insights from budget theory. *Public Budgeting & Finance, 25,* Fall, 1–19.
62. Schick, A. (1973). A death in the bureaucracy: the demise of the federal PPB. *Public Administration Review, 33,* 146–156.
63. Harper, E. L., et al. (1969). Implementation and use of PPB in sixteen federal agencies. *Public Administration Review, 29,* 634.

64. Kelley, J. (2005). A century of public budgeting reform: the "key" question. *Administration and Society, 37*, 89–109; see also Fabrizio, S., & Mody, A. (2006). Can budget institutions counteract political indiscipline? *Economic Policy, 21*, 689–739, for similar conclusions in other countries.

65. Casselman, R. C. (1973). Massachusetts revisited: chronology of a failure. *Public Administration Review, 33*, 129–135.

66. Sallack, D., & Allen, D. N. (1987). From impact to output: Pennsylvania's Planning-Programming-Budgeting System in transition. *Public Budgeting & Finance, 7*, Spring, 38–50; Tat-Kei Ho, A. (2011). PBB in American local governments: it's more than a management tool. *Public Administration Review, 71*, 391–401.

67. Wildavsky, A., & Hammann, A. (1965). Comprehensive versus incremental budgeting in the Department of Agriculture. *Administrative Science Quarterly, 10*, 321–346.

68. Phyrr, P. A. (1973). *Zero-base budgeting: a practical management tool for evaluating expenses.* New York, NY: Wiley.

69. Lauth, T. P., & Rieck, S. C. (1979). Modifications in Georgia zero-base budgeting procedures: 1973–1981. *Midwest Review of Public Administration, 13*, 225–238.

70. U.S. General Accounting Office (1979). *Streamlining zero-base budgeting will benefit decision making.* Washington, DC: U.S. Government Printing Office.

71. Schick, A. (1978). The road from ZBB. *Public Administration Review, 38*, 177–180.

72. Metzgar, J., & Miranda, R. (2001). Bringing out the dead: can information technology resurrect budget reform? *Government Finance Review, 17*, April, 9–14.

73. Posner, P. (2007). The continuity of change: public budgeting and finance reforms over 70 years. *Public Administration Review, 67*, 1018–1029.

74. Rabin, J., et al. (Eds.). (2000). *Handbook of strategic management* (2nd ed.). New York, NY: Marcel Dekker; Poister, T. H., & Streib, G. (2005). Elements of strategic planning and management in municipal government: status after two decades. *Public Administration Review, 65*, 45–56; Ugboro, I. O., et al. (2011). Strategic planning as an effective tool of strategic management in public sector organizations evidence from public transit organizations. *Administration and Society, 47*, 87–123.

75. Willoughby, K. G., & Melkers, J. E. (2000). Implementing PBB: conflicting views of success. *Public Budgeting & Finance, 20*, Spring, 105–120; Lu, Y., et al. (2011). Performance budgeting in the American states: what's law got to do with it? *State and Local Government Review, 43*, 79–94.

76. Bryson, J., et al. (2010). The state of public strategic management research: a selective literature review and set of future directions. *American Review of Public Administration, 40*, 495–521; Bryson, J. (2011). *Strategic planning for public and nonprofit organizations.* San Francisco, CA: Wiley.

77. Deming, W. E. (1983). *Quality, productivity, and competitive position.* Cambridge, MA: Massachusetts Institute of Technology Center for Advanced Engineering Study; McLaughlin, C. P., & Kaluzny, A. (Eds.) (2006). *Continuous quality improvement in health care: theory, implementations, and applications* (3rd ed.). Sudbury, MA: Jones and Bartlett.

78. Fairfax County, Virginia (2007). *Fairfax County manages for results: a guide to advanced performance management.* Retrieved October 21, 2011, from http://www.fairfaxcounty.gov/dmb/performance_measurement/manages_for_results.pdf; City of Austin, Texas (2005). *Managing for results: resource guide for business planning.* Retrieved October 21, 2011, from http://www.ci.austin.tx.us/budget/mfr.htm.

79. Moynihan, D. P. (2005). Goal-based learning and the future of performance management. *Public Administration Review, 65*, 203–216; Moynihan, D. P. (2006). Managing for results in state government: evaluating a decade of reform. *Public Administration Review, 66*, 77–89.

80. Kobrak, P. (1996). The social responsibilities of a public entrepreneur. *Administration and Society, 28*, 205–237.

81. Alderete, J. (2007). *Budget practices and state expenditures: lessons for California,* 10.

82. National Performance Review (1993). *From red tape to results: creating a government that works better and costs less.* Washington, DC: U.S. Government Printing Office.

83. Howard, M., & Kilmartin, B. (2006). *Assessment of benchmarking within government organization.* Retrieved September 15, 2011, from http://www.nasact.org/nasact/benchmarking/downloads/AssessBenchmarkGovOrg.pdf.

84. Government Performance and Results Act of 1993 (P.L. 103-62).

85. U.S. General Accounting Office (1996). *Effectively implementing the Government Performance and Results Act.* Washington, DC: U.S. Government Printing Office; Long, E., & Franklin, A. L. (2004). The paradox of implementing the Government Performance and Results Act: top-down direction for bottom-up implementation. *Public Administration Review, 64,* 309–319.

86. Government Performance and Results Modernization Act of 2010 (P.L. 111-352).

87. U.S. General Accountability Office (2004). *GPRA has established a solid foundation for achieving greater results.* Washington, DC: U.S. Government Printing Office.

88. Exec. Order No. 13450, 72 Fed. Reg. 64519 (signed November 13, 2007).

89. U.S. General Accountability Office (2011). *GPRA Modernization Act provides opportunities to help address fiscal, performance, and management challenges.* Washington, DC: U.S. Government Printing Office.

90. Joyce, P. G. (2003). *Linking performance and budgeting: opportunities in the federal budget process.* Washington, DC: IBM Center for the Business of Government.

91. U.S. Office of Management and Budget (2007). *Program Assessment Rating Tool guidance no. 2007-01* [memorandum], 1. Retrieved October 28, 2011, from archived records of the George W. Bush White House at http://georgewbush-whitehouse.archives.gov/omb/performance/fy2007/2007_guidance.pdf.

92. U.S. Office of Management and Budget (2009). *The FY 2008 performance report of the federal government.* Retrieved from http://www.govexec.com/pdfs/010809e1a.pdf.

93. U.S. Office of Management and Budget (2007). *Program Assessment Rating Tool guidance no. 2007-01,* 11–12.

94. U.S. General Accountability Office (2011). *GPRA Modernization Act provides opportunities to help address fiscal, performance, and management challenges,* 10.

95. President's Management Council (2006). *Facts about the president's management agenda.* No longer available from President George W. Bush administration White House archives online.

96. Gilmour, J. (2006). *Implementing OMB's Program Assessment Rating Tool (PART): meeting the challenges of integrating budget and performance.* Washington, DC: IBM Center for the Business of Government, 10; Joyce, P. G. (2003). *Linking performance and budgeting: opportunities in the federal budget process.* Washington, DC: IBM Center for the Business of Government.

97. Gilmour, J. B., & Lewis, D. E. (2006). Assessing performance budgeting at OMB: the influence of politics, performance, and program size. *Journal of Public Administration Research and Theory, 16,* 169–186.

98. Dull, M. (2006). Why PART? The institutional politics of presidential budget reform. *Journal of Public Administration Research and Theory, 16,* 187–215.

99. Frisco, V., & Stalebrink, O. (2008). Congressional use of the Program Assessment Rating Tool. *Public Budgeting and Finance, 28,* Summer, 1–19.

100. Rubin, I. (2009). Budgeting during the Bush administration. *Public Budgeting and Finance, 29,* Fall, 1–14.

101. U.S. Office of Management and Budget (2010). *Building a high-performing government, analytical perspectives: budget of the U.S. government, fiscal year 2010* (pp. 9–12). Washington, DC: U.S. Government Printing Office.

102. Reilly, S. (2011). Performance website underperforms. *Federal Times,* September 4. Retrieved from http://www.federaltimes.com/article/20110904//DEPARTMENTS06/10/904301.

103. U.S. Office of Management and Budget (2011). *Delivering high-performance government, analytical perspectives: budget of the U.S. government, FY 2011* (pp. 73–90). Washington, DC: U.S. Government Printing Office.

104. Joyce, P. (2011). The Obama administration and PBB: building on the legacy of federal performance-informed budgeting?

105. Head, J., & Sigritz, B. (2008). *Budget processes in the states*. Washington, DC: National Association of State Budget Officers.
106. Pew Center on the States (2009). *Performance-driven budgeting*. Retrieved October 19, 2011, from http://www.pewcenteronthestates.org/initiatives_detail.aspx?initiativeID=51276.
107. Hou, Y., et.al. (2011). State performance-based-budgeting in boom and bust years: an analytical framework and survey of the states. *Public Administration Review, 71*, 370–388.
108. Willoughby, K. G., & Melkers, J. E. (2000). Implementing PBB: conflicting views of success. *Public Budgeting & Finance, 20*, Spring, 85–120.
109. Barrett, K., & Greene, R. (2008). Grading the states: the mandate to measure. *Governing.com.* Retrieved October 28, 2011, from http://www.pewtrusts.org/uploadedFiles/wwwpewtrustsorg/Reports/Government_Performance/Grading-the-States-2008.pdf.
110. Barrett, K., & Green, R. (2008). Grading the states, 1.
111. Barrett, K., & Green, R. (2008). Grading the states, 27.
112. Coe, C. K., & Brunet, J. R. (2006). Organizational report cards: significant impact or much ado about nothing? *Public Administration Review, 66*, 90–100.
113. Kelly, J. M., & Rivenbark, W. C. (2003). *Performance budgeting for state and local governments*. Armonk, NY: M. E. Sharpe.
114. O'Toole, D. E., et al. (1996). Current local government budgeting practices. *Government Finance Review, 12*, December, 25–29.
115. Melkers, J., & Willoughby, K. (2005). Models of performance-measurement use in local governments: understanding budgeting, communication, and lasting effects. *Public Administration Review, 65*, 180–190.
116. Ho, A. (2011). PBB in American local governments: it's more than a management tool. *Public Administration Review, 71*, 391–401.
117. Barrrett, K., & Greene, R. (2000). Grading the cities: a management report card. *Governing, 13*, February, 22–88.
118. Hendrick, R. (2000). Comprehensive management and budgeting reform in local government: the case of Milwaukee. *Public Productivity & Management Review, 23*, 312–337.
119. National League of Cities (2011). *City knowledge network: database.* Accessed October 25, 2011, at http://www2.nlc.org/examples/cknsearchtest.htm.
120. ATLStat website, http://web.atlantaga.gov/atlstat/index.shtml, accessed October 28, 2011.
121. Mackie, B. (2008). *Organisational performance management in a government context: a literature review.* Retrieved October 28, 2011, from www.scotland.gov.uk/Resource/Doc/236340/0064768.pdf.
122. Wang, X. (2000). Performance measurement in budgeting: a study of county governments. *Public Budgeting & Finance, 20*, Fall, 102–118.
123. Melkers, J., & Willoughby, K. (2005). Models of performance-measurement use in local governments: understanding budgeting, communication, and lasting effects. *Public Administration Review, 65*, 180; see, more generally, the budget reform survey article Pagano, M., & Mullins, D. (2005). Local budgeting and finance: twenty-five years of developments. *Public Budgeting and Finance, 2*, Fall, 3–45.
124. Organization for Economic Cooperation and Development (2009). *Evolutions in budgetary practice: Allen Schick and the OECD senior budget officials.* Paris, France: OECD.
125. Organization for Economic Cooperation and Development (1995). *Budgeting for results: perspectives on public expenditure management* (p. 55). Paris, France: OECD; OECD (2007). *Performance Budgeting in OECD Countries.* Paris, France: OECD.
126. Audit Commission (2011). *National Indicator Set: single list for local governments.* Retrieved October 28, 2011, from www.audit-commission.gov.uk/localgov/audit/nis/pages/default.aspx.
127. Kluvers, R. (2001). An analysis of introducing program budgeting in local government. *Public Budgeting & Finance, 21*, Summer, 29–45.
128. Blondal, J. (2006). Budgeting in Singapore. *OECD Journal on Budgeting, 6*, 45–86.
129. Cunningham, G. M., & Harris, J. E. (2005). Toward a theory of performance reporting to achieve public sector accountability: a field study. *Public Budgeting & Finance, 25*, Summer, 15–42.

130. *OECD Journal on Budgeting*, various issues 2010–2011. Retrieved October 28, 2011, from http://www
.oecd.org/document/14/0,3746,en_2649_34119_2074062_1_1_1_1,00.html.
131. Barzelay, M. (2001). *The new public management.* Berkeley, CA: University of California Press; Page,
S. (2005). What's new about the new public management? Administrative change in the human
services. *Public Administration Review, 65,* 713–727; Pollitt, C., et al. (Eds.). (2007). *The new public management in Europe: adaptations and alternatives.* New York, NY: Palgrave.
132. De Vries, J. (2010). Is new public management really dead? *OECD Journal on Budgeting, 10,* 1–6.
133. Forrester, J. P., & Adams, G. B. (1997). Budgetary reform through organizational learning. *Administration and Society, 28,* 466–488; Fernandez, S., & Rainey, H. G. (2006). Managing successful organizational change in the public sector. *Public Administration Review, 66,* 168–176; Kasdin, S. (2010).
Reinventing reforms: how to improve program management using performance measures. Really.
Public Budgeting and Finance, 30, Fall, 51–78.
134. Walters, J. (2000). Raising Alabama. *Governing, 14,* October, 28–32.
135. Hou, Y. (2011). State performance-based budgeting in boom and bust years: an analytical framework and survey of the states. *Public Administration Review, 71,* 370–388.
136. U.S. General Accountability Office (2005). *Managing for results: enhancing agency use of performance
information for management decision-making.* Washington, DC: U.S. Government Printing Office.
137. Barzelay, M., & Thompson, F. (2006). Responsibility budgeting at the Air Force Materiel Command.
Public Administration Review, 66, 127–138.
138. Lu, H., & Facer, R. L., II. (2004). Budget change in Georgia counties: examining patterns and practices. *American Review of Public Administration, 34,* 67–93.
139. Andrews, M. (2005). Beyond "best practice" and "basics first" in adopting performance budgeting
reform. *Public Administration and Development, 26,* 147–161.
140. U.S. General Accounting Office (2000). *Managing for results: federal managers' views show need for
ensuring top leadership skills.* Washington, DC: U.S. Government Printing Office; Klitgaard, R.,
& Light, P. C. (Eds.) (2005). *High-performance government: structure, leadership, incentives.* Santa
Monica, CA: RAND Corporation; Ho, A. (2011). PBB in American local governments: it's more
than a management tool.
141. Ingraham, P. W., et al. (2003). *Government performance: why management matters.* Baltimore, MD: Johns
Hopkins University Press.
142. Boyne, G. A., et al. (2004). Toward the self-evaluating organization? An empirical test of the Wildavsky model. *Public Administration Review, 64,* 463–473; Swiss, J. E. (2005). A framework for assessing
incentives in results-based management. *Public Administration Review, 65,* 592–602.
143. Andrews, R., Boyne, G. A., & Walker, R. M. (2006). Strategy content and organizational performance: an empirical analysis. *Public Administration Review, 66,* 52–63.
144. Mihm, J. C., U.S. General Accounting Office (2001). *Using GPRA to assist oversight and decisionmaking.*
Testimony before the House Subcommittee on Government Efficiency, Financial Management and
Intergovernmental Relations. Washington, DC: U.S. Government Printing Office. Retrieved February 24, 2012, from http://comptrollerlegal2001.tpub.com/d01872t/d01872t0001.htm.
145. U.S. Government Accountability Office (2005). *Performance budgeting: efforts to restructure budgets to
better align resources with performance.* Washington, DC: GAO.
146. Governmental Accounting Standards Board (1994). *Concepts statement no. 2: service efforts and accomplishments reporting.* Norwalk, CT: Governmental Accounting Standards Board; Epstein, P. et al.
(2005). *Government service efforts and accomplishments performance reorts: a guide to understanding.* Norwalk, CT: Governmental Accounting Standards Board.
147. Government Finance Officers Association (2002). *Public policy statement: performance measurement and
the Governmental Accounting Standards Board.* Retrieved August 3, 2006, from http://www.gfoa.org/
services/policy/gfoapp2.shtml#ppbud8.
148. Governmental Accounting Standards Board (2008). *Concepts statements: elements of SEA reporting.*
Retrieved October 28, 2011, from http://www.seagov.org/concepts_statements/elements.shtml.
149. Yang, K., & Holzer, M. (2006). The performance-trust link: implications for performance measurement. *Public Administration Review, 66,* 114–126; Berman, B. J. (2006). *Listening to the public: adding*

the voices of the people to government performance measurement and reporting. New York, NY: Fund for the City of New York, NY: Epstein, P. D., et al. (2006). *Results that matter: improving communities by engaging citizens, measuring performance, and getting things done.* Hoboken, NJ: Jossey-Bass.

150. Nicholson-Crotty, S., et al. (2006). Disparate measures: public managers and performance-measurement strategies. *Public Administration Review, 66,* 101–113.

151. Peckenpaugh, J. (2001). Linking performance goals to budgets won't be easy, experts say. *Govexec.com.* Retrieved August 3, 2006, from http://www.govexec.com/dailyfed/0301/032201p1.htm.

152. U.S. Government Accountability Office (2009). *Hard lessons: the Iraq reconstruction experience.* Washington, DC: GAO.

153. U.S. Government Accountability Office (2006). *GAO's preliminary observations regarding preparedness, response, and recovery.* Washington, DC: GAO.

154. U.S. General Accountability Office (2011). *Overstay enforcement: additional mechanisms for collecting, assessing, and sharing data could strengthen DHS's efforts but would have costs.* Washington, DC: GAO.

155. Otterman, S. (2011). In cheating cases, teachers who took risks or flouted rules. *New York Times,* October 18. Retrieved October 29, 2011, from http://www.nytimes.com/2011/10/18/nyregion/how-cheating-cases-at-new-york-schools-played-out.html?_r=2&adxnnl=1&ref=education&pagewanted=1&adxnnlx=131896806254qgwtseUQe5lTB9njoxCg.

156. Holtzer, M., et al. (2009). *Literature review and analysis related to measurement of local government efficiency: a report to the local unit alignment, reorganization and consolidation commission (New Jersey).* Newark, NJ: Rutgers University School of Public Affairs and Administration; Berman, B. (2008). *Involving the public in measuring and reporting local government performance.* Retrieved October 28, 2011, from http://venus.fcny.org/cmgp/press/National_Civic_Review_Article.pdf.

157. Simeone, R., et al. (2005). A systems approach to performance-based management: the national drug control strategy. *Public Administration Review, 65,* 191–202.

158. U.S. General Accounting Office (1999). *Managing for results: strengthening regulatory agencies' performance management practices.* Washington, DC: U.S. Government Printing Office. For specific examples, see U.S. Government Accountability Office (2011). *Environmental Protection Agency: management challenges and budget observations.* Washington, DC: GAO.

159. Rubenstein, R., et al. (2003). Better than raw: a guide to measuring organizational performance with adjusted performance measures. *Public Administration Review, 63,* 607–615.

160. Kasdin, S. (2010). Reinventing reforms, (pp. 54–55).

161. Council of State Governments (2009). *State comparative performance measurement: overview.* Retrieved October 21, 2011, from http://www.csg.org/programs/policyprograms/documents/CPM_Overview.pdf.

162. Van Ryzin, G. G., et al. (2004). Drivers and consequences of citizen satisfaction: an application of the American Customer Satisfaction Index Model to New York City. *Public Administration Review, 64,* 331–341; Swindell, D., & Kelly, J. (2005). Performance measurement versus city service satisfaction: intra-city variations in quality? *Social Science Quarterly, 86,* 704–723.

163. Kaplan, R., & Norton, D. (2007). *Breakthrough results with the balanced scorecard: a balanced scorecard report collection* (4th ed.). Cambridge, MA: Harvard Business Review Press.

164. U.S. Government Accountability Office (2005). *Strategic budgeting: risk management principles can help DHS allocate resources to highest priorities.* Washington, DC: GAO; U.S. Government Accountability Office (2011). *GAO's perspectives on fiscal and performance challenges facing government.* Washington, DC: GAO.

Budget Preparation: The Decision Process

CHAPTER

8

Budget preparation is like a giant juggling act. Many balls are tossed up into the air—some by agencies, some by the budget office, some by the chief executive, and some by others—and surprisingly, in some years they do not all come crashing down. Instead, a proposed budget comes out of this dizzying assortment of taxing and spending initiatives, on time.

Preparing a budget in an executive budget system involves having agencies prepare requests and then assembling those requests; however, the process involves much more. Indeed, the request process is simple compared with the difficult task that remains—making decisions on the recommended levels for revenues and expenditures. Is a tax increase needed? What programs should be expanded and what programs should be reduced? In systems that do not centralize budget preparation in the executive, the same concerns prevail. A legislative committee or a joint group of executives and legislators may be responsible for weighing the citizens' joint demands for increased services and possibly lower taxes and for proposing a budget package that balances these competing demands.

This chapter includes two sections. The first section considers how a proposed executive budget is assembled. Deliberations on the revenue and expenditure sides of the budget are examined. The second section reviews the products of budget preparation—namely, the various types of budget documents and their formats.

DECISIONS ON BUDGET REQUESTS

Budget preparation involves participation by a variety of individuals and organizations, all of whom have myriad values regarding taxing and spending. In an *executive budget system*, the chief executive has the overall responsibility for the preparation process. Numerous other actors play roles as well, including the central budget office and other units such as the treasury office. Not all governments have executive systems. Many county governments do not have a county executive or manager, for example. As a consequence, their budgets are prepared jointly by several different executive and legislative officials. Legislators or their staffs may be involved in budget preparation. On occasion, state legislative staff members may be allowed to attend executive budget hearings that review the proposed budgets of line agencies. This practice helps the legislative branch become aware of the budget proposals being developed and the rationales behind these proposals prior to the budget actually reaching the legislature. In small local governments, budget preparation may be a relatively fluid process that is characterized by close links between executive and legislative officials. Even when legislative officers are not involved, their views on taxing and spending are taken into account. For example, a mayor will think twice about recommending a budget increase for a program when it is known that perhaps two-thirds of the city council has serious doubts about the program's worth.

Concerns of the Chief Executive

The chief executive—president, governor, mayor, county executive, or the like—may have official responsibility for budget preparation, but usually will have only limited direct involvement until the later stages of preparation. This system allows the chief executive time to take care of other duties. Having the budget office and other units, such as treasury, involved early in the process provides for the application of professional administrative talent in analyzing problems and options that will later come before the chief executive for review. A professional budget staff endeavors to take preliminary actions on budget requests that are in keeping with the policy objectives of the chief executive, thereby allowing the chief executive to avoid dealing with minor problems and reserving time to deal with major ones.

Strategic Concerns

The chief executive needs to convey to the departments, bureaus, and offices involved, and especially to the central budget office, a sense of priorities so that effort is not needlessly wasted on proposals that will later be rejected. Several concerns arise, with a major one at the national level being the overall philosophy of the role of government in contemporary society. What is the overall public interest, and how large should the public sector be in the total economy? Parallel questions at the regional (state or province) and local (city, county, or school district) levels are usually related to a few key issues such as the quality of the education system, the condition of roads or other infrastructure, and taxes, especially the property tax.

Another concern for many chief executives is the effect that the budget may have on the economy. Cities, counties, states, and the national government are concerned about budgetary influences on the economy, and about the economy's influences on the budget. For local and state chief executives, their concern tends to focus on whether current or proposed taxes will deter businesses from locating or expanding operations in their jurisdictions. Perhaps equally important is the quality of government services. While school districts and special districts may have little or no official role in economic development, the quality of education, water systems, sewers, and so on are critical in the location decisions of corporations. The national government has these same concerns and others as well, including international implications and price stability (see the chapter on government and the economy).

The chief executive sets ground rules on policies and program priorities. A president conveys an overall sense of priorities to the Office of Management and Budget (OMB) regarding national security and domestic spending and a sense of priorities within each of these categories. Election campaign promises are important in that chief executives usually attempt to pursue the objectives outlined in their bids for voter approval. For many chief executives, the budget serves as a vehicle for strategic planning for the government. For example, President Obama's budgets have focused on the need to create jobs in the United States, as a result of the recession he faced when coming into office. He began by proposing the 2009 American Recovery and Reinvestment Act (ultimately passed by the Congress), and has continued the process with subsequent budgets as the economy has struggled to restore the jobs lost in the recession.[1] Program priorities also can be viewed from the perspective of achieving some degree of social justice or equity (see the chapter on government and economy for a discussion of equity and equality).[2] While space constraints prohibit any extensive discussion of what constitutes social justice, it can be said that budget deliberations include an overall assessment of how different segments of the society will benefit or be burdened by governmental actions. One way of viewing this situation is to think of government as redistributing income among the various segments of society. Funding one set of programs at a high level will obviously benefit those programs' clients. If, for example, the elderly benefit from a program, then the young do not. Providing income maintenance checks to the needy redistributes money from the middle and upper classes to the poor. Redistribution also occurs through tax measures, including tax expenditures, such as the policy of not taxing home mortgage interest payments (see the chapter on budgeting for income, property, and payroll taxes). Proposed tax cuts are always debated in part based on whether the direct beneficiaries will be upper-, middle-, or lower-income individuals and households. Concerns about distributing the burden of taxes on the rich versus middle- and lower-income groups also hinge on the argument that it is the wealthier individuals who create jobs and grow the economy.[3]

A major concern of most states and particularly southern and western border states is social justice as it pertains to illegal immigrants. When taxes are high and available revenues cannot keep pace with funding needs, one view holds that illegal aliens should be denied access to government services like health care and various social services. For example, complaints from citizens began to arise when they realized that most mothers giving birth at the Los Angeles County Hospital were illegal aliens.[4] Providing free services to illegal immigrants is seen by many people as imposing an unfair burden on taxpayers. While the consensus of studies reviewed by the Congressional Budget Office in 2007 was that illegal immigration does impose a net cost on state and local governments, there is no consensus on the size of that effect.[5]

Another suggestion whose popularity is growing is that budgeting should be concerned with its generational effects—the extent to which current actions will improve or harm the conditions that older, younger, and future generations must confront.[6] For example, the federal government has reported generational effects in terms of taxes and transfers.

Today, science plays a major role in strategic decision making—namely, what scientific information can be brought to bear on problems? For example, what is the threat of an *E. coli* outbreak on the vegetable or meat industry and the health of the public, and what roles should federal, state, and local governments play in fighting it?[7] How likely is a flu pandemic, and what actions should government be taking to prevent one? Is the evidence persuasive, as most scientists would say, that the world is facing massive problems due to global warming, or is the evidence still inconclusive? Sarah Palin, the 2008 Republican vice-presidential candidate, referred to the literature on global warming as a "bunch of snake oil science" in 2010.[8]

Budget preparation also uses, to some extent, available program analyses, such as cost-effectiveness analysis and cost-benefit analysis, as is discussed in the chapter on capital assets.[9] A 2008 survey of state budget offices offers insight into the use of analysis in state budget preparation. According to the survey, 40 states have program-level performance measures, and 39 of these states require agencies to include performance data as part of their budget requests. Twenty-six states formally review or audit performance data on a regular basis, and only 14 include the review information in the budget. As for decision making, 25 states reported using a performance-budgeting process.[10]

Issues exist over how best to use analysis in decision making. Questions need to be asked, such as: Who conducted the analysis? Can the results be trusted? If an agency evaluated its own program, are the results believable, or was the analysis designed in such a way as to produce favorable results? For example, what items were included as costs and what ones as benefits? If costs are minimized and benefits maximized, the resulting cost-benefit ratio is likely to be well above the 1.0 level. When the analyses are considered valid, questions remain. If results from a program analysis are discouraging, should that be used to cut an agency's budget or to increase the budget so as to get better performance?

Surplus or Deficit?

The dynamics of decision making are greatly affected by whether a current services budget would be expected to yield a surplus or a deficit. In other words, if current revenue sources and spending patterns continue, will a surplus or a deficit result? In budget preparation, the projection of a budget deficit becomes an overriding issue that cannot be ignored. For state and local governments, chief executives are often required to submit balanced budgets, so any projections of a deficit must be resolved.[11] It is clear that federal budget decisions are being made in an environment that is dominated by concerns about the budget deficit and growing debt.

As a result of the recession that started in 2007, many state and local governments that had had budget surpluses during the early 2000s needed to make budget changes to deal with projected budget deficits. Nationwide, these deficits resulted from a combination of substantially reduced tax revenue and increases on spending for recession-driven programs such as unemployment insurance and Medicaid. The revenue reductions lasted longer and were much deeper at the state level than during the 2001–2002 recession.[12] Because the recession that started in 2007 was led by substantial reductions in the value of housing, at the local level there were substantial effects on property tax revenues.

The State of California is an extreme example of the problems faced by state governments. In California, Governor Arnold Schwarzenegger tried to reform collective bargaining for public unions (through ballot initiatives) in 2005, but ultimately failed. After that, he pushed a number of ballot initiatives to reform the budget process (reduce the vote threshold), freeze pay for elected officials, and call for a constitutional convention. All but the elected official pay measure failed. In 2009, lawmakers passed a deal to close the $26 billion budget gap. The deal contained $15.6 billion in cuts, about $2.1 billion in borrowing, $3.9 billion in new revenues, and about $2.7 billion in accounting maneuvers (like shifting a payday into the next fiscal year). New revenues included increases in the state sales tax, in addition to increases in user fees and university fees. A new budget short-fall of $26.5 billion faced the new governor, Jerry Brown, after his election in 2010. Brown cut $13.5 billion from the budget soon after taking office and sought to make up the rest in increased revenues. In order to do this, he tried to put a ballot initiative before the voters to raise various taxes.[13]

California is by no means alone. The State of Illinois also experienced severe budget dislocations in 2009 and 2010. A combination of the budget crisis and years of creative accounting to get around balanced budget requirements first came to a head in Illinois in 2010. The problems continued into 2011, when the state sought to borrow $3.7 trillion to shore up its chronically underfunded pension system.[14] At the local level, the City of Detroit perhaps best exemplifies the plight of northern rust belt cities, whose manufac-turing base had already been eroded prior to the recession, but Detroit has seen those problems deepen since the recession. In 2012, there was speculation that the severity of Detroit's fiscal problems would lead to a state takeover of the city budget, much as hap-pened in the 1970s in New York City and in the 1990s in Washington, DC. [15]

Tactical Concerns

In addition to a "philosophical" approach to taxation and expenditures, the chief executive conveys a tactical view. An assessment must be made of political reactions to any possible proposed tax increase or cut. Of course, increases are more likely to produce negative reac-tions than are tax cuts.

For governors and the president, intergovernmental relations constitute an important component of budget preparation deliberations. Presidents may prefer, where possible, to carry out policies through state and local governments rather than directly through federal agencies. Likewise, governors may prefer to work through local governments. Mandating that state and local governments deliver services, adopt standards, or otherwise implement federal programs is seen by some as a way of achieving a federal policy goal without paying for it. These *unfunded mandates* are extremely unpopular with governors, state legislatures, mayors, and city councils (see the chapter on intergovernmental relations).

Another set of considerations involves relationships with the legislative body. Stated simply, the chief executive assesses the chances of various recommendations receiving the approval of Congress, the state legislature, or the city council. Executives must decide whether to push for proposals that will meet with certain opposition from some legisla-tors in alliance with interest groups. In making such calculations, chief executives do not recommend only policies likely to be approved. A doomed recommendation may be put forth as a means of preparing the legislature to approve the proposal in some future year, or the chief executive may be strongly committed to a proposal despite legislative opposi-tion. An executive may want to score political points by advocating a proposal that has no chance with a legislature controlled by another political party, then using the disapproval of the legislature to score political points in subsequent elections. President Obama found his path substantially more difficult, to put it mildly, after the Republicans recaptured the House in the 2010 midterm elections. It seemed clear, leading up to the 2012 Presidential campaign, that proposals made by House members (such as Congressman Paul Ryan's proposal to reduce spending on Medicare) would become a target of criticism by President Obama and other Democrats. Introduced late in 2011, the proposed American Jobs Act, which had no chance of passage, seemed a clear preparatory step for the 2012 election.

Perceived citizen preferences regarding service and tax levels constitute another consideration. Chief executives have a keen sense of what the general citizenry and interest groups desire. What services do citizens demand, and what are they willing to pay for those services through either taxes or fees? Results from national and state polls are watched in an effort to identify important trends. Some cities conduct surveys of citizens and hold public hearings at which citizens may testify as a means of identifying prevailing attitudes about existing and desired services.

In preparing a budget for the upcoming fiscal year, the executive must also consider the current budget. Supplemental appropriations are standard at the federal level. Supplemental appropriations, simply called supplementals, are when an agency's budgets are selectively augmented during the fiscal year to meet unanticipated needs. During the George W. Bush administration, supplementals were the standard means for providing spending authority for the wars in Afghanistan and Iraq (see chapter on budget execution). None of the Bush administration budgets ever included the costs of those wars and the civilian reconstruction efforts in the regular departmental budget proposals. Supplemental appropriations like these may throw the existing budget out of balance (or further out of balance) as the president and the budget office begin preparing a deficit budget for the next fiscal year. This kind of situation can play into the hands of the president's political opponents.

Revenue Deliberations

Revenue Estimates

Central to deliberations on the revenue side of budget preparation are revenue estimates.[16] Revenue estimating is sometimes assigned to the organization responsible for collecting revenues, most often a treasury or revenue department. Such an arrangement may place that unit in competition with the budget office because the two may offer different revenue projections. The budget office may essentially be forced into developing a budget package that is perceived to be unnecessarily constrained because of an estimate that anticipates little or no growth in revenue or even a downturn in revenue collections. This problem is especially troublesome in some developing countries where the local treasurer is a central government appointee. At the federal level, the revenue-estimating function is handled jointly by OMB, the Council of Economic Advisers, and the Treasury Department. The Congressional Budget Office makes independent revenue estimates for congressional consideration.

Revenue estimating is, as much as anything, a technical process. If a government is required to have a balanced budget, as state and local governments are, then accurate revenue forecasts become critical. Estimates that are too high can create major crises during the execution phase, at which time expenditures must be cut so as not to exceed revenues. Low estimates also cause problems, in that programs may be needlessly reduced at the beginning of the fiscal year.

Perhaps the easiest method of revenue forecasting involves deterministic models that manipulate the revenue base and tax rate to produce a desired level of revenue. Property tax forecasts are deterministic in that a government can adjust assessments and tax rates to meet desired revenue levels. The main problems to address in such forecasting are the extent that (1) overall property values will rise or possibly decline, (2) new properties will be added to the tax rolls, and (3) properties will fall into default. Old and deteriorating properties are usually the ones most likely to fall into default, but during the recession that started in 2007, defaults were common across all types of properties. Deterministic models are useful for revenue sources over which a jurisdiction has substantial control. They are not useful for taxes on such items as personal income and retail sales, which depend on economic conditions.

In cases where jurisdictions do not have control over the revenue source, but have substantial data on past performance of the source, a more appropriate form of revenue estimate involves simple trend extrapolation. Both formal and informal trend extrapolations are used in revenue estimating. In an informal situation, an assumption may be made that a particular revenue source will increase by 5% because that is what has occurred for the past several years. In most cases, of course, revenues do not increase or decrease by a set percentage or remain constant. Revenue growth may increase on average by 5%, but in some years the growth may be 10% and in others only 1% or 2%. Given this information, what percentage estimate should be used for the upcoming budget year?

One method of dealing with this problem is to use *simple linear regression*, a statistical technique that fits a straight line to a series of historical data. The formula used is $y = mx + b$. In the equation, y, the forecast revenue, is a function of a coefficient m multiplied by a known value x plus a constant b. In the formula, m is the slope of the straight line, x is the actual revenue generated the previous year, and b is a scale factor that adjusts for orders of magnitude differences between values. Computer software is readily available for making the appropriate calculations, but such projections can also be made using a simple calculator.

Besides linear regression, other techniques exist for smoothing out fluctuations in a historical series into a straight line. The method called *moving averages* calculates an average value for each point in the historical series. Starting with a series of, say, eight years, the revenues for years 1, 2, and 3 are averaged. This average becomes the new smoothed value for year 2. Then, actual values for years 2, 3, and 4 are averaged to create a new "smoothed" year 3. Similar averages are calculated for the remaining years. A variant of this technique weighs the most recent years more heavily than the early years in calculating the moving average, on the grounds that recent years are better predictors.

Underlying these techniques is the premise that the future will be like the past. The purpose of any projection technique is to reduce historical information to a discernible pattern and then extend that pattern into the future. One way of testing how well the technique works is to "predict" several recent time periods and compare those predictions with what actually occurred. Most local governments, except large cities, still rely on one form or another of *trend extrapolation*. Evidence suggests that when used in combination with other tools, trend extrapolations produce reliable estimates for local governments.[17] Extrapolation methods are not helpful when there are significant and abrupt changes in economic conditions such as the rapid economic declines that began in late 2000 and again in 2007, causing rapid reversal from state and local budget surpluses to severe fiscal pressures.

A more complex method than simple regression or trend extrapolation involves using econometric modeling to project revenues. Several types of econometric techniques for forecasting revenues exist.[18] One of the most popular is *multiple regression*. In multiple regression models, independent variables are sought that can serve as predictors of revenue yield. The assumption is that a linear relationship exists between each predictor and the dependent variable of forecast revenue. Another assumption is that each independent variable is unrelated to the others. A model for sales tax receipts might include the independent variables of population, personal income, and the consumer price index. As the values of each of these variables increases, estimated revenues increase.

Multiple predictor variables are also used in *simultaneous equation models* (multiple regression models rely on a single equation). In simultaneous equation models, individual equations relate each independent or predictor variable to the revenue to be forecast. These individual equations are solved simultaneously. The advantage of simultaneous equation models is that, unlike multiple regression models, they do not assume that each predictor variable is independent of each other predictor variable. Because many of the variables one would use to make a revenue forecast would be expected to be related to one another, the simultaneous equation approach is both more realistic and computationally more valid.

Revenue forecasts can be made using *microsimulation models* that are dependent on large databases. Individual taxpayers and corporations are included in the models and exhibit behavior changes in response to projected changes in the economy, tax laws, price levels, personal income, and the like. The models use data based on the historical performance of actual taxpayers in the jurisdiction.

All of these models necessarily use variables that are sensitive to changes in economic conditions. Sales and income tax receipts rise and fall according to economic trends. Many user charges are affected, too. When people are unemployed, they curtail their use of public transportation, parking facilities, museums, and zoos. Therefore, these models are most vulnerable with regard to the assumptions made about future economic trends. Also critical are basic demographic shifts. Changing population patterns due to shifting birth rates and migration can undermine the effectiveness of forecasting models that previously had shown themselves to be extremely accurate.[19] Projecting national trends is quite difficult, and state and local trends are no easier to predict, especially given that each subnational jurisdiction has its own economic characteristics and is influenced by national trends.

Even though revenue estimating is a highly technical process, it is not immune from politics. Presidents, governors, and mayors are loath to forecast economic hard times and low revenue levels. Political executives tend to campaign for election in part on the promise that they will achieve economic growth. Presidents have the additional problem that the forecast of a recession may be a self-fulfilling prophecy. State and local executives must limit expenditures to available revenue. Pessimistic estimates force executives to make difficult choices as to where to cut programs so as to reduce overall expenditures. In general, there seems to be a tendency to underestimate revenues more often than to overestimate them. Apparently, politicians feel the political risks of underestimating and producing a surplus at the end of the year are less dire than the consequences of overestimating and having to make program cuts or raise taxes unexpectedly during the year.[20] Since revenue estimates can rarely, if ever, be guaranteed to come true, establishing *contingency reserves* or *rainy day funds* may be a useful method of protecting against possible shortfalls and the political problems that ensue from them (see the chapter on budget execution).

Taxing Limitations

Since the 1970s, taxing limitations have constituted a major consideration at the state and local levels.[21] Government officials, in assembling a budget proposal, may be constrained by having to present a balanced budget that allows for no increases in tax revenues. Limited in their ability to increase revenues, decision makers are sometimes forced to fund programs at less than optimal levels and even may have to cut programs.[22]

Balanced Budgets

For state and local governments, revenue estimating is particularly critical because of the standard requirement that they have balanced operating budgets. Indebtedness is possible but is typically used only for capital investments and other selected expenses. If a budget is built on revenue estimates that are too high, crises will ensue during execution as the government attempts to bring expenditures down so as to balance them against actual revenues. One of the reasons for the popularity of the property tax among revenue departments, but not taxpayers, is that in the short run, revenue from the property tax is easily forecast and budget shortfalls can be made up by resetting the property tax rate—although of course, that may be constrained by previous voter-approved limitations and may be the end of incumbents' political careers.

In addition to legal restraints, the bond markets impose some budgetary discipline on state and local governments. Some states or localities may lack structural balance between revenues and spending or may resort often to extraordinary means to bring budgets into balance. Such jurisdictions may experience lower bond ratings and higher borrowing costs, creating strong incentives for sound fiscal management (see the chapter on capital finance and debt management).

Although most states have requirements for a balanced budget, the requirements are not uniform across all states. In the first place, "balance" means that expenditures may not exceed revenues, but not all available revenues must be appropriated and spent. Coverage is not all-inclusive, and trust funds and capital expenditures are often excluded.[23] Consequently, as little as half of all state funds may be covered by the balanced budget requirement. Balancing requirements also vary as to when they apply in the budget process, such as when the budget is presented to the legislature or when it is adopted. Similar variations are found at the local level.

Achieving balance in a state budget is a political process. The obvious alternatives are to seek revenue increases or impose spending decreases, but balance can also be attained through other means. Budget reserves, rainy day funds, or savings from previous years may be drawn upon to cover expenditures.[24] It is possible that some governments may continue spending at high levels when helped by rainy day funds, at a time that budget cuts are really needed. Payments from one fiscal year may sometimes be shifted to the next, even though resources are actually used in the earlier year. Political leaders use this technique and others to make budgets appear to be balanced when the opposite is true.

Elimination of tax expenditures can yield additional revenues without officially raising tax rates. For instance, adding products or services to the list of items subject to a state sales tax can increase revenues. Decision makers are concerned with whether each tax expenditure serves any major public purpose, and all tax expenditures are particularly subject to challenge when revenues are needed to balance a budget.[25] At the federal level, one option proposed by the president's deficit commission was to broaden the tax base by substantially reducing tax expenditures and simultaneously reducing marginal tax rates (see the chapter on budgeting for income, property, and payroll taxes).

One commonly used alternative to raising taxes is raising user fees or adding new fees. A school district might consider imposing new or higher fees for student parking, school trips, lost textbooks, and physical education. Of course, there are limits on how much can be realistically collected from such fees. Could the new fee revenue cover a projected revenue shortfall and alleviate a need for a tax increase?

Budget gimmickry is also used during economic boom times. By estimating revenues to be lower than are most likely to occur, decision makers later in the year can "discover" that a budget surplus exists and then use the money for some combination of tax relief and new spending.

Tax earmarking often constrains efforts to balance budgets without necessarily helping the programs officially decreed to be beneficiaries. Receipts from state lotteries, for instance, are often earmarked for such good causes as public education or aid to senior citizens. While there are no comprehensive data on the effects of earmarking, a 2002 study found that education spending did appear to be greater in states where lottery proceeds were earmarked for education, and that this substantially exceeded the effect that earmarking had in other cases.[26] Indeed, earmarking is sometimes used as an excuse for not providing more funds to a program, because it is expected to operate within available revenue from the earmarked source. The supposed program that benefits from a lottery, then, may receive no greater funding than it would have without the lottery. Earmarking in effect "Balkanizes" governments' finances and can greatly hamper efforts to resolve budget problems when revenues decline, because monies are compartmentalized and cannot be treated as part of the total resources available for creating an overall balanced budget.[27]

In addition, revenue gaps are sometimes closed with public employee pension monies. A government may simply not make its full contribution to the employee pension funds or may even have the freedom to withdraw monies in an effort to balance the budget. Typically, financial penalties must be paid for such actions, including negative reactions by the financial markets for municipal bonds issued by jurisdictions engaging in such practices. More subtle methods involve adjusting actuarial assumptions. By making an assumption that retired employees will die comparatively early in life, fewer dollars will be needed to cover expected retirees when benefit levels are predetermined. Also, by assuming that investments on retirement monies will result in comparatively high returns, more dollars will become available to cover expected retirement benefits and the government will need to contribute less to the retirement fund.[28] The Pew Charitable Trusts estimated in 2010 that the total unfunded liability across the states for retiree pension and health benefits exceeded $1 trillion nationally.[29]

Whereas the decision makers responsible for state and local budgeting spend substantial time and energy balancing their budgets, the situation is quite different at the federal level.

Whether to require a balanced federal budget has long been a controversial issue, but a constitutional amendment requiring an annually balanced budget has yet to be adopted (see the chapter on the public sector in perspective and the chapter on budget approval and the U.S. Congress).

One general rule of thumb is that one-time revenues should not be the basis upon which long-term commitments are made.[30] This concern arose after the enactment of the American Recovery and Reinvestment Act (ARRA) when some governors expressed hesitation in accepting ARRA funds because they offered only temporary relief, and therefore put off hard decisions for the future.[31]

Spending Deliberations

Entitlements and Other Commitments

Much of the spending side of any budget is determined in advance of budget preparation deliberations. Interest on the debt must be paid, and prior commitments to employees, such as set levels of contributions to retirement plans, must be met. Entitlement programs that guarantee benefits to various groups, such as the needy, the elderly, and the ill, determine much of the spending side of a budget, where the amount spent is a function of the numbers of people qualifying for various programs, and the amount each would be paid under existing law. At the state and local levels, Medicaid and unemployment insurance spending is heavily caseload driven, and these caseloads expanded greatly during the recession that started in 2007. Local education spending, while not an entitlement in a classic sense, is still heavily driven by the size of the school-age population that a given school district needs to educate at a given point in time. The same could be said for other caseload-driven spending, such as that associated with state prisons, which is heavily driven by the size of the prison population and the sentencing behavior of judges. California, in fact, joined other states that recognized that the only way to make a significant dent in prison spending was to control the population, often through early release programs.[32]

Organizational Competition

Just as central administrative organizations compete in trying to influence revenue decisions, so organizations vie with one another on the spending side of the budget. At the top level of a government, personalities become important. The roles of various participants at the federal level depend upon a president's administrative style, his or her confidence in the abilities of key figures, and the roles that these figures seek for themselves. A president is not obligated to rely on the advice of any individual and may seek guidance from anyone inside or outside government.

Cabinet officers seek to gain acceptance and financial support for their agencies' programs. Central advisers to the president are other contenders for attention. In addition to advice provided by the White House Office staff, advice is available from the Domestic Policy Council, the National Economic Council, the Council of Economic Advisers, and the National Security Council. At these high levels of government as well as elsewhere throughout the government, heated debates occur over such topics as Social Security and health care funding.[33]

Some have suggested that at this level of government, but also at lower levels, misrepresentation and other ethically questionable behaviors prevail.[34] The competitive nature of budgeting may emphasize self-interest, both personal and collective, to the detriment of the public interest. As C. W. Lewis notes, "The process depends on and rewards deceit."[35] Agencies may misrepresent their situations to budget offices—for example, by claiming dire consequences unless budgets are increased for programs that are highly visible and favored by the public. At a higher level, political leaders may deceive the public—for example, by downplaying the importance of budget deficits and rationalizing the need for greater spending on pet projects even though the budget is out of balance. Financial managers, in serving their political bosses, are often ethically stressed during times of budget crises.[36]

Budget Office Roles

The central budget office has numerous roles. Not only does it recommend policies on spending, but it participates in the review of legislative proposals, economic policy, administrative regulations, evaluation of programs, collection of data by agencies, and agency management studies and management improvement efforts (see the chapter on budget execution). When OMB examines an agency's budget requests, all of these forces come into play. Agency budget proposals will be seen in the context of what legislative changes will be necessary, what regulatory actions will be required by the agency, and whether the agency is perceived as well managed.

Agency Expectations and Deliberations

In approaching the budget process, including the preparation phase, agencies have expectations about what constitutes success. Until the latter half of the 1970s, success was often measured in terms of budget increases approved by the executive and ultimately by the legislative body. This approach of adding increments to a base has since been discarded in many locales. Where taxing and spending limits have been imposed at the state and local levels, agencies have been forced instead to concentrate on defending their bases and minimizing the extent of cuts imposed on their budgets. The period from the late 1970s to the early 1990s was dubbed the decremental age.[37] Budgets tended to grow after that point, but the recession that began in 2007 ushered in another decremental period at all levels of government.

By the time a budget request reaches the central budget office, an extensive series of discussions has been completed within the line agency. In large agencies having several layers of organizational units, those at the bottom will have attempted to persuade their superiors to approve requests for additional funding. The force being exerted from the top downward tends to be negative—in the sense that pressure is applied to limit the growth of programs and the corresponding rise in expenditures. This does not mean that there is simply a set of petitioners and a set of rejecters who do battle within each agency or department. Middle managers up through department heads are required to take positive and negative positions, rejecting many of the proposals brought to them by subordinates and, in negotiating with their superiors, advocating those proposals that they accept.

Part of the influence within an agency is a function of superior levels attempting to determine what is likely to be salable to the budget office and the chief executive. Agencies are aware that they are likely to get less than they request. Therefore, they will avoid requesting too little, but will not ask for exorbitant sums unless an open-ended budget system is in use.

The amount eventually requested by a department is necessarily a function of the type of budget system in place. As discussed previously, some systems provide for a base budget and then permit requests for additions to that base. Others use a current services budget and require that an agency include information about possibly funding activities below and above the current services level. Some budget systems may require reductions. The challenging federal budget environment led President Obama to call for agencies to offer up reductions in spending for fiscal years 2012 and 2013. For the fiscal year 2012 process, agencies were instructed by OMB to propose budgets demonstrating how they would cut 5% from previous levels; this was increased to 10% for the fiscal year 2012 budget.[38] State and local governments have also needed to reach into the base for budget reductions. For example, Texas asked its agencies to cut their budgets by more than $3 billion during fiscal year 2010.[39]

Across-the-board cuts are sometimes imposed during budget preparation, although, as was noted previously, those can be far more harmful to some agencies than others and result in harm to the clients of the agencies that suffer reduced funding. Prioritization, therefore, is sometimes used. Washington State has used a combination of across-the-board cuts and priority funding.[40]

Budget Office and Agency Relations

Just as the interplay within an agency is extensive and vociferous during budget preparation, so is the interplay between the central budget office and the agencies. The central office, serving as the agent of the chief executive, must assert a unifying influence over the diverse interests of administrative units. These, in contrast, can be expected to favor greater autonomy. Operating departments and agencies will, of course, favor the advancement of their particular programs (seeking greater funds or defending programs against cuts), while the budget office usually will be forced to say no to program growth and to enforce needed cutbacks during times of fiscal scarcity.

When the budget office receives agency budget submissions, analysts or examiners are assigned to review these documents. The examiners serve as the main link between the budget office and line units. These professionals must balance a variety of factors, such as being expected to be thorough but having limited time available for their work, and being sensitive to political matters but serving professional values.[41] With the passage of time, examiners gain considerable knowledge about their agencies, providing substantive expertise within the budget office. They often become advocates for the agencies they review and frequently even shift their employment to an operating agency. Still, the accusation is commonly made by the agency officials that budget analysts are not program-oriented and are insensitive to the needs of operating units. Legislative analysts may also be part of the budget development process, particularly in state governments.[42] Sometimes budget office analysts may consult informally with legislative analysts during the preparation phase.

The structure of budget offices varies from government to government and from time to time. One key concern is whether the central function of examining agency budget requests should be integrated with other functions, notably management functions (discussed in the chapter on budget execution), program analysis, and planning. The argument for their integration is that it gives budget analysts much broader exposure to the operations of government and enhances the analysts' opportunities to make valuable inputs into budget deliberations. The argument against integration is that budget examination activities all too often take top priority, leaving all other activities on the sidelines.

The desire to better integrate the management and budget functions of OMB led to a reorganization, called "OMB 2000," under Director Alice Rivlin.[43] The purpose of this reorganization was to try to better integrate management improvements into the budget process. Since this reform, the budget review function at OMB has been organized into five resource management offices (RMOs):

1. Natural resources (including agriculture, energy, science, and space)
2. National security (including international affairs)
3. Education, income maintenance, and labor programs
4. General government (including housing, justice, transportation, and treasury)
5. Health

Each resource management office is responsible for budgeting, management, and planning/policy issues within its particular arena.

Budget office discussions with agencies involve how services are to be delivered to the citizenry, as well as the funding for those services. The deliberations include whether services should be provided directly by agencies, by private corporations or other governments operating under contract with government, or through some combination of these and other modes.

The nature of the dialogue between the budget office and agencies hinges in large measure on the extent to which the latter consider the former to be an important ally or an opponent. Only minimal information can be expected from an agency that is suspicious of the central budget office. A common concern is that an agency will not release data that could be used to its detriment. In contrast, if an agency can win the confidence and support of the examiner, then it in effect gains a spokesperson for its program on the chief executive's staff.

The budget office typically holds hearings with agency representatives. Whereas earlier in the process the examiners may have contacted agencies by phone, e-mail, or in person to clarify detailed items included in requests, hearings tend to focus on broader concerns. The budget office must decide whether agencies can accomplish what they propose and whether the anticipated accomplishments are worth seeking. The burden of proof rests with the agencies. The operating agency that has a reputation for requesting excessive sums and for overpromising on results will be suspect.

At the same time, winning budget office approval does not guarantee success for the agency. The resistant or recalcitrant agency may, indeed, be able to increase the caution with which the examiner makes recommendations to reduce the agency's budget.

At the federal level, the significance of OMB action is mitigated by the fact that Congress is a strong legislature that jealously guards its power to pass appropriations. It has been suggested that opposition by the budget office to any agency's request for funds may sometimes be helpful in winning legislative support.

The agencies, not the Office of Management and Budget, have had major responsibility for defending their budget requests before Congress, and therefore the OMB's utility to the agencies has been greater in the preparation phase than in the approval phase of the budget cycle. Some organizational units, such as the Federal Bureau of Investigation (FBI) in the 1950s and 1960s and the National Institutes of Health more recently, have been able to secure extensive support in Congress, thereby providing them with some autonomy vis-à-vis their departments and OMB. Of course, agencies can fall out of favor when their heads lose public and congressional confidence, making the agencies more vulnerable to OMB control. Beginning in the 1980s, OMB gained greater responsibility for explaining and defending the president's budget before Congress. This role, however, often was negative in the sense that the main task was to explain how and why reductions should be made in agencies' budgets.[44] In the Obama administration, OMB has been in the position of defending budget cuts in some areas, but also of defending the president's investment and job growth agenda before a skeptical Congress.

Legal requirements and court decisions may force increases in expenditures and preclude some decision making by agencies and the central budget office. For instance, state government mandates may require local governments to establish recycling programs for solid waste. Federal officials may require a city to upgrade its sewage treatment facilities. Federal and state court decisions may force a state government to expand prison facilities to accommodate increased numbers of prisoners or may overturn programs. Court cases may be filed against governments, forcing them to spend considerable sums on legal representation. Such suits may be filed by private citizens or corporations or by one government against another.

Budget Office Recommendations

The response of the budget office to agency requests is, in part, a function of the office's assessment of its own powers and responsibilities in relation to the operating agencies and other central units. Few would deny to a budget office the ministerial or bookkeeping functions of assembling requests and carrying out the mechanical duties of designing, tabulating, and overseeing the printing of the budget. At the same time, how many additional responsibilities the budget office has depends largely on the competition from other units and the management style of the chief executive.

In an executive budgeting system, the chief executive has the final say on what to recommend to the legislative body. Thus, the budget office attempts to formulate recommendations thought to be in keeping with the executive's priorities. As part of the calculation of what to recommend, it assesses the chances of agencies making direct appeals to the chief executive or, in the extreme case, to the legislature, and thereby overturning the budget office's recommendations. If this strategy—making an end run around the budget office—is successful, it can severely weaken the budget office's role. If an agency knows it can get what it wants by appealing directly to the chief executive or the legislature, the agency is likely to consider the budget office as merely a bookkeeper that can be largely ignored. Normally the budget director will communicate to the chief executive the importance of keeping the budget office in the loop and resisting unilateral appeals from agencies.

As a staff unit of the chief executive, the budget office is expected to develop recommendations that are consistent with executive priorities. On the other hand, as professionals, budgeters have a responsibility to report to the chief executive their views on the worthiness of programs. To report that a given program is operating well simply because the chief executive wants to hear that message does a disservice. So does recommending severe budget cuts to the chief executive when the budget office knows that these cuts could have devastating results on the affected programs or on programs that have proven to be effective. *Neutral competence* has been proposed as the appropriate role for the budget office: The office should retain its professional approach in developing its budget recommendations but simultaneously should develop recommendations in tune with executive priorities.[45]

As the budget is being developed by the budget office and when it is released, the budget office may engage in a public relations campaign that is intended to reach not only the public but also administrative agencies. At the federal level, the OMB director may issue press releases, hold press conferences, appear on Sunday television talk shows, and speak before such groups as the National Press Club. In this way, the budget director communicates on a broad scale the priorities of the administration and in effect warns agencies to beware of pushing for other priorities.

Downsizing, Rightsizing, and Spending Cutbacks

The recession that started in 2007 marked the return to a budgetary theme that first surfaced in the 1980s, referred to as "cutback budgeting." The impetus for cutbacks comes both from views that government has grown bloated and is in need of downsizing, and from the imperative that comes from reduced revenues that accompany periodic recessions. State and local governments, which are forced to balance their budgets, have led the way in making cuts during the most recent recession. Some of these governments' problems derive from extended declines in their economies. Other problems stem from a temporary lack of robustness in the national economy. When the economy slumps, state and local sales and income tax revenues fall. So-called Rust Belt states, especially Michigan, Ohio, and Pennsylvania, face a different set of economic woes—namely, a long-term erosion in their tax bases. The federal government has lagged, both because of its role in providing countercyclical assistance (much of it flowing to these subnational governments) and because it has been difficult to reach agreement on specific cutbacks because of intense and intractable political partisanship and gridlock. Pressure often exists, in such a downsizing regime, as agencies try to provide the same or even more services with fewer personnel and other resources.

The tax revolt movement, discussed in the chapter on budgeting for income, payroll, and property taxes, has imposed additional constraints on spending. In some instances, a jurisdiction's economy may have been vibrant, but the government was precluded from taxing that economic base to the extent it perceived was needed to fund government programs.

The tactics used to deal with a budget shortage depend in part upon its perceived duration. If the shortage is considered to be short term, perhaps lasting only for the current year, then modest adjustments can be made, such as imposing temporary cuts on programs and drawing on budget reserves or rainy day funds. During the recession that started in 2007, rainy day fund balances proved inadequate to shield states and local governments from substantial budget reductions. In a sense this is no surprise, as rainy day funds were never intended to permit states to weather a recession of the length and depth of the recession that started in 2007 without being required to take any policy actions. They are rather intended to buffer states against the need to take precipitous and draconian actions.

When long-term budget retrenchment is seen as necessary, then decision makers must manage the immediate problems of the current and upcoming budget years and anticipate problems in future years. When budget cuts must be imposed several years in a row, decision makers must be prepared to make extraordinarily difficult choices. Sometimes across-the-board cuts are ordered. These uniform cuts can have the effect of inappropriately freezing current priorities in place rather than taking a hard look at which lower-priority programs deserve larger reductions or even terminations.

Which budget cuts will be made ultimately hinges on the extent to which various groups in the society will suffer from program reductions or eliminations. Budget cuts are less likely to be imposed on groups that are politically organized and vocal than on other, less visible groups. Applying the budget knife to programs for the elderly is often politically dangerous, for instance, whereas cutting programs for the poor, who tend to be politically less active, may seem "safer" for decision makers. In relatively homogeneous communities, budget cutback procedures do not pit one segment of the community against another.

Budget Office Roles During Cutbacks

When jurisdictions confront fiscal stress, the decision process initially tends to be centralized. After all, without central instruction to begin a process of cutting, agencies might well submit budget requests based on unrealistic assumptions. The central budget office, working with the chief executive, attempts to instruct departments as to priorities for funding. Often some version of an across-the-board cut strategy is implemented because it is easy and perceived as fair. Such a strategy, however, is anathema to priority setting, as it makes the implicit assumptions that all programs are of equal priority, at least at the margin. If programs are set aside as immune from budget cuts, they may have few incentives to be efficient in their spending. Moreover, achieving the level of budget reductions needed to balance a budget may be impossible if many key programs are protected from cuts. In the George W. Bush administration, defense and homeland security spending was viewed by many as exempt from serious budget review in light of the wars in Iraq and Afghanistan and post–September 11, 2001, domestic security concerns. Furthermore, the American Association for Retired Persons (AARP) ran an advertising campaign during 2011 suggesting (not too subtly) that Social Security and Medicare should be immune from budget cuts unless members of Congress wanted to pay by losing their seats in the 2012 election.[46]

In a retrenchment environment, agencies normally feel fortunate if the budget office approves even their projected current services budget. In other situations, the central budget office may provide specific budget ceilings to each department. These figures, which most likely are below the current services levels, are used in preparing budget requests. This process has all the strengths and the weaknesses of fixed-ceiling budgeting. Where such approaches are taken, the process of cutting often starts earlier in the calendar than in a budget situation when growth predominates.[47] More time may be needed to determine which programs will be cut than to introduce new programs or expand existing ones, although some governments may find themselves in crisis situations in which cuts must be imposed immediately to avert a collapse of their financial situations.

Legislative Roles

If legislative preferences can be identified at the beginning of budget preparation, then cuts can be planned that are ultimately likely to meet with legislative approval. Some communities have used confidential questionnaires and other techniques for soliciting legislative input when budget cutting must be part of the preparation phase. Members of local legislative bodies, however, may prefer not to reveal their preferences until later, when more is known about the options for cutting and about citizens' attitudes. Of course, legislatures are frequently not on the "cutting" side of the budget process, in that legislatures are sometimes in the position of restoring cuts proposed by the executive, or providing their own add-ons to the budget.

Items to Cut

When reductions in expenditures become necessary, certain standard areas are considered. One of them is personnel costs. Because much of any government's operating budget covers personnel costs, it is difficult to make any appreciable reduction in expenditures without reducing personnel budgets. Several specific techniques are used for reducing personnel costs:

- Holding down general pay increases for workers
- Delaying filling of vacant positions and leaving other positions empty as they become vacant
- Laying off workers
- Providing financial incentives for workers to induce them to retire and (presumably) be replaced by lower-salaried workers
- Reducing government contributions for benefits, particularly costly retirement packages

The National Association of State Budget Offices, in its 2011 Fiscal Survey of the States, catalogued the budget reductions that had been made in the fiscal year 2011 state budget process. The most frequently used strategy was targeting cuts to individual programs (34 states), followed by across-the-board cuts (20 states) and layoffs (20 states). Interestingly, 19 of the states reporting that they had employed across-the-board cuts also employed targeted reductions. Other frequently used strategies included reducing local aid (16 states), imposing user fees (14 states), and furloughs (19 states).[48] Governments also tend to make cutbacks in equipment and facilities during times of fiscal stress. Decisions may be made to delay the purchase of major equipment and to defer maintenance, such as postponing the repair of city-owned sidewalks, roofs on government buildings, and potholes in city and state roads. The savings here can be short-lived: The failure to repair a roof, for example, might result in water damage costing many thousands of dollars. There may be a tendency to use the deferred maintenance approach on less visible facilities, especially water and sewer lines, although highways and bridges have suffered notably due to state and local fiscal problems.

In so-called tight budget periods, major emphasis is given to making operations as efficient as possible. The expectation is that organizational units should be able to operate with fewer resources while maintaining existing service levels. On the other hand, no single agency is eager to relinquish resources through increased efficiency if other agencies are not compelled to take the same route. Each agency is fearful of being the first to show how savings can be accomplished in its operations. This same attitude prevails in the approval phase among legislators, who are not eager to agree to budget cuts in their favored programs even though it is well understood that major cuts will be necessary.

Governments sometimes allow agencies to carry forward unspent money into the next fiscal year. This technique is seen as giving agencies incentives to use their resources efficiently. In a cutback period, however, the budget office and the legislature may be tempted to cancel out any carryover monies. Agencies mindful of such possible action, then, may avoid carrying forward any monies during economic recessions.

Budget cutting creates havoc, low morale, and some inefficiency in agencies. Personnel rightfully become concerned that their positions will be eliminated in the agency's budget request. Political appointees in an agency may be at odds with career personnel over which activities are essential and which are expendable. Some budget cuts necessitate agency reorganization, which disrupts operations. Uncertainty in funding can require stretching out the completion of projects. Defense is a major example of this problem, where changes in project schedules can result in billions of dollars of increased costs.

Budget Systems and Cutbacks

A final consideration regarding cutback budgeting is how the various budget systems (fixed ceiling budgeting, open-ended budgeting, and current services budgeting) assist in retrenchment efforts. As already noted, central budget offices use variations on fixed-ceiling budgeting to indicate to agencies what funding levels are acceptable in the budget preparation process. Perhaps most other budget systems have been developed on the stated or unstated premise that budgets will increase from year to year, and therefore these budget systems are less central to decision making when budget cuts must be imposed. At the same time, program budgeting and various forms of zero-base budgeting in theory should be highly useful in budget-cutting situations. During prosperous times, budgeting may be largely a process of considering possible incremental additions to the budget bases of programs. During declining times, the process may become one of subtracting increments from the base.

Final Preparation Deliberations

The chief executive and his or her staff become most active in the budget preparation phase during its final weeks, a frustrating period for the budget office. Decisions are seemingly reached but then may be reversed. The chief executive may instruct the budget office to include an agency's proposed change in the budget but later reject the proposal after considering revenue estimates. Alternatively, some spending initiative may be added at the last minute, forcing the budget office to scramble to fit that new spending in the budget. The chief executive may tentatively decide to recommend tax increases and then reverse that decision. Materials prepared during evenings and weekends by the budget office may find their way to the paper shredder as decisions are changed. The process may seem haphazard—and it probably is in many respects—but it is necessarily complicated because of the numerous factors being evaluated simultaneously.

A common complaint about the preparation phase is that only the chief executive, perhaps a top staff person (such as the governor's chief of staff), and the director of the central budget office consider the budget as a whole. An organizational unit in a department or agency is concerned primarily with its own piece of the budget, and the same is true of a department vis-à-vis other departments and the rest of the budget. Even in the central budget office, budget examiners focus mainly on one or a few segments of the budget and not on the total package. The chief executive, assisted by the budget director, must pull together pieces of information and intelligence provided by various sources into a set of decisions that can be defended as a whole. The budget that is to be submitted to the legislative body is the chief executive's creation.

The decision process necessarily involves tradeoffs. Assuming that there is a fixed budget constraint (like a balanced budget requirement), a $1 million increase in a city police department's budget means there is that much less available for other departments in the government. A one-mill increase in property taxes makes more money available to provide services that citizens want but at the same time may anger those same citizens who face an increase in their tax bills. Planning personnel layoffs may seem a reasonable choice for avoiding tax increases, but will layoffs be imposed on all agencies, including highly visible units like the police and fire departments? Chief executives take seriously the justifications that agencies make for increasing budget amounts or for avoiding budget cuts, and perceptions about the effectiveness of agencies' programs and activities influence executive decisions in the preparation phase of budgeting.

In this final stage of preparation, the chief executive must decide to what extent to include initiatives that may be ill received by the legislature. For example, with the end of the Cold War and the advent of global terrorism, the Defense Department has insisted on the need to transform itself. The argument is made that the military needs to invest in new technologies and scrap old ones. Closing unneeded military bases is part of this argument, but it runs counter to the interests of key members of Congress, who want to preserve bases in their jurisdictions. The president, then, must decide what to include in the budget on this sensitive matter, balancing the needs of national security with the reality of politics. Sustained combat operations also rapidly speed up the need for equipment replacement and spare parts, and in every war, new threats are identified that lead to research and development (R&D) expenditures for new technologies and tools to defeat the threats, such as the need to defeat or reduce damage from improvised explosive devices (IEDs).

Chief executives often include items in their budgets that they do not wholeheartedly support, because they know that the legislature is likely to fund the initiatives in any event.

In this type of situation, an executive may include the item to get a more realistic picture of ultimate expenditures and budget tradeoffs.

BUDGET DOCUMENTS

The final product of the preparation phase of budgeting is a budget document (or documents) that contains the decisions reached during the months of agency requests and executive reviews. The budget at this point is only a proposal, a set of recommended policies and programs set forth by the chief executive. It remains a proposal until the legislative body acts on it.

Number and Types of Documents

The budget for any government may consist of one or several documents. Small jurisdictions often have one-volume budgets, whereas larger governments usually package their budgets in several volumes. The size of a jurisdiction's budget, as measured in receipts or expenditures, does not always determine the size of its documents, however. Some volumes contain mainly text and tables, while others include charts, graphs, photographs, and narrative discussions of special topics and initiatives.

The preparers of budget documents are paying increasing attention to making the documents more "user friendly," reflecting the fact that these documents are expected to communicate the proposals contained within not only to technical budget analysts but also to executive and legislative political leaders, the news media, and the general citizenry. Budget documents often include glossaries that define technical terms in everyday language. Explanations are provided as to how tables should be read. Sections are sometimes color-coded and tabbed or have markings on page edges to help readers find the topics of interest to them. Since 1984, the Government Finance Officers Association has given its Award for Distinguished Budget Presentation to thousands of state and local governments.[49]

A government may produce one main document as well as one or more additional documents. A *budget-in-brief* may be prepared for general consumption that places emphasis on graphics and readability. The government can enhance its documents' interest to general readers by using attractive formats made possible by the widespread availability of affordable desktop publishing computer software. Of course, many governments have their budgets online, which increases their accessibility. Nashville has an online *Citizen's Guide to the Metro Budget*.[50]

Federal Documents

In some years, the federal government publishes numerous budget documents. In other years, it provides far fewer documents. The main budget document is the *Budget of the United States Government*,[51] which is backed up by a second and much larger document—the *Budget Appendix*.[52] In addition to preparing these documents, OMB prepares *Analytical Perspectives*, which provides more detailed information about specific aspects of the budget.[53] The content of this document varies over time but often includes discussions of crosscutting programs, such as homeland security, economic assumptions that are the foundation for the budget, budget reform proposals, and the current services budget. *Historical Tables* provides multiyear financial data on a variety of subjects.[54]

OMB produces other important documents, such as budget circulars (for example, Circular A-11 discussed in the chapter on the expenditure side of budget prepartion) and annual publications covering procurement and the midyear status of the budget. Some documents may be prepared for a few years but then are replaced or superseded by other documents. For instance, separate annual volumes have sometimes been prepared that describe the policy initiatives being advocated by the president and the information being collected by federal agencies. OMB's website (*www.whitehouse.gov/omb*) provides links to other documents it issues as well as a discussion of other sources of budget-related information.[55] The *Economic Report of the President* is prepared by the Council of Economic Advisers and is released at about the same time as the other main budget documents. The report discusses expected economic trends for the coming fiscal year and is the basis upon which the president's economic policy is formulated. The economic assumptions reflected in this report are used for estimating revenues and expenditures for the budget year.

The Treasury Department has an extensive publishing program and produces several documents specifically related to budgeting. The *Combined Statement of Receipts, Outlays, and Balances of the United States Government* reports on the financial condition of the government (see the chapter on financial management).[56] The *Treasury Bulletin*, issued quarterly, reports information about the economy, government receipts and outlays, and federal debt.[57] This document provides details on the various forms of federal securities. In addition to these documents, the Treasury Department publishes monthly and daily reports on the government's financial transactions and separate reports on trust funds, such as the unemployment, highway, and disability insurance trust funds.

Other Specialized Documents

Governments sometimes publish specialized budget-related documents in addition to those already mentioned. Some states and many local governments publish capital budgets, showing planned construction projects and major pieces of equipment to be purchased (see the chapter on capital assets), and some publish separate volumes on personnel.

The federal government and some states publish discussions of tax expenditures, which are losses in government revenue due to tax provisions that exempt some items from taxation or provide favorable tax rates. In its annual publication *Analytical Perspectives*, OMB provides an extensive discussion of the effects of various tax provisions on receipts—namely, how these provisions create tax expenditures (see the chapters on budgeting for revenues). Massachusetts publishes a separate volume on tax expenditures annually.[58]

Budget Messages

Another feature of budget documents is the budget message, in which the chief executive highlights the major recommendations in the budget. This message is sometimes presented orally to the legislature. The president's budget message is included in the *Budget of the United States Government* itself. State governments vary widely in this regard, with some having no message and others having lengthy ones, sometimes as long as 100 pages.

Exhibit 8-1 shows the budget message of Maryland Governor Martin O'Malley included with his fiscal year 2012 budget proposal. State and local jurisdictions occasionally publish their budget messages as separate documents.

Exhibit 8–1 2012 Budget Message, State of Maryland

January 21, 2011

The Senate of Maryland. The Honorable Thomas V. "Mike" Miller, President
The Maryland House of Delegates. The Honorable Michael E. Busch, Speaker
The Citizens and Families of Maryland

Dear Mr. President, Mr. Speaker, Ladies and Gentlemen of the General Assembly, and Fellow Marylanders:

These last four years, in the face of the most serious economic challenges faced by our country in modern times, we've come together as one Maryland to make progress on our shared goals. In times of adversity, the people of Maryland do not make excuses; we make progress.

Determined to move forward out of this recession, Maryland businesses chose to expand and create jobs again, and are now doing so at a rate that is twice the national rate of new job creation.

Determined to make our children winners in this new economy, together we chose to improve public education with record investments. And alone among the fifty states, we made college more affordable for more families by holding the line against any increase in college tuition for four years in a row.

Together we chose to extend affordable healthcare coverage to more families, to improve the health of the Chesapeake Bay, and to invest in job creating innovation, including biotech, renewable energy, research and development.

Despite the challenges wrought by the national recession, we remain committed to fiscal responsibility. Maryland remains one of only eight states with a Triple A bond rating certified by all three rating agencies. During the first term of the O'Malley-Brown Administration, the State adopted $5.6 billion of spending reductions and abolished 4,200 positions. And despite fiscal pressures, Maryland has preserved a healthy Rainy Day Fund.

Nearly $1 billion in additional spending reductions bring total reductions under the O'Malley-Brown Administration to $6.6 billion. Actions included in the budget improve the outlook for FY 2013 by more than $800 million.

The FY 2012 proposed budget balances a $1.4 billion budget shortfall without any new tax increases. We reduce the structural deficit by 37%, reform Maryland's

(Continued)

long-neglected pension system to put it on a path of sustainability and reduce our retiree health liability by almost $7 billion.

The FY 2012 budget, while painfully lean, protects our shared priorities and focuses new funding on job creating initiatives throughout Maryland. Progress on one of these fronts requires progress on all.

Jobs and Opportunity

In this changing new economy we are in a fight for our children's future. Together, we must move forward by creating and saving jobs through innovation, and that includes protecting our best-in-the-nation public school system. We must also be willing to continue making tough choices so that we can protect our shared priorities—priorities that will allow us to make this new economy ours and build a better future for our children.

Our FY 2012 budget proposes the creation of *Invest* Maryland, an initiative to support the growth of the state's knowledge-based industries by stimulating up to $100 million in venture capital funds and creating thousands of jobs. In addition, we include funding for the Small Business Credit Recovery Program, and further investments in job creating industries such as biotechnology, life sciences, renewable energy and research and development.

Education

For the third straight year, *Education Week* Magazine ranked Maryland the number one public school system in America. Strong public schools, world-class teachers and principals, and a workforce with the skills they need to compete in the 21st Century is essential if Maryland is to come through this national recession stronger and more quickly than other states. In order to make this new economy ours, we must protect our record investments in public schools and invest in the innovative, knowledge-based economy of today.

Together, we've chosen to protect this priority, funding public schools for the second year in a row at a record level of $5.7 billion. A record $4.9 billion in direct education aid will be distributed among Maryland's twenty-four local jurisdictions in order to maintain and build upon the progress we've already made. And as a winner in President Obama's "Race to the Top" competition, this budget proposal prioritizes innovative reform efforts to help boost student achievement, reduce achievement gaps, recruit and retain world-class teachers and students, and turn around struggling schools.

Health and Wellness

One of our solemn obligations is to protect the people of Maryland, and that means protecting the obligation we have to our most vulnerable citizens. In these tough economic times, the O'Malley-Brown Administration has expanded access to quality, affordable health care to 250,000 more Marylanders—half of whom are children; invested in the future of health care delivery; and strengthened the safety net for vulnerable families throughout our State.

Together, we've chosen to maintain and improve access to health care for over one million adults and children in our FY 2012 budget. As a result of these efforts, more than 300,000 more Marylanders—including poor children—will have access to health care in FY 2012 who five years ago did not.

Maryland will lead the nation in implementing health care reform by including funding in this budget for new technology to control administrative costs, improvements for the effectiveness and efficiency of health care, funding for better access to care for Maryland families, and ensuring that patient care is guided by the best information available at the bedside or in the operating room.

Public Safety

Even in tough times, we've protected our investments in public safety, maintaining our commitment to protecting Maryland neighborhoods and families. Thanks to these efforts, together, we've driven violent crime, property crime, and total crime to the lowest rates ever recorded.

Our FY 2012 budget proposal maintains our shared commitment to protecting our law enforcement, including those who work in Maryland's correctional facilities, while investing in advances in law enforcement technology to further support effective communication and information-sharing.

In our continued effort to make Maryland the national leader in homeland security preparedness, our budget proposal supports our state's abilities to respond to natural disasters, terrorist activities, pandemics, and other large-scale emergencies.

Environmental Protection

Together, we continue to seek a cleaner, greener, more sustainable future for the people of Maryland committed to the restoration of the Chesapeake Bay, protection of open space, preservation of our agricultural heritage, revitalization of our communities, and enhancement of our mass transit systems.

Our budget proposal increases funding for the Chesapeake Bay Trust Fund by 25%, and provides additional funding for the successful cover crop program, which experienced record levels of participation last year.

With this budget proposal, we begin a conversation that will help protect these shared priorities, reform our pension system, and make the necessary choices for better times, better opportunities, and a better future for our children. And we do so as we reaffirm the truth that we are one Maryland, united by our belief in the dignity of every individual, and united by our belief in our own responsibility to advance the greater good.

Sincerely,
Martin O'Malley, Governor

Source: Reprinted from State of Maryland (2012). *Budget Highlights: Fiscal Year 2012* (January 21). Annapolis, MD: Office of Management and Budget.

Approved Budgets

Some jurisdictions publish their approved budgets (i.e., budgets that reflect action taken by the legislative bodies). North Carolina, for example, publishes a *Post-Legislative Budget Summary*. The federal government does not provide such a volume.

Coverage

Budget documents vary with regard to the extent of their coverage. All report information about government receipts and expenditures. Likewise, intergovernmental transactions are reported. A state budget highlights the funds it receives from the federal government and the funds it provides local governments within the state. Issues arise over how much detail to provide on these items.

State and Local Budgets

Confusion is common in the handling of funds in budget documents. State and local governments are major users of special funds, which basically are financial accounts for special revenue sources, such as the Casino Revenue Fund in New Jersey, and which can be used only for specific purposes. A jurisdiction's general fund consists of revenue that can be used for all functions of the government. These different types of funds are discussed in the chapter on financial management, but here we note that many jurisdictions have a general fund budget document plus one or more documents for special funds. One result of having separate budgets can be confusion over the size of the total budget and the amount spent by any given agency, because the agency may be receiving support from several funds.

The Federal Budget

The coverage issue at the federal level is similar. Until the late 1960s, there were really three types of federal budgets: the administrative budget, the consolidated cash statement, and the federal sector of the national income accounts. Using three types of budgets resulted in much confusion. Because each type had a different coverage, total revenues and expenditures varied from one to another, leading to different statements of budget surpluses and deficits. Different pictures of federal finances—gloomy or bright—could be painted by choosing to discuss one budget statement and ignoring the other two. In response to this problem, President Johnson in 1967 appointed the President's Commission on Budget Concepts, whose eventual recommendation for a unified budget was incorporated into the budget document beginning with fiscal year 1969.[59]

In the revised format, all federal agencies and programs are included, with some important exceptions noted below. Receipts, budget authority (funds made available for obligation), outlays (expenditures), and the resulting deficit or surplus are shown. Information is supplied for the means of financing the deficit and about the size of the federal debt.

Since adoption of the unified budget, important changes have occurred. One trend was toward greater use of moving some items out of the reported budget totals, what is known as *off-budget totals*. Congress determined what was off-budget, which varied somewhat from year to year. The U.S. Postal Service, for example, was moved off-budget because it was expected to operate like a business, largely independent of the government. Other federal entities were removed from the budget because they operated largely with revolving funds rather than annual appropriations and made direct loans to the public. For example, the Rural Telephone Bank, the Federal Financing Bank, and the U.S. Synthetic Fuels Corporation were placed off-budget. Government-sponsored enterprises (GSEs), such as the Federal National Mortgage Association (Fannie Mae) and the Federal Home Mortgage Corporation (Freddie Mac), were historically neither on-budget nor off-budget. With the bailout by the government of Fannie and Freddie in 2009, they are now wholly part of the government. The Obama administration, in the fiscal year 2012 budget proposal, treats the transactions of the GSEs on a cash basis. This means that in some years there is a net cash outflow to make good on past commitments; in theory, in other years there could be a net cash inflow.[60] The Congressional Budget Office treats the transactions of the GSEs on a subsidy basis, meaning that it records the present value of the estimated costs of future commitments.[61] The Board of Governors of the Federal Reserve System is also not included in the budget. Those transactions that are not in the budget are normally described as "nonbudgetary."

Coverage—The Special Case of Credit and Insurance Liabilities

In assembling a proposed budget, both obvious and not-so-obvious expenditures must be anticipated. Much of any budget will be committed to funding the operations of government, either for direct services provided by the government's departments or through grant programs, as in the case of state aid to local school districts. Monies also must be set aside for making payments on the principal and interest for any outstanding debt. As discussed in the chapter on government and the economy, sustained federal budget deficits have yielded an increasingly large total federal debt that requires massive interest payments every year—so massive that they now constitute one of the most important components of federal expenditures. In addition to debt accumulated through borrowing by the U.S. Treasury Department, federal debt has grown through borrowing by federal agencies such as the U.S. Postal Service and the Tennessee Valley Authority.

Beginning in the late 1980s, political leaders, public administrators, leaders in private financial institutions, and the citizenry became painfully aware that the federal government had other liabilities that until then had seemed innocuous or almost nonexistent.[62] Hundreds of savings and loan institutions failed, forcing the federal government to meet its financial commitments to depositors. The Resolution Trust Corporation was established, as a temporary agency, to manage the resources of thrifts going into receivership at a staggering cost to taxpayers. Further liabilities were encountered when the government had surviving banks acquire many of the failed thrifts.[63] Similarly, the federal government during the recession that started in 2007 lent money to a wide variety of private financial institutions, issued credit guarantees to others, and took stock and other securities in exchange for loans to such private corporations as General Motors. Many of those credit programs ended by 2011 with the federal government having been repaid, or with corporations like General Motors repurchasing their stocks from the government. Loans still outstanding, however, represent contingent liabilities on future budgets. While these contingent liabilities are reported publicly, as in the Federal Reserve's reports on each of the numerous different credit programs it operates, they do not enter into the budget except in the event of default.

Types of Liabilities

Appreciating the nature of government liabilities is difficult due to the complex nature of the institutions involved. The most common method, for the federal government, of differentiating between types of liabilities is to look at them in terms of the type of instrument involved.

As outlined in **Table 8–1**, the instruments used and the consequent categories of liabilities are direct loans, guaranteed loans, insurance, and government-sponsored enterprises.

Table 8–1 Long-Term Federal Government Obligations and Risks

1. Direct Loans
   - Federal Student Loans
   - Farm Service Agency (excluding Commodity Credit Corporation), Rural Development, Rural Housing
   - Rural Utilities Service and Rural Telephone Bank
   - Housing and Urban Development
   - Export-Import Bank
   - Public Law 480—Agriculture
   - Agency for International Development
   - Troubled Asset Relief Program (TARP)
   - Disaster Assistance
   - GSE Mortgage-Backed Securities Purchase Program
   - Education Temporary Student Loan Purchase Authority
2. Guaranteed Loans
   - Federal Housing Administration–Mutual Mortgage Insurance Fund
   - Department of Veterans Affairs Mortgages
   - Federal Housing Administration—General and Special Risk Insurance Fund
   - Small Business Administration
   - Export-Import Bank
   - International Assistance
   - Farm Service Agency (excluding Commodity Credit Corporation), Rural Development, Rural Housing
   - Commodity Credit Corporation
   - Government National Mortgage Association
   - Troubled Asset Relief Program (TARP)
3. Insurance
   - Deposit Insurance—Federal Deposit Insurance Corporation
   - Pension Guarantees—Pension Benefit Guaranty Corporation
   - Disaster Insurance—Flood, Crop
   - Insurance Against Security-Related Risks—Terrorism, Airline, War
4. Government-Sponsored Enterprises
   - Federal National Mortgage Association (Fannie Mae)
   - Federal Home Loan Mortgage Corporation (Freddie Mac)
   - Farm Credit System
   - Federal Home Loan Banks

Source: Adapted from U.S. Office of Management and Budget (2011). *Analytical perspectives, budget of the United States government, fiscal year 2012* (pp. 385–402). Washington, DC: U.S. Government Printing Office.

Before discussing these instruments, we should note that other major liabilities are omitted from the table, such as the costs of environmental cleanup of nuclear weapon production plants, defense installations that are being closed both in the United States and overseas, the future unfunded liabilities of Social Security and Medicare, and other federal agency facilities. Other exclusions include federal research and development centers, such as the RAND Corporation, which are primarily the creations of the Departments of Defense and Energy, and congressionally chartered, nonprofit corporations, such as the American Red Cross.

Direct loans involve operations at home and abroad. Monies are available to help farmers acquire homes, electrify their farms, and engage in overseas commerce. International operations include loans to support the defense and economic development of other nations and to stimulate the growth of the private sectors in these countries. Immense political risks exist with such instruments because a change in a government may lead to the renunciation of previous commitments to repay loans. In other situations, developing countries may be too poor to repay loans, so these become de facto grants. *Guaranteed loans* entail agreement by the government to pay loans when customers default. A major segment of the housing mortgage market in the United States is backed by federal government loan guarantees. The category has also included student loans, which have had a history of high rates of default.[64] In the international arena, the federal government has guaranteed billions of dollars of loans made by U.S. financial institutions to developing countries under the former Housing Guaranty Loan Program and loans by host country financial institutions in other programs such as the Development Credit Authority.

During the recession that started in 2007, the most high-profile and potentially costly loan program was the Troubled Asset Relief Program (TARP), which was provided to bail out troubled financial institutions that had invested in bad loans, many of which were backed by mortgage-backed securities. TARP provided both direct loans (for example, to General Motors and Chrysler) and loan guarantees (much of which was provided to financial institutions). Originally, $700 billion was made available under the program. Only about half of that was ever provided, however, and the estimated cost, as of 2011, was only $23 billion, according to the Congressional Budget Office.[65]

Federal Insurance Programs cover deposits in financial institutions and private pension deposits. While the huge bank failures of the 1980s have been mopped up, bank failures continue to occur.[66] Pension guarantees present other problems. Corporate failures leave pensioners and employees with credits into pension plans that lack adequate financial backing. The Pension Benefit Guarantee Corporation deals with these problems, with the support of the federal government. Other programs include crop insurance for farmers.

Government-Sponsored Enterprises (GSEs) are another potential source of liability. These institutions have historically involved largely secondary credit markets, in which these institutions purchase debt instruments, such as mortgages, and in turn release funds to lending institutions for further loan activity.[67] GSEs have always had somewhat of a "neither fish nor fowl" quality. They have been owned privately, but their loans have been backed implicitly by the federal government. This implicit guarantee became an *explicit* one in 2009 when Fannie Mae and Freddie Mac were taken over by the federal government. CBO estimated in June 2011 that the total cost to the federal government from the loans guaranteed by Fannie and Freddie prior to 2009 would total $291 billion, and that there were additional losses associated with later loans.[68] It still remains to be seen what form the GSEs will take going forward. The president's 2012 budget proposed reducing the size of the portfolio for Fannie and Freddie; some bills in Congress have proposed shutting them down entirely.[69]

Federal Liability Reforms

Efforts are under way to bring some clarity to what liabilities the government has, and proposals exist for reforming this immense area of finance. The concerns about such liabilities are not new but rather date back to 1945, when Congress passed the Government Corporation Control Act.[70] At the time, there was concern that government corporations were operating without sufficient guidance and control by the government. The argument can be made that despite the numerous revisions Congress has made in the law over the years, it remains inadequate in controlling these major institutions.

The Financial Institutions Reform, Recovery, and Enforcement Act of 1989 dealt with failed thrift institutions and required the General Accounting Office (now the Government Accountability Office [GAO]) to investigate the financing of government-sponsored enterprises.[71] The GAO has designated some programs, such as the Department of the Interior's management of oil and gas resources, as "high risk."[72] The GAO's intent is to train attention on those programs that have the potential for creating large economic losses for the government.

The Federal Credit Reform Act of 1990 required the government to upgrade its accounting for credit programs.[73] OMB issued Circular A-129 (1993, rev. 2000), which provides a uniform set of procedures for agencies engaged in loan programs, both direct and guaranteed. The procedures indicate how agencies should estimate the costs of loans and loan guarantees, a function that is difficult to accomplish. The purpose of Circular A-129 is to reduce risks and place the federal government's credit operations on a better financial foundation. Agencies that guarantee loans must estimate potential defaults and include those estimates in their current appropriations requests. This requires the annual costs of credit programs to represent the present value of the long-term costs to the federal government. This reform places potential defaults in direct competition with current spending requests, a practice expected to make decision makers more cautious in extending loans and loan guarantees.

It has proved difficult, however, to obtain reliable estimates of these long-term costs because of the uncertainty associated with forecasting the long-term liabilities associated with a given program.[74] On the other hand, the Treasury Department makes estimates of country risk for some agencies, such as the Development Credit Authority, and then the U.S. Agency for International Development has little problem in calculating the appropriation it needs to cover any potential default.

Efforts are now under way to improve the collection of debts rather than simply writing off bad debts. The Debt Collection Improvement Act of 1996 strengthened the government's ability to retrieve monies owed.[75] Agencies may refer bad debts to private collection companies and may share information with one another in locating those borrowers who are in arrears.

These significant changes, however, have not addressed the main issue—namely, what should be the federal government's responsibilities in this area, and how can liabilities and risks be curtailed? One line of criticism states that the federal government has been too generous. Fostering a credit market is important to national economic growth, but should the federal government have such a major role?

Credit programs subsidize risk-taking on the part of individuals and corporations. When the federal government provides full backing for a venture, then it assumes 100% of the risk. Crop insurance, for example, is available at comparatively low cost to farms. Only about one in four farms uses the insurance, however, because when droughts, floods, and other conditions destroy crops, the government usually passes legislation that fully covers all damage. Similarly, were government to cover all of the damage from hurricanes and their related floods, then there would be little incentive to purchase insurance. The hurricanes in the mid-2000s, especially the 2005 season and Hurricanes Katrina and Rita, underscored the fact that the government was not about to cover all associated costs from storms and that property owners needed to purchase insurance.

Prescriptions for reform, therefore, tend to favor increasing the risk of the private sector and decreasing that of the public sector. Such action was taken in 1996 with the passage of the Student Loan Marketing Association Reorganization Act, which provided for the privatization of Sallie Mae (student loans) and Connie Lee (college construction loans).[76] Connie Lee was converted to a private entity in 1997, and Sallie Mae was converted in 2004.[77] In 2005, Congress passed the Terrorism Risk Insurance Extension Act, which extended coverage available through the Treasury Department.[78] The Dodd-Frank Wall Street Reform and Consumer Protection Act of 2010 included provisions that require financial institutions supervised by the Federal Reserve to increase their reporting to the Fed on their exposure to other companies and to maintain a reserve of at least 25% of such exposure, and that such institutions reveal off-balance-sheet liabilities such as participation in purchases of securities, repurchase agreements, and a long list of other types of participation in the securities market. The last provision is intended to reduce the risk of the Fed having to bail out financial institutions that engage in complex securities instruments, such as those involved in the collapse of the mortgage market (see the chapter on government and the economy).[79]

Although one line of concern insists that government credit and insurance institutions have become burdensome on government, perhaps suggesting that they should be totally privatized, the reality is that they serve important functions. Proposals exist for creating still more of these bodies. Government corporations have been proposed for air traffic services, management of petroleum reserves, and development of national infrastructure.

State and Local Governments

Similar liability and risk problems exist at the state and local levels. The Governmental Accounting Standards Board has prescribed how these governments should report risks and insurance (see the chapter on financial management). Potential losses can be due to "torts; theft of, damage to, or destruction of assets; business interruptions; errors or omissions; job-related illnesses or injuries to employees; acts of God; and any other risks of loss assumed under a policy or participation contract issued by a public entity risk pool."[80] Torts are civil wrongs that occur independent of contract, as when a city refuse truck accidentally backs into a person's vehicle and causes personal harm and property damage. Among the greatest liabilities of state and local governments are their pension systems, which are sometimes actuarially unsound.

Information Displays

Revenues

Budget documents present both revenue and expenditure data. The coverage of receipts or revenues is usually substantially less extensive than the coverage of expenditures. Budgets show receipts from taxes, such as individual and corporate income taxes; from user charges, such as water service fees; and from other governments, such as state grants to local government. Budget documents also typically discuss proposed changes in tax laws, especially proposed tax rate changes. For the federal government, some revenues are treated as expenditures. OMB treats receipts generated by an agency in the form of user fees as an *offsetting collection* and deducts them from outlays rather than treating the amount as revenue. **Table 8–2** shows the various sources used to finance the State of Utah's budget.

Expenditures

The bulk of the budget document is devoted to the expenditure side of government finance, with the main classification usually based on organizational unit. Each department presents a budget within which subunits are given separate treatment. A generally uniform format is used for each subunit, including a brief narrative description of the subunit's responsibilities and functions. Narratives contained in the federal *Appendix* also contain proposed appropriations language that may be quite specific—for the Department of

---

Table 8–2 State Fiscal Plan General Fund, State of Utah, Fiscal Year 2012 ($ thousands)

Source	Actual FY2010	Total FY2011	Total FY2012
Beginning Balance	$0	$14,886	$0
General Fund Estimate	1,780,539	2,008,582	1,964,000
Transfers from Mineral Lease	0	3,000	0
Transfers from Econ. Dev.	4,384	(6,942)	(7,230)
Transfers from Fund Balances	12,477	4,557	8,178
Legislation Impacting Revenue	0	(5)	13,636
Transfers from Nonlapsing Balances	1,450	13,394	15,252
Lapsing Balances	23,131	0	0
Other	361	0	0
Transfers from Disaster Recovery Fund	10,800	0	0
Transfers from Rainy Day Fund	83,910	5,946	0
Reserve from Prior Fiscal Year	13,217	83,388	56,559
Reserve for Following Fiscal Year	(83,388)	(56,559)	0
Total Sources of Funding	$1,846,881	$2,070,247	$2,050,396

Source: State of Utah (2011). *Budget summary fiscal year 2012* (p. 7). Retrieved December 12, 2011, from http://www.governor.utah.gov/gopb.

Agriculture's Risk Management Agency's budget of more than $82 million, not more than $1,000 was to be used for "official reception and representation expenses."[81]

In addition to the narrative are various tabular displays. Expenditures are reported by object classes, such as personnel, equipment, and travel (see the chapter on financial management). These financial tables may be primarily for informational purposes, or they may later be incorporated into the appropriation bill. When this practice is used, the legislative body is said to have adopted a *line-item budget*, which reduces the president's, governor's, or mayor's flexibility in executing the budget.

Personnel

The main component of an operating budget often consists of salaries, wages, and employee benefits. For that reason, budget documents sometimes include specific information about personnel. Sometimes the budget may even go so far as to list the number of people employed for each position title in an agency. **Table 8–3** shows budget changes in less detail by presenting the costs of personnel and other expenses for fire rescue in the City of San Diego. Carefully studying the table will give the reader a sense of the effort in calculating such budget tables and how they might be used by decision makers, both executive and legislative.

Budget presentations sometimes show for the past fiscal year the budgeted amounts and actual amounts, for both receipts and expenditures. This information is important in understanding the accuracy with which the government is able to estimate its revenues and

Table 8–3 Expenditure Detail, Fire and Rescue Department, City of San Diego, California, Fiscal Year 2010 ($ thousands)

Expenditures by Category

	FY2010 Budget	FY2011 Adopted	FY2010–2011 Change
PERSONNEL			
Salaries and Wages	$104,676	**$91,772**	($12,905)
Fringe Benefits	51,894	**62,791**	10,897
PERSONNEL SUBTOTAL	**$156,571**	**$154,563**	**($2,008)**
NON-PERSONNEL			
Supplies	$2,055	**$2,028**	($27)
Contracts	18,055	**13,135**	(4,920)
Information Technology	**2,140**	**1,784**	(356)
Energy and Utilities	3,178	**2,854**	(323)
Other	4,734	**4,778**	45
Capital Expenditures	**2,613**	1,013	(1,600)
Debt	1,747	**1,747**	–
NON-PERSONNEL	**$34,522**	**$27,339**	**($7,182)**
Total	**$191,093**	**$181,902**	**($9,191)**

Source: Modified from City of San Diego (2010). *Fire and rescue budget: fiscal year 2011* (p. 430).

keep its expenditures within budgeted amounts. Budgets typically show the most recently completed fiscal year, the estimate of how the current fiscal year will finish, and the proposed budget for the next fiscal year.

Current Services

Governments sometimes provide current services budget data, which are intended to show decision makers what receipts and expenditures will be without any changes being made in tax laws, other revenue sources, and spending levels. **Table 8–4** shows current services projections for the federal government from 2010 through 2015. In addition to receipts, the table reports outlays subdivided into discretionary spending and mandatory or entitlement spending. It also shows the differences between on-budget and off-budget receipts and outlays for each year. The off-budget surplus is due to the Social Security system bringing in more revenue than it pays out. This phenomenon will be reversed when the baby boom generation starts to draw Social Security, unless rates are substantially increased or benefits are cut.

Program Information

Increasingly over the past 50 years, budget documents have contained information on the workload and performance of programs. These program data may represent information that was used in the process of making budget decisions, or they may simply reflect information on the past performance of programs or agencies. More than 40 state governments reported in 2008 that their documents contained performance measures for their respective agencies.[82] **Table 8–5** presents performance data for the State of Maryland's Motor Vehicle Administration.

Future Years

Budget reformers have tended to advocate multiyear projections as a method for helping decision makers understand the long-term implications of policy and program issues.[83] However, given the uncertainty of the future, one might expect few governments to attempt to make projections beyond the budget year or biennium. Perhaps somewhat surprisingly, the use of multiyear projections has increased. A longitudinal study of state budgeting found that while only 2% of the states responding in 1970 said they projected effectiveness measures in budget documents, 37% responding in 2005 reported they made such projections. Comparable figures for the use of productivity measures were 8% and 38%, respectively. These 2005 figures, however, were lower than the results of the 2000 survey, perhaps suggesting that states have retrenched in their use of future-year projections.[84]

Decision makers always calculate how their actions will affect the future, so including projections in budgets seems appropriate. However, these projections can easily be faulty. A 2011 analysis found that the errors made by states in forecasting revenues for income and sales tax collections resulted in a shortfall of $49 billion in fiscal year 2009. The median error during that year was a 10.2% overestimate.[85]

Table 8–4 Current Services Estimates, Budget of the United States Government, Fiscal Year 2012 ($ billions)

	Actual	*Estimated*				
	2010	**2011**	**2012**	**2013**	**2014**	**2015**
Receipts	2,163	2,174	2,609	2,959	3,305	3,487
Outlays:						
Discretionary:						
Defense	689	746	735	735	747	758
Non-Defense	617	640	608	591	593	601
Subtotal, Discretionary	1,306	1,386	1,344	1,326	1,339	1,359
Mandatory:						
Social Security	701	727	761	802	847	895
Medicare	446	488	468	501	529	554
Medicaid and CHIP	281	285	279	299	365	406
Other Mandatory	526	676	601	547	565	600
Subtotal, Mandatory	1,954	2,177	2,109	2,150	2,306	2,455
Disaster Costs	3	7	8	9	9	10
Net Interest	196	205	240	322	421	505
Total, Outlays	3,456	3,771	3,699	3,805	4,075	4,328
Unified Deficit(+)/Surplus(−)	1,293	1,597	1,090	846	770	841
On-Budget	1,370	1,653	1,168	928	859	934
Off-Budget	−77	−56	−77	−82	−89	−93
Memorandum:						
BEA Baseline Deficit	1,293	1,593	1,036	643	463	496
Adjustments to Reflect Current Tax Policies	1	36	180	272	294	317
Adjustments to Reflect Current Spending Policies and Potential Disaster Costs	3	18	20	20	21	21
Related Debt Service	*	*	4	15	30	47
Adjusted Baseline Deficit	1,293	1,597	1,090	846	770	841

* $500 million or less.

Source: Reprinted from U.S. Office of Management and Budget (2011). *Analytical perspectives, budget of the United States Government, fiscal year 2012* (p. 360). Washington, DC: U.S. Government Printing Office.

Table 8–5 Performance Measures—State of Maryland Motor Vehicle Administration

	2009	*2010*	*2011*	*2012*
Number Enrolled in Motorcycle Safety Courses	10,358	8,902	9,233	9,464
Percent of Alcohol Fatalities	29.6%	29.6%	29.6%	29.6%
Number of Transactions at Motor Vehicle Offices	12,263,015	11,010,716	11,668,684	11,775,735
Average Customer Visit Time (minutes)	33	31	31	31
Average Wait Time at Vehicle Emissions Inspection Station (minutes)	5	4.9	4.7	4.6

Source: State of Maryland (2012). *Fiscal year 2012 proposed operating budget detail* (Vol. 1, pp. 619–620). Retrieved March 1, 2012, from http://www.dbm.maryland.gov/agencies/operbudget/Pages/2012ProposedOperBudget.aspx.

Space Limitations

Not all available program and resource information can be presented in budget documents without making the documents unwieldy. The budget formats of some jurisdictions rigidly prescribe allowed space—for example, one page for each bureau, program, or activity. This type of format may increase the readability of the document. Its disadvantage is that not all subunits are of equal importance, in terms of either budget size or political interest. Therefore, many jurisdictions use more flexible formats, providing more information on some agencies and programs and less information on others. With this type of format, larger agencies commonly receive more extensive coverage because they are more complex and engage in more varied activities. Agencies that are particularly popular or unpopular may receive more extensive coverage regardless of their size.

With the widespread use of computer technology, the space problem can be eased somewhat with some information being made available only in electronic format. Some budget offices provide their most detailed information only by CD-ROM or on their websites.

SUMMARY

In beginning the preparation phase, the chief executive conveys to agencies some sense of priorities, either formally in writing or by more subtle means. The executive's view of the role of government in society is indicated to agencies, along with more specific priorities.

The revenue side of the budget is examined carefully, especially because state and local governments are generally prohibited from having operating budgets that exceed available revenues. One of the key components of budget preparation on the revenue side is revenue forecasting, which is a technical exercise that may have intense political ramifications. Budget preparation begins in agencies and involves extensive debate. Similar debate develops between agencies and the central budget office, which in turn must compete with other central staff units. Because little formal authority is granted to a central budget office, it must always be concerned with being overruled by the chief executive.

The 1980s ushered in a new era in budgeting, where the focus was on budget cutbacks rather than program expansion. Fiscal stress, taxing and spending limitations, and an increase in anti–big government attitudes among political leaders have resulted in retrenchment efforts. A respite in cutbacks occurred in the second half of the 1990s, when the booming economy produced budget surpluses. With two recessions in the first decade of the 2000s, cutback management became necessary once again. Decision makers have come to realize that they can be forced to deal with immense problems associated with credit and insurance liabilities. The collapse of hundreds of federally backed thrift institutions amply demonstrated the risks that are involved. At the federal level, decision makers can be forced to decide whether to commit government resources to deal with the woes of private corporations, as occurred in 2007–2008 with the banking and auto industry crises.

The product of the preparation phase is a budget or a set of budget documents that reflect executive decisions on policies and programs. The federal government has what is called a unified budget. Revenue and expenditure data are treated in all budgets, but the latter receive much more extensive treatment. One common budget format has a structure based on organizational units and includes supporting narratives and tabular displays that present costs, personnel, and program data.

NOTES

1. The Recovery Act (2011). *Recovery.gov*. Retrieved April 24, 2011, from http://www.recovery.gov/About/Pages/The_Act.aspx.
2. Hampton, G. (1999). Environmental equity and public participation. *Policy Sciences, 32*, 163–174; Rubin, M. M., & Bartle, J. R. (2005). Integrating gender into government budgets: a new perspective. *Public Administration Review, 65*, 259–272; Midgley, J. (2005). *Women and the U.S. budget: where the money goes and what you can do about it*. Gabriola Island, BC, Canada: New Society. See also Clinton, W. (2011). *Back to work: why we need smart government for a strong economy*. New York, NY: Knopf.
3. Diving into the rich pool. (2011). *The Economist, 401*, September 24, 83. Hunting the rich. (2011). *The Economist, 401*, September 24, 13.
4. Mathesian, C. (1994). Immigration: the symbolic crackdown. *Governing, 7*, May, 52–57.
5. Congressional Budget Office (2007). *The impact of unauthorized immigrants on the budgets of state and local governments*, December 6. Retrieved March 1, 2012, from http://www.cbo.gov/publication/41645.
6. Williamson, J., et al. (2003). Generational equity, generational interdependence, and the framing of the debate over Social Security reform. *Journal of Sociology and Social Welfare, 30*, 3–14; Gokhale, J., & Smetters, K. (2003). *Fiscal and generational imbalances: new budget measures for new budget priorities*. Washington, DC: AEI Press.
7. Centers for Disease Control and Prevention (2011). *Investigation announcement: multistate outbreak of E. coli O157:H7 infections linked to romaine lettuce*. December 7. Retrieved December 12, 2011, from http://www.cdc.gov/ecoli/2011/ecoliO157/romainelettuce/120711/index.html.
8. See Gore, A. (2006). *An inconvenient truth: the planetary emergency of global warming and what we can do about it*. Emmaus, PA: Rodale Press; and *An inconvenient truth*, documentary movie featuring A. Gore (2006). Hollywood, CA: Paramount Classics; Palin: global warming just "snake oil." (2010). *CBS News*. Retrieved April 24, 2011, from http://www.cbsnews.com/stories/2010/02/09/politics/main6189211.shtml.
9. Weimer, D. L., & Vining, A. R. (2004). *Policy analysis: concepts and practice* (4th ed.). Upper Saddle River, NJ: Pearson Prentice Hall; Royse, D., et al. (2006). *Program evaluation: an introduction*. Belmont, CA: Thomson Brooks/Cole.
10. National Association of State Budget Officers (2008). *Budget processes in the states*, Summer, 51, 55, 57–58.
11. Balanoff, H. R., & Pinto, C. W. (1999). What do you do when your city is looking at a million-dollar deficit in the current fiscal year? *Public Productivity & Management Review, 23*, 83–88.
12. Pew Center on the States and the Nelson A. Rockefeller Institute of Government (2011). *States' revenue estimating: cracks in the crystal ball*, March. Retrieved March 1, 2012, from http://www.rockinst.org/pdf/government_finance/2011-03-01-States_Revenue_Estimating_Report.pdf.
13. Steinhauer, J. (2009). California, out of money, reels as voters rebuff leaders. *New York Times*, May 21. Retrieved April 24, 2011, from http://www.nytimes.com/2009/05/21/us/21calif.html; Nagourney, A. (2010). For California, a new month, a new deficit. *New York Times*, November 17. Retrieved April 14, 2011, from http://www.nytimes.com/2010/11/18/us/18calif.html?sq=schwarzenegger&st=cse&scp=24&pagewanted=print; Nagourney, A. (2011). Standoff in Sacramento as Brown and G.O.P lock horns over taxes. *New York Times*, April 25. Retrieved April 25, 2011, from http://www.nytimes.com/2011/04/14/us/politics/14brown.html.
14. Sector, B. (2010). Illinois stuck in "historic, epic" budget crisis. *Chicago Tribune*, January 23. http://articles.chicagotribune.com/2010-02-23/news/ct-met-state-budget-mess-20100223_1_state-budget-illinois-spending-cuts; Whorisky, P. (2011). Illinois seeks to borrow $3.7 billion to shore up pension shortfall. *Washington Post*, February 22. Retrieved April 25, 2011, from http://www.washingtonpost.com/business/illinois-seeks-to-borrow-37-billion-to-shore-up-pension-shortfall/2011/02/22/ABrXTZQ_story.htmlm.
15. Fear of state takeover hangs over Detroit budget. (2011). *Reuters*. Retrieved April 25, 2011, from http://www.reuters.com/article/2011/04/12/us-detroit-budget-idUSTRE73B5GT20110412.
16. Cornia, G. C., et al. (2004). Fiscal planning, budgeting, and rebudgeting using revenue semaphores. *Public Administration Review, 64*, 164–179.

17. Grizzle, G., & Klay, W. (1994). Forecasting state sales tax revenues: comparing the accuracy of different methods. *State and Local Government Review, 26,* 142–152.

18. Cirincione, C., et al. (1999). Municipal government revenue forecasting: issues of method and data. *Public Budgeting & Finance, 19,* Spring, 26–46.

19. Mullins, D. R., & Wallace, S. (1996). Changing demographics and state fiscal outlook: the case of sales taxes. *Public Finance Quarterly, 24,* 237–262.

20. Rodgers, R., & Joyce, P. (1996). The effect of underforecasting on the accuracy of revenue forecasts by state governments. *Public Administration Review, 56,* 48–56.

21. Mullins, D. R., & Wallin, B. A. (2004). Tax and expenditure limitations: introduction and overview. *Public Budgeting & Finance, 24,* Winter, 2–15; Mullins, D. R. (2004). Tax and expenditure limitations and the fiscal response of local government: asymmetric intra-local fiscal effects. *Public Budgeting & Finance, 24,* Winter, 111–147.

22. James, F. J., & Wallis, A. (2004). Tax and spending limits in Colorado. *Public Budgeting & Finance, 24,* Winter, 16–33.

23. Hou, Y., & Smith, D. L. (2006). A framework for understanding state balanced budget requirement systems: reexamining distinctive features and an operational definition. *Public Budgeting & Finance, 26,* Fall, 22–45.

24. Joyce, P. G. (2001). What's so magical about five percent? A nationwide look at factors that influence the optimal size of state rainy day funds. *Public Budgeting & Finance, 21,* Summer, 62–87.

25. Jen, K. I. (2002). Tax expenditures in Michigan: a comparison to federal findings. *Public Budgeting & Finance, 22,* Spring, 31–45; Brixi, H. P., et al. (2004). *Tax expenditure: shedding light on government spending through the tax system.* Washington, DC: World Bank.

26. Novarro, N. (2002). Does earmarking matter? The case of lottery profits and educational spending. *Stanford Institute for Economic Policy Research Discussion Paper 2-19,* December 9.

27. Anderson, S. H., & Smirnova, N. V. (2006). A study of executive budget-balancing decisions. *American Review of Public Administration, 36,* 323–336.

28. Schneider, M., & Damanpour, F. (2001). Determinants of public pension plan investment return. *Public Management Review, 3,* 551–573; Peng, J. (2004). Public pension funds and operating budgets: a tale of three states. *Public Budgeting & Finance, 24,* Summer, 59–73.

29. The Pew Charitable Trusts (2010). *The trillion dollar gap.* Washington, DC: Pew Center on the States.

30. Ingraham, P. W., et al. (2003). *Government performance: why management matters* (p. 34). Baltimore, MD: Johns Hopkins University Press.

31. GOP's anti-bailout South Carolina Governor Mark Sanford ordered to take federal stimulus funds. (2009). *New York Daily News,* June 5. Retrieved September 24, 2011, from http://articles.nydailynews .com/2009-06-05/news/17925331_1_stimulus-gop-presidential-bid-republican-governors-association; Condon, S. (2009). Texas gov. who refused stimulus funds asks for loan. *CBS.com,* July 16. Retrieved September 24, 2011, from http://www.cbsnews.com/8301-503544_162-5166310-503544 .html.

32. Archbold, R. (2010). California, in financial crisis, opens prison doors. *New York Times,* March 23. Retrieved September 24, 2011, from http://www.cbsnews.com/8301-503544_162-5166310-503544 .html.

33. Rivlin, A., & Sawhill, I. (Eds.) (2005). *Restoring fiscal sanity, 2005: meeting the long-run challenge.* Washington, DC: Brookings Institution.

34. Jones, L. R., & Euske, K. J. (1991). Strategic misrepresentation in budgeting. *Journal of Public Administration Research and Theory, 1,* 437–460; Peterson, P. G. (2004). *Running on empty: how the Democratic and Republican Parties are bankrupting our future and what Americans can do about it.* New York, NY: Farrar, Straus and Giroux.

35. Lewis, C. W. (1992). Public budgeting: unethical in purpose, product, and promise. *Public Budgeting and Financial Management, 4,* 667–680.

36. Miller, G. J., et al. (2005). How financial managers deal with ethical stress. *Public Administration Review, 65,* 301–312.

37. Schick, A. (1983). Incremental budgeting in a decremental age. *Policy Sciences, 16,* 1–25.

38. O' Brien, M. (2010). White House wants federal agencies to cut spending by 5 percent. *The Hill's Blog Briefing Room,* June 6. Retrieved April 29, 2011, from http://thehill.com/blogs/blog-briefing-room/news/101897-white-house-wants-agencies-to-cut-spending-by-five-percent.

39. Fikac, P. (2010). State agencies asked to find more cuts. *San Antonio Express News,* November 16. Retrieved April 29, 2011, from http://www.mysanantonio.com/default/article/State-agencies-asked-to-find-more-cuts-817261.php.

40. Government Performance Project (2003). *Washington: money.* Retrieved October 25, 2006, from http://results.gpponline.org/StateCategoryCriteria.aspx?id=139&relatedid=2 (link no longer active).

41. Goodman, D., & Clynch, E. J. (2004). Budgetary decision making by executive and legislative budget analysts: the impact of political cues and analytical information. *Public Budgeting & Finance, 24,* Fall, 20–37; Lidman, R. & Sommers, P. (2005). The "compleat" policy analysts: a top 10 list. *Public Administration Review, 65,* 628–634.

42. Hoffman, K. U. (2006). Legislative fiscal analysts: influence in state budget development. *State and Local Government Review, 38,* 41–51.

43. U.S. General Accounting Office (1995). *Changes resulting from the OMB 2000 reorganization.* Washington, DC: U.S. Government Printing Office.

44. Stockman, D. A. (1986). *The triumph of politics: how the Reagan revolution failed.* New York, NY: Harper & Row; Wildavsky, A., & Caiden, N. (2004). *The new politics of the budgetary process* (5th ed.). New York, NY: Pearson/Longman.

45. Heclo, H. (1975). OMB and the presidency: the problem of "neutral competence." *Public Interest, 38,* 80–98.

46. AARP launches ad campaign urging debt panel to steer clear of Medicare. (2011). *Kaiser Health News,* September 22. Retrieved December 12, 2011, from http://www.kaiserhealthnews.org/Daily-Reports/2011/September/22/super-committee-and-aarp.aspx.

47. Schick, A. (1986). Macro-budgetary adaptations to fiscal stress in industrialized democracies. *Public Administration Review, 46,* 124–134.

48. National Association of State Budget Officers (2011). *Fiscal survey of states,* April, 16–17.

49. Government Finance Officers Association (2009). *Distinguished budget presentation award.* Retrieved December 12, 2011, from http://www.gfoa.org/index.php?Itemid=57&id=33&option=com_content&task=view.

50. Metropolitan Government of Nashville and Davidson County (2011). *Citizens' guide to the metro budget.* Retrieved December 15, 2011, from http://www.nashville.gov/citizens_budget/2011.

51. U.S. Office of Management and Budget (2011). *Budget of the United States government, fiscal year 2012.* Retrieved December 15, 2011, from http://www.whitehouse.gov/omb/budget/overview.

52. U.S. Office of Management and Budget (2006). *Appendix, budget of the United States government, fiscal year 2007.* Retrieved December 15, 2011, from http://www.whitehouse.gov/omb/budget/appendix.

53. U.S. Office of Management and Budget (2006). *Analytical perspectives, budget of the United States government, fiscal year 2007.* Retrieved December 15, 2011, from http://www.whitehouse.gov/omb/budget/Analytical_Perspectives.

54. U.S. Office of Management and Budget (2006). *Historical tables, budget of the United States government, fiscal year 2007.* Retrieved December 15, 2011, from http://www.whitehouse.gov/omb/budget/Historicals.

55. U.S. Office of Management and Budget (2006). Website. Retrieved December 15, 2011, from http://www.whitehouse.gov/omb/.

56. U.S. Treasury Department (2010). *Combined statement of receipts, outlays, and balances of the United States government.* Retrieved September 24, 2011, from http://www.fms.treas.gov/annualreport/index.html.

57. U.S. Treasury Department (2011). *Bulletin.* Retrieved September 24, 2011, from http://www.fms.treas.gov/bulletin/index.html.

58. Department of Revenue, Commonwealth of Massachusetts (2012). *Tax expenditure budget, fiscal year 2012.* Retrieved October 10, 2011, from http://www.mass.gov/Ador/docs/dor/Stats/TEB/TEB2012.pdf.

59. President's Commission on Budget Concepts (1967). *Report* (p. 1085). Washington, DC: U.S. Government Printing Office.

60. Office of Management and Budget (2011). Credit and insurance. *Budget of the United States government, fiscal year 2012: analytical perspectives* (pp. 373–376). Washington, DC: U.S. Government Printing Office.

61. Congressional Budget Office (2011). *The budgetary cost of Fannie Mae and Freddie Mac and options for the future federal role in the secondary mortgage market. Statement of Deborah Lucas before the House Committee on the Budget,* June 2. Retrieved March 1, 2012, from http://www.cbo.gov/publication/41487.

62. Committee on the Budget, U.S. House of Representatives (1991). *Hidden exposure: the unfunded liabilities of the federal government: hearing* (102nd Cong., 1st sess.). Washington, DC: U.S. Government Printing Office.

63. Feldman, R. (1996). How weak recognition and measurement in the federal budget encouraged costly policy: the case of "supervisory goodwill." *Public Budgeting & Finance, 16,* Winter, 31–44.

64. U.S. General Accounting Office (2001). *Student loans: direct loan default rates.* Washington, DC: U.S. Government Printing Office.

65. Congressional Budget Office (2011). *The budget and economic outlook, 2012–2021: an update* (p. 18). Washington, DC: U.S. Government Printing Office.

66. Ennis, H. M., & Malek, H. S. (2005). Bank risk of failure and the too-big-to-fail policy. *Economic Quarterly* (Federal Reserve Bank of Richmond), *91*(2), 21–44.

67. U.S. General Accounting Office (2004). *Government-sponsored enterprises: a framework for strengthening GSE governance and oversight.* Washington, DC: U.S. Government Printing Office.

68. Congressional Budget Office (2011). *The budgetary cost of Fannie Mae and Freddie Mac and options for the future federal role in the secondary mortgage market. Statement of Deborah Lucas before the House Committee on the Budget,* June 2, 3.

69. Appelbaum, B. (2011). In Congress, bills to speed unwinding of two giants. *New York Times,* March 29.

70. Government Corporation Control Act of 1945, Ch. 557.

71. Financial Institutions Reform, Recovery, and Enforcement Act of 1989 (P.L. 101-73).

72. U.S. General Accountability Office (2011). *GAO's 2011 high-risk series: an update* (p. 4). Washington, DC: U.S. Government Printing Office.

73. Federal Credit Reform Act (1990). P.L. 101-508, as part of the Omnibus Budget Reconciliation Act.

74. Phaup, M. (1996). Credit reform, negative subsidies, and FHA. *Public Budgeting & Finance, 16,* Spring, 23–36.

75. Debt Collection Improvement Act of 1996 (P.L. 104-34); see also Federal Debt Collection Procedures Act of 1990 (P.L. 101-647).

76. Student Loan Marketing Association Reorganization Act of 1996 (P.L. 104-208, 2009-275), as part of the Omnibus Consolidation Appropriations Act of 1997.

77. U.S. Department of Treasury (2004). *Treasury announces successful privatization of Sallie Mae.* Retrieved August 8, 2006, from http://www.treasury.gov/press/releases/ js2173.htm (link no longer active); Corder, J. K., & Hoffman, S. M. (2004). Privatizing federal credit programs: why Sallie Mae? *Public Administration Review, 64,* 180–191.

78. Terrorism Risk Insurance Extension Act of 2005 (P.L. 109-144).

79. Wall Street Reform and Consumer Protection Act of 2010 (P.L. 111-203).

80. Governmental Accounting Standards Board (1989). *Accounting and financial reporting for risk financing and related insurance issues,* Statement No. 10. Norwalk, CT: Financial Accounting Foundation.

81. U.S. Office of Management and Budget (2011). *Budget of the United States Department of Agriculture: fiscal year 2012, appendix,* 93.

82. National Association of State Budget Officers (2008). *Budget processes in the states,* Summer, 57.

83. Jameson Boex, L. F., et al. (2000). Multi-year budgeting: a review of international practices and lessons for developing and transitional economies. *Public Budgeting & Finance, 20,* Summer, 91–112.

84. Lee, R. D., Jr., & Burns, R. C. (2000). Unpublished data from survey of state budget offices, 1975 through 2000. University Park, PA: Pennsylvania State University; Burns, R. C. (2006). Unpublished data from survey of state budget offices, 2005. University Park, PA: Pennsylvania State University.

85. Pew Center on the States and the Nelson Rockefeller Institute of Government (2011). *States' revenue estimating: cracks in the crystal ball.*

Budget Approval: The Role of the Legislature

The tradition of legislative "power of the purse" is perhaps as strong in the United States as in any other country. This means that the struggle over the budget has only begun when the budget document goes to the legislative body. Executive budget preparation at the state and federal levels will have consumed months, but the product of the process is simply a proposal. The distinction between preparation and approval is alluded to by the phrase "the executive proposes and the legislature disposes." The process of legislative disposition is often not pretty. Like the federal government (see the chapter on budget approval and the U.S. Congress), some states have had difficulty enacting their budgets on time. The State of California, for example, was 100 days late in enacting its budget for fiscal year 2010; this was the 23rd time in 24 years that the state missed the deadline.[1]

The process in the United States differs from that used in parliamentary governments such as the British one, in which the executive and legislative functions are controlled by the same political party or coalition of parties. In such systems, the approval phase is largely pro forma. Parliaments generally can alter the government's budget but are often prohibited from increasing it. Party discipline generally ensures that the changes made by a parliament are typically minor. In the United States, in contrast, the legislative body may approve a budget that diverges in important respects from the budget proposed by the executive. A 2005 study by the International Monetary Fund characterized 28 countries in terms of the relative budgetary powers of the legislature. This study ranked the United States as the one with the most legislative budgetary power, far ahead of the Westminster countries (notably Great Britain and Australia), but also more powerful than others, such as Germany, Mexico, and Spain.[2] While this study was focused on national governments, the tradition of legislative independence in the United States tends to apply to states and localities as well. In this chapter, major emphasis is given to the similarities in the approval phase across levels of government—local, state, and federal. The next chapter focuses exclusively on Congress, because that body is unique in the American political system and has unique budgetary roles, procedures, and problems.

This chapter has three main sections. The first discusses the parameters that constrain how legislative bodies operate and the processes used in approving government budgets. The second section examines the legislative budget process itself, including relationships between the legislative and executive branches, and the procedures used by the legislature. The third discusses the changing role of the legislature as an overseer of the executive branch.

CONSTRAINTS ON LEGISLATURES

General Characteristics of Legislatures

Legislative bodies—city councils, school boards, state legislatures, and Congress—sometimes have had a reputation for being relatively weak bodies (in terms of the powers granted to them or asserted by them), but that perception has changed in recent times. Legislative bodies at all levels of government are reasserting their authority to set policy and are taking measures to increase their ability to wield the powers granted to them. There are certain underlying trends and characteristics that affect the environment for legislative deliberation on the budget. These include:

- the role of the legislature as, first and foremost, a representative body,
- trends in how legislators are selected for their jobs,
- the movement toward limiting legislative terms, and
- the deep partisan divides that have developed throughout the country.

Representation of Interests

Both socioeconomic and political diversity influence legislative behavior. At the national level, Congress must deal with a broad range of issues and associated interest groups. States tend to be less diverse and tend to have fewer interest groups that press their preferences upon legislatures. This situation can allow for a relatively small number of interests to influence legislation.[3] The concentration of influence can be even greater at the local level, as in the case of a town that is dominated by a single employer.

Citizen initiatives, allowable in many states, constitute another set of parameters that can have major impacts on the legislative bodies responsible for approving budgets.[4] Under the initiative process, citizens have the power to initiate changes, often by making amendments to state constitutions. If citizens become dissatisfied with tax rates, as was frequently the case in the 1970s, voters may approve new limits on taxes that force jurisdictions to cut tax rates and spending.

Voters in some states have recall powers. When legislators take action disapproved by their constituents, they can be voted out of office before their terms expire. Michigan allows this for both local and state elective officers, including the governor as well as the legislature.[5]

The news media are also important influences on legislatures. The media bring issues to the public's attention, help frame those issues and their solutions, and focus attention on legislatures in their efforts to resolve issues. However, newspapers, local radio and television stations, and news networks vary in their abilities to understand complex budget matters and to convey information to the public.[6] As a consequence, the media can be important sources of misinformation as well as information regarding public budgeting and finance.

Though there is still a decidedly higher proportion of young adults than any other age group that uses the web as a basic source of information, the web is a rapidly increasing source of both information and misinformation for everyone. Individuals can create their own blogs, and there is considerable volunteerism creating opinions and information on the web. Sources like Wikipedia publish unvetted information on a large array of topics, and it is often difficult in these websites to distinguish fact from opinion or error. The misinformation alleging that President Obama was not born in the United States is one recent example of this phenomenon, where something that is not true—and that had been repeatedly disproved—was repeated often enough to cause some people to accept it as fact.

A responsibility—if not the chief responsibility—of legislators is to represent their constituents. Decisions on the budget can have major positive and negative effects on a legislator's constituents and on the legislator's prospects for reelection. Although a legislator may generally favor reduced government spending, one common exception arises with any budget reduction proposed for the legislator's district. Positive budget decisions—increases in government spending or fending off possible decreases in spending—are seen by every officeholder as essential for gaining reelection, which itself is seen as of paramount importance. Some research suggests that not all public preferences are for decreased spending and that decisions about capital spending are more important to voters in local elections than current operating expenditures.[7]

Legislative Apportionment

How the duty of representation is met is influenced by how legislators are elected to their jobs. In the 1960s, the U.S. Supreme Court ruled that state legislatures must draw district lines that are proportional to population. The effect of this ruling has been to apportion legislative election districts on a population basis and to reduce substantially what was once overrepresentation of rural interests and to increase representation of urban and suburban areas in states.[8]

Local governments are undergoing similar changes. City councils are changing from using at-large seats because this procedure tends to result in underrepresentation of minority interests. Instead, the movement is toward single-member districts based on neighborhood populations, or a combination of these and at-large seats.[9] Legislative bodies are increasingly diverse in terms of gender and minority representation, although the distinct influence that women and minority legislators have on the legislative process is uncertain.

In an earlier time when efforts were deliberately made to underrepresent the interests of minorities, boundaries were drawn such that minority neighborhoods were carved into small segments and then apportioned to several districts. This approach ensured that a minority candidate would never be elected to represent any of the districts. In contemporary times, efforts have been made to help ensure minority representation by drawing boundaries to encircle minority neighborhoods. The Supreme Court has held through a series of rulings that when race becomes the dominant factor in deciding on district boundaries, that action is a violation of the Equal Protection Clause of the 14th Amendment.[10] The result has been considerable confusion when state legislatures have redrawn district boundaries for their own election districts or for congressional districts.

Beyond any racial justification for redistricting, however, there is the pure political motivation for drawing or redrawing district lines. In an infamous case in advance of the 2004 election, then–House Majority Leader Tom Delay aggressively pursued the redrawing of Texas congressional boundaries in a way that would make it easier for the Republican Party to keep its majority in Congress. Democratic legislators attempted to thwart this effort by fleeing the state in an effort to prevent a vote occurring on this plan. Ultimately the U.S. Supreme Court upheld the redrawn Texas districts as constitutional, but questionable ethical behavior by Delay in his pursuit of the new congressional boundaries led to his resignation from the Congress and ultimately his conviction of laundering corporate money in an effort to influence state-level elections.[11] The takeover of state legislatures by the Republican party in the 2010 midterm elections put that party in a position to draw boundaries for the 2012 election. This clearly put the majority in a stronger position as it sought to maintain control of the House of Representatives.[12]

Redistricting plans are frequently challenged in courts for any number of reasons, and federal courts have been very active in ruling on state redistricting plans.[13] Some plans are viewed as being unfair to minorities or as overrepresenting them.[14] The U.S. Supreme Court, for example, initially found that the State of North Carolina violated the Constitution because it used race as a "predominant factor" in redrawing its congressional boundaries. Later the Court overruled a state court decision that a subsequent redrawing of the boundaries was racially (rather than politically) motivated.[15] In short, the Court seems now to be content to side with boundaries that are redrawn primarily for partisan political reasons, even if the result is a district that consists mostly of minority people where one had not existed before.[16]

Term Limits

A related concern regarding legislators is that they not become so entrenched in their positions that they lose a sense of responsibility to the citizens who elected them. One response to this concern has been a move to limit the number of years a person may serve.[17] The limits typically involve consecutive years of service, such as no more than two terms of four years in a state senate and no more than six terms of two years in a state house. Limits also can be on a lifetime basis, such as limiting the total number of years a person may serve in the house or senate for one's entire life. As of 2011, six states had lifetime limits for membership in their state legislative bodies.[18]

Term limits have been proposed at all levels of government, and many governments now have such limits. Of the ten largest cities in the United States, nine of them (all but Chicago) have term limits. Some smaller cities, such as Honolulu, Fargo, and Spokane, have term limits as well.[19] There are currently legislative term limits on the books in 15 of the 50 states, down from 16 (Utah repealed its term limit statute).[20] As for the federal government, the Supreme Court has ruled that term limits to be imposed on Congress must be carried out through a constitutional amendment.[21]

Term limits are, as one might imagine, controversial. One view is that the reform has led to more women and Latinos being elected. Between 1996 and 2007, for example, there was a 37% increase in Hispanic elected officials.[22] The academic studies on the effects of term limits on female and minority participation, however, reached rather mixed conclusions.[23] More broadly, the advocates of term limits argue that term-limited representatives are more likely to embrace the ethic of the "citizen-legislator" as opposed to a careerist politician who may lose touch with his or her constituency.

Term limits have their downside. Political bodies are automatically denied the experience that can be gained only from long years of service in a legislature. People do not automatically change their family doctors and dentists every six years, so why should they do so with their elected representatives? Effective representatives presumably should be retained in office, while ineffective ones should not be reelected. Reducing the length of time that someone may stay in office may deter some more qualified people from running for office in the first place. Term limits, in addition to denying a legislative body experienced legislators, may also increase the influence of staff who know vastly more about particular issues than inexperienced members. In fact, given the complexity of government, many legislators find that their learning curves have just reached a peak at about the time that their legislative careers are drawing to an end.

A study sponsored by the National Conference of State Legislatures concluded, after a detailed comparison of states with term limits to those without, that term limits have led to inexperienced lawmakers, polarized legislatures, and a shift in the balance of power toward the executive branch. The same study concluded that these costs have not come with the associated benefits of greater representative diversity.[24] To counter this problem, some states have established "training" and "mentoring" programs for new legislators to try to increase their effectiveness.[25] Citizens may support term limits less because of any dissatisfaction with their representatives and more because of a general cynicism about government itself.[26] A study about the effects of term limits internationally found that term limits have no significant effects on either overall spending or budget deficits, while in the United States previous studies had found that term limits tended to make government revenue and spending increase.[27]

Increased Partisanship

It has become much more difficult in recent years for legislators to reach agreement with each other on policies, as a result of the increasing polarization of politics at all levels of government. The parties have developed intractable, orthodox views on policy issues. Republicans, for example, are expected to oppose all tax increases, as a result of a pledge taken by many of them. This promise has been exacted as a result of the efforts of Grover Norquist, whose organization (Americans for Tax Reform) has argued for many years that the only way to curb the size of government is to reduce its revenue. The Tea Party movement, which was a force in the 2010 midterm congressional elections, shares a similar view of taxation. Republican candidates who did not take the pledge and who were not supported by the Tea Party had a difficult time gaining nomination in 2010; the same was true in 2012. Democrats, in contrast, have been very protective of social safety net programs and public employee unions, both of which tend to be supported by core Democratic constituencies.

In a sense, the Republican antipathy toward taxes and the Democratic protection of social programs are not new phenomena. What makes the environment different now, however, than in the past is the near vanishing of the political moderates in legislative bodies at all levels of government. Moderates, while never a majority, at one time wielded great power in legislative bodies because they represented "swing" voters whose support could mean either victory or defeat for a given initiative. Both the redistricting phenomenon and the need to adhere to party orthodoxy have made compromise almost impossible, especially at the national level.[28]

Factors Affecting Legislative Decisions

Beyond these general characteristics of legislative bodies that affect their selection and tenure in office, there are other factors that influence the manner in which they deliberate on the budget. Legislatures tend to differ from one another in terms of many of these characteristics, such as the extent of fragmentation, the role of party leadership, the amount of time available to legislate, and the availability of staff. The capacity to legislate—and consequently to budget—is heavily influenced by these factors.

Fragmentation

An overriding characteristic of state legislatures and Congress is fragmentation in budgeting. Constitutionally imposed bicameralism divides the legislature into two chambers, a house and a senate, that seek to establish their own identities and powers but that must be coordinated if a budget is to be approved. Local governing bodies, in contrast, are usually unicameral and do not face this fragmentation problem. Fragmentation is also apparent within each chamber of a legislative body and between the executive and legislative branches.

Political parties can serve as a unifying force between branches, between legislative chambers, and within chambers. According to conventional practice, whichever party wins a majority of seats in a chamber controls the leadership positions, has a majority of its members on each committee, and has each committee chaired by a member of the party. In theory, if the Republicans hold a majority of the seats in a state senate, then the Republican Party has control of that chamber in handling all legislative matters. Sometimes a ruling party may have the narrowest possible majority or no majority at all. In 2011, the Alaska Senate, the Virginia Senate, and the Oregon House were each evenly divided between Republicans and Democrats.[29] The 2006 midterm election left the U.S. Senate with a 51 to 49 Democratic majority, one so narrow that a single party switch or the death or resignation of a single Democratic senator could result in Republican control of the body.

Political Party Leadership

In the United States, political parties are weak (compared with parliamentary systems), meaning that party leadership cannot control their own party members by telling them how to vote (with notable exceptions in practice, as indicated by the above discussion on Republican positions on taxes). On any given issue there may be no guarantee that all or even most of the party's members will vote as a bloc. Many members of the legislative body, especially those who have gained seniority through numerous reelections, are not always amenable to supporting the policies pursued by their party's leadership, whether in the legislature or in the executive branch. Furthermore, in term-limited legislatures, the assistance that leaders can offer rank-and-file members with reelection is much less important. For this reason, leaders do not have as much to offer these members in exchange for toeing the party line. In addition, regional differences sometimes trump partisan differences. In the Illinois Senate, for instance, a Republican from the Chicago area may be as likely to vote with a Chicago Democrat on some issue that affects the Chicagoland region as to vote with a Republican from "downstate" Illinois. Studies have also found evidence that interpersonal ties influence legislators' votes independent of partisanship.[30] In a situation where party control is weak, leaders must try to persuade members to win their votes, unlike in earlier times when legislative leaders may have ruled with iron fists.[31]

Parties attempt to exert influence on their legislators by providing or withholding privileges or by taking party positions in caucuses. Legislative leaders have different levels of institutional control over rank-and-file members. They may, for example, differ substantially in terms of their ability to appoint members to key committees or to provide resources.[32] Republicans in a state house of representatives, for example, will meet periodically to develop party positions on issues and then attempt to exert their influence on party members to vote accordingly. The positions approved in caucus meetings do not always coincide with the views of the party's leadership.

The situation is further complicated by the fact that the two chambers can be controlled by different parties. Even if both are controlled by one party, the chief executive might be of another party. In 2010, for example, 17 states had divided governments in which the governor, the lower legislative chamber, and the upper legislative chamber were not all controlled by the same political party.[33] This condition is sometimes seen as leading to gridlock, which is one oft-cited cause for the inability of government to deal with pressing problems. While gridlock has a negative connotation, however, it should be noted that "checks and balances" (which leads to gridlock) is a principle firmly ingrained in the political philosophy of the United States and its citizens. Divided government, as will be seen in this chapter, should not be considered the sole explanation of why governments sometimes fail to address major problems.[34]

Legislative Committees

The extensive use of legislative committees is essential in that acting as a committee of the whole is impractical, but committee structures add to fragmentation. Committees become little legislatures in their own right.[35] Given that the U.S. House of Representatives has 435 members and the Senate has 100 members, a committee structure is inevitable. Among the states, New Hampshire has the largest legislature, with 424 members, and Nebraska the smallest, with 49 members in its single chamber. In 42 of the 50 states, there are at least 100 legislators.[36]

In a bicameral legislative body, legislation is handled by parallel committees in each chamber. These committees report out bills that are acted upon by the full membership of the house and senate. When differences exist in the two bills, a conference committee is usually appointed, which reports a revised bill that again is acted upon by both houses. The conference committee consists of members from the two committees that prepared the legislation. Once the chambers have passed identical bills, the legislation is ready for signing or vetoing by the governor or president.

At the local level, where unicameralism prevails, a budget committee often assumes the main responsibility for reviewing and amending the executive's proposed budget and for submitting a set of recommendations to the full legislative body, such as a city council or school board.

Committees that continue on a permanent basis are known as standing committees, whereas ad hoc committees are usually created to deal with specific problems and are then disbanded. Most standing committees consist of selected members of one house of a legislature, but standing committees can be joint in nature, consisting of selected members from both chambers. State legislatures usually had 15 to 20 standing committees in each chamber. In 2010, the range was five (the Maine House and Senate each have this number) to 55 (Illinois house).[37]

Legislators seek to serve their district's or state's interests by gaining appointment to appropriate legislative committees. Someone from a farming community may seek appointment to a state senate's agriculture committee. A member of the U.S. House of Representatives from a district that includes major military installations may seek appointment to the Armed Services Committee to help ensure that military funds continue to flow into the district. Similarly, members of the House and Senate will seek appointment to key subcommittees (organized in line with key constituencies—i.e., defense, agriculture, transportation, and so forth) of their chamber's appropriations committee.[38]

Availability of Time

How a legislative body operates is greatly influenced by whether it continues in session throughout the year. City councils usually hold meetings once, twice, or even more times per month throughout the year. Congress is in session much of each year except for holidays and recesses during election periods.

State legislatures vary widely. While about a dozen states have no limits on the length of legislative sessions, the rest control whether the legislature can meet each year, for how many days, and whether the legislature may call itself back into session after adjournment. The legislatures in California, Idaho, Illinois, Iowa, Michigan, New Jersey, New York, North Carolina, Ohio, Oregon, Pennsylvania, Rhode Island, South Carolina, Vermont, and Wisconsin hold sessions that are not limited as to their length, and thus may run during much of the year.[39] When legislatures have time limitations, procedural limits are used to "budget" the available time. For example, a common practice is to set a cutoff date for the introduction of bills, as late submission would carry deliberations beyond the required adjournment.

Similarly, time limits are set on the budget process. Some states allow their spending and taxation committees only a few weeks to consider their relevant portions of the budget, while other states allow 20 or more weeks. In some states, the entire budget approval process must be completed by the legislature within six weeks or less. Other states allow 20 weeks, 30 weeks, or even more.

A major problem facing Congress is not that it has limits on the time that it may be in session, but rather that it has difficulty approving the budget within the available time (see the chapter on budget approval and the U.S. Congress). This problem, while it may exist for some states and localities (such as California, as indicated in the beginning of this chapter), is much more the exception than the rule. The reason for this relative timeliness for states and localities may be more that they face a separate external force that does not exist at the national level. They may discover that the failure to enact bills on time can have an adverse effect on bond ratings and, therefore, increase borrowing costs. Indeed, California and Illinois, which have had recent difficulties enacting budgets on time, have the lowest bond ratings in the nation (certainly late budgets contribute only partially to this result). Lower bond ratings translate into higher borrowing costs, amounting to millions of extra dollars over the years (see discussion of bond ratings in the chapter on capital finance and debt management).[40]

Compensation and Staff

Closely associated with time limits on legislatures is the issue of compensation for their members. Annual compensation is low in many states. For example, in 2010, Maine, Mississippi, Nebraska, New Hampshire, North Carolina, Rhode Island, South Carolina, South Dakota, and Texas paid their legislators $15,000 or less.[41] In these states and others, however, members might be eligible for per diem payments, travel expenses, and other payments. Nevertheless, pay for state legislators overall is low, so most legislators need other income sources, such as from law practices or other alternative employment, in order to make ends meet. In contrast, members of Congress earn incomes and receive other benefits, such as travel expenses, that allow the legislative job to be a full-time occupation. One of the most important forms of compensation afforded members of Congress is generous pension benefits that can be an incentive for continuing to stand for reelection. Fees for speeches and other appearances are lucrative for some legislators, although these are generally prohibited to be paid to members of Congress.

Staffing is another factor that influences legislative behavior. Staff dedicated to assist legislators presumably can help them perform more effectively and reduce their reliance on the executive branch and lobbyists for information. Although local legislators, such as county commissioners or city council members, rarely have sizable staffs at their disposal, Congress does. So do many state legislatures, although some states have small staffs. A predominantly rural state, such as Wyoming, will have a legislative staff of less than 100, while a large state, such as New York, will have staff in the thousands. These personnel serve individual members, committees, and persons holding leadership positions, as in the case of the speaker of a state house of representatives. In addition, some legislative staff units serve a variety of individuals and committees in both chambers. The Congressional Budget Office (CBO) is a notable example of such a unit, but many states have similar legislative budget offices. California's Office of the Legislative Analyst, in fact, is one of the most highly regarded of such offices, and it served as a model for the development of the CBO at the national level.[42] Since the 1960s, staffs in state legislatures and Congress have greatly increased their professional training. Many staff members now have graduate degrees, including doctorates.

Legislative fiscal committee staffs provide a host of services. For example, most state legislatures' fiscal committee staffs conduct fiscal research studies, prepare reports on revenues and taxes, and prepare reports on expenditures and the budget. Other important staff functions include making revenue projections, analyzing budget trends during the fiscal year, and preparing reports on economic conditions. States also differ as to whether they maintain separate fiscal staffs for each house or one joint legislative fiscal office that serves both houses.[43]

A study published in 2000 identified the following as the most "professional" of state legislatures: Alaska, California, Florida, Illinois, Michigan, New York, Ohio, and Pennsylvania. This study measured professionalism according to several factors. Those legislatures judged to be the most professional were those with the highest level of compensation, those that spent the greatest number of days in session annually, and those that spent the most money on staff and other services.[44] A separate study, published in 2007 using 2003 data, listed the eight states above among the 14 with the most professional legislatures. It listed several other states not included above, such as Wisconsin and Massachusetts, which were judged to be third and fourth on the professionalism scale, and Arizona, which was ninth.[45] Professionalism, however, is no guarantee of a smoothly operating legislature, as has been evident in such states as California and New York. One view is that professionalism attracts better-informed individuals who inevitably clash with one another, yielding conflict that is not necessarily productive.[46]

THE LEGISLATIVE BUDGET PROCESS

This section examines what happens to the executive budget when it reaches the legislature. Legislatures are not integrated wholes but rather consist of numerous subunits, and this section considers how the executive branch relates to those subunits, especially to the two legislative chambers and their committees.

General Relations Between the Branches

The executive and legislative branches of government in the United States are typically said to be coequal.[47] The separation of powers—in this case, between the executive and legislative branches—is a fundamental feature of U.S. governments. Since political power tends to be a somewhat "zero-sum" game, the two branches tend to be wary of possible diminution of their powers and may seek strategies for demonstrating their independence. Confrontations between the two are sometimes akin to tests of strength with each branch showing it is not subservient to the other.

Authority

In earlier days, the legislature was considered to be responsible for setting policy. Today, both the legislative and executive branches are inextricably engaged in policy making. Conflicts arise, not over whether the executive should be involved in policy making, but rather to what extent and in what ways. The movement toward executive budget systems has placed the executive four-square in the policy-making process, because the preparation of budget proposals by the executive is, in effect, the drafting of proposed policies. Congress, state legislatures, and city councils have often found themselves in the position of having to react to executive recommendations instead of formulating policy. To demonstrate their independence, then, legislators may feel a compulsion to alter a proposed budget no matter how compatible its recommendations are with their own preferences.

Not all governments have executive budgeting systems. In some governments, budgeting powers overlap between the branches. In others, legislatures dominate the budgeting process. In fact, in a study of the budget practices of 13 states, only three were characterized as states where the executive is dominant, while four were judged as states where the legislature is dominant. In the rest, budgetary power was viewed as relatively equal between the branches.[48] Regardless of the distribution of powers, tensions will exist between the branches of government.

Constitutional and legal constraints greatly affect the extent of executive and legislative powers in budgeting. The Budget and Accounting Act of 1921 and comparable legislation at the state level have granted substantial budgetary powers to the president and governors. Yet, in some states, the governor must share budget-making authority with other relatively independent executive officers or legislative bodies. In most states, the legislature is free to adjust the governor's budget either upward or downward, but in three states—Maryland, Nebraska, and West Virginia—the legislature has limited or no authority to appropriate amounts above those recommended by the governor.[49]

Relationships between the branches change over time. Changes in political leadership have both short- and long-term effects. When a new executive takes office, inevitable discontinuities occur during the transition period that can last from a few weeks to months.[50] In addition, personalities and the political clout of leaders influence executive–legislative relations. The election of a highly popular political leader to the legislature can lead to diminished executive powers. A newly elected governor who is more assertive than his or her predecessor may succeed in demanding that the legislature yield some of its budgetary powers. Either the executive or the legislative branch may change its partisan makeup (as occurred, for example, in the 2010 election, when the Alabama and North Carolina legislatures turned Republican for the first time since Reconstruction, and the Minnesota Senate was taken over by the Republicans for the first time ever).[51] In periods of fiscal crisis and other challenging times, the executive may tend to garner greater budgetary powers at the expense of the legislature.[52]

Constituency Differences

The legislative and executive branches have different constituencies and, as a result, have different perspectives on the budget. One common interpretation has been that the chief executive, being elected by the jurisdiction's entire constituency, has a broader perspective on the budget. A governor will attempt to satisfy the diverse needs of citizens throughout the state. Legislative bodies, on the other hand, have been seen as consisting of parochial individuals who may be less impressed with government-wide problems and, therefore, more likely to cut budgets. The legislature, then, is seen as a protector of the treasury and as a budget cutter.

A competing view of legislative bodies is that, in their desire to represent constituents, they tend to be eager to spend resources far beyond what is financially sound and that, while the requirement for a balanced budget keeps that desire to spend in check at the state and local levels, few constraints are evident at the national level. *Pork barrel*, a basic term of U.S. politics, refers to legislatively approved government projects that are aimed at helping home districts and states.[53] In fact, some prominent political scientists have suggested that pork barrel spending and constituent casework (intervening on behalf of constituents with administrative agencies) have become more valued than legislating because they offer a more certain path to reelection.[54] A standard complaint of many pork barrel projects is that they have limited utility beyond winning votes for legislators seeking reelection. The line-item veto, discussed below, may help to reduce the wastefulness of pork barrel spending.

Factors Constraining Legislative Deliberations on the Budget

Members of the legislature or their staff often participate in budget preparation deliberations by the executive branch. When the budget reaches the legislature, it may contain relatively few surprises in terms of proposals being advanced because many of the key legislators will already be familiar with the budget's main proposals. Legislative involvement during preparation can help build support for executive budget recommendations. In addition to the political and institutional characteristics discussed previously, the deliberation of any legislature is constrained by some factors outside of its control, such as the state's economic environment and the effect of previous budget decisions. Operating within those constraints, the legislature then makes the decisions necessary for the chief executive's budget proposal to become law.

Economic and Political Environment

As with all human enterprise, legislative bodies must operate within a set of parameters that greatly constrain how they approve the budgets. One of the most important constraints is the economic environment in both the short and the long term. How a legislative body approaches the task of passing a budget is influenced greatly by whether a surplus of revenues is projected or whether sizable cuts must be made to bring expenditures down to meet anticipated reductions in revenues. During fiscal years 2009 and 2010, an average of 40 states per year needed to cut the budget in midyear.[55] Furthermore, the legislature is constrained by whether the political environment would permit additional revenues to be raised, whether the level of revenues under current law represents a revenue ceiling, or even whether tax cuts have already been promised. In the current political environment, where Tea Party activists have forced candidates for political office to pledge not to raise taxes, this can make for some very challenging budgeting.

Previous Decisions

Before a local legislative body commences considering the budget, many decisions will already have been made. As explained in previous chapters, the state will have imposed a variety of mandates. A school district will be told how many days it must operate in a school year, possibly what the minimum salaries should be for teachers at different levels, and what courses must be taught. More than half of a school district's budget typically comes from state aid, which greatly reduces what the school district can decide on its own. The state will also have imposed limits on the taxation and borrowing authority for each type of local government and may deny taxing power to some jurisdictions, as is sometimes the case with special districts.

Whether the legislative body is Congress, the state legislature, or a local legislature, many decisions will already have been made before legislative deliberations begin. Entitlement laws that provide open-ended benefits to individuals, such as guaranteed payments to all persons qualifying for disability benefits under Social Security, greatly curtail what Congress can do in a given year. Programs such as Medicaid, where many rules that affect state and local costs have been made by the federal government, may seem uncontrollable at the state or local level. In fact, one of the potential benefits from the proposal by Congressman Paul Ryan (embodied in the House-proposed fiscal year 2013 budget resolution) to reform these federal health programs is the benefit that reduced Medicaid costs could have for the states.[56] Additionally, courts force legislative bodies to take actions, such as legislatures having to revise state funding formulas for school districts to comply with court orders (see the chapter on income, property, and payroll taxes). If tax increases must be approved by voters, as is sometimes the case with sewer taxes on property, and voters reject proposed increases, then the sewer board may be faced with finding revenues in some other forms, such as raising monthly or quarterly sewer fees.

The Legislature Adopts the Budget

The legislative budget process typically involves several sequential types of actions:

- Committee action, where committees, or sometimes subcommittees, hold hearings and collect other information on proposed agency budgets, and then use their expertise to draft bills that reflect their judgment concerning funding levels for programs and agencies under their jurisdiction;
- Action by the legislature as a whole, which must vote on proposals coming out of committees, frequently modify those proposals, and resolve differences that usually exist between the chambers; and
- Action by the chief executive, whose assent is often necessary (and always necessary at the state and federal levels) in order for any budget legislation to have the force of law.

While the process is sequential, actions are simultaneous. Several committees work simultaneously on bills but report out on them at various times. Committees work on bills at the same time the full chambers act on others and the executive considers signing or vetoing others.

Committee Action

Legislatures—especially in a large government with many responsibilities—are not typically in a position to deal with the budget in a unified way. Frequently when a budget reaches a state legislature or Congress, the document is divided into numerous pieces and sent to committees. Proposals that require new substantive legislation to implement them will be sent to substantive standing committees. These committees exist for areas such as environmental protection, education, recreation, welfare, and, at the federal level, defense and international relations. For programs to be implemented, these committees must report bills that will be approved eventually by the two chambers of the legislature. Legislation of this type authorizes the existence of programs, while appropriations provide the necessary funding.

While deliberations proceed on these substantive matters, other committees deal with the financial aspects of the budget. A regular practice is to assign taxing and other revenue matters to one group of committees and spending or appropriations to another. Appropriations may be handled at the full committee level, or in subcommittees, each of which provides appropriations for a portion of the government.

Coordination problems and terrain battles among committees are common. A person typically achieves the position of chair of a committee by serving on the committee for a long time and, once made chair, is unlikely to look favorably on threats to the committee's powers. Nevertheless, some coordinating mechanisms are essential to ensure that realistic budgets are adopted. For example, if separate revenue and expenditure committees are free to act independently, then there may be little relation between how much revenue comes into the government and how much is spent.

It was precisely this situation that led the federal government to enact the Congressional Budget and Impoundment Control Act of 1974, creating the Budget Committees and budget resolution to better coordinate action on the budget (see the chapter on budget approval and the U.S. Congress). The budget resolution, which is under the jurisdiction of the Budget Committees, sought to address the fragmentation of the budget process at the federal level by requiring Congress to vote on the whole budget, rather than considering it only in pieces. This type of fragmentation may be less likely to occur at the state and local levels, particularly in smaller and less complex governmental units. Local governments are particularly unlikely to have particular budget committees.

Hearings

In local governments with elected boards or councils, hearings and budget reviews are typically conducted with the entire legislative body present. Directors of city or county departments are asked to defend budget proposals in the same way that similar officials defend their budget requests at the state and national levels. The public, however, may be more involved in local budget issues at a much greater level of detail than is the case for national or state budgets, because citizens are likely to be more knowledgeable about local issues and more directly affected by the budget.[57] In fact, specific provision for direct citizen input into the budget process is a common feature of local government budgeting.[58]

While an executive budget system provides the chief executive with control over budget preparation, there is no guarantee that all units within the executive branch will subscribe fully to the budget's recommendations. The chief executive will not be uniformly in support of all portions of the budget. Some recommendations will have been approved because of political considerations. Typically, the chief executive will single out a few major recommendations for which approval is sought, with other recommendations being considered low priority. The budget office will be expected to make general presentations on the overall recommendations contained in the budget even though it may be lukewarm toward many of those recommendations. Hearings may be held by budget or appropriations committees, or for the legislative body as a whole, in an effort to discern the overall fiscal and policy direction implied in the budget.

More detailed hearings with executive branch agencies, however, typically dominate the budget process. In advance of these hearings, executive branch agencies may be requested to provide budget justification documents to legislative committees with jurisdiction over the budget. These documents may simply be the sections of the chief executive's budget that deal with the agency, or agencies may be required to present budget data in an entirely different format than was included in the executive budget document. Agencies usually know in advance what data the committees want and in what formats and prepare accordingly during the budget preparation phase.

Hearings may generate more heat than light. It is normally the responsibility of executive branch officials to defend the chief executive's agency-by-agency budget recommendations to the legislature. The heads of the agencies in a strong executive system are the appointees of the chief executive and have an obligation to defend the budget recommendations, even though higher funding levels may be preferred.[59] Agency representatives, however, may have little enthusiasm for defending budget proposals that call for deep cuts in programs. As a result, agencies attempt to calculate the extent to which they can reveal their preferences for greater resources to the spending committees in the legislature and still remain "faithful" to the chief executive. They do not always calculate correctly. In 2002, President George W. Bush's appointed civilian head of the Army Corps of Engineers, former Representative Mike Parker, was fired for being a bit too honest in his responses to questions from Congress about the adequacy of the Corps' budget.[60] Agencies also seek to head off any budget cuts being contemplated by the appropriations committee and are willing to engage in conflict if necessary to protect their budgets.[61]

During the approval phase, central budget offices may have responsibility for exercising some control over agencies that might seek to garner financial support beyond what the executive is recommending to the legislature and may serve as a major negotiator for the executive in sensitive discussions with legislative leaders. Since the early 1980s, the Office of Management and Budget (OMB) has played a much more prominent role in legislative relations. This role includes activities not just of the OMB director, but also of individual budget examiners.[62]

Strategies

Regardless of what level of government is considered, executive–legislative relationships inevitably can be characterized as cat-and-mouse games, although it is not always clear who is the cat and who is the mouse. Strategies are devised in each branch to deal with the other. On the executive side, an almost ubiquitous strategy is to cultivate clientele who will support requests for increased funding. Agencies are sensitive to where they locate buildings and other facilities. A new facility in a key legislator's district may gain the support of that legislator. Agencies pursue such strategies continuously as a matter of course.[63]

Contingent strategies, on the other hand, are limited to particular situations. No comprehensive cataloging of them is possible because they vary from agency to agency and from circumstance to circumstance. They arise out of perceptions of what is possible in a given budget period. In growth periods, when revenue surplus or slack is evident, agencies may seek to expand existing programs or gain approval for the creation of new ones. Even when revenues are scarce, agencies whose areas are favored by the chief executive may seek expansion, as occurred with defense and homeland security in the aftermath of the September 11, 2001, terrorist attacks. Sometimes obtaining approval for a new program may be easier than obtaining approval for expansion of an existing one. Executives and legislators alike prefer being able to take credit for creation of a new program over simply improving an existing one.

A ploy used by supporters of programs may be to start a new project with a small appropriation, get the legislature accustomed to the program, and then seek much greater appropriations in subsequent years. This tactic has been referred to as the "camel's nose" strategy. Under this imagery, the majority of the "camel" (the new program) is outside the tent, and thus obscured from view. The camel's nose is visible, but the nose represents a small percentage of the total camel (the eventual cost of the program). The assumption is that once the first part (the nose) of the program is funded, funding for the rest (the remainder of the camel) will follow.[64]

When funds are less plentiful, one strategy is to defend programs against cuts and to maintain what is called the base. An agency's existing budget is often regarded as the base, with the budget process adding or subtracting increments to the base. Agencies have been known to warn that the slightest of budget cuts would necessarily diminish popular programs and thereby erode electoral support of legislators.

When cuts are perceived as inevitable, often because of declining tax revenues, one strategy is to minimize cuts in the base and to obtain fair share funding. An agency will argue, on the one hand, that its programs are essential and should not be cut at all. On the other hand, it will insist that, if cuts must be made, they be no greater than cuts imposed on programs in other agencies.

Strategies used by proponents of government programs can be highly situational. A thorough study of the strategies used by federal agencies in dealing with OMB and Congress catalogued 35 different strategies used at various times. These included some that have been well documented in the budgeting literature, such as establishing earmarked funding sources, portraying the disastrous consequences of failing to spend money, and stressing the needs of a particular group that will be served. They also include many more arcane strategies that have been less well documented: establishment of a government-sponsored enterprise, creation of a loan guarantee program, establishment of a tax expenditure, and leasing instead of purchasing a capital asset.[65] There are, in short, many different "tools" available to governments to satisfy the desire for social action. Increasingly, these tactics involve less direct means than government expenditures, for strategic as well as substantive reasons.[66] Some changes in the budget process, such as federal credit reform (see the chapter on financial management), have occurred specifically to lessen the incentives to provide resources through less direct and apparently less costly means.

While various strategies may be influential, there are limits to their effectiveness. Legislatures are influenced by personal values and committee role expectations as well as by agency budget strategies and presentations. Agency strategies may also backfire and create negative feelings on the part of members of the appropriations committees, perhaps because they suspect they are being exploited.

In response to agency pressure, legislators devise a number of strategies for dealing with their budgetary responsibilities. A major problem is the capacity of agencies to produce vast amounts of information in support of their requests—more information than the legislature can process.

Legislative hearings are often used as opportunities for members of key committees to collect what is often anecdotal information from agencies in an attempt to determine how much confidence they have in the ability of the agency to use resources effectively.

They may place much of the burden for calculation on the executive branch and demand that an agency justify its need for certain funds in response to probing questions. Detailed questions that may seem petty and trivial to outsiders are designed to determine how much confidence the subcommittee can place in the executive's stewardship of public funds. Legislators have "discernible patterns" in their line of questioning, suggesting that they have their own strategies for dealing with different agencies and that these strategies depend in part on changes in fiscal conditions.[67] How the various strategies affect the outcomes of appropriations is uncertain and no doubt varies among jurisdictions and over time.

Fiscal Notes

One important mechanism that has been adopted is the requirement that fiscal notes be developed for most draft legislation reported out of legislative committees. A fiscal note is a report that addresses the current and future costs of implementing a proposed bill. It may include analysis of the purpose of the legislation, the proposed sources of funding, and the impact on other governments, as in the case of a state law affecting local government budgets.

Fiscal notes are typically prepared by legislative staff. At the state level, appropriations committees often have this responsibility. At the federal level, the CBO prepares fiscal notes to any bill that is reported out of a House or Senate Committee. CBO is required to estimate the marginal cost of the proposed legislation to the federal government, relative to the baseline, which is the estimate of costs under current law. It also estimates the costs of legislation to state and local governments. The Unfunded Mandates Reform Act of 1995 requires that Congress consider the possible financial effects of draft legislation on state and local governments and creates hurdles to considering legislation that does not include an estimate of potential unfunded mandates (see the chapter on intergovernmental relations).[68]

The fiscal note is intended to help decision makers be better informed about the implications of draft legislation. For example, if a proposal provides for revising a state program for teenagers to include 13-year-olds, whereas only those 14 years old and older are currently included, the revision could greatly increase the number of clients served and heighten the demand on resources. Fiscal notes are also prepared for revenue proposals, as in the case of forecasting the extra income that would be generated by increasing a state sales tax by one percentage point.

Fiscal notes are particularly important at the state and local levels, where balanced budgets are required. Indeed, the revenue estimates prepared by the chief executive, coupled with any fiscal note on proposed revenue increases, will greatly influence what spending programs the legislature will be able to approve. While nearly all states require that fiscal notes be prepared,[69] the content and thoroughness of fiscal notes varies widely from state to state. Some states, for example, require that fiscal notes be prepared for tax expenditure proposals (see the chapter on income, property, and payroll taxes), while others do not.[70] The failure to prepare thorough fiscal notes may be a function of short deadlines that are impossible to meet and the lack of qualified staff in sufficient numbers to prepare the notes.[71]

In addition to fiscal notes, other mechanisms are devised to link together the work of committees and ensure that "reasonable" budgets are developed. Some states have used a system by which lump-sum amounts are assigned to program areas, and these funds then are distributed among programs within each area by standing committees and reported back to the appropriations committee for inclusion in their budget bills. Congress uses a variation of this approach. Local governments generally have less of a coordination problem because most of the budget work is handled by a single committee.

The Committee Adopts the Budget

Once committees have gathered and processed all of the information collected as a part of the hearing process, they turn to drafting and approving the budget legislation itself. This is best seen as the starting point for later legislative deliberations on the budget. The initial committee proposal can be quite influential, depending on how much interest or power the rest of the legislature has to amend bills after they emerge from committee. From the perspective of executive branch agencies and interest groups, it is highly desirable to receive favorable budget treatment in draft committee legislation.

Obtaining Overall Legislative Approval

All of the previous activity implies that legislative action is taking place in one committee of the legislature. In a bicameral legislative system, all of the previous activity takes place not in one set of legislative committees, but in committees in both chambers. Since differences almost always exist between the two legislative chambers, a bicameral system complicates the ultimate approval of the budget. Another complicating factor is that there may be multiple committees with jurisdiction over legislation that affects the budget. Thus, many different bills may be required in order to finally pass the entire budget.

One set of considerations from both the executive and the legislative branch perspectives involves the relative roles of the two chambers. At the federal level, the Constitution (Article I, Section 7) requires that revenue or tax bills begin in the House of Representatives. This means, given the current organization of the House, that revenue bills start in the Ways and Means Committee. Until the 1974 reform legislation, the normal procedure was for the Senate Finance Committee to wait until the House completed action before taking up the tax bill. Appropriations were handled in a similar manner, although the practice was based on custom and not the Constitution. Appropriation bills began in the House and were later referred to the Senate. Under that system, strategists were able to concentrate their attentions on first one committee and then another, and on one chamber and then the other, as the legislation worked its way through Congress. Since 1974, the House and Senate have simultaneously commenced work on the budget.

In either legislative house, once the budget or a component of the budget has been approved by the appropriate committee, it is considered by the relevant house where that committee is housed. The overall house may or may not substantially revise or amend the budget as approved by the relevant committee depending on the rules of that particular legislature. In some legislatures, the practice is for quite substantial amendment of committee proposals, whereas in others there is a great deal of deference to the approved committee budgets.

One factor that influences legislative deliberations on the budget is the relative roles played by the two legislative chambers. Where appropriations are handled sequentially (that is, beginning in the lower chamber and then moving to the upper chamber), the two chambers tend to take on different roles. Since a house of representatives tends to have more members than a senate, a house appropriations committee tends to have more members than its counterpart in the senate. As a result, house committee members can specialize in segments of the budget, whereas senators must attempt to become informed on a larger number of areas and consequently may be viewed as amateurs. Members of the senate committee, however, might consider themselves to have a broader awareness of total budget needs than house members. Also, given the sequencing of one chamber acting followed by the other, the house appropriations committee tends to focus on the executive's proposed budget, whereas the senate committee focuses on what the House did to the proposed budget.[72]

A vital and complicating factor in bicameral systems is the necessity to resolve the inevitable differences that result from the deliberations of the two legislative bodies. Almost invariably, because of the difference in constituencies between the houses or because the houses may be controlled by different political parties, a conference committee or some other institution will be required to work out these disputes. The conference committee process is often a delicate balancing act where the members attempt to draft legislation that can gain enough votes in each chamber without costing votes of members who may find that their preferred project or funding level did not survive in conference.

Chief Executive Action on the Budget

Once a revenue or expenditures bill has passed the legislature, it typically (at least in states and in the federal government) will go to the chief executive for approval. Deadlock between the branches is a common phenomenon. When the two cannot agree on a budget, commuters can be greatly inconvenienced due to shutdowns in public transit, welfare recipients can be forced to eke out an existence without their checks, and public employees may have to endure payless paydays. Balanced budget requirements at the state and local levels, while imposing fiscal discipline, can lead to delays in adopting budgets because neither the executive nor legislative branch wishes to take the first step toward compromise lest it be viewed as a sign of weakness. In 1992, and then again in 2009, the California state government operated for months without a budget, during which time employees were issued scrip rather than dollars.[73]

Budget offices commonly perform a clearinghouse function by reviewing all proposed legislation and bills that have been passed by the legislature and forwarded to the chief executive for signing. OMB Circular A-19, *Legislative Coordination and Clearance*, prescribes for federal agencies that they submit to OMB an annual set of proposals for legislation.[74] If these proposals are not submitted in time for consideration during budget preparation, then they are excluded from the president's budget and therefore not endorsed by the president and his administration. Circular A-19 provides that when Congress passes a bill, OMB distributes copies of the enrolled bill to affected agencies for their comments. The agencies must respond promptly, either endorsing or opposing the enrolled bill, to be considered within the president's limit of ten days. If the president does not act within the ten days (including holidays but excluding Sundays), the bill automatically becomes law.

Line-Item Veto

Once appropriation and revenue bills are adopted by the legislature, the approval phase is not completed. In more than 40 states, governors have item-veto power, which permits reductions in amounts that have been appropriated. In some cases, governors may eliminate selected language in appropriation bills that can have substantial effects on policy. State legislatures may seek to override these vetoes. Usually a two-thirds vote is required for an override. As with the general veto power, the threat of the line-item veto may be as important as its eventual use, in that legislators may avoid including some measures in an appropriation bill on the assumption that they would be excised eventually by the governor.

The line-item veto has three uses:[75]

1. It allows chief executives to keep total expenditures within the limits of anticipated available revenue.
2. The executive can reduce or even eliminate funds for projects or programs considered to be unworthy. The line-item veto can help curtail the excesses of pork barrel projects mentioned earlier.
3. The veto can be used for partisan purposes. This kind of use often occurs in situations where the governor is of one political party and one or both chambers of the legislature are of another party.

Studies have found that the item-veto power sometimes, but not always, has a negative effect on spending. This is especially true for pork barrel highway projects and can be particularly important when at least one chamber is under the control of a political party that differs from the governor's party.[76] From a practical standpoint, the line-item veto allows action by the governor without forcing the legislature to react unless it chooses to do so. Indeed, legislators may be privately pleased to have the governor veto some projects that were included in an appropriation bill to satisfy strong lobbying pressure. In spite of the constitutional foundations underlying state line-item vetoes, state courts have been very active in interpreting their application and these court decisions have had substantial effects on the "reach" of a governor's item-veto power.[77]

At the federal level, the president has always been able to exercise the standard veto power, meaning that he can veto an entire appropriation bill. When this power is exercised, the House and Senate may override the veto by a two-thirds vote. Should the veto be sustained, the legislation is referred back to the committee for further review. The disadvantage of the veto power for both Congress and the president is that much time and energy may be consumed in redrafting the legislation and negotiating an agreement between the two branches.

Every president since Ulysses S. Grant, including Barack Obama, has requested the item-veto power or a variant of it.[78] In 1996, Congress granted that wish by passing the Line Item Veto Act.[79] The law, which is discussed in the chapter on the U.S. Congress, was ultimately declared unconstitutional by the Supreme Court in 1998.[80]

LEGISLATIVE OVERSIGHT

Not only are the executive and legislative branches typically separated in U.S. governments, but each branch is also provided with powers that can be used to limit the powers of the other. The basic structure of this checks-and-balances system is set forth in the U.S. Constitution, state constitutions, and city charters. However, constitutional and statutory provisions must be implemented on a daily basis, and the extent to which one branch limits the other may fluctuate over time. In this section, we consider the increasing interest being given to the legislative body's oversight of executive operations.[81]

Influences on Oversight

When revenues are limited and the demands for expenditures are seemingly limitless, legislators perceive a need for greater efficiency and effectiveness in government operations. Such perceptions increase the interest in oversight operations, which in turn increases the pressure on administrative agencies to improve their operations while curtailing or even reducing expenditures. Agencies are required to provide masses of information to legislative committees to support their quest for ferreting out mismanagement and saving tax dollars.[82]

There are, of course, other reasons for the current legislative oversight movement. Financial crises in major cities have contributed to the interest in oversight. The Watergate scandal during the Nixon administration and subsequent scandals and abuses of government funds by federal agencies have stimulated interest in greater legislative oversight. A turnover in the party controlling the legislature, especially if it happens to both chambers and the new legislature is of a different party than the chief executive, can substantially increase oversight activities. This happened with the Democratic party takeover of both the House and Senate after the 2006 congressional election, and then again when the Republicans took over the House after the 2010 election. In this latter case, much attention was paid to promises by Representative Darryl Issa (R-FL) to use his position as chair of the House Oversight and Government Reform Committee to conduct investigations of executive branch agencies.[83] Legislators have not been immune from their own scandals, raising the question of whether they have the appropriate credentials to oversee executive branch operations.

Legislators may be sincerely interested in using government to alleviate societal problems. Frustrated by what is perceived as inept administration, they are attracted to the idea of expanding their oversight roles in the hope of improving government operations. Of course, oversight of the executive branch can also provide an opportunity for legislators to score political points. In fact, legislatures have often been criticized for engaging in oversight designed to take an agency to task for some particular perceived offense, rather than using this opportunity to attempt to understand programs in detail so that they can be reformed constructively.

This legislative interest in oversight occurs at a time when executives feel increasingly frustrated with their own efforts to control public bureaucracies. Elected executives often complain that they lack the authority needed to control and redirect agencies. Merit systems that protect civil service employees are often cited as weakening executives and protecting lazy and incompetent employees from disciplinary actions.

In states that allow strong collective bargaining for public workers, both state and local executives often complain that they cannot make needed changes in administration because of collective bargaining agreements and that unions refuse to yield to essential changes such as cutbacks in wages and benefits when revenues are down. The tensions that this creates were brought into sharp relief in 2010 and 2011 when the governors of both Wisconsin and Ohio took high-profile stands against public employee unions in their states. In Ohio, this approach seems to have led to at least a temporary backlash from voters, who approved a referendum in 2011 that repudiated a union-curbing law passed only one year earlier.[84]

Methods

Legislative oversight can be performed using numerous methods. Legislation that provides authorizations, revenues, and appropriations constitutes one set of methods. Other familiar devices are laws that prescribe the structure of executive agencies and personnel policies regarding hiring, promotion, and dismissal. An informal type of oversight occurs when a legislator or a legislative staff member contacts an agency about specific day-to-day operations. Although legislators may have no official power to command any action by an agency, their wishes will be treated carefully and with some urgency by agency personnel. Oversight is important in advise-and-consent proceedings in which a senate committee screens a nominee for an executive position. Commitments made by a nominee in response to questions asked during such nomination hearings can influence that person's actions once in office.

Legislative investigations and just the simple threat of investigation are other instruments of oversight. A legislative committee chair may greatly influence an agency by suggesting that investigative hearings will be scheduled unless certain practices are changed within the agency.

Greater specificity of legislative intent is being used to reduce executive discretion. In the past, ambiguous language was used as a deliberate tool for delegating responsibilities to the executive and increasing executive flexibility in carrying out policies. The opposite is common today. State legislatures attempt to establish legislative intent through the use of wording contained in line items, footnotes, and concluding sections to appropriation bills; the use of committee reports; and the use of letters of intent delivered to the governor.

Legislatures often find it difficult to enforce legislative intent. What if an agency stays within the legal prescriptions of legislative intent but violates its spirit? The punitive action of cutting the agency's budget often is not possible. Citizens benefiting from agency programs would be harmed as well as the agency itself. Therefore, the main punitive alternative may be to impose more restrictions on the agency, such as making legislative intent more explicit, specifically prohibiting various practices, and increasing the number of line items in the agency's budget to hamstring its flexibility.

The legislature may also attempt to enforce legislative intent by requiring agencies to collect and provide specific information to the legislature. This practice denies agencies the tactic of confessing ignorance about their own programs. If legislation indicates that an agency is to collect specific data, the agency will be expected to deliver it at designated times every year.

Congress often adopts appropriation bills that have detailed language. In fact, in 2011, the disagreements that almost resulted in a government shutdown were as much about these policy riders as about the level of appropriations. For example, House Republicans successfully included restrictions on using family planning funds for abortions in the District of Columbia, and to remove the gray wolf from the endangered species list.[85]

Sunset Legislation and Zero-Base Budgeting

Another type of oversight mechanism consists of sunset legislation coupled with zero-base budgeting (see the chapter on the expenditure side of budget preparation). Programs are authorized to exist for a given period, after which they expire (the sun sets on them). Before a program's expiration date, an agency may be required to present a zero-base budget indicating the achievements of the agency's program and the projected consequences if the program is not renewed. Depending on how these proposals are implemented, they can provide greater leverage for the legislature. For these reasons, sunset legislation is used widely by state legislatures.

Information and Analysis

Program budgeting and analysis constitute another approach to legislative oversight. Legislatures are increasingly demanding impact and output data from agencies. Such demands have reinforcing effects on chief executives' efforts to install program budgeting. There is limited evidence, however, that performance data are important in allocating resources. A recent study by Yilin Hou and his colleagues at the University of Georgia addressed this issue. The study examined the extent to which 11 states—many of which are supposedly among the leaders in performance budgeting—used performance data to inform their budget decisions between 2008 and 2010, when the recession was necessitating budget reductions for the first time in almost a decade.

The results of this research are not encouraging to supporters of performance budgeting. While this research found some evidence that some performance information was being used to inform budget decision making (for example, in the states of Maryland and Louisiana), the predominant story in the case studies was that performance information was "not necessarily very useful as a budget tool in the present fiscal climate." The essential dilemma was illustrated by the State of Utah, which was limited in its ability to reduce funding for low-rated social service programs because the recession necessitated that the state maintain the services provided by those programs and there was a lack of alternatives. The general conclusion of this study is that performance information played a greater role in these states when the economy was strong than when it was weak. Moreover, the more consistent use of performance information is found in management, rather than in budgeting.[86]

Why is performance information not being used to inform budget decisions during times of budget cutbacks? There are several possibilities. First, a given government or government agency may not yet have good measures of performance for its programs. Second, and even more likely, there may be insufficient knowledge concerning the relationship between decreases (or increases, for that matter) in funding and performance. Finally, performance data may not yet have the credibility with elected officials to allow it to be used in evidence-based decision making.

Tensions exist over which organizational units should conduct analyses. Legislatures have sometimes given little attention to oversight, and the function has fallen to audit agencies that at the state level are often headed by independently elected auditors. When legislative bodies later develop their own analytic capabilities, turf issues arise.[87] Virginia's Joint Legislative Audit and Review Commission and Florida's Office of Program Policy Analysis and Government Accountability are examples of state legislative analysis units.[88]

At the federal level, the Government Accountability Office (GAO) has an extensive ongoing research agenda that examines the full gamut of government programs.[89] The fact that the GAO works for Congress often brings it into conflict with the executive branch. One case involved the GAO's desire to obtain records of Vice President Cheney's contacts with outsiders in the process of developing the administration's energy policy. This issue became particularly salient politically after the collapse of Enron, which had ties to some high-ranking officials in the Bush administration.[90] The White House, however, maintained executive privilege, and the requested documents and names were not provided to the GAO.

Information technology also makes possible greater legislative oversight. Congress and state legislatures have developed their own information systems that allow them to tap into a variety of databases, including those maintained by agencies. The application of this technology is limited by the quality of data being maintained. Computer hardware and software cannot compensate for agency neglect in collecting important information.

Legislative Veto

Legislatures are making increased use of their power to veto proposed executive actions. For instance, an agency may be granted authority to issue regulations, but a stipulation in the legislation can require the agency to obtain legislative approval prior to implementing the regulations.[91] Depending on the governing legislation, a proposed action can be vetoed by a vote in either house or both houses of a legislature, or it can be implemented only with a vote of approval from both houses. Sometimes legislative committees have veto powers. In 16 states, legislatures can exercise some form of legislative veto over executive agency regulations.[92]

The legislative veto is used as a means of furthering policy. Legislative intent is served presumably by allowing the full legislature or designated committees to oversee executive implementation. The veto process can steer executive agencies away from actions that are contrary to what the legislature wishes to see implemented.

Not surprisingly, executives have a less positive view of legislative vetoes. The process often delays implementation of actions because the legislature is ensured a given number of weeks to consider whether to support or veto a proposal. These vetoes are seen as giving authority to legislatures to meddle needlessly in the details of administration and, more significantly, to infringe upon the constitutional administrative powers of the executive.

A crisis seemed to develop in 1983 when the Supreme Court handed down one of its most controversial decisions, in *Immigration and Naturalization Service v. Chadha*.[93] The case dealt with congressional veto power involving the deportation of aliens. What was significant was not that the Court struck down that legislative veto, but rather that it struck down most, if not all, such vetoes at the federal level. The Court's reasoning was simple: The Constitution provides for the House and Senate to set policy subject to veto by the president and does not allow for the opposite procedure.

Following the *Chadha* decision, Congress did not rush to adopt statutory measures or seek constitutional revisions that would reinstate the legislative veto. Instead, it dealt with matters as they arose and, in some instances, largely ignored the Court's ruling. For example, subsequent appropriation bills have included legislative vetoes. In 1996, Congress passed the Congressional Review Act, which provides a form of legislative veto of agency draft regulations (see the chapter on budget execution).[94] Research on the implementation of the Congressional Review Act suggests that it has been used very seldom since its enactment to veto agency regulations.[95] However, during more than half of this period, both the Congress and the presidency were under the control of the same political party, a situation in which one would not expect substantial use of a legislative veto.

Oversight Limitations

While numerous methods of oversight are available, the organizational locus of oversight remains a problem because of the fragmentation discussed earlier. A coherent approach to oversight is not possible when committee powers overlap. Every federal agency must deal with at least one (and often more) substantive committee plus the Appropriations Committee and the Budget Committee (discussed in the chapter on budget approval and the U.S. Congress) in each chamber of Congress. That is six committees at a minimum, not counting subcommittees. These committees may disagree with each other and may not have the backing of the full legislative body. Turf battles among committees are routine. Authorizing and appropriations committees frequently compete for control of spending, including earmarks. The committees responsible for transportation policy have been particularly prone to conflict over which one gets to control local transportation projects. For example, the authorizing legislation may include specific earmarks that are substantially different from those included in the appropriations bill for the same year.[96]

One approach to overcoming fragmentation might be to concentrate oversight in a staff unit of the legislature. For example, GAO at the federal level could be given greater oversight responsibilities. GAO already attempts to assist in establishing the oversight agenda for Congress, partially through establishment of its "high risk" list of federal activities.[97] Another option would be to give oversight duties to committee staffs. The problem with these suggestions is that they tend to conflict with legislators' desire to have staff units act in subordinate and inferior capacities. For a staff unit to evaluate a program enacted by the legislative body, to find the program inadequate, and to suggest means of improving it is likely to be viewed by many legislators as an affront to their authority in setting policy. For this reason, legislative analytic units tend to be cautious in program analysis and tentative in reaching conclusions and recommendations.

A final limitation on oversight is the priorities that legislators set for themselves. Reelection is always paramount, and legislators often regard oversight activities as not contributing appreciably to their prospects for winning voter approval. In that sense, the limited oversight role performed by legislatures is seen as a completely rational response to the incentives facing them. If voters are more supportive of legislators who initiate new programs than of those who serve as watchdogs over the executive branch, legislators will respond accordingly.

SUMMARY

A variety of factors constrain the budgetary role of legislatures. First and foremost, legislatures are representative bodies. As such, they are constrained by the methods through which individual members are selected, often by limits on their terms, and increasingly by the intense partisan nature of politics. In addition to these constraints, there are others that affect how they make budget decisions. The factors that may affect how legislatures budget include the extent of fragmentation, the role of party leadership, the amount of time available to legislate, and the availability of staff.

When the budget reaches the legislature, the availability of revenue greatly influences how the legislature approaches budget approval. Previously reached decisions, such as established entitlement programs, limit action, as do numerous socioeconomic and political factors, such as the influence of interest groups. The budget is approved through the work of substantive standing committees, appropriations committees, and revenue or finance committees. These committees hold hearings and produce draft legislation that is then considered by each legislative house. In interacting with these committees, agencies use numerous strategies in seeking approval of their budgets. An administrator's initial objective may be to obtain increased funding for a program. If that is not possible, then the administrator will concentrate on protecting the base and preventing budget cuts beyond those that constitute a fair share. Fiscal notes have become important tools for tracking the financial implications of proposed legislation. Once the legislature adopts the budget, it is sent to the chief executive for approval. In many states, chief executives make use of the line-item veto to strike individual projects or activities from the legislative budget.

Legislative oversight has become increasingly popular. Prior legislative approval of some administrative decisions may be required. Legislative investigative hearings serve the oversight function, along with detailed specification of legislative intent. Sunset legislation and zero-base budgeting are other oversight techniques.

NOTES

1. Goldmacher, S. (2010). State again misses budget deadline. *Los Angeles Times,* June 16.
2. Lienert, I. (2005). *Who controls the budget: the legislature or the executive?* IMF Working Paper. Washington, DC: International Monetary Fund.
3. Keefe, W. J., & Ogul, M. S. (2000). The American legislative process: Congress and the states (10th ed.). Upper Saddle River, NJ: Prentice-Hall.
4. Kurfirst, R. (1996). Direct democracy in the sunshine state: recent challenges to Florida's citizen initiative. *Comparative State Politics, 17,* August, 1–15.
5. National Conference of State Legislatures. (2011). *Recall of state officials.* Retrieved December 12, 2011, from http://www.ncsl.org/default.aspx?tabid=16581.
6. Swoboda, D. P. (1995). Accuracy and accountability in reporting local government budget activities: evidence from the newsroom and from newsmakers. *Public Budgeting & Finance, 15,* Fall, 74–90.
7. MacManus, S. (2004). "Bricks and mortar" politics: how infrastructure decisions defeat incumbents. *Public Budgeting & Finance, 24,* Spring, 96–112.
8. *Baker v. Carr* (1962). 369 U.S. 186; *Reynolds v. Sims* (1964). 377 U.S. 533.
9. *Reno v. Bossier Parish School Board* (1997). 520 U.S. 471.
10. *Shaw v. Reno* (1993). 509 U.S. 630; *Miller v. Johnson* (1995). 515 U.S. 900; *Shaw v. Hunt* (1996). 517 U.S. 899; *Bush v. Vera* (1996). 517 U.S. 952.

11. Lane, C., & Balz, D. (2006). Justices affirm GOP map for Texas. *Washington Post,* June 29, A1; Smith, R. J. (2011). Tom Delay, former U.S. House leader, sentenced to 3 years in prison. *Washington Post,* January 10.

12. Roff, P. (2010). Election 2010 redistricting gains will give GOP lasting majority. *U.S. News,* September 28. Retrieved December 12, 2011, from http://www.usnews.com/opinion/blogs/peter-roff/2010/09/28/election-2010-redistricting-gains-will-give-gop-lasting-majority.

13. Federal court involvement in redistricting litigation. (2001). *Harvard Law Review, 114,* 878–901; Bates, R. P. (2005). Congressional authority to require state adoption of independent redistricting commissions. *Duke Law Journal, 55,* 333–372; Fromer, J. C. (2005). An exercise in line-drawing: deriving and measuring fairness in redistricting. *Georgetown Law Journal, 93,* 1547–1622.

14. *Abrams v. Johnson* (1997). 521 U.S. 74; *Lawyer v. Department of Justice* (1997). 521 U.S. 567.

15. *Hunt v. Chromartie* (2001). 532 U.S. 234.

16. Savage, D. G. (2001). High court flexible on redistricting. *State Legislatures, 27,* June, 21.

17. Sundquist, J. L. (1992). *Constitutional reform and effective government.* Washington, DC: Brookings Institution, 144–198.

18. *State legislative term limits.* (n.d.). Retrieved June 6, 2011, from http://www.termlimits.org/content.asp?pl=18&sl=19&contentid=19.

19. *Term limits across America.* (2006). Retrieved August 1, 2006, from http://www.termlimits.org.

20. *State legislative term limits.* (n.d.). Retrieved June 6, 2011, from http://www.termlimits.org/content.asp?pl=18&sl=19&contentid=19

21. *U.S. Term Limits, Inc. v. Thornton* (1995). 514 U.S. 779.

22. National Association of Latino Elected Officials. (2011). *2011 Directory of Latino elected officials.* Retrieved June 6, 2011, from http://www.naleo.org/directory.html.

23. Carroll, S., & Jenkins, K. (2001). *Increasing diversity or more of the same? Term limits and the representation of women, minorities, and minority women in state legislatures.* Paper presented at the 2001 annual meeting of the American Political Science Association, San Francisco, CA, August 30.

24. National Conference of State Legislatures. (2006). Term limits erode effectiveness of legislative branch, new study finds. *NCSL.org,* August 15. Retrieved August 22, 2006, from http://www.ncsl.org.

25. Greenblatt, A. (2001). Term limits: crash course. *Governing,* November. Retrieved January 20, 2007, from http://www.governing.com/archive/2001/nov/term.txt (source no longer accessible).

26. Karp, J. A. (1995). Explaining public support for legislative term limits. *Public Opinion Quarterly, 59,* 373–391.

27. Nogare, C., & Ricciuti, R. (2008). *Term limits: do they really affect fiscal policy choices?* CESIFO working paper number 2199, January.

28. Boulard, G. (2011). The great divide. *NCSL.org,* February. Retrieved December 12, 2011, from http://www.ncsl.org/?tabid=22082; Pfiffner, J. (2006). Partisan polarization, politics, and the presidency: structural sources of conflict. In James A. Thurber (Ed.), *Rivals for power* (3rd ed., pp. 33–58). Lanham, MD: Rowman and Littlefield.

29. National Conference of State Legislatures (2011). *2011 state and legislative partisan composition.* Retrieved March 3, 2012, from http://www.ncsl.org/documents/statevote/2010_Legis_and_State_post.pdf; Vozzella, V. (2011). Democrat Edd Houck concedes Virginia Senate race; Republicans lock up hold on power. *Washington Post,* November 10. Retrieved December 12, 2011, from http://www.washingtonpost.com/local/dc-politics/democrat-edd-houck-concedes-virginia-senate-race-republicans-lock-up-hold-on-power/2011/11/10/gIQAzCOv9M_story.html.

30. Arnold, L. W., Deen, R. E., & Patterson, S. C. (2000). Friendship and votes: the impact of interpersonal ties on legislative decision making. *State and Local Government Review, 32,* 142–147.

31. Jewell, M. E., & Whicker, M. L. (1994). *Legislative leadership in the American states.* Ann Arbor, MI: University of Michigan Press.

32. Clucas, R. A. (2001). Principal-agent theory and the power of state house speakers. *Legislative Studies Quarterly, 26,* May, 319–338.

33. National Conference of State Legislatures (2011). *2011 state and legislative partisan composition.*

34. Cox, C. W., & Kernell, S. (Eds.). (1991). *The politics of divided government.* Boulder, CO: Westview Press.

35. Goodwin, G., Jr. (1970). The little legislatures: committees of Congress. Amherst, MA: University of Massachusetts Press; Deering, C., & Smith, S. (1997). *Committees in Congress.* Washington, DC: CQ Press.

36. National Conference of State Legislatures (2011). *2011 state and legislative partisan composition.*

37. Council of State Governments (2010). *The book of the states,* Table 3.23, Standing Committees Appointment and Number. Retrieved March 3, 2012, from http://knowledgecenter.csg.org/drupal/system/files/Table_3.23.pdf.

38. Gryski, G. S. (1991). The influence of committee position on federal program spending. *Polity, 23,* 443–459.

39. Council of State Governments (2010). *The book of the states,* Table 3.2, Legislative sessions: legal provisions. Retrieved March 3, 2012, from http://knowledgecenter.csg.org/drupal/system/files/Table_3.2.pdf.

40. Illinois bond rating downgraded as state seeks more borrowing. (2010). *Huffington Post,* May 31. Retrieved December 12, 2011, from http://www.huffingtonpost.com/2010/03/31/illinois-bond-rating-down_n_520671.html; Levine, D. (2010). California downgraded by S&P, weighing on states bonds. *MarketWatch,* January 13.

41. Council of State Governments (2010). *The book of the states,* Table 3.9, Legislative compensation and living expense allowances during session. Retrieved March 3, 2012, from http://knowledgecenter.csg.org/drupal/system/files/Table_3.9.pdf.

42. Joyce, P. (2011). *The Congressional Budget Office: honest numbers, power, and policymaking* (p. 26). Washington, DC: Georgetown University Press.

43. Chadha, A., et al. (2001). The consequences of independence: functions and resources of state legislative fiscal offices. *State and Local Government Review, 33,* Fall, 202–207.

44. King, J. D. (2000). Changes in professionalism in U.S. state legislatures. *Legislative Studies Quarterly, 25,* May, 327–343.

45. Squire, P. (2007). Measuring state legislative professionalism: the Squire index revisited. *State Politics and Policy Quarterly, 7,* 223–224.

46. Mahtesian, C. (1997). The sick legislature syndrome. *Governing, 10,* February, 16–20.

47. Loftus, E. (1994). The art of legislative politics. *Congressional Quarterly Press,* 61–75; Gill, J. (1995). Formal models of legislative/administrative interaction: a survey of the subfield. *Public Administration Review, 55,* 99–106.

48. Clynch E. J., & Lauth, T. P. (Eds.). (1991). *Governors, legislatures, and budgets: diversity across the American states.* New York, NY: Greenwood Press.

49. National Conferences of State Legislatures (2006). *Legislative budget procedure: a guide to appropriations and budget processes in the states, commonwealths and territories.* Retrieved August 21, 2006, from http://www.ncsl.org/programs/fiscal/ibptabls/index.htm. An explanation of a proposed constitutional amendment in Maryland suggests that the limitation on the legislature in that state exceeds that in the other two. See Maryland General Assembly, Department of Legislative Services (2011). *Fiscal and policy note, SB 632.* Retrieved March 3, 2012, from http://mlis.state.md.us/2011rs/fnotes/bil_0002/sb0632.pdf.

50. O'Lessker, K. (1992). The new president makes a budget: from Eisenhower to Bush. *Public Budgeting & Finance, 12,* Fall, 3–18.

51. Kerr, J. (2010). State elections: Republicans gain control of key state legislatures. *Huffpost Politics,* November 3. Retrieved March 3, 2012, from http://www.huffingtonpost.com/2010/11/03/state-elections-legislatures_n_778103.html.

52. Clynch, E. J., & Lauth, T. P. (Eds.). (1991). *Governors, legislatures, and budgets.*

53. Payne, J. L. (1991). *The culture of spending: why Congress lives beyond our means.* San Francisco, CA: ICS Press.

54. Fiorina, M. (1989). *Congress: keystone of the Washington establishment* (2nd ed.). New Haven, CT: Yale University Press.

55. National Association of State Budget Officers (2011). *Fiscal survey of the states.* Retrieved March 3, 2012, from www.nga.org/files/live/sites/NGA/files/pdf/FSS1106.PDF.

56. Pear, R. (2011). G.O.P. blueprint would remake health policy. *New York Times*, April 4.

57. Bland, R. L. (2007). *A budgeting guide for local governments.* Washington, DC: International City/County Management Association.

58. Ebdon, C., & Franklin, A. (2006). Citizen participation in budgeting theory. *Public Administration Review, 66*, 437–447.

59. Dobel, J. P. (1995). Managerial leadership in divided times. *Administration and Society, 26*, 488–514.

60. Rosenbaum, D. (2002). Official forced to step down after testifying on budget cut. *New York Times*, March 7, A22.

61. Johnson, C. M. (1992). *The dynamics of conflict between bureaucrats and legislators.* Armonk, NY: M. E. Sharpe.

62. Johnson, B. (1989). The OMB budget examiner and the congressional budget process. *Public Budgeting & Finance, 9*, Spring, 5–14.

63. Wildavsky, A., & Caiden N. (2000). *The new politics of the budgetary process* (4th ed., pp. 47–55, 59–64). New York, NY: Longman.

64. Wildavky, A. (1988). *The new politics of the budgetary process* (p. 115). Glenview, IL: Scott Foresman and Company.

65. Meyers, R. T. (1994). *Strategic budgeting.* Ann Arbor, MI: University of Michigan Press.

66. Salamon, L. T. (2002). *The tools of government: a guide for the new governance.* Baltimore, MD: Johns Hopkins Press.

67. Stanford, K. A. (1992). State budget deliberations: do legislators have a strategy? *Public Administration Review, 52*, 16–26.

68. Unfunded Mandates Reform Act of 1995 (P.L. 104-4). For a discussion of CBO's role in implementing the act, see Joyce, P. (2011). *The Congressional Budget Office*, 114–117.

69. Council of State Governments (2006). *The book of the states*, 109–110.

70. Snow, D. R. (1999). Do legislative procedures affect tax expenditures? *Journal of Public Budgeting, Accounting and Financial Management, 11*, 357–385.

71. Kelly, J. M. (1994). Fiscal noting reconsidered: the experience of the states with mandate cost estimation. *Public Budgeting and Financial Management, 6*, 1–27.

72. Fenno, R. F., Jr. (1966). The power of the purse: appropriations politics in Congress. Boston, MA: Little, Brown; Horn, S. (1970). *Unused power: the work of the Senate Committee on Appropriations.* Washington, DC: Brookings Institution.

73. Cash-poor California turns to IOUs. (2009). *CNNMoney.com*, July 2. Retrieved December 12, 2011, from http://money.cnn.com/2009/07/02/news/economy/California_IOUs.

74. U.S. Office of Management and Budget (2006). *Legislative coordination and clearance*, Circular A-19. Retrieved August 24, 2006, from http://www.whitehouse.gov/omb/circulars/a019/a019.html#purpose.

75. Abney, G., & Lauth, T. P. (1985). The line-item veto in the states. *Public Administration Review, 45*, 372–377; Lauth, T. P. (1996). The line-item veto in government budgeting. *Public Budgeting & Finance, 16*, 97–111.

76. Alm, J., & Evers, M. (1991). The item veto and state government expenditures. *Public Choice, 68*, 1–15; Berch, N. (1992). The item veto in the states: an analysis of the effects over time. *Social Science Quarterly, 29*, 335–346; Thompson, P., & Boyd, S. R. (1994). Use of the item veto in Texas, 1940–1990. *State and Local Government Review, 26*, 38–45.

77. Lee, R. D., Jr. (2000). State item veto legal issues in the 1990s. *Public Budgeting & Finance, 20*, Summer, 49–73.

78. Bellamy, C. (1989). Item veto: dangerous constitutional tinkering. *Public Administration Review, 49*, 46–51; Sundquist, J. (1992). *Constitutional reform and effective government*, 281–294. For the most recent proposal, see Office of Management and Budget (2011). *Budget of the United States government: fiscal*

year 2012, analytical perspectives, 156–157. Retrieved December 15, 2011, from http://www.whitehouse .gov/omb/budget/overview.

79. Line Item Veto Act of 1996 (P.L. 104-130).

80. Joyce, P. G. (1998). The line item veto act: after the Supreme Court decision, what's next? *Public Budgeting & Finance, 18,* Winter, 3–21.

81. Aberbach, J. B. (1990). *Keeping a watchful eye: the politics of congressional oversight.* Washington, DC: Brookings Institution; Evans, D. (1994). Congressional oversight and the diversity of members' goals. *Political Science Quarterly, 109,* 669–687.

82. Lewis, B. J., & Ellefson, P. V. (1996). Evaluating information flows to policy committees in state legislatures. *Evaluation Review, 20,* 29–48.

83. Crabtree, S. (2010). Issa, House GOP create new oversight sub-panels for TARP, stimulus. *The Hill,* December 17. Retrieved March 3, 2012, from http://thehill.com/homenews/house/134311-issa-gop-creates-oversight-panels-for-tarp-stimulus.

84. Bauer, S. (2011). Scott Walker's collective bargaining law keeping Wisconsin unions from seeking recertification. *Huffington Post,* September 22. Retrieved December 12, 2011, from http://www .huffingtonpost.com/2011/09/22/scott-walker-collective-bargaining_n_976376.html; Kornblut, A., & Wallsten, P. (2011). In Ohio collective-bargaining vote, Democrats see some hope for 2012. *Washington Post,* November 9. Retrieved December 12, 2011, from http://www.washingtonpost .com/politics/in-ohio-collective-bargaining-vote-democrats-see-some-hope-for-2012/2011/11/09/ gIQAJzll6M_story.html.

85. Should Congress take the gray wolf off the endangered species list? (2011). *Washington Post,* April 12. Retrieved March 3, 2012, from http://www.washingtonpost.com/opinions/should-congress-take-the-gray-wolf-off-the-endangered-species-list/2011/04/12/AFp9SlSD_story.html.

86. Hou, Y., et. al. (2011). State performance-based budgeting in boom and bust years: an analytical survey of the states. *Public Administration Review, 71,* May/June, 370–388.

87. Walton, K. S., & Brown, R. E. (1990). State legislators and state auditors: is there an inherent role conflict? *Public Budgeting & Finance, 10,* Spring, 3–12.

88. See the websites of the Joint Legislative Audit and Review Commission, Commonwealth of Virginia, at http://jlarc.state.va.us, and of the Office of Program Policy Analysis and Government Accountability, State of Florida, at www.oppaga.state.fl.us.

89. Havens, H. S. (1990). *The evolution of the General Accounting Office: from voucher audits to program evaluations.* Washington, DC: U.S. Government Printing Office; National Academy of Public Administration (1994). *The roles, mission and operation of the U.S. General Accounting Office.* Washington, DC: U.S. Government Printing Office.

90. Denniston, L. (2002). GAO sues for access to Cheney records. *Boston Globe,* February 23, A1.

91. Gibson, M. L. (1992). *Weapons of influence: the legislative veto, American foreign policy, and the irony of reform.* Boulder, CO: Westview Press.

92. Council of State Governments (2010). *The book of the states,* Table 3.26, Legislative Review of Administrative Rules/Regulations.

93. *Immigration and Naturalization Service v. Chadha* (1983). 462 U.S. 919.

94. Congressional Review Act of 1996 (P.L. 104-121).

95. Croston, S. (2010). Congress and the courts close their eyes: the continuing abdication of the duty to review agencies noncompliance with the Congressional Review Act. Washington College of Law Administration Law Review; Osorio, I. (2010). Welcome back, Congressional Review Act. *The American Spectator,* September 23; Copeland, C. (2009). Congressional Review Act: rules not submitted to GAO and Congress. *CRS Report for Congress,* December 29. Retrieved March 3, 2012, from http://www .ombwatch.org/files/regs/PDFs/CRS122909.pdf.

96. Schick, A. (2007). *The federal budget: politics, policy, process* (3rd ed.). Washington, DC: Brookings Institution.

97. Government Accountability Office (2011). *Statement of Gene Dodaro before the House Committee on Oversight and Government Reform,* February 17.

Budget Approval: The U.S. Congress

Previously, we examined the budget approval process across levels and types of government. This chapter examines the special case of the U.S. Congress, which has unique importance in the governmental system, and thus unique procedures. Rather than examining similarities among governments, this chapter considers the special budgetary processes used by Congress and the problems Congress faces. In the process, it discusses the peculiarities of the federal budget process in general.

The federal budget process has been at center stage over the past several years, both as the federal government has attempted to take action to combat the recession that began in 2007, and as it attempts to come to grips with the massive deficits that developed and expanded between 2002 and 2011. The budget battles since the beginning of the Obama administration have involved the following controversial events:

- The George W. Bush and Barack Obama proposal for a Troubled Assets Relief Program (TARP) to relieve the crisis in the financial industry, ultimately approved by the Congress.
- A second major stimulus, the $787 billion American Recovery and Reinvestment Act, aimed at job creation and support for state and local governments, proposed by President Obama and approved by the Congress.
- Presidential budget proposals that have simultaneously attempted to prop up the weak economy and at least pay lip service to deficit reduction.
- Sharply partisan disagreements between the president and the Congress, most clearly exemplified by the contrast between the Obama budgets and House Republicans, led by House Budget Committee Chairman Paul Ryan (R-WI). These disagreements increased even more, in frequency and rancor, with the rise of the Tea Party movement, which saw a great number of anti-Washington candidates elected to the Congress in 2010. These new members, who had pledged to fundamentally change the way Washington works, made it difficult for even their own party leadership to find common ground with them.

If it was not clear prior to these debates playing out, these controversies have illustrated once again the central role that the federal budget plays in both the national economy (see the chapter on government and the economy) and national politics. The battles have illustrated, going into the 2012 presidential election, that the two political parties hold sharply different visions for the country. These visions are reflected in different policy prescriptions, on both the taxing and the spending sides of the budget.

The chapter has four sections. The first section reviews the historical development of the modern budget process, from the passage of the Congressional Budget and Impoundment Control Act of 1974 to the deficit-based budget process reforms embodied in the Gramm-Rudman-Hollings reform and the Budget Enforcement Act of 1990. The second section reviews the timetable for the resulting budget process, from presidential budget submission to budget resolution to committee action, including reconciliation, authorizations, and appropriations. The third section chronicles the movement of the federal budget from deficit to surplus and then back to deficit again, by discussing the Omnibus Budget Reconciliation Act of 1993, the Balanced Budget Act of 1997, developments during the George W. Bush administration (including the tax cuts and the wars that have been fought since the terrorist attacks of September 11, 2001), and the deficit and debt debates during 2010 and 2011. The last section discusses a variety of possible reforms to the budget process.

EVOLUTION OF THE FEDERAL BUDGET PROCESS

The federal budget process has evolved since the early part of the 20th century as it has been used to achieve particular objectives and to solve particular problems. For that reason, understanding this history is crucial to demystifying the budget process. Most of the current procedures result from two laws: the Budget and Accounting Act of 1921 and the Congressional Budget and Impoundment Control Act of 1974. In addition, there were a number of deficit-based budget reforms (such as Gramm-Rudman-Hollings law in 1985, the Budget Enforcement Act in 1990, and the Budget Control Act in 2011) over roughly a quarter decade after the mid-1980s. The first of these laws, the Budget and Accounting Act of 1921, had three main purposes. First, it created a requirement that the president submit a budget to Congress each year. Prior to the Budget and Accounting Act, federal agencies submitted their budget estimates directly to Congress. Second, it created the Bureau of the Budget (now the Office of Management and Budget) to assist the president in preparing the budget.[1] Third, it created the General Accounting Office (now the Government Accountability Office), initially to help control agency spending but later to do programmatic and performance audits of federal agencies and programs.[2]

The Congressional Budget and Impoundment Control Act of 1974

Congress, like the legislatures discussed in the previous chapter, conducts its work in committees. Subcommittees are especially important in the appropriations process. One group of committees, as explained in the chapter on budget approval and the legislature, has responsibility for substantive legislation. These committees develop authorizing legislation, which establishes departments and agencies and the programs they operate. An authorization provides a dollar amount as a ceiling for spending. Approval to commit the government to spend, however, is given through the appropriations process.[3]

Another set of committees provides the wherewithal for the government to operate.[4] The Ways and Means Committee in the House and the Finance Committee in the Senate fashion legislation that generates revenue for the government. In addition to being responsible for tax legislation, these committees are responsible for some substantive measures with dedicated revenue sources, such as Social Security and Medicare. They handle legislation permitting increases in the federal debt. Such legislation is necessary because the government typically accumulates debt by spending more than it collects in revenues. As was illustrated vividly during the spring and summer of 2011, raising the debt limit is a sensitive matter partially because members of Congress assume that voting for debt increases is itself evidence of fiscal irresponsibility.

The Ways and Means Committee, as of 2011, included 37 of the 435 members of the House, and the Finance Committee included 24 of the 100 members of the Senate. The number of seats held by each party on the committees is generally proportional to total party membership in the chambers.

Discretionary, or non-entitlement, spending is under the aegis of the Appropriations Committee in each house.[5] In 2011, there were 50 members on the House committee and approximately 30 on the Senate committee. The spending side of the budget is currently divided among 12 subcommittees in the House and an identical number in the Senate that report out appropriation bills. Appropriations permit agencies to commit the government to expenditures, with some spending occurring in subsequent budget years as a result of contracts signed in the current year.

Starting in the 1940s, two major problems with this process became abundantly clear. First, because Congress dealt with the budget through a variety of bills, the budget was handled piecemeal, making it difficult to set comprehensive policy. Second, the piecemeal approach meant that various subcommittees, committees, and the two chambers had to exercise discipline over themselves to complete their work in time for the beginning of the fiscal year.

When appropriation bills are not passed on time, agencies financed through the appropriations process no longer have the funds to operate and are forced to shut down. To avoid this situation, Congress passes one or more continuing appropriation bills (often called continuing resolutions). These bills permit the affected agencies to operate for a specified time period, usually spending at the same level as they did in the just-completed fiscal year. Typically, no new programs can begin spending while the agency is operating under a continuing resolution, even if budget savings have been achieved by having proposed in the budget elimination of other programs or reduction in size of other programs. When the federal government's fiscal year began on July 1, it was common for many or most appropriation bills not to have cleared Congress by the deadline, and agencies often operated for an entire fiscal year with continuing rather than regular appropriations. Changing the fiscal year to begin October 1 was thought to be a solution, giving more time for budget preparation, congressional review, and approval. As history has demonstrated, however, appropriation bills have been approved on time no more often than before the fiscal year change.

Early Reforms and the Emergence of Backdoor Spending

Congress first attempted to deal with these problems by passing the Legislative Reorganization Act of 1946.[6] The law required Congress to agree on an overall budget package before detailed tax and spending bills were developed and approved. In 1947, the House and Senate could not reach agreement. In 1948, the chambers reached agreement and ignored it. The law's requirement for an overall budget was ignored in subsequent years.[7] Next, Congress experimented with using a single omnibus appropriation bill as a means of controlling total spending. The process seemed to work well for fiscal year 1951, but neither the Appropriations Committees nor the White House supported its continuation.[8]

During the 1960s and 1970s, the situation was complicated by what became known as "backdoor spending," in which spending authority was provided outside the appropriation process.[9] Backdoor spending may take several forms, including direct actions by substantive committees, such as contract authorizations that allow agencies to commit the government to spend and later may force the Appropriations Committees to provide the necessary funds. Substantive committees have given agencies borrowing authority, which allows them to borrow from the Treasury and spend debt receipts. Entitlement programs (Medicare and Medicaid, for example) that provide direct or mandatory spending constitute the main form of backdoor spending in that the government obligates itself to provide benefits to all qualifying applicants.

The effect of backdoor spending was that virtually all committees in Congress came to play important roles in financial decisions with no mechanism existing to coordinate their diverse activities. Many observers and participants believed that the budget was becoming increasingly uncontrollable, meaning that, barring any major readjustment in commitments to programs, much of the budget could not be altered in a given year. Contributing to this situation were multiyear government contracts with government suppliers, multiyear grants to state and local governments, entitlement programs, and interest on the national debt.[10]

As a means of controlling spending, President Nixon vetoed appropriation bills on the grounds that they included too much spending, but that action pleased neither Congress nor the agencies that were covered by the bills. Later in his administration, Nixon went ahead and signed the bills but refused to spend all of the money, a process known as impoundment. The lack of a coordinating mechanism for the budget, combined with a desire to limit impoundments, led to passage of the Congressional Budget and Impoundment Control Act of 1974.[11]

The 1974 Budget Reform

The 1974 reform legislation had many objectives.[12] One objective was to provide Congress with a means for controlling the budget as a whole—namely, linking appropriation bills with each other and linking these with revenue measures. Controlling the budget as a whole was seen as essential if Congress was to influence economic policy. Resolving conflict between Congress and the president was another important objective that required dealing with the impoundment problem. Members of Congress wished to assert their policy-making role vis-à-vis the presidency. A process was needed by which Congress could complete its work on the budget by the beginning of the fiscal year.

Taken as a whole, the Budget Act of 1974 had four main effects. First, it created a new mechanism, the budget resolution, to express the overall will of Congress on budget issues. Second, it created the Budget Committees to marshal the budget resolution through

Congress. Third, it created the Congressional Budget Office, a new agency intended to provide Congress with information on the budget and the economy. Finally, it established a new procedure for dealing with presidential impoundments.[13]

The Budget Resolution

Under the procedures established by the Budget Act of 1974, Congress would adopt a concurrent budget resolution that established the overall outline of the budget (a concurrent resolution is an action that is taken by both houses of Congress that does not require the president's signature). The resolution would represent a "blueprint" for the budget, showing aggregate budget numbers—revenues, budget authority (the authority to commit the government to spend money), outlays (the actual spending of funds out of the Treasury), the overall target (budget deficit or surplus, if any), and government debt.

Following passage of the concurrent resolution in the spring, Congress then reverted to its old procedures. Committees in Congress needed to adopt individual pieces of legislation affecting revenues and spending within the constraints imposed by the budget resolution. Subcommittees of the Appropriations Committees considered specific appropriation bills, and the revenue committees considered their portion of the budget. To allow for accommodating changes in policy, a second resolution was to be adopted by September 15. That resolution could be used for reconciliation, a process in which committees were instructed to adjust spending and revenue measures upward or downward to conform to the overall budget plan. The beginning of the fiscal year was shifted from July 1 to October 1, thereby giving Congress three additional months for its annual budgetary work.

The Budget Committees

To provide for coordination among the various components of Congress, the 1974 law established House and Senate Budget Committees, whose members are representatives from the chambers' leadership and relevant committees—the four major money committees and the substantive committees that provide authorizations. As of 2011 (the beginning of the 112th Congress), there were 38 members on the House Budget Committee and 23 on the Senate Budget Committee. The Budget Committees were to serve two functions. First, they had jurisdiction over the development of the budget resolution itself, putting them in the center of macro-level budget policy. Second, they were to serve as watchdogs, making sure that legislation was not substantially at variance with the resolution, although they lacked authority to overrule other committees. The resolution could be enforced through points of order, which would make legislation not consistent with the resolution more difficult to enact.

The Congressional Budget Office

The law also provided Congress with additional staff support by creating the Congressional Budget Office (CBO) to serve as overall staff to the Budget Committees, the other four money committees, and any other committees or individuals in Congress that need assistance in the area of budgeting. CBO's charge was to serve Congress in a nonpartisan manner.[14] Given that charge, CBO decided that it would refrain from providing policy recommendations. It was to play three main roles:

1. Developing the budget baseline (a current services estimate) that would prove to be the starting point for the resolution;
2. Estimating the costs of proposed legislation; and
3. Conducting policy research on issues before Congress.[15]

The CBO currently has a staff of about 250. It had eight directors from its creation through this writing: Alice Rivlin, Rudolph Penner, Robert Reischauer, June O'Neill, Dan Crippen, Douglas Holtz-Eakin, Peter Orszag, and Douglas Elmendorf, who was named director in early 2009 and was reappointed in 2011.

Impoundment Control

Prior to the passage of the 1974 legislation, the Nixon administration claimed it was simply following in the footsteps of virtually every president since Thomas Jefferson in deciding not to spend all of the funds that were appropriated.[16] The Anti-Deficiency Act of 1950, allowing the executive to establish agency reserves in the apportionment process (see the chapter on budget execution), was used as further justification for impounding monies.[17]

Not only did the Nixon administration use impoundment to control total spending, but the process was also used to halt spending on grant programs that the president wanted consolidated into block grants (see the chapter on intergovernmental relations). Several court suits were filed, which were generally decided in favor of releasing funds, but the Supreme Court has never addressed the issue of whether the president has the constitutional power to impound monies.

The Congressional Budget and Impoundment Control Act represented a compromise between the legislative and executive branches, albeit one that the Nixon administration was forced to accept. Two forms of impoundments were permitted: rescissions and deferrals. When in the judgment of the president part of or all funds of a given appropriation were not needed, a rescission proposal (a proposal to cancel budget authority already provided) was to be made to Congress. The rescission would not take effect unless approved by Congress within 45 working days. The other type of impoundment, deferral, was a proposal to delay obligations or expenditures. Like rescissions, deferral proposals had to be submitted to Congress, but they became effective unless either the House or the Senate passed a resolution disapproving them.

The Arrival of Large Deficits, 1981–1985

The Budget Act of 1974 established procedures and institutions to govern priority setting in Congress, but was largely silent concerning budget outcomes. That is, no assumptions were made about the appropriate size of the federal budget or budget deficit. The focus of the budget process changed substantially in the 1980s, however, largely in response to the large deficits ushered in during the administration of President Ronald W. Reagan.[18]

Reagan came into office in January 1981 following a major victory at the polls during the previous November. The 1980 election created a phenomenon not seen since the 83rd Congress of 1953: the Senate dominated by a Republican majority, the House remaining under the control of the Democrats, and a Republican president. Reagan submitted a set of budget proposals that provided for severe budget cuts in domestic programs, a shift toward the use of block grants to state and local governments (see the chapter on intergovernmental relations), an increase in defense spending, and a massive set of cuts in the personal income tax that became law in the Economic Recovery Tax Act of 1981.[19] Reagan was so popular that few political leaders, even House Democrats, dared to speak out against his recommended policies.

During the early Reagan years, OMB began to play an increasingly important role.[20] Previously, it had the job of making overall presentations on the budget before congressional committees, but the defense of specific recommended appropriations was left to the affected departments. After Reagan's election, major realignments in policies were being recommended on both the revenue and the expenditure sides of the budget, and the defense of these recommendations became the job of OMB.[21]

The 1980s Deficit

A cloud soon developed that ended the euphoria of early 1981, as the budget deficit began to grow at an alarming rate.[22] As early as 1983, Reagan budget director David Stockman famously (and accurately) predicted "$200 billion deficits as far as the eye can see."[23] The administration had championed the 1981 massive tax cuts as a means of stimulating the economy and thereby increasing revenues. Though there was a supporting theoretical tradition in economics long before the 1981 tax cuts, 1980–81 was the first time that supply-side economics specifically led to change in tax law. Tax cuts were expected to produce such simulative effects on the economy that growth in the economy would more than make up for the lost revenue from the cuts, but this proved more theory than fact (see discussion of supply-side and demand-side views in the chapter on government and the economy). The debt limit had to be raised to $1.1 trillion in 1981 and $2.1 trillion in 1985.

Stalemate

Substantive issues were partially to blame for Congress's inability to adhere to the prescribed timetable. During these years, President Reagan took a firm stand on priorities. He wanted the tax cuts that had been approved in the 1981 law, wanted a buildup in defense capability, insisted that programs like Social Security be protected from budget cuts, and at the same time sought a balanced budget.[24] All of those objectives simply could not be met simultaneously. If the budget were to be brought into balance by reducing its unprotected areas, which included an array of social programs such as Aid to Families with Dependent Children, decimation of the remaining part of the federal government would be required. As a consequence, a stalemate between the president and Congress developed, with the two occasionally reaching agreement on actions that only marginally improved the situation.

Reconciliation

As noted earlier, reconciliation was intended to provide in one resolution directed guidance to committees on how they should alter authorizing, taxing, and spending legislation. The process was envisioned as coming at the end of the budget approval phase. However, in the years following the 1974 reforms, the House and Senate Budget Committees were reluctant to use reconciliation because it would have been seen as an infringement on the domains of powerful committees and as a personal affront to the committee chairs. The reconciliation process was used for the first time in 1980, the last year of the Carter administration, and from that time forward, it became a prominent feature of congressional budgeting.[25] The current use of reconciliation is discussed below as part of the discussion of the general budget timetable.

Controllability and Policy Making

The deficit situation during the 1980s imposed constraints on Congress in regard to what it could and could not fund. The Reagan administration proposed numerous program cuts that were unpopular in Congress. While Congress had every right to reject the president's recommendations, in rejecting the proposed savings and trying to avoid adopting a budget more out of balance than that recommended by the president, Congress was forced to find offsetting measures to raise revenues, cut expenditures, or both. The end result of the back-and-forth between the president and Congress was that the spending cuts were not sufficient to offset the revenue reductions enacted in 1981. Deficits continued to grow, as there was a large structural imbalance between revenues and spending.

The Gramm-Rudman-Hollings Era, 1985–1990

The situation came to a head in the latter part of 1985. Democrats agreed with Republicans and representatives agreed with senators that the deficit situation had become intolerable. The White House did not exhibit the same level of concern but concurred that something should be done to remedy the situation.

By October 1, 1985, the beginning of the fiscal year, not a single appropriation bill had cleared Congress. A stopgap continuing appropriation bill was passed to keep the government operating. The budget resolution had been adopted on August 1 despite the official deadline of May 15. By November, both the stopgap appropriation bill was expiring and (perhaps most importantly) the debt ceiling was being reached, forcing another stopgap appropriation bill and an increase in the debt ceiling to be rushed through Congress.

Enactment of the Law

It was in this politically charged atmosphere that Congress adopted the Balanced Budget and Emergency Deficit Control Act of 1985.[26] The chief authors were Senators W. Philip Gramm (R-TX), Warren B. Rudman (R-NH), and Ernest F. Hollings (D-SC). The main objective of Gramm-Rudman-Hollings was simple: to reduce the size of the budget deficit annually until expenditures were in balance with revenues. Target figures were set, and if the president and Congress could not reach agreement on a budget package that met the target figure for a given fiscal year, then automatic across-the-board reductions in expenditures were to occur—a process known as sequestration. Senator Rudman described the law as "a bad idea whose time has come."[27]

Legal Challenge and Revision

As soon as the law was enacted, it was challenged in court. The case was brought on appeal to the Supreme Court, which ruled in July 1986 that one key provision violated the Constitution.[28] The comptroller general, who headed the General Accounting Office and as such was an officer of Congress, was found to have been granted executive powers in violation of the Constitution. After much debate, Congress, in September 1987, adopted the Balanced Budget and Emergency Deficit Control Reaffirmation Act, which modified the original Gramm-Rudman-Hollings legislation.[29]

Sequestration

Gramm-Rudman-Hollings created a new procedure—called sequestration—that was to impose budget reductions if budget deficit targets were not reached. Some cuts were to be taken from appropriated spending and some from mandatory spending. Of the appropriated cuts, half were apportioned to defense and the other half to domestic programs. On the mandatory side, special rules, limiting the reach of sequestration, applied to some domestic programs, such as Medicare and guaranteed student loans. Other parts of the budget were totally protected from sequestration. These included the basic retirement program under Social Security, Aid to Families with Dependent Children, civil service retirement funds, and the like. Gramm-Rudman-Hollings was overtaken by events in 1987. Less than a month after Congress passed the Reaffirmation Act of 1987, the stock market crashed. On Tuesday, October 19, the Dow Jones Industrial Average dropped 23% (508 points), a greater drop than the 13% decline on October 28, 1929.[30]

The crash, as would be expected, startled private and public sector leaders. Although a feared depression did not materialize, the situation served as a catalyst to force an agreement on budget deficit reduction. In November, a two-year agreement was reached by the president and Congress on cutting the deficit, but by no means eliminating it.

The 1980s closed without Gramm-Rudman-Hollings having appreciably affected the government's overall budget outlook.[31] In fact, the Gramm-Rudman-Hollings targets were routinely met by basing presidential budgets and congressional budget resolutions on unrealistically optimistic economic assumptions. Nothing in the act required the president and the Congress to do anything when (invariably) these projections did not come true.

The 1990 Budget Summit and the Budget Enforcement Act

President George H. W. Bush was elected in 1988 and almost immediately faced a rapidly deteriorating budget outlook. While the process limped along under the Gramm-Rudman-Hollings Act during 1989, by late summer 1990 the budget situation had reached another crisis stage. If Congress were to live within the constraints imposed by Gramm-Rudman-Hollings, it would have required a massive reduction in the deficit in a single year. Because this result was not credible or possible, political leaders of both parties became convinced that another approach to deficit reduction was necessary. A budget "summit" was held between Bush administration officials and key members of Congress in late 1990, which ultimately resulted in the passage of the Omnibus Budget Reconciliation Act of 1990 (OBRA 1990). OBRA 1990 included a combination of revenue increases, reductions in mandatory spending, and budget enforcement procedures estimated to reduce cumulative deficits by almost $500 billion between fiscal year 1991 and fiscal year 1995.[32]

The Budget Enforcement Act

The Budget Enforcement Act (BEA), which was established by Title XIII of OBRA 1990, provided for a new budget process that officially only temporarily replaced Gramm-Rudman-Hollings. The 1990 law shifted emphasis away from fixed annual targets for the budget deficit. In effect, it was based on the premise that Congress had little control over the total annual deficit and that the emphasis should therefore be on those areas over which control was possible. Entitlement program expenditures were allowed to fluctuate according to shifts in the eligibility pools. The law also exempted the budget from emergencies.[33] Spending limits, or caps, were set for the discretionary portion of the budget. These caps were considered to be reductions in the deficit because they did not allow discretionary spending to grow as fast as inflation.

The Budget Enforcement Act initially established so-called *firewalls* for discretionary spending, separating the three areas of defense, international aid, and domestic spending. Spending caps were set for each area for fiscal years 1991, 1992, and 1993, and overall budget caps were set for 1994 and 1995. The significance of the firewalls was that each area was protected from possible budget cuts in response to budget increases in one of the other areas. For instance, the rules prevented defense advocates from trying to avoid cuts by proposing extra cuts in domestic programs. When the Soviet Union crumbled and Eastern European nations dismantled their communist governments, the existence of a single cap after 1994 allowed the targets to be reached through cuts in the defense budget: the "peace dividend."

The BEA also created a pay-as-you-go (PAYGO) process affecting laws governing revenues and entitlement programs. The PAYGO system required that, in a given Congress, the overall effect of policies that would expand entitlement spending or decrease revenues relative to the baseline should be deficit-neutral. In practice, it was intended to focus attention not only on the cost of the policy change but also on tradeoffs with existing tax or spending programs. PAYGO gave an advantage to those programs already budgeted and made difficult the inclusion of new or expanded initiatives. The Budget Enforcement Act, along with its parent the Omnibus Budget Reconciliation Act of 1990, successfully kept the budget process under control through the 1992 presidential election, a primary objective of many political leaders. Members of Congress came to the realization that whatever proposals they wished to advance, a price was to be placed on them. Neither tax cuts nor spending increases could be advocated without taking into account their effects on the overall deficit.

THE RESULTING CONGRESSIONAL TIMETABLE

When put together, these four laws—the Budget and Accounting Act, the Budget Act of 1974, Gramm-Rudman-Hollings, and the Budget Enforcement Act—had by 1990 prescribed the rules and the timetable for enacting the federal budget each year. As will be discussed in a subsequent section, neither Gramm-Rudman-Hollings nor the BEA is currently in effect. Gramm-Rudman-Hollings was effectively superseded by the BEA, and the BEA itself was allowed to expire by Congress and President Bush after fiscal year 2002. At this point, therefore, the Budget and Accounting Act of 1921 and the Congressional Budget Act of 1974 are the remaining controlling budget process laws.

This section of the chapter summarizes the steps in the budget process as a chronology of events. Each year, the budget process begins (not quite in earnest, but it begins) with the president's budget submission in early February. It continues (with luck) only until October 1, with all appropriations enacted prior to the start of the fiscal year. Almost always, the process continues beyond October 1, as one or more bills fail to become law by the statutory deadline. **Table 10–1** shows the timetable for budgetary action as applied to the fiscal year 2012 budget process.

Submission of the President's Budget Request

As noted earlier, chief executives submit their budget proposals hoping that the legislature will "rubber stamp" the plans, but expecting (except in cases where the legislature is very weak) that significant changes will be made. Congress is an extremely strong and professional legislative body, so the president's budget is viewed as only the "first shot" in what is almost invariably an annual budgetary war.

The law provides that a president submit his budget to Congress no later than the first Monday in February. In practice, this schedule has been met except for cases where new presidents have just taken office on January 20. In this case, OMB normally submits current services estimates by the February deadline, and the new president submits policy proposals, in the form of amendments to the budget, within two months.

Table 10–1 Federal Budget Process Timetable, Fiscal Year 2012

Date	Action to Be Completed
Between the first Monday in January and the first Monday in February	President transmits the budget
Six weeks later	Congressional committees report budget estimates to Budget Committees
April 15	Action to be completed on congressional budget resolution
May 15	House consideration of annual appropriation bills may begin
June 10	House Appropriations Committee to report the last of its annual appropriations bills
June 15	Action to be completed on reconciliation
June 30	Action on appropriations to be completed by House
July 15	President transmits mid-session review of the budget
October 1	Fiscal year begins

Source: Reprinted from U.S. Office of Management and Budget (2011). *The budget system and concepts, budget of the United States government, fiscal year 2012: analytical perspectives* (p. 4). Washington, DC: U.S. Office of Management and Budget.

The Budget Resolution and Reconciliation

Congress responds to the president's budget request by producing its overall plan for the budget, in the form of its budget resolution. As noted earlier, the budget resolution, created as a coordinating mechanism by the 1974 Budget Act, serves as the overall blueprint for the budget. It also may result in reconciliation, an optional process used to make changes in revenues and mandatory spending.

The Budget Resolution

Under the current timetable, Congress is to complete work on the budget resolution by April 15 of each year. The groundwork for the development of the budget resolution is typically done by the Congressional Budget Office, whose annual report *The Budget and Economic Outlook* presents baseline budget estimates 10 years into the future.[34] This is designed to give Congress a reasonable idea of the starting point for its deliberations. The budget resolution ultimately includes aggregate budget targets (total revenue, total budget authority, and the like), functional budget targets, and allocations of budget authority and revenue authority to congressional committees. Committees are not permitted to exceed these targets—called Section 302(a) allocations—and face procedural points of order on the House and (particularly) Senate floor if they attempt to do so.[35]

The budget resolution, in practice, is a tricky annual spring ritual in which the House and Senate Budget Committees must each work with other committees and members to forge an agreement that will withstand later challenges as the details of the budget are prepared. In many years, the budget resolution has not been adopted by the statutory deadline because of difficulties in reaching agreement within one house or (in particular) between both houses. An extreme version of this problem would be the failure to adopt a budget resolution at all. For example, no budget resolution was enacted for the following fiscal years: 1999, 2003, 2005, 2007, 2011, and 2012.[36] The current budget timetable provides that, if Congress has not enacted a budget resolution prior to May 15, the appropriations committees can begin to act on appropriation bills without any limits that would have been imposed by the budget resolution.

Reconciliation

Reconciliation, an optional procedure, has been used since 1980 primarily during years when some major change is anticipated affecting either mandatory spending or revenues. When the procedure is used, reconciliation instructions are included in the budget resolution that will tell committees to produce legislation that has the effect of reducing spending and increasing revenues.[37] At least seven major observations can be made about the use of reconciliation.

1. The size and complexity of these bills defy individual comprehension. When these bills are assembled, even the members of the originating committees may not be familiar with all the details spread across hundreds of pages.
2. Large bills are open invitations to pork barrel politics. Some members will succeed in adding pet projects or programs that, if required to stand by themselves for approval, might not be accepted by Congress.

3. Large bills place presidents at a distinct disadvantage in that they must either accept or reject the bills in their entirety. On the other hand, reconciliation bills differ from appropriations in that they do not need to pass, and Congress has sometimes been hard-pressed to get the president to go along with them on reconciliation.

4. Large bills are compatible with congressional desires to avoid blame. Members of the House or Senate cannot be held accountable for their votes supporting any one aspect of a bill, because they can say they felt compelled to vote for the bill even though it admittedly was flawed in numerous respects.

5. The use of large bills and Congress's preoccupation with budgeting since the 1980s has contributed to centralization of decision making at a time when Congress had been democratized. Power was redirected to those members of Congress most closely associated with the budget process. Furthermore, because reconciliation bills cannot be filibustered, some have argued that they changed the operations of the Senate in a way that no longer gives sufficient protection to legislative minorities.[38] In fact, the protections offered by reconciliation caused the George W. Bush administration to use reconciliation bills as a means to ease passage of its legislative agenda (including tax cuts, which were passed as a result of reconciliation) without the normal hurdles that such changes would face, particularly in the Senate.[39]

6. Members of the Appropriations Committees have sometimes expressed concern that their powers are diminished through the reconciliation process, which is under the direction of the Budget Committees. In reality, reconciliation involves other members of Congress besides those who serve on the House and Senate Budget Committees. In working out a conference bill between the two chambers, the numerous subconference committees created include conferees who are not members of either the House or Senate Budget Committees. Nevertheless, the Appropriations Committees see the situation as centralizing power in the hands of the Budget Committees.

7. Because of a provision known as the "Byrd Rule" (named after former West Virginia Democratic Senator Robert C. Byrd) the House sometimes feels disadvantaged relative to the Senate by the reconciliation process. The Byrd rule (actually Section 313 of the Congressional Budget Act) limits "extraneous" matters in reconciliation legislation. A provision is considered extraneous, for example, if it does not produce a change in outlays or revenues, increases the deficit in a year beyond that covered by reconciliation, or is outside the jurisdiction of the committee proposing the change.[40]

The Authorization Process

Theoretically, federal programs must be authorized and appropriated. Authorizations play an important role in federal budgeting. They establish or change federal programs, and they create the terms and conditions under which those programs operate. Authorizations can be provided for one year (as is common for defense programs), for multiple years (Congress last passed an agriculture authorization—or "farm bill"—in 2008, when the Food, Conservation, and Energy Act was passed), or permanently (many mandatory spending programs). In the case of mandatory spending programs, authorizations provide spending directly. Major entitlement programs are authorized and appropriations are provided simultaneously. An entitlement such as Social Security, for example, is created by an authorization, and the authorization itself creates the obligation for the federal government to spend money that goes to program beneficiaries.

For discretionary spending, the authorization does not provide the appropriation directly, but rather creates a program that may or may not later be funded in the appropriation process. These authorizations typically include what are called "authorizations of appropriations," which are intended to provide guidance to the appropriations committees but are not binding on them. In fact, the appropriations committees routinely enact appropriations for programs that have no authorization at all. In fiscal year 2010, Congress appropriated $159 billion for programs whose authorizations had expired.[41] Even where there are authorizations for discretionary programs, they typically represent something like a "bid" for future resources, and the appropriations are often less than the amount that is authorized to be appropriated.

The Appropriations Process

While the reconciliation process is optional and the authorization process does not happen for all programs in all years, there is nothing optional about the process of enacting annual appropriations. In fact, enacting the regular appropriation bills is the only budget action that Congress has to take each year. Without appropriations, federal agencies cannot pay staff or contractors and cannot deliver basic benefits. For this reason, in most years the main focus of the budget process is on the fate of appropriations. The appropriations process itself involves several kinds of activities, including action in subcommittee, action in committee, action by the full House and Senate, conference committee action, and negotiation with the White House.

Subcommittee and Committee Action

Both the House and the Senate have Appropriations Committees. Historically, the Appropriations Committee in each house was divided into 13 subcommittees, which do the substantive work of crafting the detailed bills that fund each individual budget account. Each subcommittee produces a bill that funds various cabinet departments and (sometimes) related agencies. The number of subcommittees changed in 2005, when a rather contentious reform of the process created some disconnect between the House and the Senate subcommittee structure. As a result, the House had only 10 subcommittees, while the Senate had 12. This reform was allegedly driven by the desire of House Majority Leader Tom Delay (R-TX) to put NASA in a more favorable position by not having to compete for resources in the same appropriation bill with the Department of Veterans Affairs.[42]

Prior to the creation of the Department of Homeland Security, which among other things consolidated some previously independent agencies and pulled functions out of other departments into the new department, agencies' funding appeared in only one of the appropriation acts. Congress has not yet realigned its subcommittee structure and its appropriations process with the executive reorganization, and it may not ever do so. As a result, some agencies have appropriations in more than one appropriation act.

With the takeover of Congress by the Democrats in 2007, more changes were made in the makeup of committee jurisdictions. The legislative branch, which had been handled by the full committee in the House, was once again given subcommittee status in both houses. The Transportation and Treasury subcommittee was once again broken up, with separate subcommittees for Transportation, Housing and Urban Development and Related Agencies, and Financial Services and General Government. Once again this meant that both houses had parallel committee structures, and each had 12 appropriations subcommittees. Even with Republican control of the House after 2011, the number of subcommittees and jurisdictional boundaries remained largely unchanged. **Table 10–2** lists the jurisdiction of the subcommittees (that is, which federal agencies and programs are financed by which subcommittee) in the House and the Senate.

As noted earlier, the Appropriations Committees receive a 302(a) allocation as a part of the budget resolution. It effectively tells the committees how much money they have to divide up in aggregate. At an early stage of the process, the committees divide these allocations by subcommittee. These Section 302(b) allocations tell Congress how much money will be available to divide among the various agencies funded as a part of each subcommittee's bill. In other words, the 302(a) allocations establish the size of the appropriated pie, while the 302(b) suballocations tell each subcommittee how large a slice it will have.

After the suballocations have been set, the subcommittees work to produce appropriation bills. Appropriation bills become law in the same way that other bills become law. They must ultimately be passed by both houses in identical form and approved by the president. For appropriation bills, getting to this point involves a lengthy process:

- *Subcommittee action*—where hearings are held (see the previous chapter on budget approval) and initial allocations are made to each account in each appropriation bill. Each subcommittee is headed by a chairperson who exercises substantial influence over the operations of agencies under the subcommittee's jurisdiction. In fact, the subcommittee "chairman's mark" represents the starting point for deliberations on the appropriation bill, and the bill is considered by the full committee under a process known as the "mark-up," where amendments to the bill are considered in the subcommittee.

Table 10–2 Appropriations Subcommittees in Houses of Congress, 2012

Agriculture, Rural Development, and Related Agencies
Commerce, Justice, and Science and Related Agencies
Defense
Energy and Water Development and Related Agencies
Financial Services and General Government
Homeland Security
Interior, Environment, and Related Agencies
Labor, Health and Human Services, Education, and Related Agencies
Legislative Branch
Military Construction, Veterans Affairs, and Related Agencies
State, Foreign Operations, and Related Programs
Transportation, Housing and Urban Development, and Related Agencies

Source: U.S. House of Representatives, Committee on Appropriations, appropriations.house.gov/subcommittees.

- *Full committee action*—where typically the actions of the subcommittee are ratified with very little change.
- *Floor action*—where procedural limitations may (especially in the House) restrict what amendments may be proposed, and where amendments that add money normally need to be offset by reductions.
- *Conference action*—where selected members of appropriations subcommittees in each house convene to work out differences between bills.
- *Presidential action*—where the president exercises his constitutional authority to approve or veto appropriation bills.

The process of getting through these steps is time consuming, and this (coupled with the high political stakes that can accompany appropriations) means that often one or more appropriation bills do not become law prior to the beginning of the fiscal year. There were only three years between 1977 and 2011 when all appropriations cleared Congress prior to the start of the fiscal year.[43] The spectacle in 2011 that threatened a government shutdown over the failure to enact appropriations is only the most recent evidence of this failure. Although the government has not been shut down since the budgetary conflict between President Clinton and Congress in 1995 and 1996, it is now routine for appropriations to be enacted after the start of the fiscal year. Government by continuing resolution is now an annual event that creates costly disruption for federal agencies and recipients of government funds. Another source of conflict in the appropriation process has to do with items that are added to the budget by Congress but were not in the president's budget. The incentives facing Congress and the president lead them to pursue different types of priorities. While not confined to the appropriations process, "pork barrel politics" (see the earlier chapter on budget approval) is perhaps most visible in the appropriation process. The pursuit of these special-interest priorities has led to the effort to provide the president with the line-item veto, as discussed in the last section of this chapter.[44]

FROM DEFICIT TO SURPLUS TO DEFICIT, 1991–2012

The Omnibus Budget Reconciliation Act of 1990, while it did not promise a balanced budget, was projected to put the budget on a path to that budgetary promised land. But while a CBO analysis done immediately after the passage of OBRA 1990 projected a deficit of only $29 billion by fiscal year 1995, an analysis done only 13 months later projected a deficit in excess of $200 billion by mid-decade.[45] This deterioration resulted from the effects of economic recession, not because of any policy actions. It meant, among other things, that the deficit was a salient issue in the 1992 presidential campaign, which saw the election of Bill Clinton. The same election also featured the strong showing of third-party candidate Ross Perot, who was able to garner enough votes that Clinton was elected with only 43% of the popular vote. Because many of Perot's supporters had been advocates of greater deficit reduction, both political parties needed to appeal to these voters by embracing deficit reduction as a policy goal.[46]

Coming into office in January 1993, President Clinton attempted to follow through on his campaign promise to bring the budget deficit under control. In fact, the Clinton administration embraced deficit reduction as a top priority only after it failed to gain congressional approval of a proposed stimulus package to bolster a weak economy. Critics, who claimed the package was unnecessary because the economy was already on the rebound and because the government could not afford more spending at a time when the deficit was high, were successful in defeating the proposal in the Senate. The administration then turned its attention to a comprehensive deficit reduction proposal.[47]

The 1993 Budget Agreement

The Omnibus Budget Reconciliation Act of 1993, adopted in August 1993, was approved by the narrowest of margins: 218 to 216 in the House and 51 to 50 in the Senate (Vice President Gore cast the tie-breaking vote).[48] The measure was passed without any Republican votes (neither on the reconciliation bill nor on the budget resolution that preceded it) and with considerable pressure applied by Republican members to have their Democratic colleagues join them in the opposition. The Clinton administration knew that the vote would be close, so the White House lobbied members with great intensity. As a result, all members had ample opportunity to be involved in the process of adopting the budget, unlike in earlier situations, such as in 1990, when the rank and file complained that the leadership had made all of the decisions.

The 1993 law included four types of actions:

1. Tax increases, particularly increases in individual income taxes for the wealthiest Americans, gasoline taxes, and corporate taxes;
2. Spending cuts, notably cuts in Medicare, Medicaid, and defense, but in other programs as well;
3. Spending increases, such as for empowerment zones, which are designated urban and rural areas that are provided with increased services to attract business; and
4. Tax expenditures, such as tax credits for lower-income workers and tax incentives for businesses operating in empowerment zones.

Overall, the law was expected to shrink, but in no way eliminate, the deficit. The spending caps and the PAYGO process from the Budget Enforcement Act were revised and extended through fiscal 1998.[49] Annual deficits under the law were expected to approach $200 billion. Because nearly $500 billion in deficits was to be eliminated over five years, the debt was expected to increase by "only" $1.1 trillion over that same period. The total deficit reductions were expected to be equal to or somewhat less than the reductions that resulted from the Budget Enforcement Act of 1990. If the administration wanted to tackle the budget deficit in earnest, then another round of spending cuts and tax increases would be necessary. Furthermore, the budget would need to be revisited if the president and Congress could reach agreement on a plan for revising health care and its financing, a high priority of the first Clinton administration and one that failed to win congressional approval.

The 1995–1996 Debacle

The November 1994 elections set up a situation ripe for intense executive–legislative conflict that would benefit few, harm many, and add to the skepticism of the citizenry about the worthiness of government and its political leaders. The elections produced victories for the Republicans, giving them the control of both the Senate, which had been under Republican control for six years during the Reagan administration, and the House of Representatives, which had not been under Republican rule for 40 years. The House's new Speaker, Newt Gingrich (R-GA), had championed a Contract with America in the elections. Gingrich, along with a sizable group of newly elected Republican members, felt deeply committed to legislating the various components of the contract.[50] Their extensive package of proposals included a balanced budget amendment to the Constitution, the line-item veto, and the requirement of a three-fifths majority vote to raise taxes. The new House majority was also committed (at least on paper) to shrinking the size of domestic government.

The new Republican Congress and the Democratic president found themselves on an unavoidable collision track. The Republicans managed to produce a reconciliation bill in spring 1995 that included substantial reductions in many federal programs, including a $270 billion reduction over seven years (from the baseline) for Medicare spending.[51] This proposal was projected to result in a balanced budget by fiscal year 2002. When Congress sent this bill to President Clinton, however, he vetoed it as "extreme." Congress responded by holding appropriation bills hostage until or unless Clinton capitulated on reconciliation. In particular, Congress insisted that the president come up with his own balanced budget plan using the more conservative budget estimates of the Congressional Budget Office, rather than the more optimistic Office of Management and Budget projections.

When the president refused to agree to the congressional assumptions or timetable, the resulting "train wreck" led to portions of the government being forced to shut down for two extended periods (November 14 to 19, 1995; and December 16, 1995, to January 8, 1996).[52] People were inconvenienced in innumerable respects, such as not being able to visit the Grand Canyon and not being able to obtain a passport for overseas travel. While the government continued to distribute Social Security payments, processing was halted on new applications for benefits. Businesses in Washington, DC, that relied on patronage from business travelers and tourists, were hurt financially as people stayed away from the city.

Eventually, the congressional Republicans capitulated. There was no reconciliation bill and a compromise was reached on discretionary spending that did not cut appropriations by as much as was desired by the Republicans. All participants were eager to have the battles resolved, if for only a short period, to avoid having this situation continue into the 1996 presidential election. As it was, Republicans probably were blamed by the electorate for the shutdowns and overall chaos, partially explaining their losses in the House of Representatives, albeit not enough to lose control, and the win by President Clinton in his bid for reelection.[53]

The 1997 Balanced Budget Act

January 1997 ushered in the 105th Congress, with a new collective mindset, and was the beginning of President Clinton's second and final term in office. The congressional leadership realized that a balanced budget could not be achieved without Clinton's support, as it would be virtually impossible to gain enough votes to override any presidential veto. A balanced budget would inevitably involve budget cuts, which are always unpopular with anyone affected by them. As a consequence, Republicans were eager for a bipartisan budget agreement as a means for spreading the blame for cuts in programs. President Clinton, who had earlier championed the idea of a balanced budget, may well have seen 1997 as an opportunity to achieve this goal and consequently to enhance his record of achievement. Working behind the scenes was a group of largely conservative Democrats in the House, who billed themselves as the "Blue Dogs," eager to find some middle-road compromise that would avoid elimination of programs as a budget reduction effort and yet bring spending under control to balance the budget.[54]

In May 1997, President Clinton and the Republican leadership in Congress agreed on the outline for a package of decisions that was supposed to balance the budget by 2002.[55] The agreement was followed by passage of two key laws—the Balanced Budget Act and the Taxpayer Relief Act—both of which were signed by President Clinton at a special ceremony on August 5, 1997. The Balanced Budget Act was an immense piece of legislation covering such topics as food stamps, housing, communications, welfare, education, civil service retirement, and much, much more. The Taxpayer Relief Act provided tax benefits for college education, capital gains tax cuts, family tax credits for children, and other relief measures.[56] Cuts in domestic programs were included, and Medicare expenditures were shaved back. Although spending for Medicaid, which serves the needy, was reduced, the cuts were not as severe as some had advocated.

The Balanced Budget Act made permanent the requirement that budget resolutions cover a five-year period. Discretionary spending limits, to be enforced through sequestration, were extended through fiscal year 2002, as were PAYGO requirements.

The Arrival—and Disappearance—of Surpluses

The sustained growth of the economy that continued into the late 1990s accelerated the timetable for the achievement of surpluses. Fueled in large part by increases in federal revenues (which grew by an average of 8.4% per year between fiscal years 1995 and 2000 with no changes in rates), the budget surplus arrived a full four years earlier than had been projected. The federal government ran a unified budget surplus of $69 billion in fiscal year 1998. The surplus, which was the first since fiscal year 1969, grew to $129 billion in 1999 and to $236 billion in 2000.[57] Attention then turned from the question of "How do we get rid of the deficit?" to "What do we do with the surplus?" The debt held by the public at the end of fiscal year 2001, which was the last year of the budget surplus, was $3.3 trillion, or $450 billion less than it had been in fiscal year 1997, when there was a budget deficit.[58]

George W. Bush assumed the presidency in January 2001. Within a month after he had taken office, CBO projected cumulative surpluses of $5.6 trillion between fiscal years 2002 and 2011; perhaps not entirely coincidentally, OMB followed suit only one month later.[59] Three competing uses of the surplus were debated in the spring of 2001. One group wanted to use the surplus to pay down the debt as quickly as possible. A second group advocated spending the surplus on key domestic programs, including (in particular) a prescription

drug benefit for Medicare. A third group advocated a tax cut. Many supported a combination of these three approaches.

Ultimately, the Economic Growth and Tax Relief Reconciliation Act (EGTRRA) of 2001
produced a tax cut estimated to amount to $1.3 trillion over 10 years. The tax cut alterna-
tive was given substantial legs by Federal Reserve Board Chairman Alan Greenspan, who
reversed his earlier opposition to tax cuts in light of the large projected surpluses.[61] For the
personal income tax, the bill created a new 10% tax bracket, redefined the 15% bracket,
and effected a gradual reduction in other marginal rates. By the time the cut was fully
phased in, the rates for the other brackets were 25%, 28%, 33%, and 35%. In addition,
the act phased in a number of other changes, such as repealing the current restrictions on
itemized deductions and personal exemptions, doubling the child tax credit (to $1,000)
over a 10-year period, and phasing out the estate tax over a 10-year period.[62]

The estimate of $1.3 trillion tax cut understates its magnitude, since various provisions
were "turned off" in later years so as not to exceed the allowable cost of the tax cut under
reconciliation. (Under the "Byrd Rule," reconciliation provisions cannot increase the deficit in any year beyond those covered by reconciliation.) In 2010, Congress and the president agreed to extend the Bush tax cuts for two years, through fiscal year 2012. From that
point forward, CBO estimated that if some future Congress and future president do not
allow these provisions to expire (which seems likely), this action would add another $932
billion to deficits through 2016, and more than $2.9 trillion to deficits through 2021.[63]

The tax cut is one of several factors that contributed to a substantially deteriorating
budget outlook for the federal government during the first decade of the 21st century.[64]
Revenues and spending were affected by the continuing weakness of the economy in 2001.
Furthermore, the terrorist attacks of September 11, 2001, occasioned a response that will
have continuing budgetary ramifications. This response included not only the remediation
of the immediate effects of the attacks, but also a domestic and international response.
On the domestic front, Congress and the president created the Department of Homeland
Security (DHS), which combined a great many agencies that had been in separate departments under a single agency. In addition, costly wars in Afghanistan and Iraq were justified
on the basis of a continued war on terrorism. In 2011, CBO estimated that these military actions had cost almost $1.3 trillion between fiscal years 2001 and 2011.[65] Finally, an
extremely severe hurricane season in 2005 resulted in horrific death and destruction in the
Gulf Coast area, occasioning an unprecedented federal disaster relief effort.

The recession that began in 2007 had a substantial effect on the deficit outlook. This
recession, as noted earlier, was the most severe experienced by the country since the Great
Depression 80 years earlier. The lowered economic output reduced tax revenues, especially
for the individual and corporate income taxes. In fact, both revenue sources declined in
nominal terms from fiscal year 2007 to 2008, and again from 2008 to 2009. The individual
tax continued its decline between fiscal year 2009 to 2010.[66] On the spending side, a combination of increases in spending for automatic stabilizers—such as unemployment compensation, Medicaid, and food assistance under the Supplemental Nutrition Assistance
Program (SNAP—formerly food stamps)—increased budget deficits. In addition, however,
Congress and the president took a series of legislative actions to combat the recession, with

the stated goal of warding off another depression (see discussion in the chapter on government and the economy). These included:

- Spending for the Troubled Asset Relief Program (TARP), which attempted to respond to the precarious financial conditions of many large financial institutions whose greed had led them to make ill-advised investments in costly subprime mortgages. This program was later expanded to include the provision of assistance to distressed automobile manufacturers General Motors and Chrysler. While $700 billion was approved under this program, less than two-thirds of this amount was ever used. Furthermore, in the case of financial institutions, the federal government purchased stock in these banks that could later be sold. Then, when the government ultimately divested itself of these assets, this often resulted in a profit to the government. When all these factors are considered, CBO by 2011 estimated that the TARP, far from costing $700 billion, in fact cost about $20 billion. This cost included losses of $14 billion associated with the automobile bailout and another $14 billion of funds provided to the American Insurance Group (AIG). These costs were offset by profits from the sale of stock of other firms.[67]

- The American Recovery and Reinvestment Act (ARRA), which attempted to provide short-term stimulus through a combination of revenue reductions and spending increases. On the spending side, the focus was on infrastructure projects that could be started in short order, and aid to state and local governments designed to lessen the need for these governments to lay off teachers and other personnel.[68]

- The bailout by the federal government of the mortgage giants Fannie Mae and Freddie Mac, which was actually much more costly than the TARP. These firms, which guaranteed a large number of subprime mortgages and compounded that exposure by making risky investments of their own, had argued for many years that they were not creating an implicit financial risk for the taxpayer, while all the time reaping the benefit that came from Wall Street believing that they would be bailed out should they ever fail. If there ever was any question which of these two positions was correct, it was answered in September 2009 when the government was forced to take over Fannie and Freddie. As of March 2011, CBO estimated the cost of this takeover at $130 billion, although it is possible that this figure could decline if the GSEs pay more to the Treasury than they receive in payments in the future, which is a plausible scenario.[69]

- Extension of the Bush tax cuts of 2001 and 2003, most of which were scheduled to expire, for two years beginning in 2010. This measure was taken partially out of fear that raising taxes (which would have been the result of allowing them to expire) would choke off the economic recovery. This extension punted down the road (past the 2012 presidential election) the ultimate decision of what to do about these tax cuts beyond fiscal year 2013.

Table 10–3 shows the trend in deficits and surpluses for the federal government from fiscal year 1985 through fiscal year 2011. The table clearly demonstrates the rise in the deficit, the four years of budget surplus from 1998 through 2001, and the return of the deficit after 2002.

Table 10–3 Federal Deficits and Surpluses, Fiscal Year 1985 Through Fiscal Year 2011 ($ billions)

Fiscal Year	Surplus or Deficit
1985	–212.3
1986	–221.2
1987	–149.7
1988	–155.2
1989	–152.6
1990	–221.0
1991	–269.2
1992	–290.3
1993	–255.1
1994	–203.2
1995	–164.0
1996	–107.4
1997	–21.9
1998	69.3
1999	125.6
2000	236.2
2001	128.2
2002	–157.8
2003	–377.6
2004	–412.7
2005	–318.3
2006	–248.2
2007	–160.7
2008	–458.6
2009	–1,412.7
2010	–1,293.5
2011	–1,295.6

Source: Congressional Budget Office (2012). The budget and economic outlook: fiscal years 2013–2021 (p. 132). Washington, DC: U.S. Government Printing Office.

By January 2012, the Congressional Budget Office had released a revision of its budget outlook that underscored just how much the fiscal situation had deteriorated since January 2001. In this forecast, CBO estimated that the federal budget would experience cumulative deficits, in the amount of $3.1 trillion for the period of fiscal years 2013 to 2022. Under this projection, the debt held by the public as a percentage of GDP would actually drop from 75% in 2013 to 62% by 2022.[70] This forecast was quite likely optimistic, since CBO's budget projections must assume "current law," and current law does not include some likely changes in policy, such as extending the tax cuts, that would make the deficit outlook worse. In fact, CBO projected that, including extending the tax cuts and other likely policy changes, the debt held by the public would approach 100% of GDP by 2022.[71]

What to do about this? To say that the president and Congress have had difficulty devising solutions to the deficit problem seems the height of understatement. After the Bush administration punted the problem down the road for much of the first decade of the twenty-first century, the Obama administration appointed a deficit commission in 2010, headed by former Senator Alan Simpson (R-WY) and former Clinton chief of staff Erskine Bowles. They recommended a sweeping set of spending reductions and tax increases late in 2010, which were subsequently ignored by the president when his budget was put together.[72] Many other private groups have also looked at this problem, and there is a remarkable degree of consensus around imperatives to reduce the debt to a more manageable level, such as 60% of GDP.[73]

In the spring and summer of 2011, an opportunity seemed to present itself when the federal government was poised to hit its debt ceiling once again. Although many people argued that the debt ceiling is an archaic requirement (since the vote comes long after the policies that necessitate the debt have been approved), many new members of Congress refused to vote to raise the debt limit unless that vote was accompanied by other actions to reduce the national debt. Because House Republicans, in particular, were opposed to any revenue increases, the practical implication of this was to pressure Congress to enact spending reductions in order to avoid an unthinkable and economically costly fiscal insolvency. Such an insolvency would have forced the government to begin choosing, as early as early August 2011, which bills to pay and which bills to leave unpaid. Finally, on August 3, 2011, an agreement was reached with passage of the Budget Control Act of 2011. The Budget Control Act created new discretionary spending caps, covering fiscal years 2013 to 2021. In addition, it required each house to vote on an amendment to the Constitution requiring an annually balanced federal budget. Finally, it created a new committee, the Joint Select Committee on Deficit Reduction. The Joint Select Committee (or "supercommittee," as it came to be called) was a committee of 12 members (six from each house, and six from each party) tasked to identify an additional $1.5 trillion in deficit savings by November 23, 2011. The supercommittee's recommendations were to be voted on, without amendment, by the rest of Congress. Absent an agreement on at least $1.2 trillion in savings, in January 2013 a sequestration process would kick in covering a period through fiscal year 2012, that would take 50% of budget reductions from the defense budget and 50% from domestic programs (although some programs, such as Social Security, were either exempt from sequestration or the level of sequestration was limited).[74] Days before the deadline arrived, the supercommittee announced that it had failed to reach agreement.

The short-term problems pale in comparison to the long-term fiscal imbalance faced by the country. The growth in entitlement spending, fueled by demographic and cost changes, threatens to overwhelm the federal budget over the next 75 years. Because of demographics and increased costs, the major entitlement programs—Social Security, Medicare, and Medicaid—have highly uncertain fiscal futures. Since Social Security and Medicare represent transfers between current workers (who pay the payroll taxes) and current retirees (who receive the benefits financed by those taxes), the impending retirement of the baby boomers will have a substantial effect on the finances of these programs. At the same time, individuals are living longer, thus receiving benefits from these programs for a longer period of time. More importantly, Medicare and Medicaid are affected by the same cost growth as the rest of the health care system. The cost of the government's health care programs is expected to decrease slightly as a result of the Patient Protection and Affordable Care Act signed into law by President Obama in 2010, but it will come nowhere near solving the long-term fiscal problem. All told, CBO's long-term model suggests that, under plausible scenarios that would extend current law and assume other changes that seem likely to occur, spending would rise to 25% of GDP by 2035 (the historical 40-year average is 21%), revenues would remain at roughly their historical average of 18%, and debt held by the public would rise to 187% of GDP by that same year.[75]

PROPOSED REFORMS AND THEIR PROSPECTS

Congress, the president, and the nation face a complex set of interwoven problems. Tremendous uncertainty remains concerning budget priorities and the proper role of government, and this controversy will play out as the government comes to grips with the federal debt, as it inevitably must do. The current budget process seems dysfunctional, with the most basic tasks, like the adoption of a budget resolution or appropriation bills, proving elusive in a number of recent years. Given this, it is reasonable to ask what changes might be made to the budget process, and even whether the whole idea of establishing a congressional budget process was doomed from the start.[76]

The movement of the budget from deficit to surplus and back to deficit again has policy makers struggling to establish the correct goals for the budget. In addition, the nation faces what is perhaps a fundamental and expensive shift in priorities to confront threats to security both at home and abroad. In the short run, the wars in Iraq and Afghanistan seem to have given the Defense Department a blank check. However, a perennial question is: How much defense is enough? Defense policy must be rethought given the absence of the threat of nuclear attack by Russia, the potential threat of terrorism, and the instability in particular regions of the world, especially the Middle East. Unless there are conflicts that are similar in scope that replace those in Iraq and Afghanistan, there is the probability that the defense budget may be able to be downsized substantially in the coming years. At the same time, the budget faces a lurking fiscal time bomb, associated with the government's entitlement programs.[77] Can Congress better organize itself to deal effectively with this daunting set of problems?[78] If Congress's primary role is to set policy and provide leadership in furthering the nation's interests, then do means exist for improving the processes of that august body to help it meet its responsibilities? Since the budget process is at the very center of policy making, it attracts much attention from reformers and raises fundamental questions. For example, how should power be distributed between the leadership and the individual members? Placing power in the hands of those in leadership positions can help facilitate decision making, but at the same time can subjugate the voices of individual members who have been chosen by their voters to represent them.[79] This is certainly an issue that has been illustrated starkly by the creation of the supercommittee—12 members of Congress who had the power to set the budget agenda for everyone else. How should responsibilities be distributed between new members and those with seniority? How should power be shared by the two chambers of Congress? To what extent should or must Congress delegate powers, such as the power to sequester funds, to the president and to others in the executive branch of government?

These questions of process cut to the core of any congressional member's future. For example, getting appointed to the "right" committee—any committee in a position to address the needs of one's home district—is considered critical, and any plan to reorganize the committee structure is necessarily regarded as threatening. One view is that Congress will never be able to deal with fundamental problems as long as campaign funds must be obtained largely through contributions from constituent organizations. Those organizations are likely to donate substantial funds only on the condition that members provide pork barrel spending and other immediate benefits.

Budget process reform proposals are hardy perennials in Congress. Many members, convinced that the current process is fundamentally broken, propose changes in budget procedures or institutions as solutions to fiscal problems. There are many more of these proposals than can be catalogued on these pages, but among the most common are reforms that would give the president a line-item veto, would amend the Constitution to require a balanced budget, would reorganize Congress as it deals with the budget, and would convert Congress to a biennial budget process.

The Line-Item Veto

Most governors (43 out of 50) have line-item veto power, allowing them to reduce or elimi-nate line items in appropriation bills. The president of the United States has historically lacked such power. The power could be provided in a statute or, as many would advocate, in an amendment to the Constitution. Thomas Jefferson may have been the first president to refuse to spend money appropriated by Congress, and Ulysses S. Grant was apparently the first president to ask for the item-veto power. He called for the line-item veto in his fifth State of the Union address in 1873.[80]

Pros and Cons of the Line-Item Veto

One of the main justifications cited for the line-item veto is that the president needs the authority to reduce or eliminate funding of pork barrel projects that have little merit other than pleasing specific constituent groups of individual members of Congress. However, what constitutes excesses in spending is necessarily a function of one's values and priori-ties, and the executive branch is not immune from advocating spending for programs and projects of questionable utility. One aspect that is clearly not a purpose of the line-item veto is to reduce the budget deficit. The spending cuts that might be made by a president would be unlikely to have any appreciable effect on total spending.[81]

Critics of the line-item veto contend that it gives the president an unwarranted increase in power, allowing for presidential policy preferences to supplant congressional prefer-ences. If a president needed to muster senatorial votes for an initiative, he could privately threaten to item-veto favored projects of individual senators. When the White House was controlled by one political party and Congress by the other, White House priorities might prevail. One can speculate that if Presidents Reagan and George H. W. Bush had been able to wield item-veto power, then several agencies and programs would have been elimi-nated, such as the Economic Development Administration, the Appalachian Regional Commission, and urban mass-transportation formula grants.

The Rescission Process

Procedures, as initially established by the Congressional Budget and Impoundment Control Act of 1974, provide that the president submits packages of proposed rescissions in appropriations enacted by Congress. Congress has 45 days in which it is in session to approve each package or approve its own set of cuts. Before adopting an appropriation bill, Congress is made aware of what items are likely to be cut by the president. Presidential priorities are reported to Congress through budget submissions and statements of administration policy, which indicate White House opposition to provisions in draft appropriation bills. Similarly, congressional intentions are also provided to the administration, through the OMB, during the budget markup process, and the White House has an opportunity to comment and give feedback to the subcommittees marking up the bill. After appropriations, when the president does propose rescissions, a consistent pattern has been that Congress makes greater cuts than recommended by the president, albeit using a different set of priorities to determine which items will be cut.[82]

Enhanced Rescission and the Line Item Veto Act

After decades of debate, the Republican-controlled Congress enacted the Line Item Veto Act (LIVA) of 1996, which was part of the Contract with America. The act took effect in January 1997, giving President Clinton a tool to use against Congress during the 1997 legislative session. A general consensus exists that "true" item-veto power could be provided to the president only through a constitutional amendment and, therefore, the 1996 law is best viewed as enhanced rescission power. The 1996 law explicitly recognized that many "earmarks" (another name for pork barrel items) are listed not in the legislation itself (an appropriation bill or a tax bill, for example) but in committee reports accompanying those bills. Significantly, then, the LIVA gave the president power to cancel three types of provisions: (1) new items of discretionary spending (found either in appropriation bills or in committee reports accompanying these bills); (2) new entitlements or increased entitlements; and (3) tax provisions that would benefit 100 or fewer individuals or corporations. The president was required to veto an entire item and not just reduce an amount, and he could not veto existing entitlement programs and other forms of mandatory spending. The law had a sunset provision, withdrawing this power from the president on January 1, 2005.[83]

In an effort to circumvent the Supreme Court's ban on legislative vetoes (see the discussion of the *Chadha* decision in the previous chapter on budget approval), the 1996 measure provided a convoluted form of veto. The president was to submit a set of proposed budget cuts. Congress then had 30 calendar days, during a time when it was in session, to consider passing a disapproval bill. If Congress did not act, the proposed vetoes would take effect. The disapproval bill would be on an expedited schedule but would go through the standard procedure of passage in both houses and, most likely, a conference committee procedure for working out the differences between the houses. The president could then either sign or veto the disapproval bill. A veto of the disapproval bill would mean he was standing behind his original set of decisions to cut items in the budget. Congress could override the president's veto only by a two-thirds vote.

The line-item veto was first used by President Clinton to cut three items from the Balanced Budget Act of 1997 and the Taxpayer Relief Act of 1997, just five days after signing these laws. The vetoes covered (1) tax shelters for financial service companies, (2) a Medicaid provision that specifically would benefit New York State and New York City, and (3) a tax benefit that would go to a small number of agribusinesses, including large corporations that in his view did not need such a tax advantage. Clinton noted that many items were protected from his veto on the grounds that the White House had an obligation to act in good faith in retaining items that had been explicitly approved as part of the bargaining process with the Republican-controlled Congress.[84] He agreed with suggestions from the press that the vetoed items were relatively minor but noted that he expected more significant vetoes to arise when appropriation bills began to reach his desk for approval.

President Clinton also used the line-item veto power in the appropriation process. By far the most aggressive use of this power was on the military construction appropriation bill, where he cancelled 38 projects totaling $287 million. Congress used the procedures contained in the act to pass a disapproval bill, which was ultimately vetoed by President Clinton. His veto was overridden by Congress, thereby restoring funding for these projects. Clinton was much more restrained in his use of the veto on other appropriation bills, canceling only $190 million in total budget authority from those other 12 bills.[85]

The Line Item Veto Act included a section for judicial review, allowing for members of Congress and others to file suit in the U.S. District Court for the District of Columbia, with its decision being appealable directly to the Supreme Court. Well before President Clinton had an opportunity to use this new set of powers, the law was challenged in court by Senator Robert C. Byrd (D-WV), who had been the law's most outspoken critic, calling it "a malformed monstrosity."[86] The district court agreed with Byrd that the law had unconstitutionally delegated congressional powers to the president. That decision was appealed to the Supreme Court, which ruled on a procedural rather than substantive basis. In *Raines v. Byrd* (1997), the Court decided that Byrd and others lacked standing, a condition in which the party bringing suit must show that an injury has occurred or is about to occur.[87] The Court found that an injury had not occurred, as the president had not yet exercised the new power granted to him. Standing was said to be especially important in cases involving conflict between two branches of the government, in this case, between Congress and the president.

Ultimately, the constitutionality of the Line Item Veto Act was challenged on its merits by individuals with standing who had suffered injury as a result of its application. In late 1997, two suits were brought: one by the City of New York and the other by the Snake River (Idaho) Potato Growers over Clinton's cancellation of items in the Balanced Budget Act and the Taxpayer Relief Act, respectively. The law was found unconstitutional in U.S. District Court, and in 1998, the Supreme Court, in a 6 to 3 decision, sided with the District Court in the case of *Clinton v. City of New York*.[88] The Court ruled that the act ran afoul of the Presentment Clause of the Constitution because it permitted the president to unilaterally unmake law that had been made by both houses of Congress in concert with the president. The majority argued that providing the president with the kind of power envisioned in the act would require an amendment to the Constitution. Thus, the Line Item Veto Act was relegated to a one-year experiment—a blip on the federal budgeting radar screen.[89]

Subsequently, Presidents Bush and Obama each proposed a reduced form of line-item veto authority through what is referred to as "expedited rescission." Under this proposal, a president would be guaranteed a vote on rescission proposals that he proposed, and individual items would be subjected to an "up-or-down" vote on the Senate or House floor. The presumption is that these items would be subject to greater scrutiny, making it harder for the more egregious pork barrel projects to survive.[90] The House of Representatives passed a version of President Bush's proposal in June 2006.[91] In the 111th Congress, the expedited rescission approach was probably best exemplified by S. 102, sponsored by Senators Carper and McCain. No expedited rescission proposal has come to a vote in either house during the 111th Congress. Thus, as of 2012, the president still lacked any form of line-item veto authority other than the narrow authority to propose rescissions granted by the 1974 law.

Proposed Balanced Budget Requirement

A persistent proposal has been for the federal government to adopt a balanced budget requirement.[92] Proponents typically refer to the successful use of this requirement at the state level—all states except Vermont currently require some form of balanced budget.[93] Note that balanced budget requirements in most states do not preclude borrowing for capital investments, and few state budgets are annually balanced when both current and capital expenditures are taken into account. Many states also have limitations on revenue raising and spending, stemming from the Proposition 13 movement of the 1970s.

A major concern regarding implementation of a balanced budget requirement at the federal level is that the measure might impose unwarranted restrictions in times of economic hardship or national security emergencies.[94] Some form of override mechanism must be included for situations when the federal government needs to spend more to counteract economic recessions and to wage war. For the override to occur, both houses might be required to have votes of 60%, two-thirds, or a majority of all members (rather than a majority of those voting).

Having some set of enforcement mechanisms is regarded as essential for successful implementation, although such mechanisms do not exist at the state level, where the balanced budget process is regarded as generally successful. The states, however, have an externally imposed imperative for bringing revenues and expenditures into structural balance: Failing to do so would have an adverse effect on their bond ratings and borrowing costs.

Skeptics of congressional abilities to reach agreement on a balanced budget fear that Congress would resort to "smoke and mirror" techniques that merely give the illusion of a balanced budget. Such devices might include overestimating revenues to be collected and moving some expenditures off-budget so that they would be excluded from official total spending. These are, of course, precisely the kinds of tricks that resulted under Gramm-Rudman-Hollings, the federal government's prior failed experiment with fixed deficit targets. Attempting to prohibit such practices by outlawing them in the constitutional amendment would be cumbersome, and creative minds might always be able to find loopholes in the amendment's language. In addition, detailed provisions in the amendment could create an inflexibility that later might prove detrimental to the nation's best interests.

Critics of the balanced budget amendment contend that it would unduly enhance the powers of the president. A typical requirement of balanced budget proposals is that the president would have to submit a balanced budget, thereby setting the agenda from which Congress might have little latitude to veer. One line of reasoning states that for the proposal to be effective, a line-item veto for the president would be essential. Another criticism is that an annually balanced budget is not an appropriate goal for federal fiscal policy. The federal government has routinely, and appropriately, engaged in deficit spending during times of recession or when it needed to deal with other emergencies.[95] Furthermore, to the extent that the balanced budget amendment is sought as a means to avoid deficit spending, it seems useful to point out that it is not self-enforcing. The spending cuts and tax increases, and enforcement mechanisms, would still need to be enacted. It is these actions, not the Constitution, that are central to getting control of the nation's debt.[96]

Once the budget moved from deficit to surplus in 1998, the interest in a balanced budget amendment waned. But with the reemergence of budget deficits and the potential search for a new consensus for an overall goal of fiscal policy, members of Congress have begun to propose such an amendment again. As noted above, the Republican majority in the House of Representatives expressed interest in a balanced budget amendment during the 2011 budget debates. Some more conservative House members, particularly those identified with the Tea Party movement, backed a version of the balanced budget amendment that not only would require an annually balanced budget, but also would include a spending limitation (such as 18% of GDP) and a supermajority requirement to raise taxes. Ultimately, the House voted on a more traditional form of the balanced budget amendment in November 2011; it fell 23 votes short of the two-thirds necessary for passage, thus killing the amendment for the time being.

Proposed Congressional Reorganization

A perennial topic of discussion in Congress is how it could better organize itself to fulfill its responsibilities, especially its budget responsibilities. Important changes did occur as a result of passage of the Legislative Reorganization Acts of 1946 and 1970 as well as other reorganizations that affected either the House or the Senate.[97]

Committees

One typical proposal is to reduce the number of congressional committees and subcommittees. These various bodies create problems in coordination, because their domains often overlap and subject areas are needlessly segmented among committees and subcommittees. Power becomes diffuse, and setting overall policy is complicated by the split jurisdictions. The greater the number of committees, the greater the number of committee assignments members have, meaning that they can easily be scheduled to attend two or more committee meetings at the same time. This problem is even more acute in the Senate, where 100 members must handle the same work that is done by the 435 members in the House.

The large number of committees and subcommittees poses problems for the executive branch as well as for Congress. Agency administrators complain that valuable time is wasted in having to prepare for and testify before these panels. The defense area is particularly subject to comprehensive congressional involvement, with Defense Department officials having to testify before dozens of committees and subcommittees.

The size of committee membership is a related concern. Memberships are often large because members want to be placed on committees of relevance to their home districts and states. However, the larger the committee size, the greater the number of committees on which members serve and the greater the number of meetings they are unable to attend. The result is a proxy system in which another member, often the chair, casts votes for absent members on the committee.

Although considerable agreement may exist that Congress needs to reduce the number of committees and subcommittees, the task is difficult. Chairing one of these committees provides power, prestige, and perquisites, so any chairperson or other senior member on the committee is likely to defend continuance of the committee and repel efforts to diminish the committee's powers.[98] Members in both houses have historically sought seats on committees dealing with the various aspects of the budget as a means of gaining power over congressional actions.

One controversial suggestion has been that the budget process could be streamlined by eliminating the two Appropriations Committees and assigning their duties to the committees that handle authorizations. Rather than appropriation bills emanating from one committee, they would arise from the standing substantive committees in each chamber. Critics of this proposal contend that such a reform would worsen the budget situation, because the Appropriations Committees are far more likely to restrict government spending than the substantive committees, which are often seen as having been captured by the executive branch agencies that they oversee. Furthermore, the Appropriations Committees currently wield great power, and they vigorously oppose any efforts to reduce that power. They would not be abolished without a fight.

Other committee-related proposals involve reconfiguring the House and Senate Budget Committees (possibly even merging them into a joint committee) or making them into leadership committees by including chairs and other ranking members on the budget committees. The assumption behind this proposal is that including the leadership would provide greater incentives for the budget resolution to be enacted, and for other committees to make a more good-faith effort to comply with its strictures.[99] Some still argue that these committees should be eliminated on the grounds that they have merely added to the complexity of congressional budgeting, and have recently failed to accomplish their major objective in any event.[100]

Biennial Budgeting

One frequently mentioned proposal is to change over to a biennial budget.[101] Since Congress has such difficulty acting on a budget, why not simplify the problem by requiring action only every other year? The idea of moving the federal government from an annual to a biennial process is not a new one. Representative Leon Panetta (D-CA) introduced the first bill proposing such a change in 1977, and the proposal has been more or less an annual entry in the budget reform sweepstakes since then. Most biennial budgeting proposals would have the president submit the budget biennially and would also feature biennial budget resolutions and appropriations.

Perhaps the high-water mark for biennial budgeting came in 1993, when both the Joint Committee on the Organization of Congress and Vice President Gore's National Performance Review recommended that the federal government adopt a biennial timetable for the process. Most recently, biennial budgeting was the key proposed reform that the Senate Budget Committee recommended to the Joint Select Committee on Deficit Reduction, after holding hearings in the fall of 2011.[102] When the supercommittee died, so did this proposal. Despite this long history of support, in fact, no bill to create a biennial process has ever passed either the House or the Senate.

Proponents of biennial budgeting argue that the current annual process features repetitive votes on many fiscal issues that eat up valuable committee and floor time. For example, there may be three votes on the budget for defense: one associated with the budget resolution, one associated with the annual defense authorization bill, and one on the annual defense appropriation bill. Second, in a related issue, supporters note that time spent on budgeting cannot be spent on other activities, particularly detailed oversight of federal programs. In particular, these advocates of a biennial process indicate that the need for Congress to review agency performance under the Government Performance and Results Act necessitates spending more time on such detailed oversight. Third, supporters point to the dismal record of Congress and the president in enacting annual appropriation bills prior to the start of each fiscal year. Finally, executive branch officials decry the time-consuming nature of the annual process from their perspective. The sequence of developing an agency budget request, having that budget undergo review by the Office of Management and Budget and the president, and justifying the budget to Congress is continuous in an annual process.[103]

There are also numerous arguments offered by skeptics of biennial budgeting. First, the federal government has a rather checkered history of budget forecasting. Producing a budget every two years would increase the probability that budgets would be based on erroneous information. A two-year budget resolution adopted in April, for example, would be adopted a full 30 months before the end of the second fiscal year of the biennium. The agencies would have begun developing their budgets for that fiscal year at least 10 months prior to the passage of the budget resolution, or more than three years from the end of the second fiscal year of the biennium. Second, opponents argue that the benefits of biennial budgeting (decreased time on budgeting, more time for oversight) are overstated. The biennial process may degenerate into an annual process, given the uncertainties associated with budgeting for an almost $4 trillion enterprise (Congress already engages in an annual process of adopting supplemental appropriations) and the likelihood that Appropriations Committee members will want to act on the budget every year. Third, an increase in oversight under biennial budgeting would occur only if the current lack of oversight results from a lack of time. Opponents argue that even if members of Congress had more time to do oversight, they would not be likely to do more of it simply because they do not have any incentives to do so. Understanding more about how federal programs work in great detail is not politically sexy, nor does it offer any specific benefits in terms of helping members get reelected.[104]

Other Proposed Revisions in the Budget Process

While the previously mentioned changes have been the most frequently debated, they are by no means the only reform proposals put forth. One set of reforms proposes to include more performance information in the budget process. Another reform hopes to bring more accrual accounting concepts to the federal government. At least four other reforms are also worthy of discussion—automatic continuing resolutions, making the budget resolution into a joint resolution, capital budgeting, and sunset provisions for federal programs.

Automatic Continuing Resolutions

Under this proposed reform, the institution of automatic continuing resolutions for appropriations would become another possible strategy. If Congress failed to pass an appropriation bill, the agencies affected would operate with a continuing appropriation without Congress having to act. Since congressional failure to act on the budget in a timely fashion has become the norm, the obvious advantage of an automatic continuing resolution is that it would eliminate the crisis handling of appropriation bills. The disadvantage of the proposal is that incentives for Congress to adopt regular appropriation bills would be reduced.[105]

Joint Budget Resolutions

A more far-reaching proposal would eliminate the concurrent nature of budget resolutions, which do not require presidential signature, and substitute a joint resolution or law to be signed by the president.[106] In effect, budget summitry would be employed at the outset of the budget process. The hope is that the president and key congressional leaders would develop an annual budget resolution that all would support, thereby helping to ensure more timely action as the details of the budget are worked out at a later time. Budget summits bind all participants so that a president who endorsed a summit agreement could not later renege when Congress passed appropriation bills in conformance with the agreement. The downside of a joint budget resolution is that conflict would be "front loaded." Obtaining the agreement of both houses without having the president involved has often proved difficult. Allowing the president to have a veto over the budget resolution might be the practical equivalent of ensuring that no budget resolution will occur in many years.[107]

Capital Budgeting

Adoption of a capital budgeting system is yet another possibility. It is advocated as a way of helping to put the deficit into perspective, because it would show that much of federal spending is of an investment nature and not simply annual consumption. However, the federal budget has very little investment in it, if one excludes major defense systems and intergovernmental transfers to state and local governments for infrastructure (see the chapter on capital assets and capital budgeting for a discussion of the pros and cons of capital budgeting). Capital budgeting presumably would encourage better planning of expenditures. On the negative side, capital budgets could be used to downplay the true magnitude of federal budget deficits and total debt. More and more of the budget could be "capitalized" as a method of making desired spending appear to be less costly. Furthermore, if a balanced budget constitutional amendment were adopted, Congress most likely would move capital expenditures off-budget, just as states permit indebtedness for investments but not for operating expenses.[108]

Sunset Provisions

Proposals for zero-base budgeting were justified in large part by the incremental nature of the budget process, and programs, once created, tend to live forever. A relative of zero-base budgeting is sunset review, which puts government programs on a set timetable for review and possible abolition. Under some proposals, commissions would be established, similar to the base closing commissions of the 1990s, to review specified federal programs and recommend possible reorganization, expansion, or abolition. In 2010, Representative Darrell Issa (R-CA) proposed that a group of independent experts be appointed to review federal programs and make recommendations concerning which ones should be reformed or eliminated.[109] While supporters of the sunset approach trumpet it as being able to root out inefficient and ineffective programs, skeptics wonder whether the commissions would be susceptible to politicization.[110]

SUMMARY

Congress has an elaborate system for approving the budget. An authorization process exists independently of appropriations. Meanwhile, the House Ways and Means Committee and the Senate Finance Committee have power to deal not only with tax measures but also with much entitlement spending. The Appropriations Committees in the two houses operate by developing a series of bills through subcommittees.

The current budget process resulted from two main laws. The Budget and Accounting Act of 1921 prescribes the executive budget process. The Congressional Budget and Impoundment Control Act of 1974 attempted to deal with several problems, including congressional tardiness in adopting the budget, impoundments, and piecemeal handling of the budget. A budget resolution process, Budget Committees, and the Congressional Budget Office were established. Two other laws were passed in the 1980s and 1990s in an attempt to control the deficit. The Gramm-Rudman-Hollings law was a failed attempt to bring the deficit under control. Later efforts that coupled "budget summits" with a new change in process, codified in the Budget Enforcement Act, have proved much more successful. Both of these laws, however, were allowed to expire by 2002.

The resulting budget process has several stages. First, the president submits his budget on or before the first Monday in February. Congress then adopts a budget resolution that establishes a blueprint for the budget. Committee action follows the constraints established by the budget resolution. In some years, reconciliation bills, which make changes to government revenue and entitlement legislation, are enacted. In each year, much of the budget process focuses on the fate of the regular appropriation bills.

During the presidency of Bill Clinton, the budget finally moved from deficit into surplus. The improvement in the budget outlook resulted from a series of legislative actions coupled with the continued strong growth of the economy (fueling an increase in federal revenues). Fiscal year 1998 was the first year since 1969 that the federal government had a budget surplus. These surpluses lasted through fiscal year 2001, but in 2002 a combination of a tax cut advocated by President George W. Bush, a weakening of the economy, and the aftereffects of the terrorist attacks of September 11, 2001, signaled the return of deficits. These deficits, while large, paled in comparison to those that resulted after the recession that began in 2007. These deficits are projected to increase for the immediate future, and the long-term prospects for the federal budget are not good, largely because of the outlook for the major entitlement programs—Social Security, Medicare, and Medicaid. During 2011, President Obama and the Republican Congress found it difficult to agree on policy changes affecting the budget, and this almost resulted in the federal government becoming insolvent. The Budget Control Act, enacted in August 2011, promised at least a down payment on debt reduction. Failure to enact the required level of deficit reduction was to result in across-the-board reductions in many federal programs. Numerous proposals exist for further revising how the federal government adopts the budget. Major proposals include giving line-item veto power to the president, passing a constitutional amendment requiring that the budget be balanced, restructuring congressional committees, and moving the government to a biennial budget cycle. Other proposals involve establishing automatic continuing resolutions, changing the concurrent budget resolution to a joint resolution or law, separating the budget into capital and operating components, and creating a sunset review for federal programs.

NOTES

1. Tompkin, S. (1998). *Inside OMB: politics and process in the President's budget office.* Armonk, NY: M. E. Sharpe.
2. Hughes, J. (1998). General Accounting Office. In J. M. Shafritz (Ed.), *International encyclopedia of public policy and administration* (pp. 969–972). Boulder, CO: Westview Press.
3. Fisher, L. (1987). *The politics of shared power: Congress and the executive* (2nd ed., pp. 91–217). Washington, DC: Congressional Quarterly Press; Schick, A. (2000). *The federal budget: politics, policy, process* (2nd ed., pp. 105–240). Washington, DC: Brookings Institution.
4. Manley, J. (1970). *The politics of finance: the House Committee on Ways and Means.* Boston, MA: Little, Brown.
5. Fenno, R., Jr. (1966). *The power of the purse: appropriations politics in Congress.* Boston, MA: Little, Brown; Shuman, H. (1992). *Politics and the budget: the struggle between the president and the Congress* (3rd ed.). Englewood Cliffs, NJ: Prentice-Hall; Wildavsky, A., & Caiden, N. (2000). *The new politics of the budgetary process* (4th ed.). New York, NY: Longman.
6. Legislative Reorganization Act of 1946. Ch. 753.
7. Senate Committee on Government Operations, *Improving congressional control of the budget: hearings* (Part 2, 93rd Cong., 1st sess., pp. 237–239). Washington, DC: U.S. Government Printing Office.
8. Wallace, R. (1959). Congressional control of the budget. *Midwest Journal of Political Science, 3,* 151–167.
9. Kim, S. (1968). The politics of a congressional budgetary process: "backdoor spending." *Western Political Quarterly, 21,* 606–623; Schick, A. (1973). Backdoor spending authority in Senate Committee on Government Operations, *Improving congressional control over the budget: a compendium of materials* (93rd Cong., 1st sess., pp. 293–302). Washington, DC: U.S. Government Printing Office.
10. Schick, A. (1980). *Congress and money.* Washington, DC: The Urban Institute Press.
11. Congressional Budget and Impoundment Control Act of 1974 (P.L. 93–344).

12. Fisher, L. (1985). Ten years of the Budget Act: still searching for controls. *Public Budgeting & Finance, 5*, Fall, 3–28.
13. Schick, A. (2007). *The federal budget*; Joyce, P., & Reischauer, R. (1992). Deficit budgeting: the federal budget process and budget reform. *Harvard Journal on Legislation, 29*, 429–453.
14. Joyce, P. (2011). *The Congressional Budget Office: honest numbers, power and policymaking.* Washington, DC: Georgetown University Press.
15. Crippen, D. (2002). *Informing legislators about the budget: the history and role of the U.S. Congressional Budget Office.* Speech to parliamentary officials of the OECD, Washington, DC, June 7.
16. Fisher, L. (1970). The politics of impounded funds. *Administrative Science Quarterly, 15*, 361–377.
17. Anti-Deficiency Act of 1950. Ch. 510, §3, 34 Stat. 49.
18. Joyce, P. (1996). Congressional budget reform: the unanticipated implications for federal policy making. *Public Administration Review, 56*, 317–325.
19. Economic Recovery Tax Act of 1981 (P.L. 97-34).
20. Johnson, B. (1984). From analyst to negotiator: the OMB's new role. *Journal of Policy Analysis and Management, 3*, 501–515; Johnson, B. (1989). The OMB budget examiner and the congressional budget process. *Public Budgeting & Finance, 9*, Spring, 5–14; Tompkin, S. (1998). *Inside OMB.*
21. Stockman, D. (1986). *The triumph of politics: how the Reagan revolution failed.* New York, NY: Harper & Row.
22. LeLoup, L., & Hancock, J. (1988). Congress and the Reagan budgets. *Public Budgeting & Finance, 8*, Fall, 30–54.
23. A plea from David Stockman. (1983). *Washington Post*, April 20, A20.
24. Ippolito, D. (1990). *Uncertain legacies: federal budget policy from Roosevelt through Reagan.* Charlottesville, VA: University Press of Virginia.
25. Doyle, R. (1996). Congress, the deficit, and budget reconciliation. *Public Budgeting & Finance, 16*, Winter, 59–81.
26. Balanced Budget and Emergency Deficit Control Act of 1985 (P.L. 99-177), Title II; Havens, H. (1986). Gramm-Rudman-Hollings: origins and implementation. *Public Budgeting & Finance, 6*, Fall, 4–24; LeLoup, L., et al. (1987). Deficit politics and constitutional government: the impact of Gramm-Rudman-Hollings. *Public Budgeting & Finance, 7*, Spring, 83–103.
27. Rudman, W., as quoted in Wehr, E. (1985). Congress enacts far-reaching budget measure. *Congressional Quarterly Weekly Report, 43*, 2604.
28. *Bowsher v. Synar* (1986). 478 U.S. 714; Symposium: *Bowsher v. Synar* (1987). *Cornell Law Review, 72*, 421–597.
29. Balanced Budget and Emergency Deficit Control Reaffirmation Act of 1987 (P.L. 100-119), Title I.
30. Metz, T., et al. (1987). Stocks plunge 508 amid panicky selling. *Wall Street Journal*, October 20, 1.
31. Schier, S. (1992). *A decade of deficits: congressional thought and fiscal action.* Albany, NY: State University of New York Press; Thelwell, R. (1990). Gramm-Rudman-Hollings four years later. *Public Administration Review, 50*, 190–198.
32. U.S. Congressional Budget Office (1993). *The economic and budget outlook: fiscal years 1994–1998* (p. 85). Washington, DC: U.S. Government Printing Office.
33. The Budget Enforcement Act was a component of the Omnibus Budget Reconciliation Act of 1990 (P.L. 101-508); Joyce, P., & Reischauer, R. (1992). *Deficit budgeting.*
34. U.S. Congressional Budget Office (2011). *The budget and economic outlook: fiscal years 2012–2021.* Washington, DC: U.S. Government Printing Office.
35. Schick, A. (2007). *The federal budget.*
36. Lynch, M. (2011). *The deeming resolution: a budget enforcement tool* (June 9, pp. 4–5). Washington, DC: Congressional Research Service.
37. Doyle, R. (1996). *Congress, the deficit, and budget reconciliation.*
38. Dauster, W. (1998). The monster that ate the United States Senate. *Public Budgeting & Finance, 18*, Summer, 87–93.
39. Collender, S. (2001). Repeated reconciliation. *Government Executive.* Retrieved January 10, 2001, from http://www.govexec.com/dailyfed/0101/011001bb.htm.

40. U.S. Senate, Committee on the Budget, Republican Staff (2005). *Informed Budgeteer*. September. Retrieved March 17, 2012 from http://budget.senate.gov/republican/public/index.cfm/2005/9/issue-5-hurricane-katrina-the-byrd-rule.

41. U.S. Congressional Budget Office (2010). *Unauthorized appropriations and expiring authorizations* (p. 2). Washington, DC: U.S. Government Printing Office.

42. Lilly, S. (2005). Does rearranging appropriations panels make any sense? *Roll Call*, January 27.

43. Streeter, S. (2006). *Continuing appropriations acts: brief overview of recent practices* (p. 6). Washington, DC: Congressional Research Service.

44. Dennis, S., & Higa, L. (2006). Conservatives frustrated in earmarks crusade. *CQ Today*, June 14. Retrieved August 30, 2006, from http://oncongress.cq.com.

45. U.S. Congressional Budget Office (1990). *The 1990 budget agreement: an interim assessment*. Washington, DC: U.S. Government Printing Office; U.S. Congressional Budget Office (1992). *The economic and budget outlook: fiscal years 1993–1997*. Washington, DC: U.S. Government Printing Office.

46. Woodward, B. (1994). *The agenda: inside the Clinton White House*. New York, NY: Simon and Schuster.

47. Woodward, B. (1994). *The agenda: inside the Clinton White House*.

48. Omnibus Budget Reconciliation Act of 1993 (P.L. 103-66).

49. Oak, D. (1995). An overview of adjustments to the Budget Enforcement Act discretionary spending caps. *Public Budgeting & Finance, 15*, Fall, 35–53.

50. Bader, J. (1996). *Taking the initiative: leadership agendas in Congress and the "Contract with America."* Washington, DC: Georgetown University Press; Gimpel, J. (1996). *Legislating the revolution: the Contract with America in its first 100 days*. Boston, MA: Allyn and Bacon.

51. Joyce, P., & Meyers, R. (2001). Budgeting during the Clinton presidency. *Public Budgeting & Finance, 21*, Spring, 1–21.

52. Meyers, R. (1997). Late appropriations and government shutdowns: frequency, causes, consequences, and remedies. *Public Budgeting and Finance, 17*, Fall, 25–38.

53. Joyce, P., & Meyers, R. (2001). Budgeting during the Clinton presidency. *Public Budgeting & Finance, 21*, Spring, 1–21.

54. Shear, J. (1996). The tale of the dogs. *National Journal, 28*, 18–22.

55. Hager, G. (1997). Clinton, GOP Congress strike historic budget agreement. *Congressional Quarterly Weekly Report, 56*, 993, 996–997.

56. Balanced Budget Act of 1997 (P.L. 105-33) and Taxpayer Relief Act of 1997 (P.L. 105-34).

57. U.S. Congressional Budget Office (2001). *The budget and economic outlook: fiscal years 2003–2012* (p. 158). Washington, DC: U.S. Government Printing Office.

58. U.S. Congressional Budget Office (2011). *The budget and economic outlook: fiscal years 2012–2021*, 133.

59. U.S. Congressional Budget Office (2001). *The budget and economic outlook: fiscal years 2003–2012*, xiv; U.S. Office of Management and Budget (2001). *A blueprint for new beginnings* (p. 11). Washington, DC: U.S. Government Printing Office.

60. Economic Growth and Tax Relief Reconciliation Act of 2001 (P.L. 107-16).

61. Berry, J. (2001). Greenspan supports a tax cut. *Washington Post*, January 26, A1.

62. Nitschke, L., & Boudreau, W. (2001). Provisions of the tax law. *Congressional Quarterly Weekly Report, 59*, June 9, 1390.

63. U.S. Congressional Budget Office (2007). *The budget and economic outlook: fiscal years 2012–2021: an update* (p. 26). Washington, DC: U.S. Government Printing Office.

64. For an early take on the reasons for this deterioration, see Gale, W., & Orszag, P. (2003). Fiscal follies: the real budget problem and how to fix it. *The Brookings Review, 21*, 7–11.

65. U.S. Congressional Budget Office (2011). *The budget and economic outlook: fiscal years 2012–2021*, 7.

66. U.S. Congressional Budget Office (2011). *The budget and economic outlook: fiscal years 2012–2021*, 136.

67. Congressional Budget Office (2011). *Report on the Troubled Asset Relief Program*, March, 4.

68. Stolberg, S. G. (2009). Signing stimulus, Obama doesn't rule out more. *New York Times*, February 18.

69. Lucas, D. (2011). *The budgetary cost of Fannie Mae and Freddie Mac and options for the future federal role in the secondary mortgage market*. Statement before the Committee on the Budget, U.S. House of Representatives, June 2, 7.

70. U.S. Congressional Budget Office (2011). *The budget and economic outlook: fiscal years 2012–2021: an update*, xi.

71. U.S. Congressional Budget Office (2012). *The budget and economic outlook: fiscal years 2013–2022*, xii–xiv.

72. Calmes, J. (2010). Fiscal plan is expected to fall short of votes. *New York Times*, December 2; Calmes, J. (2010). Obama offers hope for debt panel's plan. *New York Times*, December 3.

73. Peterson-Pew Commission on Budget Reform (2010). *Getting back in the black*, November 10. Retrieved March 4, 2012, from http://budgetreform.org/document/getting-back-black.

74. Congressional Budget Office (2011). *Estimated impact of automatic budget enforcement procedures specified in the Budget Control Act*, September 12. Retrieved March 4, 2012, from http://cbo.gov/publication/42754.

75. U.S. Congressional Budget Office (2011). *CBO's 2011 long-term budget outlook*, June. Washington, DC: U.S. Government Printing Office.

76. Meyers, R., & Joyce, P. (2005). Congressional budgeting at age 30: Is it worth saving? *Public Budgeting & Finance, 26*, Special Issue, 68–82.

77. U.S. Congressional Budget Office (2002). *The looming budgetary impact of society's aging*. Washington, DC: U.S. Government Printing Office.

78. Rieselbach, L. (1993). *Congressional reform: the changing modern Congress*. Washington, DC: Congressional Quarterly Press.

79. Sinclair, B. (1995). *Legislators, leaders and lawmaking: the U.S. House of Representatives in the post-reform era*. Baltimore, MD: Johns Hopkins University Press.

80. Gryski, G. S. (1991). The influence of committee position on federal program spending. *Polity, 23*, 443–459.

81. U.S. General Accounting Office (1992). *Line item veto: estimating potential savings*. Washington, DC: U.S. Government Printing Office.

82. Letter from Anthony H. Gamboa to The Honorable Thad Cochran and the Honorable Robert C. Byrd (2005). *Updated rescission statistics, fiscal years 1974–2005*. Washington, DC: U.S. Government Accountability Office.

83. Line Item Veto Act of 1996 (P.L. 104-130); Joyce, P., & Reischauer, R. (1997). The federal line-item veto: what is it and what will it do? *Public Administration Review, 57*, 95–104.

84. Clinton, W. J. (1997). *Remarks by the president on the line item veto*. August 11. Retrieved December 11, 1997, from http://www.whitehouse.gov.

85. Joyce, P. (1998). The line-item veto experiment: after the Supreme Court ruling, what's next? *Public Budgeting & Finance, 18*, Winter, 3–22.

86. Byrd, R., as quoted in Taylor, A. (1996). Congress hands president a budgetary scalpel. *Congressional Quarterly Weekly Report, 54*, 866.

87. *Byrd v. Raines* (1997). 6 LW 2660 (DDC); *Raines v. Byrd* (1997). 521 U.S. 811 (1997).

88. *Clinton v. City of New York* (1998). 524 U.S. 417.

89. Joyce, P. (1998). The line-item veto experiment.

90. *Statement of Donald B. Marron before the United States Senate Committee on the Budget*, May 2, 2006.

91. A veto in the Senate? (2006). *Wall Street Journal*, July 28, A14.

92. Hager, G. (1997). Country comes full circle on balancing the budget. *Congressional Quarterly Weekly Report, 55*, 278–285.

93. Hou, Y., & Smith, D. L. (2006). A framework for understanding state balanced budget requirements systems: re-examining distinctive features and an operational definition. *Public Budgeting & Finance, 26*, Fall, 22–45.

94. Kiefer, D. W., et al. (1992). *A balanced budget constitutional amendment: economic issues*. Washington, DC: Congressional Research Service.

95. U.S. Congressional Budget Office (1993). *The economic and budget outlook: fiscal years 1994–1998*.

96. Joyce, P. (2011). Testimony before the Judiciary Committee, U.S. House of Representatives, October 5.

97. Legislative Reorganization Act of 1946. Ch. 753; Legislative Reorganization Act of 1970 (P.L. 91-510).

98. Shear, J. (1996). Power loss. *National Journal, 28*, 874–878.
99. Joyce, P. (2011). *Strengthening the budget committees*, January. Washington, DC: Pew Charitable Trusts.
100. Fisher, L. (1990). Federal budget doldrums: the vacuum in presidential leadership. *Public Administration Review, 50*, November/December.
101. Meyers, R. (1988). Biennial budgeting in the U.S. Congress. *Public Budgeting & Finance, 8*, Summer, 21–32.
102. Letter from Budget Committee Chairman Kent Conrad and Ranking Member Jeff Sessions (2011) to Senator Patty Murray and Representative Jeb Henserling of the Joint Select Committee on Deficit Reduction, October 14.
103. Joyce, P. (2000). Testimony before the Subcommittee on Legislative and Budget Process, Committee on Rules, United States House of Representatives, *Biennial budgeting: a tool for improving government fiscal management and oversight*, March 20, 268–274.
104. Joyce, P. (2000). Testimony before Subcommittee on Legislative and Budget Process.
105. H.R. 853, Comprehensive Budget Process Reform Act, Reported in House August 1999.
106. Meyers, R. (1990). The budget resolution should be a law. *Public Budgeting & Finance, 10*, Fall, 103–112; Meyers, R. (1994). *Strategic budgeting*. Ann Arbor, MI: University of Michigan Press.
107. Fulton, A. (2000). Budget reform bill faces opposition in House. *Congress Daily*, May 16.
108. U.S. General Accounting Office (1998). *Budget issues: budgeting for capital*. Washington, DC: U.S. Government Printing Office.
109. Brodsky, R. (2010). Issa calls for federal program sunset commission. *Government Executive*, October 14. Retrieved March 4, 2012, from http://www.govexec.com/oversight/2010/10/issa-calls-for-federal-program-sunset-commission/32548.
110. Mandel, J. (2006). Panel debates competing bills to "sunset" federal programs. *Government Executive*, July 19. Retrieved August 2, 2006, from http://www.govexec.com/dailyfed/0706/071906m2.htm.

Budget Execution

Once the budget has been approved, the execution phase of the budget cycle begins. Budget execution is, in one sense, just management by another name. It involves hiring and managing people, procuring capital and other resources that can be used to produce the outcomes of the organization, collecting revenues, and carrying out other activities. As there is a voluminous management literature, the focus of this chapter is on those parts of management that are most closely related to budgeting. The first section of the chapter deals with interactions between the central budget office and the line agencies. Then, four subsystems of the execution phase are discussed—tax administration, cash management, procurement, and risk management.

BUDGET OFFICE AND AGENCY RELATIONS

As would be expected, relationships—both direct and indirect—are extensive between the central budget office and the line agencies during the execution phase of the budget. These relationships involve interactions that relate directly to carrying out revenue and spending plans, but also coordinating activities that are less directly related to the overall budget, such as the organization of the government, its day-to-day management, information technology resources, and regulatory control.

Interactions on Budgeting

Every budget either explicitly or implicitly contains plans for the work to be done and the achievements to be made. Execution involves converting those plans into operations. During this phase, budget office personnel gain important insights into the operations of agencies, and this knowledge later becomes important for the next round of budget preparation.[1]

Legislative Intent

The legislature provides some indication of legislative intent through a variety of mechanisms, some legally binding and some advisory. Legislative intent is what the legislators had in mind when creating and funding programs. Legislative intent begins with the creation of a governmental unit and programs for it to administer. For example, a state legislature will have created an organization to deliver special education and one or more programs for that unit to administer. Besides these provisions are a host of other legal requirements pertaining to legislative intent. At the federal level, the Government Accountability Office has a manual known as the "Red Book" that discusses these requirements.[2]

Agencies prefer as much flexibility as they can get in budget execution, such as would occur with *lump-sum* appropriations, meaning monies that are in one overall pot and not broken into smaller ones. The more the budget is focused on detailed line items, the less flexibility the agency will have to spend money as it sees fit.

The legislative intent contained in legislation is by definition legally binding during budget execution, but beyond this is a further gray area of legislative intent. Bills reported out of legislative committee are accompanied by committee reports that explain what provisions were considered and why the committees are recommending specific provisions. These reports can run to hundreds of pages in length. In addition, the legislative history of a bill will include statements by legislators specifying how money is intended to be spent. There may be a separate explanatory report prepared after passage of the bill.

Except for two critical factors, statements contained in committee reports, statements made on the floor of the legislature, and statements made in reports subsequent to passage of bills are not legally binding on agencies—but woe to the agency that ignores these sources of information on legislative intent.

First, these statements have the effect of putting the budget office and the affected agencies on notice of what is expected in the implementation of the laws. To ignore these informal provisions, an agency runs the risk of raising the ire of legislators, people who may have the power to cut their budgets next year or to hamstring them with specific provisions in law.

The second factor involves legal challenges. Some laws and how they are administered are challenged in court by private citizens, state and local governments, interest groups, and even legislators themselves. Courts, in deciding legislative intent, first turn to the statutes involved and use a "plain language" interpretation. In other words, how does the law read using standard usage of the English language? If ambiguities remain, then courts turn to the unofficial forms of legislative intent—namely, committee reports before passage, floor debates, and committee reports after passage.

Both legislators and executives realize that legislative language needs to be worded somewhat generally so as to provide flexibility over time. Bills often cover multiple years. As time passes, executive agencies need flexibility to adapt to changes in their environments and therefore need flexibility in the laws under which they operate. This flexibility, then, creates an opening for further decision making at the onset of the new fiscal year. Once an agency's appropriation is passed by the legislature, the agency is not simply in the position of routinely commencing administration with its new funding.

Apportionments and Allotments

At the state and federal levels, an apportionment process is used in which line agencies submit plans to the central budget office for how appropriated funds will be used. The plans often indicate proposed expenditures for each month or quarter of the fiscal year.

Office of Management and Budget (OMB) Circular A-11 governs this process at the federal level. According to OMB, "Apportionment means a distribution made by OMB of amounts available for obligation in an appropriation or fund account into amounts available for specified time periods, program[s], activities, projects, objects, or any combination of these. The apportionment amount limits the obligations that may be incurred."[3]

A primary purpose of apportionment is to ensure that agencies spend at a rate that will keep them within limits imposed by their annual appropriations. A further purpose, especially at the state and local levels, may be to attempt to match spending with inflows of revenues—in other words, to promote positive cash flow. Another purpose is to guide agencies so that the desired program accomplishments are achieved. As A-11 indicates, "Apportionments may be further subdivided by an agency into allotments, suballotments, and allocations."[4] The apportionment plan, therefore, should seemingly be linked closely with performance plans, although that is not always the case. Agencies should be required to defend their proposed apportionment plans in terms of the work that they expect to accomplish over the course of the fiscal year. A third purpose may be to guide agencies in using resources efficiently. At the federal level, agencies use Standard Form 132 to submit their apportionment plans; OMB then approves, modifies, or disapproves. Spending cannot begin until approval is granted.[5]

In the apportionment process, chief executives and their budget offices have greater power to deny authority than to grant authority to agencies. The executive cannot approve apportionments for projects prohibited in the appropriation but may be able to reduce or eliminate some appropriated items. As noted in the previous chapter, presidents have impounded appropriated funds. Another executive means of denying spending authority is to exercise the line-item veto. That is common among the states and is also used in some local governments.

Initial Planning

At the outset of the fiscal year, agencies must accommodate differences between the actual appropriations and the original requests for funding. In addition, some substantive changes may be specified in the appropriations, or an informal understanding may have developed between an agency and legislators over how a program will be redirected.

For agencies that were fortunate enough to obtain increased funds for improving or expanding existing programs or for new programs, the budget office plays a key role. Mindful that the legislature will expect a detailed reporting of how these funds were used, the budget office exercises oversight in implementing the program revisions or new programs.

Control of Agencies

From the perspective of the central administration, agencies must live within their budgets. Otherwise, the budget process becomes an empty exercise. Therefore, various controls are imposed upon agencies, including the *preaudit*. After approval of an apportionment plan and granting an allotment, an agency still is not free to spend at will but rather must submit a request to obligate the government to spend resources. The request is matched against the unit's budget to determine whether the proposed expenditure is authorized and whether sufficient funds are available in the agency's budget.

Several different units may carry out the preaudit function. Not only the budget office, but also an accounting department, may be involved. At the state and local levels, independent comptrollers, controllers, treasurers, or auditors general often have preaudit responsibilities. These officials have the duty of providing another, presumably independent, check on financial transactions.

In the case of an agency proposing to hire new staff, not only will the usual preaudit procedure be used, but a central personnel office also may review the request. Such a review, known as *personnel complement control*, is used in part to avoid increasing personnel commitments and corresponding increases in budget requirements over what has been appropriated.

Midyear Changes

As the year progresses, the budget office conducts reviews of agency operations. One all-too-common problem is that the need or demand for services far exceeds the funds appropriated. Such conditions may be known at the outset of the fiscal year, with allotment plans being used in effect to ration services across the year. In other situations, the need or demand may rise unexpectedly and sharply during the year. In other cases, service demands may be as expected, but the cost of meeting those demands may change, as would occur for a state police department if gasoline prices increased suddenly. Any of these situations may prompt a request for a supplemental appropriation from the legislative branch. In other circumstances, the budget office will work with agencies to stay within funding limits.

Many governments track and report on revenues and spending throughout the year. At the federal level, each summer the Office of Management and Budget issues the *Mid-Session Review of the Budget*, which discusses economic trends and the ways in which these trends are affecting receipts, spending patterns, the activities of credit programs, and whatever other procedures are in place to attempt to limit the budget deficit. The Congressional Budget Office (CBO) issues monthly budget reviews and then in mid-summer updates its *Budget and Economic Outlook*. These reports cover some of the same ground as the OMB mid-session document. The Treasury Department issues a *Monthly Treasury Statement of Receipts and Outlays of the U.S. Government*, which is another tool for tracking government finances during budget execution.

Midyear crises may arise because of an unfavorable revenue situation. Government budgets that depend heavily on a single commodity export, like Venezuela's budget, which relies on oil, may experience significant fluctuation during the year as the world price of the commodity fluctuates. In the United States, a downturn in a state's economy can have devastating effects on sales tax and income tax receipts, forcing (because of balanced budget requirements) across-the-board cutbacks in spending, as happened in the recession that began in 2007. Because personnel costs are usually the largest single item in operating budgets, these costs must be curtailed when revenues fall below projected levels. Personnel hiring freezes are common in government. Another, more extreme, technique is to furlough employees, resulting in less pay but also less work. Depending on the chief executives' authority, they may be able to cut back on agency spending to bring outgo in line with income, or they may need approval from the legislature to take such action.

After the onset of the recession in 2007, and continuing to this writing in many cases, state and local governments found themselves in the position of needing to cut budgets in midyear. While the need to make these cutbacks, and the size of them, was moderated somewhat by the provision of the federal economic stimulus in 2009, many local governments, and most states, nonetheless found themselves in a budget-cutting stance between fiscal years 2009 and 2011. An analysis by the National Association of State Budget Officers illustrates that there were many different strategies used by states to weather this fiscal crisis. These included layoffs, furloughs, across-the-board reductions, and eliminating specific programs. In all, 43 states reduced their budgets in midyear during fiscal year 2009, 39 states did so during fiscal year 2010, and 23 did so during fiscal year 2011.[6] While some states began to find themselves in a stronger fiscal position beginning in fiscal year 2012, other states still were in a budget-cutting mode.

When more resources are needed in midyear, this frequently results in the provision of supplemental appropriations. At the state and local levels, balanced budget norms usually require the provision of supplemental funding to be offset by some reduction in another part of the budget. At the federal level, response to some natural disaster or national security emergency is less likely to be offset by other reductions. For example, the Bush administration funded the wars in Iraq and Afghanistan almost entirely through supplementals. The administration took the position that even though it was known that vast sums would be needed in these endeavors, the specific needs could not be forecast at regular budget time. Between 2001 and 2011, a total of almost $1.3 trillion was spent on the wars, and most of this was provided through supplemental appropriations.

When an agency wishes to shift existing resources to meet new needs during the fiscal year, or when an agency receives a supplemental appropriation, it must prepare a revised apportionment or reapportionment plan. The budget office then has an opportunity to exercise some guidance over how the agency will spend its monies. This process is sometimes known as *budget revision* or *rebudgeting*.

Just because a government is experiencing a downturn in revenues and needs to cut expenditures does not mean there will be no need for supplemental appropriations. In other words, budget increases and decreases occur simultaneously during budget execution. Some agencies' budgets of necessity may be augmented, while others are cut to try to make up the difference.[7] For example, many state government departments may have their budgets trimmed, while the state's labor department budget is being augmented to cope with an increased caseload of unemployed workers. During the recession that started in 2007, most states experienced an increase in Medicaid expenses at the same time that they were needing to cut budgets in other areas.

During the execution phase, agencies are required to supply periodic reports on their budgets. At the federal level, quarterly reports are required by law (Standard Form 133). Also, cabinet departments and some independent agencies must supply outlay reports that are used to monitor trends in budget deficits or surpluses.

End-of-Year Spending

As the fiscal year approaches its end, agencies will attempt to zero out their budgets. An agency having unexpended funds at the end of the fiscal year may be considered a prime candidate for cuts in the upcoming budget. Agencies with budget surpluses at the end of the year may have their budget bases reduced in the next fiscal year. Also, unexpended or unencumbered funds often lapse at the end of the budget year. From the agency's perspective, it is a now-or-never situation for spending the available money. Another factor is that an agency may have delayed some expenditures, saving a portion of its budget for contingencies. This delay results in a spurt in expenditures at the end of the year, with some spending being highly appropriate and other spending being utterly wasteful. An alternative is to allow surplus funds to be transferred to the agency's new budget without requiring a reappropriation. Some jurisdictions allow this kind of transfer within limits, such as a small percentage of each unit's total budget.[8]

Reorganizing, Downsizing, Privatizing, and Outsourcing

Budget offices have historically played central roles in examining the structures of departments and agencies, with an eye toward possible reorganization as a means for increasing the efficiency of operations. In addition to structural arrangements, budget offices often seek improvements in management processes as a means of garnering savings. When the Department of Homeland Security was created in 2002, for example, OMB played a key role in orchestrating the massive reorganization of units from various federal departments into the new department.[9] More recently, President Obama tasked OMB Deputy Director Jeffrey Zients to head up an effort to reorganize the federal government. Changes under consideration included the possibility of moving some responsibilities of the Commerce Department to other federal departments.[10]

Downsizing, rightsizing, and similar efforts may be aimed simply at reducing the size of government on the assumption that the bureaucracy is bloated and that cutbacks are possible without really altering the level of service. Other efforts to reduce the size and role of government may be based on the premise that certain functions are necessary but that most likely are not well run and could be performed better by the private sector. One option to achieve this reduced role of government in favor of the private sector is *privatization*. While definitions vary, the core of any definition of privatization or privatizing is the reassignment of government activities to the private sector. Privatization typically involves the selling of government assets to the private sector and turning the operation of these facilities over to private companies (see the chapter on capital financing).

The delivery of governmental services can be carried out to a considerable degree with the cooperation of private for-profit and nonprofit enterprises. A common mechanism used for this is *contracting* or *outsourcing*, in which a private firm provides a product or service at an agreed quantity, quality, and price. Other means of encouraging private sector involvement in the provision of public services include grants, loan guarantees, tax expenditures, social regulation, and government corporations. Outsourcing of government services is intended to increase government efficiency and reduce government spending. It should be kept in mind that outsourcing may officially result in a reduction in the number of government employees, but that many private sector employees will have jobs only because of government contracting. Outsourcing can be used for so-called business services such as janitorial housekeeping, but also for more fundamental basic services such as water, roads, prisons, and the like.[11]

Although the procedures used in contracting are reviewed later in this chapter, we note here that OMB Circular A-76, *Performance of Commercial Activities*, provides for a review process to determine when activities of the government should be contracted out. Two main criteria apply: that the activity be a "commercial" one and not "governmental," and that the cost be lower in the private sector than in government. Examples of commercial activities include guarding public buildings and providing cafeterias for employees. Policy-making activities may not be contracted out.

Contracting out has at least two types of supporters. One group wants to increase the efficiency of government operations through utilization of the private sector.[12] Circular A-76 uses an efficiency standard—namely, contracting out should be used when the unit cost for a service is lower outside government than inside it. The second group adheres to the view that the population is better served if service delivery is left, where possible, to the private sector. In 2011, presidential candidate Tim Pawlenty, former governor of Minnesota, presented a particularly vivid example of the latter, when he advocated the "Google test," arguing, "If you can find a good or service on the internet, the federal government probably doesn't need to be doing it."[13] Advocates of outsourcing contend that government should be proactive in seeking opportunities for turning functions over to the private sector.

Although critics contend that sometimes too much faith is placed in private enterprise and that outsourcing supports non-unionized firms that pay low wages, private sector contracting has become a familiar form of service delivery in the United States and abroad.[14] Contracting out is routinely used for such services as refuse pickup and towing of illegally parked vehicles. Private sector firms under government contract now handle services once thought to be exclusively the responsibility of the public sector, such as welfare services and the operation of prisons. During the wars in Iraq and Afghanistan, many security and intelligence activities, previously conducted exclusively by federal employees, have been carried out by contractors.

Several lessons have been learned as governments have ventured into outsourcing, with one of the most important being the need to conduct a thorough analysis before taking the plunge.[15] There is a need to consider whether cost efficiencies will be attained, whether the private firm will be held accountable for its performance, whether any cost efficiency is attained at the expense of quality, and whether equity or fairness in treating citizens and employees will be achieved.[16] Another important question is whether companies in the market can provide the agreed-upon services in a timely fashion and can respond to unforeseen problems that may arise. Do any legal barriers prohibit privatizing a given service? And what liability risks may be created by having a private firm deliver a government service?

The analysis needs to include projected costs for monitoring a firm in its delivery of a service. A government must be able to assure itself that a firm is abiding by its commitments and be able to respond when citizens complain about a service. Part of the monitoring process includes determining whether the cost savings that were predicted in the original analysis did, indeed, materialize. Some local governments that contract out for solid waste collection also retain some capacity inside government. In a given city, waste is collected in some areas by private contractors and in some areas by city employees. That way the city retains some capability if the private service provider does not live up to its obligations, and it ensures that there will be at least one competitor if only one private firm ventures a bid.

Management Controls

Budget offices have been assigned a variety of management-related duties beyond the core activities of assembling proposed budgets and overseeing their execution. For instance, budget offices may be partially responsible for establishing standards to be used in accounting systems (OMB Circular A-127). Of course, other units such as the Government Accountability Office (GAO) at the federal level also play major roles in this area. Information systems and procurement are other important areas in which budget offices have key roles. Procurement is discussed later in this chapter.

Some budget offices have responsibility for studying agency procedures and for recommending or prescribing new procedures. These organization-and-management (O&M) studies can recommend changes in the department's management processes.

Budget offices set ground rules for many of the routine activities of line organizations. For example, limitations are set for paying employee travel costs. Centrally imposed standards also circumscribe the use of consulting services.

Some budget offices are charged with performing a legislative clearinghouse function. Before an agency may endorse a proposal for new or revised legislation, the proposal must be vetted through the budget office. This practice helps ensure that what is proposed is consistent with the views of the chief executive, both substantively and financially (see OMB Circular A-19).

The OMB also oversees agency compliance with the Federal Managers' Financial Integrity Act of 1982, which requires safeguarding financial systems, particularly accounting and payroll, from fraud.[17] OMB Circular A-123 is used to implement the law; it was revised in 2004 and portions have been revised since then. The circular emphasizes that managers should be held accountable for producing government services that yield desired results as well as providing these services free of fraud and abuse of resources. Similar controls are established at the state and local levels.[18] Besides these areas mentioned, budget offices may have some responsibility for other management controls over agencies. For example, budget offices may be involved in some or all of the following activities:

- implementing government-wide affirmative action plans;
- ensuring compliance with right-to-know laws that require employers, both public and private, to inform their employees if they are working with hazardous materials;
- assisting with the implementation of hiring freezes and other personnel reduction plans;
- calculating the effect of federal or state laws on the budgets of lower levels of governments or the private sector;
- implementing freedom-of-information laws.

Control of Information Collection, Quality, Security, and Dissemination

Budget offices are heavily involved in government collection and dissemination of information. A chief concern is that government agencies heap huge burdens on individuals and corporations and, in the case of the federal government, on state and local governments in requiring them to submit information. The Paperwork Reduction Act (PRA), originally passed in 1980 and thoroughly rewritten in 1995, provides an elaborate process by which the federal government handles information.[19] The process is under the supervision of OMB's Office of Information and Regulatory Affairs (OIRA). The law is implemented by OMB Circular A-130. Each department is required to have a Chief Information Officer (CIO) appointed by the department head and directly accountable to the head. These officers meet periodically as the CIO Council.[20]

The Paperwork Reduction Act, as its title suggests, requires agencies to reduce the information collection burdens that they impose. Agencies are required to calculate the thousands of "burden hours" that the collection process demands of those required to submit information to them. Each year OMB publishes an *Information Collection Budget.* The document indicates both reductions and increases in burden hours. For instance, an agency may have made an administrative decision to cut back on some of the information it collected for a specific program, but that same agency may have decided to increase its collection of other information. Despite efforts to cut paperwork, the federal government has increased its information collection. According to a 2011 OMB report, "In FY 2009, the public spent an estimated 9.8 billion hours responding to Federal information collections. This figure represents a net increase of 2.9 billion burden hours from the corresponding number in FY 1995—and an increase of 85 million burden hours from the corresponding number in FY 2008."[21]

Any new collection of information must be approved by OIRA, but before that can occur, an agency must go through an elaborate analytic process. Factors to consider include the importance to the agency in collecting the information (the practical utility of the information), a realistic assessment of the burden imposed on those who would be required to submit the information, and a determination that the information does not exist already in some other form or in another agency. Once all of this activity is completed, the agency must post a notice about the proposed collection process in the *Federal Register* and then go through a period in which it accepts comments from the public. The CIO of an agency must review and certify the proposal. Only after these steps are completed may the proposal be submitted to OIRA. That office can reject the agency's proposal on grounds such as that the information is nonessential, that the information already exists, that the process would impose an undue burden, or simply that the proposed forms are unacceptable. After OMB approves a proposal, a notice must be posted once again in the *Federal Register.*

The process of disseminating information also is of concern. OMB provides guidance so that the dissemination process does not invade the privacy of citizens or reveal trade secrets of corporations. Circular A-130 provides guidance on when and how much agencies may charge for their information. The Paperwork Reduction Act requires that information be made available in a timely fashion.

Since September 11, 2001, a major concern is that information not be disseminated that could be used by terrorists, such as information about nuclear power plants that could be used to create a nuclear catastrophe. Terrorism also could come in the form of computer hackers destroying major databases. In 2000, Congress passed the Government Information Security Reform Act, which gave OMB responsibility for increasing computer security.[22] In 2002, Congress passed the Federal Information Security Management Act.[23] The law aims to protect the government's information and support systems, including computer hardware and software. The Office of Management and Budget and the National Institute of Standards and Technology, an arm of the Commerce Department, have responsibility for the law's implementation. In fiscal year 2008, OMB estimated that federal agencies spent $6.2 billion on information security. By 2012, a separate estimate was that a total of $6.5 billion, or less than 0.2% of all federal spending, was budgeted for information security.[24]

Information security has been particularly troublesome. Some cases are well publicized, such as the theft of a Department of Veterans Affairs laptop and hard drive in 2006 that contained information on 26.5 million individuals. Yet many other cases go unreported, and indeed, agencies may be unaware that their data have been compromised. Electronic filing of tax returns poses important challenges in safeguarding the security of data.[25]

Enterprise Architecture and E-Government

The term *enterprise architecture* (EA) has become widely used throughout the public and private sectors and refers in general to a framework for how business processes within an organization should relate to one another. Major emphasis is given to information technology for linking these processes. The term is defined in OMB Circular A-130, *Management of Federal Information Resources*, as follows:

> An EA is the explicit description and documentation of the current and desired relationships among business and management processes and information technology. It describes the "current architecture" and "target architecture" to include the rules and standards and systems life cycle information to optimize and maintain the environment which the agency wishes to create and maintain by managing its IT portfolio. The EA must also provide a strategy that will enable the agency to support its current state and also act as the roadmap for transition to its target environment.[26]

Protecting the privacy of individuals and organizations is central to information management. OMB is responsible for overseeing this aspect of information management and works with the CIO Council, mentioned above.[27] The office has provided guidance on such matters as information sharing among agencies. On the one hand, there is a desire to share information so as to avoid two or more agencies collecting the same information and thereby increasing the paperwork burden on individuals. On the other hand, privacy can be violated when information sharing is not handled with suitable safeguards.

Electronic government, or *E-government*, is a central concern. Information technology can be and is used in data sharing with the public, procurement, the regulatory process, and the issuance of grants and their administration. One study found FirstGov (renamed *www.USA.gov*), the intended one-stop location for searching federal websites, to be the best

E-government example at the federal level. The IRS was ranked 10th, the Treasury 19th, OMB 39th, and the Congressional Budget Office 47th. The top states were Delaware, Michigan, Maine, Kentucky, and Tennessee.[28] The Federal Funding Accountability and Transparency Act of 2006 required the government to create an extensive search engine and database accessible to the public.[29] The system, under the direction of the Office of Management and Budget, provides information about most government grants, loans, and contracts in excess of $25,000. The main means by which OMB implemented this directive was a website, *www.USAspending.gov*, where all contracts and grants awarded to organizations by federal agencies and departments are reported. For each, reports include the name of the organization, the amount of the award, and how the award will be spent. In a report released in March 2010, the GAO stated that OMB had implemented most of the programs mandated in the legislation, except it did not provide information regarding subawards of federal funds by primary contractors to subcontractors. GAO also criticized OMB for relying on the goodwill of agencies to submit timely and accurate information, and stated that much information did not meet the standards required for posting on *USAspending.gov*. OMB has since provided information on subawards, but it still apparently relies primarily on the goodwill and precision of the submitting federal agencies for timely and accurate award information.[30]

Control of Regulations

In addition to providing relief from paperwork, budget offices may be responsible for providing regulatory relief to businesses and governments. Critics of regulations view them as imposing needless expenses on corporations, which in turn pass these costs on to consumers, or to taxpayers in the case of state and local governments. However, one should keep in mind that regulations are issued pursuant to statutes and that both the regulations and the statutes presumably have important public purposes, such as ensuring the safety of a polio vaccine or the nation's food supply.

The regulatory process occurs at all levels of government and has its champions and critics at all levels.[31] Few would argue that all government regulations are worthless, but regulations can be questioned over their utility considering the costs that they impose on individuals, corporations, and other governments, as in the case of federal regulations affecting state and local governments.

Beginning in the Reagan administration, OMB was given increased powers over the regulatory process, and those powers have been greatly expanded in subsequent years. Part of this movement has probably been driven by political motivations in which presidents have sought to show their concern for keeping a potentially runaway bureaucracy in check. A central line of reasoning is that thorough analysis is needed to determine whether regulations should be issued and then whether they should be retained. In 1993, President Clinton issued Executive Order 12866, which provides for a regulatory planning and review process under OIRA. Each year, agencies must submit to OIRA their proposed plans for revising, issuing, and rescinding regulations. Any proposals for new or revised regulations must be evaluated in terms of their costs and benefits. When OMB rejects a regulation, it is sent back to the agency in the form of a "return letter." OMB also may send a "prompt letter" that need not be in a response to a submission by an agency but rather suggests that an agency has a problem with its regulations and offers suggestions for improvement.

In the Obama administration, perhaps the most important update was included in Executive Order 13497, signed by the president on January 30, 2009. It revoked two previous Executive Orders, 13258 and 13422, signed by President George W. Bush. EO 13258, signed in 2003, had taken away the authority of the vice president to help resolve regulatory reform disputes; 13422, signed in 2007, had made policy review officers in federal agencies political appointees and given them power to kill regulations at will, made agencies submit detailed and complicated paperwork on new regulations to OIRA, and forced agencies to identify specific "market failures" when issuing a new regulation. According to critics, this made the regulatory process more politicized and less effective. EO 13947 returns the OIRA regulatory review process to its format under EO 12866 of 1993.

Executive Order 13563, signed on January 18, 2011, supplements the OIRA regulatory review process. It directs agencies to increase public participation, through more consultation of state, local, and tribal officials who will be affected by new regulations, as well as posting proposed regulations online for at least 60 days before final approval. The order also promotes integration and harmonization of regulations among agencies, flexibility by providing choices to the public and avoiding "command and control" approaches when possible, and scientific objectivity in generating and interpreting evidence for or against proposed regulations. The order also specifies that agencies should perform a retrospective analysis of all regulations that might be outdated or burdensome, and should consider revising or rescinding them.

OIRA has encouraged federal agencies to post more of their regulatory material online to invite greater public participation, and implementing other policies like assigning all material related to a certain regulation a Regulation Identifier Number (RIN) to make it easier for the public to find all material. Also, OIRA and President Obama have emphasized that regulations should be made as efficient as possible and should not interfere with the operations of the private economy more than absolutely necessary. Implementing this process includes calculating a baseline scenario where the effects of not having a regulation are projected on the economy, avoiding where possible direct government interference in the market through instruments such as subsidies and bans, and making sure that regulations do not adversely affect particularly vulnerable entities, such as small businesses and governments.[32]

A major thrust for reformists has been the idea that regulations should exist only if their benefits outweigh the costs they impose on society. Circular A-4, *Regulatory Analysis*, provides ground rules for the conduct of evaluations so that some degree of standardized procedures exists from one agency to another.[33] There are major technical and political issues over what gets counted as a cost and what is counted as a benefit. The budget office was charged by the Regulatory Right-to-Know Act of 1999 with reporting to Congress on the "annual costs and benefits (including quantifiable and nonquantifiable effects) of federal rules and paperwork."[34] OMB estimated that between 2000 and 2010, it reviewed regulations that together had annual costs ranging between $44 billion and $62 billion and benefits ranging between $132 billion and $655 billion.[35]

Adopting a regulation or revising an existing one is an extremely complicated process in the federal government. OMB has identified nine basic steps that include drafting the regulation, publishing it in draft form, obtaining public comments, preparing it in final form, obtaining OMB approval, and publishing it in final form.[36] In addition, several other laws and executive orders may apply. If a regulation affects state and local governments, then analysis must be conducted to determine the financial implications of the regulation. This is in accord with the Unfunded Mandates Reform Act of 1995 (see the chapter on intergovernmental relations).[37] A draft regulation may be required to undergo special analysis of its impact on federalism as required by Executive Order 13132.

OMB has teamed with the General Services Administration in creating the website *www .RegInfo.gov*. The site contains the government's current and past regulatory plans and agendas. It has links to the *Federal Register*, which contains draft and final rules, and to the *Code of Federal Regulations*, which houses current regulations organized by subject. The other important website in this regard is *www.Regulations.gov*. This site, which includes information on proposed rules from more than 300 federal agencies, provides easy access to all documents that are open for public comment and allows searching of regulations by subject.

Controversy often arises over the fact that many regulations are written for large entities, and as a result, small organizations experience major burdens in attempting to comply with the regulations. In response to that view, Congress passed the Regulatory Flexibility Act of 1980 and made important changes in the law in 1996 through passage of the Small Business Regulatory Enforcement Fairness Act.[38] The 1980 law encourages the use of flexible regulations that require lesser amounts of information from smaller entities, including small businesses and local governments. The 1996 law, supplemented by Executive Order 13272 issued in 2002, instructs agencies to prepare guides to show small businesses how they can comply with regulations. The Small Business Administration was assigned the role of ombudsman in assisting small businesses when they encounter regulatory problems with agencies.

The 1996 law also includes within it the Congressional Review Act.[39] This law provides a form of legislative veto of administrative regulations. Before a proposed rule can take effect, it must be submitted to Congress. Congress then has 60 days, excluding days when it is in recess for four days or more, to review the regulations and can pass a joint resolution disapproving or vetoing the regulations. The president may veto the resolution, and Congress may consider overriding the president's veto. The Government Accountability Office, in a 10-year review of the law, found that the mere threat of congressional disapproval of regulations may have deterred agency rulemaking somewhat, but in general concluded that presidential oversight through OMB was more significant than congressional oversight.[40]

Beyond transparency in regulatory matters, the Obama administration has stressed open government more broadly. An "Open Government Directive" issued by OMB in late 2009 stressed three principles of open government—transparency, participation, and collaboration. Among the most important parts of this directive is an instruction to federal agencies to publish government information online and in a timely manner. Furthermore, agencies were to improve the quality of online information, and generally create a culture of open government.[41]

Given all of the items discussed here—reorganization, management controls, control of information, enterprise architecture and E-government, and control of regulations—some observers have suggested that such management tasks are too great to be left to budget offices. One suggestion is to create a separate office of management that would have nonbudgetary duties ranging well beyond what OMB currently has. The argument against creating an office of management hinges mainly on the fact that the issues addressed have budgetary implications, and to assign them to a different agency would automatically create coordination problems.

In addition to relations between the central budget office and the line agencies, several other subsystems are in operation during budget execution. Taxes and other debts must be collected, the cash needs of the government must be met, items must be purchased, and the vulnerability of the government to loss of property and other problems must be managed. These topics are discussed next.

TAX ADMINISTRATION AND DEBT COLLECTION

Tax administration, which is discussed here, and cash management, which is discussed in the next section, are two functions that are usually under the same administrative officer, typically a secretary of treasury or revenue. Having the two functions linked together administratively facilitates sharing information. The cash manager uses information generated by the tax administrator. At the federal level, the Treasury Department handles these tasks. While the two earlier chapters on budgeting for revenues discussed the nature of various taxes, here we consider how those taxes are administered over the course of the fiscal year.

Besides taxes, numerous other revenue sources must be administered. User charges are common at all levels of government. State lotteries have become important sources of revenue. Administrators responsible for lotteries focus on marketing to increase sales. As the dollar value of sales increases, the unit cost of administration declines. Governments lend billions of dollars, and loan payments frequently are delinquent. Therefore, debt collection is of great import.

Main Steps

Tax administration has four main steps:

1. Determining the objects or services to be taxed. Using the local property tax as an example, parcels of land and structures, along with their owners, must be identified.
2. Applying the tax. In the case of the property tax, this is an annual process. Governments make property tax calculations, and bills are sent to property owners. In contrast, sales tax calculations are made each time a sale occurs. Individuals have the responsibility to calculate their own income taxes.

3. Collecting the revenues. Funds are paid either directly to the government, as in the case of a corporation's paying income tax, or through a third party, as in the case of employers' remitting individual income tax withholdings to the government.
4. Enforcing the law. Audits are conducted selectively of taxpayers to verify compliance, and some taxpayers are prosecuted for tax evasion.

The chapters on budgeting for revenues have already highlighted many of the important administrative issues that are raised by initial application and collection, in the context of issues such as the determination of property tax liability and taxable income under the individual income tax. The remainder of this section highlights four issues that present challenges particular to tax administration—enforcement, the role of technology, debt collection, and taxpayer rights. Tradeoffs exist, as between collections and taxpayer rights.

Enforcement

Numerous tax enforcement measures are used, and well-trained and ethical personnel are essential for effective enforcement practices.

- The IRS verifies mathematical accuracy through the use of optical scanning. Proper design of forms and clearly written instructions contribute to improved taxpayer accuracy in filing returns.
- Tax return information supplied by individuals is compared with information supplied by banks and employers.
- Governments share computer-based data to compare information on income being reported (or not reported).[42]
- Taxpayer services are provided to help in preparing tax returns. Services may be available at designated government offices, at other facilities, by telephone, and online.[43]
- Governments draw samples of taxpayer returns to audit. Regression models are designed to identify cases that are most likely to involve noncompliance with the tax laws. In addition, some taxpayers are audited in response to tips received from the public, and others are audited at random in an attempt to encourage voluntary compliance.
- Delinquent accounts are investigated, as are accounts in which taxpayers have stopped complying altogether.
- Some taxpayers are prosecuted in court, depending on the "seriousness" of the cases and the availability of resources to pursue the cases in court.
- Special enforcement is reserved for sources of illegal income, such as gambling, prostitution, narcotics, and, more generally, organized crime.

Any government must decide how many resources to commit to these various activities and how resources should be distributed among them. The IRS has been criticized for not having a firm idea of the relative yield in tax revenue generated from these activities. Performance measures are needed to determine the relative merits of these activities.[44] Decisions must be made not only about the type of activity to conduct, but also about the distribution of tax enforcement resources across different forms of taxes. For example, a state needs to decide how many resources to commit to tax cheating on personal income, corporate income, and motor fuels taxes.[45]

Complaints often arise that some taxpayers are being audited more intensively than others. Increased auditing may be warranted where it is known that certain types of taxpayers are more likely to cheat on their returns than others. Politics also come into play, and particular types of tax cheating may be highlighted for this reason. The objective of having taxpayers comply with the law is having them report all taxable income. Failure to report income results in less money being paid in taxes. The difference between what taxpayers pay and what they should pay is known as the *tax gap*. The Internal Revenue Service estimated the tax gap for tax year 2005 to be $345 billion, which dropped to $290 billion after accounting for IRS tax collections in response to the gap. As of 2008, the IRS estimated the voluntary compliance rate to be 84%. This gap between taxes owed and taxes paid is critical considering the fact that the budget is projected to continue to be structurally out of balance in both the medium and the long term, meaning that improvements in economic conditions could not be expected to eliminate the budget deficit.[46]

Determining compliance/noncompliance with the tax laws is a difficult task. If the IRS or any other tax agency knew that taxpayers were not complying, the agency would seek to collect the delinquent taxes owed. Noncompliance data by nature, therefore, are estimates that are necessarily imprecise. The IRS for a time used a system of super-audits that required a sample of taxpayers to substantiate every item on their tax returns, but these were determined to be ineffective in detecting unreported income and identifying unauthorized or fraudulent claims for tax deductions and tax credits.

Another consideration is that tax administration would be far less complicated if tax laws were less complicated. Of course, the reason for their complexity is simple. Tax laws are replete with specific conditions to take into account the specific conditions of taxpayers. Some countries have tax withholding systems that free most taxpayers from the onerous task of preparing and filing tax returns. If tax laws were simplified, people would be better able to calculate their tax bills and would have less opportunity to cheat, and tax agencies would need to spend far less than current levels on tax administration.[47]

Technology in Tax Administration

It should come as no surprise that technology is playing increasingly important roles in tax administration:

- Besides routine recordkeeping, computers are used for drawing samples for tax auditing and for cross-checking information between different sources.
- Many businesses are required to make federal tax payments through the Electronic Federal Tax Payment System.[48]
- State and local governments electronically submit federal income tax and Social Security withholdings.
- Answers to frequently asked questions (FAQs) pertaining to tax laws are commonly available on government websites.

- Many local governments have automated tax systems that can make withdrawals for property taxes from taxpayers' bank accounts, providing that taxpayers preapprove such withdrawals.
- In many jurisdictions, taxpayers use telephone or online services to pay their taxes.
- Many governments accept credit and debit cards for payment of taxes, fees, parking tickets, and the like.
- Many states accept electronic fund transfers for corporations making tax payments.
- Electronic auctions are used by governments to sell delinquent tax properties.
- Auditors on field assignments use portable computers with wireless (Wi-Fi) Internet connections. Computers can be used to manage tax cases, providing on any one case a variety of information and prompting the case manager with reminders about the status of the case.
- Tax office employees can work at home on confidential tax files using secure, high-speed access to networks.[49]

One of the most important developments in this area relates to online tax filing and payments. The IRS Restructuring and Reform Act mandated the rapid development of electronic filing. In 2001, the Internal Revenue Service unveiled its Electronic Federal Tax Payment System–Online Service for use by individual taxpayers and businesses.[50] This system is much more user-friendly than the system originally developed for businesses. By 2011, the IRS estimated that more than three-quarters of all taxpayers filed electronically. As of 2011, 27 states accepted or were about to accept returns through "Modernized efile."[51]

Debt Collection

One of the biggest debts owed to government is taxes, but individuals and corporations also may owe several other types of debt to government. Loans, both direct and guaranteed, result in some defaults. Federal credit programs exist for college students, low-income housing, ship construction, development in other nations, and small businesses recovering from disasters, to name only a few. Various other business transactions with government result in debts, including farmers owing on crop insurance payments and foreign countries owing on purchases of agricultural commodities. Fines are another form of debt owed to the government, as in the case of a corporation being fined for not meeting environmental standards for its mining operations.

The federal government, as discussed in the chapter on budget preparation and the decision process, is attempting to deal with the "hidden liabilities" of federal credit programs. General information on credit is contained in the *Analytical Perspectives* budget document, and more detailed information is available through other documents produced by OMB and the Treasury Department.

OMB Circular A-129, *Policies for Federal Credit Programs and Non-Tax Receivables*, requires that agencies review their credit programs in terms of the costs and benefits to society. The circular establishes requirements for "sound" credit programs and specifically states that "(d)epartments and agencies shall manage credit programs and all non-tax receivables in accordance with their statutory authorities and the provisions of this

Circular to protect the Government's assets and to minimize losses in relation to social benefits provided."[52] Federal agencies must calculate expected credit losses on both direct and guaranteed loans. These losses can reduce the amount of funding available for future loans.

The Debt Collection Act of 1982, the Debt Collection Improvement Act of 1996, and OMB Circular A-129 further require that agencies take steps to improve their credit programs.[53] Loan applications must be examined with an eye toward uncovering the risks that government would take in approving the loans. Delinquent cases can be turned over to collection agencies and can be reported to consumer credit agencies. Salary offsets can be used in the case of federal employees who owe the government, and individuals may have income tax refunds withheld up to the amount owed. State governments have also used this latter technique.

In the mid-2000s, the Internal Revenue Service announced plans to turn over some tax collection to private firms.[54] The IRS, in trying to head off criticism, announced "safeguards" for taxpayers when dealing with private debt collection agencies.[55] "The private debt collection program [was] expected to bring in $1.4 billion over 10 years, with the collection agencies keeping about $330 million of that, or 22 to 24 cents on the dollars."[56]

Taxpayer Rights

In their zeal to extract as many tax dollars as possible from the public, tax administrators must keep in mind that the citizens are ultimately responsible for setting tax laws and for paying the salaries of tax administrators. In other words, administrators are employees of the citizenry. To this end, governments have adopted laws that declare a set of rights for taxpayers.

The Internal Revenue Service Restructuring and Reform Act contains more than 70 provisions that protect taxpayers and give them rights in dealing with the IRS. The law includes such important provisions as altering the burden of proof in taxpayer cases. If the IRS challenges a taxpayer on reported income tax deductions, for example, the taxpayer need only provide some credible evidence, which then shifts the burden to the IRS to disprove the evidence. An important provision is that innocent spouses can be relieved of tax fines and other penalties. Restrictions are imposed on liens and on the seizing of taxpayer property for back taxes. The IRS, as prescribed by the legislation, maintains a taxpayer advocate office, which assists taxpayers in dealing with the agency. States also have taxpayer bills of rights.[57]

The standard view in the field is that taxpayers' privacy needs to be protected, and taxpayers need to be treated equally. Some government workers have been found browsing the tax returns of celebrities and other prominent figures. The response is to restrict access to files to ensure security and avoid record tampering. One problem has been that taxpayer records are sometimes left in open areas of a tax administration office. In such situations, the records can be seen by unauthorized personnel, stolen, or lost.[58] Another concern is that the audit process not be politically motivated.

CASH MANAGEMENT

Cash management is the process of administering monies to ensure that they are available over time to meet expenditure needs and that, when temporarily not needed, they are invested at a minimum risk and a maximum yield. Cash management involves both short- and long-term investments. The latter are used mainly in the case of pension funds that try to build up reserves for future years when employees retire. The state of the art of cash management is necessarily dependent on the state of the larger financial system.

Cash Flow

An essential aspect of cash management is forecasting when revenues will be received and in what amounts, and when expenditures will occur and in what amounts over the course of the fiscal year and beyond.[59] A cash management plan will strive to accelerate the receipt of revenues and delay or minimize expenditures.

The chapter on financial management discusses the cash flows statement as one form of financial reporting.

Inflow of Revenues

Enforcement of tax laws is viewed as one means of maximizing inflow. Other techniques involve depositing government receipts as soon as possible into interest-bearing accounts. For example, when tax payments accompany tax returns, these checks can be immediately deposited in banks, and processing the returns can occur later. Governments attempt to minimize the *float time* between when checks and currency are received and when they are deposited. Accounts receivable, involving payments due from citizens, corporations, and other governments, are kept to a minimum. Inflow can be accelerated by prompt invoicing. For example, airlines may be invoiced on a monthly basis for their gate space at an airport terminal.

Lockboxes

Another technique used selectively by the federal government and some state governments is the lockbox system, which uses post office boxes that are under the control of banks. Taxpayers send their payments to designated post office boxes that are opened by banking officials, and the receipts are deposited promptly. The process reduces the amount of float time between when a check is written and when government deposits it and begins earning interest.

Governments use a variety of methods for receiving payments. A survey of state and local governments by the Government Finance Officers Association and JPMorgan Chase found that almost all received payments through the mail and by walk-ins into government offices. More than half received funds through drop boxes and automatic bank debit cards. About a third received payments via the telephone, Internet, and lockboxes.[60]

Expenditure Planning and Prompt Payment

Some techniques deal not with inflow, but with outflow. Here the concern is keeping money in interest-bearing accounts until it is needed to cover expenses and avoiding the need to borrow funds to cover expenses when revenues, such as tax receipts, are unavailable in the projected amounts. Cash flow planning is one reason that agencies are required to submit apportionment plans to the central budget office. Agencies may be instructed to shift expenditures in apportionment plans from one month or quarter to another. One rule is to pay promptly—that is, when bills are due and not before or after. This procedure is mandated at the federal level by the Prompt Payment Act of 1982, as amended.[61] Paying bills promptly saves money for the government, such as avoiding payment of late fees, and reduces a common problem encountered by government's suppliers—namely, not knowing when they will be paid. Small businesses are the most severely hurt when government agencies fail to pay their bills on time.[62]

Although the vast majority of the federal government's payments to vendors are on time, that still leaves many millions of other payments that are late.[63] The Financial Management Service within the Treasury Department has a prompt payment web page that provides for simple interest calculations for short-term tardiness and compound interest when a government agency is in arrears by months. For example, in the first half of 2011, the government paid 2.625% interest on late payments. If a payment of $6,000,000 was overdue by 31 days, then the government would owe $13,563 in addition to the principal. The web page also provides a calculator to help an agency decide when to accept a vendor's offer of a discount for early payment.[64]

Of course, another concern is to make sure that bills are not only paid on time, but paid to the right party and in the right amount. Lax disbursement systems increase the chances that errors are made in paying vendors and that fraud occurs. Fraud can happen without a government officer being aware of the situation—or with the officer's assistance.

Borrowing

If forecasted expenditures cannot be adjusted downward to be no greater than expected revenues, then short-term borrowing becomes an important option. State and local governments borrow from banks for up to one year in cases where expenditures are considered essential and funds are unavailable to cover the expenses. The backing of these bank notes consists of future receipt of revenues, and the instruments are known as BANs, RANs, and TANs—*bond, revenue,* and *tax anticipation notes.*

Governments also may spend from their own reserves and borrow from themselves. *Unrestricted fund balances,* which are in effect contingency funds, may be drawn upon to meet unanticipated expenditure needs. Short-term borrowing from one fund to meet the cash needs of another also occurs, as in the case of a local government's borrowing from its pension funds. State laws, however, may greatly restrict such borrowing as a protection against depleting the funds.

Some governments have established *rainy day funds* or *budget stabilization funds* that can be used during years when revenues decline. Statutes or state constitutional provisions require that monies be placed in these funds when the economy improves and revenues rise and that monies may be withdrawn only when revenues decline by some set percentage. It is common for governments to have in these funds something in excess of 5% of their general funds, although the appropriate amount needed depends on many factors that vary across different units of government.[65] These funds can reduce fiscal stress during recessions, such as occurred in the early 1990s, the early 2000s, and later in the first decade of the 2000s.[66] A state that dipped heavily into its rainy day fund in one year to balance its budget might then face major problems in the following year if the economy had not recovered, perhaps forcing decision makers to increase taxes. The use of budget stabilization monies also implies the replenishment of these funds when the budgetary environment becomes more favorable.

Given the severity of the recession that began in 2007, many states found that the balances in their rainy day funds were insufficient to prevent them from needing to take other actions. Indeed, it is not necessarily the intent that these funds enable states to weather all storms; rather, they are designed to either enable them to adequately confront relatively small disruptions or to buy them time in dealing with larger ones. In this recent recession, most states with rainy day funds used them at least to some extent. In Texas, Governor Rick Perry eventually agreed with the legislature to withdraw $3.1 billion to help to address a two-year shortfall of as much as $27 billion.[67] Historically, the rule of thumb for rainy day funds has been 5% of the budget, although there is no reason to believe that a fund of the same size would be appropriate for each state. In reality, there are many factors that would dictate the appropriate fund size, including the volatility of state revenues.[68]

Investment Planning

When forecasts show periods during the year when revenues will exceed expenditures, plans are made for investment. Virtually all governments encounter this situation. Often there are spurts in revenue receipts, such as when local property taxes are due or when state sales tax receipts are paid following the Christmas shopping period.

At least seven factors must be taken into account when devising an investment strategy:

1. *Security.* Financial institutions insure some deposits only up to $100,000.
2. *Maturity date.* Some instruments mature in a few months, while others mature in 30 years.
3. *Marketability or liquidity.* If cash is needed before the maturity date, may an instrument be sold to a third party, or will the issuer convert the instrument to cash?
4. *Call provisions.* May the issuer repay the investor before the date of maturity?
5. *Denominations.* Minimum amounts for investing range from $1,000 to $100,000 or more.
6. *Yield or return on investment.* Yield is measured in terms of a percentage of the investment and often expressed as an interest rate.
7. *Legal authority.* State laws may prohibit the state government and local governments from making some types of investments.

Investment Instruments

The instruments available for state and local investments consist of three general types: federal government securities, corporate securities, and money market instruments. Any government must decide to what extent it wishes to invest in each type.

Federal Securities

Fully guaranteed federal securities include Treasury bills (T-bills), notes, and bonds. T-bills mature in 4, 13, 26, and 52 weeks. They are sold at a discount by auction and consequently have no set percentage return. Treasury notes and bonds, which range in maturity from 1 to 30 years, have coupons that mature every 6 months. In the 1990s, the Treasury Department launched two instruments that are sensitive to inflation. When inflation occurs, the yield rate increases. Treasury inflation-protected securities, known as TIPS, have their interest rate set at the time of auction. Their principal rises or falls based on the consumer price index. If the consumer price index rises in a time period, the value of the note rises and then the interest is calculated based on the new principal. If deflation occurs, investors at the time of maturity are guaranteed the original purchase price.

The other inflation-sensitive instrument is the Series I savings bond. I bonds are purchased at face value, which ranges between $50 and $10,000, and have a fixed rate of return. Inflation rates, then, are added to the calculations. TIPS and I bonds have yield rates that are somewhat lower than instruments that lack the inflation protection.

Series EE/E savings bonds are guaranteed by the government, can be cashed after six months, and earn interest up to 30 years. These bonds issued before May 1, 2005, pay interest at current market rates. Bonds issued May 1, 2005, and after pay interest at a fixed rate. EE bonds come in paper and electronic form.

Other Federal-Related Securities

Other securities are issued by credit institutions created by the federal government and may have full, limited, or no backing or ambiguous backing of the government. Instruments backed by the federal government include insured notes of the Housing and Community Facilities Programs within the Agriculture Department and the Government Home Loan Mortgage Corporation, which is part of the Department of Housing and Urban Development. Instruments that do not have the expressed guarantee of the federal government but could be backed in emergency situations include Federal Home Loan Bank bonds, Federal Land Bank bonds, and Federal Intermediate Credit Bank bonds. Many of these federal-related securities involve mortgages, including mortgages on homes, farms, cooperatives, and overseas investments (Asian Development Bank notes and bonds and Export Import Bank debentures).

Corporate Securities

Corporations are another possibility for the investment of state and local monies. Corporate bonds are essentially loans made to the issuers. Stocks, in comparison, represent ownership of the corporation. In the event that a corporation goes into bankruptcy, creditors such as bondholders are paid first. If any assets remain, they are then distributed among stockholders.

Money Market Instruments

Financial institutions provide numerous investment opportunities. Interest is paid on *negotiable order of withdrawal* (NOW) checking accounts and on savings accounts. Not only can government earn interest on these deposits, but other benefits may also be negotiated through *linked deposit agreements*. In these situations, banks, as a condition of receiving government deposits, may agree to make available more loans for housing in a community or for industrial development in a targeted area.

Monies can also be invested in money market instruments, with *certificates of deposit* (CDs) being one of the most popular. Issuers include banks, offshore subsidiaries of U.S. banks, and U.S. branches of foreign banks. The latter two issue what are known as *Eurodollars* and *Yankee CDs*, respectively, which are not guaranteed by the federal government. Some, but not all, CDs are negotiable. Issuers may charge interest penalties for early withdrawal of monies. Various other instruments, used less frequently, include *bankers' acceptances and commercial paper.* Bankers' acceptances are agreements to purchase a bank's agreement to loan money on a short-term basis to a corporation (one usually involved in international trade). Commercial paper, also available through banks, is a corporate promissory note. A repurchase agreement (repo) is a pool of U.S. government securities held by a financial institution and sold temporarily to state and local governments and other purchasers. The institution agrees to repurchase the securities at a later date.

State and local governments may purchase combinations of various money market instruments. One technique is to invest in a money market fund that is a pool of securities. The Securities and Exchange Commission regulates these funds in an attempt to reduce the risks undertaken by investors. Despite these regulations, however, laws preclude many governments from investing in money market funds because they often include higher-risk investments such as Eurodollars.

Derivatives

One of the most controversial financial instruments is known as a derivative.[69] Derivatives are highly complex devices that are often poorly understood by both those who sell them and the state and local governments that buy them. A derivative's value depends upon some underlying security or a market index. In other words, the derivative is a bet on what future interest rates will be. Governments purchase swaps that trade in variable rates for fixed rates, with the underlying gamble by the government being that the return on investment will be better with the fixed rate. Some derivatives take the form of collateralized mortgage obligations, which entail investing in a pool of mortgages with the return being based on changes in interest rates and changes in mortgage prepayment rates (see discussion of the extensive use of derivatives in the subprime mortgage market in the chapter on government and the economy). Investments by state and local governments in derivatives created substantial problems during the recession that started in 2007. For example, a class action lawsuit in Texas alleged that the Teachers Retirement System in Texas lost $415 million because of investments in derivatives.[70]

Investment Pools

Another money management technique that has become popular is for jurisdictions to combine their investments into a state-authorized investment pool.[71] By pooling resources, smaller jurisdictions can take advantage of higher-yield investments that require larger investments than passbook savings or CDs. Liquidity is improved in that jurisdictions can often withdraw some of their monies from these pools without the financial loss that would be involved if they held securities themselves and had to liquidate them.

Yield Rates

Table 11–1 provides a snapshot of yield rates for some of the instruments discussed here. As can be seen from the table, the rates varied considerably between the two years reported. Rates increase with risk, with higher-risk instruments paying higher rates. The federal inflated-indexed securities paid decidedly less than other securities, indicating a price that purchasers pay for being protected from possible inflation. Bonds usually pay a higher rate than notes, and notes pay a higher rate than bills, because of the time factor involved, but this pattern does not happen to show up in the years sampled. Note the very low rates, in particular, paid on U.S. Treasury securities in 2010; these are largely a reflection of a very loose Fed monetary policy.

Table 11–1 Yield Rates of Selected Investment Instruments

Instrument	2005	2011
Federal Securities		
4-week bills	3.27	0.02
3-month bills	3.46	0.03
6-month bills	3.70	0.03
1-year	NA	0.17
Inflation indexed		
5-year	1.67	−0.34
10-year	1.77	0.79
20-year	1.86	1.54
30-year	NA	1.84
Constant maturities		
5-year	4.08	1.55
10-year	4.22	2.97
20-year	4.48	3.87
30-year	NA	4.19
Other Deposits and Securities		
3-month certificates of deposit	3.79	0.22
3-month commercial paper	3.69	0.14
3-month Eurodollars	3.79	0.35
1-year derivatives	4.29	0.40
Moody's corporate bonds, Aaa	5.07	4.96

NA–Not Available

Source: Federal Reserve Board (2005). *Statistical release.* August 29; Federal Reserve Board (2010). *Statistical release.* June 27.

Use of Investment Instruments

Most of the money (more than 90%) in state and local government trust funds, such as employee retirement systems and workers' compensation, is invested and little is kept on hand. In contrast, the money for the rest of state and local governments is kept much more fluid (one-third in cash and deposits and two-thirds invested). Retirement systems invest mainly in corporate stocks and bonds (48.8%), federal securities (6%), and foreign and international securities (18.3%).[72] In 2010, the California investment pool had 12.4% of its funds in federal agency discount notes, 11.8% in certificates of deposit, 11.3% in commercial paper, 5.5% in bank time deposits, and 3% in federal securities. California had no funds invested in corporate bonds.[73]

As noted earlier, legal constraints affect investment programs. Illinois law, for example, had barred the state from depositing funds with financial institutions that had specific ties with Sudan, but this law was declared unconstitutional by a federal judge in 2007.[74] Such laws exist in other states as well, and a New Hampshire State Supreme Court upheld that state's divestiture act in 2010.[75]

Investment Risks

Investments are not risk free. One type of risk involves the creditworthiness of the issuer of a security. Bonds issued by the federal government are nearly risk free in this sense, and bonds issued by major corporations, such as General Electric, are low risk. Another aspect of risk, however, is whether a particular instrument is volatile in terms of the yield it may produce. In this context, fixed-rate, long-term government bonds are risky investments. If a government's portfolio contains high-yield securities at a time when yield rates are declining, then the situation is generally positive. If trends reverse and yield rates climb above those in the portfolio, however, the government may have difficulty selling low-bearing securities. In that situation, a government's investments might fail to keep pace with inflation. Derivatives are often singled out as one of the most high-risk investments due to their volatility, even though the issuers of the derivatives may be creditworthy. In the 1990s, Orange County, California, was embroiled in a massive problem involving derivatives. **Exhibit 11–1** discusses that situation.

The Governmental Accounting Standards Board (GASB) has issued important directives regarding investments of government monies.[76] Statement No. 3, *Deposits with Financial Institutions, Investments (including Repurchase Agreements), and Reverse Repurchase Agreements*, mandates that governments report high-risk investments in their comprehensive annual financial reports (CAFRs). Statement No. 9, *Reporting Cash Flows of Proprietary and Nonexpendable Trust Funds and Governmental Entities that Use Proprietary Fund Accounting*, as its title suggests, sets rules for reporting cash flows for those activities within a government that are run like businesses, such as a municipal transit system or parking garage.

While an annual report showing such investments is helpful, more short-term reporting is needed. One option is to mark or report the value of each item in a portfolio on a daily basis. GASB Statement No. 31, *Accounting and Financial Reporting for Certain Investments and for External Investment Pools*, specifies that governments account for and report "fair value" for their investments in (1) participating interest-earning investment

Exhibit 11–1 Derivatives and the Case of Orange County, California

Orange County, California, the home of Disneyland and the fifth largest county in the United States, experienced a painful lesson in the risks of investing when it filed for bankruptcy protection in 1994.[1] The county had been hailed as a shrewd investor, earning close to double the rate of return on investments compared with other governments and investment pools. The county had been so successful that 180 other local governments had deposited money with Orange County with the expectation of reaping the benefits of an investment policy that was more aggressive than the typical one. In 1994, reality hit hard. This approach resulted in a loss of nearly $2 billion.

What went wrong in Orange County? First, heavy investments were placed in derivatives. Derivatives are gambles on what will happen to interest rates. When rates went in the opposite direction than expected, the county was in trouble. Second, the situation was exacerbated by the use of reverse repos. A repurchase agreement, or repo, is an instrument for investing money, while a reverse repo is a means for a government to borrow against securities that it holds. The instrument is a form of temporary debt for the issuer. Orange County used reverse repos to borrow additional money that was used in turn to purchase additional risky instruments. When the interest rates went the wrong way for the fund, the pool was stuck not only with investments that went sour, but also with the ramped-up level of investment fueled by borrowing to make still more investments. Subsequently, the Governmental Accounting Standards Board (GASB) issued Interpretation No. 3, *Financial Reporting for Reverse Repurchase Agreements*, which is intended to force governments to disclose their dealings in reverse repos and presumably rein in their use.

The Orange County debacle underscores the need for careful management of risk in developing a portfolio of investments. Derivatives may be a hedge against other investments that have low yields, but the derivatives themselves clearly entail substantial risks.[2] In addition, borrowing to make still further investments is an even more risky strategy than the derivative-based investments themselves. It is the equivalent of the individual investor borrowing money to purchase more stocks, and then having those stocks fall, leaving the investor with decreased or no earnings, but also a capital loss as the borrowed money has to be repaid out of the investor's other funds.

1.   Kearns, K. P. (1995). Accountability and entrepreneurial public management: the case of the Orange County investment fund. *Public Budgeting & Finance, 15*, Fall, 3–21.

2.   County of Orange, California (2006). *Notes to comprehensive annual financial report for year ended June 30, 2005.* Retrieved August 19, 2006, from http://www.ac.ocgov.com/200CAFR/NOTES.pdf

contracts; (2) external investment pools; (3) open-end mutual funds; (4) debt securities; and (5) equity securities, option contracts, stock warrants, and stock rights that have readily determinable fair values.

Federal Cash Management

The federal government's cash management system is considerably different from those of state and local governments. Federal monies are kept with the Federal Reserve System (see the chapter on government and the economy), which pays a form of interest for deposits, and banks, which also pay interest. The Financial Management Service (FMS) of the Treasury Department handles transactions. FMS provides extensive information on its website about the overall aspects of cash management and about specific operations. For example, the FMS "Green Book" provides detailed instructions to financial institutions as to how they are to process federal monies using automatic clearing houses (ACHs).[77] The agency's "Gold Book" gives specifics on how federal checks are to be reclaimed, as when they have been forged or have been issued to persons no longer eligible for payment.[78] Other departments and agencies handle many cash management transactions in accordance with instructions issued by the Treasury Department.

The inflow of federal receipts comes from taxes and other payments and from the sale of T-bills and other instruments discussed earlier. These sales are handled through the Federal Reserve and are limited according to the total debt ceiling set by Congress (see the chapter on budget approval and the U.S. Congress). T-bills are auctioned off weekly, and other instruments are sold less frequently. There is, of course, a secondary market for these securities.

Like state and local governments, the federal government is concerned about having needed cash on hand and minimizing the costs of money, such as avoiding late payment fees on government purchases and avoiding paying out funds any earlier than required. An additional consideration at the federal level is that the government's cash operations affect markets.[79]

The federal government operates under the Cash Management Improvement Act of 1990 in making payments to state and local governments, particularly grant payments.[80] FMS lists three objectives of the law:

1. Efficiency—to minimize the time between the transfer of funds to the states and the payout for program purposes.
2. Effectiveness—to ensure that federal funds are available when requested.
3. Equity—to assess an interest liability to the federal government and/or the states to compensate for the lost value of funds.[81]

Another important consideration is that the federal government must meet its cash needs on a global basis. Sufficient amounts of money must be available at specific times in specific countries. For example, the Defense Department (DOD) must handle large sums of foreign currency and, in doing so, exposes itself to potential problems in the value of such currency, particularly in the currency's devaluation.[82]

Currency

Since the 1990s, the federal government has been introducing redesigned currency.[83] The bills use color-shifting ink, security threads, watermarks, large off-center portraits, low-vision features, and microprinting that greatly deter counterfeiting. Nevertheless, counterfeiting remains a concern, given the sophistication of contemporary photocopying equipment.

Electronic Fund Transfers

Advances in computer technology have made possible extensive use of electronic fund transfers (EFTs). Through EFTs monies are moved via computer communication from bank to bank and from account to account. Monies received at one bank through a lock-box system, for instance, can be moved to other accounts in distant banks. Another advantage of electronic fund transfers is that they can be used for recurring payments, such as making direct deposits of Social Security payments into retirees' bank accounts. A form of electronic fund transfer is the electronic benefit transfer, which can be used to transfer funds through automatic teller machines. Some governments use electronic benefit transfers to make payments to welfare recipients. EFTs are also used by governments to transfer funds for alimony and child support in cases of divorce. The transfers, which are processed nationally by a few large banking systems, cost much less per transaction than do conventional checks.

Congress decided, in the Debt Collection Improvement Act of 1996, to phase out most check writing by January 1, 1999. This trend toward phasing out paper checks has continued, with the Treasury announcing in April 2011 that new recipients of Social Security benefits would be required to accept electronic payments—they would no longer have the option of receiving paper checks. Current check recipients will be required to switch to electronic payment by March 2013.[84]

Letters of Credit

An important cash management technique, especially for the federal government, is the use of letters of credit. As mandated by the Cash Management Improvement Act of 1990, these letters are provided to governments and nonprofit corporations that are awarded grants and contracts. The letters allow recipient organizations to establish credit at banks without the federal government having to provide money until it is needed. Funds then are transferred electronically into these accounts by the federal government.

PROCUREMENT

Procurement entails the acquisition of resources required in providing government services.[85] While this function is not at the core of budgeting, it has major budgetary implications. In fiscal year 2010, the federal government spent $535 billion (or roughly 15% of its budget) on contracted goods or services. This actually constituted a reduction in contract spending between 2009 and 2010, representing the first time since 1997 that contract spending had declined from the prior year.[86] Of course, state and local governments each year also spend billions on contracts. Some government agencies, such as the Defense Department and the National Aeronautics and Space Administration (NASA), spend a major share of their resources on contracted products and services rather than delivering services directly on their own. In addition, most other federal agencies accomplish their missions through the actions of other parties, usually through grants and other transfers of funds (see the discussion in the chapter on intergovernmental relations). Contracting, while fundamental to the operations of government, is not always handled well in budgets. Some local governments exclude contracts from their budgets and others report them only in lump sum. With the growing emphasis on results-oriented budgeting, governments have been forced to report contracts in their budgets.[87]

Procurement is extremely big business. According to *Government Executive* magazine's annual listing of the top 200 federal contractors, the top five companies in federal contracting in fiscal 2009 were Lockheed Martin, Boeing, Northrop Grumman, Raytheon, and General Dynamics. All of these companies play major roles in the defense and aerospace industries. However, also included in the top 75 were the Massachusetts Institute of Technology (42nd), the California Institute of Technology (44th), Johns Hopkins University (60th), the University of California (61st), and the University of Tennessee (73rd). All of these institutions were top contract recipients by virtue of the fact that they run large federal laboratories. Together, the top 200 contractors received contracts worth $543 billion in 2009.[88]

Organizational Configurations

Most jurisdictions have procurement systems that blend centralized and decentralized services. A central purchasing agency may be responsible for acquiring commonly used materials, such as office furniture and supplies, while line agencies have authority to purchase items used primarily by themselves. Centralization, at least in theory, has the advantage of providing overall controls to ensure that appropriate procedures are followed, resulting in fair competition among government suppliers and the purchase of quality goods and services at the lowest possible prices (due to savings arising from economies of scale). Decentralization, in contrast, presumably reduces red tape, allowing individual agencies to make purchases as needed and to tailor purchases to their specific needs. At the federal level, several major organizational units are responsible for procurement. The General Services Administration (GSA) provides overall support to departments by procuring buildings, equipment, motor vehicles, computer systems, telephone systems, supplies, day care centers for employees' dependents, and the like. Its operations are immense. In any given year, the agency operates a fleet of more than 200,000 vehicles, spends several billions of dollars on construction, manages more than 8,600 federally owned or leased buildings, and keeps many thousands of items on hand in its warehouses.[89]

Although GSA has numerous components, the main ones are the Public Buildings Service and the Federal Acquisition Service (FAS).[90] The Public Buildings unit operates with appropriated funds, while FAS operates with revolving funds by buying goods and services and then selling them to federal agencies.[91] All federal line departments and agencies carry out procurement, with the Department of Defense having one of the largest procurement operations. The Defense Logistics Agency purchases many common items centrally for the department, while the individual services and other DOD agencies also have purchasing authority.[92]

Many procurement offices can result in a hodgepodge of operations, each with its own peculiar set of regulations. In 1974, Congress attempted to deal with this problem by creating the Office of Federal Procurement Policy (OFPP) within the Office of Management and Budget.[93] The OFPP, while not conducting purchasing activities, is responsible for overall procurement policy and coordinating the activities of purchasing offices. The General Services Administration issues the Federal Acquisition Regulation (FAR), which sets standards for basically all federal acquisitions. The Defense Department and other agencies have regulations that supplement FAR.[94]

Besides a central procurement office and individual agency offices, there are other possible arrangements. In some instances, one agency may piggyback on a contract issued through another agency. At the federal level, the Department of Defense is the largest user of contracts by other agencies.[95] Another approach is for agencies to work together jointly on acquisitions. This has the advantage of increasing buying power over what any one agency would have, but has the drawback of requiring that the procurement regulations of both agencies be met. OMB has created a working group to further interagency acquisitions and resolve some of the inherent problems with the process.[96]

Procurement Objectives

A procurement program has several objectives. One chief concern is having the materials and supplies available when needed and avoiding stock outages. Every agency must focus on its mission and use procurement as a means of completing that mission in a timely fashion.

Keeping unit costs as low as possible is another objective. The lowest costs for acquiring items are often obtained by ordering large quantities, whether large amounts of office stationery or entire fleets of automobiles. Ordering large quantities, however, conflicts with another concern: keeping stocked items to a minimum. Procurement specialists strive to determine *economic ordering quantities*, or when to purchase particular types of items and in what quantities. Some purchasing offices have shifted to *just-in-time ordering*, in which items are received from vendors when needed, thereby eliminating the cost of warehousing these items. The widespread use of computer systems has greatly increased the ability of organizations—both public and private—to implement just-in-time ordering. A different concern is that lowest cost purchasing may not obtain a quality product or service. Thus, the procurement official's job is getting "best value" (considering cost, quality, and delivery).

Another objective is creating some flexibility in decision making. For example, if all personnel in a city government are on continuing appointments, then difficult choices will need to be made about possibly laying off workers during economic recessions. On the other hand, if some employees are on fixed-term contracts and expenditures need to be reduced, then these contracts simply need not be renewed when they expire. The same can be done with auxiliary services. When budget cuts are required, auxiliary contracts may not be renewed or at reduced levels.[97]

Procurement objectives often conflict with one another. Procurement policies may include numerous specific requirements that are viewed as red tape and unnecessarily hinder executives in managing their operations. At the same time, such red tape may be important in preventing fraud and waste.

Choices also must be made between purchasing, leasing, and privatizing. In some instances, there may be financial and other advantages to leasing a building rather than purchasing it. The federal government, however, may rely too heavily on leasing office space, as ownership may be less expensive in the long run. A wide range of equipment can be leased, including photocopying machines, computers, and dump trucks. The Defense Department has even considered leasing rather than buying its most expensive weapons systems.[98] *True* or *operating leases* are those in which the government pays for the specified period and gains no ownership of whatever is being leased, whereas *lease-purchase agreements* provide for ownership after a specified period. Leasing and other forms of contracting out are not necessarily an avenue for reducing costs. One survey of state governments found that only one-third reported reduced service costs.[99]

Outsourcing, as discussed earlier, is another option and may involve contracting with a private firm to use its facilities, personnel, and other resources to deliver a service. In many cases, private contractor employees and government employees work side by side to produce services in government or contracted facilities. Federal agencies must follow the guidance in Circular A-76 that covers contracts for commercial (nongovernmental) activities.[100] While many services can be contracted out, policy making is regarded as an inherently governmental function that cannot be privatized. This possibility becomes a concern in situations where government relies heavily on consulting firms to the extent that they seem to be responsible for setting policy or conducting other inherently governmental functions. A blurring of organizational boundaries occurs when a government agency works not with just one but two or more contractors on a particular program or project. In making a choice among these options, a paramount concern must be to use tax dollars effectively and efficiently, without any conflicts of interest.

The process prescribed by Circular A-76 is a complicated one.[101] OMB provides a "Supplemental Handbook" detailing the procedure to be used. Each year, OMB issues guidance on cost figures to be used in calculating anticipated pay raises and changes in the costs of supplies and equipment. An agency must identify an activity that can be contracted out (i.e., is not "inherently governmental"), must establish a process for accepting bids from both private entities and the public organization that is currently providing the service (which bids its "most efficient organization"), must review the bids and select the winner, and must implement the outcome. In the Defense Department, this process often takes 18 months or longer. These competitions tend to result in cuts in the federal workforce either because the work is contracted out or because the government unit won the bid by being more cost-effective—that is, by operating with fewer workers.[102] On average, the cost savings from A-76 competitions (no matter which sector—public or private—was the winner) are more than 30%.[103]

In addition to Circular A-76, the Federal Activities and Inventory Reform (FAIR) Act of 1998 gives priority to competitive sourcing (rather than keeping them solely in-house). Each year federal agencies, under OMB's guidance, must report what activities are "not inherently governmental in nature."[104] Upward of 50% of all jobs analyzed have been identified as potentially being outsourced. The law does not require that some or all of these jobs actually be contracted out, but certainly there is an implication that maybe they should at least be competed (public versus private, via A-76). The lists can be challenged, however. Contractors usually contend that jobs that should have been included were not. Government employees and government unions typically contend the opposite.

By the mid-2000s, there was growing concern that competitive sourcing had become too narrowly focused and that a broader approach was needed at all levels of government and in the private sector, wherever sole-source methods were present. *Spend analysis* became popular as a method for *strategic sourcing*. The underlying idea here is that careful study of existing spending patterns can provide insights into improving the efficient and effective acquisition of services and products. Both OMB and GAO have called on federal agencies to make use of spend analysis.[105] New York State has a spend analysis program for information technology acquisition that is available to state agencies and local governments.[106]

Contracting Process

Steps

Standard procedures are normally followed when contracting for products or services. Specifications for what is to be purchased are determined (this is referred to as the *requirements process*). For example, a truck might be required to have a specified ground clearance, load capacity, passenger capacity, and the like. Usually, a part of this process is *market analysis*—that is, determining what industry has available expertise. Often a formal *request for information* (RFI) is issued as a part of this process.

Then, bidding procedures begin through the issuance of *invitations for bid* (IFBs), *requests for proposal* (RFPs), and *requests for quotation* (RFQs). An IFB is used when a government has a reasonably detailed conception of what is to be purchased, such as the painting of the exterior of a building. In such cases, competitors produce largely similar products or services, so price can be the dominant discriminator. An RFP or RFQ is used in a situation where some latitude exists on the part of the bidder in terms of what is to be offered, or how it is to be provided.

Once bids are received, they are analyzed and, in the case of IFBs, awards are made to the lowest responsible qualified bidder. In a competition involving an RFP, an award might be made to a higher bidder, one that was thought to have the best approach to dealing with a problem. In this case, contracting officers are required to perform a *best value* analysis to ensure that selecting a higher price bid yields best overall value to the government. The life cycle cost of a truck, including expected maintenance costs over the life of the truck, fuel efficiency, and so forth, would generally be included in the best value analysis. For technical services, the best value analysis might take into account which bid offers the most inputs for a given price, and the award could go to a higher bidder in order to obtain better value. Also, the best value judgment would include an estimate of the risk associated with each of the bidders achieving its claimed performance, cost, and schedule.

The Office of Management and Budget has pushed agencies to use the best value approach in competitive sourcing between public and private bidders.[107] However, in a tight budget environment, there has recently been a move by some government agencies to use a less desirable procurement technique known as "low bid, technically acceptable" (LBTA). Agencies utilizing this technique, of course, run the risk of getting low-quality goods and services, especially problematic for high-tech goods or professional services, but the initial low bid makes this approach appear attractive, at least in the short term.[108]

When the government selects a firm using an RFQ, bilateral negotiations are required before a final selection may be made. In contrast, with an RFP, the government may select a firm without further negotiations. The receipt of a product or service follows the signing of a contract or the award of a grant. Additional steps include inspecting the product or service received and paying the contractor.

Congress has encouraged government agencies to buy commercial products from firms not used to doing government business. To that end, *other transactions authority* (OTA) was created. Here, the government buyer is authorized to waive all government unique regulations, and comply only with relevant general laws. Initially, this authority was provided only to the Defense Advanced Research Projects Agency (DARPA) for early research and development work. It was subsequently expanded to include other agencies and for production. Clearly, a major value of using OTA is the ability to expand the base of firms that can bid on a government procurement, by including commercially oriented firms.[109]

Not all spending is handled through the bidding process. As discussed later, many small purchases can be handled through government credit cards and no bids are required. Although restricted to small purchases, the credit card transactions amount to many billions of dollars each year and pose major challenges for auditors.

In some situations, contracts are awarded not to one company but to several firms. The federal government, because it serves the entire nation, finds it advantageous to contract with several suppliers in the same industry. This *multiple-award schedule system* makes goods and services available on a standby basis, allowing agencies to order them when needed.[110] In addition, state and local procurement agencies are permitted to take advantage of the lower prices offered in these GSA multiple-award schedules.[111] These schedules cover a wide variety of goods and services. For example, all forms of construction, ranging from simple repair and maintenance to the construction of an entire building, can be handled through a job order contracting mechanism in which suppliers agree to provide services at specified costs when needed. As another example, a painting firm might sign a contract agreeing to charge a set amount per square foot. Any agency could then hire the firm for painting services.

The federal government has experimented with *reverse auctioning* on common (interchangeable) goods and services. This technique allows bidders during the open bidding period to see the bids made by competing firms but not the identities of the firms themselves. If a company finds its bid has been undercut by another bidder, then the first bidder may consider lowering its bid to meet the competition.

Another feature of some procurement programs is specification of performance in terms of timeliness and quality. For example, a contract for a state highway construction project may stipulate that the project must be completed by a specified date, with financial penalties being imposed for each day beyond the deadline. In a cost-conscious period, the RFP may specify the desired price the government is willing to pay, and the bidders will respond with the best offer for that price.

The 1994 Federal Acquisition Streamlining Act instructs federal agencies to develop *results-oriented* or *performance contracts* for acquisitions other than standardized commercial items.[112] In other words, when an agency buys a service, such as using a firm to process grant applications from local governments, standards should be set for evaluating the firm's performance. Measurable performance is increasingly a part of federal contracts for research and development. These contracts may contain award fee incentives in which contractors achieve higher or lower fees (or profits) based on their performance. To engage in such contracting, agencies must be able to specify what work is to be accomplished, at what time, and with what degree of quality. That has been the rub of the matter. When agencies cannot precisely define their expectations of contractors, then accountability for performance can be elusive. The Services Acquisition Reform Act Advisory Panel found that to be the case at the federal level.[113]

One form of performance contracting is known as *share-in-savings*. Share-in-Savings (SiS) allows for government to contract with a private firm that takes on much of the risk of the endeavor with the promise of financial rewards later through cost savings. For example, contracting out some aspects of debt collection, as noted earlier, can enhance revenue to a government, and a contractor can be paid with some of that newly generated revenue. The E-government Act of 2002 authorizes selective use of share-in-savings contracting for information technology.[114]

Competition

Competition in procurement is considered one of the best means of ensuring quality products or services at minimum cost. Lack of competition may result from blatant favoritism in awarding contracts or from somewhat more subtle ploys, such as specifying a named product brand and model in the IFB. At the state and local levels, corporations have become more aggressive in challenging contract awards when they seem to violate legal requirements for competition.

It is important to emphasize the difference between "competition for an award" and "continuous competition during execution" (often called "competitive dual sourcing"). In the former case, there is a fierce rivalry for the initial award—the winning vendor knows that it will be a sole-source supplier from that point on, and it can bid all the changes that will come later on a monopoly pricing basis. In fact, this usually results in the winner bidding extremely low (known as a "buy-in" or sometimes more pejoratively "low-ball") and assuming that it will "get well on the changes." With continuous competition during execution, on the other hand, the best value winner (based on cost and performance) gets a larger share of each year's award, and both contractors are motivated to deliver higher and higher performance at lower and lower costs.

Not all awards are made on a competitive basis. **Exhibit 11–2** discusses *noncompetitive* or *no-bid contracting*.

Cost-plus-fixed-fee (CPFF) provisions are standard in contracting. Since the work to be done is uncertain at the outset of the contract, the award simply provides that the vendor's costs will be covered, plus the vendor will receive a fixed fee or profit on top of the costs. The fixed fee is negotiated up front and, unless the government changes the requirements, does not change even if costs go up. There is no connection between contractor performance and the fixed fee, and all costs except those determined to be unallowable are reimbursed. These provisions are often controversial, since there may seem to be insufficient incentives for vendors to keep costs down.

Cost-plus-award-fee (CPAF) provisions have been introduced to address at least part of the incentive problem. In an award fee contract, the contractor's costs are reimbursable just as in CPFF, but the amount of the award fee is not completely fixed at contract negotiation. A contractor may receive a higher or lower award fee depending on performance, and performance metrics can include cost management. CPAF has not been as widely used, at least in purchase of services, because determining appropriate and meaningful performance

Exhibit 11–2 No-Bid Contracting

No-bid or noncompetitive contracting has generally been considered anathema to contemporary procurement, but with important exceptions. The bidding process is defended as saving taxpayers' dollars by seeking out the vendors or contractors that offer the best products and services at the best prices. Without bidding, so the argument goes, government pays top dollar and often for inferior goods and services.

No-bid contracting creates opportunities for favoritism. For example, the fact that Vice President Cheney was a former head of Halliburton was the grounds for speculation that any no-bid awards going to Halliburton and its subsidiaries were based on favoritism.[1] The fact that defense contractors donate *millions* of dollars to political campaigns and then reap *billions* of dollars in no-bid defense contracts raises questions about whether these contracts were "bought" (at least indirectly) by the companies.[2] Questions were raised in 2005 when the Department of Homeland Security (DHS) announced it would enter into a no-bid contract for an intelligence analyst certificate program with a small college in Pennsylvania that just happened to have ties with Tom Ridge, the first DHS secretary and former governor of Pennsylvania.[3]

If noncompetitive contracting is considered faulty, then why use it? There are at least two main factors. One is that sometimes there is only one possible bidder, such as when government needs the services that only one company can provide. Then, going with a "sole-source" contract is the only option. The other reason is that of speed. In times of emergency, there may be no time to allow for a lengthy bidding process. A particular project needs to get under way, as in recovering from a flood or tornado.

What governments enter into no-bid contracts? Basically all of them, and basically all are challenged from time to time on their decisions to use such contracts. For example, in 2006, California entered into $51 million of no-bid contracts for sending prison inmates out of state to other facilities.[4]

Federal no-bid contracting received widespread attention with spending on the wars in Afghanistan and Iraq and for recovery from Hurricane Katrina.[5] The Department of Homeland Security awarded most of its Katrina funds with contracts valued at less than $500,000, and 55% of those awards were no-bid. Only 19% were full-and-open competitions, with the remainder falling in other categories.[6] The Government Accountability Office studied Iraq reconstruction spending between 2003 and 2006 and found that only 10% of State Department contracting was awarded competitively compared with 99% for the U.S. Agency for International Development and 82% for the Defense Department.[7] Of course, State Department spending in total was small compared with Defense Department spending. According to GAO, federal agencies obligated approximately $170 billion on noncompetitive contracts in fiscal year 2009 alone.[8]

No-bid contracting is based on negotiations. A government worker or team of workers is responsible for hammering out the details of a contract with a sole-source vendor. This process can be done in a matter of minutes or, if time allows, can extend to months. During the negotiations, there can be bargaining over prices and services. No-bid contracts often involve situations in which the quantity of services is yet unknown, as is the timeline for such services.

The immensity of no-bid contracting in the mid-2000s has resulted in some key recommendations. Both the Government Accountability Office (GAO) when looking

(continued)

at the experience with Hurricane Katrina and the Special Inspector General for Iraq Reconstruction (SIGIR) when looking at the war situation have recommended better prior planning for emergencies.[9] SIGIR recommended the creation of an enhanced Contingency Federal Acquisition Regulation (CFAR) that would be developed on an interagency basis and eventually enacted into law. When planning for emergencies, contracting staff needed to be included. The contracting staff should not be brought into a situation after the fact. Another recommendation was that responsibilities needed to be specified within agencies and across agency lines.

Adequate numbers of qualified government contracting staff are needed in all aspects of procurement but particularly in no-bid situations, where it is important to have staff alert to possible contractor failures and mismanagement. One observer said that the lack of adequate staff led to extensive waste in Iraq: "People were blowing cash around Iraq like they had leaf-blowers."[10] SIGIR recommended creation of a reserve contracting corps that could be deployed to wherever it was needed in the world.

1. Morris, D. (2003). Criticism grows of no-bid work for Iraq reconstruction. *Government Executive.* Retrieved May 21, 2012 from http://www.govexec.com/defense/2003/04/criticism-grows-of-no-bid-work-for-iraq-reconstruction/13872/; Avery, A. H. (2006). Weapons of mass construction: the potential liability of Halliburton under the False Claims Act and the implications to defense contracting. *Alabama Law Review, 57,* 827–852.

2. Strohm, C. (2004). Major defense contractors reap billions in no-bid contracts, report finds. *Government Executive.* Retrieved October 22, 2006, from http://www.govexec.com/dailyfed/0904/092904c1.htm.

3. Williams, B. (2005). No-bid contractor has deep ties to Ridge. *Center for Public Integrity.* Retrieved May 21, 2012 from http://www.iwatchnews.org/2005/03/17/3126/update-no-bid-contractor-has-deep-ties-ridge.

4. California to transfer inmates out of state (2006). *Associated Press,* October 21, 2006. Retrieved October 22, 2006, from http://www.nytimes.com/aponline/us/AP-California-Prisons.html?_r=1&oref=slogin (link no longer active).

5. Miller, T. C. (2006). *Blood money: wasted billions, lost lives, and corporate greed in Iraq.* New York, NY: Little, Brown and Company.

6. Office of the Inspector General, U.S. Department of Homeland Security (2006). *9th PCIE Hurricane Katrina Report.* Retrieved October 22, 2006, from http://www.dhs.gov/xoig/assets/katovrsght/OIG_PCIE_033106.pdf.

7. Special Inspector General for Iraq (2009). *Hard lessons: the Iraq reconstruction experience.* Washington, DC: U.S. Government Accountability Office.

8. Government Accountability Office (2010, July). *Federal contracting: Opportunities exist to increase competition and assess reasons when only one offer is received* (p.11). Retrieved March 21, 2012, from http://www.gao.gov/products/GAO-10-833.

9. U.S. Government Accountability Office (2006). *Agency management of contractors responding to Hurricanes Katrina and Rita.* Washington, DC: Author; Special Inspector General for Iraq Reconstruction, U.S. Department of Defense (2006). *Iraq reconstruction: lessons in contracting and procurement* (p. 2). Retrieved May 21, 2012 from http://www.sigir.mil/files/lessonslearned/Lessons_Learned_July21.pdf.

10. Miller, T. C., as quoted in Mandel, J. (2006). Iraq reconstruction failures tied to contracting breakdowns. *Government Executive.* Retrieved October 22, 2006, from http://www.govexec.com/dailyfed/1006/101306m1.htm.

metrics can be difficult. Governments normally have procedures that allow for challenging the costs submitted by vendors, and some costs may be determined to be unallowable, such as insufficiently documented costs; lack of evidence of prior approval by a contracting officer to incur a cost, such as in advance of travel; costs that are by regulation not reimbursable, such as interest costs; and so forth.

The Competition in Contracting Act of 1984 was passed to encourage greater competition in federal contracting and specifically enhanced the powers of losing bidders to mount legal challenges to the awards.[115] In addition to filing a protest with the contracting agency itself or with the Government Accountability Office, a losing bidder may be able to appeal to the General Services Board of Contract Appeals, the Court of Federal Claims, or a federal district court.[116] Cooperative agreements and grants awarded as the result of a competitive process are not subject to protest, and task orders in a master task order contract are not subject to protest. The original master award for the task order contract may be protested, but not subsequent task awards. In addition, the 1994 Federal Acquisition Streamlining Act contains important provisions that limit bid protests that are often perceived as needlessly delaying the awarding of contracts.

Several factors discourage competition among would-be contractors. Lack of knowledge about how contracts are awarded and how to prepare a bid excludes some companies from bidding, although that problem is somewhat mitigated today given the vast amounts of information on contracting available on government websites. The Defense Department has established Procurement Technical Assistance Centers in many states. These centers assist business firms in understanding the process by which they can sell their goods and services to the government.[117] Many procurements are so large and complex that companies would have to make major investments in personnel and technology just to become competitive in the bidding process. *Design-and-build contracts*, in which several contract awards may be made for the design phase, with the best design being selected for the build or implementation phase, enable more firms to compete for much larger, more complex contracts. But, as noted above, they become sole-source after the initial selection is made.

Competition is restricted in other ways as well. A close and long-term relationship between a government agency and a contractor can develop over time. When a contract is to be rebid for a new time period, the company already holding the contract usually has a decided advantage.

Contract bundling tends to prohibit smaller companies from competing for contracts, whether this be at the local, state, or federal level.[118] In contract bundling, several would-be small contracts are put up for bid as a single, large contract. The advantages to government are at least twofold. First, the administrative costs of handling the bidding and contracting processes are reduced. Second, the item or service being purchased is often less expensive when it is ordered in bulk as in a bundled contract than when it is purchased through several smaller contracts. Combining efforts into larger and larger contracts is often an agency response to budget cuts or cuts in personnel complement. Fewer procurement officers and fewer government staff to oversee contracts increase the pressure on the agency to make fewer but larger awards. However, such bundled contracts can involve a diverse set of products and services, many of which are beyond the scope of a single small company, thereby excluding smaller companies from the bidding process. OMB has instructed agencies to limit their use of the bundling procedure and said it would rate agencies on their efforts to avoid the practice.[119] Nonetheless, the empirical data for past competitions for bundled contracts shows clear increases in savings as the size of the effort increases.[120]

Companies become reluctant to participate in competitions when, if they win, they might have to wait for weeks or months to receive the money owed them. Delays in payments can bankrupt a small firm. Even when payments occur promptly, small firms may face other problems. If payments are made but then later an audit agency determines that the costs incurred are unallowable due to lack of adequate documentation, the small firm may be unable to comply due to weak recordkeeping. Whatever the situation, it will be costly from the standpoint of the time consumed in trying to comply with the government's requests.

Government contracting also opens up contractors to liability over their compliance with various employment laws, such as equal employment opportunity based on race, gender, and the like. The Rehabilitation Act of 1973 requires affirmative action in government hiring of people with disabilities, and this law is extended to private companies when they become government contractors.[121] Similarly, affirmative action is required in the hiring and promoting of veterans under the Vietnam Era Veterans' Readjustment Assistance Act of 1974.[122] Requirements such as these may discourage companies from bidding on federal contracts, not because the companies oppose equal opportunity or hiring veterans but because they fear lawsuits or the threat of lawsuits.

The widespread use of the Internet beginning in the 1990s has posed major challenges in the procurement arena. Expectations have developed that procurement should be an essential component of E-government. Governments at all levels have worked diligently to convert their paper-based processes for procurement to ones that include electronic processing. These efforts are complicated by the massiveness of procurement programs in large governments, by statutory restrictions that specify processes to be used, and by rapidly changing technology.

At the federal level, several websites are relevant:

- *Business.usa.gov* is intended to service all aspects of the business community and not just contracting. The site provides information on such topics as business law, taxes, and international trade as well as government procurement. The Small Business Administration maintains the site in cooperation with more than 20 other agencies.
- *Acquisition.gov* is focused specifically on procurement and provides links to a variety of government websites. This site is hosted by the E-government initiative.
- *FedBizOpps.gov*, according to its own description, is the single point of entry for federal government procurement. The site is hosted by the General Services Administration. Federal agencies have begun to post reverse auctions on this site (see above).
- *FPDS.gov* is the Federal Procurement Data System. It provides access to a wealth of information about government awards. The system is managed by a team of agencies led by the General Services Administration.
- *USASpending.gov* is an accessible, user-friendly website that allows a wide variety of queries about recipients of government awards, patterns over time, agency procurement

trends, geographic distribution of awards, and other information of interest to organizations that compete for awards and organizations and individuals who keep watch over government awards.

- *GSA e-Buy* (www.ebuy.gsa.gov) allows federal buyers to post RFQs and RFPs (see above) and vendors to respond electronically.

Increasingly, federal agencies that issue research grants have implemented online grant application systems. The National Science Foundation and the National Institutes of Health were early leaders. Once grant applications are received, agencies forward through electronic means the relevant portions of the applications to extramural panels that review the proposals. The review process in which the extramural panels evaluate proposals is also conducted online.

State and local governments and the private sector have become deeply involved in information technology as a vehicle for communicating between the business community and government procurement. For example, California maintains a website for state, federal, and local contracting.[123] One example of a commercial site is *GovCB.com*, Government Contract and Bid, which helps businesses win government contracts and find potential teaming partners online.

Computer technology is as important to government agencies that consume products and services as it is to firms that sell to government. The General Services Administration operates GSA Advantage! (gsaadvantage.gov), an online shopping center. Agencies can not only compare prices on products and place orders, but also configure products and add accessories. GSA offers to agencies similar services in the information technology realm.

Contract management is another critical component of the procurement process.[124] What good is a contract if government procurement officers fail to follow up to be sure that a business met its obligations under the contract? One occasional problem has been for contractors to meet their obligations but for government to overpay the contractors. Congress has required agencies to use recovery auditing to identify overpayments and recoup money that was misspent.[125]

Reforms

Procurement procedures become increasingly complex as additional, well-intended requirements are imposed. One prescription might be to simplify the government procurement process. Off-the-shelf purchasing of commercial items may be less expensive than specifying items that then might require special designs and types of construction. As an example of the rigidity in government purchasing, the General Services Administration once had elaborate specifications for the design and durability of "ash receiver[s], tobacco (desk type)" when commercially available ashtrays probably would have been suitable, especially given that smoking is banned in most government buildings. The Federal Acquisition Reform Act (FARA), or Clinger-Cohen Act of 1996, broadened the definition of commercial services, bringing more purchasing activities under the simplified procedures.[126] Ten years' experience with the law found that the expected cost savings were not realized.[127] In addition, numerous barriers to buying commercial goods and services were found to continue to exist.

Workforce Quality

Another reform frequently mentioned is a move to upgrade the quality and sometimes quantity of the procurement workforce. The argument is that upgrades are necessary to reflect the increasing size of contracting and its complexity, particularly in procurements for high-tech goods and in professional services. This shortage has been found across the federal government. DOD, which experienced cutbacks in the post–Cold War period but nonetheless still engages in massive contracting, has perhaps the most acute shortages. At the state level, the ongoing California Performance Review found the state's procurement workforce to be "inadequate." The review called for new civil service classifications and new training programs.[128] New York's Citywide Training Center (CTC) offers procurement classes that are recognized by the Universal Public Purchasing Certification Council and the Institute for Supply Management.[129] The Procurement and Supply Chain Benchmarking Association awards governments "best in class" status for excellence in procurement (*pasba.com*).

At the federal level, efforts are under way in dealing with perceived acquisition workforce problems. One concern is workforce turnover and retirements. One report found that 32% of contracting employees would be eligible for retirement in 2010 and 54% in 2015.[130] Another concern is that the workforce has shrunk, according to the Federal Acquisition Institute, from more than 165,000 employees in 1990 to just over 100,000 by 2009.[131] Shortages in staff may result in procurement officers devoting their time almost exclusively to the awarding of contracts at the expense of overseeing the implementation of the awards.[132] The Federal Acquisition Institute, a branch of the General Services Administration, was established in the 1970s to further the development of the procurement workforce. It delivers online and classroom training and serves as a link to other training providers.

Fraud, Waste, Abuse, and Scandals

Despite sustained efforts to improve procurement practices, the field has been plagued with scandals involving fraud, waste (as in the case of toilet seats that cost the military hundreds of dollars), and abuse (as in the case of the Federal Emergency Management Agency having hundreds of trailers sitting unused and exposed to potential flooding after Hurricane Katrina). While illegal actions represent only a very small percentage of procurement dollars, these come at a high price in terms of public faith in government. The acquisition function at several federal agencies appears on the Government Accountability Office's high-risk list, meaning that the government is exposed to the possible loss of large sums of resources, more as a result of waste than fraud.[133]

Fraud comes in many forms. Frauds involving state highway contracting occur in such ways as:

• Specifications that are written by government workers to favor particular contractors and suppliers;
• Conflicts of interest, such as acquisition officials having financial interests in road construction companies;

- Collusive bidding and price fixing (while extremely rare, these actions involve some contractors not bidding on a contract so as to swing the award to a favored company);
- Questionable documentation from contractors, such as altering or modifying critical information like the contractor's bond and pre-qualifications;
- Production substitution, such as mismarking and mislabeling products and materials; or
- Cost mischarging for materials and labor, such as cost overruns due to intentional underestimating or underbidding.[134]

Safeguards against such practices exist. Federal agencies have inspectors general offices to ferret out corruption, and similar units exist at the state and local levels. Governments sometimes cooperate with one another, as in the case of the Federal Emergency Management Agency (FEMA) working with New York State to combat fraud related to regional flooding in 2006.[135] The Procurement Integrity Act of 1996 prohibits federal employees from releasing "contractor bid or proposal information" that in some way would unfairly benefit competitors.[136] Many acquisition employees are prohibited from receiving compensation from contractors that they had direct contact with for one year or more after they leave government service. While working for government, they are to report any employment offers by contractors. Federal agency personnel in positions other than procurement are often precluded from representing their new private employer with their old agency for one year after leaving government service, although this does not prohibit their being employed by a company that does business with their old agency. Under restrictions established by the Obama administration, no former federal employee can work for a contractor for at least one year after federal employment if the position would put the former employee in direct contact with his or her agency.

One of the most notorious fraud situations in recent times involved David Safavian, who was chief of the Office of Federal Procurement Policy within OMB. Prior to joining OMB, he had been chief of staff at the General Services Administration. He was indicted and convicted for obstructing a GSA investigation into possible illegal business relations with lobbyist Jack Abramoff. He was convicted in 2006, had his conviction overturned on appeal, but then was retried and convicted in 2008. He was sentenced to 18 months in prison in late 2009.[137]

Contractors can be sanctioned. They can be suspended from government contracting for a fixed period or barred permanently. The Government Accountability Office has stepped up pressure on federal agencies to revise and use their procedures for suspending or even debarring contractors.[138] Short of these measures, they can have restrictions imposed on them on bidding on contracts and executing them.[139] Nevertheless, abuses still occur too frequently. The Government Accountability Office reported that one of the most widespread abuses of contractors was failure to pay federal taxes owed.[140] In the mid-2000s, Boeing Company engaged in bribing an Air Force contractor over tanker procurement and paid $615 million to settle the case. This largest defense contracting scandal in decades resulted in people from the Air Force and Boeing going to prison.[141] In the aftermath of the scandal, the Justice Department created a special task force against fraud in defense and homeland security.[142]

Problem Areas and Innovations

Procurement is undergoing extensive changes too numerous to discuss here, but a few can be noted. One major change is the growing importance of contracting for services as distinguished from acquisition of products. For example, in fiscal year 2010, 59% of all DOD acquisitions were contracted for services. The field has grown to such an extent that there is a professional association known as the Contract Services Association (CSA). The association promotes private contracting by government, creates opportunities for networking between companies and government agencies, and provides training for contractors in how to work with governments at all levels. Service contracting presents special challenges of determining what services of what quality, and what quantity, are to be delivered. After delivery, the challenge is in monitoring the process to ensure that the contract requirements are met and that only appropriate expenses are charged for those services.

Measuring the costs of services is particularly troublesome due to variations in accounting rules used by companies doing business in the private and public sectors. This situation complicates efforts to compare the costs of producing a service by a corporation with those done for a government agency. Furthermore, when such service contracts are awarded to nonprofit entities, important problems may arise over how government expects operations to be managed and how the nonprofits normally manage themselves.

Credit Cards and ID Cards

Government-issued credit cards have become standard components of acquisition systems. Some governments now provide employees with credit cards so that they may charge their travel expenses and be reimbursed later, rather than use travel advances or their personal funds to cover costs until being reimbursed. Credit cards are also being used for small purchases, such as $2,500 or less. The cards in the federal government are helpful in remote areas that lack ready access to General Services Administration supply centers. Today's technology allows credit cards to work or not work for specified sales. For example, the cards can be programmed not to work for liquor sales where bar code systems are used. GSA reported $17.1 billion of card purchases for fiscal year 2004 and claimed it saved nearly $54 on every transaction due to reduced processing costs—thus saving millions of dollars for the government.[143]

With millions of cards in circulation in the federal government, abuse can be expected. The Defense Department was sharply criticized when it came to light that employees had used the cards to purchase hundreds of dollars' worth of cosmetics and compact discs.[144] GAO and the Inspector General of the Department of Homeland Security found that DHS employees had purchased "a beer brewing kit, a 63" plasma television costing $8,000 which was found unused in its original box 6 months after being purchased, and tens of thousands of dollars for training at golf and tennis resorts."[145]

Affirmative Action

A continuing problem is the extent to which procurement should support affirmative action to assist minority-owned businesses, women contractors, and other special groups. In 1995, the Federal Acquisition Streamlining Act set nonbinding goals of contracting with minority-owned businesses, and Executive Order 12928 called upon agencies to develop methods for encouraging minority businesses and historically black colleges and universities to bid on contracts with the government. Executive Order 13360, issued by President George W. Bush, expects agencies to create opportunities for service-disabled veterans to contract and subcontract with the government. To avoid charges of reverse discrimination, agencies do not use quotas but rather pursue outreach and other programs to help make minority businesses aware of contracting opportunities and provide advice on how to prepare procurement proposals.

Acquisition programs are often expected to provide special opportunities to small businesses that otherwise might be locked out of selling to the government by large corporations. Executive Orders 13169 and 13170 require federal agencies to increase opportunities for small businesses, especially disadvantaged ones.[146]

Labor–Management Relations

In the contracting process, labor–management issues may arise, such as whether a contractor will enter into agreements with labor unions. Executive Order 12871 established the National Partnership Council and required federal agencies to work cooperatively with unions. In 2001, President George W. Bush revoked this order by issuing Executive Order 13202. The new order called for "neutrality towards government contractors' labor relations on federal and federally funded construction projects."

"Buy American" Concerns

International interests have always been of concern, and with economic threats to the U.S. economy has come renewed interest in requirements to "buy American." Congress from time to time has required federal agencies to report on their purchases of products made abroad but has stopped short of blocking such purchases. The purchase of defense components from overseas suppliers has been particularly sensitive.[147] In 2006, there was a brouhaha when the federal government announced plans to award a contract to manage six seaports to Dubai Ports World of the United Arab Emirates.[148] Considerable alarm was expressed over whether port security was being turned over to a Middle Eastern company, given terrorism and unrest in that part of the world. Dubai Ports World in facing the furor withdrew from the proposed contract. More generally, foreign-owned, U.S.-located firms doing national security work get special reviews and oversight. In order to do any classified work, these firms must have a government-approved board of directors with a majority of members from the United States.

Procurement During Crises

The war in Iraq after 2003 and Hurricanes Katrina and Rita in 2005 tested the limits of how procurement programs operate under extreme circumstances. Contracts for Iraq's reconstruction worth billions of dollars were awarded to be carried out in extraordinarily difficult situations. In simple terms, how can contractors be held accountable for results when shells are literally falling around them? Additionally, during these crises there were charges of favoritism in awarding contracts and just simple mismanagement. Congress created the Office of Special Inspector General for Iraq (and later Afghanistan)

Reconstruction to audit the government's activities.[149] One of the audits found "millions of reconstruction dollars stuffed casually into footlockers and filing cabinets, an American soldier in the Philippines who gambled away cash belonging to Iraq, and three Iraqis who plunged to their deaths in a rebuilt hospital elevator that had been improperly certified as safe."[150]

The 2005 hurricane season unquestionably overloaded disaster services and especially contracting systems for the federal, state, and local governments. At the federal level, the key players were FEMA, the Army Corps of Engineers, and GSA. With more than one million people displaced by the hurricanes, government offices were under extreme pressure to act quickly, resulting at the federal level in $8.1 billion in contracts being awarded in the first 90 days after the disasters.[151] GAO found such weaknesses as overall inadequate planning and preparation for disasters and lack of adequate numbers of personnel to oversee the execution of contracts.[152] FEMA was criticized as not understanding what amounts of items to order—for example, ordering twice the amount of ice needed. A survey of hurricane victims a year later gave poor marks to all levels of government. Only 30% believed the federal government had done a good or excellent job. Comparable numbers for the state and local governments were 33% and 40%. Especially dismaying was that 15% of the respondents said FEMA or the government in general had victimized them after the hurricanes.[153] FEMA was given high praise by state and local officials for the government's response in the 2011 flooding that resulted from Hurricane Irene (see discussion in the chapter on intergovernmental relations).

RISK MANAGEMENT

To provide services, governments must have property and personnel. Arising from this simple fact are a series of exposures or risks, such as the risk of property being damaged or lost owing to natural disasters, employee error, and fraud by employees and others. Property damage can lead to major repair or replacement costs and to loss of income (e.g., structural problems in a municipal stadium may force its closing). The Chicago flood of 1992, in which water from the Chicago River entered buildings throughout the downtown area, is an example of how inattention to a problem—in this case, leakage into a tunnel system caused by faulty construction under government contract—can have disastrous consequences.

Risk management considers what threats exist, the probability of each happening, and the likely consequence if the threat or disaster materializes. Until September 11, 2001, the probability of commercial aircraft being used as devices to destroy major landmark buildings would have been considered quite low. Since then, risk managers have had to reexamine the vulnerability of food supplies, water systems, nuclear power plants, ports, and the like to deliberate acts of terrorism. Anthrax in powder form was shipped in the mails in 2001, causing a shutdown of delivery to many offices, especially government offices. As of the mid-2000s, many federal agencies had systems in place to help safeguard against future anthrax attacks. Electronic government, by which much of government's work is done today, has the advantage of avoiding the anthrax threat but faces the disadvantage of malicious computer hacking.

Other risks pertain to financial guarantees. The federal government strives to identify the extent of its exposure in loan programs and other activities, such as mortgage guarantees. Perhaps the highest-profile cases associated with the financial crisis after 2007 were the costly takeovers of Fannie Mae and Freddie Mac, and the bankruptcy of the solar energy company Solyndra.

Liability

Governments are vulnerable to suits brought by employees or by corporations and private citizens. Negligence is often the basis of suits in which government is alleged not to have acted the way a "reasonable" person would and inflicted harm as a result. Court-awarded financial settlements can be extraordinarily large. In some suits against local governments, the awards have been greater than the governments' total annual budgets.

Laws govern liability cases. The federal government may be sued only in federal court. One of the most important federal laws is the Federal Tort Claims Act of 1946, which selectively permits suits against the government in cases not arising out of contract.[154] State and local governments may sometimes be sued in federal courts as well as in state courts. Antitrust cases against local governments, for example, are the domain of federal courts. Discrimination cases can be filed in federal and state courts.

Managing Risks

Governments need a management strategy for dealing with exposures. Risk management planning begins by identifying risks and, where possible, eliminating them. A faulty woodworking machine in a school shop should be repaired. The repair will improve the safety of the machine, thereby eliminating some risk when students use it. A road intersection widely known to be dangerous can be redesigned. A community that is subject to hurricanes obviously cannot avoid these fierce storms, but it can take steps to be prepared for such emergencies.

Having eliminated or reduced risks, governments must be prepared to deal with the remaining areas of exposure. Commercial insurance is used by governments and awarded through a bidding process similar to that for any other purchasing arrangement. Another option is self-insurance, where a government sets aside funds on a regular basis to cover awards or simply expends funds from the current budget to cover abnormal expenses (for example, the costs of repairing police cars damaged in the line of duty). In some instances, governments help cover each other's risks through self-insurance pooling.

Insurance premiums for liability coverage have become extremely expensive, sometimes so expensive that insurance is beyond the reach of governments—if it is available at all. Costs are a function of the nature of a policy. Salient factors include the number of employees and officials of a government, the services covered, the deductibles included, and the loss experienced. The latter is not just the experience of a particular government. A given city might have had no major suits filed against it, but because some cities have encountered major legal problems, as in cases involving landfills, all cities pay heavily for coverage.

The costs of risk management are typically handled centrally. That is, the costs of insurance premiums, court-mandated awards to injured parties, out-of-court settlements, and the like are handled by the central government budget and not charged to department budgets. Were line agencies charged for these costs, managers would be more aware of the costs of their operations and would have greater incentives to reduce risk. Faced with staggering insurance premiums, a government may choose to discontinue a service, such as operating a community swimming pool.

The Governmental Accounting Standards Board (GASB) has several pertinent statements:

- Statement No. 10, as amended by Statement No. 30, covers risks associated with torts, thefts, business interruptions, errors or omissions, job-related illnesses or injuries of employees, and acts of God.
- Statement No. 27 requires governments to report pension plan risks.
- Statement No. 31 covers the reporting of investment risks.
- Statement No. 40 requires reporting of deposit and investment risks.
- Statement No. 42 expects governments to report impairment of capital assets and insurance recoveries for situations such as when a building becomes unexpectedly unusable.[155]
- Statement No. 53 covers accounting and financial reporting for derivative investments in order to ensure that the reporting of them is done at fair market value.
- Statement No. 58 sets financial and accounting guidance for governments that have filed for Chapter 9 bankruptcy protection.

The federal government has taken steps toward integrating risk management into its overall system of management. The Office of Management and Budget drafted a proposed risk assessment bulletin that, if adopted, would establish ground rules for agencies in evaluating the risks they face.[156] The Government Accountability Office has recommended that risk assessment be used to prioritize threats and that it be used in conjunction with performance budgeting for the allocation of scarce resources.[157]

SUMMARY

Execution is the conversion of plans embodied in the budget into day-to-day operations. At stake are factors such as interpreting and complying with legislative intent as prescribed in appropriations and providing the services that have been authorized. Control over line agencies is exercised through apportionment planning and preauditing of expenditures.

Since the 1980s, there has been a resurgence of interest in achieving economy and efficiency. Outsourcing of services has been used as one means of increasing the efficiency of operations.

Budget offices are involved in a host of activities other than preparing budgets. On the federal level, OMB exercises major powers related to information collection and dissemination and to agencies issuing regulations.

Tax administration and cash management, which are usually under the direction of a secretary of treasury, are processes aimed at maximizing revenues and minimizing costs.

Numerous mechanisms are used to enforce tax laws, ranging from offering assistance in preparing tax returns to prosecuting delinquent taxpayers.

Cash management is the process of administering monies to ensure that they are available to meet expenditure needs and that monies, when temporarily not needed, are invested at a minimum risk and a maximum yield. Many instruments exist for investing state and local funds. The U.S. Treasury Department handles federal cash management through the Federal Reserve System.

Procurement entails the acquisition of resources required to provide government services, while risk management is concerned with protecting those resources. Governments often have a central purchasing office but allow individual departments some independence in purchasing products and services. A procurement program attempts to purchase only what is needed, avoid stock outages, and keep unit costs low.

Risk management attempts to eliminate or reduce risk exposure and to prepare for such events as damage to government property and liability suits arising out of government operations.

NOTES

1. Hildreth, W. B., & Khan A. (Eds.) (1999). Symposium on budget execution. *Journal of Public Budgeting, Accounting and Financial Management, 11*, 230–310; Cain, C., et al. (2004). Turnover, trust, and transfers: an examination of local government budget execution. *International Journal of Public Administration, 27*, 557–576.
2. U.S. Government Accountability Office (2008). *Principles of federal appropriations law*, 3rd ed. Washington, DC: Author.
3. U.S. Office of Management and Budget (2010). *Preparation, submission, and execution of the budget*, OMB Circular A-11, section 20. Retrieved March 20, 2012, from http://www.whitehouse.gov/sites/default/files/omb/assets/a11_current_year/a_11_2011.pdf.
4. U.S. Office of Management and Budget (2010). *Preparation, submission, and execution of the budget*, OMB Circular A-11, section 20.3, p. 750.
5. U.S. Office of Management and Budget (2010). *Preparation, submission, and execution of the budget*, OMB Circular A-11, p. 397.
6. The National Governors Association and the National Association of State Budget Officers (2011). *The fiscal survey of states* (p. 8). Retrieved March 20, 2012, from http://www.nga.org/files/live/sites/NGA/files/pdf/FSS1111.PDF.
7. Dougherty, M. J., et al. (2003). Managerial necessity and the art of creating surpluses: the budget-execution process in West Virginia cities. *Public Administration Review, 63*, 484–497.
8. Douglas, J. W., & Franklin, A. L. (2006). Putting the brakes on the rush to spend down end-of-year balances: carryover money in Oklahoma state agencies. *Public Budgeting & Finance, 26*, Fall, 46–64.
9. Peckenpaugh, J. (2002). OMB to manage Homeland Security reorganization. *Government Executive*. Retrieved August 13, 2006, from http://www.govexec.com/dailyfed/071702p1.htm (source no longer available).
10. O'Keefe, E. (2011). Trade offices targeted in reorganization plan. *Federal Eye* [*Washington Post* blog], June 9. Retrieved March 23, 2012, from http://www.washingtonpost.com/blogs/federal-eye/post/trade-offices-targeted-in-reorganization-plan/2011/06/09/AGaCQ7MH_blog.html.
11. Batley, R. (Ed.) (2006). Symposium on non-state provision of basic services. *Public Administration and Development, 26*, 193–278; Block, W. (2006). *The privatization of roads and highways: human and economic factors*. Lewiston, NY: Edwin Mellen Press; Lukemeyer, A., & McCorkle, R. C. (2006). Privatization of prisons. *American Review of Public Administration, 36*, 189–206.

12. Savas, E. S. (1982). *Privatizing the public sector.* Chatham, NJ: Chatham House; Savas, E. S. (2005). *Privatization in the city: successes, failures, lessons.* Washington, DC: CQ Press.

13. Riley, C. (2011). Pawlenty: If you can Google it, cut it. *CNN Money,* June 7. Retrieved March 23, 2012, from http://money.cnn.com/2011/06/07/news/economy/pawlenty_economic_plan/index.htm.

14. Sinn, W., & Whalley, J. (Eds.) (2006). *Privatization experiences in the European Union.* Cambridge, MA: MIT Press.

15. Avery, G. (2000). Outsourcing public health laboratory services: a blueprint for determining whether to privatize and how. *Public Administration Review, 60,* 330–337; Michel, R. G. (2004). Make or buy: using cost analysis to decide whether to outsource public services. *Government Finance Review, 19,* August, 15–21.

16. Minow, M. (2005). Outsourcing power: how privatizing military efforts challenges accountability, professionalism, and democracy. *Boston College Law Review, 46,* 989–1026.

17. Federal Managers' Financial Integrity Act of 1982 (P.L. 97-255); Robert, N., & Candreva, P. J. (2006). Controlling internal controls. *Public Administration Review, 66,* 463–465.

18. Gauthier, S. J. (2006). Understanding internal control. *Government Finance Review, 21,* February, 10–16.

19. Paperwork Reduction Act of 1980 (P.L. 96-511); Paperwork Reduction Act of 1995 (P.L. 104-13).

20. Chief Information Officers Council website, www.cio.gov.

21. Sunstein, C. (2011). *Data call for the 2011 information collection budget* [memorandum]. February 23, 1–2. Retrieved March 23, 2012, from http://www.whitehouse.gov/sites/default/files/omb/inforeg/icb/2012_icb_datacall.pdf.

22. Government Information Security Reform Act of 2000 (P.L. 106-398).

23. Federal Information Security Management Act of 2002. (P.L. 107-347).

24. U.S. Office of Management and Budget (2008). *Fiscal year 2008 report to Congress on implementation of the Federal Information Security Management Act of 2002;* Montalbano, E. (2011). Federal IT security spending called "light." *Information Week,* November 22. Retrieved March 20, 2012, from http://www.informationweek.com/news/government/security/232200045.

25. U.S. Government Accountability Office (2006). *Information security: continued progress needed to strengthen controls at the Internal Revenue Service.* Washington, DC: Author; Pulliam, D. (2006). OMB steps up data security reporting requirements. *Government Executive.* Retrieved March 20, 2012, from http://www.govexec.com/technology/2006/07/omb-steps-up-data-security-reporting-requirements/22261.

26. U.S. Office of Management and Budget (2000). *Management of federal information resources,* Circular A-130. Retrieved August 16, 2006, from http://www.whitehouse.gov/omb/circulars/a130/a130trans4.html.

27. U.S. Chief Information Officer Council (2006). *Federal enterprise architecture: security and privacy profile.* Retrieved August 16, 2006, from http://www.cio.gov/documents/Security_and_Privacy_Profile_v2.pdf.

28. Brown University (2008). *Delaware and Michigan are best states for American e-government.* July 24, 2007. Retrieved March 20, 2012, from http://news.brown.edu/pressreleases/2007/07/american-e-government.

29. Federal Funding Accountability and Transparency Act of 2006 (P.L. 109-282).

30. Government Accountability Office (2010). *Implementation of the Federal Funding Accountability and Transparency Act of 2006.* March. Retrieved March 20, 2012, from http://www.gao.gov/new.items/d10365.pdf.

31. West, W. (2005). Administrative rulemaking: an old and emerging literature. *Public Administration Review, 65,* 655–668; Teske, P. (2004). *Regulation in the states.* Washington, DC: Brookings Institution.

32. U.S. Office of Management and Budget, Office of Information and Regulatory Affairs website, http://www.whitehouse.gov/omb/international_regulatory_cooperation.

33. U.S. Office of Management and Budget (2003). *Regulatory analysis,* Circular A-4. Retrieved August 16, 2006, from http://www.whitehouse.gov/omb/circulars/a004/a-4.pdf.

34. Regulatory Right-to-Know Act of 1999, as contained in Treasury and General Government Appropriations Act for Fiscal Year 1999 (P.L. 106-58).
35. U.S. Office of Management and Budget (2011). *2011 report to Congress on the benefits and costs of federal regulation and unfunded mandates on state, local, and tribal entities.* Retrieved March 20, 2012, from http://www.whitehouse.gov/sites/default/files/omb/inforeg/2011_cb/2011_cba_report.pdf.
36. Steps available at the U.S. General Services Administration & U.S. Office of Management and Budget website, RegInfo.gov; West, W. F. (2004). Formal procedures, informal processes, accountability, and responsiveness in bureaucratic policy making: an institutional policy analysis. *Public Administration Review, 64,* 66–80.
37. Unfunded Mandates Reform Act of 1995 (P.L. 104-4).
38. Regulatory Flexibility Act of 1980 (P.L. 96-354); Small Business Regulatory Enforcement Fairness Act of 1996 (P.L. 104-121).
39. Congressional Review Act of 1996 (P.L. 104-121).
40. U.S. Government Accountability Office (2006). *Perspectives on 10 years of Congressional Review Act implementation.* Washington, DC: Author.
41. Orszag, P. (2009). *Open government directive* [memorandum]. December 8. Retrieved March 20, 2012, from http://www.whitehouse.gov/sites/default/files/omb/assets/memoranda_2010/m10-06.pdf.
42. U.S. Government Accountability Office (2005). *Tax administration: systematic information sharing would help IRS determine the deductibility of civil settlement payments.* Washington, DC: Author.
43. Gruber, A. (2006). IRS plan to close service centers based on faulty data. *Government Executive.* Retrieved December 19, 2011, from http://www.govexec.com/story_page.cfm?filepath=/dailyfed/0306/032406a1.htm.
44. U.S. Government Accountability Office (2005). *Tax administration: IRS can improve its productivity measures by using alternative methods.* Washington, DC: Author; Klun, M. (2004). Performance measurement for tax administrations: the case of Slovenia. *International Review of Administrative Sciences, 70,* 567–574; Sera, P. (2005). Performance measures in tax administration: Chile as a case study. *Public Administration and Development, 25,* 115–124.
45. Hackbart, M., & Ramsey, J. R. (2001). Estimating tax evasion losses: the road fund case. *Public Budgeting & Finance, 21,* Spring, 58–72.
46. Internal Revenue Service, U.S. Department of Treasury (2009). *Update on reducing the federal tax gap and improving voluntary compliance,* July 8. Retrieved March 20, 2012, from http://www.irs.gov/pub/newsroom/tax_gap_report_final_version.pdf.
47. U.S. Government Accountability Office (2006). *Tax compliance: opportunities exist to reduce the tax gap using a variety of approaches.* Washington, DC: Author; U.S. Government Accountability Office (2006). *Individual income tax policy: streamlining, simplification, and additional reforms are desirable.* Washington, DC: Author.
48. Internal Revenue Service, U.S. Department of Treasury (2011). *Electronic Federal Tax Payment System.* Retrieved December 19, 2011, from http://www.eftps.gov.
49. Pulliam, D. (2006). IRS gives teleworkers high-speed access to networks. *Government Executive.* Retrieved December 19, 2011, from http://www.govexec.com/story_page.cfm?filepath=/dailyfed/0306/032206p1.htm.
50. Internal Revenue Service, U.S. Department of Treasury (2006). *Electronic Federal Tax Payment System.* Retrieved August 17, 2006, from http://www.irs.gov/efile/article/0,id=98005,00.html.
51. Electronic Tax Administration Advisory Committee (2011). *Electronic tax administration advisory committee report to Congress.* June. Retrieved March 20, 2012, from http://www.irs.gov/pub/irs-pdf/p3415.pdf.
52. Office of Management and Budget (2010). *Policies for federal credit programs and non-tax receivables,* Circular A-129, revised. Retrieved March 20, 2012, from http://www.whitehouse.gov/omb/circulars_a129rev.
53. Debt Collection Act of 1982 (P.L. 97-365); Debt Collection Improvement Act of 1996 (P.L. 99-578).

54. Mandel, J. (2006). IRS announces first contracts for debt collection work. *Government Executive*. Retrieved December 19, 2011, from http://www.govexec.com/story_page.cfm?filepath=/dailyfed/0306/030906m1.htm.

55. Internal Revenue Service, U.S. Department of Treasury (2006). *Safeguards included in private debt collection initiative*. Retrieved August 17, 2006, from http://www.irs.gov/newsroom/article/0,id=155065,00.html.

56. Johnston, D. C. (2006). I.R.S. enlists help in collecting delinquent taxes. *New York Times*, August 20. Retrieved August 20, 2006, from http://www.nytimes.com/2006/08/20/business/20tax.html.

57. Internal Revenue Service, U.S. Department of Treasury (2011). *Taxpayer rights*. Retrieved March 20, 2012, from http://www.irs.gov/advocate/article/0,id=98206,00.html.

58. U.S. Government Accountability Office (2007). *Management report: improvements needed in IRS's internal controls*. Washington, DC: Author. Retrieved March 20, 2012, from http://www.gao.gov/products/GAO-07-689R.

59. Dropkin, M., & Hayden, A. (2001). *The cash flow management book for nonprofits: a step-by-step guide for managers, consultants, and boards*. San Francisco, CA: Jossey-Bass; Fight, A. (2005). *Cash flow forecasting*. Boston, MA: Elsevier.

60. Michel, R. G., & MacKenzie, M. (2005). Cash management technology in state and local government: results of a GFOA/JP Morgan Chase survey. *Government Finance Review, 21*, October, 10–15.

61. Prompt Payment Act of 1982 (P.L. 97-177).

62. U.S. Government Accountability Office (2006). *DOD payments to small business: implementation and effective utilization of electronic invoicing could further reduce late payments*. Washington, DC: Author.

63. Pulliam, D. (2006). Pentagon late payments hurt small contractors. *Government Executive*. Retrieved October 21, 2006, from http://www.govexec.com/dailyfed/0506/052206p1.htm.

64. Financial Management Service, U.S. Treasury Department (2011). *Prompt payment*. Retrieved December 17, 2011, from http://www.fms.treas.gov/prompt/ppinterest.html.

65. Joyce, P. G. (2001). What's so magical about five percent? A nationwide look at factors that influence the optimal size of state rainy day funds. *Public Budgeting & Finance, 21*, Summer, 62–87.

66. Hou, Y. (2004). Budget stabilization fund: structural features of the enabling legislation and balance levels. *Public Budgeting & Finance, 24*, Fall, 38–64; Marlowe, J. (2005). Fiscal slack and counter-cyclical expenditure stabilization: a first look at the local level. *Public Budgeting & Finance, 25*, Fall, 48–72; Schunk, D., & Woodward, D. (2005). Spending stabilization rules: a solution to recurring state budget crises? *Public Budgeting & Finance, 25*, Winter, 105–124.

67. Tan, Y. (2011). Appropriations OKs $3.1 billion from rainy day fund. *Texas Tribune*, March 15. Retrieved December 17, 2011, from http://www.texastribune.org/texas-legislature/82nd-legislative-session/appropriations-oks-31-billion-from-rainy-day-fund/.

68. Gramlich, J. (2011). Rainy day funds explained: how much money should states have in the bank? *Stateline.org*, May 4. Retrieved March 20, 2012, from www.stateline.org/live/details/story/?contentId=572171; Joyce, P. (2001). What's so magical about five percent?

69. Strong, R. A. (2005). *Derivatives: an introduction*, 2nd ed. Mason, OH: Thomson/South-Western; Hinkelmann, C., & Swidler, S. (2005). State government hedging using financial derivatives. *State and Local Government Review, 37*, 127–141; McDonald, R. L. (2006). *Derivatives markets*, 2nd ed. Boston, MA: Addison-Wesley.

70. Barton, P. (2010). Derivative disaster spreads to local governments. *CNC News*, May 10.

71. Office of the State Treasurer, State of Wisconsin (2006). *Local government investment pool*. Retrieved August 18, 2006, from http://www.ost.state.wi.us/home/lgip.htm; Treasury Department, Tennessee (2006). *Local government investment pool*. Retrieved August 18, 2006, from http://www.treasury.state.tn.us/lgip/index.htm; Sims, R. (2006). *King County investment pool receives highest rating from Standard & Poor's* [press release]. Retrieved March 23, 2012, from http://your.kingcounty.gov/exec/news/2006/0109investmentpool.aspx.

72. Percent distribution of cash and security holdings for the quarter ending December 31, 2010, and for prior quarters retrieved from U.S. Census Bureau, *Finances of state and local government employee retirement systems*, at http://www.census.gov/govs/qpr/.

73. State of California (2010). *Pooled money investment board report.* April, p. 4. Retrieved March 20, 2012, from http://www.treasurer.ca.gov/pmia-laif/reports/mnthly/2010/201001.pdf.

74. Stern, A. (2007). Judge voids Illinois law barring Sudan investment. *Reuters,* February 24. Retrieved March 23, 2012, from http://www.reuters.com/article/2007/02/24/investment-sudan-ruling-idUSN2335511320070224.

75. Wolfe, A. (2010). Court upholds Sudan Divestment Act. *Nashua Telegraph,* October 28. Retrieved March 20, 2012, from http://www.nashuatelegraph.com/news/891914-196/story.html.

76. Governmental Accounting Standards Board (2011). *Summaries/status of statements.* Retrieved December 19, 2011, from http://www.gasb.org/st/index.html.

77. Financial Management Service, U.S. Department of Treasury (2011). *Green book: guide to federal ACH payments and collections.* Retrieved December 19, 2011, from http://fms.treas.gov/greenbook/index.html.

78. Financial Management Service, U.S. Department of Treasury (2011). *Gold book: the check reclamation guide.* Retrieved December 19, 2011, from http://www.fms.treas.gov/goldbook/index.html.

79. U.S. General Accounting Office (2001). *Federal debt: debt management actions and future challenges.* Washington, DC: U.S. Government Printing Office; U.S. General Accounting Office (2004). *Debt ceiling: analysis of actions taken during the 2003 debt issuance suspension period.* Washington, DC: U.S. Government Printing Office.

80. Cash Management Improvement Act of 1990 (P.L. 101-453).

81. Financial Management Service, U.S. Department of Treasury (2011). *Cash Management Improvement Act (CMIA).* Retrieved December 2011 from http://fms.treas.gov/cmia/index.html.

82. Groshek, G. M. (2000). Foreign currency exposure in the Department of Defense. *Public Budgeting & Finance, 20,* Winter, 15–35.

83. Bureau of Engraving and Printing, U.S. Department of Treasury website, www.moneyfactory.gov.

84. Financial Management Service (2011). *U.S. Treasury to "retire" Social Security paper check option* [press release]. April 26. Retrieved March 20, 2012, from http://www.godirect.org/media/release/us-treasury-retires-paper-check-option/.

85. Cooper, P. J. (2003). *Governing by contract: challenges and opportunities for public managers.* Washington, DC: CQ Press; Seddon, N. (2004). *Government contracts: federal, state, and local,* 3rd ed. Annandale, New South Wales, Australia: Federation Press; Emanuelli, P. (2005). *Government procurement.* Markham, Ontario, Canada: LexisNexis Butterworths; Brown, T. L., et al. (2006). Managing public service contracts: aligning values, institutions, and markets. *Public Administration Review, 66,* 323–331.

86. Office of Management and Budget (2011). Obama administration succeeds in reducing contract spending for first time in 13 years. *WhiteHouse.gov.* Retrieved March 20, 2012, from http://www.whitehouse.gov/sites/default/files/contracting_reform.pdf.

87. Rubin, I. (2006). Budgeting for contracting in local government. *Public Budgeting & Finance, 26,* Spring, 1–13.

88. Top 200 federal contractors. (2010). *Government Executive,* August 15. Retrieved March 20, 2012, from http://www.govexec.com/magazine/2010/08/top-200-federal-contractors/32139/.

89. U.S. General Services Administration (2011). *GSA quick facts.* Retrieved December 19, 2011, from http://www.gsa.gov/Portal/gsa/ep/home.do?tabId=6.

90. Pulliam, D. (2006). GSA finalizes merger of contracting organizations. *Government Executive.* Retrieved December 19, 2011, from http://www.govexec.com/story_page.cfm?filepath=/dailyfed/1006/1013206p1.htm.

91. Harris, S. (2002). GSA lacks hard data on inter-agency competition. *Government Executive.* Retrieved December 19, 2011, from http://www.govexec.com/story_page.cfm?filepath=/dailyfed/1006/041102h1.htm.

92. Defense Logistics Agency, U.S. Department of Defense website, www.dla.mil.

93. Office of Federal Procurement Policy Act of 1974 (P.L. 93-400).

94. U.S. General Services Administration (2011). *Federal acquisition regulation.* Retrieved December 19, 2011, from http://acquisition.gov/far/index.html; Office of Under Secretary of Defense Acquisition Technology and Logistics, U.S. Department of Defense (2006). *Defense federal acquisition*

regulations supplement. Retrieved August 21, 2006, from http://www.acq.osd.mil/dpap/dars/dfars/index.htm.

95. U.S. Government Accountability Office (2005). *Interagency contracting: franchise funds provide convenience but value to DOD is not demonstrated.* Washington, DC: Author.

96. U.S. Office of Management and Budget (2005). *Establishing of interagency acquisition working group* [memorandum]. Retrieved August 21, 2006, from http://www.whitehouse.gov/omb/procurement/publications/ interagency_work_group.pdf (source no longer available).

97. Pallesen, T. (2006). The politics of contracting out in school districts: the case of Washington State. *State and Local Government Review, 38,* 34–40.

98. Wilson, G. C. (2002). Rent-a-weapons. *Government Executive.* Retrieved December 19, 2011, from http://www.govexec.com/story_page.cfm?filepath=/dailyfed/0202/020502db.htm.

99. Brudney, J. L., et al. (2005). Exploring and explaining contracting out: patterns among the American states. *Journal of Public Administration Research and Theory, 15,* 393–419; Nemec, J., et al. (2005). Contracting-out at local government level: theory and selected evidence from the Czech and Slovak Republics. *Public Management Review, 7,* 637–648.

100. U.S. Office of Management and Budget (2003). *Performance of commercial activities,* Circular A-76. Retrieved August 21, 2006, from http://www.whitehouse.gov/omb/circulars/a076/a76_incl_tech_correction.html.

101. U.S. Government Accountability Office (2005). *Review of OMB Circular A-76 health benefit cost factor needed.* Washington, DC: Author.

102. Peckenpaugh, J. (2001). A-76 competition may not hurt federal workers' pay. *Government Executive.* Retrieved December 19, 2011, from http://www.govexec.com/story_page.cfm?filepath=/dailyfed/0401/041801p1.

103. Gansler, J. S. (2003). *Moving toward market-based government: the changing role of government as the provider.* IBM Center for the Business of Government, June. Retrieved March 20, 2012, from http://www.businessofgovernment.org/report/moving-toward-market-based-government-changing-role-government-provider.

104. Federal Activities and Inventory Reform Act of 1998 (P.L. 105-270).

105. U.S. General Accounting Office (2004). *Federal acquisition: increased attention to vehicle fleets could result in savings.* Washington, DC: U.S. Government Printing Office; U.S. General Accounting Office (2004). *Best practices: using spending analysis to help agencies take a more strategic approach to procurement.* Washington, DC: U.S. Government Printing Office.

106. New York State Office of General Services (2005). *2005 Cronin Club Classic Innovation Award: aggregated IT procurement program.* Retrieved August 21, 2006, from http://www.naspo.org/awards/2005awards/NY_ClassicBronze.doc (source no longer available).

107. U.S. Office of Management and Budget (2006). *Competitive sourcing: report on the use of best value tradeoffs in public-private competitions.* Retrieved October 21, 2006, from http://www.whitehouse.gov/omb/procurement/comp_src/cs_best_value_report_2006.pdf (source no longer available).

108. Gansler, J. S. (2011). Shop for "best value," not "lowest price." *Federal Times,* June 12. Retrieved March 20, 2012, from http://www.federaltimes.com/article/20110612/ADOP06/106120306/1037/ADOP00.

109. Dunn, R. L. (2009). *Injecting new ideas and new approaches in defense systems: are "other transactions" an answer?* Center for Public Policy and Private Enterprise Report, July. Retrieved March 20, 2012, from http://www.acquisitionresearch.net/files/FY2009/NPS-AM-09-088.pdf.

110. U.S. Government Accountability Office (2005). *Contract management: opportunities to improve pricing of GSA multiple award schedules contracts.* Washington, DC: Author. Romzek, B. S., & Johnston, J. M. (2005). State social services contracting: exploring the determinants of effective contract accountability. *Public Administration Review, 65,* 436–449.

111. General Services Administration (2011). *GSA order 4800.2G: Eligibility to use GSA sources and supplies of services.* February 16. Retrieved March 20, 2012, from http://www.gsa.gov/graphics/fas/GSAOrder4800.2G_FSSUA_FINAL_2-2-11.pdf.

112. Federal Acquisition Streamlining Act of 1994 (P.L. 103-355).

113. Mandel, J. (2006). Panel finds performance-based contracts poorly implemented. *Government Executive.* Retrieved December 19, 2011, from http://www.govexec.com/story_page.cfm?filepath=/dailyfed/0606/062906m1.htm.

114. U.S. Government Accountability Office (2005). *Federal contracting: share-in-savings initiative not yet tested.* Washington, DC: Author.

115. Competition in Contracting Act of 1984 (P.L. 98-369), Title VII.

116. U.S. Government Accountability Office (2011). *Bid protest decisions.* Retrieved December 19, 2011, from http://www.gao.gov/decisions/bidpro/bidpro.htm.

117. U.S. Department of State (2006). *Procurement technical assistance centers.* Retrieved August 21, 2006, from http://www.dla.mil/db/procurem.htm.

118. Rubin, I. (2006). *Budgeting for contracting in local government.*

119. Mandel, J. (2006). OMB to rate agencies on efforts to break up large contracts. *Government Executive.* Retrieved August 21, 2006, from http://www.govexec.com/story_page.cfm?filepath=/dailyfed/0806/081806m1.htm.

120. Gansler, J. S. (2003). *Moving toward market-based government.*

121. Rehabilitation Act of 1973 (P.L. 93-112).

122. Vietnam Era Veterans' Readjustment Assistance Act of 1974 (P.L. 93-508); Committee on Veterans Affairs, U.S. House of Representatives (2006). *NASA extends contract proposal deadline for service-disabled veteran-owned small businesses.* Retrieved August 21, 2006, from http://veterans.house.gov/news/109/8-3-06.html.

123. Department of General Services, State of California (2006). *State, federal, and local contacts.* Retrieved August 21, 2006, from http://www.pd.dgs.ca.gov/publications/state_federal_local_contacts.htm.

124. Romzek, B. S., & Johnston, J. M. (2005). State social services contracting: exploring the determinants of effective contract accountability.

125. National Defense Authorization Act for Fiscal Year 2002 (P.L. 107-107).

126. Federal Acquisition Reform Act/Clinger-Cohen Act of 1996 (P.L. 104-106), section 4001.

127. Andrues, W. (2006). The Clinger-Cohen Act, 10 years later: measuring efficiency. *Government Executive.* Retrieved August 22, 2006, from http://www.govexec.com/story_page.cfm?filepath=/dailyfed/0706/071806cc.htm.

128. California Performance Review (2006). *The state needs to professionalize its state procurement workforce.* Retrieved August 22, 2006, from http://cpr.ca.gov/report/cprrpt/issrec/stops/proc/so61.htm (source no longer available).

129. New York City (2006). *Citywide Training Center.* Retrieved August 22, 2006, from http://www.nyc.gov/html/dcas/html/resources/ctchome.shtml.

130. Federal Acquisition Institute (2006). *Annual report on the federal acquisition workforce, fiscal year 2005.* Retrieved August 22, 2006, from http://www.fai.gov/pdfs/FAWF2005.pdf.

131. Federal Acquisition Institute (1992). *Report on the federal acquisition workforce, fiscal year 1991.* September, 2. Retrieved April 6, 2012 from http://www.fai.gov/pdfs/FAI%20report%201991.pdf; Federal Acquisition Institute (2010). *FY2009 annual report on the federal acquisition workforce* (p. 3). Fort Belvoir, VA: Federal Acquisition Institute.

132. Mandel, J. (2006). Panel agrees OMB needs official dedicated to acquisition workforce. *Government Executive.* Retrieved March 20, 2012, from http://www.govexec.com/defense/2006/07/panel-agrees-omb-needs-official-dedicated-to-acquisition-workforce/22265/.

133. U.S. Government Accountability Office (2005). *Framework for assessing the acquisition function at federal agencies.* Washington, DC: Author.

134. Compiled from Federal Highway Administration, U.S. Department of Transportation (2006). *The reporting and detecting of fraud.* Retrieved August 22, 2006, from http://www.fhwa.dot.gov/programadmin/contracts/fraud.htm.

135. Federal Emergency Management Agency, U.S. Department of Homeland Security (2006). *FEMA and state alert to fraud* [press release]. Retrieved August 22, 2006, from http://www.fema.gov/news/newsrelease.fema?id=28298.

136. Procurement Integrity Act of 1996 (P.L. 104-106).

137. Palmer, K. (2005). Former OMB official indicted. *Government Executive*. Retrieved December 19, 2011, from http://www.govexec.com/story_page.cfm?filepath=/dailyfed/1005/100505k1.htm; Palmer, K. (2006). Ex-procurement chief argues for new trial. *Government Executive*. Retrieved December 19, 2011, from http://www.govexec.com/story_page.cfm?filepath=/dailyfed/0806/081706k1.htm.

138. U.S. Government Accountability Office (2011). *Suspension and debarment: Some agency programs need greater attention, and governmentwide oversight could be improved.* November 16. Retrieved March 20, 2012, from http://www.gao.gov/products/GAO-12-245T.

139. U.S. Government Accountability Office (2005). *Federal procurement: additional data reporting could improve the suspension and debarment process.* Washington, DC: Author.

140. U.S. Government Accountability Office (2005). *Financial management: thousands of civilian agency contractors abuse the federal tax system with little consequence.* Washington, DC: Author.

141. Smith, R. J. (2006). Tanker inquiry finds Rumsfeld's attention was elsewhere. *Washington Post*, June 20. Retrieved August 22, 2006, from http://www.washingtonpost.com/wp-dyn/content/article/2006/06/19/AR2006061901090.html.

142. Cahlink, G. (2005). Justice forms procurement fraud task force. *Government Executive*. Retrieved December 19, 2011, from http://www.govexec.com/story_page.cfm?filepath=/dailyfed/0205/022305g1.htm.

143. U.S. General Services Administration (2006), *Charge card program statistics, fiscal year 2004: executive summary.* Retrieved August 22, 2006, from http://www.gsa.gov/Portal/gsa/ep/programView.do?pageTypeId=8199&ooid=11490&programPage=%2Fep%2Fprogram%2FgsaDocument.jsp&programId=10137&channelId=-13503 (source no longer available).

144. Ballard, T. N. (2002). Defense task force aims to clean up charge card abuse. *Government Executive*. Retrieved August 22, 2006, from http://www.govexec.com/story_page.cfm?filepath=/dailyfed/0302/032702t2.htm.

145. U.S. Government Accountability Office (2006). *Purchase cards: control weaknesses leave DHS highly vulnerable to fraudulent, improper, and abusive activity.* Washington, DC: U.S. GAO.

146. Gangemi, J. (2006). Winning the federal contracting game. *Businessweek Online*, July 26. Retrieved August 21, 2006, from http://www.businessweek.com/smallbiz/content/jul2006/sb20060726_724414.htm?chan=search (source no longer available).

147. Scully, M. (2006). Negotiators pressured to resolve "Buy America" dispute. *Government Executive*. Retrieved October 22, 2006, from http://www.govexec.com/story_page.cfm?filepath=/dailyfed/0906/091206cdam1.htm.

148. Bumiller, E., & Hulse, C. (2006). Panel saw no security issue in port contract, officials say. *New York Times*, February 23. Retrieved August 22, 2006, from http://www.nytimes.com/2006/02/23/politics/23port.html?ex=1298350800&en=507c0dd1d3a708e4&ei=5090&partner=rssuserland&emc=rss; Cloud, D. S., & Sanger, D. E. (2006). Dubai company delays new role at six ports. *New York Times*, February 24. Retrieved August 14, 2006, from http://select.nytimes.com/gst/abstract.html?res=F10912FC345AOC778EDDAB0894DE404482.

149. U.S. Office of the Special Inspector General for Iraq Reconstruction (2006). *SIGIR: independent and objective oversight.* Retrieved August 22, 2006, from www.sigir.mil/; U.S. General Accounting Office (2004). *Contract management: contracting for Iraq reconstruction and for global logistics support.* Washington, DC: U.S. Government Printing Office.

150. Glanz, J. (2006). New U.S. audit describes misuse of funds in Iraq projects. *New York Times*, January 25. Retrieved August 22, 2006, from http://select.nytimes.com/gst/abstract.html?res=F00F16FC3B5B0C768EDDA80894DE404482.

151. Pulliam, D. (2006). Report sheds light on hurricane fraud investigations. *Government Executive*. Retrieved December 19, 2011, from http://www.govexec.com/story_page.cfm?filepath=/dailyfed/0106/011206p1.htm.

152. U.S. Government Accountability Office (2006). *Hurricane Katrina: improving federal contracting practices in disaster recovery operations.* Washington, DC: Author.

153. USA Today/Gallup Hurricane Katrina survivors follow-up poll. (2006). *USA Today*, August 20. Retrieved August 22, 2006, from http://www.usatoday.com/news/polls/tables/live/2006-08-20-katrina-poll.htm (source no longer available).

154. Federal Tort Claims Act of 1946, Ch. 753, 60 Stat. 842.

155. Governmental Accounting Standards Board (2006). *Summaries/status: statements.* Retrieved August 22, 2006, from http://www.gasb.org/st/index.html.

156. U.S. Office of Management and Budget (2006). *Proposed risk assessment bulletin.* Retrieved August 22, 2006, from http://www.whitehouse.gov/omb/inforeg/-proposed_risk_assessment_bulletin_010906.pdf.

157. U.S. Government Accountability Office (2005). *Risk management: further refinements needed to assess risks and prioritize protective measures at ports and other critical infrastructure.* Washington, DC: Author; U.S. Government Accountability Office (2005). *Strategic budgeting: risk management principles can help DHS allocate resources to highest priorities.* Washington, DC: Author.

Financial Management: Accounting, Reporting, and Auditing

The term "creative accounting" perhaps originated with the 1968 Mel Brooks movie *The Producers*, which was later turned into a highly successful Broadway musical and a big-budget movie.[1] Both "creative accounting" and the older term "cooking the books" refer to deliberate manipulation of accounting systems and accounting reports in order to hide the actual financial condition of an entity. In the case of *The Producers*, the producers of a play deceive the backers of their play by selling many times over the total value of the enterprise. The assumption is the play will flop, the backers will expect no financial gain, and the producers will net a hefty ill-gained profit. Chaos ensues when the play unexpectedly becomes a sensation.

The Producers has provided great fun to audiences over the years, but it is not great fun when people lose their life savings in investments in companies that have used fraudulent accounting and when taxpayers must pay up through higher taxes due to accounting bad practices and fraud in their governments. In fact, a more recent (and more tragic) example of creative accounting came to light in 2008 when an unscrupulous investment adviser named Bernard Madoff defrauded investors out of billions of dollars in a Ponzi scheme involving falsified accounting records. Even if no fraud exists, an accounting error that simply fails to recognize in advance that not all taxes owed will be collected can throw a budget badly out of balance, forcing stringent measures on spending and possibly giving decision makers no choice but to adopt a tax increase in order to correct the mistake. There were also accounting scandals uncovered at the mortgage giants Fannie Mae and Freddie Mac in 2003. These scandals led to the resignations of the heads of both of these organizations after they were discovered, but they seemed even more significant in light of the costly federal bailout of both of these institutions in 2008.[2] Budget execution requires accounting systems that track projected and actual revenues and expenditures during the budget year. Accounting is the process of recording all financial transactions—revenues and expenditures—according to clear and usually precise rules, in such a manner that all transactions can be audited independently. As will be seen in the following sections, accounting serves a variety of purposes, but one of the most important has always been maintaining honesty and integrity. Accounting is also important to the functions discussed the preceding chapter—namely, tax administration, cash management, procurement, and risk management. Accounting systems provide the financial information components of more comprehensive management information systems.

This chapter has three sections. The first is devoted to accounting systems, and the second to reporting—that is, the types of documents that flow from accounting data. The third section discusses government auditing.

GOVERNMENTAL ACCOUNTING

"A standard definition of accounting is the art of analyzing, recording, summarizing, evaluating and interpreting an organization's financial activities and status, and communicating the results."[3] Accounting is one type of information system, one that contains mostly financial information on transactions involving the receipt of funds and their expenditure.

In this section, we explore several aspects of accounting systems, beginning with the purposes and standards of accounting and the organizations that shape accounting systems. Fund accounting, the structure of accounting systems, the classification of expenditures, and the bases for accounting are considered.

Organizational Responsibilities and Standards

Purposes

Accounting systems have been devised for a variety of purposes. **Exhibit 12–1** lists the main ones, including the ever-present one of ensuring honesty in the handling of public monies—keeping the rascals honest. As will be seen, accounting systems are based on details, but those who operate accounting systems should never lose sight of the main purposes. Accounting systems, in meeting the purposes noted here, are valuable tools in running the government rather than simply being additional costs of government operations.[4]

Exhibit 12–1 Purposes of Accounting

Here are some of the main purposes of accounting:

- Perhaps the primary purpose is the maintenance of honesty. Through accounting, people who have wrongly intercepted monies being paid to government or who have channeled expenditures to their own advantage can be detected. Accounting serves as a deterrent to fraud and corruption and prevents inadvertent loss.
- A related purpose is to prevent expenditures from straying beyond legal parameters. Illegal expenditures can occur that do not involve corruption, as in the case of agency expenditures that exceed an appropriation or are used for purposes other than those permitted in authorizing legislation. Accounting serves to control agencies so that they act in accordance with policy and administrative directives and appropriation legislation.

- Accounting systems are intended to provide complete, timely, and accurate information concerning receipts and expenditures. The information is used in billing taxpayers and receiving tax payments, paying employees, ordering goods, receiving goods, and paying vendors or contractors. Accounting systems help control inventory by providing accurate records of what items have been purchased.
- Another important purpose is to report on the management of funds that are held in custody or trust. For example, accounting systems are used to handle contributions to employee retirement funds and outlays to beneficiaries.
- Decision making is facilitated by accounting systems, which report historical data on revenues and expenditures that are essential for forecasting financial transactions. Without accurate information from an accounting system, decision makers are unable to determine whether a gap exists between proposed spending for the budget year and available revenue. Accounting information is important in determining whether a budget deficit exists and in what amount. Data are used in determining the size of the government's total debt, including those debts that are part of credit programs. Accounting data can help identify historical trends and current costs, and this information is essential in identifying funds required for proposed changes in service levels and service quality.
- Accounting is used internally to help managers increase efficiency and effectiveness in delivering services. The utilization of resources is monitored so as to avoid waste and to help ensure that desired programmatic outcomes are achieved. Managerial accounting focuses on calculating the costs associated with providing services to citizens. These derived costs can also be used for setting schedules for service charges. Office of Management and Budget (OMB) Circular A-123, *Management's Responsibility for Internal Control*, emphasizes that management should be held accountable for achieving results and not just for using resources efficiently and honestly.
- Information from accounting systems is used in communication between a government and its citizens, investors, and other governments. Financial reports derived from detailed accounting information can help citizens gain confidence that the government's resources are well supervised. The federal government, in making grants to state and local governments, wants to be assured that the recipient governments have accounting systems that will protect the assets being invested.
- Accounting in the public sector is being increasingly used to identify financial condition or the relative fiscal health of a government and the environment in which it operates. Investors in such commodities as state and local bonds and federal Treasury bills use accounting-based information to understand the financial condition of the governments whose bonds they are buying.

Federal Government Accounting Organizations

For accounting systems to serve these purposes, certain conventions or standards must be established, or else chaos would reign as each government or department within a government established its own standards and practices. Numerous organizations establish the ground rules for accounting.

Both the Government Accountability Office (GAO), which is an agency of Congress, and the Office of Management and Budget (OMB), which is an arm of the Executive Office of the President, set guidelines for federal agencies and to some extent compete with one another over control of accounting.[5] The Federal Managers' Financial Integrity Act of 1982, amending the Accounting and Auditing Act of 1950, requires that each executive agency establish internal accounting and administrative controls in accordance with standards prescribed by GAO and that the agency conduct annual reviews to determine the extent of compliance with those standards.[6] However, since the Supreme Court has ruled that GAO cannot be in a position of instructing agencies in what they must do (see the chapter on budget approval and the U.S. Congress), OMB has the upper hand in establishing financial management practices.

OMB's deputy director for management oversees the Office of Federal Financial Management, which is headed by the controller. The Chief Financial Officers Act of 1990 created similar offices and chief financial officer (CFO) positions within the major agencies of the government.[7] Agency CFOs have responsibility for all financial operations, including budgeting, and the CFOs, along with OMB's deputy director for management, the controller, and the fiscal assistant secretary of Treasury, meet periodically as the Chief Financial Officers Council for the purpose of coordinating their activities.[8] OMB and the council, in accordance with the law's instructions that a government-wide financial plan be developed, have launched an ambitious program to improve internal controls, lines of business, debt collection, asset management, payments to contractors and state and local governments, and the like.[9]

In addition to the Chief Financial Officers Act, 1990 also brought the formation of the Federal Accounting Standards Advisory Board (FASAB).[10] As its title suggests, this entity is strictly advisory, but its recommendations have indeed had major impacts on federal accounting. The board consists of representatives of GAO, OMB, and the Treasury Department plus a representative from the Congressional Budget Office, representatives from civilian agencies and the Department of Defense (DOD), and nonfederal members. Its mission is to develop consensus on accounting standards that can then be adopted by GAO, OMB, and the Treasury Department. FASAB has issued numerous standards, such as ones pertaining to the accounting of assets and liabilities, the first standard that it adopted, to others dealing with inventory, managerial cost accounting, and social insurance accounting. OMB reviews each standard issued and in effect incorporates all standards into government policy through Circular A-134, *Financial Accounting Principles and Standards.*

Chief financial officers are to some extent in competition with another set of key officers—namely, chief information officers (CIOs). The latter were established by the Clinger-Cohen Act (Information Technology Management Reform Act) of 1996 and have overall responsibility for information technology in their respective organizations.[11] The catch arises in that accounting systems are necessarily part of information technology operations, which creates issues over who is in charge whenever any accounting matter is at hand.[12]

The General Services Administration (GSA) is another player in the accounting game at the federal level. GSA, as described in the chapter on budget execution, is the federal government's central purchaser for buildings, materials and supplies, vehicles, and computers. In 2006, GSA had responsibility for preparing, under OMB's supervision, the Common Government-wide Accounting Code, which was expected to be the foundation for future accounting systems.[13] This effort is part of the Financial Management Line of Business

(FMLoB) Consolidation being driven by OMB. The plan is for agencies to migrate toward shared accounting systems and, in many instances, share in the use of private vendors for their accounting needs. That same year, OMB issued migration planning guidance as to how agencies were to make the transition.[14] In 2009, GAO released a report discussing progress by OMB in implementing the FMLoB consolidation, and reported that responsible officials within OMB stated that it could be 15 years or more before the standard business processes envisioned in the FMLoB initiative are in use government-wide.[15]

State, Local, and Related Organizations

State and local accounting systems are influenced by several sources. State auditors and comptrollers general set standards for their state and local systems, as do individual state legislatures. These systems also are influenced by GAO and OMB, which determine how federal grant monies are handled.

Professional organizations have periodically attempted to establish standards of accounting in the public sector. The "blue book," or GAAFR (Governmental Accounting, Auditing, and Financial Reporting), which is published by the Government Finance Officers Association, is designed to assist governments at all levels achieve what are considered the standards in the field.[16] The Government Finance Officers Association issues a variety of policy statements not only on accounting, auditing, and financial reporting, but also on budgeting, cash management, debt management, and retirement and benefits administration.

In 1984, a government counterpart to the Financial Accounting Standards Board (see below) was established. The Governmental Accounting Standards Board (GASB, usually pronounced "gas-bee") speaks for accounting practices by government entities.[17] Both the Financial Accounting Standards Board and GASB are under the umbrella of the Financial Accounting Foundation. GASB issues accounting standards, known as statements, first as exposure drafts available for public comment and then in final form. The organization also issues technical bulletins that provide guidance on the implementation of the standards. The Governmental Accounting Standards Advisory Council (GASAC) provides advice to GASB.[18]

Private Sector Accounting Organizations

The private sector has long had a well-established standards-setting organization. The Financial Accounting Standards Board issues authoritative pronouncements on accounting for profit and nonprofit organizations.[19] Also, private accounting firms have major input into determining what constitutes good accounting. The Big 4 accounting firms are Deloitte Touche Tohmatsu, Ernst & Young, KPMG, and Pricewaterhouse Coopers.[20]

Another large accounting firm, Arthur Andersen, was brought down by scandal. Energy giant Enron went bankrupt in 2001 when it came to light that the company had been cooking the books, making the firm's financial situation look far better than it actually was. Enron officials were eventually convicted. Andersen was involved, because it had been Enron's auditor. The company was found guilty of shredding key documents about Enron, and since a felon cannot be an auditor, the company was forced to relinquish its certified public accountant licensure.[21] That was effectively the end of Andersen as an accounting firm, although the consulting arm of Andersen continued as a company known as Accenture.[22]

The Enron situation and other major scandals involving accounting practices and major corporations' auditors led to widespread criticism of companies that performed both an auditing function and served as financial consultants to the corporations. At the time of the Enron collapse, Andersen was receiving more payments from Enron for consulting and financial advice than for auditing. Such situations may create conflicts of interest in which the consulting arm of a company is eager to see that the auditing arm finds no serious problems in the manner that accounting is conducted by the client. The Securities and Exchange Commission has authority in this area. The Sarbanes-Oxley Act, discussed later, limits greatly this cozy relationship between consulting and auditing. None of the major management consulting firms now has management and financial consulting practices.

Of course, Enron is not the only relatively recent accounting scandal. In the early 2000s, telecommunications behemoth WorldCom was forced to reveal that it had overstated its financial health through the use of inappropriate accounting practices to the tune of approximately $15 billion.[23] In 2006, the U.S. Justice Department decided against prosecuting Federal National Mortgage Association (Fannie Mae), a giant mortgage company and a government-sponsored enterprise (GSE). Fannie Mae was the center of a scandal involving hundreds of millions of dollars in accounting errors that extended over many years.[24] Later, the questionable practices of Fannie Mae and its associated GSE, the Federal Home Mortgage Association (Freddie Mac), were partly responsible for the subprime mortgage debacle that threatened, between 2007 and 2011, to bring down the global financial system.[25]

Standards and Principles of Accounting

While GAAFR is useful to state and local governments in evaluating their accounting systems, it is not regarded as an authoritative document. In contrast, GASB annually issues a document that is authoritative regarding the standards to be used in public accounting: Codification of Governmental Accounting and Financial Reporting Standards.[26] The Government Finance Officers Association's "blue book" includes discussions of how it is related to GASB's pronouncements.

GASB and its predecessors have recognized what are considered generally accepted accounting principles (GAAP). While space limitations do not allow a discussion of each of the 12 principles, it should be noted that they are intended as guides to establishing and modifying accounting systems. The first principle provides the foundation for the other 11 by requiring that accounting principles should be followed and that the legal requirements of a government should be met. Adhering to this first principle can be difficult in that laws can require accounting practices that are contrary to the generally accepted principles.

At the federal level, the generally accepted accounting principles are established by the Federal Accounting Standards Advisory Board (FASAB), having been granted this authority by the American Institute of Certified Public Accountants (AICPA).[27] AICPA's statement No. 91, *Federal GAAP Hierarchy*, determines what is GAAP for the federal government.[28] From that statement, FASAB has promulgated numerous statements and interpretations that constitute the first tier in the hierarchy, technical bulletins that are second, and the other documents that make up third and fourth tiers. Together, these constitute GAAP for the federal government.

Organizational Arrangements and Fraud

Creating organizational arrangements that deter fraud is of paramount interest in accounting. Fraud can be committed by workers handling receipts. An employee might hold taxpayer A's money for personal use and use taxpayer B's money to cover A's taxes and subsequently C's money to cover B's taxes. Employees may steal from petty cash or from inventory. Employees may pay vendors who are due nothing or provide travel reimbursement checks to employees who are due nothing. In Michigan, a county official was caught having filed false travel expense claims for years. What was significant was that he was the finance chairman for the county government commission, the very person who should have been alert to possible financial wrongdoings.[29] Financial control systems rely upon the principle of segregation of authority such that a person who can authorize a financial transaction cannot also approve of paying out the actual cash when it is time. A county official should not have been able to approve incurring a travel expense for himself and then approving its payment, but segregation of duties is not always complete.

Fraud can involve one or two individuals or can be systemic. The Accountant General of the Federation of Nigeria complained about public servants systematically looting the treasury, particularly through the payroll systems. He said this was done in part with the cooperation of the international community in that stolen funds were transferred overseas to international financial institutions that readily accept new deposits regardless of their source.[30] A more recent, and higher profile, example involved a lack of sufficient controls to ensure that aid provided by the United States to Afghanistan did not end up being siphoned off for personal use by Afghani officials.[31]

One prescription is that accounting systems need to be *transparent*. How they operate and the products of their operations, specifically their various reports, need to be available to interested parties and the public in general. This is of widespread concern ranging from highly developed countries to less developed ones. The International Monetary Fund uses its *Code of Good Practices on Fiscal Transparency* in working with developing nations.[32] United Way International has adopted global standards that include financial accountability and transparency as a key requirement when working with participating nongovernmental organizations.[33] Simply getting officials to make public their accounting reports can be controversial, as has been the situation in Uganda, for instance. Officials there, when called to testify about their reports, sometimes switched off their phones so as not to be reached or claimed they had gone to burials.[34] Australia's Auditor-General has called for bringing governmental accounting in line with private sector accounting. Special rules in that country's accounting allow, for example, that missiles be classified as either inventory or property, resulting in confusion over financial statements and possible opportunities for misdeeds in the handling of funds.[35]

To prevent fraud and to reduce other losses due to errors, internal controls that specify organizational arrangements and procedures are established. OMB Circular A-123, for example, "provides guidance to federal managers on improving the accountability and effectiveness of federal programs and operations by establishing, assessing, correcting, and reporting on internal control."[36] Responsibility needs to be assigned to individuals, and any delegations of responsibility need to be detailed in writing. One standard practice is to segregate duties, so that one individual may have only limited authority over monies and two or more people may be required to approve some financial transactions. The presumption is that if two or more individuals are part of a particular process, they will monitor each other's behavior and limit various abuses. For example, two or more signatures may be required in approving the issuance of checks or in transferring money through electronic funds transfers.

Employees are trained in how to enter transactions properly in accounting systems and what their ethical and legal responsibilities are in handling public resources. Individuals who handle funds may be subject to more extensive background checks before hiring and may be bonded. Downsizing can force the elimination of personnel and increase the risk that funds are vulnerable to theft or accidental loss due to the reduced oversight of financial operations.

Auditing bodies are important in preventing and detecting fraud. GAO selectively conducts financial as well as program audits and on occasion finds losses in the billions of dollars. GAO audits the financial statements for the government as a whole, for departments (for example, the Treasury Department), for independent commissions (for example, the Securities and Exchange Commission), and for federally chartered corporations (for example, the Boy Scouts of America). The heavy-duty workload of auditing at the federal level is handled by the inspectors general in their respective departments and agencies. When discrepancies are identified through audits, follow-up is necessary to determine their causes, and corrective measures need to be initiated.

Fund Accounting

One of the main differences between public and private sector accounting is the definition of the accounting entity. For the typical private sector organization, the entity is the organization itself, since accounts are designed to reflect its entire resources. Governments, in contrast, separate financial resources into distinct accounting entities called *funds*. Each fund is set up to record and account for the uses of a specific group of assets or sources of revenue or collection of specific type of costs. As provided for in generally accepted accounting principles 2, 3, and 4 and as modified by GASB, there are three general classes of public sector funds and 11 different particular types of funds.[37] These are the funds that state and local governments use.

1. *Governmental Funds* consist of five types.
   - The *general fund* is the most important governmental fund. Several revenue sources may flow into a government's general fund, such as property tax and income tax receipts at the local level. The resources in the fund are available for expenditure for virtually any purpose that the jurisdiction is legally empowered to pursue. Most municipalities, for instance, may use general fund receipts for police and road services but not schools, since the latter are the domain of independent school districts. The other fund types within the governmental class are available for what are thought of as normal government operations, but these types have receipt and/or expenditure restrictions.
   - *Special revenue funds* receive monies from special sources and are earmarked for special purposes. Gasoline taxes are typically accounted for in a special

revenue fund, with expenditures limited to transportation, especially roads and highways.

- *Capital projects funds* account for receipts and expenditures related to projects, such as construction of a new park or city hall, or for major pieces of equipment, such as vehicles for a city fire department. Monies may come into these funds from bond sales that will be paid for with general fund tax receipts.
- *Debt service funds* are used to account for interest and principal on general-purpose long-term debt. The revenue received by this type of fund is usually from the general fund.
- *Permanent funds* are used in cases where only the earnings may be expended and the principal may not. These funds earlier were part of what were called trust and agency funds.

2. *Proprietary Funds.* The second class of funds consists of those that are proprietary or business-like in nature.

- *Enterprise funds* operate as businesses whose customers are external to government. Such funds are established for toll roads, bridges, and local water systems. Numerous proposals have circulated recommending that various federal operations be converted to government corporations that would be run as enterprises.[38]
- *Internal service funds* operate as businesses whose customers are internal to government. A central purchasing office or a vehicle maintenance garage may operate as an internal service fund, with revenues coming from other departments as services are rendered.

  When bonds are sold to support the activities of a proprietary fund (for example, bond proceeds might be used to renovate a city sewage system), capital expenditures and payment of debt are handled through the proprietary fund, not through a capital project or debt service fund.

3. *Fiduciary Funds.* The third class, known as fiduciary funds, has four types. This class, often called *trust and agency funds,* consists of accounts that are dedicated to a third party.

- *Pension trusts* for government employees are often the largest set of fiduciary funds.
- *Investment trust funds* are used for tracking and reporting the external portion of local government investment pools.
- *Agency funds* pertain to government acting as a conduit for another party, such as a city government collecting taxes for the local school district.
- *Private purpose trust funds* cover all other trust-type arrangements of the government in which principal and earnings may be expended. An increasingly large set of fiduciary funds at the state level are savings held in trust for when children grow up and enroll in college or university.[39]

Account Groups

According to generally accepted accounting principles 5 through 7, governmental funds use account groups to report fixed assets and long-term liabilities, whereas proprietary and fiduciary funds report these resources and debts within the funds themselves.

Governmental funds include only financial assets—namely, assets that will be converted to cash—and therefore the general fixed asset account group (GFAAG) is used to report assets that will not be converted to cash, such as buildings, swimming pools, aircraft hangars, and airport terminals. The GFAAG is simply a reporting of assets and does not involve transactions. Fixed asset account groups are increasingly important to the description and analysis of the financial health of government agencies and entire government jurisdictions (see the chapter on capital assets).

The second account group is the general long-term debt account group. This group reports government debt that is not part of proprietary or fiduciary funds. In other words, the account group reports liabilities of the entity as a whole, as distinguished from specific funds. This account group and the fixed assets group in effect are memoranda that report assets and liabilities that otherwise would not be reported.

Structure and Rules of Accounting Systems

Ledgers

Accounting systems use ledgers as a means of organization or structure. Each fund has a general ledger and subsidiary ledgers. The general ledger records the overall status of revenues and expenditures, while subsidiary ledgers are established for each revenue source and type of expenditure. In a general fund having several tax sources of revenue, a subsidiary revenue ledger is used for each source. The Office of Management and Budget and the Treasury Department have established a U.S. Government Standard General Ledger (USSGL) that indicates how agencies are to organize their ledgers.[40] A large users manual is available online (37,131 KB). OMB Circular A-127 requires agencies to comply with the standards of the general ledger.[41]

Expenditure subsidiary ledgers control expenditures by appropriation, organizational unit, object of expenditure, and sometimes purpose or activity. Accounting systems are used to track expenditures according to provisions in appropriations. Often these appropriations are specific to organizations, as in the case of $2 million appropriated to a city housing department. The appropriation may also contain limitations on how funds will be spent, such as expenditures for personnel or equipment. This aspect of accounting is explained later. Some jurisdictions track expenditures by program or activity (this is done if a government's program budget structure does not match its organizational structure).

Accounting Formula

Accounting systems use equations that allow systematic recording of transactions and double-checking that the transactions have been properly recorded. The basic equation that is used is:

$$assets = liabilities + fund\ balance$$

In the formula, *assets* can be the revenue in a fund. *Liabilities* are the monies owed others, such as suppliers of office equipment and tires for police cars. The *fund balance* comprises the residual, uncommitted monies. Specific accounts are established for each of the three components of the formula. Asset accounts, for example, can include those showing cash on hand as well as monies owed by taxpayers (taxes receivable). FASAB has recommended standards for assets and liabilities.

In the mid-2000s, the Governmental Accounting Standards Board (GASB) began work not to revise this fundamental formula but to revise its components. GASB Concept Statement Number 4, *Elements of Financial Statements*, defines key terms that state and local governments are to use in developing their financial statements. Among the concepts defined by the statement are:

- *Assets,* which are resources that the entity presently controls.
- *Liabilities,* which are present obligations to sacrifice current resources or future resources that the entity has little or no discretion to avoid.
- An *outflow of resources,* representing a consumption of net resources by the entity that is applicable to the reporting period.
- An *inflow of resources,* representing an acquisition of net resources by the entity that is applicable to the reporting period.
- A *deferred outflow of resources,* which is a consumption of net resources by the entity that is applicable to a future reporting period.
- A *deferred inflow of resources,* which is an acquisition of net resources by the entity that is applicable to a future reporting period.
- *Net position* (fund balance) is then the residual of all other elements presented in a statement of financial position.[42]

Why go through all of this work simply defining the elements to be used in accounting? The answer is simple: unless terms are defined, there is no consistency from jurisdiction to jurisdiction and even from department to department within a jurisdiction. As a result, financial statements, to be discussed later, become largely worthless in that they are unclear as to how transactions have been recorded. Furthermore, the lack of consistency makes pointless any efforts to draw comparisons across departments, across jurisdictions, and over time. For example, it is important to handle separately resources flowing immediately into a jurisdiction as distinguished from resources that are deferred and presumably will flow into the jurisdiction at some later reporting period. Also, the inflow concept means that the resources are coming into the government and are not merely being transferred from one fund to another within the government. The latter activities are known as transfers and are discussed later.

In addition to its work on the *Elements of Financial Statements*, GASB in 2009 issued a new statement (Number 54), *Fund Balance Reporting and Governmental Fund Type Definitions*.[43] This document was the result of concerns over inconsistencies across jurisdictions as to how they were treating fund balance. Statement 54 separates fund balance between amounts that are nonspendable (such as balances that are associated with inventories, and others that are classified from more binding to less binding constraints on spending) as restricted, committed, assigned, or unassigned. It is only this last category, which can be spent for any purpose, that can add to the fund balance in the general fund.[44]

Double-entry accounting, in which any single transaction is recorded twice (at a minimum), is used as a cross-check. For instance, if taxes are received and no additional obligations are incurred, then both assets and the fund balance increase, and the accounting system will record these two events. The double-entry approach can also be used within one portion of the overall formula. If taxes are received but were already noted in an asset account called taxes receivable, then that account would be reduced while an asset account for cash would be increased. That particular set of transactions would not affect liabilities or the fund balance.

Transactions are recorded in a T, in which the left side of the T constitutes debits and the right side constitutes credits. The terms *debits* and *credits* refer only to the left and right sides of the T. Contrary to their use in everyday conversation, the term "debits" is not negative in the sense of expenses or debts owed, and the term "credits" is not positive in the sense of receipts or money to be paid to government. Rules exist as to when an account should be debited and when credited. In any transaction, the amount debited to one or more accounts must equal the amount credited to other accounts.

Specified Procedures

Flowing out of accounting standards and principles are procedures that determine how transactions will be recorded and in what accounts. These procedures are typically specified in manuals or handbooks so that employees involved in whatever aspects of accounting know how to meet their responsibilities. Manuals explain the handling of receipts and purchases, including, for example, overall purchasing policy, purchase orders, contract payments, and emergency purchases. Payroll procedures will be specified in some detail in a manual and are likely to require the approval of specific individuals, possibly including written signatures confirming which employees are to be paid what amounts.

The typical accounting cycle is as follows.[45] An event occurs and a source document is prepared. The event might be a decision to tax property, and the document might be a tax bill sent to a citizen. When the citizen pays the bill, another transaction occurs, and the accounting system needs to reflect such. On the expenditure side of the budget, one event might be placing an order for office supplies, and a later event might be receipt of the supplies and the invoice. These types of transactions will first be posted in a *journal*, which is a chronological listing of events or transactions. The journal entry indicates both the credits and the debits involved in the transaction. For example, tax monies received would increase a cash account and decrease a taxes receivable account. Entries once recorded in the journal are posted to ledgers, and from time to time the debits and credits of these accounts are totaled to obtain trial and final balances. The balances are used in preparing financial reports (which are discussed later).

Classification of Receipts and Expenditures

Receipts and expenditures are classified in a variety of ways, and elaborate coding systems are used to monitor and control financial transactions. Such coding devices help hold government officials responsible for honestly managing the government's business.

Receipts

The monies that government receives need to be recorded according to the source. The money derived from each tax source, such as property and income taxes, needs to be recorded separately and in distinction from user fees, such as charges for using a municipal golf course. The federal government treats user fees as offsetting collections. Money derived from fees, as in the case of the Tennessee Valley Authority, is used to offset expenditures for Tennessee Valley Authority operations. The net differences in such transactions are reported in the budget. The practice of netting receipts against expenditures in the budget for enterprise operations, while perfectly appropriate, hinders the transparency of financial reporting, since it means that one cannot use the government budget alone to gauge the size of government.

GASB has had to deal with a relatively recent phenomenon in the realm of revenues. Some governments strapped for cash have borrowed against outstanding receivables, such as taxes owed, and have actually sold such receivables, an act known as *securitizing* a stream of receivables (see the chapter on capital finance and debt management). In 2006, GASB released Statement Number 48, which requires these governments to report such transactions as liabilities in that they have pledged collateral against borrowed resources.[46]

Fund and Appropriation

Expenditures are accounted for in a variety of ways. One set of characteristics is the fund and appropriation. An appropriation is a legislative approval to spend from a specific fund. Since several bills may be passed that appropriate out of the general fund, the dollar stipulations in each of these bills must be observed vis-à-vis the total assets available in the general fund. Even if a jurisdiction uses only one appropriation bill, each of the expenditure limits in the bill must be observed and consequently must be monitored by the accounting system. When an expenditure is made, it is charged against the appropriated amount and the remaining available balance is shown. In this way, an accounting system can be used to keep agency expenditures within budgeted figures.

If the legislative body earmarks expenditures in detail, then the accounting system becomes increasingly complex. For example, Congress in its annual foreign assistance appropriation bill typically appropriates funds for programs within the Agency for International Development in great detail, specifying amounts to be available in each country receiving aid. The accounting system, therefore, must monitor expenditures by program (e.g., child survival) and by country to adhere to the stipulations in the appropriation bill.[47]

Organizational Unit

Expenditures are made by organizational units, and accounting systems must track expenditures accordingly. Appropriation bills are usually specific to agencies so that, instead of the government simply being authorized to spend an amount on forest preservation, a specific unit within a department is appropriated the money. Large governments, then, account for expenditures not only at the department level but also at the bureau, office, division, or regional unit level.

Objects of Expenditure

Accounting systems invariably account in terms of the objects acquired or the objects of expenditure. Broad groupings of objects are called major objects, and their subdivisions are called minor objects. **Exhibit 12–2** illustrates the object classes used by the federal government. The object series beginning with the number 11, for example, covers all

Exhibit 12–2 Federal Objects of Expenditure Classification

Code	Classification Title
10	**Personnel Compensation and Benefits**
	11 Personnel Compensation
	11.1 Full-Time Permanent
	11.3 Other Than Full-Time Permanent
	11.5 Other Personnel Compensation
	11.6 Military Personnel Basic Allowance for Housing
	11.7 Military Personnel
	11.8 Special Personal Services Payments
	11.9 Total Personnel Compensation
	12 Personnel Benefits
	12.1 Civilian Personnel Benefits
	12.2 Military Personnel Benefits
	13 Benefits for Former Personnel
20	**Contractual Services and Supplies**
	21 Travel and Transportation of Persons
	22 Transportation of Things
	23 Rent, Communications, and Utilities
	23.1 Rental Payments to General Services Administration
	23.2 Rental Payments to Others
	23.3 Communications, Utilities, and Miscellaneous Charges
	24 Printing and Reproduction
	25 Other Contractual Services
	25.1 Advisory and Assistance Services
	25.2 Other Services
	25.3 Other Goods and Services from Federal Sources
	25.4 Operation and Maintenance of Facilities
	25.5 Research and Development Contracts
	25.6 Medical Care
	25.7 Operation and Maintenance of Equipment
	25.8 Subsistence and Support of Persons
	26 Supplies and Materials
30	**Acquisition of Assets**
	31 Equipment
	32 Land and Structures
	33 Investments and Loans
40	**Grants and Fixed Charges**
	41 Grants, Subsidies, and Contributions
	42 Insurance Claims and Indemnities
	43 Interest and Dividends
	44 Refunds

Code	Classification Title
90	**Other**
	91 Unvouchered
	92 Undistributed
	94 Financial Transfers
	99 Subtotal Obligations
	99.5 Below Reporting Threshold
	99.9 Total New Obligations

Source: Adapted from U.S. Office of Management and Budget (2011). *Preparation, submission, and execution of the budget,* Circular No. A-11 (sec. 83, pp. 4–23). Washington, DC: Author. Retrieved May 6, 2012, from http://www.gpo.gov/fdsys/pkg/ERP-2011/pdf/ERP-2011.pdf.

personnel compensation expenditures, while the 12 series covers personnel benefits. The other major classes are contractual services and supplies, acquisition of assets, grants and fixed charges, and other.

Accounting systems can become unwieldy in their use of minor objects. For instance, travel as a major object can be subdivided in numerous ways:

- Mode (personal automobile, government automobile, commercial airline)
- Type of person traveling (elected official, political executive, career executive, employee, client)
- Purpose (meeting, conference, training, inspection)
- Location (in state, out of state, out of country)
- Type of expense (lodging, meals, transportation)

The number of possible permutations is great. When an accounting system uses such detail, the entry of many transactions may be delayed due to classification ambiguities.

Despite the administrative problems of detailed minor objects, legislative bodies often incorporate such details in appropriation bills. These line items in an appropriation allow control when there is concern that funds may be abused. Restrictions may be inserted regarding the purchase of newspaper subscriptions, the number of automobiles, and government employee travel. When minor object restrictions are embedded in appropriations, the limits are legally mandated, and the accounting system must ensure compliance.

Executives also use object classifications in an attempt to control agencies and increase their efficiency. Executive Order 12837 requires federal agencies to reduce their administrative costs, especially travel and other selected objects that are often viewed as luxuries.[48] Of course, many administrative expenses are central to the missions of agencies. Travel is essential for inspectors of meat and poultry processing plants, mines, and workplaces, for example.

Purpose and Activity

Program-oriented budgets that focus decision-making attention on specific program goals and objectives also require accounting-based information on how much each program costs.

The federal government uses broad functional categories, such as national defense, energy, and income security, which are divided into subfunctions. For example, energy is subdivided into supply and energy information, policy, and regulation.[49] If a budget based on program classifications cuts across agency lines, then the accounting system needs to cut across agency lines to accumulate the costs according to program. Similarly, preparing a budget that allocates funds according to detailed work activities requires an accounting system that tracks expenditures by those activities. The problem of accounting for finances by program or activity is discussed more fully in the next section in regard to cost accounting.

Performance Measurement

While practitioners and academics in the field of budgeting have long been concerned about how to measure the results of government programs, accountants only became particularly concerned starting in the 1980s.[50] They came to recognize a need for measuring outputs, outcomes, efficiency, effectiveness, and the like (see the chapter on the expenditure side of budget preparation). What is significant here is that accountants now back the notion that financial accounting should be tied to performance measurement. If one wishes to determine the efficiency of an organization in delivering a service over time, then there needs to be a measurement of the service provided (outputs) and the costs (the latter obtained through accounting).

GASB, since 1987, has had a project that encourages state and local governments to engage in *service efforts and accomplishments* (SEA) reporting as part of *general-purpose external financial reporting* (GPEFR). There have been numerous debates concerning whether such SEA reporting should be required or voluntary. GASB issued guidelines for voluntary SEA reporting in July 2010. [51]

Accounting for performance and then auditing for it require going beyond the boundaries of the organization to where results are produced. In contrast, traditional accounting systems have been structured to capture financial transactions within organizations. Once the accounting system has to take measurements outside the organization, as it must with performance accounting, major problems arise over how to collect information and how to audit it. Measurement errors inevitably occur in such systems, raising issues about their accuracy and utility.

The federal government has taken major steps in the direction of greater utilization of performance measurement. The Chief Financial Officers Act of 1990 instructs agency CFOs to develop reporting systems that provide for "the integration of accounting and budgeting information and the systematic measurement of performance." The Government Performance and Results Act (GPRA) of 1993 requires federal agencies to develop annual performance plans that are integral to the budget.[52] The GPRA Modernization Act of 2010 revised those requirements in an effort to make the reports more useful.[53] Of course, including performance information in accounting systems and having that information actually influence decision making are two different things. For the federal government, more strides have been made in performance reporting than in using performance information in decision making.

Perhaps equally difficult is the direct challenge that connecting performance and the budget creates for accounting systems themselves. Connecting performance information and cost information implies the ability to appropriately measure both. Proper cost measurement requires a level of accounting sophistication that has proved difficult for governments to achieve. They have attempted to remedy this problem through greater attention to cost accounting, as discussed later.

Basis of Accounting

The *basis of accounting* refers to the timing of transactions, or when a revenue item is recorded as received by the government and when an expenditure is recorded as having occurred. There are several methods for determining when a revenue or expenditure item is recorded, and each has a different purpose.

Cash Accounting

The oldest system is cash accounting, which is still used today, particularly in small governments. In general, all governments have a cash aspect to their accounting systems. In a cash accounting system, tax receipts are recorded when they are actually received by the government, and expenditures are recorded when payments are made. Minor variations exist. Some systems record expenditures when checks are written, but others record expenditures when checks clear the banking system. The major advantages of the cash system are that it is simple in comparison with alternatives and that it presents an accurate picture of cash on hand at any point in time.

The major disadvantage of the cash system is that it does not provide information about the future—namely, anticipated receipts and expenditures.[54] The cash on hand may seem to suggest that one's financial situation is reasonably secure, but a different picture may emerge when considering obligations that must be met, such as payrolls. Another major disadvantage of cash accounting is that it can be manipulated—for example, by making payments more quickly or more slowly—in a way that makes a government's financial condition appear better or worse at a point in time than it really is.

Encumbrance Accounting

A step in the direction of anticipating future transactions is encumbrance accounting. Expenditures are recorded when purchase orders are written or contracts are signed. Some of the cash on hand, then, is said to be encumbered and not available for covering other expenditures. In the case of a multiyear contract, all of the expenditures for a year may be encumbered at the outset of the fiscal year, or amounts may be encumbered each month as work is completed by the contractor. An encumbrance system helps ensure that a government unit will not overspend its appropriation.

Accrual Accounting

In accrual systems, financial transactions are recognized when the activities that generate them occur.[55] Revenues are recorded when the government earns the income, as when a local government sends tax bills to property owners. Expenditures are recognized when the liabilities are incurred, regardless of when payment for those goods or services might actually be made during the year.

The accrual basis has been required of federal agencies for more than 35 years, but few federal accounting systems actually use accrual accounting.[56] The obstacle has been the diversity of accounting systems. Large departments, such as the Department of Defense, for example, have many different accounting systems. Where accrual accounting is used in government, it is normally on a modified accrual basis. Not all transactions are accrued, and some remain on a cash basis. Under modified accrual accounting, revenues are recognized when they are "measurable and available" for obligation (this typically means that the revenues will be available to meet expenditures in the same fiscal year), and expenditures are recognized when an obligation to spend has occurred. Full accrual, however, is recommended for proprietary funds (enterprise and internal service funds) and pension trusts.

Despite the obstacles to implementation, the accounting profession continues to endorse strongly the accrual basis of accounting. GASB's Statement No. 11, *Measurement Focus and Basis of Accounting: Governmental Fund Operating Statements*, provides for extending the accrual process to cover items previously not covered.[57] For instance, the costs of employees' vacations are to be recognized when employees earn their vacation time. When employees are allowed to accumulate vacation leave, the accounting system needs to recognize that government's liabilities have increased. Particularly controversial is the provision that employee pension funds should recognize future payments owed to future retirees by recording them in the governmental funds rather than as normally reported in the general long-term debt account group. These provisions are controversial in that they negatively affect fund balances, pushing some governments into negative balances.

However, not recording those future obligations in the accounting system gives a false picture of the financial condition of the governmental entity. In the private sector, future pension payouts must be accounted for now to control for the possibility that the company will not have the funds to pay out the pension obligations when members of its workforce retire. Government presumably is in a somewhat different situation in that at least in principle, government can use its taxing power in the future to obtain the funds necessary to meet pension fund payout obligations. However, the fact that the government in principle can use its taxing power to meet pension obligations does not relieve government of the obligation to report what its pension fund liabilities are. Taxpayers are in for a rude shock when their jurisdiction's pension obligations have not been funded as employees earn future pension payouts and the accounting system does not record the future payouts that will be due.

Cost Accounting

While the cash, encumbrance, and accrual bases of accounting focus attention on resources coming into government and being expended, cost accounting is concerned with when resources are used, and by whom, in the production of goods and services.[58] For example, gasoline purchased for a state highway department could be accounted for when the order is made (encumbrance), when the goods are received (modified accrual method), or when the vendor is paid (cash method). The cost approach, in contrast, records the transaction when the gasoline is consumed.

Managerial cost accounting can be viewed as providing key information needed by managers in conducting their operations and, in addition to this internal function, providing information to external parties such as the legislative body, taxpayers, and investors in governmental securities.[59] In a cost accounting system, costs of providing services are matched with measures of those services. For example, a school district might want to know the average cost of graduating someone from the general population compared with the average cost of graduating a student with special needs—for instance, a student with physical disabilities.

Activity-based costing and *activity-based management* concentrate on collecting costs of delivering services to citizens.[60] The costs of delivering services can be monitored over time, thereby giving an impetus for increased efficiency of operations. Such accounting can determine the costs of producing activities, outputs, and outcomes.

The incentives for using cost accounting are different in the private and public sectors. To determine their profitability, corporations need to know the cost of providing each product or service. The costs of production can be subtracted from sales receipts to determine a corporation's profit or loss, something that every investor wants to know about a company. Governmental programs, such as police and fire departments, obviously do not seek a profit and consequently may see less need for cost accounting. Contemporary public safety managers want to know whether desired outcomes are being achieved and want to know from their accounting systems what the costs are for outputs and work (see the chapter on the expenditure side of budget preparation).

Other programs, particularly enterprise and internal service funds, while not seeking a profit, do endeavor to break even and consequently have an incentive to know the costs of their services. For example, a centralized office supplies agency has an incentive to calculate its costs so as to set appropriate fee schedules for charging departments for products. A central maintenance garage for city vehicles needs an accurate understanding of its costs for maintaining garbage trucks, police cars, and buses. Keeping costs down in each of these areas is important in linking the production of services with costs. Cost accounting systems should be able to provide insight into marginal costs, such as the extra expense of repairing each additional police car damaged in the line of duty.

Besides the reduced incentives to use cost accounting in government, several other impediments to its implementation exist. One such obstacle is that purposes and objectives are not neatly compartmentalized into organizational units, resulting in situations in which one organization may be serving multiple purposes and another organization may be serving some of those same purposes. To resolve this problem, *cost centers* must be used in which the accounting system records financial information for each activity performed within an organizational unit. In a bureau that engages in three activities and that has its personnel working at various times on the three activities, records must be maintained regarding the amount of time each worker spends on each activity. Other bureau costs, such as those for supplies, telephones, and furniture, must be distributed among the cost centers.

Other impediments to cost accounting being used in government pertain to how various financial transactions are currently conducted. Government agencies sometimes provide services to one another at no charge, resulting in a form of subsidy to the recipient agencies and a consequent understatement of the costs of the services that those agencies provide. Salaries, wages, and other personnel expenses, such as pension contributions and health benefits for employees and retirees, often appear in central budgets and not in the budgets of units that deliver services. Likewise, other support services involving budgeting, legal assistance, janitorial services, and computer support may not be charged to line agencies. The result is that organizational budgets typically fall short of fully reflecting the costs of activities.

Cost accounting requires that special attention be given to the acquisition and utilization of *fixed assets*—land, structures, and major pieces of equipment. Fixed assets are sometimes financed centrally and, as a consequence, do not appear in the budgets of the organizational units that actually use these assets. Additionally, purchases of fixed assets or capital goods should not be considered costs in the year of purchase but rather should be depreciated over the life span of the goods. From a cost standpoint, the cost of police patrol cars might be spread over three years. From a cash standpoint, the purchase will be recorded in the first year when the purchase is made. Buildings and vehicles then are depreciated over time, showing a truer picture of the cost of services than the cash method does.

The life cycle of an asset needs to be considered—that is, how long an asset has utility. Federal law and OMB Circular A-131 instruct agencies to use value engineering as a management technique in determining how long assets will be of use. The circular defines *value engineering* as "an organized effort directed at analyzing the functions of systems, equipment, facilities, services, and supplies for the purpose of achieving the essential functions at the lowest life-cycle cost consistent with required performance, reliability, quality, and safety."[61]

Depreciation is essential in cost accounting, and depreciation rules need to be applied differently according to the assets involved. FASAB has identified four types of *property, plant, and equipment* (PP&E).[62]

- The *general PP&E* category includes buildings for which a market value can be derived, such as an office building.
- The category of *federal mission PP&E* is for the uniquely federal functions of defense and space exploration. Depreciating these assets is extremely difficult because it requires estimating the assets' useful lives. How long will a weapons system be of use, or how long will a space satellite continue to operate?
- The *heritage PP&E* category includes education, culture, and artistic endeavors.[63] The Washington Monument and the White House are in this grouping, as they have special significance and are not just ordinary government buildings.
- The last category, *stewardship PP&E,* covers government holdings that are entrusted to the government for safekeeping. It includes federal land held by the National Park Service and the U.S. Forest Service.

In addition to fixed assets, other investments pose major challenges for the use of cost accounting in government. When a government bureau pays for several of its workers to attend a training program, is it an investment, and if so, what is the life of that investment? When a state government provides a grant to a local government for construction of a sewage treatment plant, how should the state record the investment given that the new plant will belong to the local government and not to the state?

Given the complexities of cost accounting, one can readily see why it is used in only limited cases in government. It is an open question whether FASAB and its participating agencies will be successful in moving the federal government toward the use of cost account-ing. The Government Accountability Office studied efforts to implement managerial cost accounting in a variety of federal agencies. One fundamental conclusion of these studies was that when leadership from the top was missing, implementation of cost accounting was spotty at best. This was the case at the Department of Health and Human Services and the Department of Education. In contrast, the Department of Transportation and the Social Security Administration were singled out as having strong leadership that fostered develop-ment of cost accounting throughout their respective component units.[64]

Project-Based Accounting

Another option that is not as elaborate as cost accounting is project-based accounting. Accounts can be established on a temporary basis to track costs for selected activities. Private firms, both for-profit and nonprofit, keep detailed accounting records for contracts, includ-ing costs at task or subtask levels. If a consulting firm has been awarded a government con-tract, a separate set of accounts is established showing which personnel worked on which tasks for what length of time in a given reporting period (weekly, biweekly, or monthly). Accounts of this type are important for reimbursement purposes. Federal cost accounting standards require strict adherence to project cost accounting. Charging time or other costs to a project when that time or other resources were not actually contributing to the proj-ect, if determined to be deliberate and significant, can result in severe penalties including debarment from future government contracting.

Project-based accounting is also used for monitoring internal operations. If a corporation is developing a new product or group of products, separate accounts can be established to gauge the developmental costs of the project. In the quasi-governmental arena, the World Bank uses account codes and employee time-reporting systems to account for project costs, enabling management to evaluate the cost of preparing, negotiating, and supervising a specific loan to a country.

Cost Finding

In some instances, governments may be satisfied with something less than a complete cost accounting system or even project-based accounting. Rather than having an ongoing cost information system, governments sometimes selectively study costs of specific activities that may be contained within a single organization or spread across several units. The cost of delivering family planning services to teenagers might be derived through analysis of expenditure records and a sampling of employee time commitments. A far more elaborate cost-finding endeavor would be to try to derive the costs of HIV/AIDS to a state govern-ment. The analysis would attempt to determine the costs of prevention and treatment activ-ities that most likely are not encoded in the accounting system. For example, AIDS may well increase health care costs for prisoners, but such costs would not routinely be segregated in the accounting system.

The analysis of cost data can be useful in identifying *fixed costs* and *variable costs*. There may be a minimum or fixed cost for providing a given service up to some particular level, above which costs increase as units of service increase. For example, a preschool program for disadvantaged children begins with a fixed set of costs for essentials such as a school room, a teacher, and some supportive services—costs that are incurred whether one or ten children are taught. As the number of children in the class increases, variable costs increase, such as those for teaching materials and supplies, and perhaps teacher aides. Fixed costs, however, do not rise unless the number of children grows to a level that another classroom, another teacher, and so forth are required.

Allowable Costs

In the awarding of grants and contracts, governments need to determine what costs are allowable. The federal government's Cost Accounting Standards Board, located within OMB's Office of Federal Procurement Policy, has attempted to set parameters for costs in defense and related contracts.[65] OMB Circular A-87 specifies in great detail what costs are allowable in grants to state and local governments.[66] Unallowable costs include entertainment, alcoholic beverages, interest on debt (such as working capital borrowings), and donations, as in the case of volunteer services.

Risk and Credit Accounting

Public sector officials have come to recognize that risks arise in carrying out public duties. Not only are revenues raised and expenditures made, but other factors create conditions that can result in major financial loss and/or expenditures. Risk management involves assessing the risk exposure of a government (see the chapter on budget execution). On the one hand, in making and guaranteeing loans, the federal government assumes risks that can have major financial consequences, as evidenced by the forced bailout of failed savings and loan associations. On the other hand, credit programs can yield savings or negative subsidies, particularly at some point in the future. Estimating such savings poses considerable technical problems, and agencies that administer such programs may be biased in favor of forecasting such savings.

The Office of Management and Budget, as prescribed by the Federal Credit Reform Act of 1990, oversaw a thorough revamping of how the government accounts for credit programs and how decisions are made about these programs. The law was intended to "place the cost of credit programs on a budgetary basis" so that they compete with all other programs for scarce resources.[67] Prior to the enactment of the Credit Reform Act, the budget "charged" costs based on the cash that would flow out of or into the budget in a given year. This meant that direct loans appeared to be the budgetary equivalent of grants, even though many of the funds would be repaid in later years. Loan guarantees, on the other hand, appeared to be cost free because third parties were disbursing the funds in the budget year (the government sometimes made money, in the budget year, because of up-front payments that came from borrowers). However, the federal government was liable for costs—sometimes substantial costs—in future years when loan recipients defaulted on their obligations. By focusing on the long-term costs to the federal government from both kinds of programs, the Credit Reform Act put them on an equivalent budgetary basis.

OMB requires agencies to supply data on direct loans, loan subsidies, guaranteed loans, and guaranteed loan subsidies as part of the agencies' budget submissions (Circular A-129). Prior to passage of the Federal Credit Reform Act, many federal agencies could borrow from the Federal Financing Bank, but they now must borrow from the Treasury

Department to finance their direct and guaranteed loan programs. When the law was implemented in the 1990s, federal agencies encountered considerable difficulty in complying, because their existing accounting systems and supporting staff were often inadequate.[68]

Generational Accounting

Of growing interest are the potential effects of government finances on different generations.[69] Expenditures for elementary and secondary education obviously help children, whereas alcohol programs help adults and programs such as Medicare help the elderly. In addition, at the federal level, generational accounting considers the effects that current budget deficits have on future generations, since those deficits represent a deferral of the costs of current benefits across generations. Although accounting systems have not been devised for identifying the costs or the benefits of government activities for different age groups, some reporting of such effects occurs.

Need for Different Bases

These different approaches to the basis of accounting are not substitutes for one another. Rather, each satisfies a different type of need.

- From the standpoint of a treasury department, a cash basis for recording receipts and expenditures is necessary because the department has the legal responsibility to receive revenue and issue checks to cover expenses. This responsibility extends to determining that there are sufficient funds to cover checks to be issued.
- The encumbrance basis is important in showing the current status of assets and liabilities, including liabilities that will place a demand on cash in the future.
- Cost accounting is valuable in identifying resources consumed, as distinguished from resources acquired and placed in inventory.
- Risk accounting provides a more comprehensive overview of obligations than is available through accounting systems that cover only revenues and expenditures.
- Generational accounting provides insights into the implications of government finances for different generations, from the elderly to the young and to those not yet born.

Private Sector Reforms in Accounting and Implications for Government Accounting

The discussion has shown that government accounting has been undergoing considerable reform, but it is worth giving special attention to efforts to extend the Sarbanes-Oxley Act to privately held companies, nonprofit organizations, and governments.

The Sarbanes-Oxley Act, formally the Public Company Accounting Reform and Investor Protection Act and commonly referred to as *SOX,* was passed in 2002 in the wake of the financial scandals involving Enron and WorldCom.[70] As its official title indicates, it was aimed at upgrading accounting practices in publicly traded companies in order to protect investors.

SOX's complex provisions include:

- Creation of the independent Public Company Accounting Oversight Board (PCAOB), which sets standards and oversees the accounting profession.
- Requirement for chief executive officers and chief financial officers of companies to take personal responsibility for the content of financial statements.
- Prohibition of ongoing use of lead auditors (that is, auditors primarily responsible for audits of particular firms) and instead required that they be rotated at least every five years.
- Internal controls and requirement that structure of such controls be audited by the company and assessed by auditors and reported to the Securities and Exchange Commission.
- Increased penalties for fraud in terms of fines and imprisonment.
- Protection to company employees who report wrongdoing (whistleblowers).
- Illegalization of the destruction of documents that are routinely needed in investigations and legal actions.

In response to Sarbanes-Oxley, the Office of Management and Budget launched a review of federal financial management. This process was already ongoing as required by the Federal Financial Management Improvement Act of 1996.[71] Circular A-123, dealing with internal controls, was revised in 2008, and subsequent guidance has been provided since. Among the specific changes over the past few years:

- Appendix B (last amended in 2009) establishes procedures to improve internal controls and eliminate fraud and waste in the use of government charge cards. The Appendix provides guidance intended to assist in avoiding improper payments and appropriately disciplining employees. It also requires that the government be reimbursed by employees or supervisors in the case of inappropriate or erroneous payments.[72]
- Appendix C, I-II (2011), outlines steps to implement the Improper Payments Elimination and Recovery Act (IPERA) of 2010. Perhaps the most important provision of this OMB guidance is the requirement that federal agencies expand "payment recapture audits to all types of payments and activities with more than $1 million in annual outlays if cost effective."[73]
- Appendix C, III (2010), implements Executive Order 13520 (November 20, 2009), on reducing improper payments. The appendix specifies responsibilities for agency officials, determines the programs subject to the executive order, establishes targets for the reduction of improper payments, lays out reporting requirements, and outlines means to deal with outstanding improper payment issues.[74]

Some have proposed scaling back the scope of Sarbanes-Oxley. Efforts have been made to reduce the liability of accounting firms in cases of wrongdoing, to direct prosecutions toward corporate wrongdoers rather than their corporations, and to reduce the scope of shareholder lawsuits. Some of these changes require congressional action, but others could be implemented through the regulatory process of the Securities and Exchange Commission.[75]

Reforms in Private Sector Pension Plans and Implications for Government Plans

The other major topic for possible reform is that of state and local pension plans. There are approximately 200 state-administered plans, some of which include local government employees as well as state employees, and about 2,000 locally administered plans.[76] In addition, there are thousands of other small plans involving annuity policies with private insurance carriers.

Retirement systems—both public sector and private sector—must comply with federal laws. The Employee Retirement Income Security Act (ERISA) of 1974 governs private sector plans.[77] Sections 415 and 457 of the Internal Revenue Code exert major controls over public retirement systems. In 1996, Congress amended these provisions to allow greater flexibility on the part of state and local systems in complying with federal law.[78]

Retirement systems are generally based on an assumption that a person will use a variety of measures to cover living expenses during retirement besides pension checks. First, living expenses may decline as the individual becomes less active and has fewer demands on income, such as support for dependents. Second, savings are used to cover expenses. Third, many government workers are covered by Social Security (including Old-Age and Survivors Insurance and disability insurance), as well as Medicare.

Defined Benefit and Defined Contribution Plans

Pension systems in the public sector historically have used *defined benefit plans,* in which benefits normally are determined according to some combination of years of services, wages or salaries (for example, average salary of the last three years of service), and age at time of retirement. The longer one has worked for a government and the higher one's salary, the higher pension benefits will be. State and local government retirement systems have historically used the defined benefit plan.

In addition to initial retirement benefits, cost-of-living allowances (COLAs) are sometimes assigned to pensioners, in some cases on an automatic basis according to an economic barometer, such as the consumer price index, and in other cases on an ad hoc basis. In the latter instance, a government might decide one year to increase retirement benefits by the same percentage as salary increases being awarded current employees. When governments face difficult financial situations, retirees may go for years without COLA increases. Other benefits are provided for disability retirement (for people who retire early because of poor health) and for survivors' benefits (covering family members who continue to live after the death of retirees). The vast majority of benefits paid each year go to elderly retirees, with the remainder divided between disability retirees and survivors.

Defined benefit plans coupled with cost-of-living allowances provide income security to employees and retirees and place investment risks on employers. Because benefits are determined in advance of retirement, employers must take steps necessary to ensure that sufficient funds will be available when employees retire. Cost accounting standards require that private sector companies "fund" the future liabilities created by these defined benefit programs. If projected earnings from investments of a company's pension fund are less than projected payouts, then the company must take an accounting adjustment, generally a write-down of profits, to cover the projected difference.

An alternative to defined benefits is the *defined contribution plan*. Under this plan, benefits are not defined in advance of retirement, but rather the employer commits to contributing regularly to an employee's retirement account (usually a percentage of compensation). The benefits received at the time of retirement are a function of the employer's and employee's contributions plus investment earnings on these contributions. 401(k) plans (named after the section of the Internal Revenue Code that defines their tax treatment) are the most common examples of defined contribution plans. 403(b) plans are the non-profit company equivalent. Both typically involve employer and individual contributions. Private companies may also have plans that are based solely on employer contributions. Most private employers use defined contribution plans, and while public employers are shifting to defined contribution plans, many still use defined benefit plans.

A key advantage of a defined contribution plan for an employer is its predictability. All that need be done each year is to set aside a percentage of salaries and wages for depositing into retirement accounts. A key disadvantage for the employee is that the benefits to be paid are not predictable and not guaranteed. Indeed many employees in defined contribution plans saw the value of their assets decline precipitously as a result of the global financial crisis that began in 2007. In many cases, this meant that these employees had to delay retirement because the value of their assets was insufficient to permit them to retire on the planned timetable. They continued to work, providing their employers had not eliminated their jobs during the recession.

Funding

Pension plans are funded by a combination of contributions from government and employees and investment earnings on those contributions. In some cases, the retirement program is financed exclusively by government, but that practice is an exception to the rule.

For the defined benefit pension plan, there are basically two methods of financing: *pay as you go* and *advance funding*. With the pay-as-you-go method, all that is required in any one budget year is to raise sufficient revenue to cover retirement benefit checks. This method is generally discouraged because it allows for the accumulation of debt. Persons in the future will be owed benefits, and taxpayers at that time will be forced to meet those costs. This is particularly problematic in cases where many employees may be eligible to retire at the same time, as will soon be the case when more baby boomers begin to retire.

The preferred method is advance funding, in which monies are accumulated for workers while they are working and those monies generate income through investments while workers are on the payroll and during retirement as well. When using this method, a retirement system must invest prudently but effectively to avoid any unfunded actuarial accrued liability so that the system is "actuarially sound." Advance funding uses the concept of present value. That is, future receipts, particularly contributions and investment earnings, are compared with anticipated costs (benefits) in terms of current dollars.

Liabilities

Until the 1970s, many public retirement systems were woefully underfunded. Over the years, governments had made pension plan commitments to employees but had failed to follow through by contributing sufficient funds to the plans. For those governments that do have underfunded pension plans, serious problems loom. Meeting current operating needs and covering the costs of retiree benefits can easily put a budget out of balance and force a tax increase. Where jurisdictions are at their legal or political limits on tax rates, severe program cuts may be the only alternative. Pension fund liabilities can increase the cost of doing business, as interest rates may be higher for jurisdictions that have large outstanding pension debts.

After the 1970s, the outlook improved for government pension plans. These were spurred by accounting requirements, such as those issued by GASB, that improved the transparency of financial reporting for pension systems. By the early 2000s, however, a new pension threat had emerged, particularly for state and local governments. This was precipitated by the chronic underfunding of pension systems by these governments, in addition to the discovery of the financial implications of the promises made to retirees for what GASB referred to as Other Post-Employment Benefits (OPEB). These OPEB benefits were mostly related to retiree health costs, which were rising rapidly because of the number of retirees and the impact of medical care inflation.

The Pew Charitable Trusts has done substantial work on the pension and OPEB financing problem at the state level. Many local pension systems, such as those for teachers and police officers, are administered at the state level. In a 2011 report, Pew estimated the total 2009 unfunded liabilities of state pension systems to be $1.26 trillion, up from $1 trillion just one year earlier. Of this amount, roughly half of the shortfall was for retirement benefits, while the other half represented OPEB liabilities.[79]

Pension assets represent about 78% of liabilities ($2.28 trillion, compared with $2.94 trillion). There is wide variation among the states in terms of their unfunded retirement liabilities. Only two states (New York and Wisconsin) had no unfunded liabilities at the end of 2009, although five other states (Delaware, North Carolina, South Dakota, Tennessee, and Washington) had unfunded liabilities of 10% or less. States with unfunded amounts of 40% or greater included Illinois, Kentucky, Louisiana, New Hampshire, Oklahoma, Rhode Island, and West Virginia.[80]

Pension systems, however, are much better funded than OPEB. At the end of 2009, OPEB assets covered only about 5% of OPEB liabilities ($31 billion, compared with $638 billion). Only two states (Arizona at 31% and Oregon at 32%) had unfunded liabilities lower than 68%. Moreover, more than half of the states (28 out of 50) effectively had no money set aside for OPEB liabilities at all—in other words, they had unfunded liabilities of 100%.[81]

The reporting, and therefore the understanding, of OPEB liabilities has been accelerated by the issuance of GASB Statement Number 45, which requires state and local governments to disclose their OPEB liabilities.[82] GASB 45 does not require these governments to fund these liabilities or even to explain how they are planning to. Once financial statements are required to disclose them, however, it is inevitable that bond rating agencies will focus attention on plans to fund them. Ignoring them, therefore, will have real costs to state and local governments. Several options are available for improving the funding situation of retirement systems and OPEB benefits:

- An obvious option is to increase government and employee contributions.
- A jurisdiction can take advantage of economies of scale by combining systems. This technique may reduce administrative costs and make possible more lucrative investments.

- Retirement systems can pool their funds for investment purposes.
- A jurisdiction can make investments that are riskier but also have higher rates of return. The stock market crash of 1987 and the Orange County, California, bankruptcy of 1994 (see the chapters on budget execution and capital finance), however, are sobering reminders of the loss that can result from nonguaranteed investments. Models are available that suggest how to balance high returns with acceptable levels of risk.
- Some jurisdictions have sold bonds to obtain the funds needed to cover retirement liabilities.
- A pension system can have its creditworthiness rated in terms of the system's ability to meet its financial obligations. This rating then can be used to back other entities for fees, consequently increasing the revenue for the pension system.
- An increasingly common response, particularly for OPEB liabilities, is to reduce the generosity of retiree health care benefits, to both current employees and current retirees. Many jurisdictions will have little choice but to take this approach as the need to finance the gap between resources available and promises made becomes more acute.

The efforts, mentioned earlier, in states such as Wisconsin and Ohio to scale back pay and benefits to public employees are certainly politically motivated. Conservative groups have financed some of these efforts. However, scale-backs have a real fiscal motivation as well. Defined benefit plans, with generous retiree health benefits, may simply prove unaffordable in the face of demographic changes and unaffordable increases in health care costs. Regardless of the outcome of the political discussion, therefore, the fiscal one is destined to continue.

Private pension plans have their own funding problems. Starting in 2006, it became woefully obvious that despite ERISA protecting private sector workers, private pension plans were underfunded. For example, giant Delphi Corporation, which was General Motors' primary parts supplier and had once been part of GM, went into bankruptcy and left in doubt the pension plans of current workers and those already retired. This caused substantial losses for the federal Pension Benefit Guaranty Corporation (PBGC), which insures private pension plans.

Congress passed the Pension Protection Act of 2006 in response to this situation. In general, the law gave private companies seven years to get their pensions up to a standard of being fully funded. The financially troubled airlines were given longer to comply. Plans that are deemed "at risk" have tougher funding standards to meet. Workers were given new incentives to save on their own through individual retirement accounts (IRAs) and 401(k) plans. The law can be seen as a balancing act of being tough with companies about their pension funding but not being so tough as to have them eliminate traditional pension systems.[83] Indeed, many companies have phased out pensions for new hires. Future funding of guaranteed health insurance benefits has also been an issue for private companies. Accounting reforms require private companies to fund through accrual the estimated costs of these health insurance payouts.

Despite this law, however, the deterioration of the economy has had substantial negative effect on private pension plans, and therefore on PBGC. In 2010 alone, PBGC assumed responsibility for 99,000 additional workers. By the end of fiscal year 2010, PBGC had a deficit of almost $23 billion, up from $11 billion in 2008. Furthermore, this represents a substantial deterioration of the PBGC situation in the past decade; in 2001, PBGC had a surplus of almost $8 billion.[84] The deterioration in PBGC's financial position caused the GAO to put the PBGC on its "high risk" list.[85] Given the fragile condition of many private pension plans, the financial condition of PBGC, and therefore its potential drain on the federal budget, remains a legitimate area of concern.

Pension Accounting and Reporting

Government requirements have influenced the reporting of both state and local governments and private firms, regarding their pension plans. Five statements and a technical bulletin issued by the Governmental Accounting Standards Board are the governing documents for accounting and reporting of state and local pension systems:

- Statement No. 25, *Financial Reporting for Defined Benefit Pension Plans and Note Disclosures for Defined Contribution Plans*
- Statement No. 26, *Financial Reporting for Postemployment Healthcare Plans Administered by Defined Benefit Pension Plans*
- Statement No. 27, *Accounting for Pensions by State and Local Governmental Employers*
- Statement No. 45, *Reporting on Post-Employment Benefits Other Than Pensions*
- Statement No. 50, *Pension Disclosures—an amendment to GASB Statements No. 25 and No. 27*
- Technical Bulletin 96-1, *Pension Disclosure Requirements for Employers*

Overall, these documents require an annual reporting of assets, changes in assets from year to year, and actuarial information on the long-term prospects of pension funds.

FINANCIAL REPORTING

Accounting systems generate reports that are used by managers, policy makers, and people outside of government. In state and local governments, generally accepted accounting principle 12 calls on jurisdictions to prepare both interim and annual reports (see above). Interim reports, such as daily and weekly reports, serve internal purposes, as in the case of checking on appropriated funds that are neither spent nor encumbered. These reports are useful in monitoring budget execution and anticipating situations in which agencies might lack sufficient funds to operate their programs throughout the fiscal year. A fundamental expectation of all financial reports is that they can be audited, meaning that accounting records back up the data in the reports.

Annual reports are particularly useful to people and organizations outside of government. They can show taxpayers how revenues have been used to support services, for example. Annual reports of local governments are helpful for businesses that are considering locating, relocating, or expanding existing facilities. Such reports are used to help discover the financial condition of governments and decide whether to purchase their bonds. The Government Finance Officers Association issues certificates of achievement for excellence in financial reporting. The association also issues awards for outstanding popular annual financial reporting (PAFRs). These reports are prepared for use by the general public and not accountants and budgeters.[86]

Financial Reports

GASB prescribes a *comprehensive annual financial report* (CAFR) that has three sections: introduction, finances, and statistics.[87] The first section includes a letter of transmittal and general information about the government. It lists the principal officials and provides an organization chart indicating lines of authority and responsibility.

The second section contains a variety of financial statements. As governments make extensive use of funds, several different types of statements may be provided on each fund. These statements by themselves can be confusing in that they do not provide an overall perspective on the finances of the government. For this reason, GASB and other professional accounting organizations prescribe the use of condensed statements that offer a comprehensive picture of a jurisdiction and omit some of the confusing detail.

One particularly troubling aspect of these statements is the use of *transfers* among funds. Monies can be moved from one fund to another without affecting the overall assets of a jurisdiction, but if transfers are not carefully noted, they may appear as expenditures in one fund and as new assets or receipts in another fund. These transfers need to be clearly identified not only to avoid confusion but also to provide important information about a government's operations. Transfers may indicate that enterprises are subsidizing general government operations, as when proceeds from a city airport are used in part to support a city's general fund. This type of transfer may be welcome relief to local taxpayers but may raise concern among holders of airport bonds. Good financial reports clearly label transfers—showing the source of receipts and the recipient of transfers—so that false impressions of asset creation or usage are avoided.

The third section of a financial report contains statistical data. Some tables present trend data assembled from earlier financial reports, such as general revenues by source over the most recent 10-year period. Other tables provide demographic data and indicate the principal taxpayers in the jurisdiction.

Balance Sheets

Of the numerous types of financial statements, balance sheets are one of the most common. A balance sheet can be thought of as a snapshot of a government's finances at a point in time, such as at the end of a quarter or fiscal year.

A balance sheet is organized according to the accounting formula discussed earlier. Assets are first listed, showing cash on hand (bank deposits) and taxes receivable. For proprietary funds and fiduciary funds, fixed assets (buildings, land, and so forth) are also reported as assets. The balance sheet then indicates liabilities—namely, accounts that are payable and bonds outstanding—followed by the fund balance, showing items such as monies that are encumbered. **Exhibit 12–3** is an example of a balance sheet from the State of Maryland. The table is just for the general fund, but the state supplies information about all other funds as well.

Exhibit 12–3 Balance Sheet, State of Maryland

<table>
<tr><td colspan="5" align="center">Governmental Funds
June 30, 2010
(Expressed in Thousands)</td></tr>
<tr>
<th></th>
<th></th>
<th>Special Revenue
Maryland
Department
of
Transportation</th>
<th>Other
Governmental
Funds</th>
<th>Total
Governmental
Funds</th>
</tr>
<tr>
<th></th>
<th>General</th>
<th></th>
<th></th>
<th></th>
</tr>
<tr><td>Assets:</td><td></td><td></td><td></td><td></td></tr>
<tr><td>Cash and cash equivalents</td><td>$ 196,138</td><td>$ 10,672</td><td></td><td>$ 206,810</td></tr>
<tr><td>Equity in pooled invested cash</td><td>1,652,469</td><td>148,336</td><td></td><td>1,800,805</td></tr>
<tr><td>Investments</td><td>10,099</td><td></td><td>$270,478</td><td>280,577</td></tr>
<tr><td>Prepaid items</td><td>408,352</td><td>90,539</td><td></td><td>498,891</td></tr>
<tr><td>Taxes receivable, net</td><td>938,646</td><td>73,281</td><td></td><td>1,011,927</td></tr>
<tr><td>Intergovernmental receivables</td><td>843,193</td><td>200,133</td><td>6,402</td><td>1,049,728</td></tr>
<tr><td>Other accounts receivable</td><td>411,499</td><td>114,391</td><td>49</td><td>525,939</td></tr>
<tr><td>Due from other funds</td><td>95,867</td><td>125,030</td><td></td><td>220,897</td></tr>
<tr><td>Due from component units</td><td>702</td><td></td><td></td><td>702</td></tr>
<tr><td>Inventories</td><td>25,987</td><td>79,089</td><td></td><td>105,076</td></tr>
<tr><td>Loans and notes receivable</td><td>14,901</td><td>1,466</td><td></td><td>16,367</td></tr>
<tr><td>Collateral for lent securities</td><td>247,824</td><td></td><td></td><td>247,824</td></tr>
<tr><td>Restricted assets:</td><td></td><td></td><td></td><td></td></tr>
<tr><td>Cash and cash equivalents</td><td></td><td>27,437</td><td></td><td>27,437</td></tr>
<tr><td>Cash with fiscal agent</td><td></td><td></td><td>13,947</td><td>13,947</td></tr>
<tr><td>Equity in pooled invested cash</td><td></td><td></td><td>105,315</td><td>105,315</td></tr>
<tr><td>Investments</td><td>2,930</td><td></td><td></td><td>2,930</td></tr>
<tr><td>Taxes receivable</td><td></td><td></td><td>26,329</td><td>26,329</td></tr>
<tr><td>Other accounts receivable</td><td></td><td></td><td>92</td><td>92</td></tr>
<tr><td>Due from other funds</td><td></td><td></td><td>2,425</td><td>2,425</td></tr>
<tr><td>Loans and notes receivable</td><td></td><td></td><td>3,256</td><td>3,256</td></tr>
<tr><td>Total assets</td><td>$4,848,607</td><td>$870,374</td><td>$428,293</td><td>$6,147,274</td></tr>
</table>

(continued)

Exhibit 12–3 Balance Sheet, State of Maryland

	General	Special Revenue Maryland Department of Transportation	Other Governmental Funds	Total Governmental Funds
Liabilities:				
Salaries payable	$ 147,411	$ 24,974		$ 172,385
Vouchers payable	255,818	38,932	$ 53,275	348,025
Accounts payable and accrued liabilities	1,392,077	349,195	25,652	1,766,924
Due to other funds	467,452	12,889	54,830	535,171
Due to component units	3,764			3,764
Accounts payable to political subdivisions	177,449	41,946	54,673	274,068
Deferred revenue	802,279	66,716	47	869,042
Accrued self-insurance costs	105,441			105,441
Collateral obligations for lent securities	247,824			247,824
Total liabilities	$3,599,515	$534,652	$188,477	$4,322,644
Fund balances:				
Nonspendable	448,982	171,094		620,076
Spendable:				
Restricted	398	3,069	151,317	154,784
Committed	1,140,676	161,559	447,295	1,749,530
Unassigned (deficit)	(340,964)		(358,796)	(699,760)
Total fund balances	$1,249,092	$335,722	$239,816	$1,824,630
Total liabilities and fund balances	$4,848,607	$870,374	$428,293	$6,147,274

The accompanying notes to the financial statements are an integral part of this financial statement.

Source: State of Maryland, Comprehensive annual financial report: fiscal year ended June 30, 2010 (p. 28).

GASB's Statement No. 11 on measurement focus and the basis of accounting requires governments to recognize items as liabilities that were previously excluded. As a result of complying with this requirement, balance sheet bottom lines went from positive to negative for many governments. When numerous governments complained about the potential political and economic harm of such balance sheets, GASB allowed governments to use the term *fund equity* for the difference between revised assets and liabilities. The term *fund balance* can be used for calculating balance sheets in the format that preceded Statement No. 11.

Although the federal government does not produce a balance sheet using the same rules as state and local governments, OMB does provide a summary of government assets and liabilities in the president's annual budget. In **Exhibit 12–4**, net liabilities for 2010 are reported at $12.1 trillion, or the equivalent of a debt of $19,163 per capita. This consists of total assets of $3.7 trillion, offset by liabilities of $15.8 trillion. The $12.1 trillion in net liabilities is more than twice the net liability level for fiscal year 2000.

Operating Statements

A second major type of financial statement is the operating statement, which shows the monies received and expended during a specified period of time. State and local governments refer to these as "statements of revenues, expenditures, and changes in fund balance." Revenues can be reported by source—sales tax and income tax. Expenditures can be reported by major objects, organizational units, or other means. **Exhibit 12–5** is an operating statement for the State of Utah. This table shows these transactions for all governmental funds. Tables such as this one and others shown in the chapter typically have notes that explain what is included and excluded in specific entries in the statements. These notes are essential components of the statements.

Cash Flow Statements

A third form of financial statement details cash flows. The purpose is to show how cash entering and leaving a fund affects an entity's operations. These statements cover cash and cash equivalents, such as short-term investments (U.S. Treasury bills; see the chapter on budget execution). Controversy exists over how these statements should be organized and whether they should be extended from just covering enterprise funds to include basically all funds. **Table 12–1** is a cash flow statement for the Commonwealth of Pennsylvania, covering the enterprise and internal service funds. Not shown in the table is Pennsylvania's detailed presentation on specific enterprise funds, which include unemployment compensation, state workers' insurance, state lottery, tuition payment, and other funds.

Other Reports and Reporting Requirements

In addition to balance sheets, operating statements, and cash flow statements, governments issue other important financial reports (e.g., disclosures on securities). Governments provide statements when issuing bonds and other securities that are intended to help would-be purchasers understand what is being offered for sale in terms of the backing of the securities and what risks are involved. GASB Statement No. 34, issued in 1999, has imposed dramatic changes on state and local government financial reporting, including the following:

- Statements must have *management's discussion and analysis* (MDA) indicating, in an objective way, the current financial situation in understandable English.
- Government-wide financial statements must be provided and must show the current and prior year.
- Full accrual accounting for all government activities is mandated.
- All capital assets must be shown and depreciated, including infrastructure assets.

(text continues on p. 436)

Exhibit 12–4 U.S. Government Assets and Liabilities

ASSETS AND LIABILITIES*

(As of the end of the fiscal year, in billions of 2010 dollars)

	1960	1965	1970	1975	1980	1985	1990	1995	2000	2005	2006	2007	2008	2009	2010
ASSETS															
Financial Assets:															
Foreign Exchange, SDRs, and Gold	12	9	20	15	22	40	53	74	50	45	38	38	38	98	96
Cash, Checking Deposits, Other Monetary Assets	53	76	47	39	60	40	53	54	77	41	60	81	380	281	313
Mortgages	33	32	48	50	93	95	121	83	94	84	85	85	90	111	107
Other Loans	123	170	213	215	276	358	253	205	234	220	214	214	217	336	471
Less Expected Loan Losses	–1	–3	–5	–11	–21	–21	–24	–30	–46	–45	–50	–46	–50	–83	–65
Other Treasury Financial Assets	63	84	62	58	82	113	191	219	292	324	323	319	304	464	420
Subtotal	284	368	385	367	512	625	648	605	701	669	670	692	980	1,207	1,341
Nonfinancial Assets:															
Fixed Reproducible Capital	1,241	1,231	1,282	1,243	1,177	1,331	1,380	1,386	1,219	1,221	1,236	1,224	1,257	1,288	1,283
Defense	1,070	1,005	1,016	928	833	969	993	970	794	769	782	777	807	822	825
Nondefense	171	226	265	315	344	363	387	416	424	452	454	446	451	466	459
Inventories	325	281	262	234	290	331	293	226	231	301	301	288	294	288	286
Nonreproducible Capital	160	212	253	413	600	700	594	442	769	1,389	1,419	1,357	1,109	782	753
Land	114	158	199	316	403	419	431	316	547	1,024	1,052	996	644	439	408
Mineral Rights	46	54	54	97	197	281	163	126	222	365	368	361	465	343	345
Subtotal	1,726	1,725	1,797	1,890	2,067	2,363	2,267	2,054	2,219	2,911	2,956	2,869	2,660	2,358	2,322
Total Assets	2,010	2,093	2,182	2,257	2,579	2,988	2,915	2,659	2,920	3,579	3,626	3,561	3,640	3,565	3,664
LIABILITIES															
Debt Held by the Public	1,417	1,457	1,297	1,319	1,639	2,710	3,689	4,900	4,259	5,076	5,169	5,240	5,886	7,634	9,019
Insurance and Guarantee Liabilities:															
Deposit Insurance	0	0	0	0	2	11	89	24	1	1	1	2	35	73	108
Pension Benefit Guarantee	0	0	0	53	39	54	54	26	50	91	79	86	75	93	102

Exhibit 12–4 U.S. Government Assets and Liabilities

	1960	1965	1970	1975	1980	1985	1990	1995	2000	2005	2006	2007	2008	2009	2010
Loan Guarantees	0	1	3	8	15	13	19	37	46	53	51	72	75	71	67
Other Insurance	39	35	27	25	33	20	25	22	20	45	21	17	21	15	15
Subtotal	39	36	30	86	90	99	186	108	118	190	153	178	206	252	293
Pension and Post-Employment Health Liabilities:															
Civilian and Military Pensions	1,070	1,345	1,609	1,823	2,242	2,224	2,172	2,105	2,201	2,398	2,479	2,514	2,646	2,739	2,896
Retiree Health Insurance Benefits	219	275	329	373	459	455	445	440	488	1,243	1,212	1,194	1,179	1,192	1,260
Veterans Disability Compensation	235	296	354	392	402	332	299	362	690	1,241	1,235	1,174	1,488	1,333	1,475
Subtotal	1,525	1,916	2,293	2,589	3,103	3,011	2,915	2,907	3,379	4,882	4,926	4,882	5,313	5,264	5,631
Environmental and Disposal Liabilities	82	104	124	140	168	200	234	309	376	287	327	356	348	346	321
Other Liabilities:															
Currency and SDRs	16	16	31	37	45	41	48	49	41	41	40	39	37	88	86
Trade Payables	18	25	26	36	69	100	145	112	102	221	229	249	289	272	289
Benefits Due and Payable	26	30	41	43	55	61	73	85	97	129	138	139	146	163	164
Subtotal	59	72	98	116	169	203	265	246	240	391	408	427	473	523	540
Total Liabilities	3,123	3,584	3,841	4,250	5,169	6,224	7,290	8,470	8,373	10,826	10,981	11,082	12,226	14,019	15,804
Net Liabilities (Liabilities Minus Assets)	1,113	1,492	1,660	1,993	2,590	3,236	4,375	5,811	5,453	7,247	7,355	7,521	8,586	10,454	12,140
Addenda:															
Ratio to GDP (in percent)	35.4	37.7	35.1	37.2	40.4	42.3	48.9	57.4	43.6	51.5	51.1	51.0	58.4	73.2	82.3

* This table shows assets and liabilities for the government as a whole excluding the Federal Reserve System. Data for 2010 are extrapolated in some cases.

Source: Reprinted from U.S. Office of Management and Budget (2010). *Analytical perspectives, budget of the United States government, fiscal year 2011* (p. 1479). Washington, DC: U.S. Government Printing Office.

Exhibit 12–5 State of Utah Receipts, Expenditures, and Changes in Fund Balance, Year Ending June 30, 2010

For the Fiscal Year Ended June 30, 2010 (Expressed in Thousands)

		Special Revenue		
	General	Education	Transportation	Transportation Investment
REVENUES				
Taxes:				
Sales and Use Tax	$ 1,416,447	$ —	$ 62,999	$ 250,158
Individual Income Tax	—	2,124,173	—	—
Corporate Tax	—	266,961	—	—
Motor and Special Fuels Tax	—	—	341,196	—
Other Taxes	275,952	36,186	9,454	—
Total Taxes	1,692,399	2,427,320	413,649	250,158
Other Revenues:				
Federal Contracts and Grants	2,642,157	636,641	421,819	—
Charges for Services/Royalties	297,494	2,719	80,704	—
Licenses, Permits, and Fees	34,540	4,982	71,633	68,792
Federal Mineral Lease	129,377	—	—	—
Federal Aeronautics	—	—	39,752	—
Intergovernmental	—	—	—	—
Investment Income	6,704	25,579	838	6,906
Miscellaneous and Other	206,666	26,591	82,609	—
Total Revenues	5,009,337	3,123,832	1,111,004	325,856
EXPENDITURES				
Current:				
General Government	288,464	—	—	—
Human Services and Youth Corrections	665,601	—	—	—
Corrections, Adult	232,235	—	—	—
Public Safety	194,314	—	—	—
Courts	136,373	—	—	—
Health and Environmental Quality	1,867,646	—	—	—
Higher Education – State Administration	52,084	—	—	—
Higher Education – Colleges and Universities	716,043	—	—	—

Exhibit 12–5 State of Utah Receipts, Expenditures, and Changes in Fund Balance, Year Ending June 30, 2010

		Special Revenue		
	General	Education	Transportation	Transportation Investment
Employment and Family Services	673,060	—	—	—
Natural Resources	158,939	—	—	—
Community and Culture	170,898	—	—	—
Business, Labor, and Agriculture	86,984	—	—	—
Public Education	—	3,002,231	—	—
Transportation	—	—	1,244,341	771,720
Capital Outlay	—	—	—	—
Debt Service:				
Principal Retirement	—	—	—	—
Interest and Other Charges	—	—	—	—
Total Expenditures	5,242,641	3,002,231	1,244,341	771,720
Excess Revenues Over (Under) Expenditures	(233,304)	121,601	(133,337)	(445,864)
OTHER FINANCING SOURCES (USES)				
General Obligation Bonds Issued	—	—	37,339	818,051
Revenue Bonds Issued	—	—	—	—
Premium on Bonds Issued	—	—	2,161	47,349
Capital Leases Acquisition	11,122	—	—	—
Sale of Capital Assets	—	32	8,016	—
Transfers In	397,162	8,664	115,904	77,117
Transfers Out	(156,098)	(322,038)	(138,550)	(239,479)
Total Other Financing Sources (Uses)	252,186	(313,342)	24,870	703,038
Net Change in Fund Balances	18,882	(191,741)	(108,467)	257,174
Fund Balances – Beginning	632,691	714,845	675,172	(8,652)
Adjustment to Beginning Fund Balances	(3,929)	—	(338,028)	338,028
Fund Balances – Beginning As Adjusted	628,762	714,845	337,144	329,376
Fund Balances – Ending	$ 647,644	$ 523,104	$ 228,677	$ 586,550

The Notes to the Financial Statements are an integral part of this statement.

Source: State of Utah. Comprehensive annual financial report for the year ended June 30, 2010 (p. 38).

Table 12–1 Statement of Cash Flows, Commonwealth of Pennsylvania

Proprietary Funds
For the Fiscal Year Ended June 30, 2010

(Amounts in thousands)

	Enterprise Funds						
	Unemployment Compensation Fund	*State Workers' Insurance Fund (Dec. 31, 2009)*	*State Lottery Fund*	*Tuition Payment Fund*	*Nonmajor Funds*	*Total*	*Internal Service Funds*
CASH FLOWS FROM OPERATING ACTIVITIES:							
Receipts from employers	$ 4,906,544	$ 196,663	$ —	$ —	$ —	$ 5,103,207	$ —
Receipts from customers	—	3,047,711	—	—	1,531,292	4,579,003	103,538
Receipts from borrowers	—	—	—	—	66,940	66,940	—
Receipts from participants	—	—	—	157,336	—	157,336	—
Receipt of premiums	—	—	—	—	5,474	5,474	—
Payments to programs for the elderly	—	—	(796,541)	—	—	(796,541)	—
Payments to prize winners	—	—	(1,900,569)	—	—	(1,900,569)	—
Payments to participants	—	—	—	(164,487)	—	(164,487)	—
Payments to claimants	(9,347,339)	(297,806)	—	—	(1,025)	(9,646,170)	—
Payments to borrowers	—	—	—	—	(76,989)	(76,989)	—
Payments for vendors, employees and other costs	—	(70,104)	(289,871)	(6,313)	(1,493,594)	(1,859,882)	(79,844)
Other receipts (payments)	—	851	(111,491)	—	660	(109,980)	61
NET CASH PROVIDED BY (USED FOR) OPERATING ACTIVITIES	(4,440,795)	(170,396)	(50,761)	(13,464)	32,758	(4,642,658)	23,755
CASH FLOWS FROM NON-CAPITAL FINANCING ACTIVITIES							
Net borrowings under advances from other funds	—	274	—	—	—	274	274
Transfers in	—	—	176,700	—	12,000	188,700	—
Transfers out	(3,500)	—	(286,597)	—	(117,377)	(407,474)	—
Grants and other revenues	4,923,537	—	111,917	—	1,372	5,036,826	—
Other	—	—	—	—	(137)	(137)	—

Table 12–1 Statement of Cash Flows, Commonwealth of Pennsylvania

(Amounts in thousands)		Enterprise Funds					Internal Service Funds
	Unemployment Compensation Fund	State Workers' Insurance Fund (Dec. 31, 2009)	State Lottery Fund	Tuition Payment Fund	Nonmajor Funds	Total	
NET CASH PROVIDED BY (USED FOR) NON-CAPITAL FINANCING ACTIVITIES	4,920,037	274	2,020	–	(104,142)	4,818,189	–
CASH FLOWS FROM CAPITAL AND RELATED FINANCING ACTIVITIES:							
Acquisition and construction of capital assets	–	–	(3,197)	–	(11,832)	(15,029)	(5,168)
NET CASH USED FOR CAPITAL AND RELATED FINANCING ACTIVITIES	–	–	(3,197)	–	(11,832)	(15,029)	(5,168)
CASH FLOWS FROM INVESTING ACTIVITIES:							
Purchase of investments	(5,612)	(850,164)	(1,289,280)	(1,583,382)	(975,942)	(4,704,380)	(373,919)
Sales and maturities of Investments	3,390	1,325,240	1,321,969	1,581,929	1,058,517	5,291,045	347,213
Investment income	50	57,569	652	31,335	3,298	92,904	155
Investment expense	–	(4,888)	–	(4,143)	–	(9,031)	–
Change in securities lending obligations	(392)	(358,618)	(1,526)	(14,481)	(8,928)	(383,945)	(1,005)
NET CASH PROVIDED BY (USED FOR) INVESTING ACTIVITIES	(2,564)	169,139	31,815	11,258	76,945	286,593	(27,556)
NET INCREASE (DECREASE) IN CASH	476,678	(983)	(20,123)	(2,206)	(6,271)	447,095	(8,969)
CASH AT JULY 1, 2009	365,281	4,712	21,706	2,283	18,122	412,104	12,114
CASH AT JUNE 30, 2010	$ 841,959	$ 3,729	$ 1,583	$ 77	$ 11,851	$ 859,199	$ 3,145

Source: Commonwealth of Pennsylvania. Comprehensive annual financial report, for the year ended June 30, 2010 (p. 54).

- Analysis must be shown of significant changes in fund balance for the various governmental, proprietary, and fiduciary funds.
- Note disclosures are required to show important accounting policies. Disclosures must show changes in long-term liabilities and in capital assets.
- GASB No. 34 reconfigured the types of funds to be used. The new configuration was presented earlier when we discussed governmental, proprietary, and fiduciary funds.[88]

In addition to GASB 34 and GASB 45 (on OPEB—discussed above), GASB has issued several other statements since 2007:

- Statement No. 51, issued in 2007, provides guidance for the classification of intangible assets, such as trademark, water, and timber rights. The statement provides that, unless specifically excluded, such intangible assets should be classified as capital assets.
- Statement No. 53, issued in 2008, and GASB No. 64 (2011) are concerned with derivatives, and specifically provide that they should be reported at fair value, with changes in fair value reported either as investment revenue, or in the statement of net assets as a deferral.
- Statement No. 56, issued in 2009, incorporates into GASB requirements specific accounting and financial reporting guidance presented by the American Institute of Certified Public Accountants (AICPA).
- Statement No. 58, issued in 2009, sets financial and accounting guidance for governments that have filed for Chapter 9 bankruptcy protection.
- Statement No. 60, issued in 2010, provides for the accounting and financial reporting of *service concession agreements* (SCAs). SCAs are public–private or public–public agreements where a government allows an operator to use public assets or infrastructure, with the operator receiving a fee.
- Statement No. 63, issued in 2011, provides financial reporting guidance for deferred outflows of resources (consumption of net assets applicable to future reporting periods) or deferred inflows of resources (acquisition of net asset to the government applicable to future reporting periods).

As of 2011, GASB had the following exposure drafts in circulation:

- *Recognition of Elements of Financial Statements and Measurement Approaches*
- *Accounting and Financial Reporting for Pensions—an amendment of GASB Statement No. 27*
- *Financial Reporting for Pension Plans—an amendment of GASB Statement No. 25*

Federal Accounting and Financial Reporting

As noted above, the Office of Management and Budget issues an annual series of tables that together report on the financial condition of the government. In addition, OMB works with federal agencies in their preparation of agency-specific reports. The Chief Financial Officers Act of 1990 and the Government Management Reform Act of 1994 required agencies to prepare a series of auditable financial statements by March 1, 1997, and every year thereafter.[89]

Circular A-136, which OMB updates annually, is the governing document in this process.[90] Federal entities are required to prepare annual performance and accountability reports (PARs). MDA is required at the outset of the report, discussing such matters as mission, organizational structure, and performance goals, objectives, and results. Next is the performance section, which provides program information. A financial section follows, covering balance sheets and several other types of financial statements. The circular also provides for quarterly and interim financial statements.

The 2010 PAR for the National Aeronautics and Space Administration is illustrative.[91] The PAR covers such issues as NASA's mission and organization, and presents detailed information on NASA's progress toward meeting performance goals, and reasons for failure to meet particular goals, where applicable. The financial statements do not begin until page 159, and the statements and accompanying audit report cover only about 25% of the total report.

Government financial reporting has clearly become much more extensive in recent decades, but this expansion has come at a cost. Questions arise regarding whether accounting systems have become overloaded and whether some of the resources spent on financial reporting might be better spent on the delivery of services to citizens. Demands for the streamlining of financial reports are increasing. To date, Congress has authorized OMB to waive some reporting requirements imposed on federal agencies. The accounting profession itself has shown some awareness that reporting requirements can create overwhelming burdens.

GOVERNMENTAL AUDITING

Auditing serves a variety of functions and consequently exists in many different forms, all over the world.[92] One distinction made is between *preaudits* and *postaudits*—that is, between reviewing transactions before and after they occur. The preaudit occurs before the government commits itself to a purchase and is used to verify, for example, that the police department has sufficient funds to purchase a piece of equipment and that the department is authorized to have that equipment. Not only the budget office but also an accounting department may be involved in preaudits. If personnel are to be hired, a personnel office may have some preaudit responsibility. Often at the state and local levels, independent comptrollers, controllers, or auditors general have preaudit responsibilities.

Postaudits generally involve more extensive procedures and often more participants. The following discussion concerns the function of postaudits in government budgeting and finance. This form of auditing has been defined as "a systematic collection of the sufficient, competent evidential matter needed to attest to the fairness of management's assertions in the financial statements, or to evaluate whether management has efficiently and effectively carried out its responsibilities."[93]

Audit Objectives and Organizational Responsibilities

Purposes

Auditing in the private sector is used largely to ensure that the financial statements issued by a firm fairly reflect its financial status, and this same concern exists in the public sector.

Auditing provides some assurance to investors in both the private and public sectors that their investments are secure and are being well managed.

Another purpose of auditing is ensuring that funds are not subject to fraud, waste, and abuse, or subject to error in reporting. When financial reports cannot be verified by checking accounting records, the opportunities for dishonesty, waste, or just poor management of funds may exist. Auditing in government is used for compliance purposes as well. As has been noted, accounting systems track receipts and expenditures to ensure that they are handled in conformance with restrictions contained in revenue and appropriation bills. Auditing helps ensure that an agency does not spend funds on an activity that, while beneficial to society, simply has not been authorized. Compliance auditing can include ensuring that an agency has accomplished programmatically what it was instructed to do. Another form of compliance auditing involves grants and contracts. The federal government, for example, needs to check that only appropriate charges have been made by a state government in the case of a federally funded project or program, such as Medicaid, or by a university in the case of funded research. Similarly, government contracts are audited regularly for compliance with financial provisions of the contracts to ensure that billed costs are within the scope of the contracts and that adequate records exist to support the legitimacy of these billed costs.

Auditing Organizations

Nationally, several organizations influence the practice of governmental auditing. The American Institute of Certified Public Accountants (AICPA) issues generally accepted auditing standards (GAAS).[94] AICPA's Attestation Standards (SSAE No. 10) instructs auditors on what records to keep and for how long. GASB, in the process of identifying standards for accounting, inevitably becomes involved in auditing. GASB Statement No. 34, discussed earlier, created several issues about auditing in state and local governments.

The Federal Accounting Standards Advisory Board (FASAB) also has a role in federal auditing. For example, its standard SFFAS No. 29 covers *Auditing Heritage Assets and Stewardship Land*.

The Government Accountability Office issues *Government Auditing Standards* (GAS, known as the "yellow book"). The standards are applied to federal agencies and may be applied to state and local governments that receive federal financial assistance.[95] GAO uses an Advisory Council on Government Auditing to assist in reviewing and revising the yellow book. The council's members come from all levels of government, the private sector, and academia. GAO and the President's Council on Integrity and Efficiency issue the *Financial Audit Manual*, which provides a methodology for federal auditing.[96]

The Office of Management and Budget is deeply involved in auditing, a relatively new role for the organization. The key documents are Circular A-123 on internal controls, Circular A-136 on reporting requirements, and Bulletin No. 06-03, *Audit Requirements for Federal Financial Statements*.[97] A-123 was revised in 2004 to bring federal standards in line with those for the private sector as required by SOX.[98] The circular took effect in fiscal year 2006. The bulletin is designed to bring federal auditing in line with private sector auditing as prescribed by the PCAOB. For example, the bulletin defines material weakness as "a significant deficiency, or combination of significant deficiencies, that results in a more than remote likelihood that a material misstatement of the financial statements will not be prevented or detected." Circular A-123 provides that agencies must give annual assurances on the accuracy and effectiveness of their internal controls for financial reporting. Agencies will eventually be required to undergo audits of their internal controls.

Auditing within a government is often performed by several organizations. Audits are conducted periodically by officers within an agency to provide information to management. These internal audits help maintain managerial control over operations. Other audits are conducted by external officers, who can be from a unit answerable to the legislative body (such as GAO being answerable to Congress), a unit headed by an independently elected officer, or an independent private corporation that has a contract to conduct an audit.

The federal government ratcheted up the auditing function during the 1970s and 1980s by creating *inspectors general* in major federal agencies. Appointed by the president with the advice and consent of the Senate, inspectors general are located within agencies but can be removed only by the president. According to the Inspector General Act of 1978 and the Chief Financial Officers Act of 1990, inspectors general are responsible for conducting audits and for investigating possible cases of fraud, waste, and abuse of government resources.[99] Most of the burden of federal auditing rests with these IGs rather than the GAO. The Chief Financial Officers Act, by creating CFOs in major agencies, greatly increased the attention that agencies devote to sound accounting practices and to the auditing of accounts. Agencies have redesigned their central staff units, consolidating considerable powers under the CFOs. Other federal agencies not covered by the 1978 legislation also have inspectors general.

Executive Order 12993 provides a process for dealing with instances of possible wrongdoing by inspectors general and their deputies. The Federal Bureau of Investigation is authorized to investigate such matters, and the President's Council on Integrity and Efficiency (PCIE) reviews the FBI's findings. The PCIE consists of department inspectors general and selected central administrators, such as representatives from OMB and the Office of Personnel Management.

All levels of government use the Big 4 and other accounting firms to conduct or assist in auditing. Depending on the state, a local government may have a choice of paying either the state auditor or a private firm for audit services. State services may be less expensive, but private services may perform audits in a more timely fashion. When a private firm is to be used, a government will employ a bidding process to give competing firms an opportunity to indicate what services they can provide, in what time frame, and at what cost.

A practice often recommended for the public sector is the use of independent *audit committees.* These bodies typically consist of administrators, legislators, and financial experts from outside the government. The committees can serve as useful interfaces between finance offices and auditors. The Sarbanes-Oxley Act required such committees of publicly traded corporations, but the committees are used only on a limited basis in the public sector.

Sometimes the number of organizations involved in auditing in a given situation can seem overwhelming. An agency may have two or more auditors. In the Department of Defense, for instance, audit functions are performed by the Defense Contract Audit Agency (which audits contractors), the inspector general, the comptroller, and the CFO.

Large state and local agencies may have similar internal auditors, and all levels of government have their central auditors, such as the Auditor General of Illinois. As noted, private accounting firms may have responsibilities as well. Additional auditing occurs because of intergovernmental financial transactions. State government agencies, for example, may be audited by federal funding agencies and GAO, although this level of auditing has changed since passage of the Single Audit Act of 1984 (see below).

Types of Audits and Standards

Audit Types

As already noted, there are preaudits and postaudits, and internal and external audits. Another means of categorizing audits is by considering the purposes to be served. The definition of auditing provided earlier suggests that audits can be directed toward finance and performance.

Financial audits focus on whether financial statements prepared by a government accurately reflect financial transactions and the government's or agency's status. The standards of auditing provide a framework for conducting an audit.

Financial audits also review how financial matters are handled or whether suitable internal controls exist to protect resources. Auditors are concerned with the vulnerability of a financial management system to potential fraud. Are organizational lines of responsibility clearly established to ensure that whoever is in charge has the authority to protect the government's or agency's finances? Are policies and procedures established for maintaining records, and are those policies and procedures adhered to in practice? Are computer systems that handle financial transactions protected against potential fraud?

Identification of risks is the first step in eliminating problems. Auditors make risk assessments to determine which accounting activities or operations to audit, as only a sample of financial activities can be audited, given the auditors' limited resources. The risk assessment determines which activities are most vulnerable to fraud, waste, and abuse and therefore should be audited.

As of 2011, the GAO's list of high-risk situations included 30 items, with some items having been on the list for many years, such as defense weapons systems acquisition. Many of the items on the list involve substantial current or future costs to the government, such as Medicare, Medicaid, the Social Security Administration's Disability Insurance programs, and the PBGC, whose problems were discussed above. The 2011 high-risk list removed two issues: the 2010 Census and DOD's personnel security clearance program.[100]

The other major auditing function served is performance or program auditing, which deals with whether resources are being used efficiently and whether results or objectives are being achieved (see the chapter on the expenditure side of budget preparation). In GAO's case, it has moved largely away from financial audits and conducts mostly performance audits. Several states have been cited as actively engaged in program audits. These include Florida's Office of Program Policy Analysis and Government Accountability (OPPAGA), Missouri's Auditor's Office and the Oversight Division of the Committee on Legislative Research, Pennsylvania's Department of the Auditor General and the Legislative Budget and Finance Committee, and Virginia's Joint Legislative Audit and Review Commission (JLARC).[101]

Any audit agency faces the difficult choice of deciding how much effort and resources should be devoted to the competing functions of financial and performance auditing. If major emphasis is given to performance auditing, fraud and other abuses may become more prevalent. Conversely, placing greater emphasis on financial auditing may keep government honest but does little to encourage agencies to fulfill their missions.

Auditing Standards

The federal Government Auditing Standards provide overall guidelines as well as standards for conducting fieldwork and preparing audit reports. Overall standards call for auditors to be independent of the agencies under review and to be fully trained in the auditing function. The Securities and Exchange Commission oversees accounting firms to ensure that private auditors are independent of the entities that they audit. Fieldwork is to be planned adequately in advance and sufficiently staffed to meet the requirements of the work plan. Auditors must keep accurate records of their fieldwork to answer questions that may arise at a later time.

Field auditing involves verifying sample transactions to ensure that transactions did occur as recorded. For example, an expense report of a trip taken by a city employee to a national conference, among numerous expense reports, might be selected for review. The auditor may (1) call the travel agent or airline to verify the ticket price, (2) check that the trip was an authorized budget expenditure, (3) interview the employee to verify unreceipted miscellaneous expenses, and (4) review other receipts and documents to determine the accuracy of the report. The purpose of this fieldwork is not particularly to find cases of fraud, waste, and abuse but rather to verify that the jurisdiction has procedures in place to protect against them.

The Single Audit Act

A concern of the federal government for many years has been the large volume of federal financial transfers to state and local governments and to nongovernmental organizations, and verification of whether these transfers are being suitably audited. The Office of Management and Budget has six circulars that detail how these organizations are to arrange their accounts:

- A-21, *Cost Principles for Educational Institutions* (2004)
- A-87, *Cost Principles for State, Local, and Indian Tribal Governments* (2004)
- A-102, *Grants and Cooperative Agreements with State and Local Governments* (1994, as amended in 1997)
- A-110, *Uniform Administrative Requirements for Grants and Agreements with Institutions of Higher Education, Hospitals, and Other Non-Profit Organizations* (1993, as amended in 1999)
- A-122, *Cost Principles for Non-Profit Organizations* (2004)
- A-133, *Audits of States, Non-Profits, and Local Organizations* (1997, with revisions and supplements in 2003 through 2007)

The Single Audit Act of 1984, as amended, requires recipients of federal assistance amounting to $500,000 or more in a fiscal year to undergo a single audit of their accounting systems and the way federal funds are handled.[102] Audits must be submitted within nine months of the audit period's close. The law applies to state and local governments as well as to nonprofit organizations. It has had the effect of requiring tens of thousands of audits annually. These audits, normally conducted by private firms, are intended to help ensure that recipients use federal resources in accordance with federal laws and regulations. The act is implemented through OMB Circular A-133. The Single Audit Act has undoubtedly improved the handling of federal financial assistance, but it may have had only a limited impact on overall financial management in these governments.

GAAS, GAS, and the Single Audit Act set standards for audit reporting. Of course, one of the chief concerns with regard to any report is that financial statements be in accordance with generally accepted accounting principles. Audit reports are expected to indicate deficiencies, such as inconsistent use of accounting procedures. Reports indicate whether internal controls exist to protect against fraud, waste, and abuse.

Four types of conclusions can be drawn by the auditing body:

1. The audit might be *unqualified,* providing an unqualified or "clean" opinion—that is, the accounting system meets all standards.
2. The report may be *qualified,* indicating there are problems but that the system generally meets standards. A qualified audit of a local or state government might be interpreted unfavorably by would-be investors in the government's bonds.
3. A *disclaimer audit* indicates that the accounting system is inadequate and that conducting an audit is impossible.
4. An audit can be *adverse* or *negative,* indicating that the financial statements fail to provide an accurate report of the entity's finances.

For fiscal year 2010, the federal government as a whole received a disclaimer of opinion from the Government Accountability Office's audit of consolidated financial statements. This was the fourteenth year of such disclaimers, covering every year since GAO carried out these audits. GAO, in its report accompanying the financial statements, highlighted the federal government's material weaknesses in internal control. In all, financial statements representing 32% of the federal government's reported assets as of September 30, 2010, either were not audited or received disclaimers of opinion. The largest single obstacle to the federal government's ability to receive a clean audit opinion is the continued financial management challenges of the Department of Defense.[103] The audit news out of federal departments has been encouraging. For fiscal year 2008, unqualified opinions were issued for all federal departments, with the important exceptions of the Departments of Defense, NASA, and Homeland Security.[104] One should keep in mind that the Defense budget is much larger and more complex than the budgets for the Department of Homeland Security or NASA. As for state governments, the Government Performance Project for 2005 reported that 36 received unqualified opinions on their comprehensive annual financial reports (CAFRs) and many on all of their financial statements as well.[105]

Improper Payments

Erroneous or improper payments have been one of the biggest problems detected through auditing. The governing legislation at the federal level was the Improper

Payments Information Act of 2002.[106] The law required federal agencies to (1) conduct risk assessments, gauging the possibility and likelihood of making improper payments, (2) estimate the annual amount of such payments, and (3) report recouped funds. This information was to be included in the agencies' performance and accountability reports (PARs; see above).

In 2009, President Barack Obama issued Executive Order 13520, discussed above, on reducing improper payments. Subsequently, in 2010, Congress passed the Improper Payments Elimination and Recovery Act. The IPERA adds to the 2002 act by (1) lowering the permitted threshold of susceptibility to improper payments over time, (2) expanding the types of programs required to be audited for payment recovery, (3) enabling agency heads to use funds they recover for additional uses such as improvement of financial management, support of their Office of Inspector General, and the original funding purpose, and (4) establishing repercussions for agencies that are noncompliant.[107] In 2011, GAO issued a report estimating that federal agencies made about $125.4 billion in improper payments during fiscal year 2010, representing approximately 3% of all federal spending during that year.[108] Of course, the federal government is not the only government subject to wrongful spending. A county treasurer in Iowa was accused, for example, of making hundreds of dollars of phone calls at government expense to a lonely-hearts telephone service.[109] State auditors check on both state spending and state grants to local governments. The federal government cannot get a handle on the extent of overpayment of federal money if such overpayments go undetected in state programs administering federal money. When state auditors find improper payment errors in the administration of state money by local governments, the grant payments can be halted. This indeed happened to a Florida opportunity council that provided services to the poor and had poorly organized accounting records, preventing the auditor from issuing an opinion.[110] In extreme cases, when local governments' finances are in disarray, states have the authority to take over the jurisdictions on a temporary basis.

Follow-up after an audit is essential to ensure that weaknesses are corrected. Without such follow-up, auditing is an empty exercise. OMB Circular A-50, *Audit Followup*, sets guidelines for checks to be made after audits have been completed at the federal level.

SUMMARY

Governmental accounting is characterized by procedures intended to prevent fraud and to guarantee agency conformance with legal requirements. Information from accounting systems is used in decision making and can help improve the efficiency and effectiveness of services. The Governmental Accounting Standards Board was established to help improve state and local government accounting systems, and the Federal Accounting Standards Advisory Board has similar responsibilities at the federal level. Generally accepted accounting principles allow the use of several different types of funds, with the general fund usually the most important for any government.

Accounting systems are structured by having a general ledger and subsidiary ledgers. They follow a relatively simple formula: assets equal the total of liabilities and fund balance. Within the ledgers, expenditures are accounted for in a variety of ways, including major and minor objects of expenditures.

Bases of accounting include cash, encumbrance, accrual, and cost. Some jurisdictions use project-based accounting and cost finding instead of the more comprehensive cost accounting methods. Regardless of the basis for accounting, reports summarizing transactions are prepared at specified intervals. Three of the most common types of reports are balance sheets, operating statements, and cash flow statements.

Auditing attempts to determine whether financial statements accurately reflect the status of accounts and/or whether an organization is operating efficiently and effectively. It is used for compliance purposes—namely, to ensure that financial transactions are in accordance with revenue and appropriation legislation. Generally accepted auditing standards constitute the guidelines for auditing in the public sector.

The field of public sector accounting, reporting, and auditing is undergoing rapid change. The stimuli for reform generally center around patent cases of fraud and waste, some on a small scale and others of huge magnitude.

NOTES

1. Brooks, M. (1968). *The Producers*. MGM Studios.
2. Joyce, P. (2011). *The Congressional Budget Office: honest numbers, power and policymaking* (p. 142). Washington, DC: Georgetown University Press.
3. Norvelle, J. W. (1997). *Introduction to fund accounting* (5th ed.). Eaton Rapids, MI: RIA Professional Publishing; see Harris, J. (2005). The discourse of governmental accounting and auditing. *Public Budgeting & Finance, 25*, Supplement 1, Winter, 154–179.
4. U.S. General Accounting Office (2000). *Executive guide: creating value through world-class financial management*. Washington, DC: U.S. Government Printing Office.
5. Mosher, F. C. (1984). *A tale of two agencies*. Baton Rouge, LA: Louisiana State University Press.
6. Federal Managers' Financial Integrity Act of 1982 (P.L. 97-255); Accounting and Auditing Act of 1950, Ch. 946, Title I.
7. Chief Financial Officers Act of 1990 (P.L. 101-576).
8. U.S. Chief Financial Officers Council website, www.cfoc.gov.
9. U.S. Office of Management and Budget (2006). *Federal financial management report, 2006*. Retrieved December 20, 2011, from http://www.whitehouse.gov/sites/default/files/omb/assets/financial_pdf/2006_report.pdf.
10. Federal Accounting Standards Advisory Board website, www.fasab.gov.
11. Clinger-Cohen Act (Information Technology Management Reform Act) of 1996 (P.L. 104-106).
12. Palmer, K. (2005). Chief financial officers highlight their job challenges. *Government Executive*. Retrieved December 20, 2011, from http://www.govexec.com/story_page.cfm?filepath=/dailyfed/0205/020805k1.htm&oref=search.
13. Mitchell, M., Deputy Associate Administrator, U.S. General Services Administration (2006). *GSA's role in implementing FMLoB government-wide*. Retrieved December 20, 2011, from http://www.gsa.gov/portal/content/102185; Mosquera, M. (2006). Financial LOB moves to standardize rules. *Government Computer News*. Retrieved December 20, 2011, from http://gcn.com/articles/2006/08/18/financial-lob-moves-to-standardize-rules.aspx?sc_lang=en.
14. U.S. Office of Management and Budget (2006). *Competition framework for financial management lines of business migrations*. Retrieved August 26, 2006, from http://www.whitehouse.gov/omb/financial/ffs/competition_framework_fmlob.pdf (source no longer available).
15. Government Accountability Office (2009). OMB's financial management line of business initiative continues but future success remains uncertain. *GAO.gov*, May 7. Retrieved March 22, 2012, from http://www.gao.gov/products/GAO-09-328.

16. Gauthier, S. J. (2005). *2005 governmental accounting, auditing, and financial reporting.* Chicago, IL: Government Finance Officers Association; Governmental Accounting Standards Board website, www.gasb.org.
17. Governmental Accounting Standards Board website, www.gasb.org.
18. Governmental Accounting Standards Board website, www.gasb.org.
19. Financial Accounting Standards Board website, www.fasb.org.
20. Gronewald, N. (2009). The big four of accounting will be among the big winners if U.S. adopts climate law. *New York Times,* July 7.
21. Andersen guilty in Enron case. (2002). BBC News, June 15. Retrieved August 26, 2006, from http://news.bbc.co.uk/2/hi/business/2047122.stm; Brown, R. E. (2005). Enron/Andersen: crisis in U.S. accounting and lessons for government. *Public Budgeting & Finance, 25,* Fall, 20–32.
22. Accenture website, www.accenture.com.
23. Report: WorldCom's problems worsen. (2002). *Associated Press,* August 8. Retrieved December 20, 2011, from http://www.highbeam.com/doc/1P1-55093311.html.
24. Hilzenrath, D. S., & Johnson, C. (2006). Fannie Mae avoids criminal charges over accounting. *Washington Post,* August 25. Retrieved December 20, 2011, from http://pqasb.pqarchiver.com/washingtonpost/access/1106727321.html?FMT=ABS&FMTS=ABS:FT&date=Aug+25%2C+2006&author=&pub=The+Washington+Post&edition=&startpage=D.1&desc=Fannie+Mae+Avoids+Criminal+Charges+Over+Accounting.
25. Wallison, P., & Calomiris, C. (2008). The last trillion dollar commitment: the destruction of Fannie Mae and Freddie Mac. *AEI.org.* Financial Services Outlook Series. September 30. Retrieved March 23, 2012, from http://www.aei.org/article/economics/monetary-policy/the-last-trillion-dollar-commitment/.
26. Governmental Accounting Standards Board (2006). *Codification of governmental accounting and financial reporting standards.* Norwalk, CT: GASB.
27. American Institute of Certified Public Accountants website, www.aicpa.org.
28. American Institute of Certified Public Accountants (2000). *Federal GAAP hierarchy,* SAS No. 91. Retrieved August 27, 2006, from http://www.cpa2biz.com/CS2000/Products/CPA2BIZ/Publications/Sub+2/Federal+GAAP+Hierarchy+-+SAS+No.+91.htm?cs_catalog=CPA2Biz&pagetype=product&cs_category=statements%5Fon%5Fauditing%5Fstandards (source no longer available).
29. Smith, J. L. (2005). Lapeer official says "sorry." *Flint Journal,* December 2, A1, A2.
30. Abuja, F. M. (2006). How public servants loot treasury—accountant general. *AllAfrica.com,* August 25. Retrieved August 27, 2006, from http://allafrica.com/stories/printable/200608250483.html.
31. Glenger, B., & Capaccio, T. (2011). Afghan aid tracking suffers on Karzai, U.S. failures, audit says. *Bloomberg,* July 20. Retrieved March 22, 2012, from http://www.bloomberg.com/news/2011-07-20/afghan-aid-tracking-suffers-on-karzai-u-s-failures-audit-says.html.
32. International Monetary Fund (2001). *Code of good practices on fiscal transparency.* Retrieved November 7, 2006, from http://www.imf.org/external/np/fad/trans/code.htm.
33. United Way International (2006). *Global standards for United Way organizations.* Alexandria, VA: United Way International.
34. Odyek, J. (2006). Uganda: accounting chiefs warned. New Vision, August 21. *AllAfrica.com.* Retrieved March 22, 2012, from http://allafrica.com/stories/200608220488.html.
35. Gettler, L. (2006). Push to get government accounting into open. *The Age,* August 3. Retrieved December 20, 2011, from http://www.theage.com.au/news/business/push-to-get-government-accounting-into-open/2006/08/02/1154198206453.html.
36. U.S. Office of Management and Budget (2004). *Management's responsibility for internal control,* Circular A-123. Retrieved December 20, 2011, from http://www.whitehouse.gov/omb/circulars_a123_rev.
37. Norvelle, J. W. (1997). *Introduction to fund accounting,* 16–18.
38. U.S. General Accounting Office (1995). *Government corporations: profiles of recent proposals.* Washington, DC: U.S. Government Printing Office; Bunch, B. S. (2000). Changes in usage of enterprise funds by large cities. *Public Budgeting & Finance, 20,* Summer, 15–29.

39. McCoskey, M. G., et al. (2003). Trust, trusts, and accountability: the role of states in college saving plans. *Public Budgeting & Finance, 23,* Fall, 49–63; College Savings Plan Network website, www.collegesavings.org.

40. Financial Management Service, U.S. Department of Treasury (2011). *USSGL implementation guidance.* Retrieved December 5, 2011, from http://www.fms.treas.gov/ussgl/approved_scenarios/index.html.

41. U.S. Office of Management and Budget (2009). *Financial management systems,* Circular A-127. Retrieved December 5, 2011, from http://www.whitehouse.gov/omb/circulars_a127.

42. Governmental Accounting Standards Board (2007). *Defining the fundamental elements of financial reporting,* June, 1. Retrieved March 22, 2012, from http://www.gasb.org/cs/BlobServer?blobcol=urldata&blobtable=MungoBlobs&blobkey=id&blobwhere=1175820452682&blobheader=application%2Fpdf.

43. Governmental Accounting Standards Board (2009). Statement No. 54, *Fund balance reporting and governmental fund type definitions.* February. Retrieved March 22, 2012, from http://www.gasb.org/st/summary/gstsm54.html.

44. Governmental Accounting Standards Board (2009). *GASB improves the usefulness of reported fund balance information.* March 11. Retrieved March 22, 2012, from http://www.gasb.org/cs/ContentServer?c=GASBContent_C&pagename=GASB/GASBContent_C/GASBNewsPage&cid=1176156695762.

45. Norvelle, J. W. (1997). *Introduction to fund accounting,* 43.

46. Governmental Accounting Standards Board (2006). Statement No. 48, *Sales and pledges of receivables and future revenues.* September 29. Retrieved March 22, 2012, from http://www.gasb.org/cs/ContentServer?c=GASBContent_C&pagename=GASB%2FGASBContent_C%2FProjectPage&cid=1176156655051.

47. Consolidated Appropriations Act of 2010 (P.L. 111-117).

48. Executive Order 12837: Deficit control and productivity improvement in the administration of the federal government, February 10, 1993.

49. U.S. Office of Management and Budget (2006). *Historical tables, budget of the United States government, fiscal year 2007,* 55. Retrieved August 27, 2006, from http://www.whitehouse.gov/omb/budget/fy2007/pdf/hist.pdf.

50. Roberts, A. (1999). Accounting for results, 1997: government-wide performance plan, fiscal year 1999. *Journal of Policy Analysis and Management, 18,* 187–191; Cunningham, G. M., & Harris, J. (2005). Toward a theory of performance reporting to achieve public sector accountability: a field study. *Public Budgeting & Finance, 25,* Summer, 15–42; Berman, B. J. (2006). *Listening to the public: adding the voices of the people to government performance measurement and reporting.* New York, NY: Fund for the City of New York.

51. Governmental Accounting Standards Board (2010). *Service efforts and accomplishments reporting.* Retrieved March 22, 2012, from http://www.gasb.org/cs/ContentServer?c=GASBContent_C&pagename=GASB/GASBContent_C/ProjectPage&cid=1176156646053.

52. Government Performance and Results Act of 1993 (P.L. 101-576).

53. Government Performance and Results Modernization Act of 2010 (P.L. 111-352).

54. Musso, D. (2006). Social Security: reliance on cash flow accounting and projections disguises an inherent upside cash flow bias. *Public Budgeting & Finance, 26,* Spring, 143–156.

55. Van der Hoek, M. P. (2005). From cash to accrual budgeting and accounting in the public sector: the Dutch experience. *Public Budgeting & Finance, 25,* Spring, 32–45; Caridad, M. (2006). Accrual budgeting: accounting treatment of key public sector items and implications for fiscal policy. *Public Budgeting & Finance, 26,* Summer, 45–65.

56. U.S. General Accounting Office (2000). *Accrual budgeting: experience of other nations and implications for the United States.* Washington, DC: U.S. Government Printing Office.

57. Governmental Accounting Standards Board (1990). *Measurement focus and basis of accounting: governmental fund operating statements,* Statement No. 11. Retrieved August 27, 2006, from http://www.gasb.org/st/index.html.

58. Kinney, M. R., & Raiborn, C. A. (2011). *Cost accounting; foundations and evolutions,* 6th ed. Mason, OH: Southwestern Cengage Learning; Brock, H. R., et al. (2007). *Cost accounting: principles and applications* (7th ed.). Boston, MA: McGraw-Hill.

59. Rivenbark, W. C. (2005). A historical overview of cost accounting in local government. *State and Local Government Review, 37,* 217–227.

60. Activity-based costing and activity-based management symposium. (1999). *Public Budgeting & Finance, 19,* Summer, 3–58; Kaplan, R. S., & Andersen, S. R. (2004). Time-driven activity-based costing. *Harvard Business Review, 82,* 131–140; Rozlocki, N. (2006). *Introduction to activity based costing (ABC): Internet ABC online presentation.* Retrieved August 27, 2006, from http://www.pitt.edu/~roztocki/abc/abctutor/ (source no longer available).

61. U.S. Office of Management and Budget (1993). *Value engineering,* Circular A-131. Retrieved December 20, 2011, from http://www.whitehouse.gov/omb/circulars_a131/.

62. Federal Accounting Standards Advisory Board (1995). *Accounting for property, plant, and equipment,* Statement of Federal Financial Accounting Standards 6. Retrieved August 27, 2006, from http://www.fasab.gov/pdffiles/vol1v4.pdf.

63. Federal Accounting Standards Advisory Board (2005). *Heritage assets and stewardship land,* Statement of Federal Financial Accounting Standards 29. Retrieved August 27, 2006, from http://www.fasab.gov/pdffiles/sffas_29.pdf.

64. U.S. Government Accountability Office (2005). *Managerial cost accounting practices: leadership and internal controls are key to successful implementation.* Washington, DC: Author; U.S. Government Accountability Office (2005). *Managerial cost accounting practices: Departments of Education, Transportation, and the Treasury.* Washington, DC: Author; U.S. Government Accountability Office (2006). *Managerial cost accounting practices: Department of Health and Human Services and Social Security Administration.* Washington, DC: Author; Government Accountability Office (2007), *Managerial cost accounting practices at the Department of the Interior* [memorandum], May 24. Retrieved March 22, 2012, from http://www.gao.gov/assets/100/94920.pdf.

65. U.S. Office of Management and Budget (2006). *Cost Accounting Standards Board.* Retrieved December 20, 2011, from http://www.whitehouse.gov/omb/procurement_casb.

66. U.S. Office of Management and Budget (2004). *Cost principles for state, local and Indian tribal governments,* Circular No. 87. Retrieved December 20, 2011, from http://www.whitehouse.gov/sites/default/files/omb/circulars/a087/a87_2004.pdf.

67. Federal Credit Reform Act of 1990 (P.L. 101-508), Title XIII.

68. U.S. General Accounting Office (1993). *Federal credit programs: agencies had serious problems meeting credit reform accounting requirements.* Washington, DC: U.S. Government Printing Office.

69. Collard, D. (2004). Generational accounting and generational transfers. *Ageing Horizons,* no. 1. Retrieved December 20, 2011, from http://www.ageing.ox.ac.uk/system/files/AH1%20Collard.pdf; Eschker, E. (2005). Generational accounting and the saving rate decline, 1960–2000. *Public Budgeting & Finance, 25,* Spring, 46–65.

70. Sarbanes-Oxley Act (Public Company Accounting Reform and Investor Protection Act) of 2002 (P.L. 107-204); McCarthy, E. (2004). *Tips for the Sarbanes-Oxley learning curve.* Retrieved August 29, 2006, from http://www.aicpa.org/PUBS/jofa/jun2004/mccarthy.htm; *Sarbanes-Oxley 101: information guide to the Sarbanes-Oxley Act of 2002.* Retrieved August 29, 2006, from http://www.sarbanes-oxley-101.com.

71. Federal Financial Management Improvement Act of 1996 (P.L. 104-208).

72. Office of Management and Budget (2009). *Circular No. A-123, Appendix B, Revised.* January 15. Retrieved March 22, 2012, from http://www.whitehouse.gov/sites/default/files/omb/circulars/a123/a123_appendix_b.pdf.

73. Office of Management and Budget (2011). *Memorandum for the Heads of Executive Departments and Agencies: Issuance of Revised Parts I and II to Appendix C of OMB Circular A-123.* April 14. Retrieved March 22, 2012, from http://www.whitehouse.gov/sites/default/files/omb/memoranda/2011/m11-16.pdf.

74. Office of Management and Budget (2010). *Appendix C, Part III: Requirements for Implementing Executive Order 13520: Reducing Improper Payments.* March 22. Retrieved March 22, 2012, from http://www.whitehouse.gov/sites/default/files/omb/assets/a123/a123_appx-c.pdf.

75. Labaton, S. (2006). Businesses seek protection on legal front. *New York Times,* October 29. Retrieved October 29, 2006, from http://www.nytimes.com/2006/10/29/business/29corporate.html?hp&ex =1162184400&en=9358599aad440557&ei=5094&partner=homepage.

76. Census Bureau, U.S. Department of Commerce (2004). *Employee retirement systems of state and local governments: 2002.* Washington, DC: U.S. Government Printing Office.

77. Employee Retirement Income Security Act of 1974 (P.L. 93-406).

78. Small Business Job Protection Act of 1996 (P.L. 104-188).

79. Pew Center on the States (2011). *The widening gap: the great recession's impact on state pension and retiree health care costs.* April, 1. Retrieved March 22, 2012, from http://www.pewcenteronthestates.org/ initiatives_detail.aspx?initiativeID=85899358839.

80. Pew Center on the States (2011). *The widening gap,* 3.

81. Pew Center on the States (2011). *The widening gap,* 6.

82. Governmental Accounting Standards Board, GASB 45.

83. Pension Protection Act of 2006 (P.L. 109-280); BNA Tax Management (2006). *Pension Protection Act of 2006.* Retrieved December 20, 2011, from http://subscript.bna.com/pic2/ppa.nsf/id/RSAR-6SSJ5X?OpenDocument; CCH (2006). *Pension Protection Act of 2006.* Retrieved August 29, 2006, from http://tax.cchgroup.com/Legislation/2006-Pension.pdf (source no longer available).

84. Pension Benefit Guarantee Corporation (2010). *PBGC annual report.* November.

85. Government Accountability Office (2009). *High-risk series: an update.* January. Retrieved March 22, 2012, from http://www.gao.gov/new.items/d09271.pdf.

86. Government Finance Officers Association (2006). *Preparing popular reports.* Retrieved December 20, 2011, from http://www.gfoa.org/index.php?option=com_content&task=view&id=1467.

87. Governmental Accounting Standards Board (2006). *Codification of governmental accounting and financial reporting standards.*

88. Governmental Accounting Standards Board (1999). *Basic financial statements—and management's discussion and analysis—for state and local governments,* Statement No. 34. Retrieved December 20, 2011, from http://www.gasb.org/cs/ContentServer?c=Pronouncement_C&pagename=GASB%2F Pronouncement_C%2FGASBSummaryPage&cid=1176156699453; Kravchuk, R. S., & Voorhees, W. R. (Eds.) (2001). Governmental Accounting Standards Board (GASB) Statement No. 34 symposium. *Public Budgeting & Finance, 21,* Fall, 1–87.

89. Government Management Reform Act of 1994 (P.L. 103-356).

90. U.S. Office of Management and Budget (2006). *Financial reporting requirements,* Circular A-136. Retrieved December 20, 2011, from http://www.whitehouse.gov/sites/default/files/omb/ circulars/a136/a136_revised_2011.pdf.

91. U.S. National Aeronautics and Space Administration (2010). *Fiscal year 2010 performance and accountability report.* November 15. Retrieved March 22, 2012, from http://www.nasa.gov/pdf/500155main_ NASA_FY_2010_PAR-11-15-10.pdf.

92. Carlos, S. (2006). Banking on accountability? Strengthening budget oversight and public sector auditing in emerging economies. *Public Budgeting & Finance, 26,* Summer, 66–100.

93. Government Finance Officers Association (1994). *Governmental accounting, auditing, and financial reporting* (p. 314). Chicago, IL: Government Finance Officers Association.

94. American Institute of Certified Public Accountants (2006). *Generally accepted auditing standards: SAS No. 95.* New York, NY: Author; Dauber, N., et al. (2005). *2006 auditing standards: including the standards of the PCAOB.* Mason, OH: Thomson.

95. U.S. General Accounting Office (2007). *Government auditing standards.* Washington, DC: U.S. Government Printing Office; U.S. Government Accountability Office (2011). *Government auditing standards: 2011 Internet version.* Retrieved December 20, 2011, from http://www.gao.gov/govaud/ iv2011gagas.pdf; Kearney, E. F., et al. (2005). *Federal government auditing: laws, regulations, standards, practices, & Sarbanes-Oxley.* Hoboken, NJ: John Wiley.

96. U.S. General Accounting Office and President's Council on Integrity and Efficiency (2004). *Financial audit manual: checklist for federal accounting, reporting, and disclosures.* Washington, DC: U.S. Government Printing Office.

97. U.S. Office of Management and Budget (2007). *Audit requirements for federal financial statements, bulletin no. 07-04.* Retrieved December 20, 2011, from http://www.whitehouse.gov/sites/default/files/omb/bulletins/fy2007/b07-04.pdf; U.S. Chief Financial Officer's Council (2005). *Implementation guide for OMB Circular A-123, management's responsibility for internal control, Appendix A, internal control over financial reporting.* Washington, DC: Author.

98. Tierney, C. E., et al. (2006). *OMB Circular A-123 and Sarbanes-Oxley: management's responsibility for internal control in federal agencies.* Hoboken, NJ: Wiley.

99. Inspector General Act of 1978 (P.L. 95-452).

100. U.S. Government Accountability Office (2011). *High-risk series: an update.* February. Retrieved March 22, 2012, from http://www.gao.gov/assets/320/315725.pdf.

101. Government Performance Project (2008). *Grading the states 2008.* Retrieved December 20, 2011, from http://www.pewcenteronthestates.org/gpp_report_card.aspx.

102. Single Audit Act of 1984 (P.L. 98-502); Single Audit Act Amendments of 1996 (P.L. 104-156).

103. U.S. Government Accountability Office (2010). *Statement of the acting Comptroller General of the United States,* December 21. Washington, DC: Author.

104. U.S. Office of Management and Budget (2009). *Federal financial management report, 2008.*

105. Government Performance Project (2006). *Grading the states 2005: A look inside.* Retrieved December 20, 2011, from http://www.pewtrusts.org/uploadedFiles/wwwpewtrustsorg/Reports/Government_Performance/GPP_Report_2005.pdf.

106. Improper Payments Information Act of 2002 (P.L.107-300).

107. Improper Payments Elimination and Recovery Act of 2010 (P.L. 111-204).

108. Government Accountability Office (2011). *Improper payments: Recent efforts to address improper payments and remaining challenges.* Statement of Kay L. Daly before the subcommittee on government organization, efficiency, and financial management, Committee on Oversight and Government Reform, House of Representatives. April 15.

109. Kompas, K. (2001). Treasurer faces charges for making calls at work. *Des Moines Register,* March 16.

110. Rousos, R. (2006). Agency under fire: a Q and A. *The Ledger,* August 25. Retrieved December 20, 2011, from http://www.theledger.com/article/20060825/NEWS/608250370.

Capital Assets: Planning and Budgeting, Analysis, and Management

This chapter examines systems for planning and budgeting for capital projects, analysis for capital project selection, and managing the government's portfolio of assets. Every year, governments spend resources on the construction of facilities or the purchase of equipment and other assets that will continue in use for many years beyond the year of purchase. The construction of a new water treatment plant will serve a community for decades, although the actual construction itself may take less than two years. By constructing the water treatment plant, the community has acquired a capital facility. It has purchased a long-term asset. This chapter focuses on the decision to build that facility or purchase an asset and related systems for managing these long-lived facilities or equipment once they are in place.

In this chapter, we examine both the rationale for public sector capital budgeting and the general form of capital plans and budgets. We see that it differs for the U.S. federal government, and most national governments, when compared with state and local governments. Furthermore, because the cost of capital projects is large, especially relative to a state or local government's operating budget, capital projects are subject to more detailed analysis, often with formal criteria for determining whether the benefits of the project are worth the cost of the project. The chapter concludes with a section on asset management. This final section focuses on how governments ensure that the capital assets they own (that they have built or purchased) are managed effectively and are maintained so that they achieve the long life cycle for which they were designed.

CAPITAL PLANNING AND BUDGETING

In this section, we define capital and capital investments, discuss the reasons for considering capital spending separately from operating budgets, describe the general form for a capital investment planning and budgeting process, and discuss the issues involved in separating capital from operating budgets. We focus mainly on state and local governments. Although there is much discussion in annual federal budgets of investments and capital expenditures, the federal government has considered several times adopting a formal capital budget. Each time, however, the arguments against a federal capital budget have outweighed the arguments for it.

Capital Investments Versus Current Expenditures

Capital Investments

The purchase or construction of a long-lasting physical asset or facility is a capital investment. Businesses invest to have new capacity, to replace assets that have reached or exceeded their usefulness, and to replace existing capacity with more efficient methods of production. These investments are intended to increase the efficiency of the businesses' output and possibly increase total output in the future. Many public sector physical facilities also represent investment in the ability to provide more or higher-quality services in the future.

Public sector assets differ in important respects from private sector assets. In conventional private sector accounting, "assets are defined as economic resources" and they are the accounting counterpart to liabilities that are "amounts owed to outside entities and employees."[1] Current assets may consist of cash, investments, and a variety of items that can be readily converted into cash, such as inventory. Capital assets in the private sector have the capacity to generate future revenues for the enterprise. In the public sector, assets typically do not have as a primary purpose the generation of future revenues.

Although a government facility that provides a service to citizens, such as a wastewater treatment plant, may not have as an objective generating future revenues, the facility once built does provide a continuing service through many future years. In that sense, an expenditure on a facility that will provide benefits for many years after its construction is an investment, and the investment creates a long-lasting asset. According to Statement No. 34 of the Governmental Accounting Standards Board (GASB; see the chapter on financial management), "infrastructure assets are long-lived capital assets that normally are stationary in nature and normally can be preserved for a significantly greater number of years than most capital assets."[2] This long-lived investment aspect helps explain why many governments distinguish capital expenditures for infrastructure from current expenditures and have capital budgeting processes, in addition to budgeting processes for current (operating) expenditures.

For governments, it is useful to distinguish among three types of investments. First, a government may purchase physical assets for its own use over many years in the future—assets such as office buildings, heavy equipment, and machinery. Second, governments may make investments in physical facilities that enhance private economic development and deliver needed public services—for example, roads and water systems. Third, governments may invest in intangibles, such as education and research. The federal government in the chapter on *federal investment* in the *Special Analyses* volume of the budget considers expenditures on physical assets, research and development, and education as investment, but excludes what may be called *social investments*, such as childhood immunization programs, which also have long-term benefits.[3] Capital budgeting processes deal only with the purchase of physical assets. Capital budgets assist in deciding how much of each type of investment is necessary, and assist in evaluating available revenues (including loans) to finance those investments.

With or without a formal capital budget, focusing some attention on the investment component of a government budget is politically useful because it draws attention to the fact that many public spending programs build for the future. Taxpayers should be informed about government spending that occurs in one year, but then has benefits over many future years. There is some evidence indicating that voters are much more sensitive to infrastructure decisions reflected in capital budgets than to operating budget decisions. The type of capital project—for maintenance and rehabilitation versus new capacity— makes a difference in voter approval in economically distressed periods. Voters tend to prefer maintenance or rehabilitation capital investments in tight budget circumstances.[4] Brick-and-mortar decisions can be decisive in whether incumbents are reelected.[5] Attention to capital assets also reminds citizens that public assets, like highways, may deteriorate to the point of uselessness if not regularly rehabilitated. Governments with formal capital budgets often draw attention in the operating budget to expenditures that are necessary to preserve the value of a previously constructed or acquired asset.

State and local governments also stress the importance of public capital investment in stimulating economic growth. Not only are obvious facilities such as convention centers or improved water services for water-intensive industries the focal point of economic development–oriented investments, but state and local governments increasingly invest in quality-of-life facilities, such as parks and other recreational facilities, and even open space to attract companies to the area.[6] A study of Pennsylvania state parks showed for every $1 spent there was a benefit of $7.62 in economic value added, considering tourism, concession sales, user charges, and other benefits.[7] States and local governments compete with each other in offering facilities, tax concessions, and other inducements to attract economic growth (see the chapter on government and the economy), requiring in many cases significant capital investments.

Sometimes it is difficult to draw the line between investment and consumption expenditures. The federal budget's definition of investment is very broad, including such human capital investments as education, research, and development expenditures, but still it does not include many other elements that it logically could. The President's 2012 budget included a discussion of social capital investments describing long-term benefits, but excluding them from the compilation of federal investments.[8] For example, mental health programs, programs for juveniles, and family counseling programs may be considered investments that help prevent future social and economic problems. A major rationale for the Child Health Insurance Program, which provides federal assistance to states for uninsured children, is that the investment in health helps prevent some future federal expenditures for Medicaid.

Although it is useful to think of government expenditures in terms of investment or consumption, for budgeting purposes the more meaningful distinction is that between capital and current or operating expenditures. Investments in social capital such as health and education do not fall into the capital category in any budgeting system. Because capital expenditures differ from current expenditures, many state and local governments therefore distinguish between capital and current budgets.

Physical Nature and Time Duration

Businesses think of capital expenditures as the purchase of physical assets or the construction of facilities that will be used over a period of several years. Public sector capital expenditures likewise involve the purchase of physical assets whose use extends over a number of years, often 30 to 50 years with proper maintenance, as in the case of sewage treatment plants.

Examples of capital expenditures are easy to find. A school building is physically present and will last for many years. In contrast, paper, pens, pencils, and staples, although physical, are used up and have to be purchased anew each year. The purchase of a laboratory is easy to classify as a capital expenditure, and the purchase of the supplies is clearly a current expenditure. Similarly, water mains extending from a treatment plant to neighborhood lines have a physical presence and will serve for many years. Their construction is a capital expenditure. In contrast, chemicals used in the water treatment process will be used up and need to be purchased again and again. Purchase of these chemicals is an operating or current expenditure.

Conventionally, debt service payments for both principal and interest for long-term bonds or loans also are included in the capital budget, as opposed to the operating budget, when the government has a capital budget separate from the operating budget. Debt service accounts may be used to segregate these payments (see the chapter on financial management), but they are regarded as capital budget items.

Classification Problems

These examples illustrate that capital expenditures normally are for purchases of physical assets that have a long life. Other examples, however, show that the distinction between capital and current expenditure is sometimes ambiguous. A big-city police department may purchase more than 50 vehicles per year, and many of those vehicles may replace vehicles purchased the previous year. That city may classify the purchase of the police cars as a current expenditure. A small town may purchase two police cars of the same type as the big city's but expect those two cars to last for three to five years. The small town probably would consider purchase of the police cars to be a capital expenditure.

Even within the same city, some classification problems occur. Books and periodicals bought for a library are expected to be used for many years, and their purchase can be treated as a capital investment. In contrast, purchase of a periodical by a department of public works, if the periodical has a short useful life, would be an operating expense.

Every government and every business establishes some kind of arbitrary cutoff point that distinguishes current from capital expenditures. In most cases, the cutoff is a combination of the size of the expenditure and the useful life of the asset. Purchase of anything expected to be consumed (or destroyed) during one year normally will be a current expenditure, no matter how large it is. In addition, small expenditures, even for goods that will last several years, also are classified as current. But the size of the government's budget usually determines how small is small. A small town may classify expenditures of less than $1,000 as current regardless of the useful life. A larger city may use $25,000 as a cutoff, and below that anything is a current expenditure regardless of its useful life. Although some purchases may be classified arbitrarily one way or the other, the issue of what constitutes a capital purchase and what constitutes a current one usually is not controversial.

Capital Decisions Versus Current Decisions

Separate Capital Budgets

The size of the expenditure and the longevity of the asset or facility purchased distinguish a capital expenditure from a current one. A third distinction of importance to decision making, the method of financing the expenditure, leads most state governments and a majority of local governments to pay at least some separate attention to capital expenditures in the annual budget decision-making process. The vast majority of states distinguish capital from current expenses in the form of either capital improvement plans or budgets or both, and most larger counties and cities as well as some smaller ones make similar distinctions.

Table 13–1 shows state and local capital expenditures for 2009 as a proportion of total expenditures. Considering only direct capital outlays, about 12% of state and local expenditures are for capital purposes. That percentage has remained about the same (10% to 13%) for more than a decade and a half. The actual expenditures do not tell the whole story, however, because most of the capital outlays at the state and local levels are financed by borrowing and hence have interest costs. With interest included, the figure is closer to 16%. Local government capital outlays are a higher proportion of total outlays than state government outlays—15% and 9%, respectively. However, these gross percentages obscure the real nature of the decisions to undertake capital projects. Capital expenditures cluster in only a few government functions. For local governments, school construction; utilities such as electricity, roads, sewerage, and water; and housing construction account for most direct capital outlays.

State government capital outlays also cluster in only a few functional categories, and decisions made in one year affect future-year budgets. More than $153 billion, or 43% of state and local public works expenditures, went to highway construction in 2008. Of that, 58% was for capital expenditures. An amount almost equal to new capital investments (43%) in highways was spent on operations and maintenance of highways built in prior years.[9]

These examples demonstrate that decisions about capital spending at the state and local levels are consequential in the year they are made and can have major consequences for future budgets. As discussed in previous chapters, it is difficult to incorporate a long-run

Table 13–1 Direct Capital Outlays as a Proportion of Total State and Local Outlays, 2009 (Billions of Dollars)

Government	Total Direct Outlays[a]	Capital Outlays	Capital as Percentage of Total	Interest on Debt[b]	Combined Capital Outlays	Combined Capital as Percentage of Total
State and Local	2,961.8	357.3	12%	117.2	474.4	16%
State	1,335.8	116.6	9%	47.2	163.8	12%
Local	1,626.0	240.7	15%	69.9	310.6	19%

(a) Outlays here exclude duplicative intergovernmental transfers so that the figures shown are for the level of government making the expenditure even if the source of finance is a transfer from another level of government.
(b) Interest on general debt plus interest on utility borrowing is attributed in this table to borrowing for capital investment.

Source: State & local government finance data query system, the Urban Institute—Brookings Institution Tax Policy Center. Retrieved December 8, 2011, from http://www.taxpolicycenter.org/slf-dqs/pages.cfm.

perspective into budget decisions, especially when the decisions tend to focus in large part on personnel expenditures and only on the current-year implications of starting new programs. The fact that current-year capital budget decisions have significant implications for future operations and maintenance suggests that the effects of capital decisions on future operating budgets must be taken into account in any budgeting process. For state and local governments, the logic of having some kind of process for examining capital spending decisions in more detail seems compelling. That does not necessarily entail separate capital budgets, however. In the next section, we illustrate a general approach to capital investment planning and budgeting that satisfies both the requirement to examine capital decisions in more detail and the requirement to consider implications for future-year operating budgets.

Capital Investment Planning

Few governmental jurisdictions simply ignore the distinction between capital costs and current. The form in which capital and current costs are planned and budgeted varies greatly across jurisdictions. For most governments, some form of long-term capital investment plan is the starting point. Even for those without formal capital budgets, capital investment planning is still the norm. Illustrating with examples from different types of institutions, the following discussion focuses on a general framework for capital investment planning that highlights the data that inform capital decisions.

Multiyear Capital Investment Plans

Most governments that distinguish between capital and current budget decisions have an established process for developing a multiyear capital investment plan (CIP) and incorporating elements of that plan into a capital budget. Likewise, governments that do not have a capital budget still have a multiyear investment plan. Five years is a common period for projecting capital expenditures, although a longer period is often included in the statements of long-range programs. For example, the Orange County (North Carolina) Water and Sewer Authority distinguishes between its 20-year capital improvements plan and its five-year capital improvements budget.[10] The long-range plan focuses on the expected needs for water supply and sewage treatment and improvements needed to develop new facilities and to replace or rehabilitate existing facilities for the next two decades, whereas the capital improvements budget includes detailed cost estimates for only the next five years.

Other jurisdictions use only a five-year time frame. California and Michigan, for example, have five-year capital investment planning cycles. Michigan's CIP is integrated into an overall asset management system. In order for a project to be included in Michigan's capital budget, it must already have gone through the investment planning process and have been included in the CIP.[11] However, not everything included in a CIP will necessarily make its way into the capital budget, as the financial resources simply may not be available for every investment that the planning process has identified. Or something in the capital investment plan may be deferred beyond the immediate five-year plan when financing, hopefully, becomes available. **Exhibit 13–1** illustrates the way a capital improvement program typically contains items for which the financing is already secured as well as items for which the financing sources are not yet known and, in some cases, may never become available.

Exhibit 13–1 City of Durham, North Carolina, Capital Improvement Program, 2011–2016

The City of Durham, North Carolina, produces a multiyear capital improvement plan (CIP) that reports on the most recent prior year's capital investments, identifies financing that already has been approved—which could be voter approved bond issues, federal grants, or other sources—and illustrates the difference between a plan and a budget. The following two tables present the plan for FY 2010–2011 through FY 2015–2016 as well as projects that will still be incomplete in FY 2015–2016, and the revenue sources for those investments. To be included in the Durham CIP, the asset must have a useful life of 10 years or more, and must have an investment value of more than $100,000.

CITY OF DURHAM

CAPITAL IMPROVEMENT PROGRAM

FY 2011–2016 CAPITAL IMPROVEMENT PROGRAM SUMMARY

SUMMARY BY PROJECT CATEGORY

Category	Prior Year	FY 2010–11	FY 2011–12	FY 2012–13	FY 2013–14	FY 2014–15	FY 2015–16	Future Years	Total Request
Water	152,076,818	24,734,000	42,009,000	11,703,000	27,700,000	10,800,000	63,870,000	41,600,000	374,492,818
Wastewater	69,838,454	21,001,000	25,760,000	19,083,000	25,965,000	21,905,000	35,295,000	9,250,000	228,097,454
Transportation	51,125,823	2,174,119	3,035,000	3,925,000	1,300,000	2,059,180	3,400,000	5,550,000	72,569,122
Technology	5,790,000	0	0	0	0	0	0	0	5,790,000
Stormwater	9,229,758	1,254,535	1,700,000	1,700,000	1,700,000	1,700,000	1,700,000	3,300,000	22,284,293
Public Protection	29,361,549	0	53,523	455,111	26,500,000	1,000,000	4,520,807	35,752,111	97,643,101
Housing & Neighborhood Revitalization	20,356,137	650,000	0	0	0	0	0	0	21,006,137
General Services	20,961,581	0	800,000	2,975,000	1,220,000	0	0	0	25,956,581
Downtown Revitalization	42,952,337	0	0	0	0	0	0	0	42,952,337
Culture & Recreation	55,475,738	0	169,303	771,867	456,123	386,825	1,095,178	0	58,355,034
	$457,168,195	$49,813,654	$73,526,826	$40,612,978	$84,841,123	$37,851,005	$109,880,985	$95,452,111	$949,146,877

(continued)

Exhibit 13–1 City of Durham, North Carolina, Capital Improvement Program, 2011–2016

SUMMARY BY REVENUE SOURCE

Source	Prior Year	FY 2010–11	FY 2011–12	FY 2012–13	FY 2013–14	FY 2014–15	FY 2015–16	Future Years	Total Funds
GOB Authorized	141,697,989	0	0	0	0	0	0	0	141,697,989
GOB Unauthorized	0	0	0	0	0	0	0	0	0
Impact Fees	14,033,366	2,050,000	2,635,000	2,925,000	0	1,559,180	2,100,000	5,050,000	30,352,546
Installment Sales	42,009,331	0	0	0	0	0	0	0	42,009,331
Intergovernmental	29,121,218	0	0	0	22,000,000	0	0	0	51,121,218
Other	36,711,924	774,119	0	0	0	0	0	0	37,486,043
Pay-As-You-Go	83,739,215	1,254,535	1,700,000	1,700,000	1,700,000	1,700,000	1,700,000	3,300,000	96,793,750
Rev Authorized	7,099,501	0	0	0	0	0	0	0	7,099,501
Rev Unauthorized	102,755,651	45,735,000	65,269,000	28,786,000	51,665,000	30,705,000	97,165,000	48,850,000	470,930,651
Unidentified	0	0	3,922,826	7,201,978	9,476,123	3,886,825	8,915,985	38,252,111	71,655,848
	$457,168,195	$49,813,654	$73,526,826	$40,612,978	$84,841,123	$37,851,005	$109,880,985	$95,452,111	$949,146,877

Source: Reproduced from *City of Durham Capital Improvement Program Process (2011).* Retrieved November 1, 2011, from http://www.durhamnc.gov/departments/bms/pdf/11-16cip_intro.pdf.

Exhibit 13–2 Capital Facilities Planning and Budgeting

1. Identify present service characteristics (inventory facilities and service levels)
   a. Coverage (quantity)
   b. Quality
   c. Cost per unit of service (efficiency)
2. Identify environmental trends
   a. Population growth projections
   b. Changing regulatory environment
   c. Employment and economic development trends
3. Develop service objectives
   a. Extension of service to new population or area (coverage)
   b. Improvement in quality of service
   c. Opportunities to stimulate economic growth
4. Develop preliminary list of capital projects and cost estimates
   a. Rehabilitation of existing facilities
   b. Replacement of existing facilities
   c. Addition of new facilities
5. Identify financial resources
   a. External assistance
   b. Projected growth in present revenue base
   c. Potential for direct cost recovery for individual projects
   d. Use of credit
6. Select subset of projects for inclusion in five-year capital investment plan (CIP)
7. Identify future recurrent cost impact of CIP on operating budget
8. Include first year of CIP in annual budget estimate

Practices vary considerably from city to city and state to state, but it is possible to outline a general format for a capital investment planning process. One such model for capital investment planning and budgeting, linked to an inventory of existing facilities, consists of eight steps (see **Exhibit 13–2**).

Step 1: Identifying Current Service Characteristics

The first step is to make an inventory of existing physical or infrastructure facilities and to assess the services provided. For a state or local government that has not previously conducted an inventory, this first step is complex and expensive, although maintaining the inventory once established need not be burdensome. Such an inventory involves listing all physical facilities and elements of the physical infrastructure and such related information as date of construction, date of last major rehabilitation, type of construction material (such as type of road surface), and, where relevant, characteristics such as size and capacity. For a building, information may be collected on electrical wiring, fiber optics for computer hookups, plumbing, and elevators. All capital asset inventory systems offered by a variety of information technology solutions providers to the public sector contain an asset inventory module.

Quantity of service includes such characteristics as the number of people served, the proportion of total population served, the geographic area covered (area, density, and spatial distribution), and various socioeconomic groupings related to coverage, such as number of clients served by a facility. Different quantity measures are appropriate for different services.

Quality of service in part is a function of the level or the type of service provided. For example, water treatment systems that remove only bacteriological contaminants are qualitatively less effective than those that remove toxins and heavy metals as well as bacteria. Quality may also be indicated by such things as the age of the facility and its condition. The latter may be measured by the frequency-of-repair record. Qualitative measures of service, including records of citizens' complaints and structured citizen satisfaction surveys, are as appropriate as other measures.

Step 2: Identifying Environmental Trends

The next step looks toward the future. Most city and state governments develop long-range planning forecasts to estimate future service requirements. These forecasts, which project population growth, commercial and industrial growth, demographic and economic changes, and so forth, are linked to the capital facilities planning process in order to develop plans for required service expansion or contraction. In addition, more detailed analyses of trends in business locations may predict possible shortages or other problems in critical areas, such as the water supply. The capital facilities planning process can provide a means for the jurisdiction to plan expansion of services in an orderly way and can help convince potential investors that the jurisdiction is anticipating future business and residential requirements.

School buildings serve as a good example. When the school-age population of a community is rising, the school district must plan for having the appropriate number of buildings of the appropriate sizes and in the appropriate locations. When the population is declining, the district must plan for decommissioning school buildings. When buildings are in surplus, should they be sold off to bring in revenue for the district, or should they be converted to other purposes? Keeping a building in inventory, even though it is not used as a school, may be advantageous if the district thinks population will increase in coming years and necessitate reopening the building.

Step 3: Developing Service Objectives

The third step is developing service objectives. The process of defining the need for capital investments can take numerous forms. Not only is the technical judgment of government staff important, but so are citizens' preferences and willingness to pay. Typical ways to include citizen input include representation on long-range planning groups, open forums to discuss the need for community facilities, and referendums to approve a specific bond issue to finance a capital investment (see the chapter on capital finance and debt management). Even in jurisdictions with established channels for citizen input, a special group often convenes every two to three years just to review the current CIP and establish new priorities. Thus, a key step is to determine the service objectives that capital investments will need to satisfy.

Step 4: Preliminary Listing of Capital Projects and Cost Estimates

Based on the service objectives established in the previous step, a preliminary list of capital projects can be developed, along with a timetable for completing the projects. Typically, the preliminary list includes the rehabilitation of existing facilities to improve the quality and/or efficiency of service; the replacement of existing facilities, also for the purpose of improving quality and efficiency; and the addition of new facilities or expansion of existing facilities to meet expansion objectives. The preliminary list typically will not be screened for financial feasibility at this stage.

Step 5: Identifying Financial Resources

With a preliminary list of projects and cost estimates in hand, identifying the financial resources potentially available to carry out the preliminary list of capital projects is a critical next step. This step involves analyzing the jurisdiction's overall financial condition and some of the individual capital projects for possible sources of financing specific to them. Since the 1980s, an important aspect of overall financial management has been the evaluation of the financial condition of local governments.[12] In the wake of public pressure to hold steady or to cut back state and local taxes, major new revenue initiatives in the form of tax increases often are not possible, even when the need to build up infrastructure and rehabilitate existing facilities is obvious. When economic conditions improve, tax bases expand, yielding more revenue. However, sustained economic problems such as those experienced after 2007 make general tax base financing for infrastructure tenuous to plan. More commonly, state and local governments (and particularly the latter) rely increasingly on revenue sources specific to individual capital projects. User fees and property assessments have traditionally been used to finance the major portion of water and other utility capital investments as well as operating expenses. More recently, cities have exacted special impact fees and other charges from residential and commercial developers to pay for roads, water, and sewer lines and drainage intended to serve new developments (see the chapter on transaction-based revenues).

Other sources of revenues tied to particular projects include grants from other levels of government and borrowing (typically involving the issuance of bonds). Although federal funding cutbacks were significant starting in the early 1980s, state aid to local governments has in some cases made up for some of the federal cutbacks, and federal funds are still available on a more limited programmatic basis (see the chapter on intergovernmental relations).

Step 6: Selecting Projects for Inclusion in Five-Year Capital Investment Plan

Step 6 involves matching available financial resources with the set of projects included in the preliminary investment plan. Steps 3 through 6 may be iterated to eventually narrow down the list of projects and select a feasible set. Reevaluation of desired service objectives sometimes is necessary during this iterative process, because financial realities can make it clear that some objectives are impossible without major new financial initiatives. For most state and local governments, the application of complex analytical tools such as cost-benefit analysis or rate-of-return analysis plays only a small role in the selection of projects. Furthermore, there is substantial disagreement over the validity of estimates of economic benefits from investments in infrastructure.[13] Instead, the ranking of priorities is often based on the principle that replacing deteriorated facilities should be the first concern, meeting population growth requirements should be the second, and improving quality of services should be last.

Contemporary management tools such as the *balanced scorecard* have been adapted to help in the project selection process. This approach emphasizes balancing selection criteria among four factors—financial information, customer requirements, internal management processes, and innovation and learning—with the notion being that a structured process to balance several criteria in different categories can lead to better choices and more successful implementation than over-reliance on any one set of factors.

Step 7: Identifying Implications for Future Recurrent Costs

Decision makers frequently neglect the recurrent cost implications of capital investments.[14] It is sometimes difficult to anticipate the costs of keeping a facility operating, and the usually valuable public relations aspects of a new project tend to overshadow the longer-run impact on the general fund's budget. The problem is exaggerated by the fact that the operating and maintenance costs of any new project or facility are lower in the early years of operation, and the heavier costs fall outside the range of normal five-year capital planning cycles. Without an analysis that takes this fact into account, a state or local jurisdiction may find itself 10 or 20 years down the road facing the dilemma of either forgoing new capital investments because of the need to budget greater funds for maintenance or neglecting maintenance in favor of more politically popular capital projects.

The analysis of future operation and maintenance costs is not all negative. If the analysis of the current capital facilities base in step 1 has been carried out well, the jurisdiction will have an idea of the current operation and maintenance costs of existing facilities. Replacing some facilities that require expensive maintenance expenditures may produce significant reductions in operation and maintenance costs in the operating budget.

Step 8: Including the First Year of the Capital Investment Plan as the Capital Budget

Once a feasible set of investments has been selected and the short- and long-term costs have been determined, the final step is to incorporate the first year of the CIP into the budget. To this point, the process, which has been one of planning and programming, may have involved input from the legislative body, but no legal appropriation of funds will have taken place. Some jurisdictions submit the CIP to the legislative body (e.g., state legislature, city council) for formal approval, but the CIP rarely includes actual appropriation of funds. Some states appropriate the full costs of capital projects, at least for smaller projects, whereas other states appropriate only the annual costs of each project. In the latter case, only a single year's cost actually shows up in the appropriation act.

The eight steps outlined in this section represent a generic process description. Governments may use different names for the various steps, and likely will combine one or more steps. Most governments will, to varying degrees of intensity, carry out some aspects of each of these steps. Some may have very involved processes for garnering input from citizens. Others may only hold a public hearing at the end of a process carried out by city staff or merely publish the capital investment plan. Office of Management and Budget

(OMB) Circular A-11 instructions to federal agencies on the preparation of capital requests contain requirements quite similar to these steps, starting with analysis of existing assets that are being used, or potentially could be used, to fulfill the function for which additional or new capital spending is being requested and concluding with required analysis of future operating costs.[15] The main difference between the federal budget preparation of capital investment requests and governments with capital budgets is that there is no overall federal capital investment plan and capital budget. Each federal agency prepares requests for capital as well as current expenditures, and a summary compilation and analysis is completed in the Office of Management and Budget, for information purposes only.

Capital Budgeting

Even though most governments of any size have some formal capital investment planning process, and the results of that process feed into budget decisions, not all governments have a formal capital budget and capital budgeting process. This section discusses capital budgeting as a decision process or budget system.

Much of the argument over the value of capital budgeting at any level of government hinges on whether there should be a separate capital budget. There is little argument over the need to examine fully the long-term implications of capital spending and not focus just on a single budget year. It is possible to have a comprehensive capital planning process that concludes with a capital investment and financing plan or capital investment statement without a separate capital budgeting process, such as that contained in the federal *Analytical Perspectives* budget document. The amount a city council, state legislature, or U.S. Congress is then asked to appropriate may be for only one year, but the budget request is made in the context of future-year requirements.

Pros and Cons of Separate Capital Budgeting

Capital budgets and statements indicate the extent to which investments are being made with current expenditures. From a political perspective, this gives capital budgets a certain public relations value because government officials can show citizens that government funds are being used for the acquisition of useful assets and not solely for the payment of bureaucrats' salaries.

On the negative side, capital budgeting can encourage political logrolling, in which various political interests agree to help each other. A capital budget can be a political grab bag, a fund where every interest can find a project. A state capital budget may provide highway projects in every county, even though real need is concentrated in a small number of counties. In providing everyone with something, some important needs will not be met, while less pressing needs will be satisfied. Furthermore, if capital costs are presented in a completely separate budget, particularly when financed by borrowing, it may appear as if capital decisions are "costless" in the current year.

On balance, however, the arguments in favor of paying special attention to capital spending, at least at the state and local levels, seem overwhelming. Although capital budget decisions are no less political than other budget decisions, the logic of focusing attention on long-run financial and economic consequences of spending or failing to spend for capital facilities is compelling. More than current operating budget decisions, decisions to invest in infrastructure help shape the future direction, location, and extent of private economic investments in the community. Local governments' capital investments may in some cases play a leading role in encouraging future local economic development, as discussed in the chapter on government and the economy. The combination of strategic planning and capital budgeting at the state and municipal levels has been found in some studies to be positively related to overall financial performance of the municipality.[16] State and local governments compete for location of major facilities, and they sometimes offer large incentive packages comprising infrastructure projects and financial assistance to induce private companies or federal agencies to locate facilities in their jurisdictions.

Once built, major facilities will largely be limited to the uses for which they were designed. Inadequate planning of facilities can result in inadequate services, major financial burdens, or the need for expensive alterations. Excess capacity built into a community sewer system cannot be converted into other uses. Too little acquisition of land for parks in a rapidly growing suburban area may later result in a shortage of recreational opportunities or may force the local government to pay far more for space than it might have earlier.

These arguments do not mandate that capital budgets be separate from operating budgets. Although capital spending requires attention to some issues that are not germane to operating budgets, capital and operating expenditures are intertwined. As noted earlier, the mistake governments often make even with separate capital budgets or a distinctive capital planning/budgeting process is not taking into account the much longer-term operation and maintenance costs. And as governments get strapped for funds, as happened in the first decade of the 2000s after several years of surpluses at all levels of government, maintenance expenditures begin to be neglected. Capital budgeting, even if formalized and well done, must clearly link back to the operations and maintenance implications in the future for current capital spending.[17]

The main reason state and local governments formally segregate capital and current into two distinct, formal budgets is related to the primary means of financing large-scale infrastructure. State and local governments rarely have sufficient revenue to finance large capital items from regular revenues, though a few do operate on a *pay-as-you-go* basis. But to appropriate the entire portion of capital facilities to be built in a given year from current revenue would typically leave insufficient funds for all the recurring expenses of state and local governments. Typically, state and local governments borrow to finance capital infrastructure, and this debt does not "count" in determining budget balance. Furthermore, operating on a *pay-as-you-use* basis, which governments do when they finance capital projects through debt, permits the annual cost of capital to be borne by the specific residents who benefit in the future from facilities as they are used to provide services each year.

Federal Capital Budgeting

For the federal government, the logic of capital budgeting is less compelling. First, about half of the "capital" side of the federal budget goes toward defense acquisitions—51% in 2010 and an estimated similar 50% in the 2012 budget proposal. The other half is divided between direct federal physical capital expenditures and grants to state and local governments for capital spending. Almost 17% for both 2010 and 2012 is for non-defense direct federal capital investments. Approximately one-third of the federal physical capital outlays are grants to state and local governments. **Table 13-2** shows the distribution of federal physical capital outlays in 2010. These percentages were stable in the preceding decade.

If one examines only those physical capital outlays undertaken directly by the federal government, excluding grants to state and local governments, defense physical acquisitions are 75% of the total.[18] These are not investments in the same sense as state and local expenditures for water systems or highways. This statement does not mean that the purchase of nuclear-powered aircraft carriers, for example, has no implications for future operations and maintenance. Rather, the need to replace a weapons system often is generated not by its wearing out, but by its inability to cope with new offensive or defensive systems of a potential enemy or its being destroyed or damaged beyond recovery in a combat or training situation.

Furthermore, the federal government may undertake many non-defense capital expenditures more for macroeconomic policy reasons than for investment purposes. Because of the federal government's role in stimulating the economy, capital spending sometimes has the primary objective of assisting a state or local economy rather than providing a needed facility. This was clearly demonstrated in the fiscal stimulus programs to address the recession that started in 2007 (see the chapter on government and the economy). So-called *shovel-ready* projects funded by federal grants to state and local governments were a major feature of the stimulus program. Federal grants for non-defense physical capital was proposed to be almost $101 billion for 2012, an almost 45% increase over federal grants to state and local governments in the pre-recession 2007 budget.[19] Unfortunately, this use of capital spending often leads to earmarking or pork-barrel decisions that place expensive projects in every congressional district.

There have been periodic calls for federal capital budgeting. At the time the unified budget was adopted at the recommendation of the 1967 President's Commission on Budget Concepts, a capital budget for the federal government was rejected.[20] There was a

Table 13-2 Federal Physical Capital Outlays, 2010 and 2012 (est.) (in Millions of Current Dollars)

| | Total Federal Physical Capital Outlays | Direct Federal | | Federal Grants to States/Local | Federal Exclusive of Intergovernmental |
		National Defense	Non-Defense		
FY 2010 actual	288.6	147.2	48.1	93.3	195.3
FY 2012 est.	302.4	151.8	49.7	100.9	201.5
FY 2010 actual	Percent of Total	51.0%	16.7%	32.3%	67.7%
FY 2012 est.	Percent of Total	50.2%	16.4%	33.4%	66.7%

Source: Compiled from U.S. Office of Management and Budget (2011). *Budget of the United States government for 2012: analytical perspectives* (p. 354). Washington, DC: U.S. Government Printing Office.

resurgence of calls for capital budgeting at the federal level in the 1980s and again in the 1990s, and the recession at the end of the first decade of the 2000s was a principal stimulus to renewed recommendations for a federal capital budget.

The federal budget for fiscal year 1996 for the first time included a capital budget presentation in the *Analytical Perspectives* chapter on investment spending. The Government Accountability Office and others argued that the federal government must adopt more contemporary financial management practices to improve the efficiency of government operations. According to these critics, federal management practices are inadequate for the task of achieving efficiency or effectiveness in government operations. This does not mean that GAO was or is in favor of a separate federal capital budget, but rather that much more systematic attention should be given to physical capital investments, to the value of those assets, and to their management.[21]

The second cause for renewed interest in federal capital budgeting is the concern that the nation as a whole—at the federal, state, and local levels—is not investing sufficiently in basic infrastructure, to the long-run detriment of the economy. Legislation in 1984 established the National Council on Public Works Improvement and gave it the mandate to assess the state of the nation's capital infrastructure and make recommendations for improvement. In 1988, the Council published the influential *Fragile Foundations: A Report on America's Public Works.*[22] In the same year, the National Academy of Sciences published the results of a major study of American cities' infrastructure facilities.[23] Both studies expressed grave concerns about the inadequate level of infrastructure investment at all levels of government in the United States.

Many of those concerned that the level of investment in infrastructure is too low have argued that the federal budget is biased against such capital investments because it must show the full cost of the capital outlays in the construction years instead of showing only the annual depreciation of the investments over their long lives.[24] A capital budgeting statement might show only one year's depreciation value in the current year budget, spreading the budget implications of such an investment over the expected years of benefits. This approach would more clearly isolate how much of the federal deficit is due to investments that will pay for themselves through future economic growth and might reduce some concern for the size of the deficit.

In 1997, President William Clinton appointed the President's Commission to Study Capital Budgeting. That commission examined primarily federal capital spending, but also considered the larger question of the nation's total investment in productive capital. The commission concluded that the federal budget process does not give sufficient attention to the long-term implications of capital spending, given that capital investments are expensed in the federal budget in the years in which the costs are incurred. However, the commission also did not recommend the creation of a separate federal capital budget, or a capital budgeting process. The recommendation focused on providing information in the annual federal budget to focus congressional decisions and public awareness on the physical infrastructure stock, the investments proposed in a given year for capital investments, especially non-defense, and the longer-term maintenance requirements implied in proposed investments, as well as the maintenance costs in the budget for previous investments.[25]

The most recent major examination of a federal capital budget, in 2008–2009, was undertaken by the Brookings Institution during the major recession and implementation of federal stimulus programs. The study evaluated both the question of the adequacy of the nation's spending on capital investments and the question of whether a federal capital budget would improve upon the way federal investments are evaluated and funded. Specifically included in the study was the possibility of creating a National Infrastructure Bank, discussed in the chapter on capital finance and debt. The study's findings were consistent with the general view of many other analyses that infrastructure investment combined across federal, state, and local governments is not keeping up with the combined effects of population and economic growth and the deterioration of aging infrastructure. However, the report concluded that a federal capital budget would add little improvement to the problems.[26]

For the most part, recent administrations have accepted the arguments and recommendations that federal budgeting must include more focus on capital spending. One section of the federal budget for fiscal year 2003 even used the (new) title Federal Investment Spending and Capital Budgeting, under which an illustrative capital budget was presented, as discussed in **Exhibit 13–3**. This one attempt to show what a federal capital and operating budget might look like, focusing entirely on capital investments that are physical in nature, has not been repeated in subsequent budgets of the George W. Bush and Barack Obama administrations.

That 2003 budget also outlined legislation that would have created capital acquisition funds and changed the way agencies that acquire physical assets would show those acquisitions in the agency budget (see below). Instead of the agency showing the full expenditure for the acquisition in the year acquired, the cost would be shown as the first year's depreciation, using straight-line depreciation. For example, if a physical asset had

Exhibit 13–3 Illustrative Federal Capital Budget

Capital, Operating, and Unified Budget Concepts, United States Government, Fiscal Year 2003 (in Billions of Dollars)

Operating Budget
Receipts	2,048	
Expenses		
Depreciation	82	
Other	2,028	
Subtotal, expenses	2,111	
Surplus or deficit (–)		–63

Capital Budget
Income: Depreciation	82	
Capital Expenditures	100	
Surplus or deficit (–)		–18

Unified Budget
Receipts	2,048	
Outlays	2,128	
Surplus or deficit (–)		–80

Source: Extracted from U.S. Office of Management and Budget (2002). *Budget of the United States government: fiscal year 2003, analytical perspectives* (p. 148). Washington, DC: U.S. Government Printing Office.

an expected life of 20 years, then 5% of the cost of that asset would show in the agency's budget, as if the agency were borrowing the full amount from the Treasury and repaying it at 5% per year for 20 years. The Treasury, however, would show the full outlay for the building, so the unified budget outlay total would not be affected by this presentation, although some agency budgets would have looked smaller.[27] Although the current version of Circular A-11, as noted above, does stress identifying the long-term budget requirements for capital acquisitions, there has been no renewal of the 2003 proposal.

The various discussions of improved presentations of capital investments and the serious concerns about underinvestment in infrastructure have not led to the adoption of capital budgeting at the federal level. Outlays for acquisition of assets or construction of facilities are still recorded fully in the year acquired or constructed. In contrast, in state and local capital budgets, full investment cost is shown, albeit in connection with the method of financing. So when a state government borrows (typically issues bonds) to finance highways, the bond issuance and construction costs are fully disclosed, but the only impact of the project in the operating or general budget is the cost of debt service—principal and interest payments (see the chapter on capital finance).

Federal capital budget presentations, by contrast, are not linked to any specific method of financing, and they do record in the budget the full construction or acquisition cost incurred in that year. That is unlikely to change in the near future. The special emphasis in the 2003 budget on capital investments was a one-time emphasis, and the illustrative capital budget presentation has not been repeated.

In the *Analytical Perspectives* volume of the annual federal budget, a chapter on federal investments continues to discuss the nature of federal expenditures on physical capital, and other types of investments such as research and development funding and education. But there has been no resurgence of interest in a federal capital budget, or capital budgeting process. **Table 13–3** is the federal investment outlays table, including all types of investments—physical capital, research and development, and education and training—from the fiscal year 2012 budget. After the one capital budget illustration in the 2003 budget, the attention to federal investments once again has taken the broad perspective of Table 13–3.

Table 13–3 Federal Investment Outlays, All Investment Purposes, 2010 and 2012(est.) (Billions of Dollars)

	Actual	Estimate
	2010	2012
Major public physical capital investment:		
Direct federal:		
National defense	147.2	151.8
Nondefense	48.1	49.7
Subtotal, direct major public physical capital investment	195.3	201.5
Grants to state and local governments	93.3	100.9
Subtotal, major public physical capital investment	288.6	302.4
Conduct of research and development		
National defense	81.1	83.0
Nondefense	59.8	66.1
Subtotal, conduct of research and development	140.9	149.1
Conduct of education and training		
Grants to state and local governments	92.6	65.3

	Actual	Estimate
	2010	2012
Direct federal:	39.3	45.0
Subtotal, conduct of education and training	131.9	110.3
Total, major federal investment outlays	**561.4**	**561.9**

Source: Compiled from U.S. Office of Management and Budget (2011). *Budget of the United States government: fiscal year 2012, analytical perspectives* (p. 354). Washington, DC: U.S. Government Printing Office.

CAPITAL PROJECT ANALYSIS

In this section, we discuss methods for analyzing prospective capital investments. Some of the tools discussed can be used for non-physical capital investments as well. Many social programs, for example, are discussed in terms of the costs of the programs and measures of effectiveness that may be output oriented (the number of participants in a workforce training program, for example) or outcome oriented (the reduction in morbidity and mortality from introducing an immunization program against a specific disease). In this chapter, we are concerned with analytical approaches to the investment and return on investment from physical capital expenditures, such as water treatment plants, highways, elementary schools, and so forth. Conceptually, the overall approach is cost-benefit analysis.

Cost-Benefit and Cost-Effectiveness Analysis

We can distinguish between cost-benefit and cost-effectiveness analysis. Both types attempt to relate costs of projects or programs to performance, and both quantify costs in monetary terms. They differ, however, in the way they measure the outcomes of programs.

Cost-effectiveness analysis measures outcomes in quantitative but nonmonetary form. For example, it might focus on the number of patients served by the construction of a new primary health care clinic, or by the introduction into existing health care facilities of new diagnostic technology. Cost-benefit analysis, by contrast, measures program outcomes in monetary form, thereby allowing for the development of ratios or other measures of the extent to which economic returns exceed economic costs, or vice versa. In the case of constructing a multilane, divided highway, for example, cost-benefit analysis would estimate the dollar value of reduced wear and tear on vehicles and time saved to travelers and would use that figure to calculate the dollar value of the gains. It would then compare those benefits to the dollar value of the cost of building and maintaining the highway.

For example, one study by a nonprofit advocacy group for transportation funding, TRIP, reported on Federal Highway Administration data that roughly one-fourth of the nation's urban roads and highways were substandard. The study estimated that drivers on urban roads in America pay an additional $402 annually in vehicle operating costs because of the poor condition of the roads.[28] This type of analysis-based estimate would be used in a cost-benefit analysis of the value of an investment in a road repaving project. Other variables necessary for the analysis would be estimates of the total vehicle miles traveled over the distance of the repaved portion, and a breakdown of the $402 per vehicle into cost per vehicle mile. The economic benefit would be the operating costs averted.

Attaching monetary value to some things, however, can be controversial. Some investments in physical infrastructure may have as the primary impact a reduction in morbidity (disease) or mortality (death), or both. For example, controlling or eliminating environmental conditions that breed mosquitoes, such as a major low-lying area drainage program, has the aim of reducing illness and death from malaria. A cost-effectiveness analysis of that program might compare the environmental intervention with an indoor residual spraying program or the issuance of insecticide-treated bed nets that intend to kill or ward off mosquitoes from being able to infect household residents. The analysis would focus on monetary costs of the various interventions, and nonmonetary results such as reduction in the number of malaria cases, deaths averted, reduction in days lost to debilitating disease, and so forth.

A cost-benefit analysis of the same investment comparisons would place monetary value on deaths averted, work days not lost to debilitating illness, and so forth. The potential technical merit of cost-benefit analysis over cost-effectiveness analysis is that the former allows for analysis across subject areas. When the expressed ratio of benefits to costs of a program is 1.0, costs are equal to benefits. As the ratio increases, the benefits accruing have increased. In theory, if government investment in a new high-efficiency airplane yielded a ratio of 1.7 and a highway traffic control program yielded a ratio of 2.5, then, based on the standard of economic efficiency (and assuming the difference in the magnitude of the programs was not great), government would be advised to favor the traffic control program over the air transportation program. Cost-effectiveness analysis, in contrast, would not allow such direct comparisons because the effects would be expressed in time saved for one program and lives saved for the other.

For a private sector company, capital projects can be evaluated and choices made in terms of the financial results to the company's owners, such as the stockholders. General Electric (GE) can make choices between investing in the aviation jet engine business and the electric turbine business, and can let the monetary returns relative to the monetary costs guide the decision.

A local government cannot as easily make the same kinds of tradeoff decisions as a private company. A local government responsible for both water and sewer service cannot just decide that because the economic returns on a water project are greater than they are for the sewer project, it will just not provide sewer service. What the local government typically has to do in this kind of comparison is decide what possibilities exist for redesigning both projects, for changing the timing of when water and sewer projects will be implemented, and what possibilities exist for more favorable financing terms. But even though compromises will be made, the local government cannot simply decide that citizens do not get sewer service the way GE can decide to go into or to exit a line of business. Regulatory matters may be more important that economic decisions. A local government may be forced to install a sewer system or upgrade an existing system because of state and federal regulations.

The following paragraphs discuss the various issues that arise in public sector decision making on capital projects within an overall economic and financial framework. We make the distinction between *economic analysis* and *financial analysis* to emphasize that there are some differences between a project being valuable (generating returns) for economic reasons and being valuable because it generates direct financial returns to the organization making the investment.

Financial benefits and economic benefits are almost never the same thing. A financial analysis is limited to the direct, actual revenue the company would be expected to earn as a result of an investment, or the increased tax revenues that are estimated to accrue to a jurisdiction as a result, for example, of a major urban renewal investment, which increases property values. An economic analysis includes the financial benefits, but also estimates other benefits, such as the financial value of dollars saved as a result of reduced workdays lost to alcohol abuse. Those dollars saved would not typically be realized in terms of some kind of additional revenue flow, and hence would not typically count as financial returns.

Every public sector capital project has both kinds of returns. Financial returns are defined as actual cash flow returns that are directly the result of the investment. Economic returns may also be measured in dollar terms, but some economic returns do not come in the form of direct cash flow to the jurisdiction making the investment. Extending the distribution of the water system has direct financial returns in the form of user payments for the water. But it also may make water using commercial activities more efficient than the means they relied upon before they got service from the utility. Economic analysis would attempt to measure the value of those efficiency gains in dollars, but these would not be cash flow to the water utility. The World Bank, in appraising a loan for a capital investment program in a developing country, would require that both economic and financial returns be measured.

Identifying Costs and Benefits

The first basic issue in an economic or financial analysis of a capital project is the decision as to what counts as a cost and what counts as a benefit. It is usually different for an economic analysis versus a financial analysis. Determining the financial costs of existing programs is often difficult because accounting systems are designed to produce information by organizational unit and not necessarily by program. Only if a program is unique to an organizational unit specified in the accounting system will the financial costs be easy to measure. For capital projects, the acquisition or purchase price and the construction costs are relatively easier in that engineering specifications precede the cost identification process, and then the specifications may be figured out.

Even when the costs are identified in this manner, all that is produced are the direct financial expenditures of government rather than costs as would be derived by a cost accounting system (see the chapter on financial management). Indeed, critics often charge that analyses overlook the costs imposed on others. Failure to consider all costs tends to weight the analysis in favor of the proposed project under review. If personal residences have to be acquired and demolished to secure the right of way for a road project, the cost of purchasing those properties can be measured, but subsequent lawsuits may award larger amounts to the property owners, and those additional costs may or may not ever be attributed back to the construction project. Furthermore, even if they are, they may be too late to influence the decision itself, as the suits likely will not be resolved before the project is finished. Similarly, the money paid to property holders for their condemned property may not fully reimburse them for their purchase of a comparable property and moving, and those additional costs imposed on the property owners never will be measured in the cost analysis. Similarly, the psychological costs of uprooting families from long-established neighborhoods will not be measured formally in economic terms.

Externalities

Indirect costs as well as benefits granted to others are called externalities, or *spillover, secondary*, and *tertiary effects*. These costs and benefits affect parties other than the ones directly involved. In the private sector, air and water pollution from industrial plants are externalities. The main concern of a private enterprise is making a profit, but part of the cost of production may be imposed on persons living in the area. Residents of areas downstream and downwind of the plant may pay the costs of discomfort, poor health, and loss of water recreation opportunities. They may also experience an actual decrease in the value of their assets, such as their homes, if the pollution is bad enough to make it difficult to sell property. If a municipality downstream has to treat water that has been polluted by the plant, the costs imposed are relatively easy to identify.

Most government capital expenditure decisions involve similar spillover effects. The costs of an urban redevelopment program are not just the financial outlays required for purchasing and clearing land, but also the costs imposed on the families and businesses that must relocate. One government's decision can affect thousands of individuals; businesses; nonprofit organizations such as churches, synagogues, and mosques; and other governments.

Some argue that there are no such things as secondary or spillover effects, that all effects of a program should be part of the explicit benefits and costs of that program. This idea is sometimes expressed as the belief that every affected individual or organization should have *standing* and should thus be taken into account in any analysis of the program.[29] Affected parties are said to be *stakeholders* in that they have interests regarding the outcomes of the program and any decisions that may change it.[30]

Redistributive Effects

Related to spillover costs and benefits are redistributive effects, which analysts once tended to ignore. Today, consideration of major infrastructure projects encompasses their potential redistributive effects. For example, the federal budget has in some administrations included a summary table of the redistributive effects of taxing and spending decisions as part of the budget presentation. But for infrastructure projects, the question is whether some groups in the society will benefit more than other groups. In the example of the high-efficiency airframe investment mentioned earlier, the program presumably would benefit middle- and upper-income groups, who would be the ones more likely to take advantage of this means of transportation. However, benefits from reduced fuel consumption, while directly benefiting airlines and passengers, indirectly benefit all of society from the reduced air pollution and reduced contributions to global warming. Other criteria for judging redistribution include race, educational level, and occupational class.[31] The effects of programs on different generations in the population have increasingly become a focus of attention.

Common tools exist for analyzing redistributive effects, including *Lorenz curves* and *Gini coefficients* of inequality. For capital infrastructure projects, an analysis of the current situation in a jurisdiction before the project is built and after the project is completed could see if the existing Gini coefficient measure of income inequality improves, worsens, or is unaffected. However, note that a project has to be large relative to the population of the jurisdiction undertaking the project to even imagine that income distribution would be affected enough to warrant the analysis. See the chapter on government and the economy for descriptions of *Gini coefficients* of inequality.

Subjective Information

Analyses often must rely on subjective, attitudinal data as distinguished from data that gauge behavior. One objective measure in the city road example discussed above might be the miles of roads resurfaced. An attitudinal measure of the same program might be citizen satisfaction with road conditions. It is indeed possible for citizens (stakeholders) to exhibit no increase in satisfaction even though road conditions may have improved markedly. The same type of situation can develop regarding police protection. Citizens' fear of being burglarized may not decrease despite a decline in the burglary rate brought on by the acquisition of city surveillance technology. In addition to not feeling safer, citizens may also feel that the surveillance system is an invasion of privacy.

Analytical models such as cost-benefit and cost-effectiveness analyses are based on rational behavior models in which individuals are presumed to respond to choices based on the desire to maximize their personal utility. Behavioral research calls into question these underlying assumptions, with the consequence that a supposedly rational result of analysis still may not be the actual preferred result of those affected by the project. Methodologies to take into account these more subjective perspectives involve surveying preferences of stakeholders or those with presumed interests in a potential project and assessing their subjective values. *Contingent valuation* surveys, discussed below, are one contemporary approach to measuring how much value survey respondents place on alternative possibilities.

The generic capital investment planning process discussed in the first section of this chapter, typical of many local governments, incorporates several opportunities for citizen involvement. For some, the CIP itself is the product of a joint government and citizen advisory committee, whereas the government's capital budget is the operationalization of that CIP.

Internal Validity

When costs, benefits, and expected relationships among them are defined, analysis must consider whether other possible variables may influence outcomes. Such influence is a threat to internal validity.[32] For example, the previous example of comparing an indoor spraying program for mosquitoes versus a low-lying area drainage program to combat malaria would be affected by the amount of rainfall after implementation of either choice, and good results may be attributed to a naturally occurring reduction in the number of mosquitoes. Similarly, a school construction program to build facilities for vocational education to increase employment among disadvantaged teenagers may seem to be effective when, in fact, it may have little influence on employment. Any increase in employment might be attributable not to school district investments but to some other program, such as one operated by a nonprofit agency or church. Whether the analysis of a capital project is rigorously quantitative in economic terms or not, every effort must be made to state clearly the causal relationships between the project(s) and the expected outcomes and then to determine the possibility of variables not related to the capital project affecting the result.

Problems of Quantification

Even if an ideal model is designed displaying all of the relevant types of costs and benefits or effects of a program, the problem of quantifying them remains. What are the monetary costs imposed on families relocated by urban redevelopment activities? Part of the costs will consist of moving expenses, perhaps higher rents, and greater costs for commuting to work. These measurements go well beyond the physical investment cost of the redevelopment program. Although these items can be measured, it is much more difficult to set a dollar value on the mental anguish of having to move and leave friends behind. For the financial analysis of the urban redevelopment project, only the direct payments to families for purchasing their homes, moving expenses, and so forth will count. For the economic analysis, the higher rents they will have to pay after the move, their greater commuting costs, and so forth will also count.

Shadow Pricing

Much of the problem of setting dollar values in the analysis stems from the fact that the results of many government investments do not have market prices. Despite various limitations, the private market does provide some standard for measuring the value of goods and services by the prices set for those. Much of analysis in the public sector, however, must impute the prices or values of programs. One such method is known as shadow pricing.[33]

Suppose an analyst is given the task of predicting the benefits of a proposed outdoor recreation project such as a community swimming facility. The average hourly value (the shadow price) to a person attending the proposed new public facility can be assumed to be what individuals on the average spend per hour for similar forms of outdoor recreation. This figure multiplied by the number attending will yield an approximate value of the recreational opportunities to be provided by the facility under study.

The geographic area presumably affected by the analysis of shadow prices can complicate the analysis. For example, if there are no nearby swimming facilities, citizens are presumed to benefit from a new facility and the shadow price analysis yields a reasonable estimate of the economic benefit. However, if there are facilities nearby that charge for use, and a new public facility is built, then the value to users of current facilities that switch to the new, public facility represents value lost to the operators of the old facilities. The economic gain to society will thus be less, and perhaps even nonexistent. In contrast, if there are consumers who could not afford to pay for the current, fee-for-service swimming facilities who use the new facilities, their use does not represent lost business to the operators of current facilities, and thus there is economic value gained from the investment. Spatial considerations have become an important feature of economic analysis of investment projects.[34]

More detailed approaches can examine each form of outdoor recreation: hiking, swimming, tennis, golfing, picnicking, and so forth. In the case of swimming, the average spent per person for one hour of swimming at a private beach can be imputed to be the value of swimming at a public beach. One danger of such an assumption, however, is that it ignores the possibility that the quality of swimming may be different at the two beaches. If such a difference exists, the shadow price should be adjusted accordingly. Another danger is that building the new public swimming facility will change the overall market value of swimming in the area. With the additional supply—the public swimming facility—people may now be less willing to pay the price charged by the private facility. In that instance, the shadow price must take into account the changes in demand.

Shadow pricing becomes increasingly difficult and the analysis more tenuous when the subject matter for study involves functions that are primarily governmental. There is no apparent method by which a dollar value can be set for the defense capability of killing via intercontinental missiles X million people of an aggressor nation within one hour. Similarly, it is difficult to calculate the dollar value of avoiding one traffic fatality. The calculations employed require assessing what kinds of people are killed in automobile accidents, how old they are, and what income they would have earned in their remaining lifetimes.

Given the sometimes questionable assumptions that must be made in estimating the dollar value of saving a life, the argument can be made that cost-effectiveness analysis is preferable to cost-benefit analysis. The former does not attempt to place a dollar value on life but leaves the estimation of that value to decision makers. The disadvantage is that cost-effectiveness analysis, unlike cost-benefit analysis, seldom will yield a single measure of effectiveness. A traffic safety program might be measured by the number of lives saved and by the dollar value of property damage caused by crashes. Like apples and oranges, these benefits cannot be compared.

Contingent Valuation

The amount the public is willing to pay for a particular benefit or to avoid a particular cost also can be measured by means of formal surveys. The methodology, known as contingent valuation, describes to survey respondents a particular service or government action and asks through various contingency statements what the respondent would be willing to pay.[35] For example, "Would you be willing to pay a $0.75 per day per family fee to avoid the smoke and other pollution emitted by a nearby power plant?" Depending on the response, subsequent questions would increase or decrease the $0.75 per day until the maximum price the individual would be willing to pay is identified, or how low the price has to go before the respondent says yes (including $0.00, meaning the respondent is not willing to pay anything to avoid the smoke). Guidelines for federal government cost-benefit analysis, contained in OMB Circular A-94, recommend willingness to pay as an appropriate concept for measuring costs and benefits.[36] Contingent valuation is used by both government and private industry in the valuation of resource losses due to damages, gaining prominence in its application to the Exxon Valdez oil spill in Alaska, and by government to assess the benefits of projected recreational and natural resource preservation programs.[37] The British Petroleum oil spill in the Gulf of Mexico in 2010 (blowout of the Deepwater Horizon rig) gave impetus to the value of the methodology in estimating the value of damage to real estate.[38] Contingent valuation studies are now almost universally required in designing multilateral donor agency-funded infrastructure construction projects that are predicated on user fees to ensure project financial viability.[39]

Discount Rates

Another problem for analysis involves the diversion of resources from the private to the public sector and from current consumption to investment in future returns. From an economic point of view, investment in a public project is warranted only if the returns are greater than they would be if the same funds were left to the private sector and if the future returns are worth the current sacrifice. Thus, the relevant concept of the cost of a public expenditure is the value of the benefits forgone by not leaving the money in the private sector to be consumed or invested.

A dollar diverted from the private sector to the public sector is not just an equivalent dollar cost or dollar benefit forgone. Presumably, had the dollar not been collected as taxes, it would have been available for the private citizen's use in some enjoyable, immediate consumption. Or it would have been available for the private citizen to invest in some kind of interest-bearing security. If the tax is used to finance a public project that produces a benefit to that citizen, or to citizens in general, then the benefit may offset the sacrifice the taxpayer had to make in private consumption or investment. This is the concept of *opportunity cost*—the public project comes at the expense of other opportunities. How do we analyze that tradeoff? If the tax is used to finance a public project that produces a benefit to citizens, then the benefit may offset the sacrifice taxpayers had to make in private consumption or investment.

The second problem is that the public benefit typically occurs at some future time, whereas the private consumption would have been in the more immediate time period. The future public benefit, even if it could be said to be exactly equal to the benefit of private consumption, will not be as valuable because of the simple fact of its being postponed. People typically are not willing to put their money in a savings account, deferring its immediate use for some future situation, without the financial institution paying interest for the privilege of holding, and using, those savings. In the project analysis situation, the analogue to interest paid to the saver, some charge must be made against the dollars removed from consumption for an investment in order to arrive at the current value of future consumption forgone. This charge is known as the discount rate.

The discount rate addresses both problems: the opportunity cost and the time value of money, two sides of the same coin. First, it is similar to an interest charge that reflects the cost of removing a dollar from private sector use and diverting it to the public sector. If a dollar could earn 4% in the private sector, investment in the public sector would be warranted (in a strictly economic sense) only if the rate of return from the public investment would be at least 4%. Second, the discount rate takes into consideration the time pattern of expenditures and returns. In general, people prefer present consumption to future consumption. A dollar that might be spent for current consumption is worth more than a dollar that might be consumed 10 years from now.

Clearly, the choice of a discount rate has an important influence on investment decisions. Too low a rate understates the value of current consumption or of leaving the money to the private sector. Too high a rate uneconomically favors current consumption over future benefits and results in less investment than is worthwhile. The choice of a discount rate may thus determine the outcome of the analysis.

Selecting appropriate discount rates is difficult. Returning to the GE example, choosing between investing in the jet engine business or in the power turbine business, the discount rate typically would be the cost of capital to the corporation. Because GE's capital includes both equity (stock values) and debt (loans, bonds), some kind of weighted cost of capital would be ascertained, and that weighted cost of capital typically would be used as the discount rate. GE then would, if evaluating strictly on financial returns, require that the returns (financial only) must exceed the cost of capital. That would be referred to as the *hurdle rate*. But a private corporation would typically have a higher hurdle rate because it would not just be comparing the investment with the cost of capital. It would be comparing the two different investments in many cases, and would more likely select the one with the higher rate of return. Of course, many other factors would go into the investment decision.

For the public sector, private market rates are inappropriate because they include calculations of the risks of loss that lenders must consider in making a loan to a private company. In contrast, interest rates charged governments are often lower because of the presumed lower risk of default (see discussion in the capital finance and debt chapter of public sector borrowing costs and risk). Also, interest cost to government often is artificially low because of various guarantees against defaults and sometimes the loan's tax-exempt status. The appropriate discount rate lies between these extremes. OMB annually provides guidance to federal agencies on the discount rates that should be used for federal projects (Circular A-94, Appendix C). In 2010, the discount rate for costs and benefits ranged from 1.4% for a 3-year period to 4.2% for a 30-year period, the equivalent nominal interest rates for federal Treasury bonds with 3- and 30-year maturities, respectively.[40]

Several discount rates may be applied to program alternatives to determine the sensitivity of the analysis to discounting. If the cost-benefit ratios of a project are well above 1.0, regardless of the discount rate used, there is little problem. A different situation arises if some plausible discount rates yield results well below 1.0. In other situations, one discount rate might result in a favorable cost-benefit ratio for alternative A and another ratio for alternative B. The point is that an arbitrary choice of a discount rate without consideration of other ranges can produce misleading results.

The relationships among costs, returns, and time are depicted graphically in **Figure 13–1**. Most investment projects involve heavy capital costs early on, followed by a tapering off to operating costs. Returns are nonexistent or minimal for the first few years and then increase rapidly. The shape of the return curve after the initial upturn depends on the nature of the particular investment and is drawn arbitrarily for illustrative purposes in the figure. The comparison of costs to benefits over time makes the necessity for discounting obvious. Higher costs occur earlier in most projects. The higher benefits that occur later are valued less because they occur later in time.

Costs and benefits must therefore be compared for each time period (usually each year), and the differences summed over the life span of the project. That is, in essence, what a discount rate accomplishes. The longer it takes for returns to occur, the more their value is discounted. In effect, the situation involves compound interest in reverse. Costs occurring earlier are subject to less discounting. Thus, for a project to be economically feasible, total discounted benefits must exceed total discounted costs. This excess of discounted benefits over discounted costs is known as the *net present value* (NPV). Government expenditures are efficient allocations of a society's resources when the net present value is positive. Any spreadsheet software contains built-in functions for calculating the net present value, the internal rate of return, and similar concepts useful in assessing the value of benefits occurring over time in comparison with the costs of the investment.

Measuring the Return on Investment (ROI)

Two forms of calculating the rate of return on investment are typically used in capital project analysis. If the project is similar to what a private company might do, such as build a parking garage for which customers will pay fees to cover the costs of the facility, then the first analysis will be a financial rate of return (sometimes called a *financial internal rate of return* or FIRR). The full costs of the project are measured on the cost side, and the financial returns in the form of charges to customers over the life span of the garage are the measures on the benefit side. The expectation is that the garage would earn revenues, taking into account the long time period over which those revenues would be earned, as exhibited in Figure 13–1, that would yield a positive FIRR.

Similarly, the extension of water lines into a new neighborhood would yield revenue in the form of hook-up charges and regular charges for water use. An FIRR analysis would inform the decision makers if the planned costs for hook-up fees and regular usage fees would yield a positive financial rate of return. Because private providers build and run parking garages and private companies may provide water services, the financial analysis of a project is important in order to evaluate whether the public investment in either facility pays for itself through future revenue generation. If it does not, then decision makers would in effect need to approve a government subsidy in order for the project to go forward.

The results of the financial analysis, if the financial return is less than an equivalent privately provided option, do not automatically mean the project should not be done. There may be good reasons to go forward anyway, including as discussed earlier positive externalities of a nonfinancial nature or redistributive benefits such as a subsidy element for low-income families. But the strict analysis of financial costs and financial returns makes the value of these other considerations apparent even if they were not directly measured.

Of course not all projects yield direct revenue. Construction of a recreation facility from which the public could not be excluded or regulated through charging fees for use would

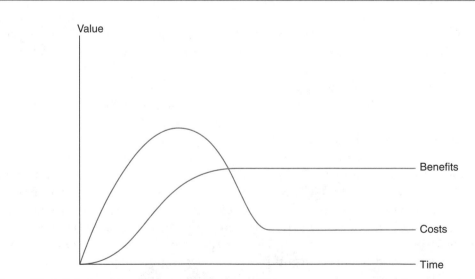

Figure 13–1 Relationship of Costs and Benefits to Time

yield benefits to the community, but if it is open to the public without charge, it would yield no revenue. As noted in the discussion of shadow pricing above, imputed prices, the prices people might pay for other recreational opportunities, may be used nonetheless to calculate a rate of return. That rate of return would be called an *economic internal rate of return* (EIRR).[41]

These examples might seem as if economic and financial rates of return are really just two names for the same thing—that an analyst may use either one or the other indifferently. For some projects, both an FIRR and an EIRR are likely to be calculated, and the results are likely to be different. For example, if the water line extension example includes health benefits to the previously unserved neighborhood whose well water contained some levels of toxic substances, then there would be value to society from the project that would be additional to the financial cash flows from the hook-up and usage fees.

If a reduction in illnesses means fewer days lost to productive work, and fewer costs for health care, then the monetary value of those additional workdays and the reduction in health care costs would be added to the financial returns, even though there would be no attempt actually to *charge* the individuals in their water rates for those health benefits. Similarly, if the project imposed costs on other individuals, or the government as a whole, such as the additional costs to people who had to relocate from their homes, then those costs would be added to the project costs. The economic rate of return analysis typically includes all of the financial costs and benefits, but also adds in economic costs and benefits that are not reflected in the financial structure of the project. The calculation methods are identical. The difference is what is put into the cost stream and the benefit stream.

ASSET MANAGEMENT

Asset management historically has not been tied directly to budgeting, not even in the context of capital budgeting. However, the increasingly sophisticated financial management systems that larger governmental jurisdictions employ may blur the lines as comprehensive systems link modules for capital budgeting, asset management, and operating (current) budgeting. Historically, asset management comes into play long after capital budget decisions have been made. Capital projects are implemented, or capital purchases are made, and the resulting physical facilities or equipment then become part of the jurisdiction's inventory of assets, whether the jurisdiction has a formal system or not. These traditionally separate processes are no longer as distinct. Two factors have contributed to the much greater emphasis now given to the role of asset management in public sector organizations—the concern beginning in the 1980s that many state and local governments had allowed critical infrastructure to deteriorate without any adequate planning for its replacement, and the 1999 release of GASB Statement No. 34, amended and updated several times since then.

Asset Decline

Asset Decline in the United States

Concern for the condition of America's deteriorating infrastructure base emerged in the early 1980s. Throughout that decade, spectacular incidents, such as the collapse of the Mianus Bridge in Connecticut and detailed studies of investment deficits, brought heightened attention to the need to rebuild and maintain the nation's physical infrastructure assets.[42] The concern continues. A study by the American Society of Civil Engineers (ASCE) estimated that the combined public infrastructure deficit in facilities such as water systems, schools, airports, and highways was a staggering $2.2 trillion in 2009.[43] That figure was close to the total amount of municipal debt outstanding that year ($2.8 trillion).[44] A study by the Urban Land Institute and Ernst & Young estimated the deficit in 2011 at $2 billion, just for replacing existing infrastructure that had completely deteriorated. This estimate notably did not include any investment for growth in systems, with the report noting that the U.S. population is growing by approximately 30 million people every decade.[45] A 2010 report by the Congressional Budget Office noted that the United States in 2007 spent only about 2.7% of GDP for infrastructure, in contrast to China's approximately 9% of GDP spent on infrastructure.[46] Federal spending increased as noted by the CBO after 2007 with the American Recovery and Reinvestment Act of 2009 providing an additional $4 billion in infrastructure spending.[47] The U.S. Treasury Department and the Council of Economic Advisors published a report in 2010 advocating the economic benefits of infrastructure investment as a means of stimulating the economy out of the recession.[48]

All of the studies define infrastructure deficit as facilities that have outlived their usefulness as well as facilities needed to address unmet needs of unserved and underserved populations. For example, some sewer systems still in use are more than 100 years old. An earlier Congressional Budget Office study noted that sewer pipes, for example, have an average asset life of 50 years, and that many systems in major U.S. cities had reached or were approaching that age.[49] In addition, when governments do not spend adequately for maintenance and rehabilitation, facilities may not come near their useful life span. But budgeting sufficient amounts in the operating budget for repairs and maintenance in order to avoid or reduce capital costs 20 years hence is not easy for elected executive and legislative officials.

Figure 13–2 illustrates the infrastructure deficit in water supply systems, comparing estimates by the U.S. Environmental Protection Agency and the Congressional Budget Office for capital investment and operation and maintenance expenditures needed between 2000 and 2019 for drinking water alone. These estimates are for expenditures to replace systems that have gone beyond their useful lives, for major rehabilitation of systems to extend their useful lives, and for systems to address the needs of population growth and quality improvements.

The two agencies' estimates are widely variant for operation and maintenance requirements, but quite close on capital investment requirements. CBO explains the differences in operation and maintenance estimates mainly to timing differences. EPA's assumption in its estimate is that most of the capital investments are needed right away, whereas CBO spreads a similar amount of capital investment over the 20-year period. The earlier capital investments (in EPA's estimate) of course then generate operation and maintenance expenditures over the time period, resulting in a larger EPA cost estimate, as the illustration shows.[50] According to the CBO and the EPA, capital investments in drinking water over that 20-year period should be between $360 billion and nearly $500 billion, respectively. If, as the EPA estimates assume, many of the investments need to be made now, then operation and maintenance costs over the period evaluated by both agencies exceed the capital investments required. Those estimates made in 2002 for investments needed urgently then were not fully met, digging the infrastructure hole deeper as the United States entered the second decade of the 2000s.[51]

Figure 13–2 Environmental Protection Agency and Congressional Budget Office Estimates for Drinking Water Investments, 2000–2019 (in Millions of Dollars)
Source: Reprinted from the U.S. Congressional Budget Office (2003). Future spending on water infrastructure: a comparison of estimates from the Congressional Budget Office and the Environmental Protection Agency (p. 2). Washington, DC: U.S. Government Printing Office.

Asset Decline in Other Countries

Concerns over infrastructure deficits are not limited to the United States, causing similar concern for improved systems for planning and budgeting and then managing the assets once built. European Union countries and especially developing and emerging market countries experience shortages of capital to construct physical facilities, and often also fail to support existing capital facilities with adequate operation and maintenance. The collapse of Asian financial markets in the 1990s and the later scandal-related collapse of Enron caused continuing problems in attracting capital to investments in power and water, leaving many countries increasingly concerned that public infrastructure cannot keep up with demand for services whether caused by aging infrastructure as in developed countries or inadequate infrastructure in the first place in developing economies. The 2007–2008 financial markets collapse exacerbated the problem for the world's industrial economies, but China, India, Brazil, and some other growing economic powers have been able to sustain needed infrastructure investments.[52] India, for example, continues to experience rapid population growth. Coupled with an inadequate infrastructure base and the more extensive infrastructure requirements of a modernizing economy, India's national investment strategy aims at not falling behind. India planned a doubling of infrastructure investments by 2017, from $500 billion to $1 trillion by 2017, about 9% of GDP, three to four times the investment levels of most western industrialized countries.[53]

Spending on Infrastructure

The U.S. physical infrastructure asset base exists primarily because of state and local government investments. As far back as the mid-1950s, state and local capital spending greatly exceeded federal capital spending. In 1956, state and local capital spending on infrastructure amounted to almost $28 billion, whereas federal capital spending was less than $10 billion. A gradual climb in federal spending led to its overtaking state and local capital spending in 1976, and it remained higher until significant federal budget cutbacks affected capital spending in 1986.[54] **Figure 13–3** documents for selected years since 1980 federal (non-defense), state, and local government expenditures for public works facilities specifically. This includes highways, airports, water transport and terminals, sewage, solid waste, water supply, and mass transit.

This figure gives some indication of the relative roles played by federal, state, and local governments in public works funding. The amounts for the three sources are all for direct spending on capital assets. By far, local governments exceed both federal and state governments, and even match federal and state combined. As can be seen in Figure 13–3, more than 50% of the total is local government spending in each of the four years after 1980. States are next, at around 24%, and federal direct (spent directly by federal agencies on capital projects) is, in all the years in the figure, less than 10%. The federal grants figure shows the contribution the federal government makes, for non-defense capital investments only, through intergovernmental grant transfers. Federal grants for physical capital investment historically were a relatively small contribution. Programs introduced in the 1970s caused federal grants to state and local governments for physical capital investments to double between 1975 and 1980, and then drop after 1980. In Figure 13–3, federal grants in 1980 for capital projects carried out at the state or local level were just over 23% of total physical capital expenditures. In the other three years depicted, federal grants have been around 15% of the total. When federal direct spending and federal grants are combined, federal finance support for capital investment in 1980 was just over 31%. For the remaining years in the figure, combined federal capital spending was 23% to 25% of total capital investment.

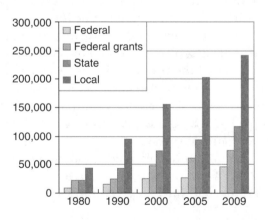

Figure 13–3 Federal State and Local Roles in Public Works Funding, 1980–2009, Selected Years (Millions of Dollars)

Sources: Compiled from Bureau of the Census, U.S. Department of Commerce (2006). *Statistical abstract of the United States: 2006* (p. 282). Washington, DC: U.S. Government Printing Office; State & local government finance data query system, the Urban Institute—Brookings Institution Tax Policy Center. Retrieved December 8, 2011, from http://www .taxpolicycenter.org/slf-dqs/pages.cfm; Federal Grants, U.S. Office of Management and Budget (2011). *Budget of the United States, FY 2012: historical tables* (Tables 9.2 and 12.1). Washington, DC: U.S. Government Printing Office.

The concern for deterioration of existing physical assets and corresponding inadequate investment levels prompted larger city governments and the more populous states as early as the early 1980s to begin developing, or purchasing from financial information services firms, more sophisticated approaches to planning and managing the infrastructure base. But the introduction of GASB Statement No. 34 in 1999 raised the bar on financial reporting standards for state and local governments, forcing more rigorous attention to the condition of the asset base in reporting on the overall health of the institution. Here we discuss its impact on capital asset reporting.

Capital Assets in GASB Statement No. 34

Statement No. 34 requires that governments report their capital assets in a *statement of net assets* and requires that the report show the depreciation in the value of those assets. Specific asset reporting requirements include:

- Depreciation of assets must begin when the asset, equipment, or facility is acquired or put in service;
- Accumulated depreciation for all assets must be reported;
- Assets acquired or built prior to 1980 are not required to be reported, but once a major renovation of an older asset has been carried out, then the rehabilitated asset must be included in the statement of net assets.[55]

The difference that this makes to capital and operating budget practices is substantial.[56] From a budgeting point of view, the cost of a capital project enters the budget in the year in which the cost is incurred whether the governmental entity has a capital budgeting process and a formal capital budget or not. GASB 34 gives visibility to the expected life span of facilities and the depreciation of the assets through the financial reporting process. In turn, citizens may observe the adequacy of the operating budget's provisions for operation and maintenance and provision for future replacement costs. In reality, citizens are unlikely to pay attention to those details unless it becomes an electoral issue. However, bond rating agencies do take into account the adequacy of operation and maintenance programs and provision for timely rehabilitation expenditures to avoid larger capital costs in the future (see the chapter on capital finance). The financial reporting requirements for physical assets more readily expose to financial institutions and bond underwriters the overall health of a jurisdiction's infrastructure and the adequacy of budget planning to preserve those assets. That in turn can affect the bond rating and therefore the interest the jurisdiction will have to pay on a bond issue. As a result, an increasing number of state and local governments have adopted comprehensive systems for assessing physical asset conditions and linking those conditions to the budgeting process, both capital budgeting and recurrent budgeting. San Diego uses a computerized inventory and mapping system to keep track of maintenance schedules on 3,000 miles of water and sewer pipes. For example, one of the features is mapping of facilities by date installed and by current condition.[57]

Requirements similar to GASB 34 in other countries also have produced similar changes. The United Kingdom Accounting Standards Board (ASB) recognizes as a Standard of Recommended Practice (SORP) local government asset accounting that includes asset inventories, depreciation of those assets, and changes in valuation of the assets.[58] Standard accounting practices in New Zealand, noted for its progressive public sector budgeting and financial management practices, "records state highways at depreciated replacement cost based on the estimated present cost of constructing the existing asset by the most appropriate method of construction."[59] Similar requirements have been proposed in Canada. The Sustainable Water and Sewage Systems Act of 2002, as amended in 2006, requires Ontario municipalities to report on the full life cycle costs of water and wastewater service. Toronto's 2005 Water and Wastewater business plan noted: "It is clear that municipalities will be required to implement asset management plans."[60]

Cities throughout developing countries that have underinvested in both maintenance and reconstruction of such critical urban infrastructure assets as paved roadways, water systems, and drainage also have begun to develop more complete systems for taking inventory of existing assets and developing CIPs based on a schedule of needed improvements.[61] These innovations in public sector asset management have begun to alter the ways some cities plan, budget, and manage their finances; capital planning and budgeting are now playing a more important role.[62]

Asset management practices are not limited to state and local governments. At the federal level, OMB Circular A-11 was modified in 2006 in Part 300 (focusing on planning, budgeting, acquisition, and management of capital assets) to give greater emphasis to the management of federal assets. When proposing in their budget to acquire a new capital asset or significantly improve an existing asset, agencies must include with their budgets a capital asset plan and business case summary.[63] The *business case summary* explains the rationale for the investment in terms of mission and alternatives considered, and provides detailed management information on the acquisition process and subsequent management of the asset. At least three viable alternatives to the asset acquisition must be presented as part of the business case. Operations and maintenance milestones are identified in the business case in order to ensure that there has been adequate planning to preserve the value of the asset once acquired and put into service. A plan for measuring the performance of the asset to be acquired provides the basis for subsequent monitoring to ensure that operations and maintenance activities are taking place to maximize the asset's useful life.

SUMMARY

Governments plan and budget for the recurring expenditures for the myriad of services they provide, and governments plan and budget for major investments in infrastructure systems and equipment. The latter investments are the focus of capital planning and budgeting. Most state and local governments have formal systems for making capital budget decisions and segregate capital investments into separate capital budgets or statements. The reasons are twofold: state and local capital investments are a major share of their total budget decisions in any given year, and state and local governments generally rely upon various forms of borrowing (discussed in the chapter on capital finance and debt) to finance capital investments. Both reasons make capital budgeting a best practice for state and local governments.

The rationale for federal capital budgeting, despite being evaluated several times in the past four decades, has never been persuasive. Capital investments are a much smaller share of the federal budget, and much of the capital costs incurred by the federal government are for defense expenditures that are not normally considered investments or grants to state and local governments to support their capital investments. Despite not adopting capital budgeting, however, the federal government has continued to adopt financial management and reporting practices to improve upon how capital costs are communicated to Congress and the public, and how they are managed.

Whether it is a formal capital budgeting process or not, federal, state, and local governments use formal analysis tools to assist in evaluating capital investments. These tools use both economic and financial measures to assess the value of the investment to the governmental jurisdiction, and take into account that these are long-term investments with long-term payoff. The analytic tools do not substitute quantitative analysis for judgment in decision making, but they do expose for decision makers and the public the underlying assumptions, costs, and benefits so that good judgments can be made.

Also independent of whether capital budgets are employed or not, other pressures since the 1980s have generated demand for better decision making and better reporting on investments. Deterioration of major infrastructure systems that might have lasted much longer before having to be replaced started creating demand in the United States for better management of infrastructure systems and more informed attention to maintenance costs and the depreciating value of infrastructure. Government cost accounting standards, particularly GASB 34, require financial reporting of physical assets that basically demand more sophisticated and integrated planning, budgeting, and financial management systems that include a focus on asset management. This has relegated arguments about whether to have capital budgets to the back seat as, regardless of formal capital budgeting, governments must do a better job of managing the entire capital investment process.

NOTES

1. Wang, X. (2010). *Financial management in the public sector: tools, applications, and cases,* (2nd ed., pp. 108–109). Armonk, NY: M. E. Sharpe.
2. Governmental Accounting Standards Board (2006). Statement of Governmental Accounting Standards No. 34, *Basic statements—and management's discussion and analysis—for state and local government* (p. 11). Norwalk, CT: Author; Governmental Accounting Standards Board (2009). S*tatement 34, 10 years later.* Retrieved November 1, 2011, from http://www.gasb.org/cs/ContentServer?c=GASBContent_C&pagename=GASB%2FGASBContent_C%2FUsersArticlePage&cid=1176156731408.
3. U.S. Office of Management and Budget (2011). *Budget of the United States government for 2012: analytical perspectives, federal investment* (p. 2). Washington, DC: U.S. Government Printing Office.
4. Zimmer, R., et al. (2011). What types of school capital projects are voters willing to support? *Public Budgeting and Finance, 31,* Spring, 37–55.
5. MacManus, S. (2004). "Bricks and mortar" politics: how infrastructure decisions defeat incumbents. *Public Budgeting & Finance, 24,* Spring, 96–112.
6. Kelly, M., & Zieper, M. (2000). Financing for the future: the economic benefits of parks and open space. *Government Finance Review, 16,* December, 23–28.

7. Penn State University (2010). *The economic significance and impact of Pennsylvania state parks: an assessment of visitor spending on the state and regional economy.* State College, PA: Penn State University, Department of Recreation, Park and Tourism Management.

8. U.S. Office of Management and Budget (2011). *Budget of the United States government for 2012: analytical perspectives, federal investment.*

9. Bureau of the Census, U.S. Department of Commerce (2011). *Statistical abstract of the United States: 2012* (p. 275). Washington, DC: U.S. Government Printing Office.

10. Orange Water and Sewer Authority (2010). *OWASA strategic plan: March 25, 2010* (p. 5). Carrboro, NC: Author.

11. Government Performance Project (2005). *State report cards: Michigan state government's grade for infrastructure management.* Retrieved September 5, 2006, from http://results.gpponline.org/StateCategoryCriteria.aspx?id=114&relatedid=5; Governance Performance Project (2008). *Grading the states: Michigan.* Retrieved November 1, 2011, from http://www.pewcenteronthestates.org/uploadedFiles/PEW_WebGuides_MI.pdf.

12. Berne, R., & Schramm, R. (1986). *The financial analysis of governments.* Englewood Cliffs, NJ: Prentice-Hall; Nollenberger, K., Groves, S., & Valente, M. (2003). *Evaluating financial condition: a handbook for local government,* (4th ed.). Washington, DC: International City/County Management Association; Governmental Accounting Standards Board (2011). *Analyzing the financial health of governments after GASB statement 34.* Retrieved November 2, 2011, from http://www.gasb.org/cs/BlobServer?blobcol=urldata&blobtable=MungoBlobs&blobkey=id&blobwhere=1175820449767&blobheader=application%2Fpdf.

13. U.S. Congressional Budget Office (1992). *How federal spending for infrastructure and other public investments affects the economy* (p. xv). Washington, DC: U.S. Government Printing Office; Haughwout, A. (2003). *Public infrastructure investments, productivity and welfare in fixed geographic areas.* New York, NY: Federal Reserve Bank of New York. Retrieved September 5, 2006, from http://www.newyorkfed.org/research/staff_reports/sr104.pdf; Vickerman, R., et al. (2008). *The wider economic benefits of transport:macro-, meso- and micro-economic transport planning and investment tools.* Paris: Organization for Economic Cooperation and Development.

14. Duscha, L. (2006). *Managing infrastructure in the 21st century Bureau of Reclamation.* Testimony before the Committee on Energy and Natural Resources, U.S. Senate, May 23, 2006. Retrieved August 15, 2006, from http://www7.nationalacademies.org/ocga/testimony/Construction_and_Infrastructure_in_the_Bureau_of_Reclamation.asp; Irving, S. (2011). *Budget process: enforcing fiscal choices.* Washington, DC: U.S. Government Accountability Office; Office of Management and Budget (2011). Circular A-11, *Capital programming guide, appendix 6: principles of budgeting for capital investments.* Washington, DC: Government Printing Office.

15. Office of Management and Budget (2011). Circular A-11, *Capital programming guide, appendix 6: principles of budgeting for capital investments.*

16. Srithongrung, A. (2008). The impacts of state capital management programs on state economic performance. *Public Budgeting & Finance, 28,* Fall, 83–107; Beckett-Camarata, J. (2003). An examination of the relationship between the municipal strategic plan and the capital budget and its effect on financial performance. *Journal of Public Budgeting, Accounting and Financial Management, 15,* 23–40.

17. City of Durham, North Carolina (2011). *Capital improvement program process: 2011.* Retrieved November 1, 2011, from http://www.durhamnc.gov/departments/bms/pdf/11-16cip_intro.pdf.

18. U.S. Office of Management and Budget (2011). *Budget of the United States government for 2012: analytical perspectives, federal investment* (p. 354).

19. U.S. Office of Management and Budget (2011). *Budget of the United States government for 2012: analytical perspectives, federal investment* (p. 354). U.S. Office of Management and Budget (2006). *Budget of the United States government for 2007: analytical perspectives, federal investment* (p. 55). Washington, DC: U.S. Government Printing Office.

20. U.S. Office of Management and Budget (1967). *Report of the President's Commission on Budget Concepts* (p. 34). Washington, DC: U.S. Government Printing Office.

21. U.S. General Accounting Office (1996). *Budget issues: budgeting for federal capital.* Washington, DC: U.S. Government Printing Office.

22. National Council on Public Works Improvement (1988). *Fragile foundations: a report on America's public works.* Washington, DC: U.S. Government Printing Office.
23. Ausubel, J., & Herman, R. (Eds.) (1988). *Cities and their vital systems: infrastructure past, present, and future.* Washington, DC: National Academy of Sciences.
24. U.S. General Accounting Office (1995). *Budget structure: providing an investment focus in the federal budget.* Washington, DC: U.S. Government Printing Office.
25. President's Commission to Study Capital Budgeting (1999). *Report.* Washington, DC: U.S. Government Printing Office.
26. Israte, E., & Puentes, R. (2009). *Investing for success: examining a federal capital budget and a National Infrastructure Bank.* Washington, DC: Brookings Institution.
27. U.S. Office of Management and Budget (2002). *Budget of the United States government: fiscal year 2003, analytical perspectives* (p. 12). Washington, DC: U.S. Government Printing Office.
28. TRIP (2010). *Hold the wheel steady: America's roughest rides and strategies to make our roads smoother.* Retrieved November 1, 2011, from http://www.tripnet.org/urban_roads_report_Sep_2010.pdf.
29. Whittington, D., & MacRae, Jr., D. (1986). The issue of standing in cost-benefit analysis. *Journal of Policy Analysis and Management 5,* 665–682; Trumbull, W. (1990). Who has standing in cost-benefit analysis? *Journal of Policy Analysis and Management, 9,* 201–218; Fuguitt, D., & Wilcox, S. J. (1999). *Cost-benefit analysis for public sector decision makers.* Westbrook, CT: Quorum Books; Whittington, D., & Hanemann, W. (2006). *The economic costs and benefits of investments in municipal water and sanitation infrastructure: a global perspective,* CUDARE Working Paper Series 1027, University of California at Berkeley, Department of Agricultural and Resource Economics and Policy.
30. Steelman, T., & Maguire, L. (1999). Understanding participant perspectives: *q*-methodology in national forest management. *Journal of Policy Analysis and Management, 18,* 361–388; Walters, L., et al. (2000). Putting more public in policy analysis. *Public Administration Review, 60,* 349–359.
31. Johnson, R., & Pierce, J. (1975). The economic evaluation of policy impacts: cost-benefit and cost effectiveness analysis. In F. Scioli & T. Cook (Eds.), *Methodologies for analyzing public policies* (pp. 131–154). Lexington, MA: Lexington Books.
32. Campbell, D., & Stanley, J. (1963). *Experimental and quasi-experimental designs for research.* Boston, MA: Houghton Mifflin; Shadish, W., et al. (2002). *Experimental and quasi-experimental designs for generalized causal inference.* New York, NY: Houghton Mifflin Harcourt.
33. Tallec, F., & Bockel, L. (2005). *Commodity chain analysis: impact analysis using shadow prices.* Food and Agricultural Organization of the United Nations. Retrieved November 1, 2011, from http://www.fao.org/docs/up/easypol/333/CCA_046EN.pdf; McKean, R. N. (1968). The use of shadow prices. In S. B. Chase, Jr. (Ed.), *Problems in public expenditure analysis* (pp. 33–65). Washington, DC: Brookings Institution.
34. Vickerman, R., et al. (2008). *The wider economic benefits of transport macro-, meso- and micro-economic transport planning and investment tools.*
35. Brubaker, E. (2004). Eliciting the public's budgetary preferences: insights from contingent valuation. *Public Budgeting & Finance, 24,* Spring, 72–95; Whittington, D. (2007). *Improving the performance of contingent valuation studies in developing countries.* EEPSEA Special and Technical Paper sp200709s1, Economy and Environment Program for Southeast Asia (EEPSEA). Retrieved November 2, 2011, from http://ideas.repec.org/p/eep/tpaper/sp200709s1.html.
36. U.S. Office of Management and Budget (2011). Circular A-94 revised, *Guidelines and discount rates for cost benefit analysis of federal programs.* Washington, DC: Author.
37. Carson, R. (2002). *Contingent evaluation: a comprehensive bibliography and history.* London, UK: Edward Elgar.
38. Lipscomb, C. (2011). Contingent valuation and real estate damage estimation. *Journal of Real Estate Literature, 19,* no. 2. Retrieved November 3, 2011, from http://papers.ssrn.com/sol3/papers.cfm?abstract_id=1943460##.
39. U.S. Department of Agriculture (2006). *Contingent valuation/recreational values.* Retrieved September 15, 2006, from http://www.economics.nrcs.usda.gov/technical/recreate/index.html.
40. U.S. Office of Management and Budget (2011). Circular A-94 revised, *Appendix C.*

41. Brigham, E., & Ehrhardt, M. (2011). *Financial management: theory and practice* (13th ed.). Mason, OH: South-Western Cengage Learning. This is a business-oriented text, as are most texts that provide detailed analysis of rates of return and related concepts, but the analytical framework is the same whether private sector or public sector oriented.

42. National Council on Public Works Improvement (1988). *Fragile foundations: a report on America's public works*. Washington, DC: U.S. Government Printing Office.

43. American Society of Civil Engineers (2009). *2009 report card for America's infrastructure*. Washington, DC: Author.

44. Securities Industry and Financial Market Association (2010). *Outstanding U.S. bond market debt*. Retrieved November 3, 2011, from http://www.investinginbonds.com/news.asp?catid=36&id=3161.

45. Miller, J. (2011). *Infrastructure 2011: a strategic priority*. Washington, DC: Urban Land Institute.

46. Congressional Budget Office (2010). *Public spending on transportation and water infrastructure*. Washington, DC: U.S. Government Printing Office; China, Miller, J. (2011). *Infrastructure 2011: a strategic priority*.

47. Congressional Budget Office (2010). *Public spending on transportation and water infrastructure* (p. 5).

48. U.S. Department of the Treasury and the Council of Economic Advisers (2010). *An economic analysis of infrastructure investment*. Washington, DC: U.S. Government Printing Office.

49. U.S. Congressional Budget Office (2002). *Future investment in drinking water and wastewater infrastructure* (p. 8). Washington, DC: U.S. Government Printing Office.

50. U.S. Congressional Budget Office (2003). *Future spending on water infrastructure: a comparison of estimates from the Congressional Budget Office and the Environmental Protection Agency* (pp. 1–3). Washington, DC: Congressional Budget Office, 1–3.

51. Congressional Budget Office (2010). *Public spending on transportation and water infrastructure* (p. 3).

52. Miller, J. (2011). *Infrastructure 2011: a strategic priority* (pp. 4–21).

53. Miller, J. (2011). *Infrastructure 2011: a strategic priority* (p. 10).

54. U.S. Congressional Budget Office (1992). *Trends in public infrastructure outlays and the president's proposals for infrastructure spending in 1993* (p. 15). Washington, DC: U.S. Government Printing Office; Congressional Budget Office (2010). *Public spending on transportation and water infrastructure* (p. 3).

55. Governmental Accounting Standards Board (2006). Statement of Governmental Accounting Standards No. 34, *Basic statements—and management's discussion and analysis—for state and local government*.

56. Bastida, F., & Benito, B. (2006). Financial reports and decentralization in municipal governments. *International Review of Administrative Sciences, 72*, 223–238. Carlson, J., et al. (2010). Government performance reforms and nonprofit human services: 20 years in Oregon. *Nonprofit and Voluntary Sector Quarterly, 39*, 630–652.

57. City of San Diego (2011). *Sewer mains by date of installation*. Retrieved November 3, 2011, from http://www.esri.com/mapmuseum/mapbook_gallery/volume19/wastewater4.html.

58. Ellwood, C. (2002). The financial reporting (r)evolution in the UK public sector. *Public Budgeting, Accounting and Financial Management, 14*, 572.

59. Santiso, C. (2006). Banking on accountability? Strengthening budget oversight and public sector auditing in emerging economies. *Public Budgeting & Finance, 26*, Summer, 57.

60. Toronto Water (2005). *2005 multi-year business plan* (p. 44). Toronto, Ontario, Canada: City of Toronto.

61. Johnson, R., & Barnett, C. (1996). *Urban services delivery in CEE and the NIS*, prepared for U.S. Agency for International Development Zagreb Conference on Local Government. Research Triangle Park, NC: Research Triangle Institute.

62. Leavitt, W., & Morris, J. (2007). Public works service arrangements in the 21st century: the multiple-sector partnership as an alternative to privatization. *Public Works Management & Policy, 12*, 325–330.

63. U.S. Office of Management and Budget (2011). OMB Circular A-11, *Capital assets* (Section 300, pp. 9–11). Washington, DC: U.S. Government Printing Office.

Capital Finance and Debt Management

In this chapter, we discuss the means for financing capital projects. As noted previously, capital investments are *lumpy*. That is, financing a large infrastructure project requires a large amount of capital up front, whereas the benefits and the revenue from that up-front investment are spread over many years—20 to 50 years in the case of significant infrastructure such as a sewer system. Not only will present taxpayers, or service charge payers, benefit from the investment, but future generations will too, and they should help pay for the investment.

For such large projects, few governments other than national governments have the capital or taxing power to finance the acquisition and construction at one time. Even national governments that have massive infrastructure needs are typically unable to finance all of their requirements without resorting to some form of long-term financing. The same is true of large private corporations wishing to undertake a major expansion of their production facilities. And the same is true of most households when it comes to purchasing something as large as a home. Few families have the cash on hand to make their first home purchase. Consequently, most governments, corporations, and households look to other sources of funds—investors or lenders—to finance up front the capital investment, and agree to pay a financial return to those investors at a future time or times.

The primary source for governments financing large capital projects is borrowing from investors: individuals and financial institutions. In the United States, state and local governments borrow from individuals and institutions such as banks, capital market funds, and other institutional investors by issuing bonds. At the end of the second quarter of 2011, the outstanding value of municipal securities held by various investors was more than $2.3 trillion.[1] That is more than 8% of total U.S. domestic debt outstanding, a figure that has held steady since the early 1990s. In the 1980s, municipal debt was 15% to 20% of total U.S. domestic debt. The growth of mortgage-related debt securities from the 1990s to the present accounts for the relative percentage decrease in municipal debt, not a decline in the absolute value of municipal debt.

Bonds and bond issuance by governments are a major focus of discussion in this chapter. In other industrialized countries, specialized lending institutions that serve as bankers for municipalities often substitute for bond issues. State infrastructure banks in the United States have increased as a source of debt financing at the U.S. state and local levels, but still do not approach the importance of the municipal bond market. It is important to stress that capital financing is not about how infrastructure is paid for. Either taxpayers of a jurisdiction in general, including the entire United States at the federal level, or the specific users of a service, or both, for the most part pay for services, and that includes the costs of financing the up-front investment. This chapter is about how the capital is raised for the initial investment in new facilities or rehabilitated existing facilities.

The second focus in this chapter is on governments' debt management practices, and what happens when the borrower does not or cannot repay. Even with robust capital markets and governments in sound financial condition, borrowing is not always sufficient, nor is it always the best way to finance infrastructure. The past 30 years have seen an increase in private equity investments in public infrastructure projects worldwide, including in the United States. Private equity investments have quite different implications for financing and managing public facilities and are the final topic of this chapter.

TYPES OF FINANCE

In the private sector, there are three sources of financing capital assets: *debt, equity*, and *retained earnings*. Retained earnings are what households think of as *savings*. Debt is available to both public and private institutions, and to households. Equity comes in the form of stock issuance in the case of publicly traded companies. Companies whose stock is traded on one of the stock exchanges—the New York Stock Exchange (NYSE), for example—sell stock in order to raise capital for investment or operating purposes. Purchasers of stock then literally *own* a fraction of the corporation. They are not entitled to any *repayment* of the money invested in purchasing the stock. Rather, they are entitled to a share of the value of the corporation. They may benefit from that value if the corporation pays dividends, or they may sell the stock at a later date. If the company has performed well in the market, the value of the shares sold will have appreciated. Equity investors of course also may experience a decline in value and actually sell their stock for less than they originally invested.

Creditors who have lent money to a public or private enterprise legally have first recourse to being repaid; they have the first claim on the assets of the borrower. Equity investors come in after all debts are satisfied. In some countries, the state owns companies that are listed on that country's stock exchange(s). For example, oil and gas companies in some countries may be owned in part by the state and in part by private investors. Public transportation companies, such as airlines, telecommunications, and some utilities such as electric power generation and water supply, may be organized as state-owned enterprises (SOE) with partial, usually minority, ownership in the hands of private investors. The SOE may also be fully owned by the state, with no shares traded in the market.

The other forms of equity capital are owners' equity investments, in the case of privately held companies, and retained earnings. In a family-owned company in which 100% of the ownership is private, not available for public sale through shares of stock, the investments these private owners have made both initially in founding the company and potentially later as additional capital is needed is *owners' equity*. Of course it need not be a family-owned company. Partnerships such as law firms are privately held, and the owners' investments are the source of equity capital. Cargill, an agribusiness company, is the largest U.S. privately held company, with revenues in 2010 of more than $108 billion.[2] When a privately held company, including a state-owned enterprise that does not offer stock shares for sale, seeks equity investment, it comes either from the current owners inviting additional private owners to put capital into the company, in exchange for partial ownership, or from the existing owners contributing additional capital from their own sources.[3]

Retained earnings, essentially profits not distributed to owners, are the third source of equity capital. For private companies, revenues in excess of cost may be distributed to the owners as their share of the profits, or they may be reinvested in the company for a variety of purposes, including capital facilities expansion. These *retained* earnings, earnings not paid out to owners but kept in the company for investment, are an important source of finance for capital investment.[4] Retained earnings may also be available to public utilities such as water authorities, but typically they are tightly regulated, or even prohibited. That is, a public water authority is not set up to make a profit, and certainly would not be expected to pay dividends to the owners (citizens). But water rates may be set up to generate revenue in excess of operating and depreciation costs in order to build up a capital reserve that then must be reinvested in the water utility. These *excess* revenues may also be referred to as *retained earnings.*

In some countries, such as the Philippines, a utility may be *owned* by the municipality it serves, and the municipality may expect dividends to be paid back into the municipal treasury. However, that practice in the 1990s almost decapitalized some water utilities because the *parent* municipality took capital out of the enterprise as dividends, capital that should have been retained to replace depreciating and deteriorating facilities.[5] This practice is common in many municipally owned utilities in developing countries. Many U.S. cities also own some of the utilities that provide services to residents, including, for example, electricity and water. However, typically these municipally owned utilities are more tightly regulated and do not subsidize general government operating costs with excess or retained earnings intended for future capital investment in the utility.

All three sources of finance—credit, owners' equity, and retained earnings—are used by public sector institutions to secure the capital needed to finance investments that may be used for rehabilitating aging infrastructure or other facilities or building new capacity in order to meet the needs of a growing population, as discussed in the capital assets chapter. Although debt is by far the most prevalent form of capital financing for public sector institutions, since the 1980s the public sector, both in industrialized countries and in developing nations, has sought private equity investments to help finance infrastructure.

STATE AND LOCAL DEBT FINANCING

State and local governments around the world rely upon debt capital to finance many types of public facilities and infrastructure. In many European countries, borrowing from banks or financing institutions especially created to lend to local governments is the most common means by which local governments secure debt capital. The Bank Nederlandse Gemeenten (Dutch Municipal Bank, BNG) is an example. In the United States, although some local governments borrow from banks for temporary operating funds, the main source of debt financing is the issuance of bonds. Commonly referred to as *municipal bonds,*

bonds are issued by state and local general-purpose jurisdictions as well as many nonprofit public institutions, such as hospitals, and single-service authorities, such as school and water districts. The exemption from federal taxes of the interest earned from many of these bonds, discussed below, is a critical feature of their success and a controversial one.[6]

Types of Bonds

Guaranteed and Non-Guaranteed Bonds

The two main categories of long-term bonds are *full faith and credit bonds* (or *general obligation bonds*) and *non-guaranteed* (or *revenue*) *bonds*. General obligation bonds are generally described as *guaranteed* because they are backed by the full faith and credit of the issuing government. That means that the issuer pledges to repay the debt using its resources (all the assets available to the issuer to satisfy the debt), including the jurisdiction's legal authority to raise taxes if necessary. Non-guaranteed bonds are those that are backed by specifically identified revenue sources and do not have the legal backing of a larger governmental entity with taxing power. If a municipality offers the full faith and credit guarantee, it is obligated to raise taxes or reduce services to pay back the credit. What happens when a municipality refuses to raise taxes or cut services is covered later in the discussion of defaults and bankruptcies.

General obligation (full faith and credit) bonds typically are considered safer investments than non-guaranteed bonds because of the full backing of the jurisdiction's resources. These bonds typically carry lower interest rates than non-guaranteed bonds. The interest rate is critical in large bond issues, for which a difference of 0.1% can affect total interest payments by millions of dollars. However, revenue bonds from a well-managed special-purpose authority, such as a water district, with an excellent record of previous borrowing are likely to have a lower interest rate than a general obligation bond from a municipality with a declining property tax base and low personal income. With states and localities facing much more severe fiscal constraints in the recession of the latter part of the first decade of the 2000s, the difference in rate or yield on general obligation versus revenue bonds started to converge.[7]

Bonds not backed by the general revenue resources of a state or local government have become much more common as special districts such as water and sewer authorities, economic development zones, and so forth have grown in number and size. In addition, state limitations on general tax revenues, such as Proposition 13 in California (see the chapter on transaction-based revenues), have forced state and local governments to favor revenue bonds over general obligation bonds. Such non-guaranteed bonds do not have the full backing of the issuing jurisdiction's resources. Whatever security is offered, such as a pledge of the revenues from the services delivered by the new facility, no other resources are available to the creditor/investor. In that case, if the revenues fail to materialize, then the investor has no recourse to other sources of repayment. For both guaranteed and non-guaranteed bonds, the investor is typically paid, except in the case of default, at a fixed rate of interest, although variable rate bonds also are increasing in frequency.

Revenue bonds are politically easier to issue, for two reasons. First, voter approval is required in almost every jurisdiction to issue a full faith and credit bond, but typically is not required for revenue bond issues. Second, revenue bonds are repaid by the charges made to only those who consume or benefit from the services provided by the debt-financed facility or infrastructure, so taxpayers not using the service are not required to help pay off the debt. As voter approval has become more difficult to achieve, the proportion of revenue bonds versus general obligation bonds has increased.

Non-guaranteed debt is generally repaid from funds restricted to the revenue earnings of the specific facility created by the investment. Many sources are used to repay these so-called non-guaranteed bonds. In the case of revenue bonds, the most common revenue, charges to users, generate the funds necessary to repay the loans. Other sources include special assessments, in which the properties affected by an investment are assessed charges. For example, property owners might be assessed hook-up charges for sewer installations.

Revenue bonds pledging the revenue from a specific tax or fee have the advantage of placing the burden for financing a facility on those who will use it. For example, using the parking fees from a parking garage to finance its construction places the burden on those who park in the garage. From an intergovernmental perspective, the revenue bond device forces nonresidents who use the parking garage or the highways to pay their fair share regardless of where they reside.

Traditionally, municipalities and local utilities issued bonds in a fairly local market with the main purchasers being local or regional banks. Bonds issued were mostly plain vanilla. A general-purpose municipal government or school district almost always issued a general obligation bond, backed by the jurisdiction, mainly by property tax proceeds. Water and other utilities issued non-guaranteed revenue bonds backed by the future revenue streams from user charges. In recent times, these conditions have changed radically. The number of different instruments for debt, while still falling within the two general categories, has increased dramatically, and banks are no longer the largest holders of municipal debt. In addition, in the electronic age, information about municipal debt issues is widely available across the country, and for that matter across the world. Large bond issues may be purchased by institutional investors who are remote from the issuing jurisdiction.

Table 14–1 shows the composition of holders of outstanding municipal debt from 1996 through 2010. Individuals held between 33% and 39% of total municipal debt during that time period. On the other hand, banking institutions held less than 10% for the same time period. This is in striking contrast to the history of municipal debt purchasers. In 1985, commercial banks held 27% of the total outstanding municipal securities. Property and casualty insurance companies also began to purchase more municipal bonds in the 1990s to diversify their investment portfolios. Mutual funds and money market funds have invested more heavily in municipal bonds too. In 2005, mutual funds and money market funds held approximately 14% and 15%, respectively, of the total outstanding municipal debt.[8] Available comparable data for Table 14–1 combines mutual and money market funds. Many of the investors in these funds are also individuals, through their pension programs or their own individual investments. If we could separate out the individual from the institutional investors in these mutual funds, the role of the individual investor in Table 14–1 would be still more prominent.

Municipal bonds are debt instruments in that the issuer incurs an obligation to repay and the buyer becomes a lender with a claim on future repayments. The buyer, however,

Table 14–1 Holders of Municipal Debt: 1996–2010 (Billions of Dollars)

	Individuals	Mutual Funds[1]	Banking Institutions[2]	Insurance Companies[3]	Other[4]	Total
1996	493	417	107	189	56	1,262
1998	499	496	120	227	61	1,403
2000	531	541	129	203	77	1,481
2002	678	642	149	203	91	1,763
2004	742	697	180	298	113	2,031
2006	872	804	242	372	113	2,403
2008	904	964	263	429	120	2,680
2010	1,090	949	297	461	131	2,928

[1] Includes mutual funds, money market funds, close-end funds, and exchange traded funds.
[2] Includes commercial banks, savings institutions, and brokers and dealers.
[3] Includes property-casualty and life insurance companies.
[4] Includes nonfinancial corporate business, nonfarm noncorporate business, state and local governments and retirement funds, government-sponsored enterprises, and foreign holders.

Source: Securities Industry and Financial Markets Association (2011). *Holders of U.S. municipal securities.* Retrieved November 7, 2011, from http://www.sifma.org/research/statistics.aspx.

---

has no direct claim on the assets of the issuer. Equity ownership, such as is purchased with corporate stocks, is not a feature of municipal bonds. Private equity ownership is a feature of build-operate-transfer and build-operate-own forms of private financing of public infrastructure facilities as discussed later in this chapter, but the main form of state and local capital financing is likely to continue to be issuance of municipal bonds, followed by borrowing from special-purpose infrastructure banks. More than 30 states now have some kind of special-purpose infrastructure bank (these will be discussed in more detail later in the chapter).

In most industrialized European economies, the banking sector is the primary source of finance to subnational governments. In some countries, municipally owned banks, such as the BNG in the Netherlands, in addition to managing the accounts and financial transactions of owner municipalities, lend long term to municipalities. In other countries, commercial and investment banks are the primary lenders. In still other European countries, specialized financing institutions somewhat similar to U.S. state revolving loan funds, and infrastructure banks have been established to provide credit to municipalities. In many emerging market countries, such as Brazil and Poland, municipalities have emerged as good credit risks, and a variety of credit systems have developed or are developing, including bond markets, specialized financing institutions, and direct lending from commercial and investment banks.[9]

Importance of Bond Financing for Infrastructure

Debt Financing Versus Pay-as-You-Go

State and local governments finance a major portion of their capital investment spending through long-term debt instruments. In 2010, state and local governments including

Table 14–2 New Bond Issues by Issuer and Type of Issue: Selected Years 1990–2010 (Billions of Dollars)

Issuer	1990	1995	2000	2005	2010
State	15.0	14.7	19.9	31.6	55.5
Special Districts, incl. School Districts	75.9	93.5	121.2	297.0	292.9
Municipality, County, or Township	32.0	37.5	39.3	80.9	86.2
Type of Issue					
General Obligation	39.5	57.0	64.5	146.2	150.6
Revenue	83.3	88.7	115.9	263.3	283.9

Source: Abstracted from Bureau of the Census, U.S. Department of Commerce (2012). *Statistical abstract of the United States: 2012* (p. 276). Washington, DC: U.S. Government Printing Office.

special districts issued $435 billion in new long-term debt. Of that amount, $150.6 billion was in the form of general obligation bonds and $283.9 billion took the form of revenue bonds.[10] **Table 14–2** illustrates the trend in issuers and type of issues since 1990. States have remained about the same, issuing about 11% of all new municipal debt. General-purpose local governments (municipalities, counties, townships), on the other hand, have declined in terms of total debt issued, with special districts such as water and sewer authorities and school districts having increased from about 62% to about 67% of all new issues. General obligation bonds during that period accounted for about one-third of all debt issues, whereas revenue bonds, at two-thirds of all issues, reflect the trends of the past 30 years for revenue bonds to dominate the issuance market.

Most state constitutions or statutes limit the issuance of long-term debt for both state and local governments to capital investment–type expenditures. Some local governments try to avoid indebtedness as much as possible and work on a pay-as-you-go system. That means saving funds in advance until there is cash sufficient to build the infrastructure facility. These governments are like the car buyers who save money until they have enough funds in the bank to purchase their cars for cash. The motivations are similar: both the government and the consumer avoid the interest costs for borrowing. If the jurisdiction can afford to wait for the facility or can plan far enough in advance to have the funds available when needed, then the prospect of financing without interest costs is attractive. Indeed, as the government is saving funds, it can invest them in interest-earning opportunities, which are becoming increasingly sophisticated for government investors.

Pay-as-you-go local governments tend to be smaller jurisdictions with relatively stable annual capital investment requirements. For example, if a small local government generally needs to spend about $500,000 per year on capital facilities and goods and that figure is not expected to change much from year to year, over time it will need to spend that same amount, plus interest, each year in debt repayment if it borrows for the capital facilities. So if the jurisdiction can plan far enough ahead or can afford to wait for the facility, by establishing a capital investment sinking fund it can accumulate the funds necessary to meet the annual $500,000 per year capital spending requirement. Future citizens of the jurisdiction will then benefit from the services and will not have to pay for the capital costs. That, of course, means that current residents/taxpayers of the jurisdiction are paying for the benefits enjoyed by others in the future.

Utilities that operate on a more or less commercial basis—capital and operating costs are financed by fees charged the users of the service—typically include a sufficient depreciation cost in the user charges to accumulate amounts to pay for rehabilitation expenses as the infrastructure wears out. But these utilities, unless small, still require large capital infusions when a major expansion or a major technology change is needed, such as shifting to a more efficient and environmentally friendly energy source. These capital infusions will most likely be through bond issues.

The pay-as-you-go approach does not work as well for larger jurisdictions, which tend to have less predictable requirements, and it does not work well for lumpy investment patterns where large amounts are needed in some years for big construction projects and smaller amounts in other years. Pay-as-you-go is also a problem during sustained periods of fiscal distress. In those times, saving for investment or even investment itself often is sacrificed to make up for declining tax revenues.[11] Some form of credit financing for most state and local jurisdictions is a necessity, especially in rapidly growing areas where, regardless of size, pay-as-you-go financing cannot keep up with population growth and service demands.[12]

Role of the Tax System and State and Local Bond Financing

A key reason for the attractiveness of bond financing for state and local government capital borrowing is that federal tax law allows deduction from the taxpayer's gross income of interest earned on many government bonds. In addition, most states with income taxes exempt interest earnings from state or local bonds for government entities within that state. Thus an individual who purchases state or local bonds retains the interest earnings tax-free in most cases, subject to alternative minimum tax limitations and a few other special cases. For individuals in the highest tax bracket, earning 6% interest on a municipal bond is equal to earning more than 9% taxable interest. If the investor purchases in-state bond issues, then for most states the interest earned is exempt from state taxes as well. Only Illinois, Iowa, Kansas, and Wisconsin do not exempt all interest earned on bonds issued by qualifying government jurisdictions in their states.[13]

Because the tax exemption for interest earnings attracts investors to the state and local bond market, a ready source of capital for infrastructure financing exists for government. The tax-exempt status of the earnings also enables jurisdictions to offer bonds at lower interest rates than they could get by borrowing from commercial lenders or issuing taxable debt securities. Tax exemption for the interest earnings on bonds, then, is the cornerstone of the U.S. system for financing public infrastructure for state and local governments. **Exhibit 14–1** illustrates the value to the investor of federal tax exemption.

Municipal bonds' tax-exempt status is somewhat controversial, however. A wave of expansion in the use of tax-exempt bonds to finance industrial development parks, incubator facilities to woo private developers to invest in local areas, and a wide variety of other essentially private endeavors led to significant curbs on state and local governments' authority to issue tax-exempt bonds in the Tax Reform Act of 1986 (TRA86). Private-purpose bonds are discussed in more detail in a following section. Other features of that tax reform also

Exhibit 14–1 Federal Tax Exemption for Municipal Bond Yields

Municipal bonds are attractive to investors in part because the earnings to the investor on the bond are exempt from federal income taxes. The wealthier the taxpayer, the more valuable the exemption is because wealthier taxpayers generally pay a higher marginal tax rate on their income. In that sense, the tax exemption on municipal bonds is a regressive feature in the federal income tax.

Arguments against this tax exemption are its regressive nature, which favors wealthier taxpayers, and the lost federal revenue that must be made up for in the form of either other taxes or higher marginal rates on the individual income tax. Arguments in favor of this exemption are that it enables badly needed public sector infrastructure to be constructed at a lower cost, and that lower cost is of greater benefit to lower-income individuals. That is because the amount lower-income people would otherwise spend on public utilities such as water and sewer would be a higher proportion of their income than it would be for wealthier households.

The table below illustrates the tax advantage, using as an example a married couple filing a joint return. For each marginal rate in the 2011 federal income tax, the cells in the table show the return (yield) the couple would have to achieve in a taxable bond to be equivalent to the value of the tax-exempt bond. The table does not take into account state taxes. Municipal bonds issued by entities in one's state of residence (state in which one files state taxes) are also exempt from state individual income taxes in almost every state with an individual income tax.

Value to Taxpayer of Federal Income Tax Exemption on Municipal Bond Yields

Marginal Tax Rate, Married Joint Return	Tax-Exempt Yield	3.00%	3.50%	4.00%	4.50%	5.00%	5.50%	6.00%
10%		3.33%	3.89%	4.44%	5.00%	5.56%	6.11%	6.67%
15%		3.53	4.12	4.71	5.29	5.88	6.47	7.06
25%		4.00	4.67	5.33	6.00	6.67	7.33	8.00
28%		4.17	4.86	5.56	6.25	6.94	7.64	8.33
33%		4.48	5.22	5.97	6.72	7.46	8.21	8.96
35%		4.62	5.38	6.15	6.92	7.96	8.46	9.23

made municipal bonds a much less attractive investment for commercial banks, accounting in part for the trend noted in Table 14–1.[14]

The securities industry clearly recognizes that there is a strong individual/household appetite for municipal bonds, as evidenced by the increasing availability of bonds as part of money market and mutual funds as well as the creation of tax-exempt bond funds. Concern for equity in taxation leads some to question whether interest on government and certain nonprofit bonds should be exempt. It is generally thought that mostly higher-income taxpayers benefit from this exemption, as they are the most likely purchasers of tax-exempt bonds and, therefore, that this exemption unfairly benefits those who can most afford to pay higher taxes. The illustration in Exhibit 14–1 seems to bear this out, at least in terms of the increasing value of the tax exemption as the marginal tax rate increases. However, the growth of mutual funds in which middle-class individuals are making more investments is mitigating this equity argument.

If and when efforts to reduce federal debt, or slow its growth, are successful, this will lead to renewed challenges to the tax exemption for interest on municipal bonds. The National Commission on Fiscal Responsibility in 2010 recommended the elimination of interest exemption for municipal debt.[15] The Obama administration in 2011 made elimination of part of the tax exemption for higher-income taxpayers one of the revenue components of a proposed jobs program.[16]

It is likely that challenges to this tax exemption will continue during serious budget deficit conditions, but unless it is replaced by other mechanisms that are equal to the challenge of financing trillions of dollars in infrastructure, it is unlikely that this fundamental feature of state and local finance in the United States will go away. At the same time, it is likely that the federal government will continue to increase regulations regarding the issuance of tax-exempt bonds in order to restrict the tax favorability to the essential purposes of financing public infrastructure. The State of South Carolina challenged the constitutionality of any federal regulation of state governments' tax-exempt debt issuance in the 1988 *South Carolina* v. *Baker* case, questioning a law that denied tax-exempt status to bearer bonds (as opposed to registered bonds; see the discussion of bond features later in this chapter).[17] The Supreme Court ruled that the Tenth Amendment did not prohibit federal regulation of state and local governments and that there is no constitutional right to state and local immunity from federal tax provisions.[18]

Nontraditional Bond Financing

Securitizing Future Revenue Streams

Securitizing the future revenue stream from some activity or of a set of receivables was an innovation in the private sector introduced in the 1980s. For example, credit card companies often issue a bond or borrow against the stream of receivables that will be flowing in from credit card users. The card company gets immediate revenue instead of waiting for the stream of repayments. This technique is called securitization because the credit card company issues a security (a bond) against the future payments that are already known because the credit card holders have already incurred the debt. Or the securitization may involve a known value for the revenue stream such as outstanding credit card debt, plus estimated additional payments for credit card debt not yet incurred. On a larger scale, banks and housing finance companies may package a group of mortgages and issue a security (a bond) that is repaid by the known stream of revenues from those future mortgage payments. It is somewhat similar to a revenue bond, except that a revenue bond is issued against future revenues that are expected and estimated.

Securitization involves a stream of payments that already are legal commitments, commitments by the credit card holder for charges already made on the card, or for mortgages already held by the institution securitizing that revenue stream. Any assured, meaning legally obligated, revenue stream that will accrue to the issuer over future years is susceptible to securitization. Securitization may involve different risks than straight revenue bonds and, therefore, may be priced higher if considered by the market as riskier investments. Or if the revenue stream is clearly known, that security may be considered less risky than a partly speculative future revenue stream. There are likely to be regulatory challenges to more esoteric forms of securitization, such as the practice of selling pieces of revenue streams to different investors in a fashion that the underlying security, such as individual mortgages, can no longer be connected to the asset (revenue stream) purchased by an investor (see the chapter on government and the economy).

An example of the use of a securitized revenue stream is a proposal for Brazil to use securitization—asset-backed securities—to finance part of the infrastructure requirements for the 2016 Summer Olympics. Brazil already has market experience in securitizing revenue streams from investment funds such as Fundo de Investimento em Direitos Creditórios, or FIDC.[19]

Because of the turmoil in the financial markets that erupted in 2007, the Securities and Exchange Commission issued new regulations in 2011 to strengthen the disclosure requirements for issuers of asset-backed securities. Some of these regulations apply to issuers of municipal asset-backed securities, though implementation for municipal issuers was delayed until 2014.[20]

Bonds issued against pools of tax liens also became popular in the late 1990s. New Jersey, Florida, and Connecticut have used this as an alternative to directly foreclosing on properties against which tax liens have been issued. Governments holding the liens capitalize on the value of those liens immediately, with the market issuer acquiring the value of the liens.[21]

A somewhat unusual revenue stream available to many states and some large cities were the proceeds from successful suits against tobacco companies. New York City issued a $709 million bond in 1999 that entitled the purchasers of the bond to the proceeds the city received under the tobacco litigation settlement funds.[22] The tobacco settlement funds are payments to states from large tobacco companies as settlement for a class action suit filed by more than 40 states to recover the costs the states were incurring for health care for illnesses and chronic conditions attributable to tobacco usage. In 1998, after a few states had won suits in court, the large tobacco companies reached a settlement with the entire class of states. That settlement assured states of a particular revenue stream into the future, and in turn that future revenue set off several securitization deals, such as New York's. California, in 2005, executed a major securitization deal of its tobacco settlement funds to help manage its significant state revenue problems.[23] Illinois successfully issued, in 2010, even in the midst of turmoil in the asset-backed securities market, a $1.5 billion securitized asset based on payments from the tobacco settlement.[24]

Airport Passenger Facility Charges

An invention in the 1990s to finance airport facilities—the pledge of specific charges for use of the airport facility collected from the airlines through increments to ticket prices—is an example of the increasingly innovative ways to use pledged revenue to finance facilities.

Airport operators (special authorities, municipalities that own the airport) apply to the Federal Aviation Administration to add a few dollars to the price of the tickets of passengers departing from or terminating their flights at the airport. Cleveland, as the owner of the Cleveland Hopkins International Airport, issued in 2011 a $75 million bond based on passenger facility charges.[25] Broward County, Florida, added another wrinkle to the passenger facility charge instrument. In 1998 and 2001, the airport issued bonds totaling more than $150 million secured by passenger facility charges. These were charges added to the price of tickets of passengers emplaning or deplaning at the airport, estimated at a cost of just over $5 per passenger. In 2012, the pledged security for the bonds will shift from the passenger facility charge to a lien on total airport system revenues until maturity in 2023. This so-called convertible lien bond device gives added security to the investors, thus presumably lowering the interest rate, and it may enable the airport to reduce the passenger facility charge later if the finances of the airport authority are sound.[26] However, plans to incur additional debt for airport runway expansion in 2012 caused the rating service Fitch to downgrade the passenger facility charge–based bonds from "A" to "A–" (see discussion on bond ratings and rating services later in this chapter).[27]

Tax Increment Financing Bonds

Tax increment bonds combine features of revenue bonds and general obligation bonds.[28] They are used to finance local economic development by pledging future increases in property taxes of areas targeted for development or redevelopment. A city may decide to redevelop an area of the inner city through construction of housing or commercial facilities and may issue a bond to finance that redevelopment. Because the redevelopment will not directly generate revenues, it is not suitable for revenue bond financing. At the same time, the city may not wish to obligate its full resources to repay the bonds, may be at state debt-limit ceilings for full faith and credit bonds, or may wish to confine the repayment obligations to the direct beneficiaries of the redevelopment. A tax increment financing bond will back up the debt issue with the pledge of increased property tax revenue from the area being developed (the property taxes will rise because the property in the redevelopment area will become more valuable).[29]

Private-Purpose Bonds

Starting in the early 1980s, considerable use was made of state and local bonds to finance private construction and ownership of facilities that were then leased back to government entities. Similar use has been made of government bonds for lease and subsequent purchase of privately constructed facilities. In some cases, government bonds have been issued to finance a facility that then is leased to or purchased by the private sector.[30] This last device has often been used to finance industrial development facilities, such as industrial parks and incubator facilities to help small businesses get started. State or local bonds issued for these largely private purposes were quite popular because the interest on the bonds was tax exempt. In 1985, more than half of a record volume in municipal debt issues involved these private-purpose activities.[31]

Pressure for reform arose amid concerns that the intention behind the tax exemption—to assist state and local governments and other eligible entities to build infrastructure for public benefit—was being diverted to benefiting private parties. The Tax Reform Act of

1986 (TRA86) contained several provisions to limit tax exemptions. Interest earned on general-purpose bonds for construction of facilities or infrastructure to provide essential services remains tax exempt. Private activity bonds for construction of facilities such as airports, docks and wharves, hazardous waste treatment plants, and water supply facilities also retain their tax-exempt status, although interest is included in the alternative minimum tax base. But the law created a distinction between *public-purpose* and *private-purpose* bonds. Unless specifically exempted under requirements spelled out in the law, the act removed the tax-exempt status of bonds for construction of industrial parks, parking garages, sports facilities, and convention or trade show facilities. In addition, each state and its local governments are limited in the amount of private-purpose bonds that can be issued in a year, and interest on any otherwise qualified bond issue is subject to tax if the bond issue exceeds the state cap.[32]

Since 1986 and the loss of the tax exemption to the investor, the issuance of private-purpose bonds has declined. States, however, continue to issue private-purpose bonds to finance facilities tied to economic development promotion, such as industrial parks and research facilities. These governments consider the economic development benefit to be worth the higher-cost, taxable bond.

Tax Credit Bonds

The U.S. municipal bond market has changed in important ways since the introduction of a variety of federal programs featuring tax credits instead of tax exemption to attract investors. **Exhibit 14–2** discusses tax credit bonds as an alternative to federal tax exemption on municipal bond interest earnings.

Exhibit 14–2 Tax Credit Bonds: An Alternative to Federal Tax Exemption on Municipal Bond Interest Earnings

Tax credit bonds are debt instruments that instead of paying the purchaser interest payments on the bond, allow the investor to subtract the equivalent of interest from the investor's federal income tax liability.[1]

Although considered several times in the 1960s and later, more serious attention was given in the late 1990s and the 2000s. A small pilot program for tax credit bonds was authorized in 1997 as an experiment for school construction. In 2000, it was proposed, unsuccessfully, as a feature of the administration's $25 billion school modernization program. The reauthorization of the Transportation Equity Act in 2003 considered tax credit bonds to finance transportation projects.

The concept of a tax credit bond is to deliver more federal support to infrastructure programs. A tax credit to the investor is worth three to four times more than the exemption of interest earnings because the tax credit directly reduces the tax liability of the taxpayer. The interest exemption reduces only taxable income. Of course the cost of the additional benefit to the investor and to the additional infrastructure that might be built would be borne directly by the federal government in the form of reduced income tax revenue.

(continued)

The first major tax credit bond programs were introduced to support school construction in distressed areas and a variety of environmental and clean energy programs. Qualified Zone Academy Bonds (QZABs) were established by the Taxpayer Relief Act of 1997 to support school construction.[2] Clean Renewable Energy Bonds (CREBs) and Forestry Conservation Bonds (FCBs) were authorized respectively in 2005 and 2008.[3] The Gulf Tax Credit Bonds (GTCB), established by the Gulf Opportunity Zone Act of 2005, served a different purpose.[4] States and cities devastated by Hurricanes Katrina and Rita needed help to finance the massive infrastructure replacement and rehabilitation investments resulting from the hurricanes. GTCBs assisted those entities with refinancing existing government debt. Exhibit 14–5 later in this chapter is a copy of part of the offer sheet for one of the bonds issued under the GTCB program.

The effects of the recession that were already being felt in 2007 have been the target of several new tax credit programs, in addition to stimulating the renewal of some of the initial four programs. Stimulus programs include Build America Tax Credit Bonds (BABs), Qualified School Construction Bonds (QSCBs), and Recovery Zone Investment Bonds (RZIBs), authorized by the American Recovery and Reinvestment Act of 2009.[5] The 2010 Hiring Incentives to Restore Employment Act subsidizes the interest cost of the issuer, as do the Build America Bonds, rather than going directly to the investor as a credit against federal tax liability.[6] The credit goes instead to the issuer. Up to 35% of the interest the issuers pay to investors is reimbursed by the federal government, thus reducing the financing cost to the issuer and reducing the purchase price to the investor. The interest on these bonds is taxable to the investor; the advantage to the investor is the purchase of a long-term, low-risk security at an attractive yield. There are both taxable and tax credit Build America Bonds. For the former, the issuer's interest costs are subsidized.[7]

Each program has its own unique features. Most of the programs described here authorize a fixed amount for tax credit or interest subsidy; once exhausted, the subsidy or the credit is no longer available unless subsequent congressional action authorizes more. In contrast, the Build America Bonds had no limit on the amount of the bonds that could be issued. Instead, the program was limited to bonds issued in 2009 and 2010.[8] For the federal government, the cost of the interest subsidy is the same as the cost of the foregone revenue from exempting from taxation the bond interest payments.

The increasing variety of programs that include a mix of tax credits to investors and interest subsidies to issuers do reduce the cost to governmental and some nongovernmental entities to invest in infrastructure for many public purposes. At the same time, they complicate the budgetary decision-making process. The traditional tax exemption of interest on municipal bonds is a *tax expenditure*. The federal government (and state governments where the interest is tax deductible) forgoes revenue equivalent to the tax that would otherwise have been due on income earned by the investor. Tax credits provided directly to investors do not reduce the amount of taxable income, but instead directly reduce tax liability. The amount of the tax credits also is revenue forgone. Thus, tax credits disguise the implicit subsidy in that it involves forgone revenues (tax expenditures) rather than more visible direct federal appropriations.[9]

1. Maguire, S. (2008). *Tax credit bonds: A brief explanation*. Washington, DC: Congressional Research Service. Provides a useful overview of the first four major tax credit bond programs.
2. P.L. 105-34.
3. P.L. 109-58 and P.L. 110-234.
4. P.L. 109-58.
5. P.L. 111-5.
6. P.L. 111-147.
7. Markus, M. (2009). *Overview of tax credit bonds*. New York, NY: Goldman Sachs. Retrieved November 5, 2011, from http://www.nast.org/2009TreasuryMgmt/Files/WED%20 MarvinMarkus.pdf.
8. Government Finance Officers Association (2010). *Issue update: taxable tax-credit bonds programs*. Retrieved November 5, 2011, from http://www.gfoa.org/downloads/taxcreditbonds.pdf.
9. U.S. Congressional Budget Office (2004). *Tax-credit bonds and the federal cost of financing public expenditures* (p. 6). Washington, DC: U.S. Government Printing Office.

Municipal Minibonds

Most purchasers of municipal bonds are large purchase investors, including financial institutions that develop tax-exempt investment funds that may then be purchased by both large and small investors. Generally it has been more difficult for all but higher-income individuals to get directly involved in purchasing bonds from their own jurisdictions because purchases often involve minimum amounts of $1,000 to $10,000 or more. Mutual funds consisting entirely of municipal bonds have brought them in reach of more investors as smaller investments may be made in these mutual funds. However, tax exemption of the earnings on these mutual funds is tricky.

Some cities have issued bonds in smaller denominations. Denver, Colorado, was one of the first issuers of *minibonds*, a $5.9 million issue in $1,000 denomination bonds in 1990.[33] The minibonds were issued directly by the city without an underwriter (see the discussion later on bond issuance), and purchase was possible only by Colorado residents. Almost 2,000 citizens purchased more than twice the amount initially expected.

While not appropriate for large-scale bond issues because it becomes uneconomical to sell and track bonds in small denominations, minibonds have proved popular for financing smaller projects that especially interest local residents. Bond issues that combine both large denomination and small denomination (mini) bonds attract different kinds of investors. A 2011 California statute authorized the sale of minibonds by lowering the statutory minimum for any government bond issue from $1,000 to $25.[34] Minibonds do not make an impact in the overall size of the municipal bond market, but they do open the door to more widespread participation, and though there is no empirical evidence to support the argument, they may have some effect on borrowing costs by introducing more competition in the investor community.[35]

Certificates of Participation

One form of municipal issuance is the use of certificates of participation (COPs). A municipality may issue a bond for the construction of a revenue-generating facility, such as a parking garage or a utility within that municipality. The issuing jurisdiction leases the facility for a specified period and sells certificates of participation to investors in the lease revenues. The investors may defer receiving their share of the lease revenues or may receive them periodically during the lease. The investors in the COPs have a legal interest in the lease facility in the event of a default. At the end of the lease period, the bond has been retired through the lease payments, investors have been paid off, and the facility belongs to the issuing jurisdiction. COPs became especially popular in California after Proposition 13 placed severe restrictions on the ability of local governments to borrow. COPs have the same legal status as revenue bonds as far as legal limitations on borrowing. COPs can be risky investments.

The Richmond County Unified School District, California, and Brevard County, Florida, provide two examples in which the governmental entity was financially unable to make the lease payments (California) and unwilling to make payments (Florida), for a time, because of dissatisfaction with the facility.[36] Richmond County Unified School District subsequently defaulted on the lease payments due on the facility built via the certificates of participation debt issue.

E-Trading Municipal Bonds

Just as online trading in the private sector has become a common practice, so securities dealers offer information about municipal bonds and offer the bonds for sale online. Issuance costs have come down somewhat compared with trading through securities dealers. Purchasing municipal bonds online is as commonplace as any other online investing. Of equal or perhaps greater importance to actually purchasing is access to online information for individual investors about possible bond investments that are then purchased either online or through regular securities dealer channels, or sometimes directly from the underwriter. Information readily available online includes trading prices and detailed information on the issuers, for both original issues and previously issued bonds offered on the secondary market. Municipal bonds of one variety or another are now as accessible an investment choice to investors as any other security. This is a far cry from the days when most municipal bonds were issued locally or regionally and known only to local or regional investors.

Bond Banks, State Revolving Funds, and Other Intermediaries

Large city and state governments, unless there are underlying problems with the jurisdictions' financial status, generally have ready access to the U.S. capital markets to issue their own bonds. However, smaller cities and municipalities, and many municipalities in developing countries where there is only a limited market in fixed-income securities, and generally no track record for municipal debt, have greater difficulty issuing debt at competitive prices. Several institutional structures are prevalent, and have been for decades, in the United States and industrialized Europe to assist smaller governments. Some of these structures have become popular in developing country public finance. The most common forms are revolving loan funds and bond banks or infrastructure banks. Several actions contributed to the invention of and growth in state revolving loan funds and bond banks in the United States. The Safe Drinking Water Act of 1974 contained provisions for the

Environmental Protection Agency to provide financial assistance to states to set up drinking water revolving funds.[37] A revolving fund is created with some initial capitalization, often grants from the federal government plus state government bond issues, to lend to municipal borrowers. The premise is that the state government can get better credit ratings both because it is in better financial condition and because it can issue debt in larger amounts than individual small local governments. Repayments from the local governments that borrow from the fund keep the capitalization intact, allowing lending and borrowing to continue on a revolving basis.

The original stimulus for many of these funds was federal environmental funding programs for water and sewerage systems. One of the model state revolving loan funds created initially with federal environmental grants is the New York State Environmental Facilities Corporation (EFC). The New York EFC is a state corporation financially independent from the state government. Its transactions are not backed by state budget authority. It operates several state revolving loan funds, the largest of which is the Clean Water State Revolving Fund, which as of 2011 had lent approximately $14 billion since its inception in 1990. Total debt outstanding for 2011 was near $7 billion, most of which was in the Clean Water Fund.[38]

Similar to the New York State facility are state bond banks or state infrastructure banks. The state bond bank may pool the borrowing needs of numerous, smaller municipal borrowers into a single state bond issue, and then finance the individual borrower's requirements from the proceeds of the single state issue. Some state bond banks issue bonds to capitalize a fund for lending, which then is a form of revolving fund. Others accumulate individual municipalities' borrowing needs until a sufficiently large amount is reached and then issue a single bond to meet those specific needs. Generally for the smaller municipal borrowers, bond banks reduce the cost of issuance.

Most state infrastructure banks were stimulated and continue to be assisted by federal programs, particularly federal transportation funding acts beginning in 1995.[39] Many of the state revolving funds and bond banks in earlier years financed federally mandated water and sewer system improvements, but since the 1990s, the main infrastructure funding through these banks has been for transportation. The original 1995 federal legislation—the National Highway System Designation Act—created a pilot program to provide federal grant funding to capitalize *state infrastructure banks* (SIBs) to finance transportation projects. Initially, 10 pilot states were authorized, but the program was later extended to all states. Subsequent reauthorizations of the Transportation Equity Act of 1998 (TEA-21) and the Safe, Accountable, Flexible, Efficient Transportation Equity Act: A Legacy for Users of 2005 (SAFETEA-LU) extended a variety of financing tools, including continued support to the SIBs.[40] Thirty-three states and Puerto Rico have some form of SIB. Two—Kansas and Georgia—are capitalized exclusively by state funds, and three—Florida, Ohio, and Pennsylvania—have separate facilities within the SIB for state and federal sources of capital.[41]

Revolving loan funds and special-purpose municipal lending institutions have been popular means in some developing countries to allow local governments access to debt financing. Beginning in the early 1980s, many developing countries began to decentralize authority and responsibility for many public services from the national to subnational governments. Along with the shift in authority and responsibility, provinces, cities, and towns were given some authority to levy user charges and raise taxes, usually accompanied by significant intergovernmental revenue transfers. To facilitate these newly more autonomous subnational jurisdictions financing capital projects, various types of lending facilities were created.

Indonesia established in 1987 the Regional Development Account (RDA), an authority within the Ministry of Finance, to make loans on a long-term basis to local authorities, primarily water authorities. Colombia established the Financiera de Desarollo Territorial (FINDETER) in 1989. Unlike Indonesia's RDA that was established as a separate account within the Ministry of Finance, FINDETER is an autonomous financial institution owned by the Ministry of Finance and regional governments. It operates as a regulated state-owned financial intermediary, channeling various sources of capital organized by the central government to local governments through loans. One study found that more than 60 financial intermediaries had been established in the 1980s and 1990s to facilitate subnational governments' access to credit in developing countries.[42]

Problems with repayment rates, the inability to move most of such institutions into lending at market competitive rates, and the overall growth of capital markets in the more advanced developing countries led, after the mid-1990s, to a de-emphasis on such financial intermediaries. The favored approach consists of governance and finance reforms that enable local governments to access credit markets through borrowing from banks and issuing municipal bonds.[43]

Overall, the use of bonds to finance state and local investments, both in the United States and in other countries, continues to increase as state and local financial conditions improve and federal transfers to assist state and local governments decrease. The recession that started in 2007 interrupted what had been a more general pattern of improvement in state and local financial conditions, and federal grants to state and local governments in several programs to combat the recession temporarily increased (see the chapters on government and the economy and intergovernmental relations). The distinction between general obligation bonds and limited revenue bonds is less important in practice than the financial condition of the borrowing entity. In fact, many water utilities and other users of more limited revenue bonds are in better financial shape than states and general-purpose local governments. All 50 states have some form of bond bank or revolving loan program.

Bond Issuance Process

The process of issuing municipal bonds involves numerous steps, and the number of participants in these steps is quite large.[44] **Exhibit 14–3** lists the major participants, ignoring some of the minor players (for example, bond printers). More detail on the main actors in the bond issuance process is included in the subsections on the major steps.

Bond Issuance Costs

With so many steps and participants in the process, the costs to the issuing jurisdiction can be high. Numerous legal steps must be followed, numerous documents must be prepared,

Exhibit 14–3 Participants in the Municipal Bond Market

Issuers: General-purpose municipalities, counties, and states; special-purpose governmental entities such as school districts and water authorities; and unique public service entities such as airports and transportation terminals.

Financial Advisers: Finance specialists increasingly used by bond issuers to structure features of the issue to increase attractiveness to borrowers and/or to address a special need of the issuer—features such as issuer options to call the bond before maturity and structuring debt retirement to match cash flow circumstances of the issuer.

Bond Counsel: Legal advisors to offer legal opinion on the legal authority of the issuer to borrow, on the tax-exempt status of the issue, and the legal obligation of the issuer to repay.

Dealers (Underwriters): Investment firms, banks, and other financial institutions licensed to trade in municipal securities who sell the issuers' bonds.

Trustee: Institution that serves mainly bondholders by securing from the issuers bond repayment cash flows and paying out to bondholders when due.

Investors: Individuals, investment banks, commercial banks, and other financial institutions.

and numerous transactions with various financial and legal institutions must occur. These transactions require considerable personnel time or the purchase of consulting services. Overall municipal issuance costs average just about 0.6%.[45] Total costs for these transactions have varied widely, from less than 0.3% (District of Columbia) to as much as 1.3% (Alaska). Mississippi analyzed bond issuance costs and found for state and local issues in 2000 an average issuance cost of just over 0.5%, but the issuance costs varied widely, with the most expensive one being more than 1.1% of the issue. The low was 0.3%.[46] Costs vary by issue based on characteristics of the issue itself—size, complexity, the issuer (financial condition, experience with previous debt issues), market conditions, and general familiarity of investors with the issuer.[47] Variations by state are affected by state policies, the general economic climate, experience with defaults or other financial troubles, and, of course, market conditions. Intense political factionalism and high turnover of elected public officials have been found to increase the borrowing costs of affected jurisdictions as investors apparently worry about the stability over time of policy decisions that may affect the issuer's financial viability.[48]

Issuers typically either secure the services of an underwriter to sell the issue or sell the bonds themselves while relying on a financial advisory service for assistance. Underwriting fees range from 0.5% to 0.75% added to the borrowing cost (usually referred to as 50 to 75 basis points, 100 basis points being equal to 1%).[49] The percentages generally are higher for smaller issues, because some of the costs are relatively fixed. Issuance costs have been declining as the market grows and becomes more competitive.

Voter Approval

In most states, a general obligation (full faith and credit) bond requires a referendum to secure voter approval. Revenue bonds and other forms of limited obligation financing generally do not require voter approval. In some cases, to avoid state limitations on general municipal borrowing, cities have established nonprofit building authorities to issue bonds and construct facilities. Such facilities are then rented to the municipality, and the rental payments secure the bond principal and interest. These special authorities, because they do not legally obligate in a direct way the general revenues of the municipality, can issue bonds without voter approval and without the debt counting as part of the municipality's overall debt. Of course, the source of funds used by the municipality to pay for renting the facility is, in fact, the general revenue fund.

Voters approve far more bond issues than they reject. In the 2011 general elections across all states, voters approved about two-thirds of the total value of all bond issues, or about $10.5 billion out of $16.5 billion.[50] This approval rate, following on several years of recession, is down considerably from historical averages. Since 1977, the average voter approval by value of the bonds is 84%.[51]

Underwriting

Typically, the authority issuing a bond will secure the services of an underwriter, whose role is to arrange the actual sale of bonds to financial institutions. The underwriter for a small issue may well be a local bank or a major regional bank. Such firms as Goldman Sachs, Merrill Lynch, Morgan Stanley Smith Barney, Citigroup, and other investment bankers and securities dealers typically handle major issues that are marketed nationally (and internationally). Individuals, banks, insurance companies, and mutual and money market funds invest in state and local bonds, as shown in Table 14–1.

Most issuers, except those with strong market recognition themselves, such as major cities, rely upon an underwriter. Underwriters have client lists and access to a wide range of investors, and typically are able to sell a borrower's bond issue more quickly than the borrower. The underwriter collects the fee from the issuer by discounting back to the issuer the value of the bonds. For example, an underwriter on a $100 million bond issue, charging 50 basis points as the underwriting fee, will actually pay to the issuer $99.5 million. The underwriter then *owns* the issue. If the market responds favorably to the bond issue, the underwriter may earn more than the 50 basis points or, in this example, $500,000. But if the underwriter has misjudged the market's appetite for the issue, or the market changes while the underwriter is still selling some of the issue, the underwriter may not achieve the planned underwriting fee.

Public Sale Versus Negotiated Sale

Issuers may approach the market to sell their bonds in one of two ways: public competitive bidding and negotiated sale. Historically, bonds have been offered for public sale, with purchasers such as larger financial institutions, which might be purchasing for their own portfolio or for resale, effectively determining the interest rate by their offers. A *public sale* is initiated by a widely published official notice of sale. The notice of sale typically includes information such as the denomination of the bonds, bid conditions and requirements, and provisions for payment. The issuer will have worked with a financial adviser to establish the amount of the issue, the maturity date(s), obtaining (typically) a rating (discussed below), and all other characteristics of the sale. Investors then in effect determine the interest rate through their bids, with the issuer free to choose the investor or potentially several investors who offer the lowest rates. More detailed information is provided in the bond prospectus.

Sealed bids are submitted by interested institutional investors, brokerage firms, and even individuals, although individuals typically purchase through intermediaries. The issuing jurisdiction then is free to accept the lowest bid interest rate or to reject the bid according to the terms and conditions of sale. Jurisdictions with good ratings prefer this method, as they are likely to attract numerous bidders and thus be able to choose lower interest rates.

The *negotiated sale*, however, is becoming increasingly common. Negotiated sales are conducted between underwriters such as the large investment banks and the issuing government. The issuer typically issues a request for proposals (RFP) specifying the objectives of the issue (amount, time period, and so forth). Responders to the RFP present to the issuer their best case for why they should be selected based on track record, fees, and so forth. Once the underwriter, or often several underwriters, is selected, the issuer then works with the underwriter to develop the bond issue. The underwriter acts as a broker between the issuing jurisdiction and the investment community. If the issuer thinks the rates quoted by potential buyers are too high, the issuer is free to reject the bids, as in a public sale.

A key advantage of a negotiated sale is that the bond issue can be spread over a longer period of time. If the interest rates in bids are high but the issuer cannot postpone the project, the issuer may sell only a portion of the total issue to start the project while the underwriter continues to seek additional bids. One disadvantage of negotiated sales is that some investors, including some pension funds, cannot purchase state or municipal securities except through public sale.

Although it has been argued that negotiated sales seem to cost about 30 basis points more than competitive bids,[52] other research has presented evidence that it is more the characteristics of the issuers that determine whether competitive versus negotiated sale is selected by the issuer, and that in turn explains any interest differences. Poor credit risk, unusually large issues, unusual financial structure or offered security, market volatility, and unusual financing terms are some of the factors that may argue for negotiated sale.[53]

Bond Features

Bonds differ from one another in a variety of ways. *Term bonds* may be due and payable to the investors on a single date. *Serial bonds* are due according to a specific schedule of payments over a number of years. In recent years, serial bonds have largely replaced term bonds, in part because of statutory prohibitions against term bonds. Investors holding term bonds obviously must be concerned with whether a jurisdiction is annually setting aside sufficient funds to be able to repay its debt. Underwriters typically require that the issuer establish a *sinking fund* and pay into that fund semiannually or annually amounts that will be sufficient at maturity to repay the principal on the bonds.

Another difference is between *coupon bonds* and *registered bonds*. Coupon bonds have coupons attached indicating the bond's maturity date and the amount of payment. Whoever presents the mature coupons receives payment. Registered bonds require that the owner register with the government issuing the bonds. The advantage of a coupon bond is that it is easily transferred from one owner to another, whereas a registered bond offers protection against loss or destruction of the bond itself.

States and municipalities historically preferred coupon bonds because the issuing jurisdiction was not responsible for keeping records of the purchasers. However, a provision of the Tax Equity and Fiscal Responsibility Act of 1982 requires that state and municipal bonds be registered to retain their tax-exempt status, and that requirement was upheld in *South Carolina* v. *Baker*. As a consequence, the use of coupon bonds has all but disappeared, although state and local governments continue to lobby for federal legislation that would permit issuing non-registered bonds that are tax exempt.

Another feature of bond sales is *discounting*. A bond is discounted when it is sold at some fraction of its face value. For example, a $10,000 bond may be sold for $9,800. It is thus discounted below par (meaning below face value). When it matures and the principal is paid out, the investor will receive $10,000 in return for the $9,800 investment in addition to the interest payments the investor would have been receiving over the years.

At times, a bond may actually be sold at a premium over its par value. This can happen when a bond whose fixed interest rate was set in a period of high interest rates becomes available for sale after interest rates have fallen. A potential investor will be attracted to the higher interest rate bond, but the seller has less incentive to sell the bond because of the low return offered by other choices now available on the market. So the seller charges the new investor, say, $10,200 for a bond that will repay principal of only $10,000 at maturity. The bond investor must consider both the selling value—discounted, at par, or at a premium—as well as the interest rate in determining the return on investment.[54] The secondary market, in which bonds already sold once are resold to other investors, rarely has bonds that are sold at their face value. Conditions at the time of sales in the secondary market are almost always different from the time of issue, causing the bonds to be valued at either more or less than their face value.

Bonds are becoming increasingly complex in the structure of their terms. Traditionally, debt issuers were concerned primarily with the *interest* or *coupon rate* of the bond and the various costs of debt issuance. Today, however, issuers are incorporating detailed features, usually with the help of financial advisory services, to vary the conditions of sale, the conditions under which the issuer may pay off the bond early, and variations in cash flows at different points in the life of the bond. For example, one feature is a collateral structure in which an asset-backed security is issued, and collateralized by a bundle of underlying securities, such as several municipal bonds. The risk and therefore pricing of those different bonds varies, and thus the new asset-backed security may smooth out the different risks. A different form or structure is when an issue is divided into different *tranches* or portions, each with different repayment schedules. This approach of designing features into a bond issue unique to the cash flow characteristics of the borrower offers ways to tailor a bond issue to its specific situation.[55]

Zero Coupon Bonds

The typical municipal bond pays interest at specified points until the maturity date, when the principal is paid. Zero coupon bonds are growing in popularity, however. The coupon rate, in finance terminology, is the interest rate that the bond will pay. A zero coupon bond pays out no interest until maturity, when both the principal and the interest are paid at once. Attractive to the issuer because they have no annual cash flow requirements, zero coupon bonds naturally require some incentive to attract investors away from the more typical municipal bond, which pays in regular installments through the years until maturity. The usual means of attracting investors to zero coupon bonds is to sell the bonds for much less than their stated value—to discount the bond from face value. Zero coupon bonds typically call for the issuer to set aside funds with a trustee, on a regular basis, sufficient to pay off the debt at time of maturity.

Interest Rates

Interest rates, of course, are one of the most critical elements of bonds for both the issuer and potential buyers. As a hedge against changing interest rates or financial condition, the state or municipal authority may sometimes use a *call feature*. This means the authority may call or repay the bond in part or in full before the maturity date. The issuer can thus take advantage of falling interest rates by paying off all or part of the bond issue. Exercising this feature usually involves the payment of some premium. Callable bonds typically carry a higher rate of interest because investors would otherwise be less attracted to an investment that may be repaid sooner and therefore at a lower profit. A similar feature that favors the bond buyer is the *put option*. It allows the buyer, at specified intervals, to require paying off the bond. For this feature, the buyer agrees to specified discount rates at the different put options.

Variable interest rate municipal bonds have become common, just as variable rate financing has become standard in the financial industry. Many state and municipal issuers have taken advantage of variable rates both at the time of original issue and to refinance bond indebtedness.

The actual interest that the jurisdiction will have to pay on a bond issue depends on many factors related to the financial condition of the jurisdiction and the general market for other investments at the time of the issue. The tax-exempt status of the interest earned by state and local bonds means that the interest rate paid will be lower than comparably safe investments that do not enjoy tax-exempt status. If the jurisdiction has a good record of previous debt management, it will be perceived as a lower risk than one that has experienced trouble meeting its financial obligations. Likewise, if the jurisdiction is located in a good regional economy with low unemployment rates and a high tax base, it will be able to sell its bonds at lower interest rates. If the issuer embodies recognized good management practices, that will have a positive impact on bond pricing.[56] The issuing jurisdiction also will provide potential investors with information about other long-term obligations, including other debt and also unfunded pension liabilities. A reputation for good financial management is cited as evidence of creditworthiness.[57]

Bond Ratings

Investors rely heavily on standard ratings provided by independent services, such as Fitch Investors Service L.P., Moody's Investor Service, and Standard & Poor's. Although the rating agencies use somewhat different labels for their ratings, they are quite similar.

The importance of bond ratings is illustrated by an upgrade for the City of Honolulu, Hawaii. In 2006, the city was upgraded by Standard & Poor's from AA– to AA. This seemingly small change would have saved the city more than $2.2 million in interest and bond insurance costs on the last two city bond issues, totaling $730 million. The factors cited in the rating change included the city having doubled its rainy day fund, institution of an improved process for regular budget review with all department heads, and other administrative and procedural improvements to the city's basic budget management practices.[58]

A downgrade in rating may come about because of the issuer's own investment practices, as in the case of the infamous Orange County, California, bankruptcy (discussed later in this chapter). State and local governments that invest their own funds, such as pension funds and short-term deposit instruments, can have their borrower status downgraded if they invest too heavily in high-risk derivatives. **Exhibit 14–4** discusses how rating agencies evaluate potential borrowers and potential debt issues.

Credit Enhancement

One device that state and local governments use to control the costs of debt and debt issuance is *insurance*. Before the financial market collapse of 2007–2008, insured municipal bond issues were insured by one of five major bond insurers—Ambac Assurance Corporation, Assured Guaranty Corporation, Financial Guaranty Insurance Company, Financial Security Assurance, and Municipal Bond Insurance Association (MBIA). As a result of all five entities' losses in the complex derivatives and structured finance fiascoes of that period, Ambac went out of business; MBIA spun off its public finance group as National Public Financial Guarantee Corporation; Assured Guaranty Corporation acquired Financial Security Assurance; and the Financial Guaranty Insurance Company effectively ceased operations in 2009. The municipal bond insurance industry, more accurately the public

---

Exhibit 14–4 How Do Rating Agencies Evaluate Municipal Bond Issues?

There are several U.S. financial services firms that rate municipal bond issues in the United States and increasingly the subnational debt issues in developing countries. Moody's, Standard & Poor's, and Fitch are among the most notable. They all use quite similar rating categories and similar criteria. The lower the grade, the more risky the bond issue, and therefore, in general, the higher the interest rate the issuer will have to pay to attract investors.

Note that the rating is for an individual bond issue, not the issuer. The same issuer may have a variety of bonds in the market, and they may be rated differently, though because overall financial condition and management of the issuer are important factors in determining a rating, issues with similar characteristics from the same issuer are likely to be rated close to each other.

The table below lists the rating categories for those three major organizations with short adjectival phrases used by the organizations to describe the rating.

Rating Categories from the Three Major U.S. Rating Organizations

Moody's	Standard & Poor's	Fitch
Aaa Strongest credit-worthiness	AAA Extremely strong capacity	AAA Highest credit quality
Aa Strong credit-worthiness	AA Very strong capacity	AA Very high credit
A Above average	A Strong capacity	A High credit
Baa Average	BBB Adequate capacity	BBB Good credit quality
Ba Below average	BBB– Lowest investment grade	
B Weak credit-worthiness	BB+ Highest speculative grade	BB Speculative
	BB Near-term less vulnerable, but long-term vulnerable	B Highly speculative
	B More vulnerable, but current capacity ok	
Caa Very weak	CCC Currently vulnerable	CCC Substantial credit risk
Ca Extremely weak	CC Highly vulnerable	CC Very high risk levels
C Weakest	C Highly vulnerable and other	C Exceptionally high risk
		RD Restricted default
	D Payment default	D Default/banktruptcy proceedings

Sources: Moody's retrieved November 9, 2011, from http://www.moodys.com/sites/products/ AboutMoodysRatingsAttachments/MoodysRatingsSymbolsand%20Definitions.pdf; Standard & Poors retrieved November 9, 2011, from http://www.standardandpoors.com/ratings/definitions-and-faqs/ en/us; Fitch retrieved November 11, 2011, from http://www.fitchratings.com/web_content/ratings/ fitch_ratings_definitions_and_scales.pdf.

Note that the rating organizations may attach + and – to above categories to indicate differences within the overall rating.

(Continued)

The terminology used by different rating organizations differs with respect to speculative and below investment grade quality. Such a rating does not mean the issuer cannot sell the bonds. It means that investors in the view of the rating agency should be cautious and aware of the considerable risk associated with the issue before purchasing. And of course the interest premium will be higher, or the issuer may have to sell the issue at below par (below face value). Issues are almost never offered at below investment grade. Of the total amount of municipal debt outstanding in 2010 ($2.93 trillion), only $.03 trillion was below investment grade.[1]

Selling at below par means the issuer will perhaps have to sell the issue at a percentage, illustratively 92 percent, of the face value of the bond. Discounting below par to 92 percent on a $100 million issue will net $92 million, but that is not what the issuer receives. Instead, the underwriter possibly might charge $500,000 in fees, netting only $91.5 million for the issuer. But at maturity, the issuer will be expected to repay the full $100 million.

In developing a rating for a specific issue, all rating agencies consider similar quantitative and qualitative information. A long list of basic information requirements from the issuer is common, such as:

1. Several recent years of annual audited financial statements
2. Several years of budget history and forecasts for the next several years
3. Capital improvement program
4. Sources of major revenues if general-purpose jurisdiction, and revenue source for the issue if a revenue bond
5. Complete statement of all outstanding debt and terms of debt
6. Basic economic conditions in the region of the issuing jurisdiction, including employment rates, employment by major employers, literacy and other education characteristics, property valuation, and sources of regular intergovernmental revenue (determined by formula)
7. Debt management policies
8. Basic institutional characteristics such as background and experience of key administrative and elected (if relevant) officials; mechanisms (electoral, appointment) and frequency for replacing key officials; and relevant national or state regulations that affect the operations of the issuer.

These are only examples drawn from the public websites and published materials of the major rating agencies. The processes by which the rating agencies combine the various types of information are proprietary, but generally are relatively transparent to the issuer in that lengthy interviews and time onsite by professionals from the rating agencies explain the information requirements and the way the information is used in constructing a rating. For a rating agency that has previously rated debt from an issuer, a new issue may require only a modest update of the previously submitted information, especially if recent.

Rating agencies periodically review bond issues because conditions may change for the issuer, and/or changes may occur in the markets that affect the outstanding bonds. Because bonds are marketable for secondary resale—original purchasers may elect to sell the bonds before maturity—a regular reconfirmation or change in the rating is necessary to secure continued investor interest.

1. Securities Industry and Financial Markets Association (2010). *Municipal bond credit report: fourth quarter and full year 2010*. Retrieved November 8, 2011, from http://www.sifma.org/research/ item.aspx?id=23188.

finance insurance industry, had all but disappeared from new bond issues. The Assured Guaranty Corporation was the only significant insurer of new issues in 2011. Only 6% of the first-quarter 2011 municipal bond new issues were insured,[59] while in the past about 50% of all issues were insured.[60] The collapse of municipal bond insurance, however, did not deter new issuances in 2010 and 2011.

Another type of credit enhancement is a *bank-issued line of credit*. The line of credit assures the bond buyer that the issuer will not be delayed in meeting payments even if short-term fluctuations in cash flow cause a temporary problem. The line of credit can be accessed if necessary to meet the short-term cash flow problem.

In some developing countries, central governments provide credit enhancements for local government borrowing through the use of an *intercept mechanism*. The central government agrees to intercept, if necessary, a stable source of revenues that otherwise would flow to the borrower, such as a portion of central revenue transfers to local government. This intercept is paid to the lender in the event of default or delayed payment by the local government. The municipal development finance agency of Colombia, FINDETER, relies heavily on the intercept of central government grants/transfers to municipal governments to collect on debt repayments. Some municipal borrowers/bond issuers, rather than repay loans, simply allow the intercept mechanism to make the payments.

Disclosure and Regulation

Municipal bond issuance is subject to the general regulatory functions of the Securities and Exchange Commission (SEC), as are all other public debt and equity issues in the U.S. financial markets. For decades, municipal debt instruments were specifically exempt from SEC regulation. Beginning in the 1970s, however, Congress began to increase the role of the SEC in regulating municipal bond issues. Amendments to the Securities Exchange Act created the Municipal Securities Rulemaking Board (MSRB) in 1975 in the wake of New York City's financial crisis and the revelation that some dealers in state and municipal securities were involved in unethical and "dangerous" conduct.[61]

SEC regulations, for all underwriting and disclosure, focus on the underwriter's role and set disclosure requirements that affect the type and quality of information that underwriters must provide to potential investors. Significant new disclosure rules were adopted in 1990 (SEC Rule 15c–12) that pertain to the consistency and timeliness of an underwriter's release of information provided by the bond issuer. The quality of the information itself and all releases by the bond-issuing jurisdiction are still considered to be the jurisdiction's responsibility. The underwriter does not assume any liability properly borne by the issuer. Evidence suggests that disclosure improves the investor's ability to judge credit, and hence improves credit ratings for creditworthy municipalities.

The Municipal Securities Rulemaking Board (MSRB) was created to provide focus to the SEC's functions in regulating financial institutions in the municipal bond market. MSRB is the standard-setting body for all municipal securities dealers. Its authority extends only to dealers and others involved in municipal bond transactions, not to the actual issuing governments themselves. MSRB functions under the general authority of the SEC to ensure that the disclosure information is as accurate and timely as possible.

It requires bond dealers to file repository copies of all official documentation on a municipal bond issue so as to make the information more widely available to all potential investors (Rule G-32).

MSRB also makes bond pricing information more widely accessible. Rule G-14 requires securities dealers to report daily to the Transactions Reporting Database all transactions in municipal securities, including both interdealer transactions and retail transactions in municipal bonds. MSRB provides a publicly accessible daily report on pricing and volume of municipal securities, enabling investors to get up-to-date information to guide investment decisions.[62]

A large step in imposing public disclosure requirements on the issuing jurisdictions themselves has been the implementation of Nationally Recognized Municipal Securities Information Repositories. These repositories are sites for mandatory registration of municipal issues, accessible to the public. Four national repositories exist, including such financial services organizations as Bloomberg Financial Markets and Standard & Poor's as well as DPC Data and FP Interactive.[63] Several state repositories exist, such as those of Texas and Ohio. Municipal debt issuers must at least annually—and more often if conditions change—report on their financial condition. This reporting requirement extends for as long as the issuer has outstanding debt in the market, providing potentially valuable information to subsequent secondary market purchasers of municipal securities. Also, municipal debt issuers are required to maintain and report regularly on their overall financial condition, not just on the status of specific debt issues.

The additional disclosure requirements initially caused considerable consternation among many of the participants in the municipal bond market.[64] One particular requirement that securities dealers thought was too vague is the requirement that brokers and dealers must judge whether a client is capable of understanding the risk involved in an investment before they issue a recommendation to the client. The requirement (Rule G-17) persists. After the landmark Orange County, California, financial fiasco (see below) there were far fewer attempts to reduce disclosure requirements of both issuers and dealers in the municipal securities market.

DEBT CAPACITY AND MANAGEMENT

Because the federal government borrows for purposes other than capital investment, we continue in this section to focus on state and local governments. Federal debt is discussed in the chapter on government and the economy. Media discussions of the federal debt and the size of the federal deficit raise citizens' consciousness of government debt, but locally people are asked officially to approve debt (bond issues) for financing everything from schools to new fire stations when it involves the pledge of all resources available to the municipality, or the *full faith and credit* of the municipality. More importantly, citizens are not given the opportunity to vote on an even larger component of state and local debt: debt that is issued by special authorities or that does not involve the pledge of full faith and credit of the jurisdiction. The questions to be addressed in this section involve how much debt can be managed safely and which debt management practices will ensure sound future financial condition.[65]

Size of Debt

The size of debt can be assessed in several ways. The total amount of debt is probably the least meaningful measure. The fact that state and local governments' total outstanding debt at the end of 2010 was nearly $3.2 trillion, although this figure may sound staggering, is not really instructive.[66] Interest payments on debt in 2010 amounted to $111.8 billion, or only 5.3% of total state and local expenditures, and interest payments have remained relatively constant over recent years at about 5% or less of total expenditures.[67] The fact that this figure is not excessive can be illustrated by considering that individuals commonly devote far more than 5% of their total expenditures on interest payments for home mortgages, car loans, and credit card debt.

Per Capita Debt

Per capita debt figures help put the total government debt in perspective. How much per capita do state and local governments owe? In 2005, they owed $6,234 per capita, up almost 65% from 1995. In 2009, state and local governments owed $8,801 per capita, an increase of 70% in 10 years.[68] Is that too much, too little, or just about right? Is it growing, declining, or remaining more or less stable? The latter question is easier to answer than the former.

Figure 14–1 charts state and local per capita debt from 1970 through 2009. Per capita debt has risen at both the state and the local government levels, with local debt rising somewhat more rapidly than state debt. In addition, the amount of increase in the five-year period 1980–1985 was almost equal to the rate of increase for the preceding 10-year period (1970–1980), and the period 1985–1990 witnessed an even faster rate of growth. Since 2000, the rate of growth is noticeably higher. Thus, state and local debt is rising faster than population, but is that cause for alarm?

Ratio of Debt to Personal Income

Relating debt to personal income instead of population clears the picture somewhat. Calculating total debt outstanding per $1,000 of personal income is one way of assessing whether debt is in danger of becoming an unreasonable economic burden. In 1992, state and local government debt per $1,000 in personal income was $184. This figure is considerably less alarming. For more than 45 years, combined state and local debt per $1,000 in personal income has remained relatively stable. Figure 14–2 charts this historical trend. State and local debt per $1,000 of personal income in the 1990s, although showing a trend toward increase after a 10-year decline from the 1970s through 1982, was no higher than the previous high of $205 back in 1972 until 2006. The rates in 2006 and 2009 were higher than at any previous point since the early 1960s, but is $222 per $1,000 in personal income too high?

To some extent, any analysis of total state and local debt is somewhat misleading in that the debt consists of both general obligations of state and local governments and revenue-backed obligations that do not encumber the taxing power of governments. The former is only approximately one-third of total debt outstanding. Thus, taxpayers are obligated for about $71 per $1,000 in personal income through taxes. There is a certain amount of

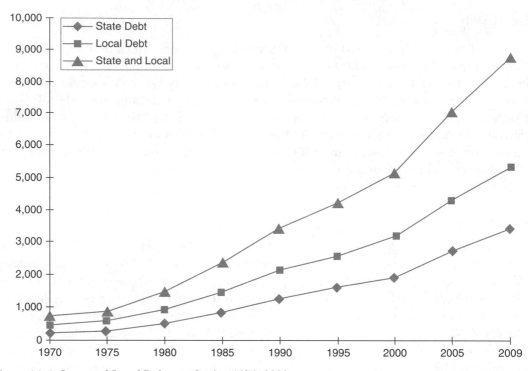

Figure 14–1 State and Local Debt per Capita, 1970–2009

Sources: Compiled from Bureau of the Census, U.S. Department of Commerce. *Statistical abstract of the United States, 1985* (p. 274); *1996* (p. 304); *2005* (Table 427); for 2009 population, Bureau of the Census, U.S. Department of Commerce (2011). *U.S. population fifty states.* Retrieved November 14, 2011, from http://www.census.gov/popest/intercensal/national/nat2010.html; for state and local debt 2009, *State and local finance data query system.* Washington, DC: Urban Institute and Brookings Institution. Retrieved November 14, 2011, from http://slfdqs.taxpolicycenter.org/pages.cfm.

discretionary obligation for the debt backed by revenue bonds, though of course other than by moving to a new location, citizens cannot easily choose among school districts, water districts, and so forth.

Distribution of Debt

Ultimately, whether the size of state and local debt is reasonable is a subjective judgment. The main factors used in making such an appraisal are the financial burden on individual taxpayers and the economy and the perceived value of the facilities and services purchased by the debt.

Generally, debt varies somewhat with income and with the amount of state and local services. The state with the highest per capita debt in 2009, Massachusetts ($11,357), also was ranked high (second) in personal income per capita ($46,394).[69] Hence, Massachusetts presumably has the income level to support a higher debt. New York ranked sixth in per capita income and eighth in per capita debt. Connecticut ranked first in per capita income and only fourth in per capita debt, although in previous years it had the opposite pattern—high in personal income per capita and low in debt per capita.

Figure 14–2 State and Local Debt per $1,000 Personal Income, 1962–2009
Sources: Compiled from Bureau of the Census, U.S. Department of Commerce (1984). *Historical statistics on governmental finances and employment* (p. 113). Washington, DC: U.S. Government Printing Office; Bureau of the Census, U.S. Department of Commerce (1988), *Government finances in 1985–86* (p. 3). Washington, DC: U.S. Government Printing Office; Bureau of the Census, U.S. Department of Commerce, *State and local government financial summary 2009* (p. 4). Washington, DC: U.S. Government Printing Office; Bureau of the Census, U.S. Department of Commerce, *Statistical abstract of the United States: 2012* (p. 443). Washington, DC: U.S. Government Printing Office.

States with higher incomes in general have higher debt, by almost any measure, and states with lower incomes have lower debt. In the end, it is a judgment call as to what state and local governments can afford, a judgment that is ultimately made by voters in general elections and referendums. In the section below on debt capacity, we discuss other measures that are often used as norms for what state and local governments should be able to afford based on government revenues and expenditures for various purposes.

Debt Default

It is important to remember that the figures on debt do not reflect the full scope of future financial obligations of governments. Pension programs for public workers constitute a form of debt and are often inadequately funded. Debt defaults are correlated with economic cycles, but it should be noted that there have been few defaults on state or local indebtedness since the Great Depression of the 1930s.[70] In that decade, about 4,800 state and local units defaulted on their obligations. While that number may seem large, the total number of governments then was 150,000. Most of the defaults involved small jurisdictions. Fewer than 50 of these defaulting governments had populations of more than 25,000.[71]

Since that time, the number of defaults has been quite low. From 1970 to 2009, the average, cumulative default rate was less than 0.1%. There were only 54 defaults during that period on debt rated by Moody's. Three of these were general obligation bonds[72]— Baldwin County, Alabama, in 1988; Jefferson County, Alabama, in 2008; and Sierra Kings Health Care District, California, in 2009.[73]

Averages can mask wide variation. Riskier issues, such as multifamily housing and non-profit health care organizations, such as some hospitals, experience much higher default rates, whereas municipal general obligation bonds and water and sewer and similar revenue-backed bonds experience default rates in the range of less than 0.05%. Even more interesting is the fact that, since the Great Depression, no state has defaulted on a debt (even then, only Arkansas postponed payments). Even municipalities that go into bankruptcy proceedings typically emerge with creditors paid off, at least on general obligation bonds. More often, the cases are ones in which the issuing jurisdiction or authority is delinquent (late) in debt payments, rather than default. That is the case in the Sierra King Health district example above.

School district issues almost never default, in part because they are typically full faith and credit bonds backed by the independent school district's taxing authority, or in the case of city or county school districts, the taxing authority of the full jurisdiction. Major events such as Hurricanes Katrina and Rita raised the specter of defaults as many jurisdictions had major portions of their tax base (primarily property) wiped out by the storms, and public utility customers in the hundreds of thousands lost homes that were previously connected to the utilities. But major federal and state intervention averted the defaults that might have happened. **Exhibit 14–5** discusses how governments responded to the potential of defaults following these disasters.

Famous or Infamous Defaults and Bankruptcies

Few public bond issuers have faced financial insolvency, although the exceptions have been noteworthy. In 1963, debt service payments on $100 million in revenue bonds for the Calumet Skyway in Chicago were interrupted.[74] In the mid-1970s, New York City came close to bankruptcy as a result of extensive borrowing to meet operating budget requirements and defaulting on some of its short-term debt. As a result, New York City was partially placed under the supervision of a financial control board (see the chapter on intergovernmental relations). Only this intervention by the state government and the banking community prevented outright default on several bond issues. Also in the 1970s, Cleveland defaulted on just over $15 million in tax anticipation notes, largely because of poor financial management practices and inadequate accounting procedures.[75]

The largest failure until the recession that started in 2007 was that of the Washington Public Power Supply System (WPPSS). In 1983, after a more than decade-long program of construction of five nuclear power generating plants, WPPSS defaulted on more than $2 billion in revenue bonds. The revenue bonds were issued in anticipation of the sale of electricity. WPPSS got caught in the situation faced by the power industry in many parts of the country in the 1970s—a combination of slower rates of growth in electricity demand, rapid escalation in the costs of nuclear power plant construction, and rising interest rates.[76] In 1993, WPPSS successfully issued $800 million in bonds to refund the debt, and was later reorganized into a new entity.[77]

In reality, defaults by state and local governments are rare. However, periodic problems arise not as much on individual bond issues but with entire jurisdictions, headlined by the Orange County, California, financial collapse in 1994. Federal legislation in 1934 permitted municipalities to declare bankruptcy, and during the Depression, many did. But it is rare now and usually associated with weak financial management practices.[78]

Notable financial collapses of entire jurisdictions have included Cuyahoga County, Ohio, in 1978; Bridgeport, Connecticut, in 1991; Orange County, California, in 1994; and Harrisburg, Pennsylvania, and Jefferson County, Alabama, in 2011. Bridgeport attempted to declare bankruptcy, although the bankruptcy was not permitted by the courts.[79] The Cuyahoga County and Orange County problems share some similarities. Neither county got into trouble as a result of overextending debt. Both counties became mired in financial difficulties as a result of their investment activities with their own pension funds and other sources of cash, plus those of numerous other local governments for which the counties acted as investment managers. Cuyahoga County lost $114 million on a

---

Exhibit 14–5 Extraordinary Events Provoke Extraordinary Responses to Prevent Municipal Default

Hurricanes Katrina and Rita in 2005 devastated the Gulf Coast of the United States, causing damages estimated in excess of $140 billion. Losses to government infrastructure alone amounted to between $13 billion on the low end and $25 billion on the high end.[1] At least $16.7 billion in face value of insured bonds was directly affected by the hurricanes, but a year after the hurricanes, only a little over $17 million in claims on insured bonds had been paid out, and most of that was thought likely to be recovered as municipalities and special districts were still struggling to get their records back in order in the immediate aftermath.[2]

The City of New Orleans and other bond issuers faced long-term problems, however, in rebuilding the lost infrastructure by issuing new debt and at the same time meeting payments on previous bonds that financed now destroyed or damaged capital assets. The Gulf Opportunity Zone Act of 2005 (P.L. 109-135) relaxed some of the restrictions on private activity bonds in order to permit tax-exempt issues for housing and other facilities that are not necessarily for public use, and waived other requirements that otherwise would potentially have impeded issuance of new bonds to refund existing bonds or to refinance infrastructure on which existing bonds already were outstanding. One provision of the act also extended authority to the affected states to issue tax credit bonds to pay interest on or to repay debt previously issued, subject to a maximum per state—$200 million for Louisiana—and requiring that the state match the tax credit issue with an equal amount of state resources, financed by debt or otherwise.

The State of Louisiana, for example, in 2006 issued $200 million in tax credit bonds to be used to pay debt service and to repay bonds issued prior to Hurricanes Katrina and Rita in affected areas. The fact sheet from this bond issue shows the debt rated AAA by Fitch and similarly by other rating agencies. While there have been major municipal bond defaults in U.S. history, they are rare, and when significant often result in solutions to work out the losses through a variety of financing options and with extended oversight by regulatory agencies or appointed oversight commissions.

1. Holtz-Eakin, D. (2005). *Macroeconomic and budgetary effects of Hurricanes Katrina and Rita* (p. 3). Washington, DC: Congressional Budget Office.
2. *Hurricane Katrina: One year later the municipal bond market remains resilient* (2006). Retrieved December 5, 2006, from http://www.dorseyco.com/documents/GKSTResearch-Hurricane KatrinaOneYearLater_000.pdf.

(Continued)

Ratings:Fitch: "AAA"
Moody's: "Aaa"
S&P: "AAA"
(CIFG Insured)
(See "RATINGS" herein)

In the opinion of Jones, Walker, Waechter, Poitevent, Carrére & Denégre L.L.P., assuming continuing compliance with certain covenants described herein, the Bonds qualify as Gulf tax credit bonds as described in Code Section 1400N(1)(4) of the Internal Revenue Code of 1986, as amended. Jones, Walker, Waechter, Poitevent, Carrére & Denégre L.L.P. is further of the opinion that, under the laws of the State, the Bonds are exempt from income and all other taxation in the State of Louisiana. See "TAX MATTERS" herein and the proposed form of opinion of Jones, Walker, Waechter, Poitevent, Carrére & Denégre L.L.P. attached hereto as Appendix D.

$200,000,000
STATE OF LOUISIANA
GENERAL OBLIGATION GULF TAX CREDIT BONDS
SERIES 2006-A

Dated: Date of Delivery   Due: July 18, 2008

The State of Louisiana (the "State") is issuing $200,000,000 principal amount of its taxable General Obligation Gulf Tax Credit Bonds, Series 2006-A (the "Bonds") pursuant to Article VII, Section 6 of the Constitution of the State of Louisiana of 1974, as amended (the "State Constitution"), Act No. 41 of the First Extraordinary Session of the Louisiana Legislature of 2006 ("Act No. 41"), and other constitutional and statutory authority, for the purpose of providing funds for the Debt Service Assistance Fund established by Act No. 41 for loans to political subdivisions of the State affected by Hurricanes Katrina and Rita, to insure the timely payment of principal of and interest on their outstanding bonds, notes, certificates of indebtedness or other written obligations for the repayment of borrowed money of local political subdivisions of the State issued prior to August 28, 2005, and to pay debt service on general obligation bonds of the State issued prior to August 28, 2005, as described under "DEBT SERVICE ASSISTANCE PROGRAM" and in "Appendix E-1 – Table of Defeased Bonds of Participating Political Subdivisions" and "Appendix E-2 – Table of Defeased Bonds of the State" attached hereto.

The Bonds are issuable only as fully registered bonds, without coupons, in the denominations of $5,000 or any integral multiple thereof within a single maturity. Except as provided below, principal of the Bonds is payable upon maturity to the registered owners thereof upon presentation and surrender of such Bonds at the designated corporate trust office of Hancock Bank of Louisiana, Baton Rouge, Louisiana, as Paying Agent and Registrar (the "Paying Agent/Registrar"). Hancock Bank of Louisiana is also acting as escrow trustee pursuant to three separate Escrow Deposit Agreements (as hereinafter defined) (the "Escrow Trustee," and, together with the Paying Agent/Registrar, the "Paying Agent").

The Bonds shall not bear interest. See "THE BONDS – Credit Allowance" herein. Initially, the Bonds will be issued in book-entry only form, registered in the name of Cede & Co., as nominee of The Depository Trust Company, New York, New York ("DTC"). DTC will act as securities depository for the Bonds. There will be no distribution of the Bonds to purchasers. Purchases of the Bonds may be made only in book-entry form in authorized denominations by credit to participating broker-dealers and other institutions on the books of DTC, as described herein. Principal on the Bonds will be payable by the Paying Agent to DTC, which will remit such payments in accordance with its normal procedures, as described herein. The State reserves the right to terminate the use of the book-entry only system and issue fully registered certificated Bonds. See "THE BONDS – Book-Entry Only System" herein. Further details of payment of the Bonds are more fully described herein.

The Bonds constitute general obligations of the State and the full faith and credit of the State is pledged to the payment of the principal of the Bonds as and when the same becomes due and payable. The Bonds, together with other general obligations of the State, are payable from monies pledged and dedicated to and paid into the Bond Security and Redemption Fund created and established in the State Treasury, have a first lien and privilege upon all State money deposited into the Bond Security and Redemption Fund, are payable on a parity with all other outstanding general obligation bonds heretofore and hereafter issued by the State under and pursuant to the State Constitution, and are secured by the monies pledged and dedicated to and paid into the Bond Security and Redemption Fund, subject to prior contractual obligations as provided in Article VII, Section 9 of the State Constitution.

The Bonds are not subject to redemption prior to maturity.

CIFG ASSURANCE NORTH AMERICA, INC. has unconditionally and irrevocably guaranteed the full and complete payment by or on behalf of the State of regular payments of principal of the Bonds.

The Bonds are offered when, as and if issued, subject to approval of legality by the Honorable Charles C. Foti, Jr., Attorney General of the State of Louisiana, and Jones, Walker, Waechter, Poitevent, Carrére & Denégre L.L.P., Baton Rouge, Louisiana, Co-Bond Counsel, and certain other conditions. Certain legal matters will be passed upon for the Underwriters by Foley & Judell, LLP, New Orleans, Louisiana, and The Boles Law Firm, APC, Monroe, Louisiana, Co-Counsel to the Underwriters. Government Finance Associates, Inc. serves as independent Financial Advisor to the State. It is expected that the Bonds in definitive form will be available for delivery at DTC in New York, New York on or about, July 19, 2006 against payment therefor.

This cover page contains certain information for quick reference only. It is NOT a summary of this issue. Investors must read the entire Official Statement to obtain information essential to making an informed investment decision.

MORGAN KEEGAN & COMPANY, INC.   GOLDMAN, SACHS & CO.

Estrada Hinojosa & Company, Inc.   Loop Capital Markets, LLC   A. G. Edwards

The date of this Official Statement is July 12, 2006.

$1.8 billion investment pool, but subsequently repaid most of the local government co-investors. Orange County invested its own pension funds and acted as the investor for almost 200 other local government units, with investments totaling more than $7 billion at the peak.[80] Orange County had a several-year history of achieving significant returns on its pension funds invested, and acted as the investor for numerous other local government pension funds. The string of successful investment years perhaps blinded the investment managers, and Orange County borrowed in order to invest still more. A series of bad market years left the county with insufficient resources to repay the borrowed funds. Taxpayers refused to increase taxes to pay off the debt, and the county entered into bankruptcy proceedings (see the financial management chapter for additional discussion). Note that the Orange County case is unrelated to municipal bond issuance.

Harrisburg, Pennsylvania, filed for bankruptcy in November 2011, owing more than $360 million, on which it had missed $65 million in payments due as of the bankruptcy filing. The debt was from financing a major renovation of a solid waste incinerator. Pennsylvania's Department of Economic and Community Development put in place an emergency plan to ensure that city services did not lapse.[81] In 2011, Jefferson County, Alabama, achieved the distinction of becoming the nation's largest municipal bankruptcy. At stake was more than $3 billion in defaulted sewer debt. Most of the debt was the result of debt refinancing packages in 2002 and 2003, swapping variable rate debt for the previous fixed debt to avoid a large increase in sewer rates.[82]

Although for residents of these various communities and investors the headlines are often dramatic, the lesson from the history of municipal bond defaults and municipal bankruptcies is that services almost always continue uninterrupted and investors typically get at least the principal back from their investments. Typically, refinancing is worked out, and investors suffer a loss on the return they had expected but do not suffer the same fate as often faced by investors in corporate bonds.

Debt Capacity

Measuring Debt Capacity

Measuring debt capacity is an art rather than a science. Since the 1980s, the public finance and budgeting profession has paid considerably more attention to improving the level of the art. Three main factors influence debt capacity: expenditure pressures, resource availability, and the commitment of government officials to use resources to meet debt requirements.[83] To these might be added voters' willingness to accept the actions of their elected officials. Expenditure analysts look at the present and potential future commitments of jurisdictions. Population growth, changing economic conditions, the state of the current capital facilities and infrastructure base, and the socioeconomic characteristics of the population are important influences on potential future expenditures.

Assessing resource availability involves analyzing all potential sources of revenue including own-source revenues; transfers from other levels of government; and types of self-financing, including user charges, special assessments, impact fees, and a variety of other measures to collect fees or revenues sufficient to support the specific project or facility (see the chapters on budgeting for revenues). The willingness of lenders to purchase debt is reflected ultimately in the interest rate they will require to lend. Revenue and expenditure analyses are used by state and local governments to support capital budgeting and debt management. Fiscal capacity analysis, focusing on the ability to generate revenues and on expenditure needs, is used to determine present fiscal conditions and estimate future conditions. Against that backdrop, the financial requirements and budgetary impact of possible capital investments and debt financing alternatives can be assessed.

Debt Burden

The most common overall measure of debt burden is the *ratio of debt to debt-carrying capacity*. Two ratios are used: the ratio of debt service (payments for principal and interest) to total expenditures of the debt issuer and the ratio of debt service to current revenues. Respectively, these measures indicate how much of the issuer's total expenditures, once the new debt is incurred, will consist of debt service and how much of current revenues will be required to pay debt service.

Although there are no hard-and-fast rules, Standard & Poor's, for example, cites a debt service to expenditure ratio of less than 5% as very good, noting in one case that a 3.7% ratio is well below the state average of 9%, which is also acceptable.[84] Another investment finance firm, Franklin Templeton, cites approvingly in a positive assessment of state debt even in the midst of the recession that debt service as a proportion of total expenditures in 2010 was less than 10% for all but three states.[85] In 2009, Massachusetts was the only state with a debt service to expenditure ratio greater than 10 (11.7%),[86] and Massachusetts is the state noted earlier that though it ranked first in state indebtedness in 2009, it also ranked second in personal income per capita.

The World Bank often looks at the ratio of debt service to current revenues, the ratio of capital expenditures to total expenditures, and the excess of current revenues over ordinary operating expenditures as indicators of the ability of a city to incur additional debt. More refined measures focus not on actual revenues but on the revenue base itself. U.S. local governments commonly use the ratio of debt to the assessed value of taxable property, because that assessed value reflects a local government's basic ability to generate revenues. These quick indicators are all useful, but ultimately they are interpretable only in the context of a jurisdiction's overall debt management strategy.

For enterprise-like operations, such as water authorities, conventional ratio measures of debt burden are in common use. The *debt-to-equity ratio* is a measure of the extent to which a utility is financing itself through debt relative to equity. The higher the ratio, the more risk there is in additional debt issues, as lenders want to see borrowers also making significant commitments of their own resources (equity). Another common ratio, *interest share of operating income*, measures the amount of debt as a percentage that operating income has to cover.

Debt Management

In general, sound debt management at the state and local levels involves restricting debt primarily to financing long-term investments. A general rule is that borrowing should not be used to meet current operating expenses. The much-publicized 1970s financial crisis experienced by New York City involved short-term borrowing to finance current expenses. State regulations and in some cases statutory limitations generally prohibit short-term borrowing for operating expenses, with the exception of good cash-flow management practices. Occasionally, short-term borrowing is used to deal with emergencies but is often refinanced as part of a long-term debt issue. Moreover, the payout period of the debt should correspond to the useful life of the facility or infrastructure financed.

The rule to restrict debt to long-term capital financing does not apply to financial emergencies resulting from major flooding or unusually heavy snows during the winter, or states' emergency responses to the Gulf of Mexico Deepwater Horizon oil spill, for example. But this rule, along with the rule to match the payout period for the debt with the expected life of the facility, should generally be followed. Adherence to these two rules ensures that the jurisdiction will more or less match the benefit flows from capital facilities with the opportunity costs. One of the major positive results of the financial difficulties of cities such as New York has been an increase in the sophistication of the tools used in analyzing the financial condition of governments. These developments have been of great value in preventing significant financial crises and almost no collapses at the state and local levels after the 2007 financial markets collapse.[87] Furthermore, state governments have become quite involved in regulating local government debt, not only by means of the more traditional statutory and constitutional provisions that govern the powers and authority of local governments but also by means of extensive state programs of technical assistance. Effective debt management requires the balancing of competing claims against the current annual budget and future annual budgets. As a consequence, state and local governments increasingly rely on methods to assess overall financial health and place potential bond issues in that context.

Debt Refinancing

From time to time, substantial swings in market conditions bring interest rates down and spur a round of refinancing bonds. The low interest rates in the 1990s brought a surge in refinancing. In 1998, of $279 billion in new debt issues, nearly $121 billion, or 43%, were refinancings. In 2000, after interest rates rose again, less than 10% of $194 billion in new issues were for refinancing.[88] In 2010, with interest rates lower again, refinancing issues were about 36% ($175 billion) of the total new issuances.[89] State and local governments also have become more sophisticated in their transactions in the financial markets. One strategy in use is to swap the interest owed on outstanding bonds for more attractive interest rates. A traditional method for accomplishing that is to call in bonds that have higher interest rates when the market changes and rates fall. That is possible only with bonds having call features.

An alternative that does not require any actual transaction with outstanding bonds is an *interest rate swap*. In this type of transaction, the borrowing authority agrees to pay a third-party financial investor a variable rate of interest over a fixed period of time in exchange for payment of a fixed rate of interest by the third party. This is a synthetic variable rate financing deal in that the bonds themselves remain as they were with the terms and conditions unchanged.

The interest rate swap works by introducing a third party into the transactions between issuers and investors. During a period of high interest rates, for example, bond issuers try several strategies to control the effects of high interest. One strategy is to issue serial bonds, breaking the total issue into several annual *tranches*. If interest rates do fall from the high at the time the choice is made to issue a bond over a series of years, then the later tranches carry lower rates. Another strategy is to issue variable interest rate bonds tied to some short-term rate index. The issuer then may enter into a contract with a third party in which, for a fee, the third party agrees to swap fixed rate payments for the variable rate payments. The issuer decides from time to time whether to take the swap. The issuer "bets" that the fee paid for the swap option over time will be less than what the issuer saves by exercising the swap option.

Interest rate swaps can help or hurt. When variable rate securities are swapped for fixed rate, and interest rates then fall, issuers find themselves with higher interest costs. Harvard University, for example, paid investors almost $500 million to get out of $1.1 billion in interest rate swaps.[90] In contrast, the Cleveland Airport bond issue described earlier in this chapter included a successful refinancing that lowered overall future interest costs for the city-owned airport.[91]

Typically a debt swap is neutral with respect to bondholders. The state or local authority is simply trading in the financial market based on judgments about future interest rates. The original bond issue is not affected, in that investors will be paid according to the original terms. The borrowing authority, through a completely separate transaction, hedges against future interest rate changes and achieves, through a third party, a gain or a loss based on the marginal interest rate differences. The risk analysis focuses on whether the overall portfolio of the borrowing authority has been exposed to higher or lower future interest payments.

Interest rate swap strategies are different from the Orange County, California, strategy for its investments. In the interest rate swap hedges, the party involved negotiates a known risk and return range, and it keeps its maximum risk exposure within bounds of good financial management practice. In the Orange County case, the county's investment manager was in effect borrowing to bet on interest rates rising. When they fell, the county could not pay off the borrowed money.

PRIVATE EQUITY FINANCING FOR PUBLIC CAPITAL ASSETS

Traditionally, state and local governments, or subnational governments in other countries, finance infrastructure as described in the preceding sections. Most rely upon access to credit to address the lumpiness of the up-front investment. Since the privatization of the formerly public water authorities in the United Kingdom during the Thatcher administration (1979–1990), however, there have been waves of private equity investments in a wide variety of what normally have been considered public facilities or public assets.[92] Of course not any one precipitating phenomenon, such as the U.K. water sector privatizations, is *the* causal factor, but what once had been primarily the province of the electric power generation industry—seeking private equity investments to pay for public facilities—spread to a wide range of other public services.

This concluding section examines the options available to governments to attract private equity investment into public service facilities. Not all forms of public-private partnerships are considered in this section. For example, contracting with private companies to perform a public service, such as contracting out solid waste collection, may not involve private equity capital investment in public infrastructure. If such a contracting arrangement does involve service contracting plus equity investment, such as contracting for solid waste collection *and* licensing a company to use its own capital to build and operate a solid waste disposal facility, then it is considered in this section. Likewise, if an arrangement involves a contract turning over the assets of an existing infrastructure system or other capital asset to a private party, either for a fixed period or permanently, it is also considered in this section.

Figure 14–3 is a schematic depicting the major institutional arrangements for financing infrastructure or other capital facilities. The specifics of contractual provisions embodied in any one category illustrated in Figure 14–3 may be so varied that some authors would depict the categories somewhat differently. And there is not a universal language in which everyone agrees on exactly what to call a given institutional structure. Our illustration focuses on the role of the private sector in bringing debt and equity financing to a public infrastructure project. Figure 14–3 is illustrative and intended to present the array of options. In the figure, the first three categories involve no direct private equity or ownership participation and were discussed in preceding sections. The figure reads from left to right with the degree of private sector equity participation increasing.

Concession Contracts

Concession contracting involves a substantial change from conventional public sector financing and operation of public service facilities. Concession contracting involves the government awarding a contract with one or more companies to operate a service, such as a water utility, for a fixed concession period.[93] For a major public utility, 15 to 30 years is a common time frame.

There are three types of concessions. First is an operating concession in which a new facility or asset is to be constructed, and the private contractor both constructs *and* operates the facility for the contract period. However, in this structure, the contractor is not involved in the capital financing. A public bond issue, for example, provides the financing, and the contractor not only constructs the works, as in conventional bond financing for infrastructure, but also has a long-term contract to operate the facility. Second is a concession contract for operating an existing infrastructure system, but also for substantial rehabilitation and expansion of the system. In this arrangement, the contractor is responsible for both debt and equity capital finance. The third concession-type contract is similar to the second, except that it involves not an existing facility or capital asset, but the construction and operation of an entirely new facility—a so-called *greenfield* project. In contrast with the first type of concession contract, the private party is responsible for the capital financing requirements, both debt and equity.

In the middle of Figure 14–3 we show all three concession variants in which the private sector is brought in to operate a facility, such as a water treatment plant or a transit system. The top category is a *Build-Operate-Transfer* (BOT) structure, in which a private company is

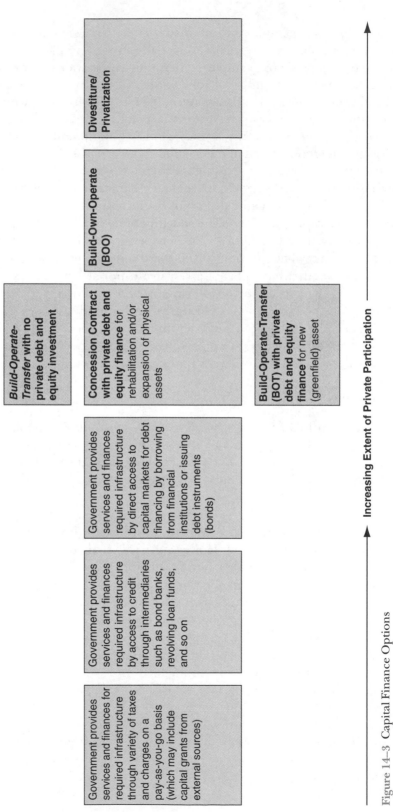

Figure 14–3 Capital Finance Options

awarded a contract to build and operate a facility for a period of time, but the government or agency that contracts with the private group provides 100% of the financing.

An example of this form of BOT is the Hudson-Bergen Light Rail (HBLR) project in New Jersey. A Phase I contract valued at $1.1 billion was awarded in 1996 to a private consortium consisting of an infrastructure construction company and two railway car and other railway products manufacturers and operators to build and operate for a 15-year period the first (9.5 miles) segment of an eventual 25-mile light rail system along the Hudson River in two counties. The private contractor was responsible for designing, building, and operating for the 15-year contract period the entire system, including construction of the railway and the stations and provision of the rolling stock. The initial concession was expanded somewhat in scope, with the contract value increased to $1.9 billion and the concession period extended to 20 years. All initial segments were completed and in operation by 2005 and 2006.[94] Subsequent contracts have been awarded to complete additional segments expanding the line.

The private consortia assumed an operating responsibility for HLBR, but assumed no responsibility for capital finance. The State of New Jersey issued bonds to finance the project, secured by a pledge of future federal transit grants—*grant anticipation note* (GAN)—authorized under TEA-21 (discussed earlier). In the event that these discretionary grants were not awarded, or were insufficient, a secondary pledge of funds in the New Jersey State transportation trust fund secured the bonds, though the secondary pledge was not needed.

The Jakarta, Indonesia, water concession contracts first executed in 1997 are examples of the second type of concession contract in Figure 14–3. With World Bank and International Finance Corporation assistance, the Jakarta public water authority and the central government of Indonesia began working on a public-private partnership in the early 1990s. Ultimately, Jakarta was split into two geographic areas, and competitive bidding resulted in two different consortia of international and Indonesian firms being awarded contracts. The lead international partners in the two concession contracts were Thames Water and Suez Lyonnaise des Eaux, respectively. Thames was one of the U.K. private water companies resulting from the divestiture of public water authority assets in the United Kingdom about a decade earlier, and Suez Lyonnaise was a French private water operator. Both lead international companies started as public utilities and by the time of the Jakarta concession were private, owning in various forms and operating water companies in their home countries as well as other countries.

In 1997, the Metropolitan Manila (Philippines) Water and Sewer Services authority (MWSS) similarly bid out and executed two contracts dividing the metro area roughly in half. The two winning companies were awarded concessions to operate the services for 25 years, and each was required to invest in significant capital facilities improvements, including rehabilitation of existing infrastructure, extension of water lines, and building of new treatment capacity. The lead international firm was Lyonnaise des Eaux, prior to its merger with Suez Water.

The two examples of developing country water concessions started in a period (late 1980s and 1990s) of great enthusiasm for privatization in the international donor finance community, including the World Bank and its financing arm the International Finance Corporation and bilateral donors such as the U.S. Agency for International Development (USAID). Collapse of the financial markets in Asia not long after those two concessions began, discussed below, cooled somewhat the ardor for concession contracting in developing country finance for a while. But these major water concessions of the late 1990s were not just phenomena in developing countries.

A U.S. example is the case of Atlanta, Georgia, which entered in 1997 into a 20-year concession contract for water services. It has been called a privatization, but as we discuss below, it is more accurately characterized as a concession contract, as Atlanta never sold or assigned the assets to the concessionaire, United Water, a subsidiary of Suez Water. The Atlanta contract was canceled after several years. In the same year, Vancouver-area authorities completed initial planning for a Richmond-Airport-Vancouver (RAV) rapid transit project. Central government financing made available in the early 2000s, emphasizing public-private partnerships, was a stimulus in financing the RAV through a concession contract, ultimately signed with a consortium, InTransitBC, formed for this specific project. The project was largely completed prior to the Vancouver 2010 Olympics, but not without cost overruns and political controversy.[95]

Characteristics of Concession Contracts

All four concessions described above reflect similar principles. First, concession contracts were selected in preference to privatization or divestiture, discussed below, largely for country-specific legal reasons, due to local political pressures, and to avoid the unfavorable perceptions that the governments were selling off the authority and responsibility to the private sector to deliver services. Public utility concessions generally are competed on the basis of bidders' proposals as to the amount of capital investment they will make, the time period over which that investment will occur, the rates they will charge consumers for the services, and the stipulation that all facilities will be properly maintained so that at the end of the concession period, a fully functional utility with fully functional capital assets will remain.

The Buenos Aires water concession awarded in 1993, one of the first major water concessions, illustrates these principles. It is an important case because long-term concession contracts are decades in planning and implementation; it would likely take a decade or more to be able to reach any conclusion concerning how they have and have not accomplished their multiple and sometimes competing goals. Under the Buenos Aires contract, all bidders were required to invest $240 million per year for the first five years in infrastructure. This compares with only about $10 million per year in capital investments in the preceding several years by the pubic sector utility. The competition was decided on the basis of which bidder offered the largest rate reduction. The winner contracted to reduce water rates by 26.9%, slightly above the 26.1% proposed by the second closest bidder.[96]

Several features of the Buenos Aires concession illustrate the features typically designed to ensure that the public sector's responsibility for the public service is treated by the concessionaire as a *public* responsibility and that consumers' interests are protected by provisions in the contract:

1. Water quality and quantity requirements such as volume and water pressure
2. Operating improvements such as installing a metering system
3. New capital facilities such as building sewage treatment plants

4. Increased population coverage for water and sewerage services
5. Tariffs fixed for five years at a time, and otherwise renegotiable only as a result of situations beyond the concessionaire's control
6. Preservation of employment and negotiation of union contracts
7. Significant capital investment; in the Buenos Aires case, this was at least $4 billion over the life of the concession, more than $1 billion of which was to be invested in the first five years. The project was subsequently augmented with the investment target just over $2 billion in the first 10 years.[97]

In this concession-type arrangement, the concessionaire is responsible for all financing, both capital and operating. The public sector is not required to provide capital grants or to raise debt capital for the program. One of the main features, aside from specific contract provisions of the type listed above, is that the concession contract stipulates the minimum amount of the capital investment that must come from concessionaire's equity participation. This has the effect of ensuring the concessionaire's performance over the concession period. The public sector is interested in seeing the concessionaire finance as large a proportion of the cost as can be negotiated as equity investment, whereas the private party is usually interested in minimizing the equity investment. Typical outcomes are 15% to 30% equity investment.

What the public sector gains from the equity investment is that the concessionaire has contributed its own capital and will not be able to make a profit unless it manages the utility efficiently and effectively to generate the return on equity. The more debt financing, the more *other people's money* other than that of the concessionaire is in the enterprise, the less incentive there is to maintain the physical infrastructure. And in the worst case, the concessionaire going bankrupt in an all debt-financed enterprise would leave the concessionaire without a significant capital loss, having no equity in the enterprise, and the public holding the bag with a dysfunctional public service.

Concession contracting, and the remaining structures for private equity financing, is not as simple as portrayed here, of course. Major concession contracts typically take three to five years to design, bid, and negotiate. To protect the public interest, the negotiating public entity spends considerable capital on legal and financial advisory fees. The concessionaires, of course, are sophisticated in the business of private investment in the specific service and in operating the business. Developing countries especially, but also smaller jurisdictions in industrialized countries, have been at a significant disadvantage in negotiating the earliest contracts, but a couple of decades are rectifying that experience gap between the public sector and private concessionaires.[98] Most of the earlier concession contracts developed problems—some quickly, and some after several years. The Jakarta concessions were awarded only months before the overthrow of the Suharto regime and less than a year before the Asia financial collapse that caused the Indonesian rupiah to devalue against the U.S. dollar from about 3,700 to 1 to about 20,000 to 1. Water consumers in Jakarta, of course, paid their water tariffs in rupiah, whereas much of the debt and equity financing the concessionaires brought to the contracts were denominated in various international currencies, mainly the dollar, pound, and franc. The immediate problem in both the Jakarta and Manila concessions was renegotiating the tariffs to allow at least cost recovery because, as in the Buenos Aires details listed above, events outside the control of the concessionaire were grounds for renegotiation of contract terms. The Vancouver RAV project was largely completed at some cost overrun, but it is regarded by local officials as a success because it contributed to success of the Winter Olympics held there in 2010 and addressed the transportation goals. We discuss a larger set of issues in the assessment section of this chapter.

Build-Operate-Transfer (BOT)

A variation in concession contracting illustrated in Figure 14–3, involving a still higher degree of private sector investment, is the Build-Operate-Transfer (BOT) structure. Contractual features are quite similar to those already discussed above in connection with the Buenos Aires concession. However, a BOT structure is more common where the intent is to build infrastructure in a geographic area in which no service currently exists, or to extend existing service to a new area, a so-called greenfield project, sometimes also called an *enclave project*, because the contractor is not dealing with an existing system. The BOT contractor is not awarded a concession to improve and operate an existing system or facility, but rather is awarded a contract to create a facility or service where no services or minimal ones previously existed, or where a new facility will be added into an existing system but can be built and operated separately from the existing system. In the BOT structure, the private party does not own the capital assets.

The BOT contracts have been common in the electric power generation and bulk water supply industries. The existing power supply is either inadequate or nonexistent. Therefore, a contract is awarded to a private contractor to build, operate, and, at the end of the contract period, transfer to the public sector the new facility. In the bulk water supply industry, the BOT contract is used to build and operate for a period of time a new impoundment, a new deep well system, or a new extraction/treatment plant to obtain bulk water from an existing source such as a river. Malaysia has used the BOT mechanism extensively for new bulk water and treatment facilities.

The BOT contracts often are characterized by what is called a *take-or-pay mechanism* for determining payments to the contractor. That is, the contractor agrees to deliver a minimum volume, for instance kilowatts of electricity or cubic meters of water, and the public utility agrees to buy at least that minimum amount. Price per unit is based on that minimum. The public utility will *take* that minimum for which the private contractor likely will be paid by tariffs paid by the consumers. But if the minimum is not actually required by the utility's customers, the utility will nonetheless *pay* the contractor for that minimum. The contractor has the assurance of the minimum, but if demand is there, the contractor may sell more than the minimum.

Other contract features are similar, especially requiring some minimum proportion of the capital investment to be the private operator's equity investment. Again, this is intended to protect the public sector against the contractor terminating the agreement early. With no equity investment, the contractor has nothing invested to lose, and should anything go wrong, the debt suppliers are the ultimate losers, along with the public utility executing the deal in the first place and its customers. The BOT structures often involve public funding as well as private funding, or they may require that the contractor finance the entire project. The contractor needs assurances of operating the facility for a period of time sufficient to achieve a return on its equity and to repay debt financing. The public agency needs to ensure that the prices charged are reasonable in the market, and that the facility is still in operating condition at the time of the transfer. Contract negotiations revolve around these two sets of provisions.

Build-Own-Operate-Transfer (BOOT)

The *Build-Own-Operate-Transfer* (BOOT) structure is a variant of the BOT. The distinguishing feature is that the private investor/operator for a period of time actually owns the capital assets. It too has a variant, the *Build-Own-Operate* (BOO). The Enron Corporation became a large multinational corporation by its innovative solutions to power problems in developing countries. One of its early successes was building generating stations on barges and bringing the barges into the metropolitan Manila harbor to add capacity to the existing system. These barges were owned by Enron. At the end of the contract, the barges could be sold to the utility or to other parties, or floated away to be used by Enron elsewhere. The most common practice where the facility is permanently located is that the contract will have provisions for the public entity's buying the facility at a negotiated price at the end of the contract period. Note that this is not a salvage price, the residual value of an asset whose useful life has for the most part been exhausted. The utility is expected to be fully operational, to have been well maintained, and to be able to provide service continuously into the future. These characteristics will be a primary feature of the concession contract. Telecommunications, transportation, and water are the traditional sectors for large BOOT contract structures for bringing private sector financing into what otherwise would have been a public responsibility.

Divestiture/Privatization

At the end of the spectrum in Figure 14–3 is divestiture or privatization. A public sector entity may decide upon divestiture of a set of assets because the facility is deteriorating, needs significant investment, or is perhaps at the periphery of what the public now thinks of as a "public sector responsibility." Not all *privatizations* involve an irrevocable sale of assets. Municipally owned parking garages are an example of an asset that sometimes is irrevocably sold to a private party, with the municipality retaining no interest in the garage. Other so-called privatizations are actually leases that for all practical purposes are seen by the public as permanent.

In 2006, Chicago executed a 99-year lease on the Skyway, an expressway connecting Chicago and Indiana, to an international consortium for $1.83 billion, and the Skyway was not the only divestiture in Chicago's plan. Morgan Stanley, an investment firm, bought four downtown parking garages for $563 million, and in 2007, the city offered Midway Airport for sale.[99] The group negotiating to purchase Midway ultimately failed to secure financing, and the sale was terminated in 2009. Tight credit markets were blamed for the inability to get financing to make the purchase.[100] Similarly, in 2006, the State of Indiana leased the Indiana Toll Road for 75 years, at a cost of $3.8 billion, to two international companies. In contrast, efforts by New Jersey to privatize the New Jersey Turnpike did not materialize.[101]

Sales of these types can be controversial in the post–September 11 era, when Americans are wary of international investors owning and/or operating major infrastructure. The Chicago Skyway, for instance, is operated by a group of Australian and Spanish investors. In 2006, a deal by a Dubai ports management firm—Dubai Ports World—to manage six U.S. seaports was killed because of the uproar over a foreign company taking over facilities vital to homeland security.

At the heart of the divestiture decision on the part a of governmental institution is whether the assets being divested are a fundamental public sector responsibility that can or should be turned over to the private sector. If a service is considered to be a fundamental public sector responsibility, why bring in the private sector, which lacks traditional public service values? But there is no clear answer in many cases, as only a few public sector goods meet the test of a *pure* public good (see the introductory chapter). Many public services may have varying degrees of private sector involvement without real consequence to the public one way or the other. Many cities own and operate parking garages, for example. Many other cities have no public parking garages but leave parking entirely in the hands of the private sector. There is no obvious criterion that says parking garages should clearly be public, or clearly be private—or at least there is no criterion upon which everyone agrees.

Appraisal of Private Equity Investment Experience

The controversy over privatization or divestiture usually arises when citizens or interest groups feel the city, or other governmental entity, is turning over a fundamental public interest to the private sector, and leaving citizens (especially poorer citizens) unprotected in the aftermath.[102] In every developing country, water sector public-private partnerships of any of the forms above lead to higher prices to some consumers. But this is often in the context of systems that have been previously heavily subsidized with the utility rarely recovering capital costs, and often not even fully recovering operating costs. The utility usually faces a major need for renovation and expansion as a result of urbanization, and the capital is just not available to the public sector.

Typically in these developing countries, the wealthy and middle-income segments have been the only ones receiving direct piped service to their residences, and they enjoy low, subsidized rates. The extremely poor segment of the population pays for bottled water or buys from vendors who travel through impoverished neighborhoods, and the price they pay per liter is generally 5 to 10 times more than the per liter cost to a middle-income household connected to the public system.

The concession or BOOT-type contract then can be quite controversial because current customers may experience rate increases, although the average rate may go down because of the addition of lower-income, low-volume users. One of the remedies for protecting the lowest income segment is what is sometimes called the *life support* tariff. The first several cubic liters of water service, an amount estimated to be the amount needed to live, is free or billed at a very low cost. Rates then go up as consumption goes up, and the middle- and upper-income groups thus pay more.

In some of the examples cited in this chapter, such as the Buenos Aires case, the concession is for services in which the existing management of the utility has become inefficient, including possibly employing a much larger workforce because the utility was serving not only to provide water, but to provide the social good of employment whether the employees were required or not. In those cases, the concession contract generally lowers the marginal cost of the service.

Certainly there are examples of high expectations not being met.[103] The two Jakarta water concessions have remained controversial, in part because at the time the contracts were awarded, both international lead firms had joint ventures with companies owned and directed by members of the then-ruling Suharto family. It has taken more than a decade to work through some of the problems built into the original contracts and to recover from the effects of the 1997 financial collapse in Indonesia as well as much of the rest of Asia. The 2007 financial market collapse similarly put a damper on long-term concession arrangements and full privatizations because of the lack of debt capital available to private investors seeking concession opportunities.

Considerable experience has amassed in both the public and private sectors in the past two decades, and sophisticated expertise is available to both sectors to protect the public interest and also to ensure a fair return on investment to the private party.[104] And public interest groups and other watchdogs are actively engaged in informing the public, sometimes dispassionately and sometimes with a strong bias. But we can confidently say that various forms of private equity financing for major capital facilities providing public services will continue to grow. The first driver is capital markets expansion. As capital markets expand, investors such as pension funds look for attractive long-term investments. The second driver is the inability of governments to find enough capital themselves to meet the demand for infrastructure. As governments face pressures to focus on vital public services, they will likely consider divesting themselves of enterprise-like operations that are easily converted to private operations.

SUMMARY

Because of the long life of capital facilities and infrastructure, extensive use is made of long-term financing in various forms. Both the public and private sectors combine debt and equity financing to satisfy capital investment needs, with equity financing for public sector infrastructure a phenomenon that has emerged in the past 30 years. Some local governments still consider it financially prudent to borrow little or not at all, but state governments and virtually all large cities are unable to provide the services demanded by citizens without resorting to some debt financing for capital investments. Although it is generally accepted that future generations should not be saddled with unreasonable debt burdens about which they have no say, most citizens recognize that capital facilities will be enjoyed by future generations. Debt financing provides a means for those future generations to share the costs as well as the benefits.

Governments typically lack the resources to fully finance the infrastructure requirements alone, although some smaller local governments do use *pay-as-you-go* financing. Governments have historically relied on private capital for financing, first to raise debt capital, and in recent years private equity capital. The municipal debt market has undergone remarkable changes in the past decade. Sophisticated structured financing tools developed for private debt and equity transactions are being applied to municipal debt issues. In addition, municipalities are using increasingly sophisticated money management techniques to minimize their cost of debt and to maximize the returns on their own investments. Occasionally these techniques result in major financial disasters. As a result, the SEC, which once had a hands-off attitude toward the municipal debt market, has adopted increasingly stringent disclosure requirements, and Congress has increased the SEC's regulatory role regarding municipal debt.

Effective debt management requires that the amount of debt incurred not impose hardships on future taxpayers and that it not force future cutbacks in operation and maintenance expenditures necessary to maintain capital facilities. State governments, through constitutional provisions and statutory requirements, regulate their own borrowing as well as that of local governments. These regulations focus mainly on the commitment of the "full faith and credit" of the jurisdiction. Partly because of the restrictions imposed on general obligation bonds and partly because of the efficiency of tying repayment of debt to specific revenues generated by the investment, there has been tremendous growth in the use of a wide variety of debt instruments. Overall, however, state and local debt has grown little over the past 30 years in relation to personal income. State and local governments also have become more sophisticated in their financial analysis of capital investments and debt financing.

Even with innovations in municipal bonds and other means for governments to access the capital markets for credit, debt financing has not been sufficient. Beginning largely with the privatization of the United Kingdom's water utilities, the involvement of public-private partnerships in financing and operating public infrastructure has become commonplace in both industrialized and developing countries. Various forms of concession contracting, including structures that feature private operating concessions only to structures that feature significant private debt and equity financing, are increasing. This industry has had significant problems with many of the earliest large concession-type contracts, but with experience, sophistication on the sides of both private investors and the public sector has made various forms of private financing more attractive to both investors and public agencies.

NOTES

1. Securities Industry and Financial Markets Association (2011). *Outstanding U.S. bond market debt*. Retrieved November 4, 2011, from http://www.sifma.org/research/statistics.aspx.
2. Industry center: Cargill Inc. profile. (2011). *Yahoo! Finance*. Retrieved November 4, 2011, from http://biz.yahoo.com/ic/40/40079.html.
3. For simplicity's sake, we do not discuss forms of ownership here. A private limited liability company (LLC) also has shares, and additional investors may be allowed to contribute equity capital by purchasing shares. But the shares are not listed publicly and are not available for sale to the public.
4. Capital investments are not the only use of retained earnings, of course. A privately held company may use retained earnings to acquire the assets of another company, including that company's capital facilities, accounts receivable and payable, and so forth. Similarly, publicly traded companies may use retained earnings for acquisitions other than capital investments.
5. Johnson, R. (1996). *Capital financing for municipal infrastructure: choices as viewed by the enterprise and the investor*. Research Triangle Park, NC: RTI International; Brinkerhoff, D., Johnson, R., & Hill, R.

(2009). *Guide to rebuilding public sector services in stability operations: a role for the military.* Carlysle, PA: Strategic Studies Institute, U.S. Army War College.

6. Maguire, S. (2011). *Tax credit bonds: overview and analysis.* Washington, DC: Congressional Research Service.

7. Kaske, M. (2011). Revenue bonds catch up to general-obligation debt: muni credit. *Bloomberg.com.* Retrieved November 5, 2011, from http://www.bloomberg.com/news/2011-09-08/revenue-bonds-catch-up-to-general-obligations-as-growth-slows-muni-credit.html.

8. For 1980s data, The Bond Market Association (2006). *Trends in the holdings of municipal securities: 1985–2006, Q2.* Retrieved December 19, 2006, from http://www.bondmarkets.com/story .asp?id=318 (site no longer accessible).

9. Martell, C., & Guess, G. (2006). Development of local government debt financing markets: application of a market-based framework. *Public Budgeting & Finance, 26,* Spring, 88–119; Liebig, K. (2008). *Municipal borrowing for infrastructure service delivery in South Africa: a critical review.* Bonn, Germany: Deutsches Institut für Entwicklungspolitik; Platz, D. (2009). *Infrastructure finance in developing countries—the potential of sub-sovereign bonds.* New York, NY: United Nations Department of Economic and Social Affairs.

10. Bureau of the Census, U.S. Department of Commerce (2012). *Statistical abstract of the United States: 2012* (p. 276). Washington, DC: U.S. Government Printing Office.

11. Wang, W., & Hou, Y. (2009). Pay-as-you-go financing and capital outlay volatility: evidence from the states over two recent economic cycles. *Public Budgeting and Finance, 29,* Winter, 90–107.

12. Wang, W., et al. (2007). Determinants of pay-as-you-go financing of capital projects: evidence from the states. *Public Budgeting and Finance, 27,* Winter, 18–42.

13. Securities Industry and Financial Markets Association (2011). *About municipal bonds: federal and state tax tables.* Retrieved November 3, 2011, from http://www.investinginbonds.com/learnmore .asp?catid=8&subcatid=60.

14. Marlin, M. (1994). Did tax reform kill segmentation in the municipal bond market? *Public Administration Review, 54,* 387–390.

15. The White House (2010). *The moment of truth: report of the national commission on fiscal responsibility and reform.* Washington, DC: U.S. Government Printing Office.

16. Hume, L., & Temple-West, P. (2011). Obama proposal stuns market: market participants weigh impact of tax-exempt interest cap. *The Bond Buyer,* September 14. Retrieved November 6, 2011, from http://www.bondbuyer.com/issues/120_177/muni-reaction-obama-jobs-bill-1031028-1.html.

17. *South Carolina* v. *Baker* (1988). 485 U.S. 505.

18. For a discussion of the history of legal actions concerning state and local tax immunity, see Wrightson, M. (1989). The road to *South Carolina:* intergovernmental tax immunity and the constitutional status of federalism. *Publius, 19,* Winter, 39–55.

19. Ossa, F. (2011). Brazil public works may turn to asset-backeds. *The Bond Buyer,* September 14. Retrieved November 6, 2011, from http://www.bondbuyer.com/idd/brazil-public-works-may-turn-to-asset-backeds-1020950-1.html.

20. National Council of State Housing Agencies (2011). *SEC approves asset-backed security rules, municipal securities implementation delayed until 2015.* Retrieved November 5, 2011, from http://www.ncsha .org/blog/sec-approves-asset-backed-security-rules-municipal-securities-implementation-delayed-until-2015.

21. Resnick, A. (2006). *Capital asset seeking to continue success with lien purchasing service.* Retrieved December 20, 2006, from http://www.lienexchange.com/Tax-Lien-Certificates-Capital-Asset-Seeking-To-Continue-Success-With-Lien-Purchasing-Service.html. This page is no longer accessible, but additional information is available at http://www.allbusiness.com/accounting-reporting/assets/565197-1.html, accessed December 13, 2011.

22. Lemov, P. (2000). Tobacco bonds draw a market. *Governing, 14,* January, 54.

23. Barrett, K., et al. (2005). Grading the states '05: the year of living dangerously. *Governing, 19,* February. Retrieved December 20, 2006, from http://www.governing.com/GPP/2005/intro.htm.

24. Seymour, D. (2010). Illinois exhales after tobacco deal. *The Bond Buyer*, December 3. Retrieved November 7, 2011, from http://www.bondbuyer.com/idd/illinois-exhales-after-tobacco-deal-1020649-1.html.

25. Deavitt, C. (2011). Cleveland airport offering $75 million in a rare deal. *The Bond Buyer*, October 31. Retrieved November 8, 2011, from http://www.bondbuyer.com/issues/120_209/cleveland-hopkins-revenue-bond-deal-1032601-1.html.

26. LeighFisher Management Consultants (2002). *Passenger facility charge convertible lien bonds for airport expansion*. Retrieved December 21, 2006, from http://www.leighfisher.com/pdfs/expertise/FLL10 .pdf (page no longer accessible).

27. Fitch downgrades Fort Lauderdale int'l airport (FL) system revs to "A" and pfc bonds to "A–." (2011). *The Bond Buyer*, April 25. Retrieved November 8, 2011, from http://www.bondbuyer.com/news/-1025905-1.html.

28. Johnson, T., & Scott, J. (2004). A comprehensive approach to the assessment of tax increment financing (TIF) projects. *Journal of Public Budgeting, Accounting & Financial Management, 16*, 394–412.

29. Indiana Department of Local Government Finance (2011). *Economic development: tax increment financing (TIF)*. Retrieved November 3, 2011, from http://www.in.gov/indot/div/projects/ i69planningtoolbox/_pdf/Tax%20Increment%20Financing.pdf.

30. Hildreth, W., & Zorn, C. (2005). The evolution of state and local government municipal debt markets over the past quarter century. *Public Budgeting & Finance, 25*, Silver Anniversary Special Edition, 127–153.

31. Hildreth, W., & Zorn, C. (2005). The evolution of state and local government municipal debt markets over the past quarter century.

32. Internal Revenue Service, U.S. Department of the Treasury (2005). *Introduction to federal taxation of municipal bonds*. Retrieved November 3, 2011, from http://www.irs.gov/pub/irs-tege/teb_phase_1_ course_11204_-2module_a.pdf.

33. Pohle, L. (1991). Marketing mini-bonds: lessons learned from Denver's successful first issuance. *Government Finance Review, 7*, June, 32–34.

34. California governor oks bill for "mini-bonds." (2011). *Reuters*, September 7. Retrieved November 8, 2011, from http://www.reuters.com/article/2011/09/08/us-economy-california-minibonds-idUSTRE78700G20110908.

35. Argument advanced in legislative analysis of the Senate version of the California bill that was signed in September 2011. Retrieved November 8, 2011, from http://www.leginfo.ca.gov/pub/11-12/bill/ asm/ab_1401-1450/ab_1408_cfa_20110816_143351_sen_floor.html.

36. Johnson, C., & Mikesell, J. (1994). Certificates of participation and capital markets: lessons from Brevard County and Richmond Unified School District. *Public Budgeting & Finance, 14*, Fall, 41–54.

37. Safe Drinking Water Act of 1974 (P.L. 95-523).

38. New York State Environmental Facility (2011). *Bonds outstanding*. Retrieved November 9, 2011, from http://www.nysefc.org/Finance/BondsOutstanding.aspx.

39. Council of State Governments (2011). *State infrastructure banks* (p. 1). Lexington, KY: Council of State Governments.

40. National Highway System Designation Act of 1995 (P.L. 104-59); Transportation Safety Act of 1998 (P.L. 105-178); Safe, Accountable, Flexible, Efficient Transportation Equity Act: A Legacy for Users (2005; P.L. 109-59).

41. Federal Highway Administration (2009). *Project finance state by state, 1998–2008: state infrastructure banks*. Washington, DC: Author. Retrieved November 1, 2011, from http://www.transportation-finance.org/tools/state_by_state/sibs.aspx.

42. Peterson, G. (2006). *Using municipal development funds to build municipal credit markets*. Washington, DC: Urban Institute.

43. Martell, C., & Guess, G. (2006). *Development of local government debt financing markets*, (pp. 88–119); Brinkerhoff, D., Johnson, R., & Hill, R. (2009). *Guide to rebuilding public sector services in stability operations: a role for the military*.

44. Feldstein, S., & Fabozzi, F. (Eds.) (2008). *The handbook of municipal bonds*. New York, NY: Wiley.

45. Quint, M. (2008). Municipal bond fees rising at fastest pace since 1981 (update 1). *Bloomberg*. Retrieved November 5, 2011, from http://www.bloomberg.com/apps/news?pid=newsarchive&refer =&sid=ajcOgJLW5ed4; Ang, A., & Green, R. (2011). *Lowering borrowing costs for states and municipalities through CommonMuni* (p. 2). Washington, DC: Brookings Institution.

46. Bloomberg Financial (2001). Municipal bond investors pay low spreads in Nevada, cited in *Las Vegas Review Online Edition*, January 23. Retrieved August 15, 2002, from http://www.lvrj.com/lvrj_home/2001/ Jan–23–Tue–2001/business/15271455.html (page no longer accessible); Mississippi Legislature Joint Committee on Performance Evaluation and Expenditure Review (2001). *Cost of issuance expenses cy 2000 state and local bond issues*. Retrieved December 20, 2006, from http://www .peer.state.ms.us/427.pdf.

47. Clinger, J., et al. (2008). Turnover, transaction costs, and time horizons: an examination of municipal debt financing. *American Review of Public Administration, 38*, 167–179.

48. Krueger, S., & Walker, R. (2008). Divided government, political turnover, and state bond ratings. *Public Finance Review, 36*, 259–286; Devitt, C. (2011). Panelists: politics play big part in analyzing governments' credit. *The Bond Buyer*, April 28. Retrieved November 10, 2011, from http://www .bondbuyer.com/issues/120_81/-1026021-1.html.

49. Marois, M., & Selway, W. (2006). Oregon taxpayers denied benefits of competitive bids for schools. *Bloomberg.com*. Retrieved December 28, 2006, from http://www.bloomberg.com/apps/news?pid =20601015&sid=aY6EMMx6FDc8&refer=munibonds#.

50. Preston, D. (2011). Voters approve at least $10.5 billion in debt. *Bloomberg.com*. Retrieved November 9, 2011, from http://www.bloomberg.com/news/2011-11-09/voters-in-u-s-pass-at-least-10-4-billion-of-debt-measures-led-by-texas.html.

51. National Conference of State Legislatures (2006). *State and municipal bond general elections 2006: voter approval rate exceeds average*. Retrieved December 27, 2006, from http://www.ncsl.org/programs/ fiscal/bonds06vote.htm (note: this report has been archived).

52. Robbins, M., & Simonsen, B. (2007). Competition and selection in municipal bond sales: evidence from Missouri. *Public Budgeting and Finance, 27*, Summer, 88–103.

53. WM Financial Strategies (2011). *Methods of sale*. Retrieved November 1, 2011, from http://www .munibondadvisor.com/SaleChoice.htm.

54. WM Financial Strategies (2011). *Municipal bond underwriting spreads: how underwriters make money*. Retrieved November 8, 2011, from http://www.munibondadvisor.com/UnderwritingSpread.htm.

55. Tavakoli, J. (2003).*Collateralized debt obligations and structured finance: new developments in cash and synthetic securitization*. New York, NY: Wiley.

56. Zhao, Z., & Guo, H. (2011). Management capacity and state municipal bond ratings: evidence with the GPP grades. *American Review of Public Administration, 41*, 562–576.

57. Krueger, S., & Walker, R. (2010). Management practices and state bond ratings. *Public Budgeting and Finance, 30*, Winter, 47–70.

58. Better bond rating is boon to Honolulu. (2006). *Honolulu Star Bulletin*, December 21. Retrieved December 27, 2006, from http://starbulletin.com/2006/12/21/editorial/letters.html.

59. Securities Industry and Financial Markets Association (2011). *Research quarterly: Q2 2011*. Retrieved November 8, 2011, from http://www.sifma.org/research/item.aspx?id=8589935096.

60. McGee, P. (2011). Experts agree to disagree on the direction of munis. *The Bond Buyer*, September 28. Retrieved November 10, 2011, from http://www.bondbuyer.com/issues/120_187/experts-municipal-bond-market-1031525-1.html?zkPrintable=true.

61. Doty, R. (1990). The role of the Municipal Securities Rulemaking Board and the central repository for public securities: dealer regulation or market regulation? *Municipal Finance Journal, 11*, 7–51.

62. Municipal Securities Rulemaking Board (2006). *Rule G-14: Reports of Sales or Purchases*. Retrieved November 8, 2011, from http://www.msrb.org/Rules-and-Interpretations/MSRB-Rules/General/ Rule-G-14.aspx.

63. U.S. Securities and Exchange Commission (2008). *SEC, MSRB: new measures to provide more transparency than ever before for municipal bond investor*. Retrieved November 7, 2011, from http://www.sec .gov/news/press/2008/2008-286.htm.

64. Lemov, P. (1996). A new investment rule requires "suitable" advice. *Governing, 10*, October, 57.

65. Denison, D., et al. (2006). State debt limits: how many are enough? *Public Budgeting & Finance, 26*, Winter, 22–39.

66. Securities Industry and Financial Markets Association (2011). *Municipal bond and credit report: fourth quarter and full year 2010.* Retrieved November 9, 2011, from http://www.sifma.org/research/item .aspx?id=23188, 16.

67. Bureau of the Census, U.S. Department of Commerce (2011). *Statistical abstract of the United States: 2012* (p. 268). Washington, DC: U.S. Government Printing Office.

68. Bureau of the Census, U.S. Department of Commerce. *Statistical abstract of the United States, 1985*, (p. 274); *1996* (p. 304); *2005* (Table 427); *State and local government financial summary 2009* (p. 4). Washington, DC: U.S. Government Printing Office.

69. Tax Foundation (2011). *Map: state debt per capita: fiscal 2009.* Retrieved November 8, 2011, from http://www.taxfoundation.org/research; Bureau of the Census, U.S. Department of Commerce (2011). *Statistical abstract of the United States: 2011* (p. 445). Washington, DC: U.S. Government Printing Office.

70. Dickson, S. (1993). Civil war, railroads, and road bonds: bond repudiations in the days of yore. In J. Lamb et al. (Eds.), *The handbook of municipal bonds and public finance* (pp. 166–173). New York, NY: New York Institute of Finance.

71. Mitchell, G. (1975). Statement before the Committee on Banking, Housing and Urban Affairs. *Federal Reserve Bulletin, 61*, 729–730.

72. Nicholas, M. (2011). Bond dealers seek to set the record straight on defaults. *The Bond Buyer*, February 28. Retrieved November 6, 2011, from http://www.bondbuyer.com/issues/120_39/ commentary_bond_dealers_america-1023761-1.html.

73. Wells Fargo Funds Management LLC (2011). *Keeping municipal default risk in perspective* (p. 3). Retrieved December 13, 2011, from http://www.wellsfargoadvantagefunds.com/pdf/whitepapers/ muni_default_risk_wp.pdf.

74. Dickson, R. (1995). *Civil war, railroads, and road bonds: bond repudiations in the days of yore* (p. 172); Collin, R. (1995). What the law says about Orange County: creditors' rights and remedies on municipal default. *Municipal Finance Journal, 16*, Summer, 52–89.

75. Cohen, N. (1989). Municipal default patterns: an historical study. *Public Budgeting & Finance, 9*, Winter, 62.

76. Leigland, J., & Lamb, R. (1986). *WPP$$: who is to blame for the WPPSS disaster?* Cambridge, MA: Ballinger.

77. Sitzer, H. (1994). The Washington Public Power Supply System: then and now. *Municipal Finance Journal, 14*, Winter, 59–78.

78. Watson, D., et al. (2005). Financial distress and municipal bankruptcy: the case of Prichard, Alabama. *Journal of Public Budgeting, Accounting & Financial Management, 17*, 129–150.

79. Park, K. (2004). To file or not to file: the causes of municipal bankruptcy in the United States. *Journal of Public Budgeting, Accounting & Financial Management, 16*, 228–256.

80. Halstead, J., et al. (2004). Orange County bankruptcy: financial contagion in the municipal bond and bank equity markets. *Financial Review, 39*, 293–315.

81. Burton, P. (2011). Attorney for Harrisburg, Pa., puts bondholders first. *The Bond Buyer*, November 9. Retrieved November 10, 2011, from http://www.bondbuyer.com/issues/120_216/harrisburg-pa-bankruptcy-1032952-1.html; Burton, P. (2011). Pa. emergency action plan ensures services for Harrisburg. *The Bond Buyer*, November 4. Retrieved November 10, 2011, from http://www.bond-buyer.com/news/harrisburg-emergency-action-bankruptcy-1032821-1.html.

82. Sigo, S. (2011). Jefferson county finally files for bankruptcy. *The Bond Buyer*, November 9. Retrieved November 10, 2011, from http://www.bondbuyer.com/news/jeffco-1032991-1.html.

83. Berne, R. (1993). Governmental accounting and financial reporting and the measurement of financial condition. In J. Lamb et al. (Eds.), *The handbook of municipal bonds and public finance* (pp. 257–315).

84. Ishpeming Public Schools, Wisconsin (2011). *Ishpeming public schools: Standard and Poor's report.* Retrieved November 8, 2011, from http://www.ishpemingschools.org/district/standard-and-poors.

85. Franklin Templeton (2011). *Five truths about municipal bonds.* Retrieved November 5, 2011, from https://www.franklintempleton.com/GWSFileServingServlet.dyn?contentType=application%2Fpdf&relativeDocPath=%2Fshare%2Fpdf%2Flit%2FTF_TRUTH.pdf.

86. McGuire, S. (2011). *State and local debt: an analysis* (p. 21). Washington, DC: Congressional Research Service.

87. McGee, P. (2011). Bankruptcy's bright side. *The Bond Buyer,* February 29. Retrieved November 10, 2011, from http://www.bondbuyer.com/issues/120_39/bankruptcys-bright-side-1023744-1.html?zkPrintable=true.

88. Bureau of the Census, U.S. Department of Commerce (2001). *Statistical abstract of the United States: 2001* (p. 275). Washington, DC: U.S. Government Printing Office.

89. Bureau of the Census, U.S. Department of Commerce (2011). *Statistical abstract of the United States: 2012* (p. 276). Washington, DC: U.S. Government Printing Office.

90. Lauerman, J., & McDonald, M. (2009). Harvard's bet on interest rate rise cost $500 million to exit. *Bloomberg.com,* October 17. Retrieved November 9, 2011, from http://www.bloomberg.com/apps/news?pid=newsarchive&sid=aHou7iMlBMN8.

91. Deavitt, C. (2011). Cleveland airport offering $75 million in a rare deal. *The Bond Buyer,* October 31. Retrieved November 8, 2011, from http://www.bondbuyer.com/issues/120_209/cleveland-hopkins-revenue-bond-deal-1032601-1.html.

92. Garvin, M., & Bosso, D. (2008). Assessing the effectiveness of infrastructure public-private partnership programs and projects. *Public Works Management and Policy, 13,* 162–178.

93. Brown, K. (2007). Are public-private transactions the future of infrastructure finance? *Public Works Management & Policy, 12,* 320–324.

94. Federal Highway Administration, U.S. Department of Transportation (2006). *Case study: Hudson-Bergen Light Rail.* Retrieved January 2, 2007, from http://www.fhwa.dot.gov/PPP/hudson.htm (page no longer accessible); Hudson-Bergen, United States of America. (2008). *Railway-Technology.com.* Retrieved November 2, 2011, from http://www.railway-technology.com/projects/hudson/.

95. Siemiatycki, M. (2008). Implications on private-public partnerships on the development of urban public transit infrastructure: the case of Vancouver, Canada. *Journal of Planning Education and Research, 27,* 137–151.

96. The World Bank (2001). *The Buenos Aires concession: the private sector serving the poor* (pp. 1–2). Washington, DC: World Bank.

97. The World Bank (2001). *The Buenos Aires concession* (p. 3); Delfino, J., et al. (2007). *How far does it go? The Buenos Aires water concession a decade after the reform* (pp. 5–6). New York, NY: United Nations Social Policy and Development Programme.

98. Ortiz, I., & Buxbaum, J. (2008). Protecting the public interest in long-term concession agreements for transportation infrastructure. *Public Works Management & Policy, 13,* 126–137; Johnston, J., & Gudergan, S. (2007). Governance of public-private partnerships: lessons learnt from an Australian case? *International Review of Administrative Sciences, 73,* 569–582.

99. Swope, C. (2007). Unloading assets. *Governing, 20,* January, 36.

100. Peterson, C. (2009). Chicago cancels Midway airport sale as cash dries up, WSJ says. *Bloomberg.com,* April 21. Retrieved November 3, 2011, from http://www.bloomberg.com/apps/news?pid=newsarchive&sid=ax26UGNat.Lg&refer=canada.

101. Bary, A. (2009). The long and binding road. *Barron's,* May 11. Retrieved November 3, 2011, from http://online.barrons.com/article/SB124183159872002803.html.

102. Hukka, J., et al. (2006). Many Ps needed for sustainable water services: expansion of the scope of public-private partnerships. *Public Works Management & Policy, 11,* 104–109.

103. Hood, J., et al. (2006). Transparency of risk and reward in U.K. public-private-partnerships. *Public Budgeting & Finance, 26,* Winter, 40–58; Erie, S., et al. (2010). Redevelopment, San Diego style: the limits of public-private partnerships. *Urban Affairs Review, 45,* 644–678.

104. Vining, A., & Boardman, A. (2008). Public-private partnerships: eight rules for governments. *Public Works Management & Policy, 13,* 149–161.

Intergovernmental Relations

Each level of government has discrete financial decision-making processes that determine matters of revenue and expenditure. Decisions about revenues and expenditures, however, are interdependent among different levels of government. Budgetary decisions made at one level are partially dependent on budgetary decisions made at other levels. Nonbudgetary decisions made at one level may also have dramatic impacts on budgets at another level of government.

This chapter examines the financial interdependencies among federal, state, and local governments.[1] The first section examines some of the basic economic and political problems that stem from having three major levels of government that provide various services and possess differing financial capabilities. The second section considers the patterns of interaction among the different levels, and the third section considers the main types of intergovernmental financial assistance programs. Key topics include devolution of responsibility from the federal government to state and local governments, especially welfare reform and health care for lower-income groups. The chapter concludes with a discussion of current issues and alternatives for restructuring these patterns of financial interaction, including the controversial issue of unfunded versus funded mandates, including, for example, state and local education programs.

STRUCTURAL AND FISCAL FEATURES OF THE INTERGOVERNMENTAL SYSTEM

In this section, we look beyond the simplified three-level model of government to consider the issues associated with having multiple levels and types of governments.

Areal and Functional Relations

Multiple Governments

Governments around the world and the organizations that they create constitute an intricate web of interjurisdictional relations. The United Nations, the European Union, NATO, and the like affect their member states and also other states throughout the world. The World Trade Organization (WTO), for example, with about 150 member states, sets ground rules for international commerce and resolves trade disputes among member nations.[2] The WTO's actions impact governments, businesses, and individuals everywhere. These interactions are about diplomacy, trade, and global concerns that extend beyond the scope of this text, but it needs to be recognized that what occurs in intergovernmental relations in the United States is within a much broader context of governments relating with one another around the world.

In the United States, governments operate within a federal system in which power is constitutionally shared between a central or national government and 50 states, which have sovereign status, meaning they are (at least technically) independent of the national government within the division of powers in the Constitution.[3] Federal systems in other countries include those in Australia, Belgium, Brazil, Canada, Germany, India, and Switzerland. In contrast is a centralized or unitary system in which all power resides in a national government, with some powers then being delegated to regional units. France and the United Kingdom are examples of this form of government.

In a federal system, the national government and states almost inevitably clash from time to time over their respective powers, and legal remedies are often available. In the United States, the states may sue in federal court when they allege federal action has abrogated their constitutionally protected powers. In a unitary system, the national government has the power to create and dissolve subunits, which may or may not have any legal recourse against adverse actions taken against them by higher authority. In other words, American states can and often do defend their rights by filing suit, claiming the federal government has usurped their powers, whereas in unitary systems, such rights are severely circumscribed at best.

Complicating the federal system in the United States is the fact that Native American tribes have independent status. The tribes exist within states but are independent of them and at least theoretically independent of the federal government. This fact has been the source of endless confusion, politicking, and legal wrangling since 1987, when the Supreme Court ruled that Native American tribes could operate gaming facilities. Congress passed the Indian Gaming Regulatory Act of 1988, which allowed for gaming and created the National Indian Gaming Commission to regulate the newly emerging industry.[4] The Supreme Court decision and the 1988 law set the stage for an elaborate set of intergovernmental actions.

Although politicians in many states opposed the introduction of casinos in their jurisdictions, the 1988 law required the states to grant licenses to Native American casinos providing certain requirements were met. Native American casinos are allowed only in states that otherwise allow other specific forms of gaming. In return, states benefit from tax receipts. The law has led to states having to negotiate with tribes over the construction, operation, and expansion of casinos, regardless of whether they wanted such casinos to exist at all.[5]

Indian gaming has grown dramatically. Revenues were $5.4 billion in 1995 and reached $26.5 billion in 2009.[6] Of the 419 casinos in operation in 2009, 120 were in the region consisting of Iowa, Michigan, Minnesota, Montana, North Dakota, Nebraska, South Dakota, Wisconsin, and Wyoming. Another 113 were in Kansas, Oklahoma, and Texas.[7] Casinos bring employment and perhaps some improvement in Native American health, due to citizens being better able to afford health care, but casinos also yield higher crime rates, which impose law enforcement costs on local governments.[8] In other words, actions at the federal level forced state and local governments to interact with tribes, and these interactions produced both costs to governments and revenues.

In addition to the federal government, the 50 state governments, and more than 560 Native American tribal entities,[9] the United States includes more than 89,000 local governments and the District of Columbia.[10] The local "level" is not a single level in that most states have county governments (more than 3,000 nationwide), and within their boundaries exist such general-purpose governments as municipalities and sometimes townships (more than 19,000 municipalities and 16,500 townships). Superimposed over these are numerous independent school districts and special-purpose districts such as irrigation and sewer districts. Special districts, of which there are more than 37,000, are the most numerous. There are more than 13,000 school districts.

These various local governments have a decidedly different legal status from that of the states. Although the states created the national government and preserved their sovereignty through the Constitution, local governments are creatures of their respective states. They were created by the states and can be destroyed by the states.

Whether federal or unitary, many countries are granting greater autonomous authority to regional, provincial, or local governments. This autonomy does not necessarily mean shifts from unitary to federal systems. India, for example, enacted in 1991 constitutional reforms to establish certain powers and responsibilities for local governments as a matter of national constitutional authority, effectively removing some aspects of state government control over local government. In most of the Central and Eastern European states formerly part of the Soviet Union, central authority over all governmental functions has given way to increased responsibility at the regional and city levels, and that authority is defined and delimited by the central government. In Russia itself, an initial movement toward some degree of decentralization under President Boris Yeltsin lost ground to a strong recentralization under Prime Minister Vladimir Putin, who retrieved most authority from oblasts (regions) granted in previous administrations.

Having myriad governments at different levels within a nation can be defended in several ways. By having multiple governments, an omnipotent, despotic type of government may be avoided. Another advantage is that the diversity of governments allows for differing responses according to the divergent needs of citizens in different locales. For instance, some communities may place greater emphasis than others on amenities, such as flower beds and other decorations along city streets, whereas other communities may prefer more utilitarian, and presumably less expensive, streets. The Federalist framers and advocates for the U.S. Constitution defended a federal structure using three arguments:

- It would promote a sense of community and affinity between citizens and the government.
- It would promote efficiency by assigning functions that had mainly local importance to local governments and functions of national importance to the federal government.
- It would promote liberty by avoiding concentration of power in the hands of a few.[11]

The existence of numerous units of government increases the probability that individuals will be able to find communities to live in that suit them. For example, people may locate in communities that offer desirable mixes of taxes and services. Of course, we do not suggest that such economic calculations are the sole criteria on which people base their location decisions, but the existence of multiple governments enhances that important aspect of quality of life.[12]

Another advantage is that having multiple governments allows the achievement of *economies of scale.* Functions may be performed by the size of government that is most efficient in carrying out the functions. Just as it may be advantageous from the standpoint of efficient resource use for private, profit-oriented organizations to grow to a large scale, so it also may be advantageous for one unit of government to conduct some government activities on a large scale.

On the other hand, to perform all government functions at the central level might result in inefficient conduct of some activities. Not only did the economic woes of the former Soviet Union demonstrate that overly centralized planning of the productive sector of the economy produced many inefficiencies, but the overly centralized administrative and fiscal systems also left a legacy of weak decision making not well adapted to provision of basic local public services.[13] Lessened flexibility of operations and other diseconomies suggest the need for some functions to be performed by units of government smaller than the central government. Geographically and economically smaller-scale activities are more efficient when carried out by smaller governments. Probably many services can be provided most efficiently at the local level.

No government, no matter what the level, is free to do whatever it pleases. The U.S. Constitution enumerates the federal government's powers (especially Article I, Section 8) and reserves all other powers to the states (10th Amendment). In some countries, the reverse is true, with the states, regions, or provinces having enumerated powers and the national government having the remainder. In the United States, each state constitution provides for the powers of that government. Local governments have fewer constitutional protections, because these governments have been created by their states. Within these constitutional and legal parameters, a higher-level government may impose standards upon lower levels.

Coordination Problems

The existence of thousands of governments results in coordination problems both geographically and functionally. Municipalities in a metropolitan area need some coordinative mechanisms. Road networks, for example, need to be planned in accordance with commuting patterns within a metropolitan area, and such plans should not be restricted to the geographical boundaries of each municipality. Before the federal government became involved in highway programs, many highways did not connect sensibly across state lines. Recreation and parks programs may be provided on a metropolitan or area basis and thereby achieve economies of scale. Numerous regional planning agencies, regional or metropolitan transportation planning groups, and regional economic development programs exist so as to consolidate an otherwise fragmented approach to interjurisdictional overlaps.[14]

The need to avoid excessive fragmentation at the local level in a decentralized system has led some to argue for consolidation of the local governments in a metropolitan area, such as in Miami–Dade County, Florida, and Nashville–Davidson County, Tennessee. However, some studies have shown that the savings expected from metropolitan consolidation have not been achieved. Rather, greater efficiencies seem to result from competition among the various local governments in a metropolitan area.[15] Where coordination is needed among the local governments of a metropolitan area, it seems achievable through cooperation and shared decision making rather than consolidation. Nevertheless, there does seem to be evidence that consolidation has benefits in the case of very small local units of government.

Federal-state, interstate, and interlocal arrangements have been developed for the provision of services (as distinguished from forums for discussion), including metropolitan councils of governments that involve officials from various communities in a region. One of the most successful interstate organizations is the Port Authority of New York and New Jersey, established in 1921 by the two participating states.[16] The authority operates terminals, bridges, and tunnels. It operated the World Trade Center until its destruction in 2001. Subsequently, the Port Authority and the Lower Manhattan Development Corporation approved plans for rebuilding on the site.

At the local level, numerous types of cooperative arrangements exist. Some counties provide services such as water and sewage treatment on a contract basis for municipalities within their jurisdictions. The choice of such an arrangement may be at the discretion of municipalities, as in the case of the Lakewood Plan, whereby communities can contract with Los Angeles County for virtually all city services (see the chapter on budget execution). In some instances, state governments may require city-county cooperation for services, such as police and fire departments having standby aid agreements during large civil disturbances or fires.

Functional coordination among different levels is also necessary because the three main levels of government share responsibilities for some of the same functions. Criminal justice, for instance, is a shared function. Some type of police, court, and prison system exists at each government level. Environmental protection similarly is a function in which federal, state, and local jurisdictions all have a stake, and all but the smallest local governments have some formal unit involved in addressing environmental problems. The independent pursuit of similar objectives by different governments can result in wasted resources and ineffective services.

Multilevel overlapping and shared responsibility can make it difficult to design federal programs to achieve national objectives. Any given federal assistance program may be a good fit for local governments in one state and not in another state given the differences in how states allocate responsibilities between themselves and their respective local governments. Therefore, emphasis has been given to developing mechanisms for functional integration. Although program specialists stress functional integration, however, policy generalists may stress areal integration. This conflict was popularized by Deil S. Wright as "picket fence federalism"—each picket represents a function, such as mental health or education, and all three levels of government make up part of each picket.[17] Another analogy used is that of silos, that program areas are compartmentalized within each of many silos. As with pickets of a fence, silos discourage the crossover of information and integration of services that so often is needed in government operations.

Exhibit 15–1 illustrates how complicated the mosaic of intergovernmental relations can be. The exhibit uses as its focus the efforts made to control air emissions in an intergovernmental context. The particular device illustrated in the exhibit, an interstate compact among 12 states and the District of Columbia, is one mechanism that can be used to coordinate efforts by multiple jurisdictions to combat problems that span jurisdictional boundaries. More generally, all problems dealing with the environment, whether they involve air, land, or water, more or less need to be handled on a multijurisdictional basis, including internationally.[18]

Exhibit 15–1 Coordinating Air Emissions as a Case Study in Interstate Compacts

Like watersheds, airsheds respect no political boundaries. Emissions from private vehicles, public facilities, and factories within the boundaries of one political jurisdiction effectively go where the winds blow. Unlike water, which has a stable pattern of flows, emissions into the air over time span the full 360 degrees of the map.

In purely self-interested terms, it may not be rational for a local government with a strong "smokestack" industry that is employing a large percentage of the work force to regulate emissions from that industry, especially if the prevailing winds for the most part blow the polluted air away from the jurisdiction. For this reason, the federal government has for several decades played a significant role in setting limits on emissions. However, federally imposed limits rely on states and localities to develop policies and practices to meet the standards. Increasingly, states and the local jurisdictions within metropolitan areas realize that they cannot act unilaterally to solve the problems if their neighbors are not also taking care of the problems. They then act to create coordinated policies and programs to impose and enforce stronger controls.

One such example is an interstate compact among New England and mid-Atlantic states to control ground-level ozone concentrations.[1] Members of this Ozone Transport Commission (OTC) agreed on a "budget" or a total amount of nitrous oxide emissions that would be allowed from sources within the states in the compact.[2] States then allocate the allowable emissions among the major producers/sources, rewarding those that come in "below budget." Individual emitters and even states may trade in these permitted levels. Those falling below the levels may trade for various compensations with those who cannot meet the allocated amount.

Although substantial cutbacks in emissions have been achieved (more than a 50% reduction from 1990 to 1999), the scenario has not been all rosy. Midwestern states did not join the Commission, and prevailing winds bring large problems eastward, so the attorneys general of eight states and New York City sued the top five coal-burning power plants in the United States, all located in several Midwestern states.[3] That suit progressed to the U.S. Supreme Court, which ruled against the Midwestern states on the grounds that the legal authority of states was preempted by various federal statutes, including the Clean Air Act (as amended numerous times), notwithstanding the fact that EPA had not established or enforced regulations.[4]

Air quality has improved in the Northeast, although OTC's specific contribution is impossible to determine. Adoption in 1999 by OTC states of a cap and trade program setting a budget or "cap" on NOx emissions (nitric oxide and nitrogen dioxide gases)

requiring electric utilities to reduce NOx emissions below 1990 levels achieved a 60% reduction in NOx emissions in 2002, with further reductions in 2003 and 2004.[5] Although interstate compacts can be effective in addressing cross-jurisdictional issues, they are not easy to set up. Article I, Section 10, of the Constitution requires congressional approval of any interstate compact. Despite this step, this approach has proved a useful mechanism for creating interjurisdictional authority to address mutual interests.

1. Ozone Transport Commission website, http://www.otcair.org/.
2. Ozone Transport Commission (2005). *Final OTC multipollutant program development strategy.* Retrieved September 27, 2006, from http://www.otcair.org (document no longer accessible).
3. Office of the Governor of Vermont (2011). *Vermont joins efforts to fight greenhouse gas emissions.* Retrieved November 26, 2011, from http://governor.vermont.gov/newsroom-vermont-joins-efforts-to-fight-greenhouse-emissions.
4. *Connecticut v. American Electric Power; American Electric Power v. Connecticut.* 564 U.S. __, slip opinion (2011).
5. U.S. Environmental Protection Agency (2011). *Cap and trade: multi-state NOx programs.* Retrieved November 27, 2011, from http://www.epa.gov/captrade/documents/nox.pdf.

The September 11 Disasters

The terrorist attacks of September 11, 2001, dramatically underscore the need for intergovernmental cooperation and coordination. One fact that immediately became painfully obvious was the lack of sharing of information and coordination within federal agencies and among them. Equally important were the weak linkages existing among federal intelligence gathering and law enforcement agencies on the one hand and similar units internationally and at the state and local levels within the United States.

The federal government responded to its immediate problems by creating a Department of Homeland Security that pulled together a variety of agencies that had been located throughout the federal bureaucracy. Among other things, Homeland Security provided grants for upgrading law enforcement and fire protection at the state and local levels. Noticeably absent, however, from Homeland Security's ranks was the Federal Bureau of Investigation (FBI), which remained within the Department of Justice. The FBI continues to be the federal government's primary criminal investigation and law enforcement unit, having responsibility for international investigations such as tracking international conduits for funding terrorist activities. The U.S. Treasury Department also has a key role in investigating international financial crimes.[19]

Although it is impossible to assess how effective intergovernmental cooperation has been in preventing acts of terrorism and other major incidents, because many threats averted are never made public, it is probably safe to conclude that improvements have been made in intergovernmental cooperation on intelligence gathering. Major news coverage of some significant events averted, such as an attempted car bombing in Times Square in New York City in 2010, suggests that intelligence gathering and sharing has paid off.[20] No doubt, however, much work in this endeavor lies ahead. Do local, state, and federal law enforcement organizations routinely share relevant information about possible terrorists? Is such information shared on a timely basis? Is there a system for following up on leads about possible terrorist activities? These are fundamental intergovernmental questions for which there are no simple answers.

Additionally, the events of September 11 made apparent the need for governments to work cooperatively in responding to major national disasters. Fire services, emergency rescue assistance, and law enforcement were called upon to handle situations of vast proportion. In New York City, the drama was played out in a situation where communications systems were largely destroyed by the collapse of the twin towers of the World Trade Center. Therefore, there was need to coordinate intergovernmental and interorganizational disaster recovery efforts in a context of poor communications links. Police and fire communication units were largely blocked from communicating with one another, underscoring the importance of intergovernmental and interorganizational coordination.

Hurricanes and Other Disasters

September 11 dramatized the need for all levels of government to cooperate in the event of catastrophic disasters. Such major events include natural disasters like the devastation inflicted in 2005 by the Gulf Coast Hurricanes Katrina, Rita, and Wilma. The Gulf hurricanes were the worst natural disasters in the history of the United States. All half-million of New Orleans' residents had to flee the city, and tens of thousands more were displaced along the coast. One stark item of evidence of the failure of the intergovernmental system was that thousands of people arrived at the New Orleans Superdome having nowhere else to go, and federal, state, and local officials were left clueless as to how to get these people out of the city to safety as water broke through the levees and inundated the city. The need to evacuate thousands had been played out in an intergovernmental exercise in the spring of 2005, but plans were not put in place for the disaster that came to pass that same year in August, September, and October.

State and local governments were overwhelmed. First responders, particularly the police, were at a loss to control order. Thousands needed help at a time when the revenue coming into governments was cut off, and yet governments were expected to operate on balanced budgets. Roads, sewers, water systems, schools, and other government facilities were destroyed, creating need for massive rebuilding.

The people who were displaced typically sought help from governments other than their own.[21] New Orleans could not help its residents who had been evacuated to other locales in Louisiana, Texas, and other states. People were unable to work and needed cash assistance in the form of unemployment insurance or welfare. People were without housing and were temporarily placed in shelters, some operated by the Red Cross, and later in hotels and motels paid for by the Federal Emergency Management Agency (FEMA). On the positive side, state and local governments and charitable organizations from areas not ravaged by the storms received evacuees with little expectation of being reimbursed for their expenses.

Health hazards were common.[22] Sewage and industrial pollutants had poured into New Orleans. Houses were flooded and mold grew, posing health dangers to people trying to restore their homes. Meanwhile, many hospitals and clinics were knocked out of operation, while those that remained in operation were overwhelmed with demands on their services. Many of the displaced people were poor and needed Medicaid assistance.

Congress eventually made available $109 billion in relief funding and another $8 billion in tax relief.[23] The money was for use in the five affected states from Texas to Florida and included coverage of damage from Hurricane Wilma in Florida. FEMA disaster recovery grants continued to be awarded in 2011 for continuing reconstruction. The Katrina disaster caused a collapse in the intergovernmental system, at least in the short run.[24] During and after the disaster, accusations flew about as to who was to blame, and surely there were plenty of major blunders on the part of many participants. One conclusion that emerged from the disaster was that roles need to be better spelled out before a disaster hits.[25] There is general agreement that in the early hours of a disaster, those on the ground locally—state and local officials and local voluntary groups such as the Red Cross and the Salvation Army—have primary responsibility. As time passes, the federal government can be expected to step in, but in what ways is yet to be determined. For example, one knotty issue is whether the federal government should be able to declare marshal law and bring in regular Army troops or take command of state National Guard troops. State and local officials, as would be expected, are wary of federal control, but a counterargument is that the federal government is likely to get the blame for whatever goes wrong and therefore should have the authority to get the job done, whatever that may require. The argument is that in crisis times, one organization whose authority spans the geographical region—namely, the federal government—should have responsibility, with state and local governments assuming secondary roles.

FEMA had been an independent agency until it was brought into the newly formed Homeland Security Department in response to the September 11 disasters. Arguments have been made for retaining FEMA within Homeland Security or spinning it off once again as an independent agency, reporting directly to the president. The arguments are not especially persuasive on either side. What is persuasive is the need for a clear role for FEMA. That would seem to be one of a coordinator for all federal, state, and local units when major national disasters occur.[26]

The Deepwater Horizon oil spill of 2010 in the Gulf of Mexico was the worst oil spill in U.S. history, overshadowing the infamous Exxon Valdez oil spill of 1989 off the Alaskan coast. The problems it caused put major strains on the intergovernmental system. The intergovernmental aspects of it, and the political arguments that ensued, were exacerbated by the apparently lax regulatory framework, entirely a federal responsibility because the well was outside the limits of state authority.[27] On the other hand, the conflicts among federal, state, and local governments were not as rancorous as those in the Hurricanes Katrina and Rita disasters.

The largest hurricane of the 2011 season, Irene, caused massive flooding along the east coast of the United States, and was particularly devastating to inland areas in New England. The FEMA response to Irene, in marked contrast to the 2005 Gulf coast storms, was generally praised by governors of the affected states.[28] Federal, state, and local officials were much better prepared, and coordination among governmental and nongovernmental organizations was markedly improved since 2005.

Fiscal Considerations

Vertical Fiscal Imbalance

The conflict between the organizing principles of geographic area and program function plays out within the context of need for services and the corresponding need for revenues, with differences in capabilities existing both within and among levels of government.[29] *Vertical fiscal imbalance,* or *fiscal noncorrespondence,* refers to the relative abilities of different levels of government to generate needed revenue and to produce specific public services. The intergovernmental fiscal problem is deciding on assignment of expenditure responsibilities, and then designing an intergovernmental fiscal system of revenue authority, shared revenue sources, and transfers to match the expenditure assignments. Although one level of government may have a comparative advantage in providing a particular service efficiently, it may not have the same advantage in obtaining revenue. Conversely, another level of government may possess sufficient revenue capability but is not the most efficient unit to provide certain services.

In the United States, it is typically the federal government that possesses the greatest revenue capacity, but not the comparative advantage in providing many government services. State and local governments, on the other hand, have functional expenditure obligations that exceed their ability to raise revenue.

This disparity is due largely to the different revenue sources used by governments. The federal government, relying on personal and corporate income taxes, has a more elastic tax structure in which revenues increase with any increase in economic activity. Although state and local revenue sources are relatively more inelastic, the demand for services provided by these governments is quite elastic. For example, the property tax does not change when the economy swings up and down. As discussed in the chapter on transaction-based revenue sources, the property tax is based on the assessed value of the property. Assessments are expensive to carry out, so they are not changed frequently. Hence, we describe the property tax as inelastic with respect to changing economic conditions. When income falls, property taxes still must be paid, but the amount of tax paid on income drops. Of course, when property taxes increase or even remain stable and the economy takes a significant downturn, as happened in 2001–2003, and again in 2007–2011, property owners who have lost their jobs may experience extreme difficulty in making their property tax payments.

Superior fiscal capacity can be used by one level of government to entice or persuade another to provide a given service. For example, the federal government used its tremendous fiscal capacity to persuade the states to build an interstate network of freeways. Had the federal government not been willing to pay 90% of the cost of the system, there would be far fewer freeways today. Federal programs created by the Clean Water Act and the Safe Drinking Water Act, discussed in the chapter on capital finance and debt management, initially provided grant funding for water and sewer systems, and then after some years of grant funding, provided capitalization funding for state revolving loan funds to lower the borrowing costs for water and sewer systems. Similar federal assistance to capitalize state education loan programs to induce more school construction have been proposed, but not implemented. States also induce local activities through grants and loans.

Horizontal Fiscal Differences

Problems caused by differences in fiscal capacity also exist for governments at the same level. From state to state, there clearly are differences in income and wealth, which are the basic sources of government revenue. For example, U.S. per capita personal income in 2009 was $39,138, but Connecticut's was $54,397, or 139% of the national average, and Mississippi's was $30,103, or only 76% of the national average.[30] Differences in income and wealth lead to differences in revenue-generating abilities, tax burdens, and levels of public services, although no simple correlation exists between income on the one hand and taxing and spending on the other hand.

There is disagreement over whether per capita income differences are a good measure, however, of the differing fiscal capacities of the states. Per capita income has been widely used since the 1930s to differentiate among the states' relative needs for federal assistance. However, this measure does not fully capture ability to pay for services within states. Other measures include retail sales and gross state product. Analysts often use full market property value to assess debt repayment capacity, but this measure reflects accumulated wealth and not necessarily the direct ability to generate revenues.

The ability of a state to raise revenue to meet its spending requirements is called the *fiscal capacity* of the state. The *total taxable resources* (TTR) index, as calculated by U.S. Department of the Treasury, is an estimate of a state's gross state product, similar to the concept of gross domestic product calculated for a national economy, as compared with the nation as a whole (see the chapter on government and the economy). The index is set with the national score of 100, and states with scores above that level presumably have high abilities to generate revenues and states with scores below have low abilities. For 2009, Connecticut and Delaware scored high on the index (148 and 149, respectively), whereas Mississippi was at the bottom (69). Other low states were Arkansas and West Virginia (77 and 72, respectively). Near the middle point of 100 were California, Illinois, Rhode Island, and Washington (in the 105 to 108 range).[31] The TTR is used by the Department of Health and Human Services in distributing Community Mental Health Service and Substance Abuse Prevention and Treatment block grant programs' funds to the states. Were the index to become widely accepted as an effective measure of states' capacity, it might well be used for a host of grant formulas.

The extent to which a state actually taps into its available resources is called the *tax burden*. Before it was eliminated in federal budget cutting, the U.S. Advisory Commission on Intergovernmental Relations (ACIR) calculated a measure that estimated the revenues a state would raise if it were to use the average tax system employed throughout the country. This *representative tax system* (RTS) measured tax capacity and, when divided by population, provided a gauge of a state's fiscal effort.[32] The ACIR subsequently added the concept of representative expenditures, including information about costs for public services, to help measure different states' financial abilities.[33]

There has been some reconstruction of the ACIR's work since its demise,[34] though scholars and governments in other countries have shown more interest than have those in the United States in the concepts of the representative tax system and fiscal capacity.[35] Canada has an official Expert Panel on Equalization and Territorial Formula Financing that calculates *representative tax* burdens.[36]

Several other measures are used to gauge the tax burden in the states. These include total state and local taxes as a share of personal income, as a share of total taxable resources, or as a share of gross state product. Similar measures are derived using state and local own-source revenue. Using the own-source revenue figure as a share of total taxable resources, Alaska in 2009 was ranked first, at 19%, compared with middle-ranked Minnesota and Louisiana (each 11%) and lowest-ranked Wisconsin (5%).[37] It should be noted that Alaska is sometimes excluded from state comparisons because of its unusual economic conditions.

Overall, although there are plenty of arguments about the adequacy of any one measure or group of measures, the empirical research corresponds to commonsense expectations. Some poorer states in the country have greater needs for spending on services than they have the fiscal capacity to respond, and some richer states have greater fiscal capacity than their expenditure requirements. In addition, some states make more of an effort to use their own taxable resources to meet expenditure needs than others. Federal formulas such as the TTR index are used by some federal programs to calculate distribution of grant funds to states to guard against the federal government rewarding states that do not make the effort with their own tax resources while penalizing other states that do make the effort. However, politics sometimes interferes with this principle, and as a result few federal programs use a measure of tax effort of any kind in calculating grant distributions.

Any comparisons among states or localities, whether based on income, wealth, or tax effort, cannot capture an essential feature determining levels of services and levels of taxation. Residents of each state do not make uniform demands for services. Even if the ability to tax or charge for services were distributed evenly across the country, expenditures would differ because citizens desire different levels of services. From a strict demand point of view, a state would provide only those services for which citizens are willing to pay. But willingness to pay for services, as measured by tax effort, still may not solve the problem. The need for many government services is greatest in those states where the fiscal capacity to meet those needs is lowest. Mississippi is a good example of a state that has high needs and falls short despite making a better-than-average effort to meet those needs. In the measure discussed above, Mississippi is ranked 10th in its actual use of its own source revenues as a percentage of its total taxable resources. The problem is even more acute with respect to different local jurisdictions in the same state. Central city governments in large metropolitan areas face demands for services that increase at a faster rate than does the value of their revenue sources.

Fiscal Responsibilities

Another issue is the extent to which one government with greater revenue-generating capacity should be responsible for aiding other lower-level governments. The issue is whether and to what extent governments should redistribute resources among different segments of the population and geographic areas. Since the 1980s, there seemingly has been less support for redistributive activities, especially at the federal level, than in the decades beginning with the Johnson administration's War on Poverty. The two decades from 1960 through 1980 witnessed the largest effort ever by the federal government to redress disparities among the states and among regions within states. On one index measure, income inequality in the United States has been rising (income inequality is discussed in the chapter on government and the economy).

By 1979, questions had been raised about the ability of the federal government to sustain such a redistributive effort. In response, the New Federalism of President Reagan implemented significant reductions in federal programs to transfer funds to impoverished individuals and low-income states and localities. In the 1990s, balanced federal budgets came at the same time as economic prosperity produced state budget surpluses, so there was no great pressure to increase programs to equalize disparities among the states. The return to federal deficits after 2000 discouraged such efforts, even in the face of severe state budget crises. The exceptions to that are the temporary measures undertaken to combat the recession that began in 2007, including particularly the American Recovery and Reinvestment Act. These temporary measures included significant federal grants to state and local governments (see the chapter on government and the economy). In fact, federal grants to state and local governments during the two recessions since 2000 brought federal grants as a proportion of state and local revenues well above the previous peak in 1980. We discuss this in some detail later in this chapter.

One governing principle is that a government should engage in such funding only when the problem addressed corresponds to its level of responsibility—that is, the federal government should deal with national problems and the states with state problems. Oates made this argument in a classic work in the 1970s.[38] The principle was articulated quite clearly by President Ronald Reagan's Executive Order 12612: "It is important to recognize the distinction between problems of national scope (which may justify Federal action) and problems that are merely common to the States (which will not justify Federal action because individual States, acting individually or together, can effectively deal with them)."[39] Though there have been differences in preference for various programs since then, both Democratic and Republican administrations since have tended toward devolution of responsibility. The Obama administration made one of its main proposed fiscal policies a more equitable distribution of the tax burden by eliminating the George W. Bush administration tax reduction for the top income bracket, but was unable to get the measure through Congress.

Disparities in fiscal capacity among governments at the same level lead directly to another problem, that of *external costs* and *external benefits* of government functions. People of low income moving from states with low services to states with high services create new burdens on the high-service states. This occurred, for example, with the population migration of the 1930s from impoverished areas to the West Coast and in later migrations from the rural South to cities in the North and West. Proportionately more people who move from lower-income to higher-income states receive welfare payments and generate greater demands on other public services than do those moving from states with similarly high levels of income and services. The flow of illegal immigrants into some states exacerbates those states' difficulties in financing social services and education.

Some of the costs of the failure to provide comparable levels of service across state lines are borne by those outside the low-service states. But the situation has positive aspects as well. Providing services at the most economical level may result in the benefits' spilling over into other areas. The most obvious example is education. Higher levels of education generally yield higher levels of income. Given the mobility of the population, the benefits produced by one local education system may spread far beyond its geographic boundaries.

Economic Competition

Governments compete with each other in trying to attract businesses and industries.[40] Firms locate for a variety of reasons, such as access to markets, a good labor supply, and availability of other resources. Furthermore, they locate where there are clusters of related industries and suppliers. Because businesses seek to minimize production costs, the advantage lies with jurisdictions that have a high service level and low taxes on industry. Whether these are the main reasons businesses actually move or not is irrelevant. As long as governments compete on the basis of taxes and services, the fiscal effects are the same.

Competition for businesses among political jurisdictions can have important consequences, including distortions in revenue and expenditure patterns. When special concessions are granted to firms, needed revenues must be obtained elsewhere or the level of services must be reduced. Devoting resources to special facilities, such as industrial parks, which are frequently financed by long-term debt instruments, may affect a community's ability to finance other capital projects, such as a civic center or a new sewage treatment plant.

The package of tax forgiveness, direct subsidies, and free services that Alabama gave Daimler-Benz in return for locating its first U.S. manufacturing facility in the state was a gamble. The state provided a direct subsidy of $42 million, forgave corporate taxes to the extent the forgone taxes were used by Daimler-Benz for debt service on its physical plant investments, and allowed the company to keep up to 5% of the state income tax withheld from employee salaries, again if the withheld taxes were used instead to pay debt service.[41] In return, Daimler-Benz has built additional factories in Alabama since the 1993 plant, including plans announced in 2011 to invest $2 billion to upgrade and expand the Tuscaloosa plant.[42] In addition, other automotive companies such as Honda subsequent to the Daimler investment located facilities there, although each of those decisions was accompanied by additional tax concessions.[43]

Although intense competition among some states for industrial relocation does cause problems, there are important benefits from this competition. First, it serves as a market-like regulator, preventing state and local governments from over-taxation. Second, it increases the efficiency of the allocation of public sector resources. States and localities that offer uneconomical incentives to businesses ultimately cannot sustain those incentives. There is a tendency toward equilibrium in the balance of incentives and the taxes and other charges necessary to make services available to support industrial development. Some states have backed away from the use of high-cost incentives. For example, Michigan backed away from giving breaks to production companies that shot movies in the state.[44]

Overlapping Taxes

The taxes of jurisdictions overlap with each other, and ultimately the same people and firms must pay the various governments. Tax overlapping also occurs when all levels of government tax the same specific source, such as when federal, state, and local governments all tax income. Overlapping or multiple taxation is unavoidable and not necessarily undesirable. It causes serious problems only when a government at one level in effect preempts another government's ability to raise sufficient revenue. This can occur if the state sales tax rate is so high that it discourages local jurisdictions from levying such a tax. Indeed, states may preclude their local governments from having sales taxes but may provide them with alternative sources of revenue. On the other hand, some states have begun allowing local governments to have sales taxes to support transportation, but only after obtaining voter approval.[45]

The same kind of crowding-out problem occurs as a result of heavy federal personal and corporate income taxes. State and local governments, although often criticized for failing to raise sufficient revenue to meet needs, may be largely preempted by the federal government from major reliance on income taxes.

One proposal would cause a major reallocation of governmental responsibilities among federal, state, and local governments to address tax overlapping directly by introducing a new shared tax—a value-added tax (see the chapter on transaction-based revenue sources)—and sharing corporate income and gasoline taxes. Differences in the latter two taxes among the states would be eliminated.[46] Shared taxes also would reduce tax competition among states. The value-added tax idea was floated again in 2010 by the Obama administration, though the motive was to address the federal deficit more than to address intergovernmental tax competition.[47] Shared taxes are common in developing countries, where decision makers typically revamp their countries' fiscal systems to support decentralization and devolution.

PATTERNS OF INTERACTION AMONG LEVELS OF GOVERNMENT

The structural and fiscal features of the U.S. intergovernmental system ensure that there will be numerous interactions among the different levels of governments. Multiple governments within the same nation interact in numerous ways that directly involve budgetary and other financial decisions as well as each government's fiscal condition. Intergovernmental revenue transfers, such as grants, are a common form of interaction, but they are by no means the only important form. Federal direct expenditures and taxes that occur within a state or local jurisdiction are also important, as is the financial assistance that one level of government gives to another. Finally, regulations, statutes, and other actions that do not directly involve taxing and spending, but nevertheless affect taxing and spending, shape budgetary decisions.

Direct Expenditures and Taxes

Discussions of intergovernmental finance too often concentrate exclusively on financial assistance and neglect the importance of direct expenditures. How much the federal government spends in a state and, in turn, how much a state spends in specific local areas have large impacts. Direct federal expenditures have varying geographical impacts, and the same is true for state expenditures.

Nongrant Spending

Locating government-owned or government-built facilities in a jurisdiction can substantially affect the jurisdiction's economy. Political considerations are crucial at the state level in regard to the location of highways, state hospitals, prisons, and parks. Local and state governments work actively to obtain federal projects in their jurisdictions as one means of guaranteeing future prosperity. At the federal level, military installations, the awarding of defense contracts to corporations (which are geographically based), and other civilian installations inspire intensive lobbying.

In an attempt to reduce the political bargaining over which military facilities to close during defense downsizing, Congress has several times created temporary commissions to make recommendations on base closings that then must be approved by the president and Congress. The most recent Defense Base Closure and Realignment Commission made 180 such recommendations in 2005. The recommendations were greater than all previous commissions' recommendations combined.[48]

Although some of the political bargaining was reduced in the past by the existence of these commissions, members of Congress still fight to save facilities in their home districts or states. The reality is that communities sometimes benefit more from the base closing than from the previous operations of the base. Facilities and space are turned over to the local community for economic development, and that new activity often proves more valuable. Portsmouth, New Hampshire, for example, turned the former Pease Air Force Base into an industrial park, and more than 10 times the number of people are employed in the industrial park than formerly worked at the Air Force base. Charleston, South Carolina's, economy grew after a naval base closing, with new companies occupying old Navy sites. With so many closings and downsizings having occurred, a body of knowledge has developed over how communities can adjust—although painfully—to the loss of defense dollars.[49] The end of the Space Shuttle program in 2011 is a painful example of what happens when federal spending ceases. Thousands of workers directly and indirectly lost their jobs on Florida's east coast and in the Houston, Texas, area because of the decision to end this program.[50]

Beyond the physical items are various programs that disburse loans and grants to individuals and corporations. At the federal level, these programs include Social Security, Medicare, support to farmers, and small business loans. Social Security, Medicare, and Medicaid alone accounted for nearly 40% of all federal expenditures in 2011.[51] States also distribute large welfare and other human services payments among local jurisdictions.

Federal spending other than grants to individuals, organizations, and governments includes significant salaries and wages paid to federal employees and members of the military, most of whom live in one state or another. States having more than 100,000 federal civilian workers include California, Maryland, Texas, and Virginia plus the District of Columbia.[52] Defense payrolls in states ranged in 2009 from as low as $262 million in Vermont to as high as $18 billion in Virginia and $19 billion in Texas. Texas, which is a major beneficiary of federal defense spending, had in 2009 approximately 131,500 active duty military troops stationed in the state, along with 56,000 Reserve and National Guard people and another 48,000 defense civilian personnel.[53] Contracts with private firms and individuals for defense work totaled $303 billion, with California getting 14% of that very large pie.[54] These contracts, federal salaries, and miscellaneous other small programs are of far greater economic significance than are actual federal grants given to state and local governments.

Tax Collections

In addition to spending, tax collections have varying effects on locales, and the resulting balance between federal tax collections and expenditures has significant effects on jurisdictions. Generally, federal revenues raised in the Northeast and the Midwest have tended to be greater than the federal expenditures in these regions. The opposite pattern has existed in the South and the West, with the exception of states like Texas, California, Colorado, Nevada, and Oregon, where the federal tax burden has been greater than total federal expenditures.[55] The typical historical pattern changed with the federal programs put in place to combat the effects of the recession that started in 2007. In 2009, only Connecticut, Delaware, Minnesota, and New Jersey had more federal taxes collected in their states than federal expenditures in and grants to those states. Of course, this discussion in no way suggests that federal taxes should be equal to expenditures.

Table 15–1 indicates the states with the highest and lowest ratios of federal spending per dollar of taxes for 2009. Hawaii topped the list. The federal government spent $3.65 in Hawaii for every $1.00 extracted in taxes. Delaware was at the other extreme. For every $1.00 in taxes, only 59 cents flowed back into the state. Because of the deficit-financed federal spending, the data in Table 15–1 are somewhat misleading when compared with earlier years. In 2007 and 2008, for example, the federal government collected more taxes in 19 states than it spent in those states, but in 2009, this happened in just four states."[56] Where the balance is less than even, federal finance has a negative impact on a state's economy. This has been the case historically in the Great Lakes states, which are part of the so-called Rust Belt. Federal tax collections from each of the following Northeastern and Midwestern states exceeded federal expenditures in these states in 2004: Illinois, Indiana, Michigan, Minnesota, New York, and Wisconsin. By contrast, in 2009, of those six states,

Table 15–1 States with Highest and Lowest Ratios of Federal Spending per Dollar of Federal Taxes, 2009

Highest Ratios of Spending per Dollar of Taxes			Lowest Ratios of Spending per Dollar of Taxes		
Rank	State	Ratio	Rank	State	Ratio
1.	Hawaii	3.65	41.	Arkansas	1.06
2.	Mississippi	3.42	42.	Rhode Island	1.06
3.	New Mexico	3.35	43.	Ohio	1.04
4.	West Virginia	3.13	44.	Nebraska	1.02
5.	Alaska	3.04	45.	New York	1.01
6.	Alabama	2.72	46.	Illinois	1.00
7.	Virginia	2.65	47.	Connecticut	.95
8.	Montana	2.64	48.	New Jersey	.78
9.	South Carolina	2.63	49.	Minnesota	.68
10.	Maine	2.33	50.	Delaware	.59

Source: Data for 2009 compiled from Internal Revenue gross collections, by type of tax and state, fiscal year 2009. Retrieved November 18, 2011, from http://www.irs.gov/taxstats/article/0,,id=206488,00.html; and Bureau of the Census, U.S. Department of Commerce (2011). *Statistical abstract of the United States: 2012* (p. 316). Washington, DC: Government Printing Office.

only in Minnesota did federal tax collections exceed federal expenditures. Clearly, whether a federal budget deficit is incurred for economic stimulus reasons, war expenditures, or just unwillingness to balance the budget, states generally have more federal funds spent in their states than they pay in taxes in recession years.

Table 15–1 compares federal spending with federal taxing without regard to estimates of need or ability to pay. If one federal responsibility is to redistribute income from wealthier areas of the country to poorer areas, then it should not be surprising that some states send more taxes to Washington than the federal government spends in those states. **Figure 15–1** illustrates the relationship between the net revenue flow of federal expenditures and federal taxes, for all 50 states, and state per capita income. If this net federal flow is generally redistributive, then we would expect the pattern to be generally downward sloping to the right, which indeed is what Figure 15–1 demonstrates. The lower the per capita income, the greater the net flow of federal funds to the state.

We inserted the overall, linear trend line in the figure. The correlation between net flow and per capita income is –0.34, the negative sign consistent with the expectation. Although the trendline is consistent with the hypothesis that net federal revenue and expenditure actions are redistributive across the states, there is considerable variation, visible in the scatterplot with its numerous large outliers. In other years, the trend is the same, consistent with the hypothesis, and the correlation is stronger. In 2004, for example, the correlation coefficient was –0.61. Of course, numerous other factors are involved. Figure 15–1 merely

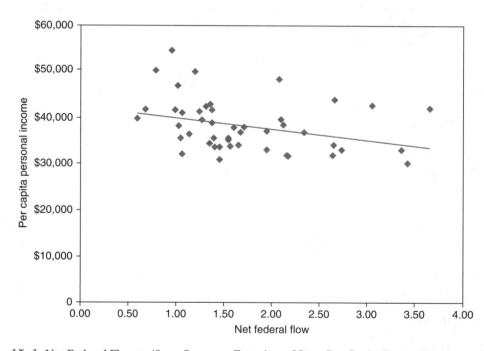

Figure 15–1 Net Federal Flow to/from State as a Function of State Per Capita Personal Income, 2009.
Sources: Compiled from *Internal Revenue gross collections, by type of tax and state, fiscal year 2009.* Retrieved November 18, 2011, from http://www.irs.gov/taxstats/article/0,,id=206488,00.html; Bureau of the Census, U.S. Department of Commerce (2011). *Statistical abstract of the United States: 2012* (p. 316). Washington, DC: Government Printing Office.

illustrates the general tendency of total federal activities in the states to be redistributive. Figure 15–1 is important, however, because it includes not just federal grants, but all federal spending in states. It would appear that total federal spending is more redistributive than federal grants alone.

Intergovernmental Assistance

State Aid

The literature on intergovernmental relations tends to overemphasize federal aid to state and local governments and underemphasize state aid to local government. In 2008, federal aid to states was $423 billion and to local governments was $58 billion. State aid to local governments was $467 billion.[57] State support of local governments for most states is the largest element in the state budget. Of course, state aid probably would be much smaller were states not receiving substantial federal support. As noted in the chapter on the public sector in perspective, states receive more than one-fourth of their revenue from the federal government. Local governments receive about 33% of their revenue from other governments, almost all of it from state governments, with only 4% from the federal government. Except for school districts, each type of local government obtains half or more of its revenue from its own sources. Differences in federal and state support exist among the types of local governments.

Figure 15–2 illustrates intergovernmental revenues provided to the different types of local government entities, as a proportion of those entities' total general revenues. For example, in the middle column, county revenues for 2007 were 64% from their own sources. The remaining 36% came from intergovernmental transfers—3% from federal government, 31% from states, and 2% from other local entities. Similarly, one can see that school districts are the only local entities that receive more than half of their revenue from other governments—state governments provided a majority of the funds that school districts spent (53%).

Another way to look at intergovernmental aid is to consider where most of the federal intergovernmental transfers go, and similarly for state and local transfers. As of 2007, about 36% of all federal aid to local governments went to municipalities, but these monies constituted only about 5% of municipal revenues. Special districts such as sewer and water districts were the most dependent on federal aid, which constituted 16% of their budgets. Slightly more than half (56%) of state aid went to school districts, with these monies accounting for just under half of school district revenues. Most of the other state aid went to counties and municipalities, 24% and 16%, respectively.[58]

These summary figures, of course, do not convey the great variety in patterns of state aid. Some states provide much greater assistance to local governments than other states. Some states may provide a given service and thereby make direct expenditures, whereas other states may fund local governments to provide the service. Tennessee's local governments, for example, receive about 25% of their revenues from other governments, almost all from the state government. This is much less than New Mexico's local governments, which get 53% of their revenues from other governments, again almost all from the state government.[59] Hawaii's intergovernmental transfers to local governments are low because the state directly operates schools, unlike the other states, which funnel elementary and secondary school money to local districts.

Federal Aid		State Aid	Local Aid
3.3% →	Counties 64.1%		
		30.8% ←	
			1.9% ←
5.3% →	Municipalities 73.9%		
		18.7% ←	
			2.1% ←
1.2% →	Townships 77.7%		
		18.6% ←	
			2.4% ←
15.8% →	Special Districts 68.1%		
		8.8% ←	
			7.3% ←
1.0% →	School Districts 44.7%		
		53.2% ←	
			1.2% ←

Figure 15–2 Intergovernmental Sources of General Revenue for Types of Local Governments, 2007. Data may not equal 100% due to rounding.

Source: Compiled from Bureau of the Census, U.S. Department of Commerce (2009). *Table 2. Local government finances by type of government and state: 2006–07.* Retrieved November 26, 2011, from http://www.census.gov/govs/estimate/historical_data_2007.html#state_local.

State Aid to Education

Aid to elementary and secondary education, as noted, constitutes the largest portion of state aid to local governments. Local school districts have not always depended as heavily on state and federal aid. **Figure 15–3** shows that local sources in the early part of the 20th century accounted for more than 80% of total funding, whereas it had declined to only 43% by 1980. Since then, local financing for education has varied, rising to 48% by the mid-1990s but then falling again to about 43% in 2000 and 2009. Just as state aid to local governments in general varies considerably from state to state, so too does state aid to education, with Florida, Illinois, Nebraska, and South Dakota providing the lowest percentage of funding (low to mid-30% range).[60]

Because of the importance of external—mainly state—funding, the manner in which funds are distributed to local school districts is often a matter of some controversy. States use a formula for distributing these funds. Historically known as the *foundation plan*, such formulas are geared toward guaranteeing a minimum amount of educational expenditures either per pupil or per classroom. The word *foundation* suggests equality of educational opportunity, meaning that every student should have a minimum level of education—a foundation program. Formulas typically have been tied to real estate property assessments, with districts having low assessments per pupil receiving more aid than districts having high assessments.

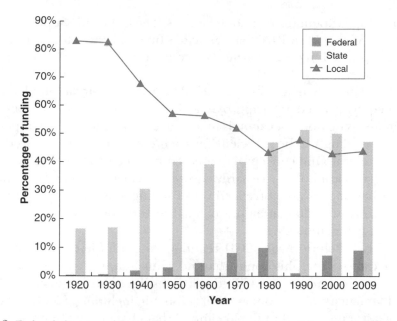

Figure 15–3 Federal, State, and Local Support for Elementary and Secondary Education, 1920–2009 (in Percent).

Sources: Compiled from Monk, D. H. (1991). *Educational finance: an economic approach* (p. 101). New York, NY: McGraw-Hill; Bureau of the Census, U.S. Department of Commerce (1991). *Government finances: 1989–90* (p. 7). Washington, DC: U.S. Government Printing Office; Bureau of the Census, U.S. Department of Commerce (2002). *Public education finances, 2000* (p. 1). Washington, DC: U.S. Government Printing Office; Bureau of the Census, U.S. Department of Commerce (2011). *Public elementary-secondary school system finance data.* Retrieved November 14, 2011, from http://www.census.gov/govs/www/school.html.

Although relatively rare, some state formulas even have recapture provisions in which state aid to wealthier districts can be negative, with the funds the state receives from wealthier districts being used to support the poorer districts.[61] Separate formulas may be used for programs serving preschool, disadvantaged, and handicapped children as well as elementary-level children and secondary-level children.

Foundation formulas were attacked in the courts starting in the 1970s as discriminatory. Foundation plans were accused of failing to equalize educational opportunity among jurisdictions. While recognizing the great importance of education, the Supreme Court in 1973 decided in a Texas case, *San Antonio School District v. Rodriquez,* that the allocation of funds for education was a state responsibility and was not controlled by the Constitution.[62] The Court, in that case, was concerned that basing the formula on a macro measure such as the property tax base may not represent circumstances at the micro or individual level (e.g., extremely poor families might live in a wealthy district and not be receiving equal educational opportunity). Thus, the Court ruled that the reliance on the property tax did not create any inequality challengeable on constitutional grounds.

Despite the Court's conclusion in *Rodriquez,* other cases have been won in state courts, so that many states have been required to alter their education financing schemes to minimize disparities in per-pupil expenditures among districts. The California Supreme Court ruled in *Serrano v. Priest* (*Serrano II*) in 1976 that the state's finance system for education violated California's equal protection clause in the state constitution because it created disparities in per-pupil spending.[63]

A National Academy of Sciences study concluded that the foundation plan notion and its emphasis on equity defined as an approximately equal funding amount per pupil is no longer useful in assessing how education is financed and provided.[64] Equal spending does not ensure that spending will be sufficient for each child to achieve desired outcomes. Adequacy is a more profound concept that links equity to educational achievement. The equal opportunity to learn is not necessarily ensured by equal funding. Some have argued that student performance is not correlated with funding amounts, calling into question both formula systems and states' attempts to equalize educational opportunity using various measures of equal spending.[65]

The No Child Left Behind Act of 2001 reauthorizing the Elementary and Secondary Education Act expresses the philosophy that individuals should have equal chances for educational achievement and mandates individual testing to measure success.[66] Reauthorization of the Elementary and Secondary Education Act, including No Child Left Behind, was delayed at least until 2012, and the likelihood that changes to the present act will be made in the national election year is slender. Major reform proposals for the reauthorization focus primarily on the student achievement testing provisions, and pay little attention to questions of equitable funding.[67]

Rose v. Council for Better Education, a 1989 Kentucky Supreme Court case, is often considered the landmark case in litigation using the adequacy concept. The court decided that the Kentucky legislature had failed to live up to the state's constitutional requirement to "provide an efficient system of common schools throughout the state."[68] That forced the state to change its school funding scheme. At least 43 states have faced suits in their respective state courts over state funding schemes for education.[69] One of the issues in determining an adequate funding level is differential costs in achieving approximately equal student performance in schools that have predominantly higher-income families versus districts with predominantly lower-income families. Schools in lower-income areas generally have difficulty hiring the more experienced, and therefore more expensive, teachers, whereas schools in upper-income areas are more likely to be saturated with the more experienced teachers. When states attempt to adjust funding formulas to provide comparable funding, the likelihood is that school districts previously getting more funds when distribution was based on teaching positions rather than actual teacher salaries face funding cuts, whereas lower-income districts receive increases. In 2007–2009, Oakland, California, and New York City introduced "hold harmless" provisions that increase funding for lower-income districts, but hold districts that otherwise would receive substantial cuts harmless from having to let teachers go.[70] The recession that started in 2007 and the 2010 elections that put more conservative Republicans in control of many state legislatures brought on additional cuts in state aid to education, and the likely result will be new rounds of lawsuits in some state courts as funding cuts potentially increase disparities among school districts.

Other State Aid

Other state aid programs are comparatively small. Education is followed in size by expenditures for welfare and highways. Aid for these programs is usually handed out based on some type of formula (welfare programs are often per-client reimbursement programs). Virtually all states have some form of motor fuels tax–sharing formula that benefits local government road programs as well as state roads.[71] General local government support, as opposed to specific functional aid, is higher than support for any functions other than education and welfare.

Overall, state assistance has been more predictable than federal aid because of the extensive use of formulas, though the efforts in 2011 in some states following the 2010 elections to reduce state aid to local governments may change that. Formulas facilitate budget planning at the local level because jurisdictions from year to year have some knowledge of what state funds will be. The only major controversies have centered on the factors used in the formulas. Aid to local governments in many states rises and falls depending on the states' economic health. Local governments have shown resiliency in making up for state and federal decreases by drawing on their own resources and by placing greater reliance on user charges and other charges aimed at direct beneficiaries of programs (see the chapter on budgeting for transaction-based revenues).

Local governments particularly were at the bottom of the food chain in 2001–2002 and again after 2007 when state budget deficits were redressed in most states at least in part by drastic cuts in aid to local governments. In some cases, states failed to live up to legislated formulas.[72]

When state funding, even though it is supposedly guaranteed, seems threatened, local school districts take various measures in anticipation of possible funding problems. Expenditures may be reduced to some extent, and then later may be boosted when state funds are released to the districts. Districts sometimes may deliberately overestimate their local revenue receipts in order to be able to have a balanced budget, at least on paper.[73]

Federal Aid

Federal grants have been aimed at inducing state and local governments to increase the level of services in specified functions and are not intended to replace state or local spending with federal revenues. The inducement effect is based on the theory that the more separation exists between taxing and spending, the more taxpayers will not perceive the full costs of local services. This is known as the *fiscal illusion hypothesis*.

Matching Requirements, Fungibility, and the Flypaper Effect

Matching provisions are usually required as a means of ensuring that grants will not merely result in a lessened tax effort by the recipients of the grants. For example, a grant might require that a state government match federal aid dollar for dollar, that a particular project funded by a grant be funded 50% by each level of government. Without a matching provision, a $1 million federal grant could be offset by an equal reduction in state or local revenues supporting a program, thereby producing no increase in the level of services.

The ability to replace local or state money for a program with grant money is known as *fungibility*. The government providing the grant usually does not want this to occur because its intent is to increase funding in a targeted area. For example, if grant money is targeted at crime, then the intent is to boost law enforcement expenditures and not to have federal dollars simply supplant some of the state and local money that otherwise would have been spent on law enforcement. The freed-up funds then might be used to support other programs, to reduce taxes, or for a combination of these. However, sometimes substituting spending by a recipient government with a grant or transfer from another government may be the goal. States may want local governments to accept state aid and decrease reliance on the property tax. A related matter is the extent of earmarking of grant money for specific purposes, a topic addressed later in this chapter. When grants are earmarked in detail, flexibility is decreased. In the case of helping small businesses recover from the September 11 disaster in New York City, the New York City Investment Fund found it important to avoid earmarking and to provide small businesses with the flexibility that they needed in the use of the assistance.[74] In the case of donations, for example, people who donate to the Red Cross in the wake of hurricanes and tornadoes, such as the 2011 Joplin, Missouri, tornado disaster, often earmark their donations specifically for particular disasters and reduce the flexibility of the agency in meeting other needs.

Fungibility poses a major threat to analyses of the effectiveness of programs and the use of such analyses in budgetary decision making. If state or local dollars are replaced one-for-one with grant money, then no increase in funding has occurred, and any identified change in program results clearly is not associated with funding. The extent to which governments take advantage of possible fungibility relates to another concept known as the *flypaper effect*. When private citizens receive increased funding, say bonuses of $1,000 each, the typical pattern will be to spend some and save some. A family with a tight budget might spend all or almost all of the $1,000, but other families might spend only $700 and put the remaining $300 in savings. The question for state and local governments is whether they tend to do the same or if there is a flypaper effect in which the money received gets spent for the intended purpose (that is, whether the money "sticks" to the grant area as planned by the donor government).

Research tends to support the flypaper effect. Recipient governments tend to spend the money received for the intended purpose, and in some cases the governments even spend more of their own funds than they otherwise would have spent.[75] Financially strapped jurisdictions, however, may view fungibility as an opportunity to free up money for other pressing services, and to do so may even use what amounts to subterfuge to hide such transactions from the granting agency.

One study of state general grants to local education agencies found that grants do induce increased local spending for education, but not by as much as the amount of the grant funds.[76] The fiscal effect, inducing more local spending, is less when the grants are provided without any minimum requirements for tax effort or expenditure requirements. When there is no matching requirement, the greater effect may be on local tax relief—mainly property taxes in the case of education—rather than on increasing spending. The opposite situation arises also. Research shows that some increases in state aid for education forced by having to meet legal challenges result in reduced state aid to local governments in other functional areas.[77]

Where the objective is more clearly weighted toward redistributive effects, such as welfare assistance, there is the risk that states with less fiscal capacity may choose to spend less than what is considered nationally desirable. The various low-income assistance programs with which the federal government helps states and localities exhibit a range of federal involvement. The Supplemental Nutrition Assistance Program (known more colloquially as food stamps) is fully federally funded. The Supplemental Security Income (SSI) program for the low-income elderly and disabled is mainly federally funded. The Temporary Assistance to Needy Families (TANF) program is a block grant program with major contributions from both the federal government and the states.[78] State fiscal responses to this package of programs has been somewhat mixed, with apparent reduced efforts for cash assistance programs and overall increased state and local spending for various welfare programs, especially Medicaid.

For grant programs aimed at inducing behavior changes and not necessarily fiscal responses, the task is more difficult. To accomplish changes in program emphasis at the state and local levels with grants, one has to believe that state and local preferences for service modes, such as transportation, arc primarily driven by the cost and revenue availability. The Intermodal Surface Transportation Efficiency Act of 1991 (ISTEA) and the Transportation Enhancement Act of 1998 (TEA) were intended in part to encourage development and use of transportation modes other than cars on highways. In reality, states and localities are more likely to choose to repair and rehabilitate deteriorating highways and bridges than to fund mass transit.[79] The federal Children's Health Insurance Program (CHIP) was designed to induce states to implement programs to insure low-income children. It was designed with a punitive "use it or lose it" provision that gave states limited time to meet all the provisions. As a result, most states lost millions in unspent CHIP money—California in the first year forfeited nearly $600 million.[80]

Federal Aid and Functional Areas

During the 1960s, about 80% of all federal aid went for transportation and income security. As can be seen in **Table 15–2**, there have been substantial shifts since that time. Transportation, which accounted for more than 40% of the aid in the 1960s, declined to just under 20% in 1970, and then continued to fall to 10% in 2010. Aid for health programs rose to 48%. Income security accounted for about 19% of the aid. It has fluctuated widely, up in the 1960s (38%), down to 20% in 1980, back up again around 25% in the 1990s, and down again to just less than 20% in 2010. The last decrease is in part due to welfare reforms limiting the number of years during which an individual can receive assistance (TANF program). Generally, the effects of rapidly rising health care costs and the number of individuals qualifying for income security programs explain most of the shifts that occurred between 1980 and 2010.

The amount of federal aid given to state and local governments varies among federal agencies. As can be seen in **Table 15–3**, the Department of Health and Human Services disburses the most aid by far, accounting for 57% of all federal grants.[81] A different perspective, however, is gained by looking at the portion of an agency's budget committed to grants. Although the Department of Health and Human Services spends about 41% of its funds on grants, the Department of Education spends more than 80%, and the Department

Table 15–2 Percentage Function Distribution of Federal Grants-in-Aid, 1960–2010

	1960	1970	1980	1990	2000	2010
Administration of Justice	*	*	1	*	2	1
Agriculture	3	3	1	1	0	0
Community and Regional Development	1	8	7	4	3	3
Education, Employment, Training, and Social Services	7	27	24	16	13	16
General Government	3	2	9	2	1	1
Health	3	16	17	33	44	48
Income Security	38	24	20	27	24	19
Natural Resources and Environment	1	2	6	3	2	2
Transportation	43	19	14	14	11	10
Other	*	*	1	1	1	1
Total	100	100	100	100	100	100

Totals may not equal 100 percent due to rounding.
*0.5 percent or less

Source: Calculated from U.S. Office of Management and Budget (2011). *Analytical perspectives, budget of the United States government, 2012* (p. 297). Washington, DC: U.S. Government Printing Office.

Table 15–3 Federal Agency Outlays and Grants to State and Local Governments, 2010 (in Billions of Dollars)

Agency	Total Outlays	Grant Outlays	Grants as Percentage of Total
Agriculture	129.5	32.5	25.1
Commerce	13.2	0.5	3.8
Education	92.9	75.1	80.8
Energy	30.8	2.2	7.1
Environmental Protection Agency	11.0	6.9	62.6
Health and Human Services	854.1	347.1	40.6
Homeland Security	44.5	8.9	20.1
Housing and Urban Development	60.1	44.4	73.9
Interior	13.2	4.5	34.1
Justice	29.6	4.6	15.5
Labor	173.1	11.6	6.7
Social Security Administration	754.2	0.0	0.0
Transportation	77.8	61.0	78.4
Treasury	444.3	3.9	0.9
Veterans Affairs	108.3	0.8	0.8
Other Agencies	620.0	4.4	0.7
Total*	3,456.2	608.4	17.6

*Total does not include allowances and undistributed offsetting receipts (on-budget and off-budget).

Source: Compiled from U.S. Office of Management and Budget (2011). *Analytical perspectives, budget of the United States government, 2012* (pp. 285–295, 440). Washington, DC: U.S. Government Printing Office.

of Transportation and the Department of Housing and Urban Development spend 78% and 74% on grants, respectively.

Regional Differences

Just as total federal outlays are not uniform from state to state, so too do grants vary. In 2009, the national average was $1,765 per capita in federal grants to state and local governments, up from $533 in 1990 and $1,169 in 2005. The states receiving the highest per capita grants, other than Alaska, were Wyoming ($4,067), New Mexico ($3,301), North Dakota ($2,792), Vermont ($2,687), and New York ($2,670). With the exception of New York, the other top five per capita recipients were all very sparsely populated states. The group with the lowest per capita grants consisted of Virginia ($1,138), Nevada ($1,189), Florida ($1,223), Colorado ($1,260), and Georgia ($1,317). The lowest-ranking recipients were a mix of less and more populous states. Alaska was the highest state, with $5,188, but it commonly is an outlier and is typically excluded from comparisons.[82]

These per capita grant figures must not be interpreted simply as revealing which areas are winners and losers in the federal aid game. As noted in the previous section, a state and its local governments might receive comparatively small amounts of grants, but extensive economic support as a result of direct federal expenditures. Virginia receives relatively little in grants, but benefits from having a great many federal offices and facilities.

Assuming that the federal graduated income tax has the effect of drawing proportionately greater resources from wealthy states than from less wealthy states, federal aid could amplify or dampen this effect. For example, per capita federal aid to state and local governments might increase as per capita personal income declines, which would amplify the effect. This pattern, however, is not evident. Nonetheless, as already discussed, there is a general redistributive effect when the total flows to states from all federal actions and flows of taxes from the states are compared to per capita income. Other factors explaining the distribution of federal grants include the number of Medicaid recipients and the amount of federal land in the state, which brings money from minerals, timber, and grazing rights. Again, caution is necessary when interpreting only one measure of federal economic impact on states. The lack of a clear pattern is explained by the numerous federal grant programs that tend to offset each other in benefiting particular types of states.

Studies that have compared federal aid and state aid to urban areas have concluded that, although both are responsive to need, state aid is more responsive. Cities with greater fiscal problems receive greater per capita state assistance. An important factor in this area is local initiative itself. Some cities are much more aggressive and adept at securing federal and state aid, and this ability is not necessarily correlated with the extent of need. In recent years, state governments have tried to offset some of the decline in federal aid to local governments, particularly by targeting their assistance to cities with the severest problems measured in terms of need, such as prevalence of poverty and low fiscal capacity. However, state budget crises during the recent two recessions, as noted above, resulted in serious cutbacks in state assistance to all local governments, both rural and urban.

In metropolitan areas, fiscal imbalances can cause problems in the pattern of services and the ability to pay for those services. Capital flight out of central cities in the form of wealthier households and businesses moving to the suburbs exacerbates differences, especially in the older cities of the Northeast and the Midwest. One way that some metropolitan areas have combated this problem is to develop metropolitan area tax base sharing and other fiscal equalization strategies, although few governments across the country willingly share their tax bases. Some multiple municipal jurisdictions within the same metropolitan area have begun to see advantages in increased coordination as some city regions look to their potential fate in a global economy. Greater metropolitan area coordination and cooperation is likely to be an important outgrowth of the recent recessions, the likelihood of a weak federal budget for years to come, and state governments' recent cutback responses.[83]

Federal aid to local communities can be provided directly to these communities or indirectly through the states. In the latter case, state officials are allowed some discretion in distributing federal funds, although federal regulations may require that a given amount pass through to localities and that some of this money be distributed according to set criteria, such as population. State *enabling legislation* often is required before a local government can receive funds directly from the federal government.

Devolution and Future Trends

The dollar volume of federal grants-in-aid continues to climb each year, but federal aid as a percentage of state and local expenditures reached a peak in 1980, as shown in **Figure 15–4**, and is not expected to grow again in the foreseeable future. Both 2008 and 2009 are shown in the figure to provide a before/after comparison. The effects of the stimulus programs to combat the recession did not have a significant impact until budget year 2009. Federal grants as a percentage of state and local expenditures increased from what had been an almost steady 16% since 1980 to 19% in 2009. Later in the chapter, we discuss federal aid as a share of state and local revenues. Because of the two recessions between 2000 and 2011, federal aid to state and local governments as a proportion of state and local revenues jumped up substantially, falling between the two recessions. The trend to low levels of federal assistance except in a major crisis as in the recent recession, and the size of the federal deficit, are changing the character of intergovernmental relations in the United States.

Figure 15–4 illustrates three other comparative measures of federal grants. Grants as a percentage of federal outlays grew from 8% in 1960 to 15% in the 1975–1980 period, then fell for the next decade to 11%. From 1995 to 2009, the proportion of grants in total federal outlays has varied around 15% to 16%. Federal aid hovered between 2% and 4% of gross domestic product throughout the period covered by Figure 15–4.[84]

Figure 15–4, in addition to tracking changes in federal grants vis-à-vis state and local expenditures and total federal outlays, also indicates the substantial change in the character of federal aid to state and local governments. The most prominent change has been the growth in the percentage of federal grants that are payments to individuals. As Figure 15–4 shows, beginning in 1985, payments to individuals have grown from the mid-30% range to above 60%. The other noticeable trend is the decline in federal grants for physical capital. In the 1960s, nearly 50% of federal grants were for physical capital. That percentage dropped below 25% in 1975, and has continued to decline to below 14% in 2009.

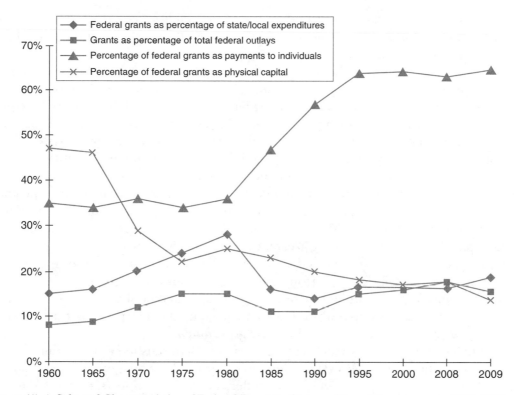

Figure 15–4 Selected Characteristics of Federal Grants to State and Local Governments, 1960–2009.
Source: Office of Management and Budget (1998). *Budget of the United States government, fiscal 1997* (p. 194). Washington, DC: U.S. Government Printing Office; Office of Management and Budget (2004). *Budget of the United States government: historical tables, fiscal year 2012, table 12-1.* Retrieved November 28, 2011, from http://www.gpoaccess.gov/usbudget/fy12/hist.html; Bureau of the Census, U.S. Department of Commerce (2011). *Statistical abstract: 2012* (pp. 268, 269, 310). Washington, DC: U.S. Government Printing Office; and *State and local finance data query system.* Washington, DC: Urban Institute and Brookings Institution. Retrieved November 28, 2011, from http://slfdqs.taxpolicycenter.org/pages.cfm.

The shift from grants to states and local governments for physical capital investments toward payments to individuals has meant a change for state and local governments. Rather than serving as active agents in implementing federally funded programs, they now play more of a role as conduits for channeling federal funds to individuals. During the 1960s, which saw extensive federal assistance to capital infrastructure programs, state governments mainly (but also local governments) were heavily involved in selection, design, and contracting for public works financed by federal dollars. The shift toward payments to individuals channeled by the states has meant hiring more staff to determine eligibility, to verify information, and to track benefits paid to recipients.

Federal aid cutbacks in many states have created difficulties for many governments and have proved nearly devastating for others, especially when combined with reductions in revenue due to economic recessions and taxing limitations. The recessionary period of 1990–1992 caused enormous hardships for state and local governments. That was repeated in the two recessions since 2000. Prior to the 1960s, state and local governments had primary financing responsibility for domestic programs. Beginning with the 1960s and the antipoverty programs of the Johnson administration, the financial role of the federal government came to equal and, by the mid-1970s, even exceed the financial role of state and local governments. Although state and local spending has not yet caught up with federal domestic spending despite the substantial shifts in spending patterns of the past decade, growth in state and local government spending has been more rapid than growth in federal spending. Not only have federal grants for capital declined, but state and local spending for capital investment as a percentage of gross domestic product has declined as well. Thus, states have been forced to scramble to keep services operating and in many situations have had little or no choice but to cut and sometimes eliminate programs.

State and local governments have responded by improving management and efficiency, increasing their own-source revenue generation, and moving toward employment of user charges and other mechanisms that limit expenditures more to what people are actually willing to pay. This change is yielding greater overall allocative efficiency in the economy—that is, producing goods and services that citizens value the most and thereby maximizing net benefits. The change signals a stronger role for state and local governments as determinants of domestic policy, and for many it represents a welcome shift back toward a more decentralized political system in which federal management expertise is no longer seen as significantly greater than that of state and local governments.

Nevertheless, the federal government has been less than satisfied that its grant monies are being well administered. President George W. Bush's 2009 budget proposal reported that of the 280 grant programs evaluated under the PART system (see the chapter on budget preparation and the decision process), only 88 were rated moderately effective or effective. Sixteen were considered ineffective, and 97 were rated as "results not demonstrated." Results such as these are the basis for recommendations that various grants be eliminated and others be scaled back in funding. Budgets of the Obama administration have not included systematic analysis of the effectiveness of federal grant programs comparable to the PART rating system put in place by the George W. Bush administration.

Devolution has meant a fundamental shift in responsibility for policy, programs, and financing. Devolution involves outright reductions in federal aid to state and local governments, changes in some programs from matching to nonmatching grants, and, of course, greater flexibility. In response to the challenges, state and local governments have taken on much more activist roles in policy formulation, program design, and program implementation in assuming responsibilities that have been determined by federal policy and program design since their origins. States have become more activist in developing and implementing environmental programs, including some that exceed mandatory federal standards.[85] They have also taken the initiative in developing policies and programs in child health insurance, despite some of the disasters initially experienced as a result of rigid federal design.[86]

Exhibit 15–2 discusses welfare reform as an example of devolution. Massive changes were initiated in 1996 with passage of the Personal Responsibility and Work Opportunity Reconciliation Act (PRWORA).[87] The law gave states considerable authority in devising programs for the needy. In the more than 10 years of experience under the law, successes have been achieved but problems remain.

Exhibit 15–2 Welfare Reform as a Case Study in Devolution

The most prominent shift in devolving policy and program design in the past three decades has been the reconfiguring of the nation's welfare system. Several changes in parts of the system were made in the decade leading up to passage of the Personal Responsibility and Work Opportunity Reconciliation Act (PRWORA) of 1996. The earned income tax credit was changed to increase disposable income among low-income, basically welfare-eligible households and individuals. Medicaid coverage was expanded to include adults with dependent children, affecting mainly families with incomes that previously had put them above welfare eligibility.

The big change in the intergovernmental system introduced by PRWORA was the shift of federal responsibility for setting welfare standards and the long-standing approach of federal matching grants to a fixed block grant program.[1] States were given wide latitude in designing programs. From the point of view of welfare recipients, the major change was a maximum lifetime eligibility of five years for public financial assistance. This change involved the replacement of the Aid to Families with Dependent Children (AFDC) program with Temporary Assistance for Needy Families (TANF). Some states, such as North Carolina, chose to take devolution one step further by delegating the administration of TANF to local governments.[2]

PRWORA provided for considerable relaxation in federal requirements through granting states waivers, thereby exempting them from many federal requirements, to develop their own policies and system designs.[3] Some states secured waivers to contract out to private organizations such previously state functions as eligibility determination, job counseling and training, and administration of the program.[4] Others consolidated numerous programs. States were allowed to determine eligibility, set benefit levels, and design their own program administration.

State programs are funded through a combination of federal funds (through the TANF block grant) and state funds. Federal funding exceeded $21.7 billion in 2010.

The law provided for limitations as to how long people could be eligible for cash assistance. Recipients of AFDC (TANF's predecessor) in 1990 totaled 11.5 million. That number had increased to 13.4 million in 1995. The numbers started coming down in 1997 to 8.9 million, 5.4 million in 2001, and 4.5 million in 2005. Since 2005, with the exception of 2008, the number of people receiving assistance under TANF has been relatively steady around 4.5 million (3.7 million in 2008).[5] One continuing problem and one addressed explicitly in the 2007 budget is that cash assistance all too often goes to people who should have been ineligible for benefits.[6] This is the *improper payments* problem.[7]

Innovative policy and program reforms in welfare-to-work transition, teen pregnancy reduction, health screening, and single-parent family issues have been developed as a result of the "experiments" conducted across the states. Welfare recipients themselves have had varying experiences. Clearly, some have found productive employment and are unlikely to return to public assistance. However, much of the decline in welfare rolls has been attributed to individuals and households being declared ineligible because they could not, or did not, meet the work requirements. One report of an official federal study showed that in 2005, only 40% of those who met the poverty threshold to qualify for assistance actually received assistance. This was in contrast to the previous AFDC program, which provided assistance to up to 80% of the qualified individuals.[8]

(continued)

A study comparing former welfare recipients in terms of job retention with otherwise similar individuals not previously on welfare found that former welfare recipients were more likely to retain their jobs.[9] To reduce clients' dependence on cash assistance and increase their employability, states have used a variety of programs, including job training, technical-postsecondary education, assistance in entrepreneurship through formation of self-owned businesses, and training in money management and savings.[10]

Some states have developed supplemental forms of assistance to address the group of individuals who are no longer on the welfare rolls and are working, but are earning wages that would otherwise qualify them for public assistance. Measuring whether people are working has proved troublesome because of the latitude afforded states by devolution. Some states have been more inclusive in counting people as working. For instance, some states considered people working if they were at home tending to disabled family members.[11] Congress restricted the definition of worker participation, and in 2006, the Department of Health and Human Services, which administers the program, issued regulations dealing with this problem.[12]

Children, who had been the focus of the old AFDC program, slipped through the cracks in some instances under TANF. The share of poor children receiving support had dropped from more than 60% in the 1990s to about 30% by the mid-2000s.[13] That number remained about the same through 2011.[14]

States, in some cases, have adjusted their income taxes to benefit poor families. Minnesota, for example, implemented a state earned income tax credit and supplemental programs for child care subsidies and child care credits.[15] Problems persist over how best to assist people with disabilities. These people are eligible for Supplemental Security Income (SSI) and can be eligible for TANF as well.[16]

Congress reauthorized PRWORA in 2002. Reauthorization in 2011 was lost in the overall impasse in the Congress, but the program was extended. One continuing issue is whether the Congress should authorize what are called "superwaivers." As noted above, federal officials have authority to waive various requirements at the request of state governments. The superwaiver would simply broaden that authority. The plus side of the argument is that the superwaiver would allow states to have the flexibility they need. The Obama administration supported greater flexibility in state administration of the program. The negative side is that state programs would evolve into widely divergent activities, losing any semblance of being a national program. Indeed, were that to happen, some fear that could be the grounds for eliminating or reducing TANF funding.[17]

A continuing problem is obtaining systematic information across the states as to how they are using TANF funding. Because the states have great flexibility in the spending of federal dollars, evaluating the effectiveness of such spending is a challenging endeavor.[18]

1. Personal Responsibility and Work Opportunity Reconciliation Act of 1996 (P.L. 104-193).
2. Berner, M. (2005). A race to the bottom? Exploring county spending shortfalls under welfare reform in North Carolina. *Public Budgeting & Finance, 25,* Winter, 86–104.
3. Meyer, B. D., & Rosenbuam, D. T. (2000). Making single mothers work: recent tax and welfare policy and its effects. *National Tax Journal, 53,* 1027–1061.
4. Arsnault, S. (2000). Welfare policy innovation and diffusion: Section 1115 waivers and the federal system. *State and Local Government Review, 32,* 49–60.

5. Administration for Children and Families, U.S. Department of Health and Human Services (2011). *Temporary Assistance for Needy Families and Children: caseload data.* Retrieved November 27, 2011, from http://www.acf.hhs.gov/programs/ofa/data-reports/caseload/caseload_current. htm#2011.

6. U.S. Office of Management and Budget (2006). *Analytical perspectives, budget of the United States government, 2007* (p. 100). Washington, DC: U.S. Government Printing Office.

7. U.S. Government Accountability Office (2004). *TANF and child care programs: HHS lacks adequate information to assess risk and assist states in managing improper payments.* Washington, DC: Author.

8. Schott, L. (2011). *Policy basics: an introduction to TANF.* Washington, DC: Center on Budget and Policy Priorities. Retrieved November 28, 2011, from http://www.cbpp.org/cms/?fa=view&id=936.

9. Gooden, S. T., & Bailey, M. (2001). Welfare and work: job-retention outcomes of federal welfare-to-work employees. *Public Administration Review, 61,* 83–91.

10. U.S. Government Accountability Office (2005). *Welfare reform: more information needed to assess promising strategies to increase parents' incomes.* Washington, DC: Author.

11. U.S. Government Accountability Office (2005). *Welfare reform: HHS should exercise oversight to help ensure TANF work participation is measured consistently across states.* Washington, DC: Author.

12. Greenberg, M., & Parrott, S. (2006). Summary of TANF work participation provisions in the budget reconciliation bill. Retrieved October 3, 2006, from http://www.cbpp.org/1-18-06tanf .htm; Lower-Basch, E., et al. (2006). An analysis of new interim final TANF rules. Retrieved October 3, 2006, from http://www.cbpp.org/7-21-06tanf.htm.

13. Parrott, S., & Sherman, A. (2006). *TANF at 10: program results are more mixed than often understood.* Center on Budget and Policy Priorities. Retrieved April 13, 2012, from http://www.cbpp.org/cms/?fa=view&id=600.

14. Administration for Children and Families, U.S. Department of Health and Human Services (2011). *Temporary Assistance for Needy Families and Children: caseload data.*

15. Wilson, P. (2000). Tax implication of welfare reform: the Minnesota experience. *National Tax Journal, 53,* 417–437.

16. U.S. Government Accountability Office (2004). *TANF and SSI: opportunities exist to help people with impairments become more self-sufficient.* Washington, DC: Author.

17. Nivola, P. S., Noyes, J. L., & Sawhill, I. V. (2004). Waive of the future? Federalism and the next phase of welfare reform. Retrieved October 3, 2006, from http://www.brookings.edu/es/research/projects/wrb/pulications/pb/pb29.htm.

18. U.S. Government Accountability Office (2006). *Welfare reform: better information needed to understand trends in states' uses of the TANF block grant.* Washington, DC: Author.

Other Elements Affecting Intergovernmental Patterns

Direct expenditures and financial assistance provided by one level of government to another level are not the only factors in the U.S. system of intergovernmental relations that affect budgeting. In addition to restrictions and requirements built into most financial assistance, the programs financed by the assistance contain various requirements that influence how state and local governments plan and budget. Another element derives from the fact that state governments are the constitutional authorities for establishing local governments within their jurisdictions and thus have significant roles in determining which revenue sources local governments may use, which services local governments are responsible for providing, and under which circumstances local governments may enter into debt.

Features Associated with Financial Assistance

The preceding sections discussed the targeting aspects of grants provided by one level of government to another level. Additional controls often are built into the assistance arrangement. One of the fastest-growing budgetary components for all levels of government is the Medicaid program, which offers health assistance to the poor. Major health care reform legislation in 2010 significantly expanded eligibility for Medicaid, and altered federal-state relationships in health care for low-income individuals and families.[88] It was accomplished with significant Republican opposition, and opposition by many Republican-controlled state governments. The longer-term outlook for health care reform, labeled by some opponents as *Obamacare*, rests in part in the courts and in part on whether Democrats retain control of at least one chamber in the Congress.

Medicaid is a federal-state matching grant program. Prior to 1991, some states adopted taxes on health providers as one means to raise the state funds required by the state matching provision. In 1991, the Health Care Financing Administration (HCFA), now the Centers for Medicare and Medicaid Services (CMS), prohibited the use of health provider taxes and prohibited counting private donations to health providers as part of the state match.[89] This particular regulation was aimed at increasing the likelihood that state matches would be additive, rather than federal funds substituting for state efforts.

In the early 2000s, Congress clamped down on states manipulating their finances so as to qualify for greater federal Medicaid funds. The states, using a variety of accounting techniques, were able to circumvent the "upper payment limit" that was supposed to put a cap on federal support.[90] A point not wasted on federal officials—both elected and appointed—is that federal aid is a high-stakes game that many states play with great assertiveness so as to maximize their financial benefits. **Exhibit 15–3** illustrates federal-state relationships in the evolution of Medicaid, including the significant changes introduced by the Patient Protection and Affordable Care Act of 2010.[91]

Exhibit 15–3 Federal Health Care Reform and Medicaid

Medicaid is a federal-state program administered at the federal level by the Centers for Medicare and Medicaid Services in the Department of Health and Human Services. The program provides medical insurance to the categorically needy, including people who qualify for cash assistance under the Temporary Assistance for Needy Families (TANF) program, pregnant women and children below the poverty level, children at the poverty level, caregivers of children, disabled people receiving benefits under the Supplemental Security Income (SSI) program, and others. Beyond the categorically needy are the medically needy who cannot qualify for assistance because their incomes are too high but they cannot afford medical insurance. The Patient Protection and Affordable Care Act of 2010 greatly expanded eligibility, increasing the income threshold and including most uninsured adults under 65 who meet the poverty threshold.[1]

All states participate in the Medicaid program. States are allowed considerable flexibility in designing their programs. Some states, prior to the 2010 health care reform, covered few adults; others have more extended adult coverage, some including both parents and childless adults. States may also participate in the State Children's Assistance Program (CHIP or SCHIP), which provides additional support and is intended to expand coverage of children beyond the standard Medicaid program, particularly to children whose families otherwise do not qualify for Medicaid.[2]

Eligibility for Medicaid was expanded in the 2010 health care reform. Previously, eligibility requirements included income at or below 64% of the poverty level. The Patient Protection and Affordable Care Act increased the threshold to 133%. It also extended (effective 2014) coverage to childless adults. More than 50 million people were covered by Medicaid prior to health care reform in 2010.[3] A Congressional Budget Office estimate of the eventual impact of the reform, when all provisions are implemented, is that an additional 15 to 20 million may become eligible.[4] An Urban Institute analysis concluded that the number was likely to be closer to 15 million additional enrolled, with the federal government paying for almost all of the costs of the additional coverage for the first several years.[5]

Enrollment patterns and benefit patterns before the reform provisions are put into place have varied widely across the states under Medicaid. About 75% of enrollees are children and their parents. The major beneficiaries of medical care, as measured in dollars, however, are the elderly and disabled clients—accounting for about 70% of expenditures. At the time of patients' discharge from nursing homes, about two-thirds of those patients are on Medicaid.[6]

The federal government spent about $247 billion on Medicaid in 2009; the states' share was $127 billion. State shares were lower as a result of supplemental federal funding to assist state budgets in the American Recovery and Reinvestment Act.[7] Federal spending in 2010 was up somewhat, to $273 billion. CBO projected that the federal share would stay around that figure until 2014 when all of the reform provisions kicked in. At that point, the projected federal spending would jump about 20% to $329 billion, and grow about 10% a year for the next several years.[8]

The 2010 health care reform legislation changed the picture considerably, both for federal and state spending. Estimating state expenditures is more difficult, because states have considerable design latitude. An Urban Institute analysis compared several estimates of the costs to states of the new provisions for Medicaid included in the health care reform legislation.[9] All agree that states initially will experience little if any additional cost due to expanded coverage, because the federal government will cover the incremental increase, explaining the federal jump of 22% in 2014. After that, estimates vary depending on the assumptions about the actual number of new individuals who will seek out the program and, the most controversial element, the amount that states will save from reducing their costs for indigent care of the uninsured. The table shows five estimates included in the Urban Institute Health Policy Center analysis. Three— the Lewin Group, Center for Medicare and Medicaid Services (CMS; the government's official estimate), and Dorn and Buettgens (DB; health care consultants) account for savings. Two—the Congressional Budget Office (CBO) and the Urban Institute (UI)—do not.

	Lewin	CMS	DB	CBO	UI
Estimated cost or (savings) in $billions	($106.7)	($33.0)	($40.9)	$20.0	$21.1

(continued)

The UI and CBO estimates do not maintain that no savings are possible, but did not attempt to estimate them.

Some regard the health care reform as a major breakthrough in both health care financing and federal-state relations; others are particularly disbelieving that any savings to government (both federal and state) will materialize from increased insurance coverage.[10] The latter concern, plus the view that the federal government's substantial expansion of the program regardless of states' preferences, had led as of mid-2011 almost 30 states to file suit challenging the constitutionality of provisions of the act. Some suits made their way through the circuit court system to the Supreme Court in 2012.[11] If the Supreme Court upholds the constitutionality of key provisions, a new landmark will have been set in intergovernmental relations. If the hypothesized savings from states no longer paying as much for uninsured health care do materialize, then the states that are most upset will be in the somewhat ironic position of having opposed on states' rights principles legislation that has a positive impact on state budgets. If the Supreme Court rejects key provisions, then intergovernmental relations will not have changed much as a result of major health care reform legislation.

1. P.L. 111-148.
2. Centers for Medicare and Medicaid Services, U.S. Department of Health and Human Services (2005). *Medicaid at-a-glance, 2005.* Washington, DC: U.S. Government Printing Office.
3. U.S. General Accounting Office (2004). *Medicaid: intergovernmental transfers have facilitated state financing schemes.* Washington, DC: U.S. Government Printing Office.
4. U.S. Congressional Budget Office (2009). *Likely effects of substantially expanding eligibility for Medicaid.* Retrieved November 27, 2011, from http://www.cbo.gov/doc.cfm?index=10445&zzz=39234.
5. Kaiser Commission on Medicaid and the Uninsured (2010). *Medicaid coverage and spending in health reform: national and state results for adults at or below 133% FPL.* Retrieved November 28, 2011, from http://www.kff.org/healthreform/upload/Medicaid-Coverage-and-Spending-in-Health-Reform-National-and-State-By-State-Results-for-Adults-at-or-Below-133-FPL.pdf.
6. Marron, D. B. (2006). *Medicaid spending growth and options for controlling costs* (p. 1). Washington, DC: U.S. Government Printing Office.
7. Center for Medicare and Medicaid Systems (2011). *National health expenditure web tables: table 3.* Retrieved November 25, 2011, from https://www.cms.gov/NationalHealthExpendData/downloads/tables.pdf.
8. Congressional Budget Office (2011). *The budget and economic outlook: fiscal years 2011–2021* (p. 54). Washington, DC: U.S. Government Printing Office.
9. Bovbjerg, R. (2011). *State budgets under federal health care reform: the extent and causes of variations in estimated impacts* (p. iv). Washington, DC: Kaiser Commission on Medicaid and the Uninsured. Retrieved November 27, 2011, from http://www.kff.org/healthreform/upload/8149.pdf.
10. Gamkhar, S., & Pickerell, J. (2011). The state of American federalism 2010–2011: the economy, healthcare reform and midterm elections shape the intergovernmental agenda. *Publius, 41,* 361–394.
11. Dinan, J. (2011). Shaping health reform: state government influence in the Patient Protection and Affordable Care Act. *Publius, 41,* 395–420.

Features Not Directly Associated with Financial Assistance

The federal government's authority under the Constitution has been used to *preempt* or supersede state authority, and state governments frequently preclude local action in various arenas. Since the late 1960s, coinciding with the development of many of the federal assistance programs, federal preemptions of state and local authority have increased at a rapid pace. From 1960 through 1995, more than 800 statutory actions were implemented preempting state policy or action in favor of federal policy or action.[92] Examples include the Clean Water Act amendments in 1987 and the Safe Drinking Water Act amendments of 1996. The former retained the regulatory requirements, but reduced federal financial assistance to state and local governments and shifted it to assisting states to set up revolving loan funds to finance systems. The 1996 amendments to the Safe Drinking Water Act strengthened the regulatory requirements to mandate stronger scientific studies of health risks. The result of those additional requirements has been increased costs to states. A recent change was the 2010 health care reform discussed in Exhibit 15–3.

Judicial strengthening of the federal government's preemptive right to regulate is often traced to the 1985 case of *Garcia v. San Antonio Metropolitan Transit Authority.*[93] The case focused on whether the federal Fair Labor Standards Act applied to a local government entity. The Supreme Court ruled that because the transit authority had received considerable funding from federal programs (Urban Mass Transportation Act of 1965), it must adhere to fair labor standards requirements. In this case, the Court narrowly interpreted the extent to which the Constitution protects the powers and authority of the states.

The Court in recent times has not always ruled in favor of preemption, which is welcome on the parts of states and local governments, but is unsettling to all parties involved in that the Court has not delineated any clear doctrine as to when preemption should be upheld and when denied. In *Printz v. United States* (1997), the U.S. Supreme Court ruled that the provision of the Brady Handgun Violence Prevention Act requiring chief law enforcement officers of local jurisdictions to conduct background checks until a national system was in place was an unconstitutional requirement of state officials to enforce federal law.[94] In contrast, the Court in *Geier v. American Honda Motor Company* (2000) upheld preemption, which had the effect of protecting the automobile manufacturer from tort suits claiming that vehicles should have been equipped with airbags.[95] In 2000 and 2001, the Court ruled that the Age Discrimination in Employment Act and the Americans with Disabilities Act (ADA) did not apply to the states.[96] In 2011, the Supreme Court was asked to review whether the federal government had preemptive powers over the states regarding immigration. Arizona and other states had taken actions against undocumented immigrants.[97]

The National Conference of State Legislatures (NCSL) regards preemption as such a threat to state sovereignty that it has a project devoted to analyzing proposed federal legislation and working against would-be preemptions. Despite its efforts, preemptions march on. In 2005, Congress passed a law that preempted state courts from hearing lawsuits stemming from alleged injuries caused by defective vaccines. In 2006, Congress preempted the states regarding the registry of sex offenders.[98] Despite stating in the overview page of the NCSL *Preemption Monitor* website that federal preemptive legislation is increasing, the 2010 and 2011 issues of the *Monitor* identified only two pieces of federal legislation judged to contain provisions preempting state authority in almost two years, both relatively minor statutes, in terms of states' rights, dealing with tobacco products transportation and distribution and public smoking.[99]

State Control of Local Governments

These issues are not limited to federal effects on state and local governments. Because state governments have full constitutional authority over local governments, significant limitations on local authority may stem from state actions. Statutory debt limitations, usually expressed as a maximum debt to the property tax base ratio, are common (see the chapter on capital finance and debt management), as are requirements that state legislatures approve through formal legislative enactment some local taxes, such as sales taxes.

A state also may assume direct control of a local government if it cannot exercise the capacity to govern itself. Instances of state takeover of municipal functions have been associated with some aspect or another of financial failure, but not usually bond debt failures. State governments watch local situations to see whether intervention is needed, although they do not consistently use specific indices of financial condition in making their decisions.[100]

State takeovers are not restricted to cities of a certain size. In December 1996, the State of Florida appointed a State Control Board to supervise for a five-year period the City of Miami's budget and finances after the City was unable to balance its budget in two successive years, which is against state law. Although the City experienced considerable political turbulence, including a mayoral election that was invalidated several months after the mayor took office, by the end of the oversight board's commission, in 2002, the City had regained sound financial footing, and even was able to sell $32 million in bonds to refinance bonds sold previously at higher interest rates.[101]

In 2011, the city of Harrisburg, Pennsylvania, filed for bankruptcy after falling behind on $65 million in payments on financing for a solid waste incinerator facility. The state took action with a state-supervised emergency plan to ensure that all city essential services continued.[102] Jefferson County, Alabama, in late 2011, gained the dubious distinction of being the largest municipal bankruptcy filing in U.S. history.[103] At issue was failure to honor debt repayment obligations on a $3 billion sewer bond. State takeover or direct supervision was being considered as a likely outcome. Detroit also faced imminent state takeover in 2011; Michigan took initial steps late in the year to take over the city's finances and operation of services.[104]

Examples of full state takeovers include the 1997 assumption of control by the State of North Carolina over the small town of Princeville, under a previously never used state statute dating back to 1931. The state's Local Government Commission took over town finances and revenue collections, and the town commissioners continued to govern otherwise. Town officials had been unable, or unwilling, to collect taxes due, and the town sewer system was overflowing into the streets due to neglected maintenance.[105] Under the commission's financial oversight, Princeville began to correct its situation, but hurricanes Dennis and Floyd in 1999 severely flooded the town, overtaking the town's own fiscal crisis.

Somewhat analogous was the situation with the nation's capital, except that it is the federal government that statutorily controls the District of Columbia. Like cities in many states, the District operates under the auspices of a home rule charter that grants considerable autonomy to the District, albeit subject to change by the Congress. In 1995, a financial control board was appointed to supervise the finances of the District of Columbia, similar to one created by the New York legislature to supervise New York City's finances in 1975. As part of the 1997 Balanced Budget Act (see the chapters on government and the economy, and budget approval and the U.S. Congress), Congress also developed a financial assistance package for the District of Columbia. The aid package focused on relieving the District of its unfunded pension liability, a tax credit package, Medicaid, and prison system financial relief. To end the oversight of the Financial Responsibility and Management Assistance Authority, the District had to become current with bond debt service, repay U.S. Treasury loans, restore access to short- and long-term credit, and achieve a balanced budget for four consecutive years. In 2001, the District of Columbia met all four conditions and the assistance authority ceased operations.[106]

The State of Michigan appointed a temporary financial manager in late 2011 to take over Flint, which previously had been under state supervision from 2002 to 2004.[107] State takeover of a general-purpose jurisdiction such as a city or town is not the only kind of state control over substate entities. School systems are a target of state action. Texas passed a law in 1995 that would allow the state to take over schools that failed to meet specified state standards. The law was challenged in the courts, but the Supreme Court determined in 1998 that there was no need for a ruling at the time because no school takeover was imminent.[108] By the mid-2000s, school takeovers were more common. In 2006, St. Louis schools, the City of Los Angeles, and the City of San Bernadino were among the governments under pressure to perform or face possible takeovers.[109] In recent years, school district takeovers have occurred in many states and the District of Columbia. The reasons for taking over a district are financial, academic, financial and academic, or all encompassing.[110] The No Child Left Behind Act requires states to implement corrective actions for schools that fail in repeated years to meet student performance expectations.[111] The Obama administration in 2010 proposed in the reauthorization of the Elementary and Secondary Education Act provisions to allow states more flexibility in determining standards for low performance and for determining the appropriate steps.[112] By early 2012, Congress had not acted on the reauthorization.

A state's assuming complete control over a city or a school district is still a rare event, but it serves as a reminder that local governments are statutorily governed by state governments. Local governments have nothing comparable to the states' protection from the federal government as guaranteed by the Constitution's 10th Amendment reserving a broad array of powers to states.

TYPES OF FISCAL ASSISTANCE

Grant Characteristics

Of the numerous aspects of grants-in-aid, at least four are particularly important: (1) the purpose of the award, (2) the recipient, (3) the amount, and (4) the method of distribution. The purposes of awards will be discussed in some detail in the next subsection, but for the moment it should be noted that purposes range from narrowly defined functions to general support.

Recipients can be individuals or families who receive financial aid, as in the case of welfare payments made directly to clients or Medicaid payments made to medical providers to cover the health needs of the poor and medically needy. When programs provide guarantees of aid to individuals and families, they are referred to as entitlements. Sometimes the term *entitlement* is used for programs providing funds to state and local governments, as in the instance of the Community Development Block Grant program (CDBG), in which 1,209 states and local units of governments received funds on a formula basis in 2011—funds that are predictable by the cities in advance of their receipt.[113]

The third aspect is the amount of aid that is made available. Some programs are open-ended in the sense that aid is provided to all persons who qualify. All persons meeting a needs test based on income, for instance, might qualify for aid. If the number of qualified applicants increases, then the amount of aid available must also increase. This type of grant, of course, complicates budgeting, because administrators do not know in advance the amount of funds that will be needed. An alternative is for the legislature to predetermine an amount that will be available regardless of the number of potential recipients.

The Women, Infants, and Children (WIC) supplemental food program is an example of a program in which the amount that eligible families may receive is determined by a needs test, but funding may or may not be made available for everyone who is eligible. Once the funding limit in a particular state is reached, other eligible candidates are placed on a waiting list. For this program, the Food and Nutrition Service in the U.S. Department of Agriculture must annually estimate the number of eligible individuals so that federal appropriations can cover the number of people who are eligible. Some studies have shown that more people participate than are eligible, leading some in Congress to call for funding cuts, but other evidence indicates that there are more people who are eligible than who participate. For example, in one county in Washington State, only 28% of the estimated eligible 50,000 children participate, "because no one knows about it."[114]

Fourth, various methods are used in deciding whether applicants will receive funding and in what amounts. In one method, would-be recipients compete for awards by submitting proposals to indicate how funds will be used. This method is common for demonstration grants available to private and nonprofit institutions and several categories of grants available to state and local governments. Another method is to use a formula that allocates funds among eligible recipients. Formulas can be used to help target money where it is needed most. Gaining agreement on specific provisions in a formula among legislators can be difficult. For example, members of Congress evaluate proposed provisions of a formula in terms of how their home districts or states will be affected. Sometimes the distribution is set by the legislative body, particularly in instances in which funds are provided for specified public works projects.

At the federal level, the process of awarding and administering grants is spelled out in OMB Circular A-102, *Grants and Cooperative Agreements with State and Local Governments*.[115] *Cooperative agreements* are used when "substantial involvement" by federal agencies is planned, unlike *grants*, in which activities are carried out primarily by state and local governments.

Categorical Aid

At the federal level, hundreds of grant programs exist. **Table 15–4**, based on data from the 2011 online *Catalog of Federal Domestic Assistance*, provides a count of various grant programs, by type of grant, and an illustration of each type. There are more than 2,000 federal domestic assistance programs in the catalog, of which only the grant programs (as opposed to loans and other programs) are listed in Table 15–4. It needs to be noted that the listings in the table are not mutually exclusive; a program is sometimes listed in two or even more categories. Also, not all items listed flow directly through state and local governments; some grants, such as research grants, go directly to individuals, businesses, and nonprofit organizations.

Categorical grants are a historically common designation, although not used in the *Catalog*. The meaning of "categorical" was that funds were targeted for expenditure in specified areas. This broad type is now separated into three in the *Catalog*: (1) The category of *project grants*, of which there were 1,475 in 2011, covers such items as scholarships, research grants, and construction grants. (2) The category of *direct payments for specified use*, of which there were 213, is for comparatively narrowly defined projects. The category does not include contracts, such as when the federal government contracts with a local government to carry out an activity on its behalf. (3) The category of *direct payments with unrestricted use*, of which there were 47, is broader than the second grouping. As the table indicates, payments for a broad range of vocational rehabilitation services for veterans falls into this category.

The last three entries in Table 15–4 are of a different character. *Sale, exchange, or donation of property and goods* covers such activities as the government donating surplus food to a food bank. *Use of property, facilities, and equipment* includes lending or donating surplus military equipment (tanks, artillery, and clothing) to state-run military museums. *Provision of specialized services* covers the direct support by federal agencies in pursuit of state and local activities, such as ensuring accuracy in weights and measures.

Table 15–4 Federal Grant Programs by Type, with Examples, 2011

Type of Program	Number of Programs	Example
Formula Grants	238	School Breakfast Program
Project Grants	1,475	Small Business Innovation Research
Direct Payments for Specified Use	213	Food Stamps
Direct Payments with Unrestricted Use	47	Vocational Rehabilitation for Disabled Veterans
Sale, Exchange, or Donation of Property and Goods	26	Food Donation
Use of Property, Facilities, and Equipment	34	Donation/Loans of Obsolete Department of Defense Property
Provision of Specialized Services	98	Weights and Measures Service

Source: Adapted from U.S. General Services Administration (2011). *Catalog of federal domestic assistance.* Retrieved November 18, 2011, from https://www.cfda.gov/index?s=program&mode=list&tab=list.

The number of these various types of aid, of course, does not signify the amount of assistance available, but it does indicate the diversity of programs. Indeed, one frequent complaint over the years has been that there are too many specific grant programs and that they should be reduced in number. As a result, various consolidations have occurred from time to time, but later new programs are added, resulting in an ever-fluctuating number of grants.

Categorical programs have a narrow focus and target aid to deal with perceived problems. If rat infestations are seen as a major problem in poor neighborhoods, an aid program can be established to support efforts to eliminate or control rat populations. Categorical programs presumably allow the federal government to target aid to deal with problems that are perceived to be national in scope and allow the state governments to do the same in regard to state problems. Many categorical programs were created during the War on Poverty initiated by President Johnson in the late 1960s. Part of the motivation for creating categorical programs was that state legislatures, then dominated in many states by politicians from rural areas, were unresponsive to urban needs, especially the problems of large center cities. Many categorical grant programs were intended to channel funds directly to cities, bypassing the state legislatures.[116]

Another reason for creating categorical programs was to target and restrict assistance in various ways in an effort to control the recipients' behavior.[117] For example, assistance for community development projects required extensive community participation to ensure that low-income groups had an influence over program design.

Categorical grants typically require would-be recipients to apply for aid by preparing proposals. These proposals indicate what problems exist, how the problems will be addressed, and what the expected benefits will be. During the application process, applicants must engage in considerable preplanning that is expected to help increase the chances that the money will be spent effectively. Funding agencies, by means of an application review process, presumably can weed out unsound projects.

Criticisms of categorical aid programs abound. Grants may skew local priorities. A jurisdiction might apply for funds for one type of project even though some other project, for which no grant funding was available, would provide greater benefits to the jurisdiction. Another criticism is that much time and energy are consumed in drafting grant proposals. Still another is that some jurisdictions do not obtain their "fair share" of federal dollars simply because they lack adequate staff for proposal writing. Small jurisdictions, in particular, may have little "grantsmanship" capability. Categorical grants make budget planning difficult because proposals may be held pending for months. Another problem is that grants are not coordinated. Furthermore, state legislatures dislike being bypassed, and many grant recipients—whether governmental or private organizations—resent some of the restrictions that are attached to the use of funds.

Critics frequently propose that the application process be simplified. Simplification includes reducing the amount of paperwork involved and standardizing some forms and procedures to make the process more comprehensible to applicants who may wish to seek funds from two or more agencies. OMB Circular A-102 and subsequent legislation reducing duplicative audit requirements have standardized some forms and procedures, but preparing individual grant applications is no less time consuming. Most federal agencies have automated some or all of their application processes, making it possible for applications to be submitted online. Of course, that step has not eliminated the actual proposal writing, but processing time has been reduced.

Revenue Sharing

A dramatic alternative that has none of the application process and restricted purpose features of categorical grant is General Revenue Sharing (GRS), which at the federal level was created by the State and Local Fiscal Assistance Act of 1972.[118] Under the original legislation, the federal government shared some of its revenue with states, counties, cities, and townships. In subsequent years, the states were dropped from the list of beneficiaries, in part because many had surpluses in their budgets and could hardly claim to be in need of general federal support.

Although general revenue sharing was allowed to expire in 1986, it is worthy to note in that it represents the opposite end of the spectrum from categorical grants. GRS also continues to be proposed from time to time, along with shared tax systems, as a more radical overhaul to the intergovernmental fiscal system. The now-defunct program had three key characteristics:

- Pre-established amounts of aid
- Use of formulas for distributing the aid
- Considerable latitude to spend funds in terms of local priorities

GRS expired because a compelling case could not be made for its continuation. As the federal government faced annual budget deficits in excess of $200 billion, federal officials could convincingly argue that there simply was no revenue to share with local governments. Additionally, proponents faced the difficult task of identifying a national purpose being served by GRS. In the short run, eliminating the program caused serious budgetary problems for municipalities with shrinking tax bases. In addition, many local governments shifted to user charges, which in some cases were regressive (see the chapter on transaction-based revenue sources). User charges are typically based on the cost of the service rather than the ability to pay.

Although revenue sharing is no longer in operation at the national level, it persists at the state level. Many states provide funds to local governments using formulas based on population and income. Fiscal pressures on state governments in the early 1990s caused many to reduce the amounts allocated to revenue sharing. Then, after almost a decade of surpluses, a return in 2001 to severe state budget pressures again caused states to drastically reduce funding.[119] These fund-sharing programs were not restored, and with the fiscal pressures on states since 2007–2012, they are not likely to be restored in the near future.[120]

Revenue sharing is still the most common means of central government financial assistance to lower-level governments in other countries in the wake of major decentralization of governmental responsibilities. For example, in the 1990s, the Philippines underwent a major shift from central government responsibilities for almost all services to extensive devolution of responsibility to local governments. Functions such as health and education, which previously were entirely central government responsibilities, were devolved to provincial and various levels of local government. Former central ministry of health and education employees were transferred to province or local payrolls. To equalize the financial impacts, the Internal Revenue Allotment (IRA) was created, allocating almost all of the proceeds of the national income tax to local levels of government.[121] The IRA allotment continues to be the main revenue source for local government units in the Philippines.

Block Grants

A form of compromise between GRS and categorical grants is special revenue sharing, or block grants. Under this system, a higher-level government shares part of its revenue with lower-level governments, but the use of funds is restricted to specified functions, such as law enforcement or social services. A distinction is sometimes made between block grants and special revenue sharing, with the former requiring submission of an application and the latter not. More often, however, the terms are used interchangeably or the term "block grant" is used to cover both types of revenue sharing. State aid to education, using various formulas, is an example of a block grant, with the funds coming largely from state general revenue. State aid for local roads is another form of block grant, with monies coming from earmarked taxes on motor fuels. The Temporary Assistance to Needy Families program discussed earlier is a federal example.

Block grants at the federal level have been used as a method for consolidating categorical grant programs. These "categoricals" are grouped together so that jurisdictions have greater flexibility in specified program areas. The application process is greatly reduced, because a jurisdiction applies for only one grant instead of several. Early block grant legislation included the Partnership for Health Act of 1966, the Law Enforcement Assistance Act of 1968, and the Comprehensive Employment and Training Act of 1973.

The landmark in block grant legislation was the Housing and Community Development Act of 1974, which created the Community Development Block Grant (CDBG) program, the longest running program of the Department of Housing and Urban Development.[122] This program provides entitlement funding to medium and large cities through the use of a formula and gives funds to states to award small cities on a discretionary basis. Changes in the program from time to time reflect current priorities. For example, the law phased out programs for open space, public facility loans, water and sewer grants, urban renewal, model cities, and rehabilitation loans. Under the original legislation, entitlement cities were required to submit an application for funding. The process was considerably less detailed than had been required for the previous categorical programs. Later, the application process was dropped for the entitlement cities.

Some federal block grants awards are based on metropolitan areas, which are defined by the Office of Management and Budget. An area that is not classified as metropolitan may be excluded from funding, and the amount of funding to a given area may be dependent on its population size or other key characteristics. Therefore, the definition of an area becomes critical for funding purposes. In 1999, OMB redefined the concept of metropolitan area.[123] In 2010, the government again revised the standards for defining metropolitan areas, effective in 2013. The CDBG grants are affected by the metropolitan definition.[124]

Various consolidations of categorical grants into block grants have taken place over recent decades. The first wave started with the Omnibus Budget Reconciliation Act of 1981, which among other things consolidated many existing categorical grant programs and created nine new block grants, four in health-related services, to be administered by the states.[125] The most recent round of consolidation and relaxation of federal control created the Temporary Assistance to Needy Families (1996), the initial major reform of welfare assistance, in an attempt to devolve responsibilities from the federal government to states, as discussed earlier. President George W. Bush's 2006 budget called for consolidating 18 community development grants into one and cutting back their funding. The proposal met with opposition from both Democrats and Republicans.[126] Though smaller block grants were included in the stimulus programs starting in 2007 (see the chapter on government and the economy), there have been no major proposals for additional grant program consolidation from the White House or Congress since the 2006 proposal.

The programmatic feature of federal block grants is that monies are granted in lump sums to states, which determine how the money is to be used and, when it involves local government assistance, how funds are to be divided among governments within each state. This approach has been championed as restoring power to the states. The fiscal feature of federal block grants, each time they are introduced, has been a substantial reduction in funds. These cuts are defended in part in the name of efficiency. Allowing states and localities to select the desired mix of activities and levels of quality and quantity, block grants reduce the costs of "one size fits all" categorical grants, which substitute federal judgments for those at the state and local levels. Furthermore, because the block grants provide more flexibility to state and local governments, fewer federal officials are needed to administer the programs and fewer state officials are needed to oversee local government operations. Given that block grants almost always result in some degree of reduced federal financing because they are consolidating previous categorical programs, state and local governments have to achieve the supposed efficiencies, make up for the losses, or reduce quality or quantity of services. This may account for the fact that there have been no further major consolidations since the 1990s.

Figure 15–5 illustrates the pattern of state and local revenues and federal assistance. In the figure, state and local total revenues are shown in billions of dollars on the left *y*-axis, and the percentage of state and local general revenues constituted by federal aid is shown on the right *y*-axis. From 1950 through the first decade of the 2000s, state and local governments generally maintained their overall revenue growth despite relative declines in federal grants, with the exceptions of the recessions in 2001–2002 and 2007 and subsequent years. In those two periods, state and local revenues dropped significantly, as the figure illustrates. In the 2001–2002 recession, federal grants increased significantly, reaching 20% in 2002 of total state and local revenues, higher than the previous peak (1980). In the post-recession period, they fell back to 17%. However, they immediately went back up in 2009 as the stimulus programs had substantial effects and as state revenues fell. The drop in state and local revenues was precipitous—from $2.7 billion in 2008 to $2.1 billion in 2009, or 24%.[127] Aided primarily by programs included in the various stimulus packages, federal aid to states increased 20% in 2009 over 2008, and the federal share of state and local revenues jumped from 17% to 27%, by far the highest share in the 1950 through 2009 period.

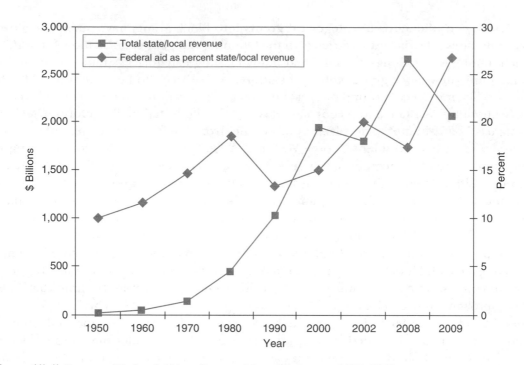

Figure 15–5 Impact of Federal Aid on State and Local Revenues, 1950–2009.
Sources: Compiled from Bureau of the Census, U.S. Department of Commerce (1952). *Statistical abstract, 1952* (p. 353). Washington, DC: U.S. Government Printing Office; *Statistical abstract, 1962*; *Statistical abstract, 1982* (p. 416)/ (p. 275); *Statistical abstract, 2006* (p. 280); and Tax Policy Center (2011). *State and local finance data query system (SLF-DQS).* Washington, DC: Urban Institute–Brookings Institution. Retrieved November 28, 2011, from http://slfdqs.tax-policycenter.org/pages.cfm.

HOMELAND SECURITY: A CASE STUDY IN INTERGOVERNMENTAL RELATIONS

Homeland security is a complex problem that is overseen by a complex federal department and a myriad of other state, federal, and local governments. Following the September 11, 2001, attacks, decision makers in both Congress and the executive branch agreed that a major federal response was required. Not everyone agreed that a separate federal department should be created, but that was the outcome. The U.S. Department of Homeland Security was formed by pulling together a variety of agencies from other executive departments, resulting in what some would consider a hodgepodge organization.[128] Much of the focus of the department is on combating terrorism, but it is also responsible for helping during natural disasters such as floods, hurricanes, and the like. As the enormity of the 9/11 attacks recedes in memory, combating terrorism has become less publicly visible as an issue, and security of U.S. borders has come to mean, at least in the media and in political rhetoric, as much about preventing illegal immigration and the influx of illegal drugs as about preventing terrorism.

Focusing on homeland security is a good illustration of intergovernmental relations, given its importance in all aspects of daily living and given that it is the most recent major change in the organization of the U.S. intergovernmental system.

Table 15–5 Organizational Units and Percent of Budget, U.S. Department of Homeland Security, Fiscal Year 2010

Departmental Operations	1
Analysis and Operations	1
Office of the Inspector General	*
U.S. Customs and Border Protection	20
U.S. Immigration and Customs Enforcement	10
Transportation Security Administration	14
U.S. Coast Guard	19
U.S. Secret Service	3
National Protection and Programs Directorate	4
Office of Health Affairs	*
Federal Emergency Management Agency	11
FEMA: Grant Programs	7
U.S. Citizenship and Immigration Services	5
Federal Law Enforcement Training Center	1
Science and Technology Directorate	2
Domestic Nuclear Detection Office	1
TOTAL BUDGET AUTHORITY**	**100**

* Less than 0.5%
** Figures may not total to 100 due to rounding.

Source: U.S. Department of Homeland Security (2012), *Homeland Security: budget-in-brief, fiscal year 2012* (p. 19). Washington, DC: U.S. Government Printing Office.

Organization of Homeland Security and Intergovernmental Relations

Table 15–5 shows the main organizational units within the Department of Homeland Security (DHS) and their portions of the department's budget. The table is useful in understanding the diversity within the department, how funds are distributed across a wide variety of activities, and how components of DHS must interact with state and local governments. Indeed, virtually all aspects of DHS have an intergovernmental component. The table also illustrates the relative emphases in DHS complex functions, though in generalizing from broad budget allocations, caution is appropriate because many of the major organizational units within DHS have overlapping contributions to the missions assigned to the department.

- The single largest unit in terms of budget (20%) is U.S. Customs and Border Protection. Linked closely to Customs and Border Protection is another unit, the U.S. Immigration and Customs Enforcement unit. Together, they have a 30% share of the DHS budget. A proposal was floated in 2006 to merge the two entities, but it went nowhere.[129] The latter unit is the main investigative arm of the department, but noticeably absent from the department is the Federal Bureau of Investigation, which remains in the U.S. Department of Justice. State and local governments are involved with DHS in terms of investigating illegal smuggling of people, drugs, and other commodities into the nation. The 30% share of the two units reflects the growing concern in the United States with border security from illegal immigration in addition to security against acts of political violence. Of the two, the political rhetoric of Republican presidential candidate debates in 2011 and 2012 at least suggests that illegal immigration is a greater concern for the public than terrorism.

The other issue that has emerged challenges interdepartmental coordination at the federal, state, and local levels. The number of incidents, at least those publicized, of acts of political violence attempted or planned that have their primary roots inside the United States appears to have increased relative to threats originating from outside the United States. For domestic violence threats, the FBI has the primary lead in investigation and prevention, and some major metropolitan areas, such as New York City, take fairly independent roles in identifying and neutralizing threats.

- The U.S. Coast Guard, which during wartime is under the Navy in the U.S. Department of Defense, has the next largest share of the DHS budget, 19%. The Coast Guard interacts with state and local governments in terms of harbors and international waters, including the Great Lakes. Drug interdiction is one of the Coast Guard's major tasks, but illegal drugs flowing across inland borders is much more a border protection and state and local responsibility.

- The Transportation Security Administration (TSA, 14%) is responsible for airport screenings, among other duties. State and locally operated airports must interact with TSA. TSA sets the standards and requirements for passenger screening and manages the entire function, more or less independently of state and local jurisdictions.

- The Federal Emergency Management Agency plus FEMA grants programs have an 18% share of the budget—11% for FEMA itself and 7% for the grants program. FEMA is responsible for preparing for and responding to disasters. Its handling of the Katrina and Rita hurricane disasters brought into question its ability to respond effectively to national disasters. However, its handling of Hurricane Irene and the Joplin, Missouri, tornado in 2011 substantially redeemed its reputation. Hurricanes and other disasters underscore the need for FEMA to work with state and local governments.

- Besides these main units, there are other, smaller ones in DHS.

The department carries out its functions through a mix of approaches. Unlike some departments, which are mainly in the business of achieving objectives through awarding money, such as the Department of Housing and Urban Development, DHS spends a good portion of its own funds. As noted earlier in the chapter (Table 15–3), about 20% of homeland security money is in grants and cooperative agreements, compared with HUD, 74% of whose budget consists of grants and contracts. The DHS 20% grants figure is down from almost a third in 2007. It should be noted that the grant figure can fluctuate annually depending on the amount of funding appropriated to restore and rebuild after major disasters. Additionally, DHS is a primary user of contracting for services (see the chapter on budget execution). For example, FEMA and other units contract extensively for both services and products. FEMA has special needs to be able to enter into contracts on a speedy basis.[130]

Grants

DHS administers a wide variety of grants programs, as shown in **Table 15–6**. One cluster, the Homeland Security Grant Program (HSGP), provides grants to state governments, local governments (mainly large metropolitan and urban areas), and some private and nonprofit entities. All states have counterparts to DHS and receive federal funding, some of which is dispersed further to state and local units. Similarly, all states share in the Citizen Corps grants, which support activities similar to the old Civil Defense.

These grant programs vary considerably in magnitude. In 2010, for example, the Mississippi Department of Public Safety was awarded a $100 million grant for pilot programs across the state to enhance public safety. The San Francisco Fire Department received a grant for $3.6 million to support adequate staffing for fire and emergency response. Overall, governments were by far the largest type of recipient—$6.7 billion in awards. The next closest were nonprofits, at just under $700 million in grant awards.[131]

The other two sets of grants under HSGP do not go to every state. The Urban Areas Security Initiative had just over $662 million in award funding in 2011 that by law goes to 31 high-risk urban areas. Of that amount, 82% was designated for 11 *Tier One* areas (annually determined highest risk urban areas).[132]

The funding amounts for the five subprograms under HSGP in 2011 broke out as follows: (1) state homeland, $526.9 million; (2) Operation Stonegarden (formerly law enforcement), $54.9 million; (3) urban areas, $662.6 million; (4) metropolitan medical response,

---

Table 15–6 Grant Programs Operated by the U.S. Department of Homeland Security, 2011

Program

Assistance to Fire Fighter Grants
Driver's License Security Grant Program (DLSGP)
Emergency Management Performance Grant (EMPG)
Emergency Operations Center (EOC)
Freight Rail Security Grant Program (FRSGP)
Homeland Security Grant Program (HSGP)
   State Homeland Security Program (SHSP)
   Urban Areas Security Initiative (UASI)
   Operation Stonegarden (OPSG)
   Metropolitan Medical Response Grants (MMRS)
   Citizen Corps Program (CCP)
Intercity Bus Security Grant Program (IBSGP)
Intercity Passenger Rail Security Grant Program (IPR)
Non-Profit Security Grant Program (NSGP)
Port Security Grant Program (PSGP)
Regional Catastrophic Preparedness Grant Program (RCPGP)
Transit Security Grant Program (TSGP)
Tribal Homeland Security Grant Program (THSGP)

Source: Compiled from U.S. Department of Homeland Security (2011). Website. Retrieved November 14, 2011, from http://www.dhs.gov.

$34.9 million; and (5) Citizen Corps, $10.0 million. All of those amounts are lower than five years earlier, with law enforcement grants reduced the most, from $396 million in 2006.[133]

A variety of grant programs focus on protecting vital facilities, most notably the Intercity Security Programs, aimed at ports and transit systems. Buffer zone grants are used by state and local governments to create protection areas around high-risk areas such as nuclear and other power plants, chemical facilities, and dams.[134] In addition, the department awards grants and contracts in other security areas. For example, it has award programs for radiation detection and information technology.

Awards are made for the Homeland Security Grant Program through a combination of formula and categorical processes. Monies do not flow automatically to state and local governments, so therefore they must apply for funding. That is done exclusively online through the cross-agency portal *Grants.gov*. In order to apply, a government needs some savvy in understanding the language and forms of grantsmanship, though the increasingly standardized grant application processes across many federal departments and agencies has simplified the process.

Some of the HSGP, as prescribed by Congress, must be distributed among the states at a minimum of 0.355% of total funds. This is akin to the floor that was set under General Revenue Sharing, ensuring a minimum amount of funding across governmental boundaries. The minimum share has declined from 0.75%.[135]

The remaining money is awarded on a risk-based program. DHS is required to employ a threat- or risk-based methodology to determine the distribution of funding for a majority of its preparedness and planning programs (more than 90% of DHS grants, excluding post-disaster recovery grant programs). The risk-based methodology naturally is controversial, because no one likes to think their area is at lower risk and therefore lower priority for protection than other areas of the country. For that reason, Congress requires the Government Accountability Office to review the methodology and the results of its application by DHS. The GAO concluded in its most recent review: "Generally DHS has constructed a reasonable methodology to assess risk and allocate funds within a given year."[136]

This translated to the department cutting back on the number of metropolitan areas eligible for Urban Areas Security Initiative grants from 50 in 2005 to 31 in 2011. Recipients in urban areas eliminated from funding were eligible for continuation awards to complete the projects they had begun but were ineligible for new awards. This was called "sustained" funding. California lost two areas—Sacramento and San Diego. Others eliminated included Phoenix, Arizona; Las Vegas, Nevada; and Toledo, Ohio. Two Florida areas were added—Orlando and Fort Lauderdale.

The change in the funding process met with vociferous opposition from some members of Congress and state and local government officials. Critics challenged Homeland Security's decision making, questioning the basis on which risk was assessed. Las Vegas officials noted that its being a major tourist destination and known around the world made it a likely target for a massive terrorist event. San Diego officials noted that the extensive military installations in the area made that city a target for terrorists. New York City, although not eliminated, was cut back in funding. Critics questioned why the city would be cut when it was the focal point of September 11. Senator Charles Schumer (Democrat of New York) said Secretary Chertoff had "promised to fight to increase New York's formula, and here it is, we're being whacked with a two-by-four and we don't hear a peep out of Secretary Chertoff."[137]

Congress as is its rightful role has set funding constraints on Homeland Security grants, but those priorities are sometimes questioned. One is the 0.355% requirement for each state to receive some funding. Examples of wasteful spending are often used by critics to indict the whole program. For example, some of the law enforcement grants have been spent on physical fitness training for law enforcement and the purchase of treadmills and other training machines, seemingly aimed at making law enforcement officers buff. Homeland Security officials have winced over such spending but have noted that it is specifically authorized by Congress.[138]

But the biggest concern is that Congress sets priorities on spending by allocating money to the various grant programs independent of what the "experts" in Homeland Security think makes sense. For example, Congress determines how much money will be spent on ports versus other forms of infrastructure. Congress, as the representative of the people, has the right and responsibility to set priorities and allocate funds, but in an era in which the United States seemingly faces multiple internal and cross-border threats, should greater flexibility be afforded the Department of Homeland Security? Should the department have flexibility in allocating funds among ports, law enforcement, and the like? If yes, how much flexibility? This is the age-old problem of trying to reach an appropriate balance in decision making between the legislative and executive branches.

RESTRUCTURING PATTERNS OF INTERGOVERNMENTAL RELATIONS

Tax Laws

Tax Deductions and Exemptions

A substantive change that could be made is to adjust taxes in ways that would reduce the need for financial assistance. By increasing the taxing powers of lower-level governments, the need for grants-in-aid may be reduced. For example, taxpayers currently may deduct many state and local taxes from gross income before computing federal tax liabilities. Included are state and local income taxes, property taxes, and some other lesser taxes. Excluded are state sales, gasoline, and similar consumption and excise taxes. The Tax Reform Act of 1986 (TRA86) is responsible for removing the deductibility of some state and local taxes, such as sales taxes.[139] Since 2005, taxpayers may choose to deduct either state sales or state income taxes, if they itemize deductions. Federal tax law could be altered to either increase or decrease deductibility. Such tax policies affect disposable income, affect government revenue, and alter the distribution of taxing power among levels of government. Some of those reforms, such as eliminating the deductibility of interest on two home mortgages and property taxes paid on those homes, will no doubt be considered not so much as an intergovernmental fiscal reform but as one of the elements in addressing the federal budget deficit.

Economists have been particularly critical of deductions for property taxes in that this benefit is largely enjoyed by middle-income families. Lower-income families are less likely to own homes and therefore are unable to benefit from the deductibility, and higher-income families do not benefit appreciably from such deductions. The importance of the home building industry to the overall economy, however, has been used by lobbyists to argue in favor of property tax deductibility.

On the other side of the argument, tax deductions do provide some measure of latitude for state and local taxation. They reduce somewhat the differentials among states and among localities, and they mitigate some of the problems of tax overlapping. At least overlapping taxes may be held to a level that is not confiscatory. The strongest argument in favor of tax deductibility is that the practice is firmly entrenched and that any effort to eliminate deductibility for property taxes, for example, would be politically unacceptable without compensating tax relief.

Some states, such as New York, offer exemptions on property taxes for school financing, but not property taxes imposed by general-purpose local governments such as cities. The state exemptions involve excluding the first $30,000 value of the home from calculation of school district property tax, for couples earning less than $500,000. New York also provides an additional benefit, up to the first $62,200 value of the home, to senior citizens. The state then reimburses the local school district for the full amount.[140] The exemptions make homeownership more affordable without denying school districts the money they need for their operations. Some analysis has indicated that when exemptions exist, districts are likely to be less efficient in their operations because they can raise taxes and let the state government, rather than local taxpayers, foot much of the bill.[141]

Tax Credits

The institution of tax credits would be likely to cause a more substantial shift in revenue sources than would result from changes in tax deductibility. Tax credits would allow individual taxpayers to use taxes paid to one jurisdiction to reduce the tax liability owed to another jurisdiction. A tax credit reduces tax liability dollar for dollar, whereas a deduction of taxes paid to another jurisdiction from one's taxable income is worth only the marginal tax bracket percentage, the highest being 35%. One proposal sometimes made is to allow such credits for the federal income tax. The effect would be to redistribute revenue from the federal government to state and local governments. A tax credit on income taxes could encourage those states without income taxes to adopt them because the taxpayers would be less affected. However, if the tax credit is uniform regardless of income, it would benefit the wealthier states even more than the poorer ones. Tax credits instead of tax deductions have become a feature of some federal programs to stimulate infrastructure construction. Instead of the traditional deduction of interest earned on municipal bonds, tax credits for mortgage interest earned from particular types of bonds directly reduce the federal income tax owed.

Unemployment Insurance

The federal government has enticed or forced states to impose unemployment insurance taxes on employers by providing that most monies from such taxes may stay within each state. In the event that a state did not have an approved system, a tax presumably would be imposed by the federal government. All states adopted unemployment insurance programs because failure to do so would have made those states without such programs less attractive as places to live and conduct business. In that case, the federal government used its taxation power effectively to force a policy action at the state level.

Until TRA86, unemployment benefits were not treated as income under federal tax law, thereby providing an important benefit to individuals and creating a costly tax expenditure for the federal government. These benefits are now taxable, though many states exempt them from state income taxation. For 2009 only, the first $2,400 in unemployment income was exempt from federal taxation, a provision in the American Recovery and Reinvestment Act (see the chapter on government and the economy). Inheritance taxes are practically forced on states by a federal tax provision deducting 80% of any state inheritance tax paid. Any state that did not adopt an inheritance tax would lose considerable appeal to retirees and other older citizens. The first $5 million in the value of an estate is not subject to federal taxes.

Tax Exemptions on Bonds

Another important benefit afforded state and local governments through federal tax law is the tax exemption on interest earned on bonds issued by these governments. Tax exemption has had the effect of allowing governments to pay lower interest rates to bondholders than if the bonds were taxable.

Shared Taxes

Currently, the federal, state, and local governments in the United States have either exclusive or overlapping jurisdiction over various tax sources. Only the federal government may tax imports and exports. The federal government does not have a property tax or general sales tax. Federal, state, and local governments overlap in the use of personal and corporate income taxes. Some states benefit from linking their own personal income tax systems to the federal system. Individuals in North Carolina, for example, can file a state income tax form that bases taxes on the federal taxable income. This simplifies administration of the system and reduces state tax administration costs. When changes in federal tax provisions occur, such as TRA86's expansion of the federal tax base, it automatically expanded the base for most states because their systems are tied in one form or another to the federal system. However, there is no shared link between the two—the federal Internal Revenue Service collects only federal income taxes, and state and local governments collect their own income taxes. State and local governments typically share a sales tax. It is collected by the state, but revenues are allocated to local governments that levy such taxes.

A. M. Rivlin, the first director of the Congressional Budget Office and later the director of the Office of Management and Budget, proposed a value-added tax that would be shared among levels of government.[142] This idea still has currency, but it is discussed more in terms of its potential for reforming the overall federal tax system to address the debt crisis than as an approach to intergovernmental fiscal reform. Sharing the tax means that it would be a common tax, eliminating competition between states over the level of taxation. It would also mean shared administration, reducing the collection costs, and it would minimize the ability of one level of government to preempt other levels' use of a particular tax. State and local finance in the German federal system, for example, relies heavily on shared taxation. A national shared sales tax also would resolve the issues around states' inability to develop an effective way to tax e-commerce (see the chapter on budgeting for revenues: income, payroll and property taxes). Any major realignment of responsibilities among levels of government must include changes in revenue systems as well.

Grant Requirements

Strings

State and local officials are all too familiar with the strings that come attached to grants. The solicitation announcements in which governments are encouraged to apply for grants are replete with notifications as to how the money may and may not be used and other requirements. For example, grants must be audited and the audit reports supplied to the funding agency. Other progress and final reports are required. These reporting requirements for the federal government have grown as federal agencies needed to comply with the Government Performance and Results Act and President Bush's PART system before it was eliminated in the Obama administration. The end of PART, however, did not reduce grantee reporting requirements.

Grants administration sometimes involves gray areas in which funding agencies say something *should* be done but lack authority to say it *must* be done. Officials of recipient governments are wary of not following such guidance even though they think the funding agency may be stepping out of bounds. No one wants to jeopardize possible future funding by failing to follow unofficial guidance. The situation has been referred to as "soft governance."[143]

Mandates

Other proposals to improve intergovernmental fiscal relations pertain to mandates. For instance, when a state legislature passes a law requiring school districts to adopt certain procedures in dealing with gifted children or children with learning disabilities, a mandate has been established that has budgetary implications. Typically, federal mandates on state and local governments are tied to grants or other forms of federal assistance and contracts, making the stipulation that a government (or private party) must meet specified conditions to qualify for funds.

Notable federal crosscutting mandates—requirements that apply to the work of most federal agencies and grant programs—require recipients to pay locally prevailing wages, meet Americans with Disabilities Act standards for removing architectural barriers for persons with disabilities, and prevent discrimination based on race, gender, and the like. These mandates are at a basic level unrelated to the purpose of the grant or contract or other funding. That is, a local government carrying out an activity funded under the Community Development Block Grant program related to building a community facility would be required to pay minimum wages and would be required to adhere to provisions of the Fair Labor Standards Act and the Davis-Bacon Act. The various requirements imposed have to do with federal policy as stated in the legislation and regulations toward work and employment conditions including fair wages. These regulations would apply to the entire local government, not just the particular department involved with the facility.

Other mandates are directly related to the grant program objectives. As noted earlier, continued TANF funding to states is contingent on their reducing the number of people on their welfare rolls. How the states accomplish that goal is open to wide latitude in this block grant program, but the states are required to achieve specific, quantitative reductions, as discussed in Exhibit 15–2.

Medicaid is a categorical grant program that is always on the firing line because of the high and increasing costs of health care and because of the state funds that have to be committed along with the federal funds. Federal mandates limit state control of Medicaid by specifying in great detail who is eligible and what costs are reimbursable. As a result of these mandates, states have felt they are less able to make their own budgetary decisions.

Unfunded Mandates

Another category for reform has been eliminating what many term "unfunded mandates." These are federal or state mandates that are not necessarily tied to particular financial assistance programs. For example, federal laws and court rulings have set standards for state prison systems that in many cases require additional prisons to be built without federal assistance. These requirements are not associated with any program of financial assistance, and they are mandatory for all states (in the case of federal requirements) regardless of whether the state is a recipient of federal programs related to the justice system. They are a matter of a federal determination that it is in the national interest to require states to meet certain standards, but no help to do so is available from the federal government.

The Disabilities Education Act of 1975, later known as the Individuals with Disabilities Education Act, is implemented by regulations that include detailed requirements for states to accommodate students with disabilities to enable successful educational outcomes.[144] The act promises federal funding assistance up to 40% of the amount states spend. In principle, one might call that a "funded mandate." However, appropriations have never come close to meeting that 40% promise. Hence, the mandate is unfunded.

Clean air and water standards have forced local governments to build new solid waste treatment facilities, substantially change wastewater treatment systems, and adopt numerous other practices. OMB determined in 2006 that over a 10-year period, seven rules imposed costs of greater than $100 million on states, local governments, and tribes. Air emission standards for waste combustors alone cost $320 million per year in constant (inflation-adjusted) 1990 dollars.[145] One cannot argue that local governments would otherwise spend nothing and attribute the total spending to federal, unfunded mandates.

State and local officials argue that these mandates should be accompanied by federal funding because they appear to be attempts to achieve goals previously set by the federal government through financial assistance programs and now, with federal aid being cut due to budgetary pressures, have become regulatory means to the same end. The contrary view argues that there are genuine national goals that relate to such public purposes as health and safety, environmental regulation, minimum living standards for every family, and so forth, and that these require federal action. Just because a national purpose exists, it does not necessarily mean there should be a matching federal payment to assist in achieving that purpose. The same line of reasoning is employed by states in their use of mandates for local governments.

In 1995, Congress passed the Unfunded Mandates Reform Act (UMRA), which requires draft legislation to be analyzed as to what unfunded mandates might be imposed on other governments or the private sector.[146] Bills below certain thresholds that are adjusted annually do not fall under the law. For a bill in 2011 to be covered by UMRA, it had to have an impact on state and local governments of $72 million or more, and on the private sector, $142 million or more.[147] The Congressional Budget Office, a staff arm of Congress, prepares the estimates, which are attached to committee reports on the bills. If the threshold is reached, a member of the House of Representatives may raise a point of order, which then requires the full House to vote on whether to consider the bill. If a point of order is raised in the Senate, the chamber is barred from considering the bill unless a vote is taken to waive the order or the presiding officer overrules the point of order. Note that this provision goes into effect only when a point of order is raised. Otherwise, the bill's consideration proceeds with the unfunded mandate included.

Four features restrict the law's applicability. The first three are provisions of the act itself. First is that of the threshold cost figure. Second, any new conditions imposed on grant programs are excluded. Thus, if the federal government required states to change state law in order to receive federal highway money (as it did by requiring each state to enact a 21-year-old drinking age), this would not count as a mandate. Third, a wide variety of topics are outside the law, such as national security, constitutional rights, and part of the Social Security program. Included here are the statutory rights protecting against discrimination, such as in voting and employment. Fourth, the Congressional Budget Office determined that programs like Medicaid have sufficient flexibility for state implementation that the provisions of UMRA do not apply.[148] Some critics have argued that the law is too restrictive in its application.[149]

President Clinton in 1999 issued Executive Order 13132, Federalism, to implement the law.[150] Federal agencies are required to estimate mandates contained in legislation they wish to see passed and estimate the mandates contained in regulations that they draft. The Government Accountability Office has responsibility for reviewing the regulation estimates.

Mandates Since Passage of the Unfunded Mandates Reform Act

As might be expected, most proposed federal legislation does not include mandates. In its 2011 report on 2010 reviews, CBO noted that of 474 bills and legislative proposals reviewed, only 64 contained intergovernmental mandates at all. Of these, only three bills had mandates exceeding the 2010 threshold ($70 million in 2010).[151] In the period since the law became effective through 2010, CBO identified mandates in excess of applicable thresholds in less than 1% of federal laws and less than 5% of private sector mandates.[152] Among some of the mandates have been:

- an increase in the minimum wage,
- a reduction in federal funding to administer the Food Stamp program,
- a preemption of state taxes on premiums for certain prescription drug plans,
- a temporary preemption of state authority to tax certain Internet services and transactions, and
- a requirement that state and local governments meet certain standards for issuing driver's licenses.[153]

Not included in the list is the No Child Left Behind Act of 2001, which greatly reconfigured how the federal government relates to state and local governments regarding elementary and secondary education. That law is discussed at length in **Exhibit 15–4**. As that discussion indicates, there has been lengthy and heated debate over whether the law contains unfunded mandates.

Exhibit 15–4 No Child Left Behind: Reform and Revolution?

The No Child Left Behind Act (NCLB) of 2001 is the most important piece of education legislation to pass Congress since the Elementary and Secondary Education Act of 1965.[1] The law dramatically altered the role of the federal government in public education and how the federal government interacts with states and local school districts.

Summary of the Law

This complex law, sprawled across more than 1,000 pages, can be summarized as follows:

- The law stresses accountability in the sense that schools are to test children to measure their progress in reading and mathematics. The aim is to have all students at or above proficiency by the year 2014. To determine whether success is achieved, schools are required to engage in annual testing of children from grades 3 through 8.
- Greater flexibility was afforded the states by allowing for shifting of some federal monies among grants so as to further NCLB objectives.
- Because reading is the foundation of most learning, the subject was given priority, with the expectation that all children be able to read by the end of third grade. A Reading First initiative was created to this end.
- The quality of teachers was to be increased so as to improve the quality of instruction.
- The law strives to eliminate the "achievement gap" between general population whites on the one hand and minorities on the other, particularly Hispanics, African Americans, and Native Americans.
- Limited English proficient (LEP) students are given priority—namely, students whose families routinely speak a language other than English.[2]
- States are required to establish standards of "adequate yearly progress" (AYP) and to impose sanctions when a school fails to meet its objectives two years in a row. In such cases, students may transfer to another school. In some instances, school districts are required to offer children the opportunity to transfer to other school districts, a fact that requires the creation of intergovernmental agreements to accommodate these children.
- Schools not meeting their AYPs for three years are required to provide students with supplemental education services (SES), such as tutoring.[3]
- The law guarantees full funding so that it supposedly contains no unfunded mandates. "Nothing in this Act shall be construed to authorize an officer or employee of the federal government to mandate, direct, or control a state, local education agency, or school's curriculum, program of instruction, or allocation of state or local resources, or mandate a state or any subdivision thereof to spend any funds or incur any costs not paid for under this act."

(continued)

Measuring Achievement

How best to measure the academic progress of students has long been debated in the education profession, but under the No Child Left Behind Act, two basic models are used. The U.S. Department of Education, which administers NCLB, presumes states will use the *status model* unless there is agreement to use the other model. The status model is aimed at determining whether students are meeting AYP. The model is akin to a pass-fail system—students in any given school are either passing or failing.

The alternative is the *growth model*, which gauges progress that is being achieved from year to year even though some students may remain below the proficiency level. In growth models, schools typically look not only at total progress but at the progress of subgroups, such as minority students and students who have English as a second language. Student achievement in effect can be graded, unlike the pass-fail system of the status model.[4]

Besides state-level testing, a national test is administered every two years on a sample of fourth- and eighth-grade children so as to be able to compare student academic achievement across state boundaries. This is known as the National Assessment of Educational Progress (NAEP).

So what have the results been? They have been mixed. In 2009, the NAEP fourth-grade reading score was not appreciably better than in 2007. However, it was higher than in all assessment years between 1992 and 2005. Eighth-grade reading scores were barely higher from 2007 to 2009, but they were noticeably higher than in 1992. Twelfth-grade reading scores showed similar minimal improvement between 2005 and 2007, but they were effectively higher between 1992 and 2009. The gaps between white and black students on the fourth-grade reading assessment was smaller in 2009 than in any previous assessments since 1992. That was not the case for Hispanics.

Findings for math achievement scores were basically similar to reading scores. That is, the 2009 assessment results were not higher than the 2007 results but were higher than all previous assessments, starting with the 1990 math achievement testing. Similarly, math achievement gaps between black and white students improved since 1990, but gaps between white and Hispanic students did not.[5] As of 2011, it is clear that the achievement gap will not be closed by the 2014 deadline.

State officials have tended to defend their school operations on the ground that the tests are faulty. The contention is that multiple measures of student learning and progress should be used.

Mandates

The law does expect states and school districts to accomplish a great deal, but this is done through funding and not official mandates in the sense of requiring compliance. State and local governments need not participate, but to do so means forgoing much-needed federal dollars. "Bundling" occurs in which governments are told they must comply with NCLB if they want federal funding of any sort.[6] The governments cannot pick and choose among grants.

In reality, the federal government has not provided full funding. That is true by one measure: how much has been appropriated versus how much was authorized. Congress has never appropriated funds at the level provided for in authorizing legislation.[7]

However, that is a weak test in that appropriations are typically less than authorizations. A better measure is, what does it cost to implement, and how much of that is covered? One study estimated that in implementing NCLB, administrative costs were increased by 2% and program costs by 27%, for a total of 29%, but federal assistance was nowhere close to that.[8]

Legal Challenges

Claims that the law unconstitutionally mandates states to act have been unsuccessful, with the federal courts simply holding that no one is putting an NCLB gun to the heads of state and local governments.[9] A three-judge panel of the Sixth Circuit Court of Appeals overturned the District Court, but upon a full Circuit Court review, the District Court ruling was upheld, that NCLB did not constitute an unfunded mandate. The Supreme Court later declined to review, and the original conclusion that NCLB did not represent an unfunded mandate stands. Indeed, the Republican Policy Committee has insisted that the law is "neither unfunded nor a mandate."[10]

The Complaints About NCLB

The complaints against the No Child Left Behind Act are far too numerous to list here, but a few should be noted. These are in addition to the repeatedly stated need for full funding of the law.

- Testing is too rigid and states are not given flexibility in designing systems to meet their specific needs.
- Although the Department of Education has authority to issue waivers and exempt states in some aspects of the law and 40 states have made such requests, these were rarely granted in the early years of the law's implementation, at least in the eyes of critics.[11] Such action, contend the critics, makes a joke of claims that the law is flexible. The counterargument is that were every requested waiver and exemption to be granted, the law would be gutted.
- The system tends to emphasize penalties for schools and teachers, who are stigmatized when they fail to meet adequate yearly progress (AYP) standards. One is reminded of the old saw: "The beatings will continue until morale improves."
- Too much emphasis is given to reading and mathematics at the expense of other subjects, such as high-level thinking skills, global understanding, and communication skills. Art and music instruction tend to get set aside to make room in the school day for reading and math instruction.
- The program diverts class time away from learning and wastes classroom time with test preparation and testing.
- For Native Americans and others, the law tends to drub out cultural and heritage learning.
- The emphasis on raising test results has led to the encouragement of low-achieving students to drop out of school. The process has been seen as a positive factor in recruiting for the military, especially during the time when troops were needed for combat in Afghanistan and Iraq.

Critics of the law are almost legion, though opinion seems to be shifting, particularly as American student achievement continues to fall behind that of students in many other countries. Early polls suggested that public opinion was highly against the act.

(continued)

For example, one poll of Americans who knew about NCLB found that 60% of the respondents thought the act had no positive effect or had been harmful.[12] However, an Education Testing Service (ETS) opinion poll in 2007 found that "parents, teachers and administrators strongly support No Child Left Behind (NCLB) reauthorization, despite limited knowledge about the law's provisions. They also favor greater flexibility in assisting students and schools struggling to meet high standards and call for increased funding for poorly performing schools to make adequate yearly progress."[13]

NCLB's Future

The law was due for reauthorization in 2007. Congress was unable to achieve that goal, and extended the act to 2012. As noted above, the deep partisan divides in Congress and the fact that 2012 is a national election year make it unlikely that the 2012 deadline will be met, and the act will likely be extended again until the new Congress and perhaps a new administration take office.

The Obama administration proposed significant changes in its position on the reauthorization, particularly emphasizing greater flexibility for the states both in terms of implementation and in terms of determining whether standards are being met and what remedies should be taken if they are not. The major nod toward less centralization in federal control and influence over education was the Race to the Top grants competition. The American Recovery and Reinvestment Act (ARRA) provided more than $4 billion in competitive grant funding, through several rounds of competition, for states to implement new programs to meet the NCLB and state-determined goals.[14] Delaware and Tennessee were the successful state applicants in round one, garnering $100 and $500 million, respectively. Ten states—Florida, Georgia, Hawaii, Maryland, Massachusetts, New York, North Carolina, Ohio, and Rhode Island—and the District of Columbia were the successful round two competition winners. Up to $3.3 billion in funding was awarded in round two, ranging from several grants of $75 million to grants of $700 million each to New York and Florida. The round three competition was announced in November 2011, with up to $200 million available for the nine unfunded finalists in round two, and an additional $500 million for additional states.[15]

The Race to the Top program was established in late 2011 by the Obama administration to move from the temporary status established by the ARRA to permanent status. Overall, the intergovernmental system for education was altered as a result of the administration using the political impetus behind recession recovery programs to put in place a *funded mandates* approach to education improvement in the states.[16] Whether it will survive the prevailing political climate and the severe budget problems during the 2012 election year is highly uncertain.

1. Elementary and Secondary Education Act of 1965 (P.L. 89-10); No Child Left Behind Act of 2001 (P.L. 107-110).
2. U.S. Government Accountability Office (2006). *No Child Left Behind Act: assistance from education could help states better measure progress of students with limited English proficiency.* Washington, DC: Author.
3. U.S. Government Accountability Office (2006). *No Child Left Behind Act: education actions needed to improve implementation and evaluation of supplemental education services.* Washington, DC: Author.
4. National Association for Gifted Children (2011). *Growth models position statement.* Retrieved December 1, 2011, from http://www.nagc.org/index.aspx?id=6296.

5. Aud, S., & Hanes, G. (2011). *The condition of education in 2011 in brief.* National Center for Education Statistics. Retrieved November 30, 2011, from http://nces.ed.gov/pubs2011/2011034.pdf.
6. No Child Left Behind and the political safeguards of federalism. (2006). *Harvard Law Review, 119,* 885–906.
7. New America Foundation (2009). *No Child Left Behind financing.* Retrieved December 1, 2011, from http://febp.newamerica.net/background-analysis/no-child-left-behind-funding.
8. Mathis, W. J. (2005). The cost of implementing the federal "No Child Left Behind Act": different assumptions, different answers. *Peabody Journal of Education, 80,* no. 2, 90–119; see Imazeki, J. (2006). Does No Child Left Behind place a fiscal burden on states? Evidence from Texas. *Education Finance and Policy, 1,* 217–246.
9. *School District of the City of Pontiac v. Spellings* (2005). 2005 U.S. Dist. LEXIS (E.D.Mich.) 29253.
10. Republican National Committee (2004). *The "No Child Left Behind Act": neither unfunded nor a mandate.* Retrieved October 8, 2006, from http://rpc.senate.gov/_files/Ap2104UnfundedJG.pdf (document no longer accessible).
11. Civil Society Institute (2006). *NCLB left behind: understanding the growing grassroots rebellion against a controversial law.* Retrieved October 8, 2006, from http://www.nclbgrassroots.org/landscape.php (document no longer accessible).
12. *Phi Delta Kappa/Gallup poll reveals public and NEA in sync about No Child Left Behind* (2006). Retrieved October 8, 2006, from http://www.nea.org/newsreleases/2006/nr060822.html (document no longer accessible on that site).
13. ETS (2011). *Standards, accountability and flexibility: Americans speak on No Child Left Behind reauthorization.* Retrieved December 1, 2011, from http://www.ets.org/americans_speak/nclb.
14. American Recovery and Reinvestment Act of 2009 (P.L. 111-5).
15. U.S. Department of Education (2011). *Race to the Top.* Retrieved December 2, 2011, from http://www2.ed.gov/programs/racetothetop/index.html.
16. Conlan, T., & Posner, P. (2011). Inflection point? Federalism and the Obama administration. *Publius: The Journal of Federalism, 41,* 421–446.

The fifth "official" mandate (from the above list) to be passed between 1996 and 2005 was the Real ID Act of 2005.[154] Following the September 11 disasters, there was general consensus that government needed to have better identification of people, but whereas many countries require adults to have passports regardless of any plans to travel overseas, that notion was anathema in the United States. Instead, the view was that the country would stay with state identification systems, but Congress wanted more careful attention devoted to confirming that people were who they said they were when applying for driver's licenses and identification cards. Congress also wanted more secure state cards in order to thwart counterfeiters.

The 2005 legislation, therefore, required extensive revamping of state driver's license and identification card systems. Congress did not have authority to require states to comply, and indeed some states even voiced interest in rebelling. However, there was considerable clout behind the legislation. If a state did not comply, its licenses and identification cards would be unacceptable by the federal government. In just one simple example, people with such licenses would be prohibited from passing security at airports and boarding aircraft.

The CBO estimated that Real ID would cost $100 million to implement, and Congress appropriated $40 million in fiscal 2006.[155] The states found both the CBO number and the appropriation to be wildly underestimated. Implementation was estimated to cost $11 billion according to a study done by the National Governors Association, National Conference of State Legislatures, and American Association of Motor Vehicle Administrators.[156] Implementation of the act was delayed for several years. Implementing regulations were not issued until 2008, setting 2011 as the date by which states were to have complied with the act. That deadline was later extended to January 2013.[157]

The Courts

The courts also have become somewhat involved in addressing federal mandates, although in cases not involving significant state and local financial issues. In 1995, in *U.S. v. Lopez*, the Supreme Court struck down a federal statute that regulated possessing a gun in a school zone. In 1997, it ruled that the provisions of the Brady Handgun Act requiring state and local law enforcement officers to conduct criminal background checks on persons applying to purchase guns were not enforceable.[158] In *Citizens United v. Federal Election Commission*, the Supreme Court struck down provisions of the McCain–Feingold Act that prohibited corporations from producing and broadcasting overt messages in support of political positions or candidates.[159] This opened the door to virtually unlimited corporate funding of political campaigns.

Civil Rights

One area of controversy concerns the extent to which a jurisdiction's operations must comply with civil rights stipulations. In 1984, the Supreme Court ruled in *Grove City College v. Bell* that only that portion of an organization affected by federal dollars had to comply with standards protecting against discrimination based on race, gender, age, and handicapping condition.[160] In that instance, the college's only federal support was for student-aid activities, so only those activities had to comply. In 1988, Congress reversed that decision by passing the Civil Rights Restoration Act, which provides that all operations of a recipient government must meet federal standards.[161] The law was passed despite a veto by President Reagan.

Title IX of the Education Amendments of 1972 addressed the same issue: the applicability of the prohibitions against discrimination in educational institutions on the basis of gender to all activities of an institution, whether or not those activities received any federal funding.[162] Title IX is applicable across the entire institution, without regard to specific links to federal funding. If a university, for example, participates in a federal student financial aid program or receives funding directly from the federal government or indirectly from state government agencies for construction of a library, then the university may not discriminate on the basis of gender in any program.

Thus, women's sports programs have to be supported if men's sports programs are funded by the university. Sometimes schools have had to eliminate some sports due to funding constraints; for example, in 2006, James Madison University had to eliminate 10 sports teams. In 2011, the University of Maryland announced the elimination of eight teams due to lack of sufficient funds.

Streamlining and Paperwork Reduction

Related to mandates are various reporting requirements that create paperwork and thereby create costs. Reporting requirements may be associated with a single federally funded program, or identical information is often required for many programs funded by the same federal agency. States require local governments to submit numerous reports each year, and the federal government requires the same of state and local governments.

The Paperwork Reduction Act, a 1995 revision of the 1980 statute, regulates agency requests for information from state and local governments, and from private corporations and individuals. Office of Management and Budget approval is required for any information form that is to be administered to 10 or more individuals or institutions. OMB reports to Congress periodically on progress in meeting the targets in the reduction of paperwork (see the chapter on budget execution).

The Regulatory Flexibility Act of 1980 and Executive Order 12866 of 1993 require agencies to conduct regulatory impact analyses to determine the effects of proposed rules or regulations, including the effects on state and local governments. Agencies are required to develop annual regulatory plans that must be submitted to OMB, which in effect has a veto power over regulations. The Clinton, George W. Bush, and Obama administrations all have emphasized the importance of cost-benefit analysis in the regulatory process.

The Single Audit Act of 1984, amended in 1996, is an additional paperwork reduction device (see the chapter on financial management).[163] Implemented through OMB Circular A-133, the act allows a state or local government receiving funds through numerous different federal programs to comply with those programs' audit provisions by using a single financial compliance audit.[164]

The 1990 Cash Management Improvement Act introduced prompt payment provisions that require the federal government to pay interest to the recipient when a transfer is late. A related provision requires states withdrawing federal funds early to pay interest to the federal government. Streamlining cash flow has been achieved through the provisions of this act.

The Federal Financial Assistance Management Improvement Act of 1999, among other things, was passed to "simplify federal financial assistance application and reporting requirements."[165] The act and its implementing regulations aim to create a standard format for applications for federal financial assistance. These are analogous to the National Science Foundation's and National Institutes of Health's online research grant applications. The Financial Assistance Management Improvement Act of 1999 involves the work of 26 agencies in developing a unified plan.

An outgrowth of these efforts is the creation of the website *Grants.gov*.[166] The purpose of the site is to provide one-stop shopping for grants. The site is searchable for possible grants, and application can be made online. In order for a state or local government agency to apply, it must obtain a DUNS number, which stands for "Data Universal Number System," and must file with the Central Contractor Registry. The Department of Health and Human Services is the contact point for Grants.gov, and all federal agencies are required to post their grant announcements and other solicitations on the site. OMB, in accordance with the Federal Funding Accountability and Transparency Act of 2006, developed a search engine and database on government grants, contracts, and loans, accessible at *www.usaspending.gov*.[167]

Another useful tool is the *Catalog of Federal Domestic Assistance*, mentioned earlier. The *Catalog*, which gives capsule descriptions of grant programs, can help a local government determine whether it might be able to secure federal funding for a contemplated project, even though applications may not be being received at that particular time.

Grant Coordination

Another concern is how to coordinate federal grants at regional and statewide levels. If a community is applying for a federal grant to assist elderly citizens, how would that grant complement other programs for the elderly in the region, and how would it relate to state-level programs?

In response to this type of question and as an outgrowth of the Intergovernmental Cooperation Act, the Bureau of the Budget (now OMB) in 1969 issued Circular A-95, which provided for the establishment of area-wide and state clearinghouses responsible for reviewing and commenting on proposed projects. The review and comment process offered the potential for eliminating waste in the use of federal funds. Jurisdictions applying for these funds were expected to respond to any objections made by the clearinghouses and, where appropriate, to modify the proposed projects. Circular A-95 was later rescinded and replaced by various executive orders, the most recent being Executive Order 12372— Intergovernmental Review of Federal Programs. Ultimately, the state- and area-wide reviews proved slow and cumbersome. As of 2011, nine states and five territories had active single points of contacts registered.[168]

Awarding Grants and Grants Administration

All too often applicants for grants worry about possible bias on the part of those responsible for making awards. The fear is that regardless of the merits of grant proposals, awards will be made based on favoritism.

Nightmares along this line became reality in 2006. The Inspector General Office in the U.S. Department of Education issued a scathing report about the handling of the Reading First program, part of the No Child Left Behind program.[169] The report stated that people chosen to serve on review panels for state applications were often biased, favoring particular textbook publishers and curriculum vendors.

All governments experience problems in administering grants. Communication problems are routine—for example, between what a local government thinks it needs to report to its funding agencies at the state and federal levels and what they think needs to be reported. As time passes during a grant, recipient governments frequently need to make adjustments to accommodate changes in their environment, but these adjustments may not meet with approval of funding agencies.

Management Capacity

With the increasing emphasis on block grants, greater attention has been focused on the abilities of state and local governments to manage themselves. Devolving to these governments' decision-making authority over the use of federal funds has been accompanied by a concern that they improve their management capabilities. There have been suggestions that the federal government should assume responsibility for management capacity building, but the federal government has shown only a limited inclination to accept any such obligation. In fact, management improvements and other innovations at the state and local levels in recent years have led many to look to them as a source of management ideas for the federal government.

SUMMARY

Fundamental issues arise in regard to the question of how to structure intergovernmental relations. Functional integration results in picket fence arrangements that may deter geographic integration. Fiscal capacities differ among and within levels of government, so that the government that perhaps should provide services often lacks the necessary funding capability. Failure to provide services results in externality problems.

Both direct spending and grants-in-aid are important for intergovernmental relations. Decisions by federal and state agencies on the location and expansion of capital facilities affect the economic viability of local jurisdictions. Despite more extensive attention often being devoted to federal aid programs, state aid to local government is actually larger. Some states provide much of their local governments' revenue while others provide little, a point that should be stressed to avoid unwarranted generalizations. Aid to education constitutes the largest portion of state aid, with monies typically allocated on a formula basis. Federal aid is concentrated in the areas of education, income security, health, and transportation.

Major changes are occurring in the intergovernmental fiscal landscape, with substantial responsibilities for welfare reform already having been devolved to state governments, and numerous other proposals up for consideration. Health care reform significantly altered the joint federal-state Medicaid program. Furthermore, substantial concern has prompted legislative and executive action to mitigate the impacts of unfunded federal mandates. Little fiscal impact from these actions occurred until the massive stimulus programs to address the effects of the recession starting in 2007. The American Recovery and Reinvestment Act of 2009 in particular provided massive funding for grants to states and local governments, and most of those programs came with additional flexibility in state program design and administration. The Race to the Top initiative altered, albeit perhaps temporarily, the federal-state relationship in implementing the No Child Left Behind Act.

Intergovernmental grants have at least four aspects: their purpose (narrow, broad, or general), the type of recipient, the amount, and the method of distribution. Categorical grants are criticized as deterring coordination, skewing local priorities, and needlessly wasting time in their proposal preparation. On the positive side, these grants are said to force planning in the preparation of their proposals and to allow for screening out poorly conceived projects. General revenue sharing supported local priorities and provided funds to jurisdictions that did not have staff available to apply for categorical grants. It was criticized as not targeting any national purpose and giving funds to many undeserving jurisdictions. Ultimately, the program was terminated at the federal level, but some states continue to engage in revenue sharing with their local governments. Block grants, a cross between categorical grants and GRS, have advantages and disadvantages of both.

In addition to grant programs, numerous other intergovernmental devices are employed. They include provisions in federal tax law that benefit state and local governments and review and comment processes for grant proposals. Proposals have been made for major reconfiguring of program responsibilities among the federal, state, and local governments. Since the 1980s, many state and local governments have shown a resurgence in this area, resulting in what many see as a healthy redress of balance between the federal level and the state and local levels.

NOTES

1. Gamkhar, S., & Pickerell, J. (2011). The state of American federalism, 2010–2011: The economy, healthcare reform and midterm elections shape the intergovernmental agenda. *Publius, 41,* 361–394.
2. World Trade Organization (2011). *Members and observers.* Retrieved November 25, 2011, from http://www.wto.org/english/thewto_e/whatis_e/tif_e/org6_e.htm; Roberts, A. (2004). A partial revolution: the diplomatic ethos and transparency in intergovernmental organizations. *Public Administration Review, 64,* 410–424.
3. Lacroix, A. (2010). *The ideological origins of American federalism.* Cambridge, MA: Harvard University Press; Nivola, P. S. (2005). *Why federalism matters.* Washington, DC: Brookings Institution; Conlan, T. (2006). From cooperative to opportunistic federalism: reflections on the half-century anniversary of the Commission on Intergovernmental Relations. *Public Administration Review, 66,* 663–676; McGuire, M. (2006). Intergovernmental management: a view from the bottom. *Public Administration Review, 66,* 677–679.
4. Indian Gaming Regulatory Act of 1988 (P.L. 100-497); National Indian Gaming Commission website, www.nigc.gov.
5. Mays, G. L. (2005). Intergovernmental relations and Native American gaming. *American Review of Public Administration, 35,* 74–93.
6. National Indian Gaming Commission (2005). *Growth in Indian gaming, 2004.* Retrieved September 28, 2006, from http://www.nigc.gov/TribalData/GrowthinIndianGamingGraph19952004/tabid/114/Default.aspx; National Indian Gaming Commission (2011). *NIGC gaming revenues: 2005–2010.* Retrieved November 25, 2011, from http://www.nigc.gov/linkclick.aspx?fileticket=1P8h79gnJOU%3d&tabid=67.
7. National Indian Gaming Commission (2010). *Tribal gaming revenues (in thousands) by region: fiscal years 2008–2009.* Retrieved November 26, 2011, from http://www.nigc.gov/linkclick.aspx?fileticket=goZC PYPDuT4%3d&tabid=67.
8. Evans, W. N., & Topoleski, J. H. (2002). The social and economic impact of Native American casinos. *NBER.* Retrieved November 28, 2011, from http://papers.nber.org/papers/w9198.
9. Bureau of Indian Affairs, U.S. Department of Interior (2010). *Federally recognized Indian tribes.* Retrieved November 25, 2011, from http://www.artnatam.com/tribes.html.
10. Bureau of the Census, U.S. Department of Commerce (2011). *Statistical abstract: 2012* (p. 267). Washington, DC: U.S. Government Printing Office.
11. Walker, D. B. (1995). *The rebirth of federalism: slouching toward Washington.* Chatham, NJ: Chatham House.
12. Tiebout, C. M. (1956). A pure theory of public expenditures. *Journal of Political Economy, 44,* 416–424; Howell-Moroney, M. (2008). The Tiebout hypothesis 50 years later: lessons and lingering challenges for metropolitan governance in the 21st century. *Public Administration Review, 68,* 97–109.
13. Ter-Minassian, T. (1997). *Fiscal federalism in theory and practice.* Washington, DC: International Monetary Fund.
14. Hall, J. (2008). The forgotten regional organizations: creating capacity for economic development. *Public Administration Review, 68,* 110–125.
15. Pineda, C. (2005). *City-county consolidation and diseconomies of scale: summary of selected literature.* Harvard University Ash Institute for Democratic Governance. Retrieved November 25, 2011, from http://www.innovations.harvard.edu/cache/documents/9331.pdf; Wood, C. (2006). Scope and patterns of

metropolitan governance in urban America: probing the complexities in the Kansas City region. *American Review of Public Administration, 36*, 337–353.

16. Port Authority of New York and New Jersey website, http://www.panynj.gov/.

17. Wright, D. S. (1988). *Understanding intergovernmental relations* (3rd ed., pp. 83–86). Pacific Grove, CA: Brooks/Cole.

18. Sapat, A. (2004). Devolution and innovation: the adoption of state environmental policy innovations by administrative agencies. *Public Administration Review, 64*, 141–151; U.S. General Accounting Office (2004). *Columbia River Basin: a multilayered collection of directives and plans guide federal fish and wildlife activities.* Washington, DC: U.S. Government Printing Office; Intergovernmental Panel on Climate Change website, http://www.ipcc.ch/.

19. U.S. Government Accountability Office (2006). *International finance crime: Treasury's roles and responsibilities relating to selected provisions of the USA PATRIOT Act.* Washington, DC: Author.

20. Baker, A., & Rashbaum, W. (2010). Police find car bomb in Times Square. *New York Times*, May 1. Retrieved November 27, 2011, from http://www.nytimes.com/2010/05/02/nyregion/02timessquare.html?pagewanted=print.

21. Winston, P., et al. (2006). *Federalism after Hurricane Katrina.* Retrieved September 28, 2006, from http://www.urban.org/UploadedPDF/311344_after_katrina.pdf.

22. U.S. Government Accountability Office (2005). *Hurricane Katrina: providing oversight of the nation's preparedness, response, and recovery activities.* Washington, DC: Author.

23. Fellowes, M., & Liu, A. (2006). *Federal allocations in response to Katrina, Rita and Wilma: an update.* Washington, DC: Brookings Institution.

24. Derthick, M. (2009). *The transformation that fell short: Bush, federalism, and emergency management.* Albany, NY: Nelson A. Rockefeller Institute of Government. Retrieved November 26, 2011, from http://www.rockinst.org/pdf/disaster_recovery/gulfgov/gulfgov_reports/2009-08-Transformation_That_Fell.pdf.

25. Bea, K. (2007). *Federal Emergency Management policy changes after Hurricane Katrina: a summary of statutory provisions.* Washington, DC: Congressional Research Service.

26. U.S. Government Accountability Office (2006). *Catastrophic disasters: enhanced leadership, capabilities, and accountability controls will improve the effectiveness of the nation's preparedness, response, and recovery system.* Washington, DC: Author.

27. Birkland, T., & DeYoung, S. (2011). Emergency response, doctrinal confusion and federalism in the *Deepwater Horizon* oil spill. *Publius, 41*, 471–493.

28. Terkel, A. (2011). FEMA praised by governors for response to Hurricane Irene. *Huffington Post*, August 28. Retrieved November 27, 2011, from http://www.huffingtonpost.com/2011/08/28/hurricane-irene-fema-response_n_939545.html; West, P. (2011). Washington shows off its progress in hurricane response. *Los Angeles Times*, August 28. Retrieved November 27, 2011, from http://articles.latimes.com/2011/aug/28/nation/la-na-hurricane-irene-obama-20110829.

29. Katz, B., et al. (2010). *Delivering the next economy: the states step up.* Washington, DC: Brookings Institution. Retrieved November 26, 2011, from http://www.brookings.edu/papers/2010/1117_states_next_economy.aspx; *Financing governments in the 21st century: intergovernmental collaboration can promote fiscal and economic goals.* Washington, DC: National Academy of Public Administration.

30. Bureau of the Census, U.S. Department of Commerce (2011). *Statistical abstract: 2012* (p. 445).

31. Office of Economic Policy, U.S. Department of Treasury (2005). *Total taxable resources, 2004.* Retrieved November 28, 2011, from http://www.treasury.gov/resource-center/economic-policy/taxable-resources/Documents/tables%202011.pdf.

32. U.S. Advisory Commission on Intergovernmental Relations (1992). *Significant features of fiscal federalism, vol. 2, revenues and expenditures: 1992.* Washington, DC: U.S. Government Printing Office.

33. U.S. Advisory Commission on Intergovernmental Relations (1990). *Representative expenditures: addressing the neglected dimension of fiscal capacity.* Washington, DC: U.S. Government Printing Office.

34. Wong, J. D. (2004). The fiscal impact of economic growth and development on local government revenue capacity. *Journal of Public Budgeting, Accounting, and Financial Management, 16*, 413–423.

35. Sobarzo, H. (2004). *Tax effort and tax potential of state governments in Mexico: a representative tax system.* Retrieved November 28, 2011, from http://kellogg.nd.edu/publications/workingpapers/WPS/315.pdf.

36. Expert Panel on Equalization and Territorial Formula Financing (2006). *Achieving a national purpose: putting equalization back on track.* Canada Office of the Prime Minister. Retrieved November 28, 2011, from http://www.eqtff-pfft.ca/english/EQTreasury/index.asp.

37. Authors' calculations from Tax Policy Center (2011). *State and local government finance data query system (SLF-DQS).* Washington, DC: Urban Institute–Brookings Institution. Accessed November 28, 2011, at http://www.taxpolicycenter.org/slf-dqs/pages.cfm; http://www.treasury.gov/resource-center/economic-policy/taxable-resources/Documents/tables%202011.pdf.

38. Oates, W. E. (1972). *Fiscal federalism.* New York, NY: Harcourt Brace Jovanovich.

39. Executive Order 12612—Federalism. 52 FR 41685, 3 CFR, 1987 Comp., p. 252.

40. Ulbrich, H. (2002). Economic aspects of business tax incentives. *Public Policy and Practice, 2,* October. Retrieved October 25, 2011, from http://ipspr.sc.edu/ejournal/businesstax.asp.

41. Gardner Jr., E. (2001). Moving into global competition: a case study of Alabama's recruitment of Mercedes-Benz. *Review of Policy Research 18,* 80–93.

42. Cremer, A. (2011). Daimler spends $2 billion on Mercedes-Benz site in Alabama as demand rises. *Bloomberg.com,* July 21. Retrieved November 28, 2011, from http://www.bloomberg.com/news/2011-07-21/daimler-spends-2-billion-on-mercedes-benz-site-in-alabama-as-demand-rises.html.

43. McCracken, J. (2000). Mercedes to build 2nd plant in Alabama. *Auto.com.* Retrieved August 2002 from http://www.auto.com/industry/merc26_20000826.htm; this citation no longer archived on *Auto.com.*

44. With film incentive capped, Michigan's movie jobs face an uncertain future. (2011). *Huffpost Detroit,* November 17. Retrieved December 6, 2011, from http://www.huffingtonpost.com/2011/11/17/michigan-film-incentive-jobs_n_1098247.html.

45. Goldman, T., & Wachs, M. (2003). A quiet revolution in transportation finance: The rise of local option transportation taxes. *Transportation Quarterly, 57,* 19–32; Crabbe, A. E., et al. (2005). Local transportation sales taxes: California's experiment in transportation finance. *Public Budgeting & Finance,* Fall, 91–121; Green, A. D. (2006). Life in the fast lane: transportation finance and the local option sales tax. *State and Local Government Review, 38,* 92–103.

46. Rivlin, A. M. (1992). *Reviving the American dream: the economy, the states, and the federal government* (pp. 126–152). Washington, DC: Brookings Institution, 126–152.

47. Murphy, C. (2010). VAT: will the U.S. adopt a Value-Added Tax? *CBS Money-Watch.com, April 7, 2010.* Retrieved November 28, 2011, from http://www.cbsnews.com/8301-503983_162-20001918-503983.html.

48. Defense Base Closure and Realignment Commission (2005). *Report.* Retrieved November 25, 2011, from http://www.brac.gov/docs/final/Volume1BRACReport.pdf; see U.S. Department of Defense (2006). *BRAC: base realignment and closure.* Retrieved November 25, 2011, from http://www.dod.mil/brac/.

49. Crock, S. (2004). A tale of two military bases. *BusinessWeek.com.* Retrieved September 29, 2006, from http://www.businessweek.com/bwdaily/dnflash/dec2004/nf2004128_9707_db056.htm?chan=search.

50. Crock, S. (2004). A tale of two military bases. *BusinessWeek.com.* Retrieved September 29, 2006, from http://www.businessweek.com/bwdaily/dnflash/dec2004/nf2004128_9707_db056.htm?chan=search.

51. U.S. Office of Management and Budget (2011). *Budget of the United States government, 2012* (p. 174). Washington, DC: U.S. Government Printing Office.

52. Bureau of the Census, U.S. Department of Commerce (2011). *Statistical abstract, 2012* (p. 326).

53. Bureau of the Census, U.S. Department of Commerce (2011). *Statistical abstract, 2012* (p. 334).

54. Bureau of the Census, U.S. Department of Commerce (2011). *Statistical abstract, 2012* (p. 333).

55. Dubay, C. S. (2006). *Federal tax burdens and expenditures by state.* Washington, DC: Tax Foundation.

56. Data for 2009 compiled from Internal Revenue gross collections, by type of tax and state, fiscal year 2009. Retrieved November 18, 2011, from http://www.irs.gov/taxstats/article/0,,id=206488,00.html; and Bureau of the Census, U.S. Department of Commerce (2011). *Statistical abstract of the*

United States: 2012 (p. 316). Washington, DC: Government Printing Office. Data for earlier years are from the same sources, corresponding to the dates.

57. Bureau of the Census, U.S. Department of Commerce (2011). *State and local government finances summary: 2007–2008* (p. 6–11). Retrieved October 16, 2011, from http://www2.census.gov/govs/estimate/08statesummaryreport.pdf.

58. Compiled from Bureau of the Census, U.S. Department of Commerce (2009). *Table 2. Local government finances by type of government and state: 2006–07.* Retrieved November 26, 2011, from http://www.census.gov/govs/estimate/historical_data_2007.html#state_local.

59. Bureau of the Census, U.S. Department of Commerce (2011). *Statistical abstract, 2012* (p. 292).

60. Bureau of the Census, U.S. Department of Commerce (2009). *Public education finances, 2009* (p. 1). Washington, DC: U.S. Government Printing Office.

61. Benson, E. D., & Marks, B. R. (2005). "Robin Hood" and Texas school district borrowing costs. *Public Budgeting & Finance, 25*, Summer, 84–105; Texas Education Agency (2011). *Chapter 41: wealth equalization.* Retrieved November 27, 2011, from http://www.tea.state.tx.us/index2.aspx?id=6796&menu_id=645.

62. *San Antonio School District v. Rodriquez* (1973). 411 U.S. 1.

63. *Serrano v. Priest (Serrano II)* (1976). 557 P.2d 929 (Calif.).

64. Ladd, H. F., & Hansen, J. S. (Eds.) (1999). *Making money matter: financing America's schools.* Washington, DC: National Academy of Sciences; Ladd, H. F., et al. (Eds.) (1999). *Equity and adequacy in education finance: issues and perspectives.* Washington, DC: National Academy of Sciences.

65. Hanushek, E., & Landseth, A. (2009). *Schoolhouses, courthouses, and statehouses: solving the funding-achievement puzzle in America's public schools.* Princeton, NJ: Princeton University Press.

66. No Child Left Behind Act of 2001 (P.L. 107-110).

67. U.S. Department of Education (2011). *Blueprint for reform: the reauthorization of the Elementary and Secondary Education Act.* Retrieved November 26, 2011, from http://www2.ed.gov/policy/elsec/leg/blueprint/publicationtoc.html.

68. *Rose v. Council for Better Education* (1989). 7090 S.W.2d 186 (Ky.).

69. Yinger, John (2004). *Helping children left behind: state aid and the pursuit of educational equity.* Cambridge, MA: MIT Press.

70. Bireda, S. (2011). *Funding education equitably: the "comparability provision" and the move to fair and transparent school budgeting systems.* Washington, DC: Center for American Progress.

71. See Federal Highway Administration, U.S. Department of Transportation (2011). *Highway statistics, 2010.* Retrieved November 28, 2011, from http://www.fhwa.dot.gov/policyinformation/statistics/2010/index.cfm.

72. Klas, M. (2011). Teachers sue state over "unconstitutional" pay cut to balance the budget. *Miami Herald,* June 20. Retrieved November 26, 2011, from http://www.miamiherald.com/2011/06/20/2275364/teachers-sue-state-over-unconstitutional.html#ixzz1PtlsaIr1.

73. Reschovsky, A. (2004). The impact of state government fiscal crises on local governments and schools. *State and Local Government Review, 36*, 86–102; Vanylos, I. (2005). Fiscal reaction to state aid uncertainties: evidence from New York State. *Public Budgeting & Finance, 25*, Winter, 44–58.

74. New York City Investment Fund (2003). *Lessons learned: an analysis of the New York City Investment Fund's financial recovery fund for small businesses affected by 9/11.* Retrieved October 1, 2006, from http://www.nycif.org/RECOVERYFUND/LessonsLearned_FRF.pdf (document no longer accessible online).

75. Deller, S. C., & Maher, C. (2005). Categorical municipal expenditures with a focus on the flypaper effect. *Public Budgeting & Finance, 25*, Fall, 73–90; Deller, S. C., & Maher, C. S. (2006). A model of asymmetries in the flypaper effect. *Publius, 36*, 213–230.

76. Fisher, R. C., & Papke, L. E. (2000). Local government responses to education grants. *National Tax Journal, 53*, 153–168.

77. Baicher, K., & Gordon, N. (2006). The effect of state education finance reform on total local resources. *Journal of Public Economics, 90*, 1519–1535.

78. Chernick, H. (2000). Federal grants and social welfare spending: do state responses matter? *National Tax Journal, 53*, 143–152; Rodgers, H. R., & Tedin, K. L. (2006). State TANF spending: predictors of state tax effort to support welfare reform. *Review of Policy Research, 23*, 745–759.

79. U.S. Government Accountability Office (2008). *Surface transportation: restructured federal approach needed for more focused, performance-based, and sustainable programs.* Washington, DC: Government Printing Office.

80. Fossett, J., & Thompson, F. J. (2006). Administrative responsiveness to the disadvantaged: the case of children's health insurance. *Journal of Public Administration Research and Theory, 16,* 369–392; Johnson, T. J., et al. (2006). The effects of cost-shifting in the state children's health insurance program. *American Journal of Public Health, 96,* 709–775.

81. Compiled from U.S. Office of Management and Budget (2011). *Analytical perspectives, budget of the United States government, 2012* (pp. 285–295, 440). Washington, DC: U.S. Government Printing Office.

82. Calculated from Bureau of the Census, *Statistical abstract of the United States: 2012* (pp. 18, 269).

83. Katz, B., & Bradley, J. (2011). Metro connection: cities, competitiveness, growth through innovation, job creation, U.S. economic growth. *Democracy: A Journal of Ideas,* March (Brookings Institution online journal). Retrieved November 25, 2011, from http://www.brookings.edu/articles/2011/03_metros_katz_bradley.aspx.

84. U.S. Office of Management and Budget (2006). *Historical tables: budget of the United States government, 2007* (p. 312). Washington, DC: U.S. Government Printing Office; Council of Economic Advisers (2011). *Economic Report of the President: 2011* (p. 188). Washington, DC: U.S. Government Printing Office.

85. Arrandale, T. (2002). The pollution puzzle. *Governing, 16,* August, 22–26.

86. Buntin, J. (2001). The increasingly expansive Medicaid machine. *Governing, 15,* October, 30–32.

87. Personal Responsibility and Work Opportunity Reconciliation Act of 1996 (P.L. 104–193).

88. Holahan, J., & Headen, I. (2011). *Medicaid coverage and spending in health reform: national and state-by-state results for adults at or below 133% FTL.* Washington, DC: Kaiser Commission on Medicaid and the Uninsured. Retrieved November 24, 2011, from http://www.kff.org/healthreform/upload/8149.pdf.

89. Eckl, C. L., et al. (1991). *State budget and tax actions: 1991* (p. 13). Washington, DC: National Conference of State Legislatures.

90. U.S. General Accounting Office (2004). *Medicaid: improved federal oversight of state financing schemes is needed.* Washington, DC: U.S. Government Printing Office; U.S. General Accounting Office (2004). *Medicaid: intergovernmental transfers have facilitated state financing schemes.* Washington, DC: U.S. Government Printing Office.

91. P.L. 111-148.

92. Walker, D. B. (1996). The advent of an ambiguous federalism and the emergence of New Federalism II. *Public Administration Review, 56,* 271–280.

93. *Garcia v. San Antonio Metropolitan Transit Authority* (1985). 469 U.S. 528.

94. *Printz v. United States* (1997). 521 U.S. 98.

95. *Geier v. American Honda Motor Company* (2000). 529 U.S. 861; Andrews, J. L. (2006). Saving preemption: a conflict preemption quandary resolved in *Geier v. American Honda Motor Co., Inc. Transportation Law Journal, 32,* 221–284.

96. *Kimel v. Florida Board of Regents* (2000). 528 U.S. 62; *Board of Trustees of Alabama v. Garrett* (2001). 531 U.S. 356.

97. Tough Arizona-style immigration laws pose new issues for high court. *International Business Times,* December 6. Retrieved December 6, 2011, from http://www.ibtimes.com/articles/262064/20111206/tough-arizona-stlye-immigration-laws-pose-new.htm.

98. National Conference of State Legislatures (2006). *Preemption monitor.* Retrieved October 3, 2006, from http://www.ncsl.organ/sclaw/PreemptionMonitor_Index.htm (no longer archived); see Galligan, T. C. (2006). U.S. Supreme Court tort reform: limiting state power to articulate and develop tort law—defamation, preemption, and punitive damages. *University of Cincinnati Law Review, 74,* 1189–1264; Kaulukukui, K. L. (2006). The brief and unexpected preemption of Hawaii's humpback whale laws: the authority of the states to protect endangered marine mammals under ESA and MMPA. *Environmental Law Reporter News and Analysis, 36,* 10712–10725.

99. Authors' review of all issues of *Preemption Monitor* for mid-2009 through mid-2011.

100. Kloha, P., et al. (2005). Someone to watch over me: state monitoring of local fiscal conditions. *American Review of Public Administration, 35*, 236–255.

101. Dluhy, M. J., & Frank, H. A. (1999). Miami's fiscal crisis: two years later. *Municipal Finance Journal, 20*, Spring, 1–19; Once in financial straits, Miami sells $32.5 million in bonds. (2002). *Naples Daily News.* Retrieved August 2002 from http://www.naplesnews.com/02/03/florida/d755883a.htm.

102. Burton, P. (2011). Attorney for Harrisburg, Pa., puts bondholders first. *The Bond Buyer*, November 9. Retrieved November 10, 2011, from http://www.bondbuyer.com/issues/120_216/harrisburg-pa-bankruptcy-1032952-1.html; Burton, P. (2011). Pa. emergency action plan ensures services for Harrisburg. *The Bond Buyer*, November 4. Retrieved November 10, 2011, from http://www.bondbuyer.com/news/harrisburg-emergency-action-bankruptcy-1032821-1.html.

103. Sigo, S. (2011). Jefferson county finally files for bankruptcy. *The Bond Buyer*, November 9. Retrieved November 10, 2011, from http://www.bondbuyer.com/news/jeffco-1032991-1.html.

104. Detroit faces state takeover. (2011). (*Wilmington, NC) Star News*, December 3, 5.

105. Kirkpatrick, C. (1997). State seizes town drowning in debts, failed infrastructure. *Durham Herald-Sun*, February 5, 1, 8.

106. *The District of Columbia Financial and Responsibility Management Assistance Authority will suspend operations.* Retrieved August 2002 at http://www.cdfra.gov.

107. Pierog, K. (2011). Michigan governor approves state takeover of Flint. *Reuters*, November 30. Retrieved December 2, 2011, from http://www.reuters.com/article/2011/11/30/us-flint-michigan-emergency-idUSTRE7AS2YN20111130.

108. *Texas v. United States* (1998). 523 U.S. 296.

109. Heath, B., et al. (2005). Mayor: fix Detroit or risk takeover. *Detroit News*, January 13. Retrieved October 3, 2006, from http://www.detnews.com/2005/metro/0501/13/A01-58735.htm; Fisher, R. (2006). State still has option to takeover St. Louis schools. *Missouri Digital News.* Retrieved October 3, 2006, from http://www.mdn.org/2006/STORIES/NODLER12.HTM; Kennedy-Ross, S., & Vivanco, L. (2006). City takeover talk irks school officials. *San Bernardino County Sun*, September 21. Retrieved October 3, 2006, from http://www.sbsun.com/search/ci_4371038.

110. Wong, K. K., & Shen, F. X. (2002). *Do school district takeovers work? Assessing the effectiveness of city and state takeovers as a school reform strategy.* National Association of State Boards of Education. Retrieved November 28, 2011, from http://www.nasbe.org/Standard/9_Spring2002/Takeover.pdf; Burns, P. (2003). Regime theory, state government, and a takeover of urban education. *Journal of Urban Affairs, 25*, 285–303.

111. National Association of State Boards of Education (2008). Meeting the challenge: the states' role in improving low-performing schools through restructuring—2007 Study Group. Retrieved November 28, 2011, from http://nasbe.org/index.php?option=com_zoo&task=item&item_id=184&Itemid=1033.

112. U.S. Department of Education (2010). A blueprint for reform: the reauthorization of the Elementary and Secondary Education Act. Retrieved November 28, 2011, from http://www2.ed.gov/policy/elsec/leg/blueprint/blueprint.pdf.

113. U.S. Department of Housing and Urban Development (2011). *Community Development Block Grant Program—CDBG.* Retrieved November 28, 2011, from http://portal.hud.gov/hudportal/HUD?src=/program_offices/comm_planning/communitydevelopment/programs.

114. Cull, I. (2011). WIC program highly underutilized in Spokane County. *KXLY.com*, November 17. Retrieved November 29, 2011, from http://www.kxly.com/news/29799930/detail.html.

115. U.S. Office of Management and Budget (1997). *Grants and cooperative agreements with state and local governments*, Circular A-102. Retrieved November 28, 2011, from U.S. Office of Management and Budget (1997). *Grants and cooperative agreements with state and local governments*, Circular A-102 (revised periodically, last complete revision 1997). Retrieved October 4, 2006, from http://www.whitehouse.gov/omb/circulars/a102/a102.html.

116. McDowell, B. D. (1991). Grant reform reconsidered. *Intergovernmental Perspective, 17*, Summer, 8–11.

117. Givel, M. (1991). *The War on Poverty revisited: the Community Services Block Grant Program in the Reagan years.* Lanham, MD: University Press of America; U.S. Government Accountability Office (2006).

Community Services Block Grant Program: HHS should improve oversight by focusing monitoring and assistance efforts on areas of high risk. Washington, DC: Author.

118. State and Local Fiscal Assistance Act of 1972 (P.L. 92-512).

119. Greenblatt, A. (2002). Enemies of the State. *Governing, 16,* June, 26–31.

120. Scott, D. (2011). Detroit Mayor, Mich Gov. at odds over shared revenue. *Governing*, November 17. Retrieved November 28, 2011, from http://www.governing.com/news/local/Detroit-Mayor-Mich-Gov-At-Odds-Over-Shared-Revenue.html#.

121. Philippines Institute for Development Studies (1992). *LGUs slice of internal revenue allotment from the national pie.* Retrieved November 9, 2006, from http://serp-p.pids.gov.ph/details.php3?tid=2913.

122. Housing and Community Development Act of 1974 (P.L. 93-383); U.S. Government Accountability Office (2006). *Community Development Block Grants: program offers recipients flexibility but oversight can be improved.* Washington, DC: Author; U.S. Government Accountability Office (2006). *Community Development Block Grants: options for improving the targeting of funds.* Washington, DC: Author; U.S. Government Accountability Office (2010). *Community Development Block Grants: entitlement communities' and states' methods of distributing funds reflect program flexibility.* Washington, DC: Author.

123. U.S. Office of Management and Budget (1999). *Revised statistical definitions of metropolitan areas (MA) and guidance on use of MA definitions,* Bulletin 99–04. Retrieved November 30, 2011, from http://www.whitehouse.gov/omb/bulletins/b99-04.html.

124. U.S. General Accounting Office (2004). *Metropolitan statistical areas: new standards and their impact on selected federal programs.* Washington, DC: U.S. Government Printing Office.

125. Omnibus Budget Reconciliation Act of 1981 (P.L. 97-35).

126. Gruber, A. (2005). Hanging on. *Government executive.* Retrieved October 5, 2006, from http://www.govexec.com/features/0505-01/0505-01na1.htm.

127. Bureau of the Census (2011). *Statistical abstract of the United States: 2010* (p. 273); and Tax Policy Center (2011). *State and local finance data query system.*

128. Homeland Security Act of 2002 (P.L. 107-296).

129. Office of Inspector General, U.S. Department of Homeland Security (2005). *An assessment of the proposal to merge Customs and Border Protection with Immigration and Customs Enforcement.* Retrieved November 28, 2011, from http://www.dhs.gov/interweb/assetlibrary/OIG_06-04_Nov05.pdf.

130. U.S. Government Accountability Office (2006). *Department of Homeland Security's use of special streamlined acquisition authorities in Section 833 of the Homeland Security Act of 2002.* Washington, DC: Author.

131. All grant awards from queries on http://www.usaspending.gov.

132. Department of Homeland Security (2011). *FY 2011 Homeland Security Grant Program (HSGP): Urban Areas Security Initiative.* Retrieved November 30, 2011, from http://www.fema.gov/government/grant/hsgp/#2.

133. Department of Homeland Security (2011). *FY 2011 Homeland Security Grant Program (HSGP): Urban Areas Security Initiative;* U.S. Department of Homeland Security (2006). DHS announces $1.7 billion in homeland security grants. Retrieved November 30, 2011, from http://www.dhs.gov/dhspublic/display?content=5667.

134. Department of Homeland Security (2011). *Chemical security.* Retrieved November 30, 2011, from http://www.dhs.gov/files/programs/chemical-security.shtm.

135. U.S. Department of Homeland Security (2011). *FY 2011 Homeland Security Grant program.* Retrieved November 30, 2011, from http://www.fema.gov/government/grant/hsgp/.

136. U.S. Government Accountability Office (2008). *Homeland Security: DHS risk-based grant methodology is reasonable, but its current version's measure of vulnerability is limited* (p. 1). Washington, DC: Author.

137. Schumer, C., as quoted in Bohn, K. (2006). Homeland Security grants rile DC, NYC. *CNN.com.* Retrieved October 5, 2006, from http://edition.cnn.com/2006/US/05/31/homeland.grants/index.html. (no longer accessible from archives).

138. Hudson, A. (2006). Homeland Security grants spent on clowns and gyms. *Washington Times,* April 21.

139. Tax Reform Act of 1986 (P.L. 99-514).

140. New York State Department of Taxation and Finance (2011). *STAR program.* Retrieved November 30, 2011, from http://www.tax.ny.gov/pit/property/star/index.htm.

141. Eom, T. H., & Rubenstein, R. (2006). Do state-funded property tax exemptions increase local government inefficiency? An analysis of New York State's STAR program. *Public Budgeting & Finance, 26,* Spring, 66–87.

142. Rivlin, A. M. (1992). *Reviving the American dream: the economy, the states, and the federal government* (pp. 126–152). Washington, DC: Brookings Institution.

143. Bradson, T., et al. (2006). Soft governance, hard consequences: the ambiguous status of unofficial guidelines. *Public Administration Review, 66,* 546–553.

144. P.L. 108-446.

145. U.S. Office of Management and Budget (2006). *Draft 2006 report to Congress on the costs and benefits of federal regulations.* Retrieved November 9, 2006, from http://www.whitehouse.gov/omb/inforeg/reports/2006_draft_cost_benefit_report.pdf.

146. Unfunded Mandates Reform Act of 1995 (P.L. 104-4); see Gullo, T. (2004). History and evaluation of the Unfunded Mandates Reform Act. *National Tax Journal, 57,* 559–570.

147. Congressional Research Service (2011). *Unfunded Mandates Reform Act: history, impact and issues* (p. 13). Washington, DC: Author.

148. U.S. Congressional Budget Office (2009). *Cost estimate for the Patient Protection and Affordable Care Act.* Retrieved November 30, 2011, from http://www.cbo.gov/ftpdocs/107xx/doc10731/Reid_letter_11_18_09.pdf.

149. Congressional Research Service (2011). *Unfunded Mandates Reform Act: history, impact and issues.*

150. Executive Order 13132—Federalism. 64 FR 43255.

151. U.S. Congressional Budget Office (2011). *A review of CBO's activities in 2010 under the Unfunded Mandates Reform Act* (p. 3). Washington, DC: Author.

152. U.S. Congressional Budget Office (2011). *A review of CBO's activities in 2010 under the Unfunded Mandates Reform Act* (p. 67).

153. U.S. Congressional Budget Office (2011). *A review of CBO's activities in 2010 under the Unfunded Mandates Reform Act.*

154. Real ID Act of 2005 (P.L. 109-13).

155. U.S. Congressional Budget Office (2006). *A review of CBO's activities under the Unfunded Mandates Reform Act, 1996 to 2005* (p. 5).

156. National Governors Association, National Conference of State Legislatures, and American Association of Motor Vehicle Administrators (2006). *The Real ID Act: national impact analysis.* Washington, DC: Author.

157. Department of Homeland Security (2011). *Real ID final rule.* Retrieved December 2, 2011, from http://www.dhs.gov/files/laws/gc_1172765386179.shtm.

158. *U.S. v. Lopez* (1995). 514 U.S. 549; *Printz v. U.S.* (1997). 521 U.S. 898.

159. *Citizens United v. Federal Election Commission* (2010). 558 U.S. 08-205; Bipartisan Campaign Reform Act of 2002 (P.L. 107-55).

160. *Grove City College v. Bell* (1984). 465 U.S. 555.

161. Civil Rights Restoration Act of 1988 (P.L. 100-259).

162. Education Amendments of 1972 (P.L. 92-318).

163. Single Audit Act of 1984 (P.L. 98-502).

164. U.S. Office of Management and Budget (2011). *Audit of states, local governments, and non-profit organizations,* Circular A-133. Retrieved December 2, 2011, from http://www.whitehouse.gov/sites/default/files/omb/assets/a133/a133_revised_2007.pdf.

165. Federal Financial Assistance Management Improvement Act of 1999 (P.L. 106-107).

166. U.S. Department of Health and Human Services (2011). *Grants.gov.* Retrieved December 2, 2011, from http://grants.gov/.

167. Federal Funding Accountability and Transparency Act of 2006 (P.L. 109-282).

168. Office of Management and Budget (2011). *Intergovernmental review (SPOC list).* Retrieved December 2, 2011, from http://www.whitehouse.gov/omb/grants_spoc/.

169. Office of the Inspector General, U.S. Department of Education (2006). *The Reading First program's grant application process: final inspection report.* Washington, DC: U.S. Government Printing Office.

Concluding Remarks

Public budgeting, because it involves allocating scarce public resources, will always be at the center of debates about government. This is likely to be particularly true over the next decade (if not longer) as governments of all kinds, domestically and internationally, come to grips with the need to develop a sustainable fiscal policy. In many cases, governments will find that the promises they have made outstrip their capacity to pay for these promises. This will necessarily mean scaling back on expenditures, augmenting revenues, or probably both. In the United States, to the extent that the federal government is forced to finally deal with its mounting debt, this will have ripple effects not only on the state and local sectors, but on the private sector as well.

In this general environment of resource scarcity, and although any predictions about the future should always be attempted with some humility, recent experience leads us to conclude that the field of public budgeting and finance in the coming years will be characterized by sustained or increased attention given to several areas:

- Disagreements about the appropriate roles of government in the economy and society
- Disagreements about the level and type of taxes, who pays them, and the viability of various revenue sources
- Integration of planning, budgeting, accounting, performance measurement, and evaluation systems
- Financial management and financial reporting, including accounting rules for governments and nonprofit agencies
- Legislative–executive conflict over budgetary roles
- Setting priorities for the nation within the intergovernmental system, including the continuing need to consider the tradeoffs between the costs of security versus other pressing needs
- Promotion of economic growth in an international context
- Coming to grips with the fiscal implications of an aging society and with the consequences of promises that have been made to the elderly
- Dealing with the demands placed on public budgets from an aging infrastructure

In concluding, we would like to give brief attention to each of these areas in order to encourage readers to follow these debates for themselves.

Proper Role of Government

The first decade of the new century closed with considerable debate about the proper role of government—the extent to which government should be involved in addressing income and social disparities and the extent to which government should bail out large corporations that find themselves in financial jeopardy as a result of their own decisions.

The United States entered the second decade of the 2000s with the greatest disparities in income levels between top- and bottom-income earners in perhaps more than a century, and with middle-income households realizing little income growth in more than a decade. To what extent are these disparities the proper province of government intervention, or should these matters be resolved by private markets? That question is complicated by the rapidity with which government intervened in the recession that started in 2007 to save large corporations in the financial industry from the consequences of risks they had taken themselves, with the by-product that compensation of senior executives in that industry suffered only a short-term drop. Is government intervention in the economy either deliberately or inadvertently exacerbating disparities among different economic groups?

Resources for Financing Public Services

The financing of services is another controversial aspect of government. The resources that finance government do not just appear. In a democratic society, decisions must be made by the populace and their elected leaders to provide these resources. In a country founded in response to concerns about "taxation without representation," however, even taxation *with* representation has proved to be controversial.

There are many sources of this controversy. First, there is the question of the level of taxation. This question, although difficult, is often driven by consensus over how much money it would be necessary to raise in order to finance the desired level of services. This decision itself is quite difficult and controversial. Even after the decision about "how much" has been resolved, it does not tell us which taxes will be employed by a given government. The individual income tax and the property tax have provoked the most hostility, which has taken the form of specific limitations on the level of taxation and how taxes are administered. It is likely that these kinds of movements will continue, with the "taxpayer bills of rights" (TABORs) as perhaps the most prominent current example of efforts to limit government revenues. More recently, the rise of the Tea Party movement and opposition to all taxes, and support of most (if not all) tax reductions, regardless of their fiscal consequences, is a good example of anti-tax sentiment.

Second, the question of who will pay what level of tax will remain the subject of great debate. Disagreements about whether a given tax should be progressive or proportional, or even how progressive it should be, are really debates about how the tax burden will be distributed across the population. If tax increases are part of the federal government's solution to its current fiscal imbalance, this will lead to questions about whether the deficit should be reduced by taxing mainly higher-income people or whether there should be relatively equal sacrifice among income groups. Perhaps the best example of this during the Obama presidency has been about whether the Bush tax cuts should be extended for everyone, or only for those below a particular income level, such as $250,000. Republican members of Congress generally have taken the former position, while the Obama administration and most Democratic members of Congress have for the most part taken the latter position.

Third, there is the question of the viability of certain revenue sources, particularly the state and local sales tax. The popularity of Internet sales has threatened the sales tax, as states and localities find it difficult to collect the tax on items sold over the Internet and through mail-order catalogs. As more sales shift from traditional brick-and-mortar venues, states and localities that rely heavily on the sales tax will find their revenue streams increasingly at risk. This may eventually put pressure on these governments to turn to alternative revenue sources. Other taxes, such as those on certain forms of gambling and on corporations, may be somewhat risky as well, because the tax base for these sources is a bit less stable than for some other sources of revenue.

Integrating Planning, Budgeting, Accounting, and Measurement

Although budget reform, focused on better integration of budget and performance data, has been a hardy perennial over at least the past 50 years, it seems obvious to even the most casual observer that the trend in government has been toward greater availability of information that will permit elected officials and citizens to evaluate the success of public services. The next logical step, already in evidence in many governments, is that budgetary decision systems will have increased capabilities to use this program information when resources are allocated. Whether the use of program information is desirable has been a moot question for years. The issue today is how to use program information, how to create the right incentives for improving government performance through its use, and where its use is likely to have the most positive effects—not whether to use it.

Advancements in computer technology—both hardware and software—will help strengthen the trend toward use of program data. Where 30 years ago the impediments to wider use of program data were both conceptual and technical, the technical limitations have largely disappeared. Wider accessibility to computer technology also is spurring the rapid growth of tools that can help decision makers use the technology. Knowledge management systems and decision support systems will increase the capacities of decision makers to consider information even under tight deadline pressures.

Increasingly, the conceptual framework for the use of performance information for budgeting is becoming more widely accepted as well. Most governments recognize the need for some enterprise-wide strategic planning effort, informed by the desires of program or agency stakeholders. Furthermore, the development of performance and cost measures that are directly related to the programs or activities listed in these plans is viewed as essential to understanding how well these programs or agencies are functioning.

The integration of planning and budgeting, with the goal of informing the budget process with data on expected performance, is recognized as the crucial last step in making budgeting more performance-focused. It is fair to say that many—perhaps the majority of—governments have made substantial progress in planning and in the supply of relevant measurements, but many still fall short when it comes to the use of those measures for budgeting and management. The trend toward using performance measures does not mean that political realities will be removed from budgetary decision making, as some critics have contended. Rather, a greater array of information will be more readily available than in the past, and decision makers will have the option of considering that information in determining what positions to take on difficult problems. The desire—quite attainable—is not to have resource allocation driven by performance information in some kind of automatic sense, but to have more resource allocation decisions *informed* by considerations of performance.

Regardless of exactly how these connections are made, the movement toward performance-informed budgeting is unlikely to abate, largely because it focuses on the major budgeting question: Does the value that society receives from the public expenditure match or exceed the cost of the program or service? Growth in government programs will be accepted grudgingly, if at all, by taxpayers, who remain skeptical of the ability of governments to do many things well. Increasingly, this will mean that justifying government spending requires demonstration that "value for money" is being delivered.

Financial Management and Financial Reporting

Financial management—defined as the stewardship of public resources after they are received—can hardly avoid being an important focus for the budget process. Particularly because these are public resources, the accountability for their use is even more important. Economic problems at the local, state, and federal levels have continued to make for "tight" budget situations that call for frugal measures. Governments frequently need to engage in midyear "rebudgeting" in response to unanticipated spending pressures or inadequate revenues. Budget execution, therefore, will receive greater attention in the future. Can savings be achieved through closer monitoring of program spending? Can improvements in accounting systems lead to savings? What alternative financial arrangements hold promise for reducing costs? To what extent should governments pursue contracting out of services, privatization, and leasing arrangements?

The past 30 years have seen major additional requirements for accounting and financial reporting for state and local governments. In large part, these have been spurred by the need for those external to government to have a better understanding of government's financial position. For example, potential investors in municipal bonds desire to understand the underlying fiscal health of a given state, locality, or government enterprise. Prior to the institution of common accounting standards by the Governmental Accounting Standards Board (GASB), it was difficult to draw any valid conclusions about the fiscal health of these jurisdictions based on information contained in their financial statements. Citizens and bond purchasers view as vital the overall performance of the entire jurisdiction, such as the local government, in maintaining and preserving the assets that have been the result of previous capital investment, much of it debt financed. At the federal level, successive presidential administrations since 1990 have made improving federal financial management and reporting a priority, even without the same kinds of accounting standards. Complying with these rules and guidelines, however, can be complicated and costly for governments at all levels. For example, the requirement under GASB No. 45 that states and localities report the full accrued cost of employee benefits may ultimately cost these governments significant resources not in reporting costs, but in order to fund these benefits more fully in the interest of improving their stated financial position.

Legislative and Executive Roles in Budgeting

Executive and legislative bodies will continue their struggles with one another over their relative roles in budgetary decision making. Both executives and legislatures may be less than assertive in dealing with the most intractable problems. Gridlock existed largely from 1981 to 1993 when Republican Presidents Reagan and Bush controlled the White House and Democrats largely controlled Congress. Gridlock developed again in 1995 when the president was a Democrat, Bill Clinton, and Congress came under the control of Republicans. With the Republicans regaining control of the House of Representatives in 2010 after four years in the minority, gridlock resurfaced. In fact, according to many observers, the level of partisanship and the difficulty in reaching consensus is worse than it has ever been at the federal level. This is largely the result of a vanishing "middle" in American politics— the extremes of the political spectrum have become increasingly dominant.

State and local governments have their own share of legislative–executive conflict. These conflicts are made more or less important in a given jurisdiction by the relative budgetary power of the branches. Although some state governments have strong legislatures similar to the Congress, in other cases the legislatures are weaker because of short legislative sessions, term limits, limited staff, or a combination of all of these. It is probably the trend toward term limits that has weakened state legislatures the most. It remains to be seen whether this trend will continue into the future or whether the appeal of term limits has ebbed. Although the 2006 and 2008 elections saw substantial gains for the Democratic party in control of both legislatures and governorships, this trend was reversed in elections held at the state level, starting in 2009 and extending to 2011. Similarly, the local "legislative branch" differs in power from government to government, especially between those governments that are council–manager versus strong mayor systems.

Priority Setting in an Intergovernmental System

Governments will continue to be confronted with competing programmatic needs that must be met in a context of limited resources and intergovernmental relationships. Homeland security is likely to have the highest priority on limited resources for the foreseeable future. Small wars, special military operations, and rebuilding at least conventional weapons systems that have been heavily depleted by the Iraq and Afghanistan wars also seem likely to continue putting pressure on the federal budget. For the defense budget, a key question will be whether forward basing of heavily armored divisions and air power in Europe and elsewhere is affordable. Programs for the elderly (especially Social Security) and health care will continue to demand the attention of the federal government (see more on this below), while all levels of government will be called upon to deal with such intractable problems as HIV/AIDS and other infectious diseases, drug trafficking and drug abuse, and poverty and related conditions, such as homelessness. If Congress and the president ever get around to making real spending reductions in order to lower the federal deficit, this may squeeze the funding available for all levels of government.

State and local governments, in contrast, will continue to find that financing elementary and secondary education will require new approaches as traditional sources of finance decline or are limited by taxpayer resistance. The pressures to improve the quality of education are likely to continue, both because of federal initiatives like the No Child Left Behind Act (or whatever may follow it) and because of similar state-level accountability efforts. Although there is not necessarily a direct relationship between spending more money and education quality, it is nonetheless true that these efforts will put more pressure on the budgets of state and local governments. Difficult choices must be made over how other programs will operate and how they will be financed. Presidents, governors, and mayors may all lament the afflictions of AIDS and drug dependency, but where are funds to be obtained for dealing with these problems? Local governments may be willing to provide programs for the poor, but only if state and federal funds are available to support these efforts. The intergovernmental finance system will come under increasing scrutiny as the different levels of government vie for the same tax dollars.

Continued conflict among national, state, and local levels of government may be expected as new problems emerge that challenge existing intergovernmental divisions of authority and responsibility. Nowhere are the intergovernmental roles more complex than in attempting to ensure homeland security. How are security agencies at the federal level best able to relate to state and local agencies, especially given the long-standing tension that has existed among the levels of government? The budget systems of all governments allocate large sums of money to security efforts, but how are agencies to be held accountable for results when buck-passing for any failures can easily be done in such a decentralized environment? Other continuing intergovernmental concerns include preemptions of authority by the federal government over areas claimed by state and local governments, and mandates by the federal government to state and local governments and by states to local governments.

Promoting Economic Growth in an International Context

Promoting economic growth for the nation will continue to be a priority. In addition, Rust Belt states will continue their struggle to reorient their economies in search of new industrial niches. Other regions, such as those dependent on the price of petroleum, will continue through periods of boom and bust as petroleum supplies and prices and worldwide demand fluctuate. The extent to which state and local governments can affect their economic futures will remain uncertain because all governments are subject to the ups and downs of the business cycle.

One of the most important sources of the uncertainty in promoting economic growth by all levels of government is the interdependence of the U.S. economy with the international economy. If there was ever any question that this interdependence existed, the global financial upheaval that was precipitated by U.S. economic factors in 2007 and 2008, and the financial market problems created by the European debt crisis in 2011 and 2012, should have resolved it once and for all. What the U.S. economy makes and sells is intimately influenced by the economies of other nations. Perhaps none of these events will have a greater impact on the United States and the world than the rapid changes in the Brazilian, Chinese, Indian, and even Russian economies. The industrial mix of the U.S. economy and its labor force will inevitably change. These changes will arise at a time when the U.S. labor force is growing older as a whole due to the aging of the baby boomers. In addition, to the extent that more manufactured goods are produced abroad, the number of higher-wage U.S. manufacturing jobs will continue to decline. How budget systems will be able to respond to these challenges is unknown.

Dealing with the Budgetary Implications of an Aging Society

The U.S. population is getting older. As this happens, it will place pressure on the entire society—public, private, and nonprofit sectors—to deal with the budgetary implications of an older population. The most obvious implication for public budgets is at the federal level, where both Social Security and Medicare face mounting financial pressures. These pressures largely result from the nature of these programs, which transfer resources from current workers (through payroll taxes) to current retirees (through benefits). As the baby boomers retire and begin receiving benefits, the ratio of workers paying into these systems to individuals receiving benefits will decline. For Social Security, dealing with this imbalance is conceptually easy, because the federal government controls both sides of the Social Security equation—the taxes paid and the benefits received. A wide variety of fixes is possible, including tax increases and benefit cuts, but each of these is politically difficult because of the dislike for higher taxes and the popularity of the program. This comes at a time when public sentiment leans toward restricting immigration as a source of labor force growth in younger age groupings—a less restrictive immigration policy could improve the Social Security outlook.

Medicare is a different story. The financing problems of Medicare are driven in part by the aging of the population, but a more important factor affecting the future fiscal imbalance for the program is the generally high level of medical care inflation across the entire economy. This, in turn, is driven by factors such as increased life expectancy and the availability of often expensive drugs and procedures to prolong life. Medicaid—the shared federal/state/local program providing health benefits for the poor—is also substantially affected by the cost of health care. The solutions for financing both Medicare and Medicaid are also politically difficult, but perhaps the larger problem is that they are analytically insoluble. Simply put, it is hard to know how to bring down the cost of medical care without sacrificing other things that Americans hold dear, such as the choice of doctors and unfettered access to procedures.

In addition to these federal programs, state and local governments will find themselves needing to deal with rapidly increasing costs associated with employee retirement. In addition to the traditionally underfunded pension systems, the requirement that state and local governments report their "Other Post-Employment Benefit" (OPEB) liabilities (mainly for retiree health) has highlighted the huge gap between needs and current funding streams. As health costs continue to increase, this problem will only increase, and it will be compounded by the need for governments to provide health benefits to current employees, in addition to retirees.

Problems of an Aging Infrastructure

Particularly for state and local governments, the implications of an aging infrastructure will have important fiscal implications. The scope of this challenge is a wide one, and includes roads, bridges, schools, university buildings, prisons, utilities, and numerous other capital projects. This problem has been almost continuously discussed by economists and civil engineers over the past 20 years, but little has been done to address it, with the exception of the temporary programs put in place to address the effects of the recession that started in 2007. The infrastructure aging problem has only become worse. To the extent that the tight future fiscal situation over the next several years hampers the ability of these governments to keep up with the rising infrastructure needs, this mismatch will be an ever-expanding problem. This, in turn, will create pressures for assistance from higher levels of government (federal and state governments) to assist with financing this infrastructure. In addition to the problem of having to build more infrastructure, there is the related, and costly, problem of maintaining what has already been constructed. Maintenance is an expense that is frequently underfunded, thus compromising the condition of infrastructure and accelerating the need for its replacement.

At the same time that there will be more pressure to increase spending on infrastructure, the traditional sources of revenue to finance this spending may be particularly constrained. In the face of rising energy prices, federal and state governments will find it difficult to increase the gasoline tax at all; it will be even more difficult to raise it to a level that would be sufficient to meet the expected need. This will mean that governments will face tough choices as to whether to build new and maintain existing infrastructure at the expense of funds for other important functions.

As a result, governments will increasingly turn to creative financing arrangements—especially public–private partnerships (P3s). Although in some quarters controversial, public–private partnerships will grow in number simply because many elected officials will otherwise have to cut budgets or raise taxes to maintain and build infrastructure. In addition to P3s, state and local governments will likely seek additional privatization or leasing strategies to provide needed infrastructure. This will increase substantially the need for governments to have qualified contract management staff.

These themes do not capture all that is likely to transpire over the coming years. Based on history, the thing that is the surest is that the budgetary conflicts and decisions will mirror the conflicts and debates about priorities within the society. This is both appropriate and inescapable because the budget represents the priorities of the government expressed in dollar terms.

Bibliographic Note

This bibliographic note is intended to assist the reader in finding materials for further reading on public budgeting systems. Because the preceding chapters have extensive notes, we make no attempt here to recapitulate everything cited. Readers will find the index to be a handy guide to note references. This note is meant as an aid in identifying general references as well as sources that have produced and can be expected to continue to produce literature on public budgeting.

Numerous periodicals provide information about the theory and practice of administration in general, and budgeting and finance in particular. Researchers frequently have a choice today of locating journal articles in print or on the Web. Although many journals are available online, they are seldom free. Publishers commonly will provide only a free sample or abstract online, and then researchers must rely on print or electronic subscriptions, or access through public or university library subscriptions. Online databases such as EBSCOhost or ProQuest Direct offer full-text access to collections of journals for subscribers. Researchers need to check with their local libraries for access to these or other full-text databases or for print copies of the journals described below.

Periodical indexes, once available in print and on CD-ROM, are now generally available online. Researchers may still need to rely on print indexes when searching for topics in older issues. As with the journals themselves, these online indices are not free. Researchers should check with local libraries for access or may be able to pay a per-search fee individually for some databases. Periodical indices include *Current Contents* (New York, NY: Thomson Reuters), *Economic Literature* (Nashville, TN: American Economic Association), *Ingenta Connect* (Providence, RI: Ingenta), *Public Affairs Information Service (PAIS) International* (New York, NY: ProQuest [part of Cambridge Information Group]), and *TOC Premier* (Ipswich, MA: EBSCO). *Current Contents* and *TOC Premier* provide table of contents information for academic journals. *EconLit* is the American Economic Association's electronic bibliography of economics literature, containing abstracts, indexing, and links to full-text articles in economics journals. *PAIS*, as its title suggests, indexes journal articles in the field of public administration and public affairs. *Ingenta* is a subscription service that provides for searches and full texts of articles.

Some of the most important journals that produce articles on budgeting and finance include the following. *Public Administration Review* (Wiley-Blackwell Publishing for the American Society for Public Administration) often publishes scholarly articles on budgeting. *Policy Studies Journal* (Policy Studies Organization) includes occasional articles related to budgeting in its regular issues and in special symposia issues. *State and Local Government Review* (University of Georgia) frequently includes budget-related articles that are particularly helpful to practitioners as well as scholars.

Public Budgeting & Finance (Wiley-Blackwell Publishing for the Association for Budgeting and Financial Management and the American Association for Budget and Program Analysis), *Journal of Public Budgeting, Accounting, and Financial Management* (PrAcademics Press), *OECD Journal on Budgeting* (Organisation for Economic Co-operation and Development), and *Public Finance and Management* (Southern Public Administration Education Foundation) focus especially on financial management and budgeting. *Government Finance Review* (Government Finance Officers Association) provides brief analytic pieces and news items on budgeting and finance.

Numerous journals cover the fields of public finance, policy analysis, and policy evaluation. Although occasional articles related specifically to budgeting systems appear in these journals, their usual focus is on specific budgetary subtopics. *National Tax Journal* (National Tax Association) and *Public Finance Review* (Sage) publish empirical and theoretical analyses of economic policy concerns, including government growth and size, tax policy, and fiscal and monetary policy, as well as economic analysis. Numerous journals are devoted to policy analysis and policy evaluation. In addition to *Policy Studies Journal*, the journals *Evaluation Review* (Sage), *Evaluation and Program Planning* (Elsevier), *Journal of Policy Analysis and Management* (Wiley for the Association for Public Policy Analysis and Management), and *Public Performance and Management Review* (M. E. Sharpe) all share that focus.

Besides the periodicals concentrating on budgeting or related topics, other professional journals publish occasional articles of relevance. These include *Administration and Society, Administrative Science Quarterly, American Economic Review, American Political Science Review, Journal of Public Administration Research and Theory, Management Science,* and *Public Management Review*. The Washington-based *National Journal* (http://nationaljournal.com) and *Government Executive* (http://www.govexec.com) provide news and analysis of the federal government, including budgetary events, and *C. Q. Weekly* (Washington, DC: Congressional Quarterly; www.cqrollcall.com/CQ-Weekly) covers congressional actions in particular. Most of the journals listed have annual or occasional indices to facilitate general searches.

Another major source of up-to-date analysis and data consists of government publications. An annual index to many local, state, and federal documents is *Bibliographic Guide to Government Publications—U.S.* (Boston, MA: Hall). Federal documents can be located through the Government Printing Office and its Government Information Locator Services website (http://www.access.gpo.gov) and through the federal government's main Web portal, *USA.gov* (http://www.usa.gov). For statistical information, refer to the *American Statistics Index*, which indexes federal documents, and the *Statistical Reference Index*, which indexes state government publications. Both indices are published by the Congressional Information Service owned by LEXIS/NEXIS (Washington, DC).

Congressional documents can be identified and obtained through a variety of sources. A useful index is the *CIS Index to Publications of the United States Congress* (Washington, DC:

Congressional Information Service, LEXIS/NEXIS). Many congressional documents are available through the *Thomas* database of the U.S. Library of Congress's website (http://thomas.loc.gov). The Government Accountability Office, which is an arm of Congress, has its reports available online as well (http://www.gao.gov).

Congress in 2006 passed the Federal Funding Accountability and Transparency Act, which provided for the creation of a federal spending database. The database, called *USAspending.gov*, is a central entry point for obtaining information about all aspects of federal government spending, including contracts and grants, by geographic area and recipient.

There are numerous online subscription databases related to government. One of the most valuable is *LEXIS/NEXIS* (Reed Elsevier). Four major databases that are part of LEXIS/NEXIS are *Congressional Universe*, for information about Congress; *Academic Universe*, for legal research; *State Capital Universe*, for information about state governments; and *Statistical Universe*, for data searches. *Westlaw* (St. Paul, MN: West Publishing) is comparable to LEXIS/NEXIS Academic Universe.

Students of budgeting and finance will find themselves returning regularly to several key government sources. The Office of Management and Budget (http://www.whitehouse.gov/omb), Council of Economic Advisers (http://www.whitehouse.gov/cea), Treasury Department (http://www.treasury.gov), Congressional Budget Office (http://www.cbo.gov), Government Accountability Office (http://www.gao.gov), and the Federal Reserve (http://www.federalreserve.gov) produce publications and data of major import to the field. Reports from these agencies are available in print and on the Web. Data related to international budgeting and economic issues are found in a variety of sources, including the World Bank (http://www.worldbank.org), the Organisation for Economic Co-operation and Development (http://www.oecd.org), the International Monetary Fund (http://www.imf.org), and the International Finance Corporation (http://www.ifc.org).

Several annual volumes from various agencies contain basic data on revenues and expenditures for local, state, and federal levels and intergovernmental transfers among levels. Considerable care must be exercised when working from more than one source, as the figures do not always agree. For instance, some sources dealing with government and the economy use national income as a measure, whereas others use gross domestic product. In other words, users must be cautious when data are combined from two or more sources. The Census Bureau in the Department of Commerce has published the annual *Statistical Abstract* since 1978 and a host of materials on government finances. However, the home page for the 2012 *Statistical Abstract* (http://www.census.gov/compendia/statab/) contains the disappointing news to what must be millions of users of the most comprehensive single compendium of statistics on the United States:

> The U.S. Census Bureau terminated the collection of data for the Statistical Compendia program effective October 1, 2011. The Statistical Compendium program is comprised of the Statistical Abstract of the United States and its supplemental products—the State and Metropolitan Area Data Book and the County and City Data Book. In preparation for the Fiscal Year 2012 (FY 2012) budget, the Census Bureau did a comprehensive review of a number of programs and had to make difficult proposals to terminate and reduce a number of existing programs in order to acquire funds for higher priority programs. The decision to

eliminate this program was not made lightly. To access the most current data, please refer to the organizations cited in the source notes for each table of the Statistical Abstract.

Readers and authors, including the three authors of this book, will in the future have to search in every federal agency, and other sources, that have collected the statistical series compiled in the *Statistical Abstract* the kinds of data from which many of the tables and figures in *Public Budgeting Systems* have been composed.

Similarly, readers and authors accustomed to accessing the entire U.S. federal budget, including all its appendices and special analyses, for any year since 1996 through the site *GPOaccess* (http://www.gpoaccess.gov/usbudget/) as of 2012 are redirected to the GPO site *FDsys* (http://www.gpo.gov/fdsys/). For the pdf format, all of the information in the federal budget as it appears in the print documents is available unchanged. For users accustomed to downloading files for analysis, such as in popular spreadsheets, it appears at least as of early in 2012 that one may have to download files one table at a time, rather than all of the tables at once, such as in the "Historical Tables" chapter of *Special Analyses.*

Another important source, the *Census of Governments*, is conducted every five years by the Bureau of the Census, U.S. Department of Commerce, and is required by law. It contains not only financial data but also a wealth of organizational information. State and local government budget information is almost always three to four years out of date, except right after the Census of Governments. The Census Bureau is located on the Web at http://www.census.gov. Publications in print and online of the Federal Reserve contain more up-to-date information on state and local government, but these publications do not disaggregate local from state. The Federal Reserve has been an important source of information for this ninth edition of *Public Budgeting Systems* for analysis of the recession that began in 2007.

Besides the Census Bureau, other providers of statistical information are located on the Web. They include *Statistical Resources on the Web*, maintained by the University of Michigan (http://www.lib.umich.edu/clark-library) and the *Government Information Locator Service*, maintained by the U.S. Government Printing Office (http://www.access.gpo.gov).

Analyses of federal budgeting and finance are published by private organizations such as the American Enterprise Institute (Washington, DC; http://www.aei.org), the Committee for Economic Development (Washington, DC; http://www.ced.org), the Heritage Foundation (Washington, DC; http://www.heritage.org), the National Bureau of Economic Research (Cambridge, MA; www.nber.org), the Conference Board (New York, NY; http://www.conference-board.org), and the Tax Foundation (Washington, DC; http://www.taxfoundation.org). The Brookings Institution (Washington, DC; http://www.brookings.edu) publishes numerous books on budgeting and taxation, as does the Urban Institute (www.urban.org). Brookings and the Urban Institute have, over the past decade, collaborated to form the Urban-Brookings Tax Policy Center (www.taxpolicycenter.org), which publishes high-quality research related to taxation. Two useful private sources of information on state and local government borrowing and the municipal bond market are the *Bond Buyer*, available in print and online by subscription only, and the public access website of the *Securities Industry and Financial Markets Association (SIFMA)* at http://www.sifma.org/. Some data are limited access to members only, but all of the data from this source in Chapters 13 and 14 were available for non-member public access.

Books, of course, are an important source of information. Five of the classics in public budgeting, no longer subject to revision and updating, are:

- Willoughby, W. F. (1918). *The problems of a national budget.* New York, NY: Appleton.
- Buck, A. E. (1919). *Public budgeting.* New York, NY: Harper and Brothers.
- Smithies, A. (1955). *The budgetary process in the United States.* New York, NY: McGraw-Hill.
- Burkhead, J. (1956). *Government budgeting.* New York, NY: Wiley.
- Wildavsky, A. (1964). *The politics of the budgetary process.* Reading, MA: Addison-Wesley.

Histories of budgeting include:

- Browne, V. J. (1949). *The control of the public budget.* Washington, DC: Public Affairs Press.
- Gross, B. M. (1969). The new systems budgeting. *Public Administration Review, 29,* 113–137.
- Lewis, C. W. (1989). History of federal budgeting and financial management from the Constitution to the beginning of the modern era. *Public Budgeting and Financial Management, 1,* 193–213.
- Meyer, A. E. (2002). *Evolution of the United States budget,* rev. ed. Westport, CT: Praeger.
- Rubin, I. S. (1993). Who invented budgeting in the United States? *Public Administration Review, 53,* 438–444.
- Webber, C., & Wildavsky, A. (1986). *A history of taxation and expenditure in the Western World.* New York, NY: Simon & Schuster.

Works on budgeting with a special focus, such as on the federal government, state governments, budget theory, and budget politics, include the following:

- Allen, R., & Tommasi, D. (2001). *Managing public expenditure: A reference book for transition countries.* Paris: Organisation for Economic Co-operation and Development.
- Bland, R. L. (2007). *A budgeting guide for local government.* Washington, DC: International City/County Management Association.
- Forsythe, D. W., and Boyd, D. (2012). *Memos to the governor: An introduction to state budgeting,* 3rd ed. Washington, DC: Georgetown University Press.
- Gosling, J. L. (2009). *Budgetary politics in American governments,* 5th ed. New York, NY: Routledge.
- Joyce, P. (2011). *The Congressional Budget Office: Honest numbers, power and policymaking.* Washington, DC: Georgetown University Press.
- Konigsberg, C. (2007). *America's priorities: How the U.S. government raises and spends $3,000,000,000,000 (trillion) per year.* Bloomington, IN: AuthorHouse.
- Koven, S. G. (1999). *Public budgeting in the United States.* Washington, DC: Georgetown University Press.
- McCaffery, J. L., & Jones, L. R. (2001). *Budgeting and financial management in the federal government.* Greenwich, CT: Information Age.
- Michel, R. G. (2002). *Organization and design of an effective budget function.* Chicago, IL: Government Finance Officers Association.
- Mikesell, J. L. (2010). *Fiscal administration,* 8th ed. Belmont, CA: Wadsworth.

- Nice, D. C. (2002). *Public budgeting*. Belmont, CA: Wadsworth.
- Reed, B. J., & Swain, J. W. (1996). *Public finance administration*, 2nd ed. Thousand Oaks, CA: Sage.
- Rubin, I. (2003). *Balancing the federal budget*. New York, NY: Chatham House.
- Rubin, R. (2010). *The politics of public budgeting: Getting and spending, borrowing and balancing*, 6th ed. Washington, DC: CQ Press.
- Schick, A. (2007). *The federal budget: Politics, policy, process*, 3rd ed. Washington, DC: Brookings Institution Press.
- Smith, R. W., & Lynch, T. D. (2003). *Public budgeting in America*, 5th ed. Upper Saddle River, NJ: Pearson Prentice Hall.
- Steiss, A. W., & Cyprian Nwagwu, E. O. (2001). *Financial planning and management in public organizations*. New York, NY: Marcel Dekker.
- Thurmaier, K. M., & Willoughby, K. G. (2001). *Policy and politics in state budgeting*. Armonk, NY: M. E. Sharpe.
- Vogt, A. J. (2004). *Capital budgeting and finance: A guide for local governments*. Washington, DC: International City/County Management Association.
- Wildavsky, A. (2001). *Budgeting and governing*, ed. Brendon Swedlow. New Brunswick, NJ: Transaction.
- Wildavsky, A., & Caiden, N. (2001). *The new politics of the budgetary process*, 5th ed. New York, NY: Longman.

Edited volumes provide reprints of journal articles and originally prepared pieces. Among these are:

- Rabin, J., Hildreth, W. B. & Miller, G. J. (Eds.) (1996), *Budgeting formulation and execution*, Athens, GA: Carl Vinson Institute of Government, University of Georgia.
- Khan, A., & Hildreth, W. B. (Eds.) (2003), *Case studies in public budgeting and financial management*, 2nd ed., New York, NY: Marcel Dekker.
- Menifield, C. (Ed.) (2011), *Comparative budgeting: A global perspective*, Sudbury, MA: Jones & Bartlett Learning.
- Bartle, J. R. (Ed.) (2001), *Evolving theories of public budgeting*, New York, NY: Emerald Group.
- Hyde, A. C. (Ed.) (2001), *Government budgeting: Theory, process, and politics*, 3rd ed., Fort Worth, TX: Harcourt College.
- Meyers, R. T. (Ed.) (1999), *Handbook of government budgeting*, San Francisco, CA: Jossey-Bass.
- Aronson, J. R., & Schwartz, E. (Eds.) (2004), *Management policies in local government finance*, 5th ed., Washington, DC: International City/County Management Association.
- Banovetz, J. M. (Ed.) (1996), *Managing local government finance: Cases in decision making*, Washington, DC: International City/County Management Association.
- Golembiewski, R. T., & Rabin, J. (Eds.) (1997), *Public budgeting and finance*, 4th ed., New York, NY: Marcel Dekker.

A variety of simulations is available to assist students in appreciating the dynamics of decision making. Numerous simulations, directly or indirectly related to budgeting and finance, are listed on the website of the Association for Budgeting and Financial Management (http://www.abfm.org). ABFM has developed a teaching database that includes syllabi, assignments and projects, lectures and handouts, and readings. The *Public Budgeting Laboratory* is a comprehensive set of materials prepared by Jack Rabin, W. Bartley Hildreth, and Gerald J. Miller. It consists of a book of readings, noted above, by Rabin, Hildreth, and Miller, plus a *Workbook,* a *Data Sourcebook,* and an *Instructor's Manual* (Athens, GA: Carl Vinson Institute of Government, University of Georgia, 1996). There are also simulations on reducing federal debt that can be used. A good one is *Principles and Priorities,* sponsored by the Concord Coalition (www.concordcoalition.org); there is also an online version of this exercise.

For literature on decision making, program budgeting, zero-base budgeting, accounting, economic policy, program evaluation, and the like, the reader is encouraged to turn to the notes for each chapter.

Happy reading.

Index